Mastering Go

Fourth Edition

Leverage Go's expertise for advanced utilities, empowering you to develop professional software

Mihalis Tsoukalos

BIRMINGHAM—MUMBAI

Mastering Go

Fourth Edition

Senior Publishing Product Manager: Denim Pinto

Acquisition Editor – Peer Reviews: Swaroop Singh

Project Editor: Meenakshi Vijay

Content Development Editor: Deepayan Bhattacharjee

Copy Editor: Safis Editing

Technical Editor: Aniket Shetty

Proofreader: Safis Editing

Indexer: Manju Arasan

Presentation Designer: Ajay Patule

Developer Relations Marketing Executive: Vipanshu Parashar

First published: April 2018

Second edition: August 2019

Third edition: August 2021

Fourth edition: March 2024

Production reference: 1250324

Published by Packt Publishing Ltd.

Grosvenor House

11 St Paul's Square

Birmingham

B3 1RB, UK.

ISBN 978-1-80512-714-7

www.packt.com

Contributors

About the author

Mihalis Tsoukalos is a UNIX systems engineer and a technical writer. He is the author of *Go Systems Programming*, *Time Series Indexing*, and *Mastering Go*. He holds a BSc in mathematics from the University of Patras and an MSc in IT from University College London, UK. He has written more than 300 technical articles for magazines including *Sys Admin*, *MacTech*, *Linux User and Developer*, *Usenix ;login:*, *Linux Format*, and *Linux Journal*. His research interests include times series, databases, and indexing.

As authoring a book is a team effort, I would like to thank the people at Packt Publishing, including Denim Pinto, Amit Ramadas, Aniket Shetty, and Meenakshi Vijay, for answering all my questions and helping me write this book. I would also like to thank Ricardo Gerardi and Derek Parker, the technical reviewers of the book, for their great work.

Finally, I would like to thank you, the reader of the book, for choosing this book. I hope you find it helpful and that it will keep you good company in your Go journey.

About the reviewers

Derek Parker is the author of *Delve*, the Go debugger, and is an active open source maintainer, contributor, speaker, and a longstanding member of the Go community.

I would like to thank my amazing wife, Erica Parker, and my children, for allowing me the time to work on this during the review process.

Ricardo Gerardi is an experienced IT professional with over 25 years of experience in the industry. He has worked in both large and small companies in Brazil and Canada, and he is currently serving as a Principal Consultant at Red Hat. Ricardo has been a Linux and open-source enthusiast and contributor for over 20 years. He is currently interested in IT automation, Kubernetes, and exploring innovative solutions using the Go programming language. He's the author of *Powerful Command-Line Applications in Go* and *Automate Your Home Using Go*. Ricardo also writes regularly about Go, Linux, and other technologies for several online community publications.

I would like to thank Mihalis Tsoukalos for writing such a great Go reference, and I would like to thank my daughters for allowing me the time to work on this project.

Join our community on Discord

Join our community's Discord space for discussions with the authors and other readers:

https://discord.gg/FzuQbc8zd6

Table of Contents

Chapter 2: Basic Go Data Types   47

Chapter 4: Go Generics   133

Chapter 10: Working with TCP/IP and WebSocket   427

Chapter 12: Code Testing and Profiling　　　　　519

Appendix: The Go Garbage Collector

Other Books You May Enjoy   689

Index   693

Preface

Welcome to the fourth edition of *Mastering Go*! As the Go programming language continues to evolve and gain popularity, I am delighted to present an updated edition of this book.

In the rapidly changing landscape of technology, Go has emerged as a language of choice for building scalable, performant, and maintainable software. Whether you are a seasoned Go developer looking to deepen your expertise or a newcomer eager to master the intricacies of the language, this book is your comprehensive guide.

If you have an older edition of *Mastering Go,* apart from the first edition, which is now pretty old, do not throw it away just because *Mastering Go, Fourth Edition,* is out. Go has not changed that much and both the second and third editions can still be useful and relevant. However, *Mastering Go, Fourth Edition,* is better in many aspects than all previous editions and includes information about the latest Go versions, which you are not going to find in the previous editions of the book.

There exist many exciting topics in this latest edition, including writing RESTful services, writing a statistics application, and working with eBPF, as well as an entirely new chapter on fuzz testing and observability.

I tried to include the right amount of theory and hands-on content—but only you, the reader, can tell if I have succeeded or not. Try to do the exercises located at the end of each chapter and do not hesitate to contact me about ways or ideas to make future editions of this book even better.

Thank you for choosing to pick up *Mastering Go, Fourth Edition*. Let us dive in and unlock the full potential of Go together. Happy coding!

Who this book is for

This book is for amateur and intermediate Go programmers who want to take their Go knowledge to the next level, as well as developers in other programming languages who want to learn Go.

If this is your first programming book ever, you might have some issues following it and a second reading might be required to fully absorb all the presented knowledge.

Learning by doing is a fundamental principle of studying any programming language. Throughout the book, you will find practical examples and hands-on exercises that illustrate key concepts and encourage you to apply your knowledge to real-world scenarios.

One way or another, prepare to work and learn and fail and then work and learn and fail some more. After all, life is not that different from programming.

What this book covers

Chapter 1, A Quick Introduction to Go, begins by discussing the history of Go, important characteristics of Go, and the advantages of Go, before describing the godoc and go doc utilities and explaining how we can compile and execute Go programs. Then, the chapter discusses about controlling program flow, printing output and getting user input, working with command line arguments, and using log files. In the last part of *Chapter 1*, we develop a basic version of a statistics application that we are going to keep improving in forthcoming chapters.

Chapter 2, Basic Go Data Types, discusses the basic data types of Go, both numeric and non-numeric; arrays and slices that allow you to group data of the same date; Go pointers; constants; and working with dates and times. The last part of the chapter is about generating random numbers and populating the statistics application with random data.

Chapter 3, Composite Data Types, begins by teaching you about maps, before going into structures and the struct keyword. Additionally, it talks about regular expressions, pattern matching, and working with CSV files. Last, it improves the statistics application by adding data persistency to it.

Chapter 4, Go Generics, is about Generics and how to use the new syntax to write generic functions and define generic data types. This chapter also presents the cmp package, the slices package, and the maps package, which are all implemented using generics to work with as many data types as possible.

Chapter 5, Reflection and Interfaces, is about reflection, interfaces, and type methods, which are functions attached to data types. The chapter also covers the use of the sort.Interface interface for sorting slices, the use of the empty interface, type assertions, type switches, and the error data type. Additionally, we discuss how Go can mimic some object-oriented concepts before improving the statistics application. This chapter also compares generics with interfaces and reflection.

Chapter 6, Go Packages and Functions, is all about packages, modules, and functions, which are the main elements of packages. Among other things, we create a Go package for interacting with a SQLite3 database, create documentation for it, and explain the use of the sometimes-tricky `defer` keyword. Last, we talk about Workspaces, which is a relatively new Go feature.

Chapter 7, Telling a UNIX System What to Do, is about Systems Programming, which includes subjects such as working with command line arguments, handling UNIX signals, file input and output, the `io.Reader` and `io.Writer` interfaces, and the use of the `viper` and `cobra` packages. Last, we update the statistics application to use JSON data and convert it into a proper command line utility with the help of the `cobra` package.

Chapter 8, Go Concurrency, discusses goroutines, channels, and pipelines. We learn about the differences between processes, threads, and goroutines, the `sync` package, and the way the Go scheduler operates. Additionally, we explore the use of the `select` keyword and we discuss the various *types* of Go channels as well as shared memory, mutexes, the `sync.Mutex` type, and the `sync.RWMutex` type. The rest of the chapter talks about the `context` package, the `semaphore` package, worker pools, how to time out goroutines, and how to detect race conditions.

Chapter 9, Building Web Services, discusses the `net/http` package, the development of web servers and web services, the creation of web clients, and the timing out of HTTP connections. We also convert the statistics application into a web service and create a command line client for it.

Chapter 10, Working with TCP/IP and WebSocket, is about the `net` package, TCP/IP, the TCP and UDP protocols, as well as the WebSocket protocol and working with RabbitMQ. We develop lots of practical servers and clients in this chapter.

Chapter 11, Working with REST APIs, is all about working with REST APIs and RESTful services. We learn how to define REST APIs and develop powerful concurrent RESTful servers as well as command line utilities that act as clients to RESTful services.

Chapter 12, Code Testing and Profiling, discusses code testing, code optimization, and code profiling, as well as cross compilation, creating example functions, the use of `go:generate`, and finding unreachable Go code.

Chapter 13, Fuzz Testing and Observability, talks about fuzz testing, which is a relatively new addition to the Go programming language, and about observability, which refers to the ability to understand, measure, and analyze the internal state and behavior of a system based on its external outputs or observable signals.

Chapter 14, Efficiency and Performance, is about benchmarking Go code, understanding the Go memory model, and eliminating memory leaks. The chapter also includes the development of an eBPF utility—eBPF has become a foundational technology for improving observability, security, and performance in modern Linux systems.

Chapter 15, Changes in Recent Go Versions, is about the language changes, additions, and improvements in the latest Go versions and it will help you understand how Go is evolving over time.

Appendix, The Go Garbage Collector, talks about the operation of the Go Garbage Collector and illustrates how this Go component can affect the performance of your code.

To get the most out of this book

This book requires a modern computer with a relatively recent Go version installed, which includes any machine running Mac OS X, macOS, or Linux, as well as familiarity with your operating system, its filesystem, and git(1). Most of the presented code also runs on Microsoft Windows machines without any changes.

As you embark on your journey to mastering Go, I encourage you to experiment, ask questions, and engage with the material actively. The Go programming language offers a refreshing blend of simplicity and power, and I am confident that this book will provide you with the knowledge and skills needed to become a proficient Go developer.

Download the example code files

The code bundle for the book is hosted on GitHub at https://github.com/mactsouk/mGo4th. We also have other code bundles from our rich catalog of books and videos available at https://github.com/PacktPublishing/. Check them out!

Download the color images

We also provide a PDF file that has color images of the screenshots/diagrams used in this book. You can download it here: https://packt.link/gbp/9781805127147.

Conventions used

There are a number of text conventions used throughout this book.

CodeInText: Indicates code words in text, database table names, folder names, filenames, file extensions, pathnames, dummy URLs, user input, and Twitter handles. For example: "Mount the downloaded WebStorm-10*.dmg disk image file as another disk in your system".

A block of code is set as follows:

```
package main
import "fmt"
func doubleSquare(x int) (int, int) {
    return x * 2, x * x
}
```

When we wish to draw your attention to a particular part of a code block, the relevant lines or items are set in bold:

```
fmt.Println("Double of", n, "is", d)
fmt.Println("Square of", n, "is", s)

anF := func(param int) int {
    return param * param
}
```

Any command line input or output is written as follows:

```
$ go run namedReturn.go 1 -2
-2 1
-2 1
```

Bold: Indicates a new term, an important word, or important information. For instance, words in menus or dialog boxes appear in the text like this. For example: "The wordByWord() function uses *regular expressions to separate the words* found in each line of the input file".

Warnings or important notes appear like this.

Tips and tricks appear like this.

Get in touch

Feedback from our readers is always welcome.

General feedback: Email feedback@packtpub.com and mention the book's title in the subject of your message. If you have questions about any aspect of this book, please email us at questions@packtpub.com.

Errata: Although we have taken every care to ensure the accuracy of our content, mistakes do happen. If you have found a mistake in this book, we would be grateful if you reported this to us. Please visit http://www.packtpub.com/submit-errata, click **Submit Errata**, and fill in the form.

Piracy: If you come across any illegal copies of our works in any form on the internet, we would be grateful if you would provide us with the location address or website name. Please contact us at copyright@packtpub.com with a link to the material.

If you are interested in becoming an author: If there is a topic that you have expertise in and you are interested in either writing or contributing to a book, please visit http://authors.packtpub.com.

Share your thoughts

Once you've read *Mastering Go, Fourth Edition*, we'd love to hear your thoughts! Scan the QR code below to go straight to the Amazon review page for this book and share your feedback.

https://packt.link/r/1805127144

Your review is important to us and the tech community and will help us make sure we're delivering excellent quality content.

Download a free PDF copy of this book

Thanks for purchasing this book!

Do you like to read on the go but are unable to carry your print books everywhere?

Is your eBook purchase not compatible with the device of your choice?

Don't worry, now with every Packt book you get a DRM-free PDF version of that book at no cost.

Read anywhere, any place, on any device. Search, copy, and paste code from your favorite technical books directly into your application.

The perks don't stop there, you can get exclusive access to discounts, newsletters, and great free content in your inbox daily

Follow these simple steps to get the benefits:

1. Scan the QR code or visit the link below

https://packt.link/free-ebook/9781805127147

2. Submit your proof of purchase
3. That's it! We'll send your free PDF and other benefits to your email directly

1

A Quick Introduction to Go

Despite its name, this chapter is more than just a quick introduction to Go, as it is also going to be the foundation for the rest of the book. The basics of Go, some design decisions, and the philosophy of Go are explained in this chapter so that you can get the big picture before learning the details of Go. Among other things, we present the advantages and disadvantages of Go so that you know when to use Go and when to consider other alternatives.

In the sections that follow, we cover a number of concepts and utilities in order to build a solid foundation of Go, before building a simplified version of the which(1) utility, which is a UNIX utility that locates program files by searching the directories of the PATH environment variable. Additionally, we explain how to write information in log files, as this can help you store error messages and warnings while you are developing software in Go.

At the end of the chapter, we develop a basic command line utility that computes basic statistical properties. It is that command line utility that we are going to improve and expand in the remaining book chapters as we learn more advanced Go features.

The contents of this chapter are:

- Introducing Go
- When to use Go
- Hello World!
- Running Go code
- What you should know about Go
- Developing the which(1) utility in Go

- Logging information
- Developing a statistics application

Introducing Go

Go is an open-source systems programming language, initially developed as an internal Google project that went public back in 2009. The spiritual fathers of Go are Robert Griesemer, Ken Thomson, and Rob Pike.

 Although the official name of the language is Go, it is sometimes (wrongly) referred to as *Golang*. The official reason for this is that `https://go.org/` was not available for registration and `golang.org` was chosen instead—however, nowadays, the official Go website is `https://go.dev/`. Keep in mind that when you are querying a search engine for Go-related information, the word *Go* is usually interpreted as a verb; therefore, you should search for *golang* instead. Additionally, the official Twitter hashtag for Go is *#golang*.

Let us now discuss the history of Go and what that means for someone who wants to learn Go.

The history of Go

As mentioned earlier, Go started as an internal Google project that went public back in 2009. Griesemer, Thomson, and Pike designed Go as a language for professional programmers who want to build reliable, robust, and efficient software that is easy to manage. They designed Go with simplicity in mind, even if simplicity meant that Go was not going to be a programming language for everyone or everything.

The figure that follows shows the programming languages that directly or indirectly influenced Go. As an example, Go syntax looks like C, whereas the package concept was inspired by Modula-2.

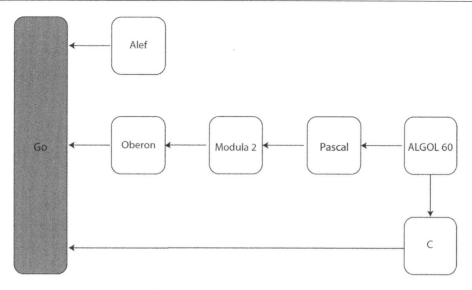

Figure 1.1: The programming languages that influenced Go

The deliverable was a programming language with tools and a standard library. What you get with Go, apart from its syntax and tools, is a rich standard library and a type system that tries to save you from easy mistakes, such as implicit type conversions, unused variables, and unused packages. The Go compiler catches most of these easy mistakes and refuses to compile until you do something about them. Additionally, the Go compiler can find difficult-to-catch mistakes such as race conditions.

If you are going to install Go for the first time, you can start by visiting `https://go.dev/dl/`. However, there is a big chance that your UNIX variant has a ready-to-install package for the Go programming language, so you might want to get Go by using your favorite package manager.

As Go is a portable programming language, almost all presented code is going to work fine on any modern Microsoft Windows, Linux, or macOS machine without any changes. The only Go code that might need some small or big adjustments is the code that deals with the operating system. Most of that code is covered in *Chapter 7, Telling a UNIX System What to Do*.

The advantages of Go

Go comes with some important advantages for developers, starting with the fact that it was designed and is currently maintained by real programmers. Go is also easy to learn, especially if you are already familiar with programming languages such as C, Python, or Java. On top of that, due to its simplified and elegant syntax, Go code is pleasant to the eye, which is great, especially when you are programming applications for a living and you have to look at code on a daily basis. Go code is also easy to read, which means that you can make changes to existing Go code easily, and offers support for Unicode out of the box. Lastly, Go has reserved only 25 keywords, which makes it much easier to remember the language. Can you do that with C++?

Go also comes with concurrency capabilities, using a simple concurrency model that is implemented using *goroutines* and *channels*. Go manages OS threads for you and has a powerful runtime that allows you to spawn lightweight units of work (goroutines) that communicate with each other using channels.

Although Go comes with a rich standard library, there are really handy Go packages, such as cobra and viper, that allow Go to develop complex command line utilities such as docker and hugo. This is greatly supported by the fact that executable binaries are statically linked, which means that once they are generated, they do not depend on any shared libraries and include all required information. In practice, this means that you can transfer an existing executable file to a different machine with the same architecture and be sure that it is going to run without any issues.

Due to its simplicity, Go code is predictable and does not have strange side effects, and although Go supports pointers, it does not support pointer arithmetic like C, unless you use the unsafe package, which can be the root of many bugs and security holes. Although Go is not an object-oriented programming language, Go interfaces are very versatile and allow you to mimic some of the capabilities of object-oriented languages, such as polymorphism, encapsulation, and composition. However, Go offers no support for classes and inheritance. *Chapter 5, Reflection and Interfaces*, provides more information on the subject.

Additionally, the latest Go versions offer support for *generics*, which simplifies your code when working with multiple data types. You can learn more about Go generics in *Chapter 4, Go Generics*. Finally, Go is a garbage-collected language, which means that no manual memory management is needed.

When to use Go

Although Go is a general-purpose programming language, it is primarily used for writing system tools, command line utilities, web services, and software that works over networks and the internet. You can use Go for teaching programming, and it is a good candidate as your first programming language because of its lack of verbosity and clear ideas and principles.

Go can help you develop the following kinds of applications:

- Professional web services
- Networking tools and servers such as Kubernetes and Istio
- Backend systems
- Robust UNIX and Windows system tools
- Servers that work with APIs and clients that interact by exchanging data in myriad formats, including JSON, XML, and CSV
- WebSocket servers and clients
- gRPC (Remote Procedure Call) servers and clients
- Complex command line utilities with multiple commands, sub-commands, and command line parameters, such as docker and hugo
- Applications that exchange data in the JSON format
- Applications that process data from relational databases, NoSQL databases, or other popular data storage systems
- Compilers and interpreters for your own programming languages
- Database systems such as CockroachDB and key/value stores such as etcd

Although Go is a very practical and competent programming language, it is not perfect:

- This is a personal preference rather than an actual technical shortcoming: Go has no direct and full support for object-oriented programming, which is a popular programming paradigm.
- Although goroutines are lightweight, they are not as powerful as OS threads. Depending on the application you are trying to implement, there might exist some rare cases where goroutines will not be appropriate for the job. The Apache web server creates UNIX processes with fork(2) to serve its clients—Go does not support the functionality of fork(2). However, in most cases, designing your application with goroutines and channels in mind will solve your problems.

- Although garbage collection is fast enough most of the time, and for almost all kinds of applications, there are times when you need to handle memory allocation manually, such as when developing an operating system or working with large chunks of memory and want to avoid fragmentation—Go cannot do that. In practice, this means that Go will not allow you to perform any memory management manually.

- Go does not offer the full functionality of a functional programming language.

- Go is not good at developing systems with high availability guarantees. In such cases, use Erlang or Elixir instead.

There are many things that Go does better than other programming languages, including the following:

- The Go compiler catches a large set of silly errors that might end up being bugs. This includes imported Go packages and variables that are not being used in the code.

- Go uses fewer parentheses than C, C++, or Java, and no semicolons, which makes Go source code more human-readable and less error-prone.

- Go comes with a rich and reliable standard library that keeps improving.

- Go has support for concurrency out of the box through goroutines and channels.

- Goroutines are lightweight. You can easily run thousands of goroutines on any modern machine without any performance issues.

- Unlike C, Go considers functions as first-class citizens.

- Go code is backward compatible, which means that newer versions of the Go compiler accept programs that were created using a previous version of the language without any modifications. This compatibility guarantee is limited to major versions of Go. For example, there is no guarantee that a Go 1.x program will compile with Go 2.x.

The next subsection describes my personal Go journey.

My personal Go journey

In this subsection, I am going to tell you my personal story of how I ended up learning and using Go. I am a UNIX person, which means that I like UNIX and prefer to use it whenever possible. I also love C, and I used to like C++; I wrote a command line FTP client in C++ for my M.Sc. project. Nowadays, C++ is just a huge programming language that is difficult to learn. Although C continues to be a decent programming language, it requires lots of code to perform simple tasks and suffers from difficult-to-find and correct bugs, due to manual memory management and extremely flexible conversion between different data types without any warnings or error messages.

As a result, I used to use Perl to write simple command line utilities. However, Perl is far from perfect for writing serious command line tools and services, as it is a scripting programming language and is not intended for web development.

When I first heard about Go, that it was developed by Google, and that both Rob Pike and Ken Thomson were involved in its development, I instantly became interested in Go.

Since then, I have used Go to create web services, servers, and clients that communicate with RabbitMQ, MySQL, and PostgreSQL, create simple command line utilities, implement algorithms for time series data mining, create utilities that generate synthetic data, etc.

Soon, we are going to move on to actually learn some Go, using *Hello World!* as the first example, but before that, we will present the go doc command, which allows you to find information about the Go standard library, its packages, and their functions, as well as the godoc utility.

    If you have not already installed Go, this is the right time to do so. To do that, visit
`https://go.dev/dl/` or use your favorite package manager.

The go doc and godoc utilities

The Go distribution comes with a plethora of tools that can make your life as a programmer easier. Two of these tools are the go doc subcommand and godoc utility, which allow you to see the documentation of existing Go functions and packages without needing an internet connection. However, if you prefer viewing the Go documentation online, you can visit `https://pkg.go.dev/`.

The go doc command can be executed as a normal command line application that displays its output on a terminal, and it is similar to the UNIX man(1) command, but for Go functions and packages only. So, in order to find out information about the Printf() function of the fmt package, you should execute the following command:

```
$ go doc fmt.Printf
```

Similarly, you can find out information about the entire fmt package by running the following command:

```
$ go doc fmt
```

As godoc is not installed by default, you might need to install it by running go install golang. org/x/tools/cmd/godoc@latest. The godoc binary is going to be installed in ~/go/bin, and you can execute it as ~/go/bin/godoc unless ~/go/bin is in your PATH environment variable.

The godoc command line application starts a local web server. So you need a web browser to look at the Go documentation.

Running godoc requires executing godoc with the -http parameter:

```
$ ~/go/bin/godoc -http=:8001
```

The numeric value in the preceding command, which in this case is 8001, is the port number that the HTTP server will listen to. As we have omitted the IP address, godoc is going to listen to all network interfaces.

 You can choose any port number that is available if you have the right privileges. However, note that port numbers 0–1023 are restricted and can only be used by the root user, so it is better to avoid choosing one of those and pick something else, if it is not already in use by a different process. Port number 8001 is usually free and is frequently used for local HTTP servers.

You can omit the equals sign in the presented command and put a space character in its place. So the following command is completely equivalent to the previous one:

```
$ ~/go/bin/godoc -http :8001
```

After that, you should point your web browser to http://localhost:8001/ in order to get the list of available Go packages and browse their documentation. If no -http parameter is provided, godoc listens to port 6060.

If you are using Go for the first time, you will find the Go documentation very handy for learning the parameters and the return values of the functions you want to use — as you progress in your Go journey, you will use the Go documentation to learn the gory details of the functions and variables that you want to use.

The next section presents the first Go program of the book and explains the basic concepts of Go.

Hello World!

The following is the Go version of the *Hello World!* program. Please type it and save it as hw.go:

```
package main
import (
    "fmt"
)
```

```
func main() {
    fmt.Println("Hello World!")
}
```

 If you are eager to execute hw.go, type go run hw.go in the same directory where you save it. The file can also be found in the ch01 directory of the GitHub repository of the book.

Each Go source code begins with a package declaration. In this case, the name of the package is main, which has a special meaning in Go—autonomous Go programs should use the main package. The import keyword allows you to include functionality from existing packages. In our case, we only need some of the functionality of the fmt package that belongs to the standard Go library, implementing formatted input and output with functions that are analogous to C's printf() and scanf(). The next important thing if you are creating an executable application is a main() function. Go considers this the entry point to the application, and it begins the execution of an application with the code found in the main() function of the main package.

hw.go is a Go program that runs on its own. Two characteristics make hw.go a source file that can generate an executable binary: the name of the package, which should be main, and the presence of the main() function—we discuss Go functions in more detail in the next subsection, but we will learn even more about functions and methods, which are functions attached to specific data types, in *Chapter 6, Go Packages and Functions*.

Introducing functions

Each Go function definition begins with the func keyword, followed by its name, signature, and implementation. Apart from the main() function, which has a special purpose, you can name the rest of your functions anything you want—there is a global Go rule that also applies to function and variable names and is valid for all packages except main: *everything that begins with a lower-case letter is considered private and is accessible in the current package only*. We will learn more about that rule in *Chapter 6, Go Packages and Functions*. The only exception to this rule is package names, which can begin with either lowercase or uppercase letters. Having said that, I am not aware of a Go package that begins with an uppercase letter!

You might now ask how functions are organized and delivered. Well, the answer is in packages—the next subsection sheds some light on that.

Introducing packages

Go programs are organized in packages—even the smallest Go program should be delivered as a package. The package keyword helps you define the name of a new package, which can be anything you want, with just one exception: if you are creating an executable application and not just a package that will be shared by other applications or packages, you should name your package main. You will learn more about developing Go packages in *Chapter 6, Go Packages and Functions*.

Packages can be used by other packages. In fact, reusing existing packages is a good practice that saves you from having to write lots of code or implement existing functionality from scratch.

The import keyword is used for importing other Go packages into your Go programs to use some or all of their functionality. A Go package can either be a part of the rich Standard Go library or come from an external source. Packages of the standard Go library are imported by name, for example, import "os" to use the os package, whereas external packages like github.com/spf13/cobra are imported using their full URLs: import "github.com/spf13/cobra".

Running Go code

You now need to know how to execute hw.go or any other Go application. As will be explained in the two subsections that follow, there are two ways to execute Go code: as a compiled language, using go build, or by mimicking a scripting language, using go run. So let us find out more about these two ways of running Go code.

Compiling Go code

To compile Go code and create a binary executable file, we need to use the go build command. What go build does is create an executable file for us to distribute and execute manually. This means that when using go build, an extra step is required to run the executable file.

The generated executable is automatically named after the source code filename without the .go file extension. Therefore, because of the hw.go source filename, the executable will be called hw. If this is not what you want, go build supports the -o option, which allows you to change the filename and the path of the generated executable file. As an example, if you want to name the executable file a helloWorld, you should execute go build -o helloWorld hw.go instead. If no source files are provided, go build looks for a main package in the current directory.

After that, you need to execute the generated executable binary file on your own. In our case, this means executing either hw or helloWorld. This is shown in the following output:

```
$ go build hw.go
```

```
$ ./hw
Hello World!
```

Now that we know how to compile Go code, let us continue using Go as if it were a scripting language.

Using Go like a scripting language

The go run command builds the named Go package, which in this case is the main package implemented in a single file, creates a temporary executable file, executes that file, and deletes it once it is done—to our eyes, this looks like using a scripting language while the Go compiler still creates a binary executable. In our case, we can do the following:

```
$ go run hw.go
Hello World!
```

 Using go run is a better choice when testing code. However, if you want to create and distribute an executable binary, then go build is the way to go.

Important formatting and coding rules

You should know that Go comes with some strict formatting and coding rules that help a developer avoid rookie mistakes and bugs—once you learn these few rules and Go idiosyncrasies as well as the implications they have on your code, you will be free to concentrate on the actual functionality of your code. Additionally, the Go compiler is here to help you follow these rules with its expressive error messages and warnings. Last, Go offers standard tooling (gofmt) that can format your code for you, so you never have to think about it.

The following is a list of important Go rules that will help you while reading this chapter:

- Go code is delivered in packages, and you are free to use the functionality found in existing packages. There is a Go rule that says that if you import a package, you should use it in some way (call a function or use a datatype), or the compiler is going to complain. There exist exceptions to this rule that mainly have to do with packages that initialize connections with database and TCP/IP servers, but they are not important for now. Packages are covered in *Chapter 6, Go Packages and Functions*.

- You either use a variable or you do not declare it at all. This rule helps you avoid errors such as misspelling an existing variable or function name.

- There is only one way to format curly braces in Go.

- Coding blocks in Go are embedded in curly braces, even if they contain just a single statement or no statements at all.

- Go functions can return multiple values.

- You cannot automatically convert between different data types, even if they are of the same kind. As an example, you cannot implicitly convert an integer to a floating point.

Go has more rules, but the preceding ones are the most important and will keep you going for most of the book. You are going to see all these rules in action in this chapter as well as in other chapters. For now, let's consider the only way to format curly braces in Go because this rule applies everywhere.

Look at the following Go program named `curly.go`:

```
package main
import (
    "fmt"
)
func main()
{
    fmt.Println("Go has strict rules for curly braces!")
}
```

Although it looks just fine, if you try to execute it, you will be disappointed because the code will not compile and, therefore, you will get the following syntax error message:

```
$ go run curly.go
# command-line-arguments
./curly.go:7:6: missing function body
./curly.go:8:1: syntax error: unexpected semicolon or newline before {
```

The official explanation for this error message is that Go requires the use of semicolons as statement terminators in many contexts, and the compiler implicitly inserts the required semicolons when it thinks that they are necessary. Therefore, putting the opening curly brace ({) in its own line will make the Go compiler insert a semicolon at the end of the previous line (`func main()`), which is the main cause of the error message. The correct way to write the previous code is the following:

```
package main
import (
```

```
        "fmt"
    )
    func main() {
        fmt.Println("Go has strict rules for curly braces!")
    }
```

After learning about this global rule, let us continue by presenting some important characteristics of Go.

What you should know about Go

This big section discusses important and essential Go features including variables, controlling program flow, iterations, getting user input, and Go concurrency. We begin by discussing variables, variable declaration, and variable usage.

Defining and using variables

Imagine that you want to perform basic mathematical calculations. In that case, you need to define variables to keep the input, intermediate computations, and results.

Go provides multiple ways to declare new variables to make the variable declaration process more natural and convenient. You can declare a new variable using the var keyword, followed by the variable name, followed by the desired data type (we are going to cover data types in detail in *Chapter 2, Basic Go Data Types*). If you want, you can follow that declaration with = and an initial value for your variable. If there is an initial value given, you can omit the data type and the compiler will infer it for you.

This brings us to a very important Go rule: if no initial value is given to a variable, the Go compiler will automatically initialize that variable to the zero value of its data type.

There is also the := notation, which can be used instead of a var declaration. := defines a new variable by inferring the data of the value that follows it. The official name for := is *short assignment statement*, and it is very frequently used in Go, especially for getting the return values from functions and for loops with the range keyword.

The short assignment statement can be used in place of a var declaration with an implicit type. You rarely see the use of var in Go; the var keyword is mostly used for declaring global or local variables without an initial value. The reason for the former is that every statement that exists outside of the code of a function must begin with a keyword, such as func or var.

This means that the short assignment statement cannot be used outside of a function environment because it is not permitted there. Last, you might need to use var when you want to be explicit about the data type. For example, when you want the type of a variable to be int8 or int32 instead of int, which is the default.

Constants

There are values, such as the mathematical constant Pi, that cannot change. In that case, we can declare such values as constants using const. Constants are declared just like variables but cannot change once they have been declared.

 The supported data types for constants are character, string, Boolean, and all numeric data types. There's more about Go data types in *Chapter 2, Basic Go Data Types*.

Global variables

Global variables are variables that are defined outside of a function implementation. *Global variables* can be accessed from anywhere in a package without the need to explicitly pass them to a function, and they can be changed unless they were defined as constants, using the const keyword.

Although you can declare local variables using either var or :=, only const (when the value of a variable is not going to change) and var work for global variables.

Printing variables

Programs tend to display information, which means that they need to print data or send it somewhere for other software to store or process it. To print data on the screen, Go uses the functionality of the fmt package. If you want Go to take care of the printing, then you might want to use the fmt.Println() function. However, there are times when you want to have full control over how data is going to be printed. In such cases, you might want to use fmt.Printf().

fmt.Printf() is similar to the C printf() function and requires the use of control sequences that specify the data type of the variable that is going to be printed. Additionally, the fmt.Printf() function allows you to format the generated output, which is particularly convenient for floating point values because it allows you to specify the digits that will be displayed in the output (%.2f displays two digits after the decimal point of a floating point value). Lastly, the \n character is used for printing a newline character and, therefore, creating a new line, as fmt.Printf() does not automatically insert a newline—this is not the case with fmt.Println(), which automatically inserts a newline, hence the ln at the end of its name.

The following program illustrates how you can declare new variables, how to use them, and how to print them—type the following code into a plain text file named variables.go:

```
package main
import (
    "fmt"
    "math"
)
var Global int = 1234
var AnotherGlobal = -5678

func main() {
    var j int
    i := Global + AnotherGlobal
    fmt.Println("Initial j value:", j)
    j = Global

    // math.Abs() requires a float64 parameter
    // so we type cast it appropriately
    k := math.Abs(float64(AnotherGlobal))

    fmt.Printf("Global=%d, i=%d, j=%d k=%.2f.\n", Global, i, j, k)
}
```

Personally, I prefer to make global variables stand out by either beginning them with an uppercase letter or using all capital letters. As you are going to learn in *Chapter 6, Go Packages and Functions*, the case of the first character of a variable name has a special meaning in Go and changes its visibility. So this works for the main package only.

This above program contains the following:

- A global int variable named Global.
- A second global variable named AnotherGlobal—Go automatically infers its data type from its value, which in this case is an integer.
- A local variable named j of type int, which, as you will learn in the next chapter, is a special data type. j does not have an initial value, which means that Go automatically assigns the zero value of its data type, which in this case is 0.
- Another local variable named i—Go infers its data type from its value. As it is the sum of two int values, it is also an int.

- As math.Abs() requires a float64 parameter, you cannot pass AnotherGlobal to it because AnotherGlobal is an int variable. The float64() *type cast* converts the value of AnotherGlobal to float64. Note that AnotherGlobal continues to have the int data type.

- Lastly, fmt.Printf() formats and prints the output.

Running variables.go produces the following output:

```
Initial j value: 0
Global=1234, i=-4444, j=1234 k=5678.00.
```

This example demonstrated another important Go rule that was also mentioned previously: *Go does not allow implicit data conversions like C*. As presented in variables.go, the math.Abs() function that expects (requires) a float64 value cannot work with an int value, even if this particular conversion is straightforward and error-free. The Go compiler refuses to compile such statements. You should convert the int value to a float64 explicitly using float64() for things to work properly.

For conversions that are not straightforward (for example, string to int), there exist specialized functions that allow you to catch issues with the conversion, in the form of an error variable that is returned by the function.

Controlling program flow

So far, we have seen Go variables, but how do we change the flow of a Go program based on the value of a variable or some other condition? Go supports the if/else and switch control structures. Both control structures can be found in most modern programming languages, so if you have already programmed in another programming language, you should already be familiar with both if and switch statements. if statements use no parenthesis to embed the conditions that need to be examined because Go does not use parentheses in general. As expected, if has support for else and else if statements.

To demonstrate the use of if, let us use a very common pattern in Go that is used almost everywhere. This pattern says that if the value of an error variable as returned from a function is nil, then everything is OK with the function execution. Otherwise, there is an error condition somewhere that needs special care. This pattern is usually implemented as follows:

```
err := anyFunctionCall()
if err != nil {
    // Do something if there is an error
}
```

err is the variable that holds the error value as returned from a function and != means that the value of the err variable is not equal to nil. You will see similar code multiple times in Go programs.

Lines beginning with // are single-line comments. If you put // in the middle of a line, then everything after // until the end of the line is considered a comment. This rule does not apply if // is inside a string value.

The switch statement has two different forms. In the first form, the switch statement has an expression that is evaluated, whereas in the second form, the switch statement has no expression to evaluate. In that case, expressions are evaluated in each case statement, which increases the flexibility of switch. The main benefit you get from switch is that when used properly, it simplifies complex and hard-to-read if-else blocks.

Both if and switch are illustrated in the following code, which is designed to process user input given as command line arguments—please type it and save it as control.go. For learning purposes, we present the code of control.go in pieces in order to explain it better:

```go
package main
import (
    "fmt"
    "os"
    "strconv"
)
```

This first part contains the expected preamble with the imported packages. The implementation of the main() function starts next:

```go
func main() {
    if len(os.Args) != 2 {
        fmt.Println("Please provide a command line argument")
        return
    }
    argument := os.Args[1]
```

This part of the program makes sure that you have a single command line argument to process, which is accessed as os.Args[1], before continuing. We will cover this in more detail later, but you can refer to *Figure 1.2* for more information about the os.Args slice:

```go
    // With expression after switch
    switch argument {
    case "0":
```

```go
        fmt.Println("Zero!")
    case "1":
        fmt.Println("One!")
    case "2", "3", "4":
        fmt.Println("2 or 3 or 4")
        fallthrough
    default:
        fmt.Println("Value:", argument)
    }
```

Here, you see a switch block with four branches. The first three require exact string matches and the last one matches everything else. The order of the case statements is important because only the first match is executed. The `fallthrough` keyword tells Go that after this branch is executed, it will continue with the next branch, which in this case is the default branch:

```go
    value, err := strconv.Atoi(argument)
    if err != nil {
        fmt.Println("Cannot convert to int:", argument)
        return
    }
```

As command line arguments are initialized as string values, we need to convert user input into an integer value using a separate call, which in this case is a call to `strconv.Atoi()`. If the value of the `err` variable is `nil`, then the conversion was successful, and we can continue. Otherwise, an error message is printed onscreen and the program exits.

The following code shows the second form of `switch`, where the condition is evaluated at each case branch:

```go
    // No expression after switch
    switch {
    case value == 0:
        fmt.Println("Zero!")
    case value > 0:
        fmt.Println("Positive integer")
    case value < 0:
        fmt.Println("Negative integer")
    default:
```

```
            fmt.Println("This should not happen:", value)
        }
    }
```

This gives you more flexibility but requires more thinking when reading the code. In this case, the default branch should not be executed, mainly because any valid integer value would be caught by the other three branches. Nevertheless, the default branch is there, which is good practice because it can catch unexpected values.

Running `control.go` generates the following output:

```
$ go run control.go 10
Value: 10
Positive integer
$ go run control.go 0
Zero!
Zero!
```

Each one of the two switch blocks in `control.go` creates one line of output.

Iterating with for loops and range

This section is all about iterating in Go. Go supports `for` loops as well as the `range` keyword to iterate over all the elements of arrays, slices, and (as you will see in *Chapter 3, Composite Data Types*) maps, without knowing the size of the data structure.

An example of Go simplicity is the fact that Go provides support for the `for` keyword only, instead of including direct support for `while` loops. However, depending on how you write a `for` loop, it can function as a `while` loop or an infinite loop. Moreover, `for` loops can implement the functionality of JavaScript's `forEach` function when combined with the `range` keyword.

 You need to put curly braces around a `for` loop even if it contains just a single statement or no statements at all.

You can also create `for` loops with variables and conditions. A `for` loop can be exited with a `break` keyword, and you can skip the current iteration with the `continue` keyword.

The following program illustrates the use of for on its own and with the range keyword—type it and save it as forLoops.go to execute it afterward:

```go
package main
import "fmt"
func main() {
    // Traditional for loop
    for i := 0; i < 10; i++ {
        fmt.Print(i*i, " ")
    }
    fmt.Println()
}
```

The previous code illustrates a traditional for loop that uses a local variable named i. This prints the squares of 0, 1, 2, 3, 4, 5, 6, 7, 8, and 9 onscreen. The square of 10 is not computed and printed because it does not satisfy the 10 < 10 condition.

The following code is idiomatic Go and produces the same output as the previous for loop:

```go
i := 0
for ok := true; ok; ok = (i != 10) {
    fmt.Print(i*i, " ")
    i++
}
fmt.Println()
```

You might use it, but it is sometimes hard to read, especially for people who are new to Go. The following code shows how a for loop can simulate a while loop, which is not supported directly:

```go
// For loop used as while loop
i = 0
for {
    if i == 10 {
        break
    }
    fmt.Print(i*i, " ")
    i++
}
fmt.Println()
```

The break keyword in the if condition exits the loop early and acts as the loop exit condition. Without an exit condition that is going to be met at some point and the break keyword, the for loop is never going to finish.

Lastly, given a slice, which you can consider as a resizable array, named aSlice, you iterate over all its elements with the help of range, which returns two ordered values: *the index of the current element in the slice and its value*. If you want to ignore either of these return values, which is not the case here, you can use _ in the place of the value that you want to ignore. If you just need the index, you can leave out the second value from range entirely without using _:

```
// This is a slice but range also works with arrays
aSlice := []int{-1, 2, 1, -1, 2, -2}
for i, v := range aSlice {
    fmt.Println("index:", i, "value: ", v)
}
```

If you run forLoops.go, you get the following output:

```
$ go run forLoops.go
0 1 4 9 16 25 36 49 64 81
0 1 4 9 16 25 36 49 64 81
0 1 4 9 16 25 36 49 64 81
index: 0 value:  -1
index: 1 value:  2
index: 2 value:  1
index: 3 value:  -1
index: 4 value:  2
index: 5 value:  -2
```

The previous output illustrates that the first three for loops are equivalent and, therefore, produce the same output. The last six lines show the index and the value of each element found in aSlice.

Now that we know about for loops, let us see how to get user input.

Getting user input

Getting user input is an important part of the majority of programs. This section presents two ways of getting user input, which read from standard input and use the command line arguments of the program.

Reading from standard input

The fmt.Scanln() function can help you read user input while the program is already running and store it to a string variable, which is passed as a pointer to fmt.Scanln(). The fmt package contains additional functions for reading user input from the console (os.Stdin), files, or argument lists.

 The fmt.Scanln() function is rarely used to get user input. Usually, user input is read from command line arguments or external files. However, interactive command line applications need fmt.Scanln().

The following code illustrates reading from standard input—type it and save it as input.go:

```go
package main
import (
    "fmt"
)
func main() {
    // Get User Input
    fmt.Printf("Please give me your name: ")
    var name string
    fmt.Scanln(&name)
    fmt.Println("Your name is", name)
}
```

While waiting for user input, it is good to let the user know what kind of information they have to give, which is the purpose of the fmt.Printf() call. The reason for not using fmt.Println() instead is that fmt.Println() automatically appends a newline character at the end of the output, which is not what we want here.

Executing input.go generates the following kind of output and user interaction:

```
$ go run input.go
Please give me your name: Mihalis
Your name is Mihalis
```

Working with command line arguments

Although typing user input when needed might look like a nice idea, this is not usually how real software works. Usually, user input is given in the form of command line arguments to the executable file. By default, command line arguments in Go are stored in the os.Args slice.

The standard Go library also offers the flag package for parsing command line arguments, but there are better and more powerful alternatives.

The figure that follows shows the way command line arguments work in Go, which is the same as in the C programming language. It is important to know that the os.Args slice is *properly initialized by Go and is available to the program when referenced*. The os.Args slice contains string values:

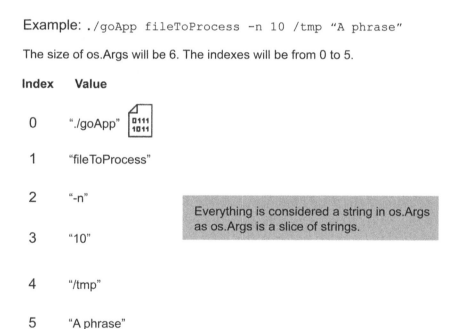

Figure 1.2: How the os.Args slice works

The first command line argument stored in the os.Args slice is always the file path of the executable. If you use go run, you will get a temporary name and path; otherwise, it will be the path of the executable as given by the user. The remaining command line arguments are what come after the name of the executable—the various command line arguments are automatically separated by space characters unless they are included in double or single quotes; this depends on the OS.

The use of os.Args is illustrated in the code that follows, which is to find the minimum and the maximum numeric values of its input while ignoring invalid input, such as characters and strings. Type the code and save it as cla.go:

```
package main
import (
    "fmt"
    "os"
    "strconv"
)
```

As expected, cla.go begins with its preamble. The fmt package is used for printing output, whereas the os package is required because os.Args is a part of it. Lastly, the strconv package contains functions for converting strings to numeric values. Next, we make sure that we have at least one command line argument:

```
func main() {
    arguments := os.Args
    if len(arguments) == 1 {
        fmt.Println("Need one or more arguments!")
        return
    }
```

Remember that the first element in os.Args is always the path of the executable file, so os.Args is never totally empty. Next, the program checks for errors in the same way we looked for them in previous examples. You will learn more about errors and error handling in *Chapter 2, Basic Go Data Types*:

```
var min, max float64
var initialized = 0
for i := 1; i < len(arguments); i++ {
    n, err := strconv.ParseFloat(arguments[i], 64)
    if err != nil {
        continue
    }
```

In this case, we use the error variable returned by strconv.ParseFloat() to make sure that the call to strconv.ParseFloat() was successful and there is a valid numeric value to process. Otherwise, we should continue to the next command line argument.

The for loop is used to iterate over all available command line arguments except the first one, which uses an index value of 0. This is another popular technique for working with all command line arguments.

The following code is used to properly initialize the value of the min and max variables after the first valid command line argument is processed:

```
if initialized == 0 {
    min = n
    max = n
    initialized = 1
    continue
}
```

We are using initialized == 0 to test whether this is the first valid command line argument. If this is the case, we process the first command line argument and initialize the min and max variables to its value.

The next code checks whether the current value is our new minimum or maximum—this is where the logic of the program is implemented:

```
        if n < min {
            min = n
        }
        if n > max {
            max = n
        }
    }
    fmt.Println("Min:", min)
    fmt.Println("Max:", max)
}
```

The last part of the program is about printing your findings, which are the minimum and maximum numeric values of all valid command line arguments. The output you get from cla.go depends on its input:

```
$ go run cla.go a b 2 -1
Min: -1
Max: 2
```

In this case, a and b are invalid, and the only valid inputs are -1 and 2, which are the minimum value and maximum value, respectively:

```
$ go run cla.go a 0 b -1.2 10.32
Min: -1.2
Max: 10.32
```

In this case, a and b are invalid input and, therefore, ignored:

```
$ go run cla.go
Need one or more arguments!
```

In the final case, as cla.go has no input to process, it prints a help message. If you execute the program with no valid input values, for example, go run cla.go a b c, then the values of both Min and Max are going to be zero.

The next subsection shows a technique for differentiating between different data types, using error variables.

Using error variables to differentiate between input types

Now, let me show you a technique that uses error variables to differentiate between various kinds of user input. For this technique to work, you should go from more specific cases to more generic ones. If we are talking about numeric values, you should first examine whether a string is a valid integer before examining whether the same string is a floating-point value, because every valid integer is also a valid floating-point value.

The first part of the program, which is saved as process.go, is the following:

```go
package main

import (
    "fmt"
    "os"
    "strconv"
)

func main() {
    arguments := os.Args
    if len(arguments) == 1 {
        fmt.Println("Not enough arguments")
```

```
        return
    }
```

The previous code contains the preamble and the storing of the command line arguments in the arguments variable.

The next part is where we start examining the validity of the input:

```
    var total, nInts, nFloats int
    invalid := make([]string, 0)
    for _, k := range arguments[1:] {
        // Is it an integer?
        _, err := strconv.Atoi(k)
        if err == nil {
            total++
            nInts++
            continue
        }
```

First, we create three variables for keeping a count of the total number of valid values examined, the total number of integer values found, and the total number of floating-point values found, respectively. The invalid variable, which is a slice of strings, is used for keeping all non-numeric values.

Once again, we need to iterate over all the command line arguments except the first one, which has an index value of 0, because this is the path of the executable file. We ignore the path of the executable, using arguments[1:] instead of just arguments—selecting a continuous part of a slice is discussed in the next chapter.

The call to strconv.Atoi() determines whether we are processing a valid int value or not. If so, we increase the total and nInts counters:

```
        // Is it a float
        _, err = strconv.ParseFloat(k, 64)
        if err == nil {
            total++
            nFloats++
            continue
        }
```

Similarly, if the examined string represents a valid floating-point value, the call to `strconv.ParseFloat()` is going to be successful, and the program will update the relevant counters. Lastly, if a value is not numeric, it is appended to the `invalid` slice with a call to `append()`:

```
        // Then it is invalid
        invalid = append(invalid, k)
    }
```

The last part of the program is the following:

```
    fmt.Println("#read:", total, "#ints:", nInts, "#floats:", nFloats)
    if len(invalid) > total {
        fmt.Println("Too much invalid input:", len(invalid))
        for _, s := range invalid {
            fmt.Println(s)
        }
    }
}
```

Presented here is extra code that warns you when your invalid input is more than the valid one (`len(invalid) > total`). This is a common practice for keeping unexpected input in applications.

Running `process.go` produces the following kind of output:

```
$ go run process.go 1 2 3
#read: 3 #ints: 3 #floats: 0
```

In this case, we process 1, 2, and 3, which are all valid integer values:

```
$ go run process.go 1 2.1 a
#read: 2 #ints: 1 #floats: 1
```

In this case, we have a valid integer, 1, a floating-point value, 2.1, and an invalid value, a:

```
$ go run process.go a 1 b
#read: 1 #ints: 1 #floats: 0
Too much invalid input: 2
a
b
```

If the invalid input is more than the valid one, then `process.go` prints an extra error message.

The next subsection discusses the concurrency model of Go.

Understanding the Go concurrency model

This section is a quick introduction to the Go concurrency model. The Go concurrency model is implemented using *goroutines* and *channels*. A goroutine is the smallest executable Go entity. To create a new goroutine, you have to use the go keyword followed by a predefined function or an anonymous function—both these methods are equivalent as far as Go is concerned.

 The go keyword works with functions or anonymous functions only.

A channel in Go is a mechanism that, among other things, allows goroutines to communicate and exchange data. If you are an amateur programmer or are hearing about goroutines and channels for the first time, do not panic. Goroutines and channels, as well as pipelines and sharing data among goroutines, will be explained in much more detail in *Chapter 8, Go Concurrency*.

Although it is easy to create goroutines, there are other difficulties when dealing with concurrent programming, including goroutine synchronization and sharing data between goroutines—this is a Go mechanism for avoiding side effects by using global state when running goroutines. As main() runs as a goroutine as well, you do not want main() to finish before the other goroutines of the program because once main() exits, the entire program along with any goroutines that have not finished yet will terminate. Although goroutines cannot communicate directly with each other, they can share memory. The good thing is that there are various techniques for the main() function to wait for goroutines to exchange data through channels or, less frequently in Go, use shared memory.

Type the following Go program, which synchronizes goroutines using time.Sleep() calls (this is not the right way to synchronize goroutines—we will discuss the proper way to synchronize goroutines in *Chapter 8, Go Concurrency*), into your favorite editor, and save it as goRoutines.go:

```
package main
import (
    "fmt"
    "time"
)
func myPrint(start, finish int) {
    for i := start; i <= finish; i++ {
        fmt.Print(i, " ")
```

```
    }
    fmt.Println()
    time.Sleep(100 * time.Microsecond)
}
func main() {
    for i := 0; i < 4; i++ {
        go myPrint(i, 5)
    }
    time.Sleep(time.Second)
}
```

The preceding naively implemented example creates four goroutines and prints some values on the screen using the myPrint() function—the go keyword is used for creating the goroutines. Running goRoutines.go generates the following output:

```
$ go run goRoutines.go
2 3 4 5
0 4 1 2 3 1 2 3 4 4 5
5
3 4 5
5
```

However, if you run it multiple times, you will most likely get a different output each time:

```
1 2 3 4 5
4 2 5 3 4 5
3 0 1 2 3 4 5
4 5
```

This happens because *goroutines are initialized in a random order and start running in a random order*. The Go scheduler is responsible for the execution of goroutines, just like the OS scheduler is responsible for the execution of the OS threads. *Chapter 8, Go Concurrency*, discusses Go concurrency in more detail and presents the solution to that randomness issue with the use of a sync.WaitGroup variable—however, keep in mind that Go concurrency is everywhere, which is the main reason for including this section here. Therefore, as some error messages generated by the compiler discuss goroutines, you should not think that these goroutines were created by you.

The next section shows a practical example that involves developing a Go version of the which(1) utility, which searches for an executable file in the PATH environment value of the current user.

Developing the which(1) utility in Go

Go can work with your operating system through a set of packages. A good way of learning a new programming language is by trying to implement simple versions of traditional UNIX utilities— in general, the only efficient way to learn a programming language is by writing lots of code in that language. In this section, you will see a Go version of the which(1) utility, which will help you understand the way Go interacts with the underlying OS and reads environment variables.

The presented code, which will implement the functionality of which(1), can be divided into three logical parts. The first part is about reading the input argument, which is the name of the executable file that the utility will be searching for. The second part is about reading the value stored in the PATH environment variable, splitting it, and iterating over the directories of the PATH variable. The third part is about looking for the desired binary file in these directories and determining whether it can be found or not, whether it is a regular file, and whether it is an executable file. If the desired executable file is found, the program terminates with the help of the return statement. Otherwise, it will terminate after the for loop ends and the main() function exits.

The presented source file is called which.go and is located under the ch01 directory of the GitHub repository of the book. Now, let us see the code, beginning with the logical preamble that usually includes the package name, the import statements, and other definitions with a global scope:

```
package main
import (
    "fmt"
    "os"
    "path/filepath"
)
```

The fmt package is used for printing onscreen, the os package is for interacting with the underlying operating system, and the path/filepath package is used for working with the contents of the PATH variable that is read as a long string, depending on the number of directories it contains.

The second logical part of the utility is the following:

```
func main() {
    arguments := os.Args
    if len(arguments) == 1 {
        fmt.Println("Please provide an argument!")
        return
    }
```

```
file := arguments[1]
path := os.Getenv("PATH")
pathSplit := filepath.SplitList(path)
for _, directory := range pathSplit {
```

First, we read the command line arguments of the program (os.Args) and save the first command line argument into the file variable. Then, we get the contents of the PATH environment variable and split it using filepath.SplitList(), which offers a portable way of separating a list of paths. Lastly, we iterate over all the directories of the PATH variable using a for loop with range, as filepath.SplitList() returns a slice.

The rest of the utility contains the following code:

```
fullPath := filepath.Join(directory, file)
// Does it exist?
fileInfo, err := os.Stat(fullPath)
if err != nil {
    continue
}

mode := fileInfo.Mode()
// Is it a regular file?
if !mode.IsRegular() {
    continue
}

// Is it executable?
if mode&0111 != 0 {
    fmt.Println(fullPath)
    return
}
}
}
```

We construct the full path that we examine using filepath.Join(), which is used for concatenating the different parts of a path using an OS-specific separator—this makes filepath.Join() work on all supported operating systems. In this part, we also get some lower-level information about the file—keep in mind that UNIX considers everything as a file, which means that we want to make sure that we are dealing with a regular file that is also executable.

Executing `which.go` generates the following kind of output:

```
$ go run which.go which
/usr/bin/which
$ go run which.go doesNotExist
```

The last command could not find the `doesNotExist` executable—according to the UNIX philosophy and the way UNIX pipes work, utilities generate no output onscreen if they have nothing to say.

Although it is useful to print error messages onscreen, there are times that you need to keep all error messages together and be able to search for them later when it is convenient for you. In this case, you need to use one or more log files.

The next section discusses logging in Go.

Logging information

All UNIX systems have their own log files for writing logging information that comes from running servers and programs. Usually, most system log files of a UNIX system can be found under the `/var/log` directory. However, the log files of many popular services, such as Apache and Nginx, can be found elsewhere, depending on their configuration.

Logging and storing logging information in log files is a practical way of examining data and information from your software asynchronously, either locally, at a central log server, or using server software such as Elasticsearch, Beats, and Grafana Loki.

Generally speaking, using a log file to write some information used to be considered a better practice than writing the same output on screen for two reasons. Firstly, because the output does not get lost, as it is stored on a file, and secondly, because you can search and process log files using UNIX tools, such as `grep(1)`, `awk(1)`, and `sed(1)`, which cannot be done when messages are printed in a terminal window. However, writing to log files is not always the best approach, mainly because many services run as Docker images, which have their own log files that get lost when the Docker image stops.

As we usually run our services via `systemd`, programs should log to `stdout` so that `systemd` can put logging data in the journal. `https://12factor.net/logs` offers more information about app logs. Additionally, in cloud-native applications, we are encouraged to simply log to `stderr` and let the container system redirect the `stderr` stream to the desired destination.

The UNIX logging service has support for two properties named *logging level* and *logging facility*. The logging level is a value that specifies the severity of the log entry. There are various logging levels, including debug, info, notice, warning, err, crit, alert, and emerg, in reverse order of severity. The log package of the standard Go library does not support working with logging levels. The logging facility is like a category used for logging information. The value of the logging facility part can be one of auth, authpriv, cron, daemon, kern, lpr, mail, mark, news, syslog, user, UUCP, local0, local1, local2, local3, local4, local5, local6, or local7 and is defined inside /etc/syslog.conf, /etc/rsyslog.conf, or another appropriate file depending on the server process used for system logging on your UNIX machine. This means that if a logging facility is not defined correctly, it will not be handled; therefore, the log messages you send to it might get ignored and, therefore, lost.

The log package sends log messages to standard error. Part of the log package is the log/syslog package, which allows you to send log messages to the syslog server of your machine. Although by default log writes to standard error, the use of log.SetOutput() modifies that behavior. The list of functions for sending logging data includes log.Printf(), log.Print(), log.Println(), log.Fatalf(), log.Fatalln(), log.Panic(), log.Panicln(), and log.Panicf().

 Logging is for application code, not library code. If you are developing libraries, do not put logging in them.

In order to write to system logs, you need to call the syslog.New() function with the appropriate parameters. Writing to the main system log file is as easy as calling syslog.New() with the syslog.LOG_SYSLOG option. After that, you need to tell your Go program that all logging information goes to the new logger—this is implemented with a call to the log.SetOutput() function. The process is illustrated in the following code—type it into your favorite plain text editor and save it as systemLog.go:

```
package main
import (
    "log"
    "log/syslog"
)
func main() {
    sysLog, err := syslog.New(syslog.LOG_SYSLOG, "systemLog.go")
```

```
        if err != nil {
            log.Println(err)
            return
        } else {
            log.SetOutput(sysLog)
            log.Print("Everything is fine!")
        }
    }
```

After the call to log.SetOutput(), all logging information goes to the syslog logger variable which sends it to syslog.LOG_SYSLOG. Custom text for the log entries coming from that program is specified as the second parameter to the syslog.New() call.

 Usually, we want to store logging data in user-defined files because they group relevant information, which makes them easier to process and inspect.

Running systemLog.go generates no output. However, if you execute journalctl -xe on a Linux machine, you can see entries like the following:

```
Jun 08 20:46:05 thinkpad systemLog.go[4412]: 2023/06/08 20:46:05
Everything is fine!
Jun 08 20:46:51 thinkpad systemLog.go[4822]: 2023/06/08 20:46:51
Everything is fine!
```

The output on your own operating system might be slightly different, but the general idea is the same.

Bad things happen all the time, even to good people and good software. So the next subsection covers the Go way of dealing with bad situations.

log.Fatal() and log.Panic()

The log.Fatal() function is used when something erroneous has happened and you just want to exit your program as soon as possible after reporting that bad situation. The call to log.Fatal() terminates a Go program at the point where log.Fatal() was called after printing an error message. In most cases, this custom error message can be Not enough arguments, Cannot access file, or similar. Additionally, it returns a non-zero exit code, which in UNIX indicates an error.

There are situations where a program is about to fail for good and you want to have as much information about the failure as possible—log.Panic() implies that something really unexpected and unknown, such as not being able to find a file that was previously accessed or not having enough disk space, has happened. Analogous to the log.Fatal() function, log.Panic() prints a custom message and immediately terminates the Go program.

Keep in mind that log.Panic() is equivalent to a call to log.Print(), followed by a call to panic(). This is a built-in function that stops the execution of the current function and begins panicking. After that, it returns to the caller function. Conversely, log.Fatal() calls log.Print() and then os.Exit(1), which is an immediate way of terminating the current program. Both log.Fatal() and log.Panic() are illustrated in the logs.go file, which contains the following Go code:

```go
package main
import (
    "log"
    "os"
)
func main() {
    if len(os.Args) != 1 {
        log.Fatal("Fatal: Hello World!")
    }
    log.Panic("Panic: Hello World!")
}
```

If you call logs.go without any command line arguments, it calls log.Panic(). Otherwise, it calls log.Fatal(). This is illustrated in the following output from an Arch Linux system:

```
$ go run logs.go
2023/06/08 20:48:42 Panic: Hello World!
panic: Panic: Hello World!

goroutine 1 [running]:
log.Panic({0xc000104f60?, 0x0?, 0x0?})
    /usr/lib/go/src/log/log.go:384 +0x65
main.main()
    /home/mtsouk/code/mGo4th/ch01/logs.go:12 +0x85
exit status 2
$ go run logs.go 1
```

```
2023/06/08 20:48:59 Fatal: Hello World!
exit status 1
```

So the output of log.Panic() includes additional low-level information that, hopefully, will help you resolve difficult situations that arise in your Go code.

 Please keep in mind that both of these functions terminate the program abruptly, which may not be what the user wants. As a result, they are not the best way to end a program. However, they can be handy for reporting really bad error conditions or unexpected situations. Two such examples are when a program is unable to save its data or when a configuration file is not found.

The next subsection is about writing to custom log files.

Writing to a custom log file

Most of the time, and especially on applications and services that are deployed to production, you need to write your logging data in a log file of your choice. This can be for many reasons, including writing debugging data without messing with the system log files, or keeping your own logging data separate from system logs to transfer it or store it in a database or software, like Elasticsearch. This subsection teaches you how to write to a custom log file that is usually application-specific.

Writing to files and file input and output are both covered in *Chapter 7, Telling a UNIX System What to Do*—however, saving information to files is very handy when troubleshooting and debugging Go code, which is why this is covered in the first chapter.

The path of the log file (mGo.log) that is used is stored on a variable named LOGFILE—this is created using the os.TempDir() function, which returns the default directory used on the current OS for temporary files, in order to prevent your file system from getting full in case something goes wrong.

Additionally, at this point, this will save you from having to execute customLog.go with root privileges and putting unnecessary files into precious system directories.

Type the following code and save it as customLog.go:

```
package main
import (
    "fmt"
    "log"
    "os"
```

```
    "path"
)
func main() {
    LOGFILE := path.Join(os.TempDir(), "mGo.log")
    fmt.Println(LOGFILE)
    f, err := os.OpenFile(LOGFILE, os.O_APPEND|os.O_CREATE|os.O_WRONLY,
0644)
// The call to os.OpenFile() creates the log file for writing,
// if it does not already exist, or opens it for writing
// by appending new data at the end of it (os.O_APPEND)
    if err != nil {
        fmt.Println(err)
        return
    }
    defer f.Close()
```

The defer keyword tells Go to execute the statement just before the current function returns. This means that f.Close() is going to be executed just before main() returns. We will go into more detail on defer in *Chapter 6, Go Packages and Functions*:

```
    iLog := log.New(f, "iLog ", log.LstdFlags)
    iLog.Println("Hello there!")
    iLog.Println("Mastering Go 4th edition!")
}
```

The last three statements create a new log file based on an opened file (f) and write two messages to it, using Println().

 If you ever decide to use the code of customLog.go in a real application, you should change the path stored in LOGFILE to something that makes more sense.

Running customLog.go on an Arch Linux machine prints the file path of the log file:

```
$ go run customLog.go
/tmp/mGo.log
```

Depending on your operating system, your output might vary. However, what is important is what has been written in the custom log file:

```
$ cat /tmp/mGo.log
iLog 2023/11/27 22:15:10 Hello there!
iLog 2023/11/27 22:15:10 Mastering Go 4th edition!
```

The next subsection shows how to print line numbers in log entries.

Printing line numbers in log entries

In this subsection, you will learn how to print the filename as well as the line number in the source file where the statement that wrote a log entry is located.

The desired functionality is implemented with the use of log.Lshortfile in the parameters of log.New() or SetFlags(). The log.Lshortfile flag adds the filename as well as the line number of the Go statement that printed the log entry in the log entry itself. If you use log.Llongfile instead of log.Lshortfile, then you get the full path of the Go source file—usually, this is not necessary, especially when you have a really long path.

Type the following code and save it as customLogLineNumber.go:

```go
package main
import (
    "fmt"
    "log"
    "os"
    "path"
)

func main() {
    LOGFILE := path.Join(os.TempDir(), "mGo.log")
    fmt.Println(LOGFILE)
    f, err := os.OpenFile(LOGFILE, os.O_APPEND|os.O_CREATE|os.O_WRONLY,
0644)
    if err != nil {
        fmt.Println(err)
        return
    }
    defer f.Close()
    LstdFlags := log.Ldate | log.Lshortfile
    iLog := log.New(f, "LNum ", LstdFlags)
    iLog.Println("Mastering Go, 4th edition!")
```

```
        iLog.SetFlags(log.Lshortfile | log.LstdFlags)
        iLog.Println("Another log entry!")
}
```

In case you are wondering, you are allowed to change the format of the log entries during program execution—this means that when there is a reason, you can print more analytical information in the log entries. This is implemented with multiple calls to iLog.SetFlags().

Running customLogLineNumber.go generates the following output:

```
$ go run customLogLineNumber.go
/var/folders/sk/1tk8cnw50lzdtr2hxcj5sv2m0000gn/T/mGo.log
```

It also writes the following entries in the file path that is specified by the value of the LOGFILE global variable:

```
$ cat /var/folders/sk/1tk8cnw50lzdtr2hxcj5sv2m0000gn/T/mGo.log
LNum 2023/06/08 customLogLineNumber.go:25: Mastering Go, 4th edition!
LNum 2023/06/08 20:58:09 customLogLineNumber.go:28: Another log entry!
```

The first error message is from source code line 25, whereas the second one is from source code line 28.

You will most likely get a different output on your own machine, which is the expected behavior.

Writing to multiple log files

This subsection shows a technique for writing to multiple log files—this is illustrated in multipleLogs.go, which can be found in the GitHub repository of the book under directory ch01 and comes with the following code:

```
package main

import (
    "fmt"
    "io"
    "log"
    "os"
)

func main() {
    flag := os.O_APPEND | os.O_CREATE | os.O_WRONLY
```

```
    file, err := os.OpenFile("myLog.log", flag, 0644)
    if err != nil {
        fmt.Println(err)
        os.Exit(0)
    }
    defer file.Close()

    w := io.MultiWriter(file, os.Stderr)
    logger := log.New(w, "myApp: ", log.LstdFlags)
    logger.Printf("BOOK %d", os.Getpid())
}
```

The `io.MultiWriter()` function is what allows us to write to multiple destinations, which in this case are a file named `myLog.log` and standard error.

The results of running `multipleLogs.go` can be seen in the `myLog.log` file, which is going to be created in the current working directory, and to standard error, which is usually presented on screen:

```
$ go run multipleLogs.go
myApp: 2023/06/24 21:02:55 BOOK 71457
```

The contents of `myLog.log` are the same as before:

```
$ at myLog.log
myApp: 2023/06/24 21:02:55 BOOK 71457
```

In the next section, we are going to write the first version of the statistics application.

Developing a statistics application

In this section, we are going to develop a basic statistics application stored in `stats.go`. The statistical application is going to be improved and enriched with new features throughout this book.

The first part of `stats.go` is the following:

```
package main

import (
    "fmt"
    "math"
    "os"
    "strconv"
```

```
    )

    func main() {
        arguments := os.Args
        if len(arguments) == 1 {
            fmt.Println("Need one or more arguments!")
            return
        }
    }
```

In this first part of the application, the necessary Go packages are imported before the main()
function makes sure that we have at least a single command line parameter to work with, using
len(arguments) == 1.

The second part of stats.go is the following:

```
        var min, max float64
        var initialized = 0

        nValues := 0
        var sum float64
        for i := 1; i < len(arguments); i++ {
            n, err := strconv.ParseFloat(arguments[i], 64)
            if err != nil {
                continue
            }

            nValues = nValues + 1
            sum = sum + n

            if initialized == 0 {
                min = n
                max = n
                initialized = 1
                continue
            }

            if n < min {
                min = n
            }
```

```
        if n > max {
            max = n
        }
    }

    fmt.Println("Number of values:", nValues)
    fmt.Println("Min:", min)
    fmt.Println("Max:", max)
```

In the previous code excerpt, we process all valid inputs to count the number of valid values and find the minimum and the maximum values among them.

The last part of stats.go is the following:

```
    // Mean value
    if nValues == 0 {
        return
    }
meanValue := sum / float64(nValues)
    fmt.Printf("Mean value: %.5f\n", meanValue)

    // Standard deviation
    var squared float64
for i := 1; i < len(arguments); i++ {
        n, err := strconv.ParseFloat(arguments[i], 64)
        if err != nil {
            continue
        }
        squared = squared + math.Pow((n-meanValue), 2)
    }
    standardDeviation := math.Sqrt(squared / float64(nValues))
    fmt.Printf("Standard deviation: %.5f\n", standardDeviation)
}
```

In the previous code excerpt, we find the *mean value* because this cannot be computed without processing all values first. After that, we process each valid value to compute the *standard deviation* because the mean value is required in order to compute the standard deviation.

Running `stats.go` generates the following kind of output:

```
$ go run stats.go 1 2 3
Number of values: 3
Min: 1
Max: 3
Mean value: 2.00000
Standard deviation: 0.81650
```

Summary

At the beginning of this chapter, we discussed the advantages, disadvantages, philosophy, and history of Go. Then, the basics of Go were presented, which include variables, iterations, and flow control as well as how to log data.

After that, we learned about logging, implemented `which(1)`, and created a basic statistics application.

The next chapter is all about the basic Go data types.

Exercises

Test out what you have learned by trying to complete the following exercises:

- Read the documentation of the `fmt` package using `go doc`.
- In UNIX, an exit code of 0 means success, whereas a non-zero exit code usually means failure. Try to modify `which.go` to do so with the help of `os.Exit()`.
- The current version of `which(1)` stops after finding the first occurrence of the desired executable. Make the necessary code changes to `which.go` in order to find all possible occurrences of the desired executable.

Additional resources

- The official Go website: `https://go.dev/`
- The Go Playground: `https://go.dev/play/`
- The `log` package: `https://pkg.go.dev/log`
- Elasticsearch Beats: `https://www.elastic.co/beats/`
- Grafana Loki: `https://grafana.com/oss/loki/`
- Standard deviation: `https://en.wikipedia.org/wiki/Standard_deviation`

- Microsoft Visual Studio: `https://visualstudio.microsoft.com/`
- The Standard Go library: `https://pkg.go.dev/std`
- The godoc utility: `https://pkg.go.dev/golang.org/x/tools/cmd/godoc`

Leave a review!

Enjoying this book? Help readers like you by leaving an Amazon review. Scan the QR code below to get a free eBook of your choice.

2

Basic Go Data Types

Data is stored and manipulated in variables—all Go variables should have a data type that is either determined implicitly or declared explicitly. Knowing the built-in data types of Go allows you to understand how to manipulate simple data values and construct more complex data structures when simple data types are not enough or not efficient for a job. ***Go being a statically typed and compiled programming language*** allows the compiler to perform various optimizations and checks prior to program execution.

The first part of this chapter is all about the basic data types of Go, and the second part logically follows, covering the data structures that allow you to group data of the same data type, which are arrays and the much more powerful slices.

But let us begin with something more practical: imagine that you want to read data as command line arguments. How can you be sure that what you have read was what you expected? How can you handle error situations? What about reading not just numbers and strings but dates and times from the command line? Do you have to write your own parser for working with dates and times?

In *Chapter 1, A Quick Introduction to Go*, we included the entire code of the presented source files. However, starting from this chapter, this will not always be the case. This serves two purposes: the first one is that you get to see the code that really matters, and the second one is that we save book space.

This chapter will answer all these questions and many more, such as working with the unsafe package, the internals of slices and how slices are connected to arrays, and how to work with pointers in Go. Additionally, it implements utilities that generate random numbers and random strings and updates the statistics application. So, this chapter covers:

- The error data type
- Numeric data types
- Non-numeric data types
- Constants
- Grouping similar data
- Pointers
- Data types and the unsafe package
- Generating random numbers
- Updating the statistics application

We begin this chapter with the error data type because errors and error handling play a key role in Go.

The error data type

Go provides a special data type, named error, for representing error conditions and error messages—in practice, this means that Go treats errors as values. *To program successfully in Go, you should be aware of the error conditions that might occur with the functions and methods you are using and handle them accordingly.*

As you already know from the previous chapter, Go follows a particular convention concerning error values: if the value of an error variable is nil, then there is no error. As an example, let us consider strconv.Atoi(), which is used for converting a string value into an int value (Atoi stands for *ASCII to Int*). As specified by its signature, strconv.Atoi() returns (int, error). Having an error value of nil means that the conversion was successful and that you can use the int value if you want. Having an error value that is not nil means that the conversion was unsuccessful and that the string input is not a valid int value.

 If you want to learn more about strconv.Atoi(), you should execute go doc strconv.Atoi in your terminal window.

You might wonder what happens if you want to create your own error messages. Is this possible? Should you wish to return a custom error, you can use errors.New() from the errors package. This usually happens inside a function other than main() because main() does not return anything to any other function. Additionally, a good place to define your custom errors is inside the Go packages you create.

You will most likely work with errors in your programs without needing the functionality of the errors package. Additionally, *you are not going to need to define custom error messages unless you are creating big applications or packages*.

If you want to format your error messages in the way fmt.Printf() works, you can use the fmt.Errorf() function, which simplifies the creation of custom error messages—the fmt.Errorf() function returns an error value just like errors.New().

Now, we should talk about something important: you should have a global error-handling tactic in each application that should not change. In practice, this means the following:

- All error messages should be handled at the same level, which means that all errors should either be returned to the calling function or be handled at the place they occurred.
- The handling of critical errors should be clearly documented. This means that there will be situations where a critical error should terminate the program and other times where a critical error might just create a warning message onscreen and continue.
- It is considered a good practice to send all error messages to the log service of your machine because this way the error messages can be examined later. However, this is not always true, so exercise caution when setting this up—for example, cloud-native apps do not work that way. For cloud-native apps it is better to send the error output to standard error so that the error messages do not get lost.

 The error data type is defined as an interface—interfaces are covered in *Chapter 5, Reflection and Interfaces*.

Type the following code in your favorite text editor and save it as error.go in the directory where you put the code for this chapter. Using ch02 as the directory name is a good idea.

```
package main
import (
    "errors"
```

```
        "fmt"

        "os"

        "strconv"

    )
```

The first part is the preamble of the program—error.go uses the fmt, os, strconv, and errors packages.

```
    func check(a, b int) error {

        if a == 0 && b == 0 {

            return errors.New("this is a custom error message")

        }

        return nil

    }
```

The preceding code implements a function named check() that returns an error value. If both input parameters of check() are equal to 0, the function returns a custom error message using errors.New()—otherwise it returns nil.

```
    func formattedError(a, b int) error {

        if a == 0 && b == 0 {

            return fmt.Errorf("a %d and b %d. UserID: %d", a, b, os.Getuid())

        }

        return nil

    }
```

The preceding code implements formattedError(), which is a function that returns a formatted error message using fmt.Errorf(). Among other things, the error message prints the user ID of the user who executed the program with a call to os.Getuid(). When you want to create a custom error message, using fmt.Errorf() gives you more control over the output.

```
    func main() {

        err := check(0, 10)

        if err == nil {

            fmt.Println("check() executed normally!")

        } else {

            fmt.Println(err)

        }

        err = check(0, 0)
```

```go
    if err.Error() == "this is a custom error message" {
        fmt.Println("Custom error detected!")
    }

    err = formattedError(0, 0)
    if err != nil {
        fmt.Println(err)
    }

    i, err := strconv.Atoi("-123")
    if err == nil {
        fmt.Println("Int value is", i)
    }

    i, err = strconv.Atoi("Y123")
    if err != nil {
        fmt.Println(err)
    }
}
```

The preceding code is the implementation of the main() function where you can see the use of the if err != nil statement multiple times as well as the use of if err == nil, which is used to make sure that everything was OK before executing the desired code.

Bear in mind that although the preceding code compares an error message, this is considered a bad practice. It is better to print an error message when it is not nil.

Running error.go produces the following output:

```
$ go run error.go
check() ended normally!
Custom error detected!
a 0 and b 0. UserID: 501
Int value is -123
strconv.Atoi: parsing "Y123": invalid syntax
```

Now that you know about the error data type, how to create custom errors, and how to use error values, we will continue with the basic data types of Go that can be logically divided into two main categories: *numeric data types* and *non-numeric data types*. Go also supports the bool data type, which can have a value of true or false only.

Numeric data types

Go supports integer, floating-point, and complex number values in various versions depending on the memory space they consume—this saves memory and computing time. Integer data types can be either signed or unsigned, which is not the case for floating-point numbers.

The table that follows lists the numeric data types of Go.

Data Type	Description
int8	8-bit signed integer
int16	16-bit signed integer
int32	32-bit signed integer
int64	64-bit signed integer
int	32- or 64-bit signed integer
uint8	8-bit unsigned integer
uint16	16-bit unsigned integer
uint32	32-bit unsigned integer
uint64	64-bit unsigned integer
uint	32- or 64-bit unsigned integer
float32	32-bit floating-point number
float64	64-bit floating-point number
complex64	Complex number with float32 parts
complex128	Complex number with float64 parts

The int and uint data types are special as they are the most efficient sizes for signed and unsigned integers on a given platform and can be either 32 or 64 bits each — their size is defined by Go itself based on the CPU register size. The int data type is the most widely used numeric data type in Go due to its versatility.

The code that follows illustrates the use of numeric data types—you can find the entire program as numbers.go inside the ch02 directory of the book GitHub repository:

```go
func main() {
    c1 := 12 + 1i
    c2 := complex(5, 7)
    fmt.Printf("Type of c1: %T\n", c1)
    fmt.Printf("Type of c2: %T\n", c2)
```

The preceding code creates two complex variables in two different ways—both ways are perfectly valid and equivalent. Unless you are into mathematics, you will most likely not use complex numbers in your programs. However, the direct support for complex numbers shows how modern Go is.

```
var c3 complex64 = complex64(c1 + c2)
fmt.Println("c3:", c3)
fmt.Printf("Type of c3: %T\n", c3)
cZero := c3 - c3
fmt.Println("cZero:", cZero)
```

The preceding code continues to work with complex numbers by adding and subtracting two pairs of them. Although cZero is equal to zero, it is still a complex number and a complex64 variable.

```
x := 12
k := 5
fmt.Println(x)
fmt.Printf("Type of x: %T\n", x)
div := x / k
fmt.Println("div", div)
```

In this part, we define two integer variables named x and k—their data type is identified by Go based on their initial values. Both are of type int, which is what Go prefers to use for storing integer values. Additionally, when you divide two integer values, you get an integer result even when the division is not perfect. Therefore, if this is not what you want, you should take extra actions—this is shown in the next code excerpt:

```
var m, n float64
m = 1.223
fmt.Println("m, n:", m, n)
y := 4 / 2.3
fmt.Println("y:", y)
divFloat := float64(x) / float64(k)
fmt.Println("divFloat", divFloat)
fmt.Printf("Type of divFloat: %T\n", divFloat)
}
```

The preceding code works with float64 values and variables. As n does not have an initial value, it is automatically assigned with the zero value of its data type, which is 0 for the float64 data type. Additionally, the code presents a technique for dividing integer values and getting a floating-point result, which is the use of float64(): divFloat := float64(x) / float64(k).

This is a type conversion where two integers (x and k) are converted to float64 values. As the division between two float64 values is a float64 value, we get the result in the desired data type.

Running numbers.go creates the following output:

```
$ go run numbers.go
Type of c1: complex128
Type of c2: complex128
c3: (17+8i)
Type of c3: complex64
cZero: (0+0i)
12
Type of x: int
div 2
m, n: 1.223 0
y: 1.7391304347826086
divFloat 2.4
Type of divFloat: float64
```

The output shows that both c1 and c2 are complex128 values, which is the preferred complex data type for the machine on which the code was executed. However, c3 is a complex64 value because it was created using complex64(). The value of n is 0 because the n variable was not initialized, which means that Go automatically assigned the zero value of its data type to n.

Avoiding overflows

As each variable is stored in memory (bits), there is a limit to how much information we can store in the memory space of a variable. Although in this subsection we are going to talk about integers, similar rules apply to all numeric data types. Go comes with constants in the math package that represent the maximum and minimum values of integer data types. For example, for the int data type, there exist the math.MaxInt and math.MinInt constants that represent the maximum and minimum allowed values of an int variable, respectively.

The important part of overflows.go can be found in two for loops. The first one concerns determining the maximum int value:

```
for {
    if i == math.MaxInt {
        break
```

```
    }
    i = i + 1
}
```

In the preceding code, we keep increasing the value of i until it reaches math.MaxInt.

The next for loop is about finding out the minimum int value:

```
for {
    if i == math.MinInt {
        break
    }
    i = i - 1
}
```

This time, we keep decreasing the value of i until it reaches math.MinInt.

Running overflows.go produces the following output:

```
$ go run overflows.go
Max: 9223372036854775807
Max overflow: -9223372036854775808
Min: -9223372036854775808
```

Therefore, the maximum int value on the current platform (MacBook Pro with M1 Max CPU) is 9223372036854775807 and the minimum int value is -9223372036854775808. When we try to increase the maximum int value, we will get the minimum int value instead!

After learning about numeric data types, it is time to learn about non-numeric data types, which is the subject of the next section.

Non-numeric data types

Go has support for strings, characters, runes, dates, and times. However, Go does not have a dedicated char data type. In Go, dates and times are the same thing and are represented by the same data type. However, it is up to you to determine whether a time and date variable contains valid information or not.

We begin by explaining the string-related data types.

Strings, characters, and runes

Go supports the `string` data type for representing strings—strings are enclosed within either double quotes or back quotes. A Go string is just *a collection of bytes* and can be accessed as a whole or as an array. A single byte can store any ASCII character—however, ***multiple bytes are usually needed for storing a single Unicode character***.

Nowadays, supporting Unicode characters is a common requirement—Go was designed with Unicode support in mind, which is the main reason for having the rune data type. A rune is an `int32` value that is used for representing a single Unicode code point, which is an integer value that is used for representing single Unicode characters or, less frequently, providing formatting information.

 Although a rune is an `int32` value, you cannot compare a rune with an `int32` value. Go considers these two data types as totally different.

You can create a new *byte slice* from a given string by using a `[]byte("A String")` statement. Given a byte slice variable b, you can convert it into a string using the `string(b)` statement. ***When working with byte slices that contain Unicode characters, the number of bytes in a byte slice is not always connected to the number of characters in the byte slice, because most Unicode characters require more than one byte for their representation***. As a result, when you try to print each single byte of a byte slice using `fmt.Println()` or `fmt.Print()`, the output is not text presented as characters but instead integer values. If you want to print the contents of a byte slice as text, you should either print it using `string(byteSliceVar)` or using `fmt.Printf()` with %s to tell `fmt.Printf()` that you want to print a string. You can initialize a new byte slice with the desired string by using a statement such as `[]byte("My Initialization String")`.

 We will cover byte slices in more detail in the *Byte slices* section.

You can define a rune using single quotes: `r := '€'` and you can print the integer value of the bytes that compose it as `fmt.Println(r)`—in this case, the integer value is 8364. Printing it as a single Unicode character requires the use of the %c control string in `fmt.Printf()`.

As strings can be accessed as arrays, you can iterate over the runes of the string using a for loop or point to a specific character if you know its place in the string. The length of the string is the same as the number of characters found in the string, which is usually not true for byte slices because Unicode characters usually require more than one byte.

The following Go code illustrates the use of strings and runes and how you can work with strings in your code. You can find the entire program as text.go in the ch02 directory of the GitHub repository of the book.

The first part of the program defines a string literal that contains a Unicode character. Then it accesses its first byte as if the string were an array:

```go
func main() {
    aString := "Hello World! €"
    fmt.Println("First byte", string(aString[0]))
```

The next part is about working with runes:

```go
    r := '€'
    fmt.Println("As an int32 value:", r)
    // Convert Runes to text
    fmt.Printf("As a string: %s and as a character: %c\n", r, r)
    // Print an existing string as runes
    for _, v := range aString {
        fmt.Printf("%x ", v)
    }
    fmt.Println()
```

First, we define a rune named r. What makes this a rune is the use of single quotes around the € character. The rune is an int32 value and is printed as such by fmt.Println(). The %c control string in fmt.Printf() prints a rune as a character. Then we iterate over aString as a slice or an array using a for loop with range and print the contents of aString as runes.

```go
    // Print an existing string as characters
    for _, v := range aString {
        fmt.Printf("%c", v)
    }
    fmt.Println()
}
```

Lastly, we iterate over aString as a slice or an array using a for loop with range and print the contents of aString as characters.

Running text.go produces the following output:

```
$ go run text.go
First byte H
As an int32 value: 8364
As a string: %!s(int32=8364) and as a character: €
48 65 6c 6c 6f 20 57 6f 72 6c 64 21 20 20ac
Hello World! €
```

The first line of the output shows that we can access a string as an array whereas the second line verifies that a rune is an integer value. The third line shows what to expect when you print a rune as a string and as a character—the correct way is to print it as a character. The fifth line shows how to print a string as runes and the last line shows the output of processing a string as characters using range and a for loop.

Converting int to string

You can convert an integer value into a string in two main ways: using string() and using a function from the strconv package. However, the two methods are fundamentally different. The string() function converts an integer value into a Unicode code point, which is a single character, whereas functions such as strconv.FormatInt() and strconv.Itoa() convert an integer value into a string value with the same representation and the same number of characters.

This is illustrated in the intString.go program—its most important statements are the following. You can find the entire program in the GitHub repository of the book.

```
input := strconv.Itoa(n)
input = strconv.FormatInt(int64(n), 10)
input = string(n)
```

Running intString.go generates the following kind of output:

```
$ go run intString.go 100
strconv.Itoa() 100 of type string
strconv.FormatInt() 100 of type string
string() d of type string
```

The data type of the output is always string, however, string() converted 100 into d because the ASCII representation of d is 100.

Now that we have looked at converting integers into strings, it is time to learn how to work with Unicode text and code points.

The unicode package

The unicode standard Go package contains various handy functions for working with Unicode code points. One of them, which is called unicode.IsPrint(), can help you to identify the parts of a string that are printable using runes.

The following code excerpt illustrates the functionality of the unicode package:

```
for i := 0; i < len(sL); i++ {
    if unicode.IsPrint(rune(sL[i])) {
        fmt.Printf("%c\n", sL[i])
    } else {
        fmt.Println("Not printable!")
    }
}
```

The for loop iterates over the contents of a string defined as a list of runes ("\x99\x00ab\x50\x00\x23\x50\x29\x9c") while unicode.IsPrint() examines whether the character is printable or not—if it returns true then a rune is printable.

You can find this code excerpt inside the unicode.go source file in the ch02 directory in the GitHub repository of the book. Running unicode.go produces the following output:

```
Not printable!
Not printable!
a
b
P
Not printable!
#
P
)
Not printable!
```

This utility is very handy for filtering input or filtering data before printing it on screen, storing it in log files, transferring it on a network, or storing it in a database.

In the next subsection, we continue working with text with the help of the strings package.

The strings package

The strings standard Go package allows you to manipulate UTF-8 strings in Go and includes many powerful functions. Many of these functions are illustrated in the useStrings.go source file, which can be found in the ch02 directory of the book GitHub repository.

If you are working with text and text processing, you need to learn all the details and functions of the strings package, so make sure that you experiment with all these functions and create many examples that will help you to clarify things.

The most important parts of useStrings.go are the following:

```go
import (
    "fmt"
    s "strings"
    "unicode"
)
var f = fmt.Printf
```

As we are going to use the strings package multiple times, we create a convenient alias for it named s – note that this is considered a bad practice and that we are just doing that here to prevent the lines from getting too long. We do the same for the fmt.Printf() function where we create a global alias using a variable named f. These two shortcuts reduce the amount of long, repeated lines of code. You can use them when learning Go, but this is not recommended in any kind of production software as it makes the code less readable.

The first code excerpt is the following:

```go
        f("To Upper: %s\n", s.ToUpper("Hello THERE"))
        f("To Lower: %s\n", s.ToLower("Hello THERE"))

        f("%s\n", s.Title("tHis wiLL be A title!"))
        f("EqualFold: %v\n", s.EqualFold("Mihalis", "MIHAlis"))
        f("EqualFold: %v\n", s.EqualFold("Mihalis", "MIHAli"))
```

The strings.EqualFold() function compares two strings without considering their case and returns true when they are the same and false otherwise.

```go
        f("Index: %v\n", s.Index("Mihalis", "ha"))
        f("Index: %v\n", s.Index("Mihalis", "Ha"))
```

```
f("Count: %v\n", s.Count("Mihalis", "i"))
f("Count: %v\n", s.Count("Mihalis", "I"))
f("Repeat: %s\n", s.Repeat("ab", 5))


f("TrimSpace: %s\n", s.TrimSpace(" \tThis is a line. \n"))
f("TrimLeft: %s", s.TrimLeft(" \tThis is a\t line. \n", "\n\t "))
f("TrimRight: %s\n", s.TrimRight(" \tThis is a\t line. \n", "\n\t "))
```

The `strings.Index()` function checks whether the string of the second parameter can be found in the string that is given as the first parameter and returns the index where it was found for the first time. On an unsuccessful search, it returns -1.

```
f("Prefix: %v\n", s.HasPrefix("Mihalis", "Mi"))
f("Prefix: %v\n", s.HasPrefix("Mihalis", "mi"))
f("Suffix: %v\n", s.HasSuffix("Mihalis", "is"))
f("Suffix: %v\n", s.HasSuffix("Mihalis", "IS"))
```

The `strings.HasPrefix()` function checks whether the given string, which is the first parameter, begins with the string that is given as the second parameter. In the preceding code, the first call to `strings.HasPrefix()` returns true, whereas the second returns false. Similarly, `strings.HasSuffix()` checks whether the given string ends with the second string. Both functions consider the case of the input string and the case of the second parameter.

```
t := s.Fields("This is a string!")
f("Fields: %v\n", len(t))
t = s.Fields("ThisIs a\tstring!")
f("Fields: %v\n", len(t))
```

The handy `strings.Fields()` function splits the given string around one or more whitespace characters as defined by the `unicode.IsSpace()` function and returns a slice of substrings found in the input string. If the input string contains whitespace characters only, it returns an empty slice.

```
f("%s\n", s.Split("abcd efg", ""))
f("%s\n", s.Replace("abcd efg", "", "_", -1))
f("%s\n", s.Replace("abcd efg", "", "_", 4))
f("%s\n", s.Replace("abcd efg", "", "_", 2))
```

The `strings.Split()` function allows you to split the given string according to the desired separator string—the `strings.Split()` function returns a string slice. Using "" as the second parameter of `strings.Split()` allows you to *process a string character by character*.

The strings.Replace() function takes four parameters. The first parameter is the string that you want to process. The second parameter contains the string that, if found, will be replaced by the third parameter of strings.Replace(). The last parameter is the maximum number of replacements that are allowed to happen. If that parameter has a negative value, then there is no limit to the allowed number of replacements.

```
f("SplitAfter: %s\n", s.SplitAfter("123++432++", "++"))
trimFunction := func(c rune) bool {
    return !unicode.IsLetter(c)
}
f("TrimFunc: %s\n", s.TrimFunc("123 abc ABC \t .", trimFunction))
```

The strings.SplitAfter() function splits its first parameter string into substrings based on the separator string that is given as the second parameter to the function. The separator string is included in the returned slice.

The last lines of code define a trim function named trimFunction that is used as the second parameter to strings.TrimFunc() in order to filter the given input based on the return value of the trim function—in this case, the trim function keeps all letters and nothing else due to the unicode.IsLetter() call.

Running useStrings.go produces the following output:

```
To Upper: HELLO THERE!
To Lower: hello there
THis WiLL Be A Title!
EqualFold: true
EqualFold: false
Prefix: true
Prefix: false
Suffix: true
Suffix: false
Index: 2
Index: -1
Count: 2
Count: 0
Repeat: abababab
```

```
TrimSpace: This is a line.
TrimLeft: This is a        line.
TrimRight:        This is a        line.
Compare: 1
Compare: 0
Compare: -1
Fields: 4
Fields: 3
[a b c d   e f g]
_a_b_c_d_ _e_f_g_
_a_b_c_d efg
_a_bcd efg
Join: Line 1+++Line 2+++Line 3
SplitAfter: [123++ 432++ ]
TrimFunc: abc ABC
```

Visit the documentation page of the strings package at https://pkg.go.dev/strings for the complete list of available functions. You will see the functionality of the strings package in other places in this book.

Enough with strings and text, the next section is about working with dates and times in Go.

Times and dates

Often, we need to work with date and time information to store the time an entry was last used in a database or the time an entry was inserted into a database.

The king of working with times and dates in Go is the time.Time data type, which represents an instant in time with nanosecond precision. Each time.Time value is associated with a location (time zone).

If you are a UNIX person, you might already know about the UNIX epoch time and wonder how to get it in Go. The time.Now().Unix() function returns the popular UNIX epoch time, which is the number of seconds that have elapsed since 00:00:00 UTC, January 1, 1970. If you want to convert the UNIX time to the equivalent time.Time value, you can use the time.Unix() function. If you are not a UNIX person, then you might not have heard about the UNIX epoch time before, but now you know what it is!

The time.Since() function calculates the time that has passed since a given time and returns a time.Duration variable—the duration data type is defined as type Duration int64. Although a Duration is, in reality, an int64 value, you cannot compare or convert a duration to an int64 value implicitly because Go does not allow implicit data type conversions.

The single most important topic about Go and dates and times is the way Go parses a string in order to convert it into a date and a time. The reason this is important is that usually such input is given as a string and not as a valid date variable. The function used for parsing is called time. Parse() and its full signature is Parse(layout, value string) (Time, error), where layout is the parse string and value is the input that is being parsed. The time.Time value that is returned is a moment in time with nanosecond precision and contains both date and time information.

The next table shows the most widely used strings for parsing dates and times.

Parse Value	Meaning (examples)
03	12-hour value (12pm, 07am)
15	24-hour value (23, 07)
04	Minutes (55, 15)
05	Seconds (5, 23)
Mon	Abbreviated day of week (Tue, Fri)
Monday	Day of week (Tuesday, Friday)
02	Day of month (15, 31)
2006	Year with 4 digits (2020, 2004)
06	Year with the last 2 digits (20, 04)
Jan	Abbreviated month name (Feb, Mar)
January	Full month name (July, August)
MST	Time zone (EST, UTC)

The previous table shows that if you want to parse the 30 January 2023 string and convert it into a Go date variable, you should match it against the 02 January 2006 string because this string indicates the expected format of the input—you cannot use anything else in its place when matching a string like 30 January 2023. Similarly, if you want to parse the 15 August 2023 10:00 string, you should match it against the 02 January 2006 15:04 string because this specifies the expected format of the input.

The documentation of the time package (https://pkg.go.dev/time) contains even more detailed information about parsing dates and times—however, the ones presented here should be more than enough for regular use.

Now that we know how to work with dates and times, it is time to learn more about working with time zones.

Working with different time zones

The presented utility accepts a date and a time and converts them into different time zones. This can be particularly handy when you want to preprocess log files from different sources that use different time zones to convert these different time zones into a common one. Once again, you need time.Parse() in order to convert a valid input into a time.Time value before doing the conversions. This time the input string contains the time zone and is parsed by the "02 January 2006 15:04 MST" string.

In order to convert the parsed date and time into New York time, the program uses the following code:

```
loc, _ = time.LoadLocation("America/New_York")
fmt.Printf("New York Time: %s\n", now.In(loc))
```

This technique is used multiple times in convertTimes.go.

 If a command line argument contains any space characters, you should put it in double quotes for the UNIX shell to treat it as a single command line argument.

Running convertTimes.go generates the following output:

```
$ go run convertTimes.go "14 December 2023 19:20 EET"
Current Location: 2023-12-14 19:20:00 +0200 EET
New York Time: 2023-12-14 12:20:00 -0500 EST
London Time: 2023-12-14 17:20:00 +0000 GMT
Tokyo Time: 2023-12-15 02:20:00 +0900 JST
$ go run convertTimes.go "14 December 2023 19:20 UTC"
Current Location: 2023-12-14 21:20:00 +0200 EET
New York Time: 2023-12-14 14:20:00 -0500 EST
London Time: 2023-12-14 19:20:00 +0000 GMT
```

```
Tokyo Time: 2023-12-15 04:20:00 +0900 JST
$ go run convertTimes.go "14 December 2023 25:00 EET"
parsing time "14 December 2023 25:00 EET": hour out of range
```

In the last execution of the program, the code must parse 25 as the hour of the day, which is wrong and generates the hour out of range error message.

There is a known Go issue related to the parsing of times and dates that you can learn about at https://github.com/golang/go/issues/63345.

The next subsection is about constant values.

Constants

Go supports constants, which behave like variables but cannot change their values. Constants in Go are defined with the help of the const keyword. Constants can be either *global or local*. However, if you are defining too many constant values with a local scope, you might need to rethink your approach.

The main benefit you get from using constants in your programs is the guarantee that their value will not change during program execution. Strictly speaking, the value of a constant variable is defined at compile time, not at runtime—this means that it is included in the binary executable. Behind the scenes, Go uses Boolean, string, or numeric as the type for storing constant values because this gives Go more flexibility when dealing with constants.

Some possible uses of constants include defining configuration values such as the maximum number of connections or the TCP/IP port number used and defining physical constants such as the speed of light or the gravity on earth.

The next subsection discusses the constant generator iota, which is a handy way of creating sequences of constants.

The constant generator iota

The *constant generator iota* is used for declaring a sequence of related values that use incrementing numbers without the need to explicitly type each one of them.

The concepts related to the const keyword, including the constant generator iota, are illustrated in the constants.go file.

```
type Digit int
type Power2 int
```

```
const PI = 3.1415926
const (
    C1 = "C1C1C1"
    C2 = "C2C2C2"
    C3 = "C3C3C3"
)
```

In this part, we declare two new types named Digit and Power2 that will be used in a while, and four new constants named PI, C1, C2, and C3.

 A Go type is a way of defining a new named type that uses the same underlying type as an existing type. This is mainly used for differentiating between different types that might use the same kind of data. The type keyword can also be used for defining structures and interfaces, which is not the case here.

```
func main() {
    const s1 = 123
    var v1 float32 = s1 * 12
    fmt.Println(v1)
    fmt.Println(PI)
    const (
        Zero Digit = iota
        One
        Two
        Three
        Four
    )
```

The preceding code defines a constant named s1. Here you also see the definition of a constant generator iota based on Digit, which is equivalent to the next declaration of five constants:

```
const (
    Zero = 0
    One = 1
    Two = 2
    Three = 3
    Four = 4
)
```

Although we are defining constants inside `main()`, constants can normally be found outside of `main()` or any other function or method.

The last part of `constants.go` is as follows:

```
        fmt.Println(One)
        fmt.Println(Two)
        const (
            p2_0 Power2 = 1 << iota

            _

            p2_2

            _

            p2_4

            _

            p2_6
        )
        fmt.Println("2^0:", p2_0)
        fmt.Println("2^2:", p2_2)
        fmt.Println("2^4:", p2_4)
        fmt.Println("2^6:", p2_6)
    }
```

There is another constant generator iota here that is different than the previous one. Firstly, you can see the use of the underscore character in a `const` block with a constant generator iota, which allows you to skip unwanted values. Secondly, the value of iota always increments and can be used in expressions, which is what occurred in this case.

Now let us see what really happens inside the `const` block. For p2_0, iota has the value of 0 and p2_0 is defined as 1. For p2_2, iota has the value of 2 and p2_2 is defined as the result of the expression `1 << 2`, which is `00000100` in binary representation. The decimal value of `00000100` is 4, which is the result and the value of p2_2. Analogously, the value of p2_4 is 16 and the value of p2_6 is 64.

Running `constants.go` produces the following output:

```
$ go run constants.go
1476
3.1415926
1
2
2^0: 1
```

```
2^2: 4
2^4: 16
2^6: 64
```

Typed and untyped constants

Constant values can have a data type. This can be restrictive because a constant value with a data type can only operate with values and variables of the same data type, but it can save you from bugs because the compiler can catch such situations.

The code excerpt from `typedConstants.go` is going to show the difference between *typed* and *untyped constants*:

```
const (
    typedConstant   = int16(100)
    untypedConstant = 100
)

func main() {
    i := int(1)
    fmt.Println("unTyped:", i*untypedConstant)
    fmt.Println("Typed:", i*typedConstant)
}
```

So, `untypedConstant` does not have a data type associated with it whereas `typedConstant` does. If you try to run `typedConstants.go`, the compiler is not going to be able to compile it and it is going to produce the following error output:

```
$ go run typedConstants.go
# command-line-arguments
./typedConstants.go:13:24: invalid operation: i * typedConstant
(mismatched types int and int16)
```

The cause of the error condition can be found in the generated output: `mismatched types int and int16`. Put simply, `i` is an `int` variable whereas `typedConstant` is an `int16` value and Go is unable to perform their multiplication because the data types of the variables do not match. On the other hand, there are no issues with the `i*untypedConstant` multiplication because `untypedConstant` does not have a data type.

Having data is good but what happens when you have lots of similar data? Do you need to have lots of variables to hold this data or is there a better way to do so? Go answers these questions by introducing arrays and slices.

Grouping similar data

There are times when you want to keep multiple values of the same data type under a single variable and access them using an index number. The simplest way to do that in Go is by using arrays or slices. *Arrays* are the most widely used data structures and can be found in almost all programming languages due to their simplicity and speed of access. Go provides an alternative to arrays that is called a *slice*. The subsections that follow help you understand the differences between arrays and slices so that you know which data structure to use and when. The quick answer is that *you can use slices instead of arrays almost anywhere in Go,* but we are also demonstrating arrays because they can still be useful and because slices are implemented by Go using arrays!

Arrays

We are going to begin our discussion about arrays by examining their core characteristics and limitations:

- When defining an array variable, you must define its size. Otherwise, you should put [...] in the array declaration and let the Go compiler find out the length for you. So you can create an array with 4 string elements either as [4]string{"Zero", "One", "Two", "Three"} or as [...]string{"Zero", "One", "Two", "Three"}. If you put nothing in the square brackets, then a slice is going to be created instead. As it contains four elements, the (valid) indexes for that array are 0, 1, 2, and 3.

- You cannot change the size of an array after you have created it.

- When you pass an array to a function, *Go creates a copy of that array* and passes that copy to that function—therefore any changes you make to an array inside a function are lost when the function exits.

As a result, arrays in Go are not very powerful, which is the main reason that Go has introduced an additional data structure named slice that is like an array but is dynamic in nature, as explained in the next subsection. However, data in both arrays and slices is accessed the same way.

Slices

Slices in Go are more powerful than arrays mainly because they are dynamic, which means that they can grow or shrink after creation as needed. Additionally, any changes you make to a slice inside a function also affect the original slice. Keep in mind that this is usually the case, but it is not always true—as discussed in a while, all slices have an underlying array for storing the data. Only changes that do not cause an allocation of the underlying array are reflected back to the caller function. However, functions working with slices do not usually change the size of the slice.

But how does this happen? Strictly speaking, *all parameters in Go are passed by value*—there is no other way to pass parameters in Go. However, you can explicitly pass a pointer to a variable in order to pass by reference. A *slice value is a header that contains a pointer to an underlying array where the elements are actually stored, the length of the array, and its capacity*—the capacity of a slice is explained in the next subsection. Note that the slice value does not include its elements, *just a pointer to the underlying array*. So, when you pass a slice to a function, Go makes a copy of that header and passes it to the function. This copy of the slice header includes the pointer to the underlying array. That slice header is defined in the `reflect` package (`https://pkg.go.dev/reflect#SliceHeader`) as follows:

```
type SliceHeader struct {
    Data uintptr
    Len  int
    Cap  int
}
```

 A side effect of passing the slice header is that it is faster to pass a slice to a function because Go does not need to make a copy of the slice and its elements, just a copy of the slice header.

You can create a slice using `make()` or like an array without specifying its size or using `[...]`. If you do not want to initialize a slice, then using `make()` is better and faster. However, if you want to initialize it at the time of creation, then `make()` cannot help you. As a result, you can create a slice with three `float64` elements as `aSlice := []float64{1.2, 3.2, -4.5}`. Creating a slice with space for three `float64` elements with `make()` is as simple as executing `make([]float64, 3)`. Each element of that slice has a value of `0`, which is the zero value of the `float64` data type.

Both slices and arrays can have many dimensions—creating a slice with two dimensions with `make()` is as simple as writing `make([][]int, 2)`. This returns a slice with two dimensions where the first dimension is 2 (rows) and the second dimension (columns) is unspecified and should be explicitly specified when adding data to it.

If you want to define and initialize a slice with two dimensions at the same time, you should execute something similar to `twoD := [][]int{{1, 2, 3}, {4, 5, 6}}`.

You can find the length of an array or a slice using `len()`. You can add new elements to a full slice using the `append()` function. `append()` automatically allocates the required memory space. Keep in mind that you should assign the return value of `append()` back to the desired variable as this is not an in-place change.

The example that follows clarifies many things about slices—feel free to experiment with it. Type the following code and save it as goSlices.go:

```go
package main
import "fmt"
func main() {
    // Create an empty slice
    aSlice := []float64{}
    // Both length and capacity are 0 because aSlice is empty
    fmt.Println(aSlice, len(aSlice), cap(aSlice))
    // Add elements to a slice
    aSlice = append(aSlice, 1234.56)
    aSlice = append(aSlice, -34.0)
    fmt.Println(aSlice, "with length", len(aSlice))
```

The append() commands add two new elements to aSlice. As stated before, the result of append() is not in-place and must be assigned to the desired variable.

```go
    // A slice with a length of 4
    t := make([]int, 4)
    t[0] = -1
    t[1] = -2
    t[2] = -3
    t[3] = -4
    // Now you will need to use append
    t = append(t, -5)
    fmt.Println(t)
```

Once a slice has no place left for more elements, you can only add new elements to it using append().

```go
    // A 2D slice
    twoD := [][]int{{1, 2, 3}, {4, 5, 6}}
    // Visiting all elements of a 2D slice
    // with a double for loop
    for _, i := range twoD {
        for _, k := range i {
            fmt.Print(k, " ")
        }
```

```
                fmt.Println()
    }
```

The preceding code shows how to create a 2D slice variable named twoD and initialize it at the same time.

```
    make2D := make([][]int, 2)
    fmt.Println(make2D)
    make2D[0] = []int{1, 2, 3, 4}
    make2D[1] = []int{-1, -2, -3, -4}
    fmt.Println(make2D)
}
```

The previous part shows how to create a 2D slice with make(). What makes the make2D a 2D slice is the use of [][]int in make().

Running goSlices.go produces the following output:

```
$ go run goSlices.go
[] 0 0
[1234.56 -34] with length 2
[-1 -2 -3 -4 -5]
1 2 3
4 5 6
[[] []]
[[1 2 3 4] [-1 -2 -3 -4]]
```

About slice length and capacity

Both arrays and slices support the len() function for finding out their length. However, slices also have an additional property called *capacity* that can be found using the cap() function. The capacity of a slice is important when you want to select a part of a slice or when you want to reference an array using a slice.

The capacity shows how much a slice can be expanded without the need to allocate more memory and change the underlying array. Although after slice creation the capacity of a slice is handled by Go, a developer can define the capacity of a slice at creation time using the make() function—after that, the capacity of the slice doubles each time the length of the slice is about to become bigger than its current capacity. The first argument of make() is the type of the slice and its dimensions, the second is its initial length, and the third, which is optional, is the capacity of the slice. Although the data type of a slice cannot change after creation, the other two properties can change.

Writing something like make([]int, 3, 2) generates an error message because at any given time the capacity of a slice (2) cannot be smaller than its length (3).

The figure that follows illustrates how length and capacity work in slices.

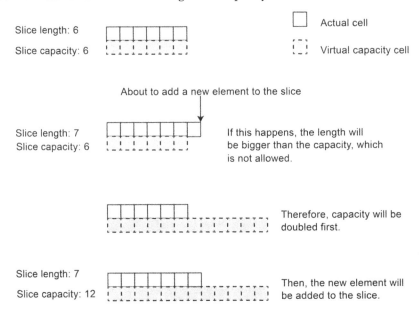

Figure 2.1: How slice length and capacity are related

For those of you that prefer code, here is a small Go program that showcases the length and capacity properties of slices. Type it and save it as capLen.go:

```
package main
import "fmt"
func main() {
    // Only length is defined. Capacity = length
    a := make([]int, 4)
```

In this case, the capacity of a is the same as its length, which is 4.

```
    fmt.Println("L:", len(a), "C:", cap(a))
    // Initialize slice. Capacity = length
    b := []int{0, 1, 2, 3, 4}
    fmt.Println("L:", len(b), "C:", cap(b))
```

Once again, the capacity of slice b is the same as its length, which is 5 because this is the default behavior.

```
// Same length and capacity
aSlice := make([]int, 4, 4)
fmt.Println(aSlice)
```

This time the capacity of slice aSlice is the same as its length, not because Go decided to do so but because we specified it in the make() call.

```
// Add an element
aSlice = append(aSlice, 5)
```

When you add a new element to slice aSlice, its capacity is doubled and becomes 8.

```
fmt.Println(aSlice)
// The capacity is doubled
fmt.Println("L:", len(aSlice), "C:", cap(aSlice))
// Now add four elements
aSlice = append(aSlice, []int{-1, -2, -3, -4}...)
```

The ... operator expands []int{-1, -2, -3, -4} into multiple arguments and append() appends each argument one by one to aSlice.

```
fmt.Println(aSlice)
// The capacity is doubled
fmt.Println("L:", len(aSlice), "C:", cap(aSlice))
}
```

Running capLen.go produces the following output:

```
$ go run capLen.go
L: 4 C: 4
L: 5 C: 5
[0 0 0 0]
[0 0 0 0 5]
L: 5 C: 8
[0 0 0 0 5 -1 -2 -3 -4]
L: 9 C: 16
```

Setting the correct capacity of a slice, if known in advance, will make your programs faster because Go will not have to allocate a new underlying array and have all the data copied over. This is important when dealing with very large slices.

Working with slices is good but what happens when you want to work with a continuous part of an existing slice? Is there a practical way to select a part of a slice? Fortunately, the answer is yes—the next subsection sheds some light on selecting a continuous part of a slice.

Selecting a part of a slice

Go allows you to select parts of a slice, provided that all desired elements are next to each other. This can be handy when you select a range of elements and you do not want to give their indexes one by one. In Go, you select a part of a slice by specifying (directly or indirectly) two indexes, where the first one is the beginning of the selection and the second one is the end of the selection, without including the element at that index, separated by :.

 If you want to process all the command line arguments of a utility apart from the first one, which is its file path, you can assign it to a new variable (arguments := os.Args) for ease of use and use the arguments[1:] notation to skip the first command line argument.

However, there is a variation where you can add a third parameter that controls the capacity of the resulting slice. So, using aSlice[0:2:4] selects the first 2 elements of a slice (at indexes 0 and 1) and creates a new slice with a maximum capacity of 4. The resulting capacity is defined as the result of the 4-0 subtraction where 4 is the maximum capacity and 0 is the first index—if the first index is omitted, it is automatically set to 0. In this case, the capacity of the result slice will be 4 because 4-0 equals 4.

If we had used aSlice[2:4:4], we would have created a new slice with the aSlice[2] and aSlice[3] elements and with a capacity of 4-2. Lastly, the resulting capacity cannot be bigger than the capacity of the original slice because in that case, you would need a different underlying array.

Type the following code into your favorite editor and save it as partSlice.go:

```go
package main
import "fmt"
func main() {
    aSlice := []int{0, 1, 2, 3, 4, 5, 6, 7, 8, 9}
```

```
        fmt.Println(aSlice)
        l := len(aSlice)
        // First 5 elements
        fmt.Println(aSlice[0:5])
        // First 5 elements
        fmt.Println(aSlice[:5])
```

In this first part, we define a new slice named aSlice that has 10 elements. Its capacity is the same as its length. Both the 0:5 and :5 notations select the first 5 elements of the slice, which are the elements found at indexes 0, 1, 2, 3, and 4.

```
        // Last 2 elements
        fmt.Println(aSlice[l-2 : l])
        // Last 2 elements
        fmt.Println(aSlice[l-2:])
```

Given the length of the slice (l), we can select the last two elements of the slice either as l-2:l or as l-2:.

```
        // First 5 elements
        t := aSlice[0:5:10]
        fmt.Println(len(t), cap(t))
        // Elements at indexes 2,3,4
        // Capacity will be 10-2
        t = aSlice[2:5:10]
        fmt.Println(len(t), cap(t))
```

Initially, the capacity of t will be 10-0, which is 10. In the second case, the capacity of t will be 10-2.

```
        // Elements at indexes 0,1,2,3,4
        // New capacity will be 6-0
        t = aSlice[:5:6]
        fmt.Println(len(t), cap(t))
}
```

The capacity of t is now 6-0 and its length is going to be 5 because we have selected the first five elements of slice aSlice.

The output of partSlice.go is presented in small chunks:

```
$ go run partSlice.go
[0 1 2 3 4 5 6 7 8 9]
```

The previous line is the output of fmt.Println(aSlice).

```
[0 1 2 3 4]
[0 1 2 3 4]
```

The previous two lines are generated from fmt.Println(aSlice[0:5]) and fmt.Println(aSlice[:5]).

```
[8 9]
[8 9]
```

Analogously, the previous two lines are generated from fmt.Println(aSlice[1-2 : 1]) and fmt.Println(aSlice[1-2:]).

```
5 10
3 8
5 6
```

The last three lines print the length and the capacity of aSlice[0:5:10], aSlice[2:5:10], and aSlice[:5:6].

Byte slices

A byte slice is a slice of the byte data type ([]byte). Go knows that most byte slices are used to store strings and so makes it easy to switch between this type and the string type. There is nothing special in the way you can access a byte slice compared to the other types of slices. What is special is that *Go uses byte slices for performing file I/O operations because they allow you to determine with precision the amount of data you want to read or write to a file*. This happens because bytes are a universal unit among computer systems.

 As Go does not have a data type for storing single characters, it uses byte and rune for storing character values. A single byte can store a single ASCII character only whereas a rune can store Unicode characters. As a result, a rune can occupy multiple bytes.

The small program that follows illustrates how you can convert a byte slice into a string and vice versa, which you need for most file I/O operations—type it and save it as byteSlices.go:

```go
package main
import "fmt"
func main() {
```

```go
    // Byte slice
    b := make([]byte, 12)
    fmt.Println("Byte slice:", b)
```

An empty byte slice contains zeros—in this case, 12 zeros.

```go
    b = []byte("Byte slice €")
    fmt.Println("Byte slice:", b)
```

In this case, the size of b is the size of the string "Byte slice €", without the double quotes—b now points to a different memory location than before, which is where "Byte slice €" is stored. *This is how you convert a string into a byte slice.*

As Unicode characters like € need more than one byte for their representation, the length of the byte slice might not be the same as the length of the string that it stores.

```go
    // Print byte slice contents as text
    fmt.Printf("Byte slice as text: %s\n", b)
    fmt.Println("Byte slice as text:", string(b))
```

The preceding code shows how to print the contents of a byte slice as text using two techniques. The first one is by using the %s control string and the second one using string().

```go
    // Length of b
    fmt.Println("Length of b:", len(b))
}
```

The preceding code prints the real length of the byte slice.

Running byteSlices.go produces the following output:

```
$ go run byteSlices.go
Byte slice: [0 0 0 0 0 0 0 0 0 0 0 0]
Byte slice: [66 121 116 101 32 115 108 105 99 101 32 226 130 172]
Byte slice as text: Byte slice €
Byte slice as text: Byte slice €
Length of b: 14
```

The last line of the output proves that although the b byte slice contains 12 characters, it has a size of 14.

Deleting an element from a slice

There is no default function for deleting an element from a slice without using a package such as
slices, which means that if you need to delete an element from a slice, you must write your own
code. However, starting with Go 1.21, you can use slices.Delete() for that purpose. Therefore,
this subsection is relevant when using an older Go version or when you want to manually delete
an element.

Deleting an element from a slice can be tricky, so this subsection presents two techniques for doing
so. The first technique virtually divides the original slice into two slices, split at the index of the
element that needs to be deleted. Neither of the two slices includes the element that is going to
be deleted. After that, it concatenates these two slices and creates a new one.

The second technique copies the last element at the place of the element that is going to be deleted
and creates a new slice by excluding the last element from the original slice. However, this particular technique changes the order of the slice elements, which in some cases might be important.

The next figure shows a graphical representation of the two techniques for deleting an element
from a slice.

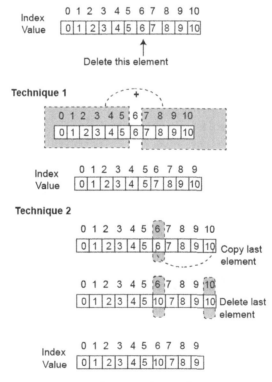

Figure 2.2: Deleting an element from a slice

The following program shows the two techniques that can be used for deleting an element from a slice. Create a text file by typing the following code—save it as deleteSlice.go.

```go
package main
import (
    "fmt"
    "os"
    "strconv"
)
func main() {
    arguments := os.Args
    if len(arguments) == 1 {
        fmt.Println("Need an integer value.")
        return
    }
    index := arguments[1]
    i, err := strconv.Atoi(index)
    if err != nil {
        fmt.Println(err)
        return
    }
    fmt.Println("Using index", i)
    aSlice := []int{0, 1, 2, 3, 4, 5, 6, 7, 8}
    fmt.Println("Original slice:", aSlice)
    // Delete element at index i
    if i > len(aSlice)-1 {
        fmt.Println("Cannot delete element", i)
        return
    }
    // The ... operator auto expands aSlice[i+1:] so that
    // its elements can be appended to aSlice[:i] one by one
    aSlice = append(aSlice[:i], aSlice[i+1:]...)
    fmt.Println("After 1st deletion:", aSlice)
```

Here we logically divide the original slice into two slices. The two slices are split at the index of the element that needs to be deleted. After that, we concatenate these two slices with the help of . . . .

Go supports the . . . operator, which is used for exploding a slice or an array into multiple arguments before appending it to an existing slice.

Next, we see the second technique in action:

```go
    // Delete element at index i
    if i > len(aSlice)-1 {
        fmt.Println("Cannot delete element", i)
        return
    }
    // Replace element at index i with last element
    aSlice[i] = aSlice[len(aSlice)-1]
    // Remove last element
    aSlice = aSlice[:len(aSlice)-1]
    fmt.Println("After 2nd deletion:", aSlice)
}
```

We replace the element that we want to delete with the last element using the aSlice[i] = aSlice[len(aSlice)-1] statement and then we remove the last element with the aSlice = aSlice[:len(aSlice)-1] statement.

Running deleteSlice.go produces the following kind of output, depending on your input:

```
$ go run deleteSlice.go 1
Using index 1
Original slice: [0 1 2 3 4 5 6 7 8]
After 1st deletion: [0 2 3 4 5 6 7 8]
After 2nd deletion: [0 8 3 4 5 6 7]
```

As the slice has nine elements, you can delete the element at index value 1.

```
$ go run deleteSlice.go 10
Using index 10
Original slice: [0 1 2 3 4 5 6 7 8]
Cannot delete element 10
```

As the slice has only nine elements, you cannot delete an element with an index value of 10 from the slice.

How slices are connected to arrays

As mentioned before, behind the scenes, *a slice is implemented using an underlying array.* The length of the underlying array is the same as the capacity of the slice and there exist pointers that connect the slice elements to the appropriate array elements.

You can understand that by connecting an existing array with a slice, Go allows you to reference an array or a part of an array using a slice. This has some strange capabilities including the fact that the changes to the slice affect the referenced array! However, when the capacity of the slice changes, the connection to the array ceases to exist! This happens because when the capacity of a slice changes, so does the underlying array, and the connection between the slice and the original array does not exist anymore.

Type the following code and save it as `sliceArrays.go`:

```go
package main
import (
    "fmt"
)
func change(s []string) {
    s[0] = "Change_function"
}
```

This is a function that changes the first element of its input slice.

```go
func main() {
    a := [4]string{"Zero", "One", "Two", "Three"}
    fmt.Println("a:", a)
```

Here we define an array named a with 4 elements.

```go
    var S0 = a[0:1]
    fmt.Println(S0)
    S0[0] = "S0"
```

Here we connect S0 with the first element of the array a and we print it. Then we change the value of S0[0].

```go
    var S12 = a[1:3]
    fmt.Println(S12)
    S12[0] = "S12_0"
    S12[1] = "S12_1"
```

In this part, we associate S12 with a[1] and a[2]. Therefore S12[0] = a[1] and S12[1] = a[2]. Then, we change the values of both S12[0] and S12[1]. These two changes will also change the contents of a. Put simply, a[1] takes the new value of S12[0] and a[2] takes the new value of S12[1].

```
fmt.Println("a:", a)
```

And we print variable a, which has not changed at all in a direct way. However, due to the connections of a with S0 and S12, the contents of a have changed!

```
// Changes to slice -> changes to array
change(S12)
fmt.Println("a:", a)
```

As the slice and the array are connected, any changes you make to the slice will also affect the array even if the changes take place inside a function.

```
// capacity of S0
fmt.Println("Capacity of S0:", cap(S0), "Length of S0:", len(S0))
// Adding 4 elements to S0
S0 = append(S0, "N1")
S0 = append(S0, "N2")
S0 = append(S0, "N3")
a[0] = "-N1"
```

As the capacity of S0 changes, it is no longer connected to the same underlying array (a).

```
// Changing the capacity of S0
// Not the same underlying array anymore!
S0 = append(S0, "N4")
fmt.Println("Capacity of S0:", cap(S0), "Length of S0:", len(S0))
// This change does not go to S0
a[0] = "-N1-"
// This change goes to S12
a[1] = "-N2-"
```

However, array a and slice S12 are still connected because the capacity of S12 has not changed.

```
fmt.Println("S0:", S0)
fmt.Println("a: ", a)
```

```
        fmt.Println("S12:", S12)
    }
```

Lastly, we print the final versions of a, S0, and S12.

Running sliceArrays.go produces the following output:

```
$ go run sliceArrays.go
a: [Zero One Two Three]
[Zero]
[One Two]
a: [S0 S12_0 S12_1 Three]
a: [S0 Change_function S12_1 Three]
Capacity of S0: 4 Length of S0: 1
Capacity of S0: 8 Length of S0: 5
S0: [-N1 N1 N2 N3 N4]
a:  [-N1- -N2- N2 N3]
S12: [-N2- N2]
```

The next subsection shows a technique for catching out of bound errors on slices as early as possible.

Catching out of bounds errors

In this subsection, we present a technique for catching out of bounds errors. The technique is illustrated with the help of two functions. The first function is the next:

```
func foo(s []int) int {
    return s[0] + s[1] + s[2] + s[3]
}
```

In the case of foo(), no bound checking is performed on slice s. This means that we can use any index on it without being sure that we will get that index in the first place and without the compiler performing any checks.

The second function is the following:

```
func bar(slice []int) int {
    a := (*[3]int)(slice)
    return a[0] + a[1] + a[2] + a[3]
}
```

Keep in mind that the compiler is not going to check the slice provided as a parameter to the function. However, the compiler is going to refuse to compile the preceding code. The generated error is going to be `invalid argument: index 3 out of bounds [0:3]`. The reason that the error was caught is that although we get three elements from `slice` and put them into a, we are using four elements from array a, which is clearly not allowed.

Let us now discuss the use of the copy() function in the next subsection.

The copy() function

Go offers the copy() function for copying an existing array to a slice or an existing slice to another slice. However, the use of copy() can be tricky because the destination slice is not auto-expanded if the source slice is bigger than the destination slice. Additionally, if the destination slice is bigger than the source slice, then copy() does not empty the elements from the destination slice that did not get copied. This is better illustrated in the figure that follows.

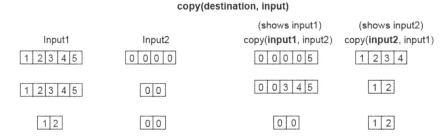

Figure 2.3: The use of the copy() function

The following program illustrates the use of copy()—type it in your favorite text editor and save it as copySlice.go:

```go
package main
import "fmt"
func main() {
    a1 := []int{1}
    a2 := []int{-1, -2}
    a5 := []int{10, 11, 12, 13, 14}
    fmt.Println("a1", a1)
    fmt.Println("a2", a2)
    fmt.Println("a5", a5)
    // copy(destination, input)
```

```
    // Len(a2) > Len(a1)
    copy(a1, a2)
    fmt.Println("a1", a1)
    fmt.Println("a2", a2)
```

Here we run the copy(a1, a2) command. In this case, the a2 slice is bigger than a1. After copy(a1, a2), a2 remains the same, which makes perfect sense as a2 is the input slice, whereas the first element of a2 is copied to the first element of a1 because a1 has space for a single element only.

```
    // Len(a5) > Len(a1)
    copy(a1, a5)
    fmt.Println("a1", a1)
    fmt.Println("a5", a5)
```

In this case, a5 is bigger than a1. Once again, after copy(a1, a5), a5 remains the same whereas a5[0] is copied to a1[0].

```
    // Len(a2) < Len(a5) -> OK
    copy(a5, a2)
    fmt.Println("a2", a2)
    fmt.Println("a5", a5)
}
```

In this last case, a2 is shorter than a5. This means that the entire a2 is copied into a5 as there is enough room. As the length of a2 is 2, only the first 2 elements of a5 change.

Running copySlice.go produces the following output:

```
$ go run copySlice.go
a1 [1]
a2 [-1 -2]
a5 [10 11 12 13 14]
a1 [-1]
a2 [-1 -2]
```

The copy(a1, a2) statement does not alter the a2 slice, just a1. As the size of a1 is 1, only the first element from a2 is copied.

```
a1 [10]
a5 [10 11 12 13 14]
```

Similarly, copy(a1, a5) alters a1 only. As the size of a1 is 1, only the first element from a5 is copied to a1.

```
a2 [-1 -2]
a5 [-1 -2 12 13 14]
```

Last, copy(a5, a2) alters a5. As the size of a5 is 5, only the first two elements from a5 are altered and become the same as the first two elements of a2, which has a size of 2.

Sorting slices

There are times when you want to present your information sorted and you want Go to do the job for you. In this subsection, we are going to see how to sort slices of various standard data types using the functionality offered by the sort package.

The sort package can sort slices of built-in data types without the need to write any extra code. Additionally, Go provides the sort.Reverse() function for sorting in reverse order. However, what is really interesting is that sort allows you to write your own sorting functions for custom data types by implementing the sort.Interface interface—you will learn more about sort. Interface and interfaces in general in *Chapter 5, Reflection and Interfaces.*

 With Go generics, the slices package was introduced in the standard Go library— the slices package is discussed in *Chapter 4, Go Generics.*

So, you can sort a slice of integers saved as sInts by typing sort.Ints(sInts). When sorting a slice of integers in reverse order using sort.Reverse(), you need to pass the desired slice to sort.Reverse() using sort.IntSlice(sInts) because the IntSlice type implements the sort. Interface internally, which allows you to sort in a different way than usual. The same applies to the other standard Go data types.

Create a text file with following the code that illustrates the use of sort and name it sortSlice.go:

```
package main
import (
    "fmt"
    "sort"
)
func main() {
    sInts := []int{1, 0, 2, -3, 4, -20}
```

```
    sFloats := []float64{1.0, 0.2, 0.22, -3, 4.1, -0.1}
    sStrings := []string{"aa", "a", "A", "Aa", "aab", "AAa"}
    fmt.Println("sInts original:", sInts)
    sort.Ints(sInts)
    fmt.Println("sInts:", sInts)
    sort.Sort(sort.Reverse(sort.IntSlice(sInts)))
    fmt.Println("Reverse:", sInts)
```

As sort.Interface knows how to sort integer values, it is trivial to sort them in reverse order.

```
    fmt.Println("sFloats original:", sFloats)
    sort.Float64s(sFloats)
    fmt.Println("sFloats:", sFloats)
    sort.Sort(sort.Reverse(sort.Float64Slice(sFloats)))
    fmt.Println("Reverse:", sFloats)
    fmt.Println("sStrings original:", sStrings)
    sort.Strings(sStrings)
    fmt.Println("sStrings:", sStrings)
    sort.Sort(sort.Reverse(sort.StringSlice(sStrings)))
    fmt.Println("Reverse:", sStrings)
}
```

The same rules apply when sorting floating point numbers and strings.

Running sortSlice.go produces the following output:

```
$ go run sortSlice.go
sInts original: [1 0 2 -3 4 -20]
sInts: [-20 -3 0 1 2 4]
Reverse: [4 2 1 0 -3 -20]
sFloats original: [1 0.2 0.22 -3 4.1 -0.1]
sFloats: [-3 -0.1 0.2 0.22 1 4.1]
Reverse: [4.1 1 0.22 0.2 -0.1 -3]
sStrings original: [aa a A Aa aab AAa]
sStrings: [A AAa Aa a aa aab]
Reverse: [aab aa a Aa AAa A]
```

The output illustrates how the original slices were sorted in both normal and reverse order.

The next section discusses pointers in Go. Although Go does not support pointers in the same way that C does, Go allows you to work with pointers and pointer variables.

Pointers

Go has *support for pointers but not for pointer arithmetic,* which is the cause of many bugs and errors in programming languages like C. A pointer is the memory address of a variable. You need to *dereference a pointer* in order to get its value—dereferencing is performed using the * character in front of the pointer variable. Additionally, you can get the memory address of a normal variable using an & in front of it.

The next diagram shows the difference between a pointer to an int and an int variable.

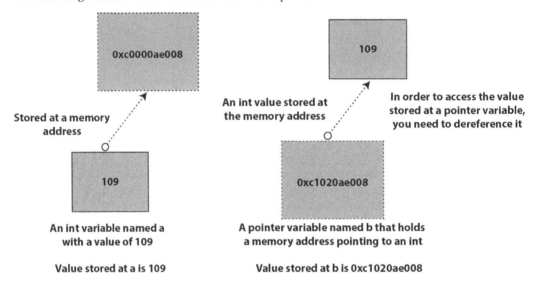

Figure 2.4: An int variable and a pointer to an int

If a pointer variable points to an existing regular variable, then any changes you make to the stored value using the pointer variable will modify the regular variable.

 The format and the values of memory addresses might be different between different machines, different operating systems, and different architectures.

You might ask, what is the point of using pointers when there is no support for pointer arithmetic? The main benefit you get from pointers is that passing a variable to a function as a pointer (we can call that by reference) does not discard any changes you make to the value of that variable inside that function when the function returns. There exist times where you want that functionality because it simplifies your code, but the price you pay for that simplicity is being extra careful with what you do with a pointer variable.

Remember that slices are passed to functions without the need to use a pointer—it is Go that passes the pointer to the underlying array of a slice and there is no way to change that behavior.

Apart from reasons of simplicity, there exist three more reasons for using pointers:

- Pointers allow you to share and manipulate data between functions without explicitly returning values back to the caller. However, when sharing data between functions and goroutines, you should be extra careful with *race condition* issues. This allows multiple functions to try to alter the value of the same pointer variable at the same time, which causes unpredictable behavior in the final state of that pointer variable.

- Pointers are also very handy when you want to tell the difference between the zero value of a variable and a value that is not set (nil). This is particularly useful with structures because pointers (and therefore pointers to structures, which are fully covered in the next chapter) can have a nil value, which means that you can compare a pointer to a structure with a nil value, which is not allowed for normal structure variables.

- Having support for pointers and, more specifically, pointers to structures allows Go to support data structures such as linked lists and binary trees, which are widely used in computer science. Therefore, you are allowed to define a structure field of a Node structure as Next *Node, which is a pointer to another Node structure. Without pointers, this would have been difficult to implement and possibly too slow.

The following code illustrates how you can use pointers in Go—create a text file named pointers.go and type the following code:

```
package main
import "fmt"
type aStructure struct {
    field1 complex128
    field2 int
}
```

This is a structure with two fields named field1 and field2.

```
func processPointer(x *float64) {
    *x = *x * *x
}
```

This is a function that gets a pointer to a float64 variable as input. As we are using a pointer, all changes to the function parameter inside the function will be persistent. Additionally, there is no need to return something.

```
func returnPointer(x float64) *float64 {
    temp := 2 * x
    return &temp
}
```

This is a function that requires a float64 parameter as input and returns a pointer to a float64.
To return the memory address of a regular variable, you need to use & (&temp). In this case, Go
is smart enough to realize that the pointer to temp escapes, so its value will be heap allocated,
ensuring that the caller has a valid reference to work with as opposed to stack allocation where
the reference is invalid when the function returns and the stack frame is eliminated.

```
func bothPointers(x *float64) *float64 {
    temp := 2 * *x
    return &temp
}
```

This is a function that requires a pointer to a float64 as input and returns a pointer to a float64
as output. The *x notation is used for getting the value stored in the memory address stored in
x and is called dereferencing.

```
func main() {
    var f float64 = 12.123
    fmt.Println("Memory address of f:", &f)
```

To get the memory address of a regular variable named f, you should use the &f notation.

```
    // Pointer to f
    fP := &f
    fmt.Println("Memory address of f:", fP)
    fmt.Println("Value of f:", *fP)
    // The value of f changes
    processPointer(fP)
    fmt.Printf("Value of f: %.2f\n", f)
```

fP is now a pointer to the memory address of the f variable. Any changes to the value stored in
the fP memory address influence the f value as well. However, this is only true for as long as fP
points to the memory address of the f variable.

```
    // The value of f does not change
    x := returnPointer(f)
    fmt.Printf("Value of x: %.2f\n", *x)
```

The value of f does not change because the function only uses its value.

```
// The value of f does not change
xx := bothPointers(fP)
fmt.Printf("Value of xx: %.2f\n", *xx)
```

In this case, the value of f, as well as the value stored in the fP memory address, do not change because the bothPointers() function does not make any changes to the value stored in the fP memory address.

```
// Check for empty structure
var k *aStructure
```

The k variable is a pointer to an aStructure structure. As k points to nowhere, Go makes it point to nil, which is the zero value for pointers.

```
// This is nil because currently k points to nowhere
fmt.Println(k)
// Therefore you are allowed to do this:
if k == nil {
    k = new(aStructure)
}
```

As k is nil, we are allowed to assign it to an empty aStructure value with new(aStructure) without losing any data—new() allocates the required memory and sets the pointer to that memory. Now, k is no longer nil but both fields of aStructure have the zero values of their data types.

```
    fmt.Printf("%+v\n", k)
    if k != nil {
        fmt.Println("k is not nil!")
    }
}
```

The preceding code is just making sure that k is not nil. You might consider that check redundant, but it does not hurt to double-check because if you try to dereference a nil pointer, your program is going to crash.

Running pointers.go generates the following kind of output:

```
Memory address of f: 0x140000180d8
Memory address of f: 0x140000180d8
Value of f: 12.123
```

```
Value of f: 146.97
Value of x: 293.93
Value of xx: 293.93
<nil>
&{field1:(0+0i) field2:0}
k is not nil!
```

We are going to revisit pointers in the next chapter when we discuss structures.

Converting a slice to an array or an array pointer

In this subsection, we are going to learn how to convert a slice to an array or an array pointer. The first part of slice2array.go is the following:

```go
func main() {
    // Go 1.17 feature
    slice := make([]byte, 3)
    // Slice to array pointer
    arrayPtr := (*[3]byte)(slice)
    fmt.Println("Print array pointer:", arrayPtr)
    fmt.Printf("Data type: %T\n", arrayPtr)
    fmt.Println("arrayPtr[0]:", arrayPtr[0])
```

In the preceding code we convert slice into an array pointer that points to an array with 3 elements.

The rest of the slice2array.go code is the following:

```go
    // Go 1.20 feature
    slice2 := []int{-1, -2, -3}
    // Slice to array
    array := [3]int(slice2)
    fmt.Println("Print array contents:", array)
    fmt.Printf("Data type: %T\n", array)
}
```

In the preceding code we converted a slice into an array with 3 elements.

Running slice2array.go produces the following output:

```
$ go run slice2array.go
Print array pointer: &[0 0 0]
```

```
Data type: *[3]uint8
arrayPtr[0]: 0
Print array contents: [-1 -2 -3]
Data type: [3]int
```

The first three lines of output have to do with the slice-to-array-pointer conversion whereas the last two have to do with the slice-to-array conversion. The second line of output verifies that we are dealing with a pointer to an array with three elements (*[3]uint8) and the last line verifies that we are dealing with an array with three elements ([3]int).

Next, we discuss data types and the unsafe package.

Data types and the unsafe package

The unsafe package in Go provides facilities for performing operations that break the type safety guarantees of Go. It is a powerful but potentially dangerous package, and its use is discouraged in most Go code. Therefore, the unsafe package is intended for specific situations where low-level programming is necessary, such as interfacing with non-Go code, dealing with memory layout, or implementing certain advanced features.

In this section, we are going to discuss four functions of the unsafe package that are related to strings and slices. You might not have to use any of them on a regular basis, but it is good to know about them because they provide speed when dealing with large strings or slices that take lots of memory because they **deal with memory addresses directly**, which might be very dangerous if you do not know what you are doing. The four functions that we are going to discuss are unsafe.StringData(), unsafe.String(), unsafe.Slice(), and unsafe.SliceData(). You can learn more details about their usage using go doc.

 Please bear in mind that the unsafe package is called unsafe for a reason, and that in most cases you should not use this package!

The first part of typeUnsafe.go comes with two functions:

```
func byteToString(bStr []byte) string {
    if len(bStr) == 0 {
        return ""
    }
    return unsafe.String(unsafe.SliceData(bStr), len(bStr))
```

```go
    }

    func stringToByte(str string) []byte {
        if str == "" {
            return nil
        }
        return unsafe.Slice(unsafe.StringData(str), len(str))
    }
```

These two particular functions convert a byte slice to a string and vice versa using unsafe.String()
and unsafe.Slice(), respectively.

The unsafe.String() function requires a pointer parameter and a length value in order to know
how far from the pointer it is going to go for the data. The unsafe.SliceData() function returns
a pointer to the underlying array of the function argument slice.

unsafe.Slice() operates in an analogous way and returns a slice whose underlying array starts
at the given pointer value and whose length and capacity are equal to the integer value that is
passed as its second parameter—it is important to understand that when working with memory
addresses via pointers and the unsafe package, we need to specify how far in memory we need
to go.

 As Go strings are immutable, the bytes returned by unsafe.StringData() should
not be modified.

The second part of typeUnsafe.go is the following:

```go
    func main() {
        str := "Go!"
        d := unsafe.StringData(str)
        b := unsafe.Slice(d, len(str))
        // byte is an alias for uint8
        fmt.Printf("Type %T contains %s\n", b, b)

        sData := []int{10, 20, 30, 40}
        // Get the memory address of sData
        fmt.Println("Pointer:", unsafe.SliceData(sData))
```

The last part of typeUnsafe.go is as follows:

```
    // String to Byte slice
    var hi string = "Mastering Go, 4th edition!"
    myByteSlice := stringToByte(hi)
    fmt.Printf("myByteSlice type: %T\n", myByteSlice)

    // Byte slice to string
    myStr := byteToString(myByteSlice)
    fmt.Printf("myStr type: %T\n", myStr)
}
```

The output of typeUnsafe.go is the following:

```
$ go run typeUnsafe.go
Type []uint8 contains Go!
Pointer: 0x1400001e0c0
myByteSlice type: []uint8
myStr type: string
```

 Remember that the most common purpose for using the unsafe package is speed when dealing with large amounts of data because it allows you to perform pointer arithmetic and conversions between different pointer types without type safety checks. When dealing with large amounts of data, pointer arithmetic can speed up things.

Next, we discuss generating random numbers and random strings.

Generating random numbers

Random number generation is an art as well as a research area in computer science. This is because computers are purely logical machines, and it turns out that using them to generate random numbers is extremely difficult!

Go can help you with that using the functionality of the math/rand package. Each random number generator needs a seed to start producing numbers. The seed is used for initializing the entire process and is extremely important because if you always start with the same seed, you will always get the same sequence of pseudo-random numbers. This means that everybody can regenerate that sequence, and that particular sequence will not be random after all.

However, this feature is very handy for testing purposes. In Go, the rand.Seed() function is used for initializing a random number generator.

 If you are really interested in random number generation, you should start by reading the second volume of *The Art of Computer Programming* by Donald E. Knuth (Addison-Wesley Professional, 2011).

The following function, which is part of randomNumbers.go found in ch02 in the book's GitHub repository, is what generates random numbers in the [min, max) range.

```
func random(min, max int) int {
    return rand.Intn(max-min) + min
}
```

The random() function does all of the work, which is generating pseudo-random numbers in the min to max-1 range by calling rand.Intn(). rand.Intn() generates non-negative random integers from 0 up to the value of its single parameter minus 1.

The randomNumbers.go utility accepts four command line parameters but can also work with fewer parameters by using default values. By default, randomNumbers.go produces 100 random integers from 0 up to and including 99.

```
$ go run randomNumbers.go
Using default values!
39 75 78 89 39 28 37 96 93 42 60 69 50 9 69 27 22 63 4 68 56 23 54 14 93
61 19 13 83 72 87 29 4 45 75 53 41 76 84 51 62 68 37 11 83 20 63 58 12 50
8 31 14 87 13 97 17 60 51 56 21 68 32 41 79 13 79 59 95 56 24 83 53 62 97
88 67 59 49 65 79 10 51 73 48 58 48 27 30 88 19 16 16 11 35 45 72 51 41 28
```

In the following output, we define each of the parameters manually (the minimum value, maximum value, number of random values, and seed value):

```
$ go run randomNumbers.go 1 5 10 10
3 1 4 4 1 1 4 4 4 3
$ go run randomNumbers.go 1 5 10 10
3 1 4 4 1 1 4 4 4 3
$ go run randomNumbers.go 1 5 10 11
1 4 2 1 3 2 2 4 1 3
```

The first two times the seed value was 10, so we got the same output. The third time the value of the seed was 11, which generated a different output.

Generating random strings

Imagine that you want to generate random strings that can be used for difficult-to-guess passwords or for testing purposes. Based on random number generation, we create a utility that produces random strings. The utility is implemented as genPass.go and can be found in the ch02 directory of the book's GitHub repository. The core functionality of genPass.go is found in the next function:

```go
func getString(len int64) string {
    temp := ""
    startChar := "!"
    var i int64 = 1
    for {
        myRand := random(MIN, MAX)
        newChar := string(startChar[0] + byte(myRand))
        temp = temp + newChar
        if i == len {
            break
        }
        i++
    }
    return temp
}
```

As we only want to get printable ASCII characters, we limit the range of pseudo-random numbers that can be generated. The total number of printable characters in the ASCII table is 94. This means that the range of the pseudo-random numbers that the program can generate should be from 0 to 94, without including 94. Therefore, the values of the MIN and MAX global variables, which are not shown here, are 0 and 94, respectively.

The startChar variable holds the first ASCII character that can be generated by the utility, which, in this case, is the exclamation mark, which has a decimal ASCII value of 33. Given that the program can generate pseudo-random numbers up to 94, the maximum ASCII value that can be generated is 93 + 33, which is equal to 126, which is the ASCII value of ~. All generated characters are kept in the temp variable, which is returned once the for loop exits. The string(startChar[0] + byte(myRand)) statement converts the random integers into characters in the desired range.

The genPass.go utility accepts a single parameter, which is the length of the generated password. If no parameter is given, genPass.go produces a password with 8 characters, which is the default value of the LENGTH variable.

Running genPass.go produces the following kind of output:

```
$ go run genPass.go
Using default values...
!QrNq@;R
$ go run genPass.go 20
sZL>{F~"hQqY>r_>TX?O
```

The first program execution uses the default value for the length of the generated string whereas the second program execution creates a random string with 20 characters.

Generating secure random numbers

If you intend to use these pseudo-random numbers for security-related work, it is important that you use the crypto/rand package, which implements a cryptographically secure pseudo-random number generator. You do not need to define a seed when using the crypto/rand package.

The following function that is part of the cryptoRand.go source code showcases how secure random numbers are generated with the functionality of crypto/rand.

```
func generateBytes(n int64) ([]byte, error) {
    b := make([]byte, n)
    _, err := rand.Read(b)
    if err != nil {
        return nil, err
    }
    return b, nil
}
```

The rand.Read() function randomly generates numbers that occupy the entire b byte slice. You need to decode that byte slice using base64.URLEncoding.EncodeToString(b) in order to get a valid string without any control or unprintable characters. This transformation takes place in the generatePass() function, which is not shown here.

Running cryptoRand.go creates the following kind of output:

```
$ go run cryptoRand.go
Using default values!
Ce30g--D
$ go run cryptoRand.go 20
AEIePSYb13KwkDnO5Xk_
```

The output is not different from the one generated by genPass.go, it is just that the random numbers are generated more securely, which means that they can be used in applications where security is important.

Now that we know how to generate random numbers, we are going to revisit the statistics application.

Updating the statistics application

In this section, we are going to improve the functionality and the operation of the statistics application. When there is no valid input, we are going to populate the statistics application with ten random values, which is pretty handy when you want to put lots of data in an application for testing purposes—you can change the number of random values to fit your needs. However, keep in mind that this takes place when all user input is invalid.

 I have randomly generated data in the past in order to put sample data into Kafka topics, RabbitMQ queues and MySQL tables.

Additionally, we are going to *normalize* the data. Officially, this is called *z-normalization* and is helpful for allowing sequences of values to be compared more accurately. We are going to use normalization in forthcoming chapters.

The function for the normalization of the data is implemented as follows:

```
func normalize(data []float64, mean float64, stdDev float64) []float64 {
if stdDev == 0 {
    return data
}

normalized := make([]float64, len(data))
for i, val := range data {
    normalized[i] = math.Floor((val-mean)/stdDev*10000) / 10000
}
return normalized
}
```

From the parameters of the function, you can see that `normalize()` needs the mean value and the standard deviation of the sample before normalizing it. Apart from that, there is a small trick with `math.Floor()` for defining the accuracy of the normalized `float64` values, which in this case is four digits. To get two digits of accuracy, you should change the code to `math.Floor((val-mean)/stdDev*100)/100`.

Additionally, the function for generating random floating-point values is implemented as follows:

```
func randomFloat(min, max float64) float64 {
    return min + rand.Float64()*(max-min)
}
```

The `rand.Float64()` function returns values from `0` to `1.0`, without including `1.0`. The `randomFloat()` function returns values from `min` to `max`, without including `max`.

You can review the source code of `stats.go` to learn about the remaining implementation details. The main difference with the version of the previous chapter is that we are now using a slice called `values` for storing all the valid values that we are processing.

Running `stats.go` produces the following kind of output:

```
$ go run stats.go 3 5 5 8 9 12 12 13 15 16 17 19 22 24 25 134
Number of values: 16
Min: 3
Max: 134
Mean value: 21.18750
Standard deviation: 29.84380
Normalized: [-0.6095 -0.5425 -0.5425 -0.4419 -0.4084 -0.3079 -0.3079
-0.2744 -0.2074 -0.1739 -0.1404 -0.0733 0.0272 0.0942 0.1277 3.78]
```

Although randomly generated values might not be perfect at all times, they are usually more than enough for testing purposes.

Summary

In this chapter, we learned about the basic data types of Go, including numerical data types, strings, and errors. Additionally, we learned how to group similar values using arrays and slices. Lastly, we learned about the differences between arrays and slices and why slices are more versatile than arrays, as well as pointers and generating random numbers and strings in order to generate random data.

One thing that you should remember from this chapter is that a slice is empty if its length is equal to 0. On the other hand, a slice is `nil` if it is equal to `nil`—this means that it points to no memory address. The `var s []string` statement creates a `nil` slice without allocating any memory. A `nil` slice is always empty—the reverse is not always true.

As far as Go strings are concerned, remember that double quotes define an interpreted string literal whereas back quotes define a raw string literal. Most of the time, you need double quotes.

Last, keep in mind that the use of the `unsafe` package can lead to subtle bugs and memory safety issues. The Go language encourages type safety, and the use of `unsafe` should be limited to situations where there is a clear understanding of the risks and where no safer alternative exists.

The next chapter discusses the composite data types of Go, namely, maps and structures. Maps can use keys of different data types whereas structures can group multiple data types and create new ones that you can access as single entities. As you will see in later chapters, structures play a key role in Go.

Exercises

Try to do the following exercises:

- Correct the error in `typedConstants.go`.
- Create and test a function that concatenates two arrays into a new slice.
- Create a function that concatenates two arrays into a new array. Do not forget to test it with various types of input.
- Create a function that concatenates two slices into a new array.
- Run `go doc errors Is` in order to learn about `errors.Is()` and try to create a small Go program that uses it. After that, modify `error.go` to use `errors.Is()`.
- Modify `stats.go` in order to accept the number of randomly generated values as a command line argument.
- Modify `stats.go` in order to always use randomly generated data.

Additional resources

- The `sort` package documentation: `https://pkg.go.dev/sort`
- The `time` package documentation: `https://pkg.go.dev/time`
- The `crypto/rand` package documentation: `https://pkg.go.dev/crypto/rand`
- Go 1.20 release notes: `https://tip.golang.org/doc/go1.20`
- The `math/rand` package documentation: `https://pkg.go.dev/math/rand`

Join our community on Discord

Join our community's Discord space for discussions with the authors and other readers:

https://discord.gg/FzuQbc8zd6

3

Composite Data Types

Go offers support for maps and structures, which are composite data types and the main subject of this chapter. The reason that we present them separately from arrays and slices is that both maps and structures are more flexible and powerful than arrays and slices. Each map can use keys of a given predefined data type, whereas structures can group multiple data types and create new data types.

Maps and slices are used for completely different reasons. Arrays and slices are used to store contiguous data and benefit from memory locality and indexing. Maps are useful when you do not need the locality of data but still need a way to reference it in constant time.

The general idea is that if an array or a slice cannot do the job, you might need to look at maps. If a map cannot help you store your data the way you want, then you should consider creating and using a structure—you can also group structures of the same type using arrays or slices. Keep in mind that maps and structures are distinct in their use case. You can easily have a map of structures, as well as an array or slice of structures. However, a structure is useful when you need to combine multiple pieces of logically grouped data and/or variables.

Additionally, the knowledge of this chapter will allow us to read and save data in the CSV format using structures.

Also, we are going to improve the statistics application we originally developed in *Chapter 1, A Quick Introduction to Go*. The new version of the utility is going to be able to load data from disk, which means that you no longer need to hardcode your data or generate random numbers.

This chapter covers:

- Maps
- Structures
- Regular expressions and pattern matching
- Improving the statistics application

Without further ado, let us begin by presenting maps.

Maps

Both arrays and slices limit you to using positive integers as indexes, which start from 0 and cannot have gaps in them—this means that even if you want to put data in the slice element at index 99 only, the slice is still going to occupy 100 elements in memory. Maps are more powerful data structures because they allow you to use indexes of various data types as keys to look up your data, as long as these keys are *comparable*. Comparable means that Go should be able to tell if two values are equal or which value is bigger (or smaller) than the other.

 Although Boolean variables are comparable, it makes no sense to use a bool variable as the key to a map because it only allows for two distinct values. Additionally, although floating point values are comparable, precision issues caused by the internal representation of such values might create bugs and crashes, so you might want to avoid using floating point values as keys to maps.

You might ask, why do we need maps, and what are their advantages? The following list will help clarify things:

- Maps are very versatile. You can even create a database index using a map, which allows you to search and access elements based on a given key or, in more advanced situations, a combination of keys.
- Although this is not always the case, working with maps in Go is fast, as you can access all elements of a map in constant time. Inserting and retrieving elements from a map is a constant time operation.
- Maps are easy to understand, which often leads to clear designs.

You can create a new map variable using either make() or a map literal. Creating a new map with string keys and int values using make() is as simple as writing make(map[string]int) and assigning its return value to a variable. On the other hand, if you decide to create a map using a map literal, you need to write something like the following:

```
m := map[string]int {
    "key1": -1
    "key2": 123
}
```

The map literal version is faster when you want to add data to a map at the time of creation. The previous map literal contains two keys and two values—two pairs in total.

 You should make no assumptions about the order of the elements inside a map. Go randomizes keys when iterating over a map— this is done on purpose and is an intentional part of the language design.

You can find the length of a map, which is the number of keys in the map, using the len() function, which also works with arrays and slices; also, you can delete a key and value pair from a map using the delete() function, which accepts two arguments: the name of the map and the name of the key, in that order.

How to tell whether a key exists on a map

You can tell whether a key k exists on a map named aMap by the second return value of the v, ok := aMap[k] statement. If ok is set to true, then k exists, and its value is v. If it does not exist, v will be set to the zero value of its data type, which depends on the definition of the map.

Now, a very important detail: *if you try to get the value of a key that does not exist in a map, Go will not complain about it and return the zero value of the data type of the value.*

Now, let us discuss a special case where a map variable has the nil value.

Storing to a nil map

You are allowed to assign a map variable to nil. In that case, you will not be able to use that variable until you assign it to a new map variable. Put simply, if you try to store data on a nil map, your program will crash. This is illustrated in the next bit of code, which is the implementation of the main() function of the nilMap.go source file that can be found in the ch03 directory of the GitHub repository of this book:

```
func main() {
    aMap := map[string]int{}
    aMap["test"] = 1
```

This works because aMap points to an existing map, which is the return value of map[string]int{}.

```
fmt.Println("aMap:", aMap)
aMap = nil
```

At this point, aMap points to nil, which in Go is a synonym for nothing.

```
fmt.Println("aMap:", aMap)
if aMap == nil {
    fmt.Println("nil map!")
    aMap = map[string]int{}
}
```

Testing whether a map points to nil before using it is a good practice. In this case, if aMap == nil allows us to determine whether we can store a key/value pair to aMap or not—we cannot, and if we try it, the program will crash. We correct that by issuing the aMap = map[string]int{} statement.

```
    aMap["test"] = 1
    // This will crash!
    aMap = nil
    aMap["test"] = 1
}
```

In this last part of the program, we illustrate how your program will crash if you try to store data on a nil map—never use such code in production!

 In real-world applications, if a function accepts a map argument, then it should check that the map is not nil before working with it.

Running nilMap.go produces this output:

```
$ go run nilMap.go
aMap: map[test:1]
aMap: map[]
nil map!
panic: assignment to entry in nil map

goroutine 1 [running]:
```

```
main.main()
        /Users/mtsouk/Desktop/mGo4th/code/ch03/nilMap.go:21 +0x17c
exit status 2
```

The reason the program crashed is shown in the program output: panic: assignment to entry in nil map.

Iterating over maps

When for is combined with range, it implements the functionality of the *foreach loops* found in other programming languages and allows you to iterate over all the elements of a map without knowing its size or its keys. In that case, range returns key and value pairs, in that order.

Type the following code and save it as forMaps.go:

```go
package main
import "fmt"
func main() {
    aMap := make(map[string]string)
    aMap["123"] = "456"
    aMap["key"] = "A value"

    for key, v := range aMap {
        fmt.Println("key:", key, "value:", v)
    }
```

In this case, we use both the key and the value that returned from range.

```go
    for _, v := range aMap {
        fmt.Print(" # ", v)
    }
    fmt.Println()
}
```

In this case, as we are only interested in the values returned by the map, we ignore the keys.

 As you already know, you should make *no **assumptions about the order*** that the key and value pairs of a map will be returned in from a for/range loop.

Running forMaps.go produces this output:

```
$ go run forMaps.go
key: key value: A value
key: 123 value: 456
 # 456 # A value
```

Having covered maps, it is time to learn about Go structures.

Structures

Structures in Go are both very powerful and very popular and are used for organizing and grouping various types of data under the same name. Structures are the more versatile data type in Go—they can even have associated functions, which are called methods.

Structures, as well as other user-defined data types, are usually defined outside the main() function or any other package function so that they can have a global scope and be available to the entire Go package. Therefore, unless you want to make clear that a type is only useful within the current local scope and is not expected to be used elsewhere, you should write the definitions of new data types outside functions.

The type keyword

The type keyword allows you to define new data types or create aliases for existing ones. Therefore, you are allowed to say type myInt int and define a new data type called myInt, which is an alias for int. However, Go considers myInt and int as totally different data types that you cannot compare directly, even though they store the same kind of values. Each structure defines a new data type, hence the use of type.

Defining new structures

When you define a new structure, which is called a struct in the Go documentation, you group a set of values into a single data type, which allows you to pass and receive this set of values as a single entity. *A structure has fields, and each field has its own data type*, which can even be another structure or a slice of structures. Additionally, as a structure is a new data type, it is defined using the type keyword, followed by the name of the structure, and ending with the struct keyword, which signifies that we are defining a new structure.

The following code defines a new structure named Entry:

```
type Entry struct {
```

```
    Name    string
    Surname string
    Year    int
}
```

 Although you can embed a structure definition into another structure, it is generally a bad idea and should be avoided. If you even think about doing so, you might need to think about your design decisions. However, it is perfectly acceptable to have existing structs as types inside a struct.

For reasons that will become evident in *Chapter 6, Go Packages and Functions*, the fields of a structure usually begin with an uppercase letter—this depends on what you want to do with the fields and how their visibility outside of the current package might affect that. The Entry structure has three fields, named Name, Surname, and Year. The first two fields are of the string data type, whereas the last field holds an int value.

These three fields can be accessed with the *dot notation* as V.Name, V.Surname, and V.Year, where V is the name of the variable holding an instance of the Entry structure. A structure literal named p1 can be defined as p1 := Entry{"Joe", "D.", 2012}.

Two ways exist to work with structure variables. The first one is as regular variables, and the second one is as pointer variables that point to the memory address of a structure. Both ways are equally good and are usually embedded into separate functions, because they allow you to initialize some or all of the fields of structure variables properly and/or do any other tasks you want before using the structure variable.

As a result, there exist two main ways to create a new structure variable using a function. The first one returns a regular structure variable whereas the second one returns a pointer to a structure. Each one of these two ways has two variations. The first variation returns a structure instance that is initialized by the Go compiler, whereas the second variation returns a structure instance that is initialized by the developer.

Last, keep in mind that the order in which you put the fields in the definition of a structure type is significant for the type identity of the defined structure. Put simply, *two structures with the same fields will not be considered identical in Go if their fields are not in the same order*. This mainly has to do with exchanging data between server and client software because variables of different structures cannot be compared, even if they have the exact same list of fields with the exact data types in the exact same order, as they belong to different data types.

Using the new keyword

Additionally, you can create new structure instances using the new() keyword with statements
such as pS := new(Entry). The new() keyword has the following properties:

- It allocates the proper memory space, which depends on the data type, and then it zeroes it.

- It always returns a pointer to the allocated memory.

- It works for all data types except channels and maps.

All these techniques are illustrated in the code that follows. Type the following code in your favorite text editor and save it as structures.go:

```
package main
import "fmt"


type Entry struct {
    Name     string
    Surname string
    Year     int
}


// Initialized by Go
func zeroS() Entry {
    return Entry{}
}
```

Now is a good time to remind you of an important Go rule: *if no initial value is given to a variable,*
the Go compiler automatically initializes that variable to the zero value of its data type. For structures,
this means that a structure variable without an initial value is initialized to the zero values of
the data type of each one of its fields. Therefore, the zeroS() function returns a zero-initialized
Entry structure.

```
// Initialized by the user
func initS(N, S string, Y int) Entry {
    if Y < 2000 {
        return Entry{Name: N, Surname: S, Year: 2000}
    }
    return Entry{Name: N, Surname: S, Year: Y}
}
```

In this case, the user initializes the new structure variable. Additionally, the initS() function checks whether the value of the Year field is smaller than 2000 and acts; if it is smaller than 2000, then the value of the Year field becomes 2000. This condition is specific to the requirements of the application you are developing—what this shows is that the place where you initialize a structure is also good for checking your input.

```go
// Initialized by Go - returns pointer
func zeroPtoS() *Entry {
    t := &Entry{}
    return t
}
```

The zeroPtoS() function returns a pointer to a zero-initialized structure.

```go
// Initialized by the user - returns pointer
func initPtoS(N, S string, Y int) *Entry {
    if len(S) == 0 {
        return &Entry{Name: N, Surname: "Unknown", Year: Y}
    }
    return &Entry{Name: N, Surname: S, Year: Y}
}
```

The initPtoS() function also returns a pointer to a structure but also checks the length of the user input. Again, this kind of checking is application specific.

```go
func main() {
    s1 := zeroS()
    p1 := zeroPtoS()
    fmt.Println("s1:", s1, "p1:", *p1)
    s2 := initS("Mihalis", "Tsoukalos", 2024)
    p2 := initPtoS("Mihalis", "Tsoukalos", 2024)
    fmt.Println("s2:", s2, "p2:", *p2)
    fmt.Println("Year:", s1.Year, s2.Year, p1.Year, p2.Year)
    pS := new(Entry)
    fmt.Println("pS:", pS)
}
```

The new(Entry) call returns a pointer to an Entry structure. As a rule of thumb, when you have to initialize lots of structure variables, it is considered good practice to create a function for doing so, as this is less error-prone.

Running `structures.go` creates the following output:

```
s1: {   0} p1: {   0}
s2: {Mihalis Tsoukalos 2024} p2: {Mihalis Tsoukalos 2024}
Year: 0 2024 0 2024
pS: &{   0}
```

As the zero value of a string is the empty string, s1, p1, and pS do not show any data for the Name and Surname fields.

The next subsection shows how to group structures of the same data type and use them as the elements of a slice.

Slices of structures

You can create slices of structures to group and handle multiple structures under a single variable name. However, accessing a field of a given structure requires knowing the exact place of the structure in the slice.

Have a look at the following figure to better understand how a slice of structures works and how you can access the fields of a specific slice element.

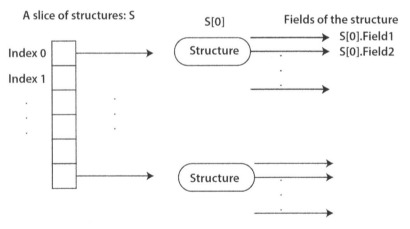

Figure 3.1: A slice of structures

So each slice element is a structure that is accessed using a slice index. Once we select the slice element we want, we can select any one of its fields.

As the whole process can be a little perplexing, the code that follows sheds some light and clarifies things. Type the following code and save it as `sliceStruct.go`. You can also find it by the same name in the ch03 directory in the GitHub repository of the book.

```
package main
import (
    "fmt"
    "strconv"
)

type record struct {
    Field1 int
    Field2 string
}

func main() {
    s := []record{}
    for i := 0; i < 10; i++ {
        text := "text" + strconv.Itoa(i)
        temp := record{Field1: i, Field2: text}
        s = append(s, temp)
    }
```

You still need append() to add a new structure to a slice.

```
    // Accessing the fields of the first element
    fmt.Println("Index 0:", s[0].Field1, s[0].Field2)
    fmt.Println("Number of structures:", len(s))
    sum := 0
    for _, k := range s {
        sum += k.Field1
    }
    fmt.Println("Sum:", sum)
}
```

Running sliceStruct.go produces the following output:

```
Index 0: 0 text0
Number of structures: 10
Sum: 45
```

We revisit structures in *Chapter 5*, where we discuss reflection, as well as *Chapter 7, Telling a UNIX System What to Do*, where we learn how to work with JSON data using structures. For now, let us discuss regular expressions and pattern matching.

Regular expressions and pattern matching

You might wonder why we are talking about regular expressions and pattern matching in this chapter. The reason is simple. In a while, you will learn how to store and read CSV data from plain text files, and you should be able to tell whether the data is valid or not.

Pattern matching is a technique for searching a string for some set of characters, based on a specific search pattern that is based on regular expressions and grammars.

A regular expression is a sequence of characters that defines a search pattern. Every regular expression is compiled into a recognizer by building a generalized transition diagram called a finite automaton. A finite automaton can be either deterministic or nondeterministic. Nondeterministic means that more than one transition out of a state can be possible for the same input. A recognizer is a program that takes a string x as input and can tell whether x is a sentence of a given language or not.

A grammar is a set of production rules for strings in a formal language—the production rules describe how to create strings from the alphabet of the language that are valid according to the syntax of the language. A grammar does not describe the meaning of a string or what can be done with it in whatever context—it only describes its form. What is important here is to realize that grammars are at the heart of regular expressions because, without a grammar, you cannot define and therefore use a regular expression.

About regexp.Compile and regexp.MustCompile

The Go package responsible for defining regular expressions and performing pattern matching is called regexp. Inside that package exists regexp.Compile() and regexp.MustCompile(), which have similar capabilities.

Both the regexp.MustCompile() and regexp.Compile() functions parse the given regular expression and return a pointer to a regexp.Regexp variable that can be used for matching—regexp.Regexp is the representation of a compiled regular expression. The re.Match() method returns true if the given byte slice matches the re regular expression, which is a regexp.Regexp variable, and false otherwise.

The main and crucial difference between regexp.Compile() and regexp.MustCompile() is that the former returns a *regexp.Regexp pointer and an error variable, whereas the latter returns a *regexp.Regexp pointer only. As a result, if there is some kind of error in the parsing of the regular expression, regexp.MustCompile() is going to panic and therefore crash your program!

However, `regexp.MustCompile()` panicking is not necessarily a bad thing because if a regular expression cannot be parsed, you will know that your expression is invalid early in the process. At the end of the day, it is the developer that decides the overall policy regarding regular expression parsing.

There are times when we want to find only those matches for a pattern that are followed or preceded by another given pattern. These kinds of operations are called lookahead and lookbehind, respectively. Go offers no support for either lookahead or lookbehind and will throw an error message when used. The general syntax of lookahead is `X(?=Y)`, which means, match `X` only if it is followed by `Y`. The difference between `regexp.Compile()` and `regexp.MustCompile()` is illustrated in the `main()` function of `diffRegExp.go`, which is going to be presented in two parts.

```
func main() {
    // This is a raw string literal
    var re string = `^.*(?=.{7,})(?=.*\d)$`
```

What is wrong with the preceding regular expression? The problem is that it is using lookahead, which is not supported in Go.

The second part is next:

```
    exp1, err := regexp.Compile(re)
    if err != nil {
        fmt.Println("Error:", err)
    }
    fmt.Println("RegExp:", exp1)

    exp2 := regexp.MustCompile(re)
    fmt.Println(exp2)
}
```

In this second code segment, the use of `regexp.Compile()` and `regexp.MustCompile()` is illustrated.

Running `diffRegExp.go` produces the next output:

```
$ go run diffRegExp.go
Error: error parsing regexp: invalid or unsupported Perl syntax: `(?=`
RegExp: <nil>
panic: regexp: Compile(`^.*(?=.{7,})(?=.*\d)$`): error parsing regexp:
invalid or unsupported Perl syntax: `(?=`
```

```
goroutine 1 [running]:
regexp.MustCompile({0x100a0c681, 0x15})
    /opt/homebrew/Cellar/go/1.20.6/libexec/src/regexp/regexp.go:319 +0xac
main.main()
    /Users/mtsouk/Desktop/mGo4th/code/ch03/diffRegExp.go:20 +0xf8
exit status 2
```

So, in the first case, we know that there is an error in the regular expression because of the return value of `regexp.Compile()`, whereas when using `regexp.MustCompile()` with an erroneous regular expression, the program panics and automatically terminates.

The next subsection shows how to define regular expressions.

Go regular expressions

We begin this subsection by presenting some common match patterns used to construct regular expressions.

Expression	Description
.	Matches any character
*	Means any number of times—cannot be used on its own
?	Zero or once—cannot be used on its own
+	Means one or more times—cannot be used on its own
^	This denotes the beginning of the line
$	This denotes the end of the line
[]	[] is for grouping characters
[A-Z]	This means all characters from capital A to capital Z
\d	Any digit in 0-9
\D	A non-digit
\w	Any word character: [0-9A-Za-z_]
\W	Any non-word character
\s	A whitespace character
\S	A non-whitespace character

The characters presented in the previous table are used for constructing and defining the grammar of a regular expression.

Creating separate functions for pattern matching can be handy because it allows you to reuse the functions without worrying about the context of the program.

Keep in mind that although regular expressions and pattern matching look convenient at first, they are the root of lots of bugs. *My advice is to use the simplest regular expression that can solve your problem*. However, avoiding using regular expressions while still doing your job would be much better in the long run!

About raw string and interpreted string literals

Although we discussed strings in the previous chapter, it is in the definition of the regular expression in diffRegExp.go that we have used a *raw string literal* for the first time, so let us talk a little bit more about raw string literals, which are included in back quotes instead of double quotes. The advantages of raw string literals are the following:

- They can keep huge amounts of text inside them without the need for control characters, such as \n, for changing lines.

- They are handy when defining regular expressions because you do not need to use backquotes (\) to escape special characters.

- They are used in structure tags, which are explained in *Chapter 11, Working with REST APIs*.

So, in summary, *raw string literals are for storing strings without any escape processing, whereas interpreted string literals are processed when the string is created*.

The next subsection presents regular expressions for matching names and surnames.

Matching names and surnames

The presented utility matches names and surnames—according to our definition, these are strings that begin with an uppercase letter and continue with lowercase letters. The input should not contain any numbers or other characters.

The source code of the utility can be found in nameSurRE.go, which is in the ch03 folder. The function that supports the desired functionality is named matchNameSur() and is implemented as follows:

```
func matchNameSur(s string) bool {
    t := []byte(s)
    re := regexp.MustCompile(`^[A-Z][a-z]*$`)
```

```
    return re.Match(t)
}
```

The logic of the function is in the `` `^[A-Z][a-z]*$` `` regular expression, where ^ denotes the beginning of a line and $ denotes the end of a line. What the regular expression does is to match anything that begins with an uppercase letter ([A-Z]) and continue with any number of lowercase letters ([a-z]*). This means that Z is a match, but ZA is not a match because the second letter is in uppercase. Similarly, Jo+ is not a match because it contains the + character.

Running nameSurRE.go with various types of input produces the following output:

```
$ go run nameSurRE.go Z
true
$ go run nameSurRE.go ZA
false
$ go run nameSurRE.go Mihalis
True
```

This technique can help you check the validity of user input. The next subsection is about matching integers.

Matching integers

The presented utility matches both signed and unsigned integers—this is implemented in the way we define the regular expression. If we want to match unsigned integers only, then we should replace [-+]? in the regular expression with [+]?.

 A better alternative than using a regular expression for matching integer values would have been the use of strconv.Atoi(). As a piece of advice, if you can avoid using regular expressions, opt for the alternative method. However, regular expressions are invaluable when you do not know in advance the kind or the amount of data to expect in the input. In general, regular expressions are invaluable for separating the various parts of the input. Keep in mind that regular expressions are always matching strings, and you can also find digits in strings.

The source code of the utility can be found in intRE.go, which is in the ch03 directory. The matchInt() function that supports the desired functionality is implemented as follows:

```
func matchInt(s string) bool {
    t := []byte(s)
```

```
    re := regexp.MustCompile(`^[-+]?\d+$`)
    return re.Match(t)
}
```

As before, the logic of the function is found in the regular expression that is used for matching integers, which is `^[-+]?\d+$`. In plain English, what we mean here is that we want to match something that begins with – or +, which is optional (?), and ends with any number of digits (\d+)—it is required that we have at least one digit before the end of the string that is examined ($).

Running intRE.go with various types of input produces the following output:

```
$ go run intRE.go 123
true
$ go run intRE.go /123
false
$ go run intRE.go +123.2
false
$ go run intRE.go +
false
$ go run intRE.go -123.2
false
```

Later in this book, you will learn how to test Go code by writing testing functions—for now, we will do most of the testing manually.

Improving the statistics application

It is time to update the statistics application. The new version of the statistics utility has the following improvements:

- It uses functions to simplify the main() function and improve the overall design.
- It can read CSV files that contain the numeric input.

But first, we need to learn how to work with CVS files in Go, which is the subject of the next subsection.

Working with CSV files

Most of the time, you do not want to lose your data or have to begin without any data every time you execute your application. There exist many techniques for doing so—the easiest one is by saving your data locally. A very easy-to-work-with plain text file format is CSV, which is what is explained here and used in the statistics application later on.

The good thing is that Go provides a dedicated package for working with CSV data, named encoding/csv (https://pkg.go.dev/encoding/csv). For the presented utility, both the input and output files are given as command line arguments.

 When reading or writing CSV data from disk, everything is considered a string. Therefore, if you have numeric data that you want to treat as such during the reading phase, you might need to convert it to the proper data type on your own.

There exist two very popular Go interfaces, named io.Reader and io.Write, that relate to reading and writing files, respectively. Almost all reading and writing operations in Go use these two interfaces. The use of the same interface for all readers allows readers to share some common characteristics, but most importantly, it allows you to create your own readers and use them anywhere that Go expects an io.Reader reader. The same applies to writers that satisfy the io.Write interface. You are going to learn more about interfaces in *Chapter 5, Reflection and Interfaces*.

The main tasks that need to be implemented are the following:

- Loading CSV data from disk and putting it into a slice of structures
- Saving data to disk using the CSV format

The encoding/csv package contains functions that can help you read and write CSV files. As we are dealing with small CSV files, we use csv.NewReader(f).ReadAll() to read the entire input file at once. For bigger data files, or if we wanted to check the input or make any changes to the input as we read it, it would have been better to read it line by line using Read() instead of ReadAll().

Go assumes that the CSV file uses the comma character (,) for separating the different fields of each line. Should we wish to change that behavior, we should change the value of the Comma variable of the CSV reader or the writer, depending on the task we want to perform. We change that behavior in the output CSV file, which separates its fields using the tab character.

 For reasons of compatibility, it is better if the input and output CSV files use the same field delimiter. We are just using the tab character as the field delimiter in the output file to illustrate the use of the Comma variable.

As working with CSV files is a new topic, there is a separate utility named csvData.go in the ch03 directory of the GitHub repository of this book that illustrates the techniques for reading and writing CSV files. The source code of csvData.go is presented in chunks. First, we present the preamble of csvData.go that contains the import section as well as the Record structure and the myData global variable, which is a slice of Record.

```go
package main
import (
    "encoding/csv"
    "log"
    "os"
)

type Record struct {
    Name        string
    Surname     string
    Number      string
    LastAccess  string
}
var myData = []Record{}
```

Then, we present the readCSVFile() function, which reads the plain text file with the CSV data.

```go
func readCSVFile(filepath string) ([][]string, error) {
    _, err := os.Stat(filepath)
    if err != nil {
        return nil, err
    }
    f, err := os.Open(filepath)
    if err != nil {
        return nil, err
    }
    defer f.Close()

    // CSV file read all at once
    // lines data type is [][]string
    lines, err := csv.NewReader(f).ReadAll()
    if err != nil {
        return [][]string{}, err
    }
    return lines, nil
}
```

Note that we check whether the given file path exists and is associated with a regular file inside the function. There is no right or wrong decision about where to perform that checking—you just have to be consistent. The readCSVFile() function returns a [][]string slice that contains all the lines we have read. Additionally, keep in mind that csv.NewReader() does separate the fields of each input line, which is the main reason for needing a slice with two dimensions to store the input.

After that, we illustrate the writing to a CSV file technique with the help of the saveCSVFile() function.

```
func saveCSVFile(filepath string) error {
    csvfile, err := os.Create(filepath)
    if err != nil {
        return err
    }
    defer csvfile.Close()
    csvwriter := csv.NewWriter(csvfile)
    // Changing the default field delimiter to tab
    csvwriter.Comma = '\t'
    for _, row := range myData {
        temp := []string{row.Name, row.Surname, row.Number, row.
LastAccess}
        err = csvwriter.Write(temp)
        if err != nil {
            return err
        }
    }
    csvwriter.Flush()
    return nil
}
```

Note the change in the default value of csvwriter.Comma to match our needs.

Lastly, we can see the implementation of the main() function.

```
func main() {
    if len(os.Args) != 3 {
        log.Println("csvData input output!")
        os.Exit(1)
    }
```

```
    input := os.Args[1]
    output := os.Args[2]
    lines, err := readCSVFile(input)
    if err != nil {
        log.Println(err)
        os.Exit(1)
    }

    // CSV data is read in columns - each line is a slice
    for _, line := range lines {
        temp := Record{
            Name:       line[0],
            Surname:    line[1],
            Number:     line[2],
            LastAccess: line[3],
        }
        myData = append(myData, temp)
        log.Println(temp)
    }
    err = saveCSVFile(output)
    if err != nil {
        log.Println(err)
        os.Exit(1)
    }
}
```

The main() function puts what you have read with readCSVFile() in the myData slice—remember that lines is a slice with two dimensions and that each row in lines is already separated into fields. In this case, each line of input contains four fields. So we process that [][]string slice and put the desired information in the slice of structures (myData).

The contents of the CSV data file used as input are as follows:

```
$ cat ~/csv.data
Dimitris,Tsoukalos,2101112223,1600665563
Mihalis,Tsoukalos,2109416471,1600665563
Jane,Doe,0800123456,1608559903
```

Running `csvData.go` produces the following kind of output:

```
$ go run csvData.go ~/csv.data /tmp/output.data
{Dimitris Tsoukalos 2101112223 1600665563}
{Mihalis Tsoukalos 2109416471 1600665563}
{Jane Doe 0800123456 1608559903}
```

The contents of the output CSV file are the following:

```
$ cat /tmp/output.data
Dimitris        Tsoukalos       2101112223      1600665563
Mihalis Tsoukalos       2109416471      1600665563
Jane    Doe     0800123456      1608559903
```

The `output.data` file uses tab characters to separate the different fields of each record, hence the generated output. The `csvData.go` utility can be handy for performing conversions between different types of CSV files.

The updated version of the statistics application

In this subsection, we are going to show the updated code of the statistics application. The `normalized()` function has not changed, so it is not presented again.

The first code excerpt from `stats.go` is the implementation of the function that reads the CSV file as text and converts it into a slice of `float64` values.

```go
func readFile(filepath string) ([]float64, error) {
    _, err := os.Stat(filepath)
    if err != nil {
        return nil, err
    }

    f, err := os.Open(filepath)
    if err != nil {
        return nil, err
    }
    defer f.Close()
    lines, err := csv.NewReader(f).ReadAll()
    if err != nil {
        return nil, err
    }
```

```go
    values := make([]float64, 0)
    for _, line := range lines {
        tmp, err := strconv.ParseFloat(line[0], 64)
        if err != nil {
            log.Println("Error reading:", line[0], err)
            continue
        }
        values = append(values, tmp)
    }

    return values, nil
}
```

Once the specified CSV file is read, its data is put into the `lines` variable. Keep in mind that, in our case, each line in the CSV file has a single field. Nevertheless, `lines` has two dimensions.

As we want to return a slice of `float64` values, we have to convert the `[][]string` variable into a `[]float64` variable, which is the purpose of the last `for` loop. The most important task of the `for` loop is to make sure that all strings are valid `float64` values, in order to put them in the `values` slice—this is the purpose of the `strconv.ParseFloat(line[0], 64)` call.

Next, we have the implementation of the function that computes the standard deviation:

```go
func stdDev(x []float64) (float64, float64) {
    sum := 0.0
    for _, val := range x {
        sum = sum + val
    }

    meanValue := sum / float64(len(x))
    fmt.Printf("Mean value: %.5f\n", meanValue)

    // Standard deviation
    var squared float64
    for i := 0; i < len(x); i++ {
        squared = squared + math.Pow((x[i]-meanValue), 2)
    }
```

```
    standardDeviation := math.Sqrt(squared / float64(len(x)))
    return meanValue, standardDeviation
}
```

First, stdDev() computes the sum of all given values and, after that, the mean value of the data. Last, the standard deviation is computed. You can remove the fmt.Printf() call inside the stdDev() function when you are sure that everything works as expected.

Lastly, here is the implementation of main():

```
func main() {
    if len(os.Args) == 1 {
        log.Println("Need one argument!")
        return
    }

    file := os.Args[1]
    values, err := readFile(file)
    if err != nil {
        log.Println("Error reading:", file, err)
        os.Exit(0)
    }
    sort.Float64s(values)

    fmt.Println("Number of values:", len(values))
    fmt.Println("Min:", values[0])
    fmt.Println("Max:", values[len(values)-1])

    meanValue, standardDeviation := stdDev(values)
    fmt.Printf("Standard deviation: %.5f\n", standardDeviation)

    normalized := normalize(values, meanValue, standardDeviation)
    fmt.Println("Normalized:", normalized)
}
```

Although the core functionality of the updated version of stats.go is the same as the version developed in the previous chapter, the use of functions simplifies the implementation of main().

Running stats.go produces the following output:

```
$ go run stats.go csvData.txt
Error reading: a strconv.ParseFloat: parsing "a": invalid syntax
Number of values: 6
Min: -1.2
Max: 3
Mean value: 0.66667
Standard deviation: 1.54883
Normalized: [-1.2053 -1.0761 -0.4305 0.2797 0.9254 1.5065
```

The previous output shows that csvData.txt contains an invalid line—the contents of csvData. txt are the following:

```
$ cat csvData.txt
1.1
2.1
-1.2
-1
0
a
3
```

Despite being much better than the previous version, the new version of the statistics utility is still not perfect. Here is a list of things that can be improved:

- The ability to process multiple CSV data files.
- The ability to sort its output based on a predefined statistics property, such as the mean value when dealing with multiple CSV data files.
- The ability to use JSON records and JSON slices for the data instead of CSV files.

The statistics application will keep improving, starting from *Chapter 5, Reflection and Interfaces*, where sorting slices with structure elements is implemented.

Summary

In this chapter, we discussed the composite data types of Go, which are maps and structures. Additionally, we talked about working with CSV files as well as using regular expressions and pattern matching. We can now keep our data in proper structures, validate it using regular expressions, and store it in CSV files to achieve data persistency.

Always keep in mind that *if you try to get the value of a key that does not exist in a map, Go will not complain about it and will return the zero value of the data type of the value.*

The next chapter is about Go generics, which is a relatively new Go feature.

Exercises

- Write a Go program that converts an existing array into a map.

- Write a Go program that converts an existing map into two slices—the first slice containing the keys of the map whereas the second one containing the values. The values at index n of the two slices should correspond to a key and value pair that can be found in the original map.

- Make the necessary changes to nameSurRE.go to be able to process multiple command line arguments.

- Change the code of intRE.go to process multiple command line arguments and display totals of true and false results at the end.

- Make changes to csvData.go to separate the fields of a record based on the # character.

- To understand how difficult regular expressions might end up, look on the internet for a regular expression to match email addresses.

- The regexp package includes the MatchString() method. Try to understand its main difference from the Match method and create a working example.

- Write a Go utility that converts os.Args into a slice of structures, with fields for storing the index and the value of each command line argument—you should define the structure that is going to be used.

- Make changes to csvData.go to separate the fields of a record, using a single character that is given as a command line argument.

- Modify the stdDev() function of stats.go, in order to save the mean value of the sample into a global variable and delete the fmt.Printf() call from it.

Additional resources

- The encoding/csv documentation: https://pkg.go.dev/encoding/csv
- The runtime package documentation: https://pkg.go.dev/runtime
- The regexp package documentation: https://pkg.go.dev/regexp

Join our community on Discord

Join our community's Discord space for discussions with the authors and other readers:

https://discord.gg/FzuQbc8zd6

4

Go Generics

This chapter is about generics and how to use the new syntax to write generic functions and define generic data types. Generic programming is a programming paradigm that allows the developer to implement a function using one or more data types that are going to be provided at a later time.

The Go generics support came with Go 1.18, which was officially released in February 2022. As a result, Go generics is now old news! Nevertheless, the Go community is still trying to make sense and good use of generics. In fact, most Go developers are already doing their job without the help of generics.

 If you feel that this chapter does not interest you at this point of your learning journey, feel free to skip it and come back at a later stage. However, I suggest that you read it even though it might not interest you right now.

This brings us to the following fact: *you do not have to use Go generics if you do not want to, have doubts about the usefulness of generics, or have a different approach in mind*. After all, you can still write wonderful, efficient, maintainable, and correct software in Go without using generics! Additionally, the fact that you can use generics and support lots of data types, if not all available data types, does not mean that you should do that. Always support the required data types, no more, no less, but do not forget to keep an eye on the future of your data and the possibility of supporting data types that were not known at the time of writing your code.

This chapter covers:

- An introduction to generics
- Constraints

- Defining new data types with generics
- When to use generics
- The cmp package
- The slices package
- The maps package

An introduction to generics

Generics is a feature that allows you the capability of not precisely specifying the data type of *one or more function parameters*, mainly because you want to make your functions as universal as possible. In other words, generics allow functions to process several data types without the need to write any special code, as is the case with the empty interface and interfaces in general. Interfaces are covered in *Chapter 5, Reflection and Interfaces*.

 When working with interfaces in Go, you must write extra code to determine the data type of the interface variable you are working with, which is not the case with generics.

Let me begin by presenting a small code example that implements a function that clearly shows a case where generics can be handy and save you from having to write lots of code:

```
func PrintSlice[T any](s []T) {
    for _, v := range s {
        fmt.Println(v)
    }
}
```

So, what do we have here? There is a function named PrintSlice() that accepts a slice of any data type. This is denoted by the use of []T in the function signature, which specifies that the function accepts a slice, in combination with the [T any] part that specifies that all data types are accepted and therefore supported. The [T any] part tells the compiler that the data type T is not going to be determined at execution time but it is still going to be determined and enforced at compile time based on the type provided by the calling code. We are also free to use multiple (generics) data types using the [T, U, W any] notation—after which we should use the T, U, and W data types in the function signature.

The any keyword tells the compiler that there are no constraints about the data type of T. We are going to discuss constraints in a bit—for now, we will just learn about the syntax of generics.

Now, imagine writing separate functions to implement the functionality of PrintSlice() for slices of integers, strings, floating-point numbers, complex values, and so on. So, we have found a profound case where using generics simplifies the code and our programming efforts. However, not all cases are so obvious, and we should be very careful about overusing any.

Hello, generics!

The following (hw.go) is a piece of code that uses generics, to help you understand more about them before going into more advanced examples:

```go
package main
import (
    "fmt"
)

func PrintSlice[T any](s []T) {
    for _, v := range s {
        fmt.Print(v, " ")
    }
    fmt.Println()
}
```

PrintSlice() is similar to the function that we saw earlier in this chapter. PrintSlice() prints the elements of each slice in the same line and prints a new line at the end with the help of fmt. Println().

```go
func main() {
    PrintSlice([]int{1, 2, 3})
    PrintSlice([]string{"a", "b", "c"})
    PrintSlice([]float64{1.2, -2.33, 4.55})
}
```

Here, we call the same PrintSlice() with three different data types: int, string, and float64. The Go compiler is not going to complain about that. Instead, it is going to execute the code as if we had three separate functions, one for each data type.

Therefore, running hw.go produces the following output:

```
1 2 3
a b c
1.2 -2.33 4.55
```

So, each slice is printed as expected using a single generic function.

With that information in mind, let us begin by discussing generics and constraints.

Constraints

Let us say that you have a function that works with generics that multiplies two numeric values. Should this function work with all data types? Can this function work with all data types? ***Can you multiply two strings or two structures?*** The solution for avoiding that kind of issue is the use of constraints. *Type constraints* allow you to specify the list of data types that you want to work with in order to avoid logical errors and bugs.

Forget about multiplication for a while and think about something simpler. Let us say that we want to compare variables for equality—is there a way to tell Go that we only want to work with values that can be compared? Go 1.18 came with predefined type constraints—one of them is called comparable and includes data types that can be compared for equality or inequality.

 For more predefined constraints, you should look at the constraints package (https://pkg.go.dev/golang.org/x/exp/constraints).

The code of allowed.go illustrates the use of the comparable constraint.

```
package main
import (
    "fmt"
)

func Same[T comparable](a, b T) bool {
    // Or
    // return a == b
    if a == b {
        return true
    }
    return false
}
```

The Same() function uses the predefined comparable constraint instead of any. In reality, the comparable constraint is just a predefined interface that includes all data types that can be compared with == or !=.

We do not have to write any extra code for checking our input as the function signature makes sure that we are going to deal with acceptable and functional data types only.

```
func main() {
    fmt.Println("4 = 3 is", Same(4,3))
    fmt.Println("aa = aa is", Same("aa","aa"))
    fmt.Println("4.1 = 4.15 is", Same(4.1,4.15))
}
```

The main() function calls Same() three times, using different data types, and prints its results.

Running allowed.go produces the following output:

```
4 = 3 is false
aa = aa is true
4.1 = 4.15 is false
```

As only Same("aa","aa") is true, we get the respective output.

If you try to run a statement like Same([]int{1,2},[]int{1,3}), which tries to compare two slices, the compiler is going to generate the following error message:

```
# command-line-arguments
./allowed.go:19:10: []int does not satisfy comparable
```

This happens because we cannot directly compare two slices—this kind of functionality should be implemented manually. Note that you are allowed to compare two arrays!

The next subsection shows how to create your own constraints.

Creating constraints

This subsection presents an example where we define the data types that are allowed to be passed as parameters to a generic function using an interface. The code of numeric.go is as follows:

```
package main
import (
    "fmt"
)

type Numeric interface {
    int | int8 | int16 | int32 | int64 | float64
}
```

Here, we define a new interface called `Numeric`, which specifies the list of supported data types. You can use any data type you want as long as it can be used with the generic function that you are going to implement. In this case, we could have added `string` or `uint` to the list of supported data types, if that makes sense. In this case, adding `string` to the `Numeric` interface does not make any sense.

```
func Add[T Numeric](a, b T) T {
    return a + b
}
```

This is the definition of the generic function with two generic parameters that use the `Numeric` constraint.

```
func main() {
    fmt.Println("4 + 3 =", Add(4,3))
    fmt.Println("4.1 + 3.2 =", Add(4.1,3.2))
}
```

The previous code is the implementation of the `main()` function with the calls to `Add()`.

Running `numeric.go` produces the following output:

```
4 + 3 = 7
4.1 + 3.2 = 7.3
```

Nevertheless, the Go rules still apply. Therefore, if you try to call `Add(4.1,3)`, you are going to get the following error message:

```
# command-line-arguments
./numeric.go:19:15: default type int of 3 does not match inferred type
float64 for T
```

The reason for this error is that the `Add()` function expects two parameters of the same data type. However, `4.1` is a `float64` whereas `3` is an `int`, so not the same data type.

There is an additional issue with constraints that we have not discussed so far. As we already know, *Go treats different data types differently even if the underlying data type is the same*. This means that if we create a new data type that is based on `int` (`type aType int`), it is not going to be supported by the `Numeric` constraint as this is not specified. The next subsection shows us how to deal with it and overcome that limitation.

Supporting underlying data types

With supertypes, we are adding support for the underlying data type—the real one—and not the data type at hand, which might be an alias for an existing Go data type. Supertypes are supported by the ~ operator. The use of supertypes is illustrated in supertypes.go. The first part of the code in supertypes.go is the following:

```
type AnotherInt int

type AllInts interface {
    ~int
}
```

In the previous code, we define a constraint named AllInts that uses a supertype (~int) as well as a new data type that is named AnotherInt and is in reality int. The definition of the AllInts constraint allows AnotherInt to be supported by AllInts.

The second part of supertypes.go is the following:

```
func AddElements[T AllInts](s []T) T {
    sum := T(0)
    for _, v := range s {
        sum = sum + v
    }
    return sum
}
```

In this part, we have defined a generic function. The function comes with a constraint as it supports slices of AllInts only.

The last part of supertypes.go is the following:

```
func main() {
    s := []AnotherInt{0, 1, 2}
    fmt.Println(AddElements(s))
}
```

In this last part, we call AddElements() using a slice of AnotherInt as its parameter—this capability is offered by the use of the supertype in the AllInts constraint.

Running supertypes.go produces the following output:

```
$ go run supertypes.go
3
```

So, *the use of supertypes in type constraints allows Go to deal with the actual underlying data type*.

Supporting slices of any type

In this subsection, we are going to specify that a function parameter can only be a slice of any data type. The relevant code in sliceConstraint.go is as follows:

```
func f1[S interface{ ~[]E }, E interface{}](x S) int {
    return len(x)
}

func f2[S ~[]E, E interface{}](x S) int {
    return len(x)
}

func f3[S ~[]E, E any](x S) int {
    return len(x)
}
```

All three generic functions are equivalent. The use of ~[ ]E specifies that the underlying data type should be a slice even if it is a type by a different name.

The f1() function is the long version of the function signature. interface{ ~[]E } specifies that we only want to work with slices of any data type (E interface{}). The f2() function replaces interface{ ~[]E } with just ~[]E because Go allows you to omit the enclosing interface{} for interfaces in the constraint position. Last, the f3() function replaces the commonly used interface{} with its predefined equivalent any, which we have already seen in action. I find the implementation of f3() much simpler and easier to understand.

The next section shows us how to use generics when defining new data types.

Defining new data types with generics

In this section, we are going to create a new data type with the use of generics, which is presented in newDT.go. The code of newDT.go is the following:

```
package main
```

```
import (
    "fmt"
    "errors"
)


type TreeLast[T any] []T
```

The previous statement declares a new data type named TreeLast that uses generics.

```
func (t TreeLast[T]) replaceLast(element T) (TreeLast[T], error) {
    if len(t) == 0 {
        return t, errors.New("This is empty!")
    }

    t[len(t) - 1] = element
    return t, nil
}
```

replaceLast() is a method that operates on TreeLast variables. Apart from the function signature, there is nothing else that shows the use of generics.

```
func main() {
    tempStr := TreeLast[string]{"aa", "bb"}
    fmt.Println(tempStr)
    tempStr.replaceLast("cc")
    fmt.Println(tempStr)
```

In this first part of main(), we create a TreeLast variable with the aa and bb string values and then we replace the bb value with cc, using a call to replaceLast("cc").

```
    tempInt := TreeLast[int]{12, -3}
    fmt.Println(tempInt)
    tempInt.replaceLast(0)
    fmt.Println(tempInt)
}
```

The second part of main() does a similar thing to the first part using a TreeLast variable populated with int values. So, TreeLast works with both string and int values without any issues.

Running newDT.go produces the following output:

```
[aa bb]
```

```
[aa cc]
[12 -3]
[12 0]
```

The first two lines of the output are related to the `TreeLast[string]` variable whereas the last two lines of the output are related to the `TreeLast[int]` variable.

The next subsection is about using generics in Go structures.

Using generics in Go structures

In this section, we are going to implement a linked list that works with generics—this is one of the cases where the use of generics simplifies things because it allows you to implement the linked list once while being able to work with multiple data types.

The code of `structures.go` is the following:

```
package main
import (
    "fmt"
)

type node[T any] struct {
    Data T
    next *node[T]
}
```

The node structure uses generics in order to support nodes that can store all kinds of data. This does not mean that the next field of a node can point to another node with a `Data` field with a different data type. The rule that a linked list contains elements of the same data type still applies—it just means that if you want to create three linked lists, one for storing `string` values, one for storing `int` values, and a third one for storing JSON records of a given `struct` data type, you do not need to write any extra code to do so.

```
type list[T any] struct {
    start *node[T]
}
```

This is the definition of the root node of a linked list of node nodes. Both `list` and `node` must share the same data type, `T`. However, as stated before, this does not prevent you from creating multiple linked lists of various data types.

You can still replace any with a constraint in both the definition of node and list if you want to restrict the list of allowed data types.

```
func (l *list[T]) add(data T) {
    n := node[T]{
        Data: data,
        next: nil,
    }
```

The add() function is generic in order to be able to work with all kinds of nodes. Apart from the signature of add(), the remaining code is not associated with the use of generics.

```
    if l.start == nil {
        l.start = &n
        return
    }

    if l.start.next == nil {
        l.start.next = &n
        return
    }
```

These two if blocks have to do with the addition of a new node to the linked list. The first if block is when the list is empty whereas the second if block is when we are dealing with the last node of the current list.

```
    temp := l.start
    l.start = l.start.next
    l.add(data)
    l.start = temp
}
```

The last part of add() has to do with defining the proper associations between nodes when adding a new node to the list.

```
func main() {
    var myList list[int]
```

First, we define a linked list of int values in main(), which is the linked list that we are going to work with.

```
    fmt.Println(myList)
```

The initial value of myList is nil, as the list is empty and does not contain any nodes.

```
myList.add(12)
myList.add(9)
myList.add(3)
myList.add(9)
```

In this first part, we add four elements to the linked list.

```
// Print all elements
cur := myList.start
for {
    fmt.Println("*", cur)
    if cur == nil {
        break
    }
    cur= cur.next
}
}
```

The last part of main() is about printing all the elements of the list by traversing it with the help of the next field, which points to the next node in the list.

Running structures.go produces the following output:

```
{<nil>}
* &{12 0x14000096240}
* &{9 0x14000096260}
* &{3 0x14000096290}
* &{9 <nil>}
* <nil>
```

Let us discuss the output a little more. The first line shows that the value of the empty list is nil. The first node of the list holds a value of 12 and a memory address (0x14000096240) that points to the second node. This goes on until we reach the last node, which holds the value of 9, which appears twice in this linked list, and points to nil, because it is the last node. Therefore, the use of generics makes the linked list able to work with multiple data types.

The next three sections present three packages that use generics—feel free to look into their implementations for details (see the *Additional resources* section).

The cmp package

The cmp package, which became part of the standard Go library in Go 1.21, contains types and functions for comparing ordered values. The reason for presenting it before the slices and maps packages is that it is used by the other two. Keep in mind that in its current version, the cmp package is simplistic but it might get enriched in the future with more functionality.

> Under the hood, the cmp, slices, and maps packages use generics and constraints, which is the main reason for presenting them in this chapter. So, generics can be used for creating packages that work with multiple data types.

The important code of cmpPackage.go can be found in the main() function.

```
func main() {
    fmt.Println(cmp.Compare(5, 4))
    fmt.Println(cmp.Compare(4, 5))
    fmt.Println(cmp.Less(4, 5.1))
}
```

Here, cmp.Compare(x, y) compares two values and returns -1 when x < y, 0 when x=y, and 1, when x > y. cmp.Compare(x, y) returns an int value. On the other hand, cmp.Less(x, y) returns a bool value that is set to true when x < y and false otherwise.

Note that in the last statement, we are comparing an integer value with a floating point value. However, the cmp package is clever enough to convert the int value into a float64 value and compare the two values!

Running cmpPackage.go produces the following output:

```
$ go run cmpPackage.go
1
-1
true
```

The output of cmp.Compare(5, 4) is 1, the output of cmp.Compare(4, 5) is -1, and the output of cmp.Less(4, 5) is true.

The slices package

The slices package has been part of the standard Go library since Go 1.21 and offers functions for slices of any data type. Before continuing our discussion of the slices package, let us talk about the *shallow copy* and *deep copy* functionality, including their differences.

Shallow and deep copies

A *shallow copy* creates a new variable and then it assigns to it all the values that are found in the original version of the variable. If we are talking about a map, then this process assigns all keys and values using ordinary assignment.

A *deep copy* first creates a new variable and then, it inserts all the values that are found in the original variable. However, each value must be copied recursively—this might not be an issue if we are talking about a string, but it might become an issue if we are talking about a structure, a reference to a structure, or a pointer. Among other things, this process might create never-ending circles. The key word here is *recursively*—this means that we need to go through all the values (if we are talking about a slice or a map) or fields (if we are talking about a structure) and find out what needs to be copied, recursively.

Therefore, the main difference between a shallow copy and a deep copy is that in the deep copy, *the actual values are being copied recursively* whereas in the shallow copy, *we assign the original values using ordinary assignment*.

We are now ready to continue with the presentation of the functionality of the slices package. The first part of the implementation of main() in slicesPackage.go is the following:

```go
func main() {
    s1 := []int{1, 2, -1, -2}
    s2 := slices.Clone(s1)
    s3 := slices.Clone(s1[2:])
    fmt.Println(s1[2], s2[2], s3[0])
    s1[2] = 0
    s1[3] = 0
    fmt.Println(s1[2], s2[2], s3[0])
```

The slices.Clone() function returns a shallow copy of the given slice—the elements are copied using assignment. After the s2 := slices.Clone(s1) call, s1 and s2 are equal, yet have separate memory spaces for their elements.

The second part is the following:

```go
    s1 = slices.Compact(s1)
    fmt.Println("s1 (compact):", s1)
    fmt.Println(slices.Contains(s1, 2), slices.Contains(s1, -2))

    s4 := make([]int, 10, 100)
    fmt.Println("Len:", len(s4), "Cap:", cap(s4))
```

```
    s4 = slices.Clip(s4)
    fmt.Println("Len:", len(s4), "Cap:", cap(s4))
```

The slices.Compact() function replaces consecutive appearances of equal elements with a single copy. Therefore, -1 -1 -1 is going to become -1 whereas -1 0 -1 is not going to change. As a rule of thumb, slices.Compact() works best on sorted slices.

The slices.Contains() function reports whether a given value is present in a slice.

The slices.Clip() function removes unused capacity from a slice. Put simply, the capacity of the slice becomes equal to the length of the slice. This can save you lots of memory when the capacity is much larger than the length of a slice.

The last part comes with the following code:

```
    fmt.Println("Min", slices.Min(s1), "Max:", slices.Max(s1))
    // Replace s2[1] and s2[2]
    s2 = slices.Replace(s2, 1, 3, 100, 200)
    fmt.Println("s2 (replaced):", s2)
    slices.Sort(s2)
    fmt.Println("s2 (sorted):", s2)
}
```

The slices.Min() and slices.Max() functions return the minimum and maximum values in a slice, respectively.

The slices.Replace() function replaces the elements in the given range, which in this case is s2[1:3], with the provided values, which in this case are 100 and 200, and returns the modified slice. Last, slices.Sort() sorts a slice with values of any ordered type in ascending order.

Running slicesPackage.go produces the following output:

```
$ go run slicesPackage.go
-1 -1 -1
0 -1 -1
s1 (compact): [1 2 0]
true false
Len: 10 Cap: 100
Len: 10 Cap: 10
Min: 0 Max: 2
s2 (replaced): [1 100 200 -2]
s2 (sorted): [-2 1 100 200]
```

You can see the effect of slices.Clip() in the capacity of the slice and the effect of slices. Replace() in the values of the s2 slice.

The next section presents the maps package.

The maps package

The maps package has been part of the standard Go library since Go 1.21 and offers functions for maps of any type—its use is illustrated in mapsPackage.go.

The mapsPackage.go program uses two helper functions that are defined as follows:

```go
func delete(k string, v int) bool {
    return v%2 != 0
}

func equal(v1 int, v2 float64) bool {
    return float64(v1) == v2
}
```

The purpose of the delete() function is to define which pairs are going to be deleted from the map—this function is called as a parameter to maps.DeleteFunc(). The current implementation returns true for all odd values. This means that all odd values along with their keys are going to be deleted. The first parameter of delete() has the data type of the keys of the map whereas the second one has the data type of the values of the map.

The purpose of the equal() function is to define how the equality of the values of the two maps is defined. In this case, we want to compare int values to float64 values. For this to be legitimate, we need to convert the int values to float64 values, which takes place inside equal().

Let us now continue with the implementation of the main() function. The first part of the main() function as found in mapsPackage.go is the following:

```go
func main() {
    m := map[string]int{
        "one": 1, "two": 2,
        "three": 3, "four": 4,
    }

    maps.DeleteFunc(m, delete)
    fmt.Println(m)
```

In the previous code, we define a map named m and call maps.DeleteFunc() in order to delete some of its elements.

The second part is as follows:

```
n := maps.Clone(m)
if maps.Equal(m, n) {
    fmt.Println("Equal!")
} else {
    fmt.Println("Not equal!")
}

n["three"] = 3
n["two"] = 22

fmt.Println("Before n:", n, "m:", m)
maps.Copy(m, n)
fmt.Println("After n:", n, "m:", m)
```

The maps.Clone() function returns a shallow clone of its argument. After that, we call maps.Equal() to make sure that maps.Clone() works as expected.

The maps.Copy(dst, src) function copies all pairs in src into dst. When a key in src already exists in dst, then the value in dst will be overwritten by the value associated with the respective key in src. In our program, we copy n to the m map.

The last part is the following:

```
t := map[string]int{
    "one": 1, "two": 2,
    "three": 3, "four": 4,
}

mFloat := map[string]float64{
    "one": 1.00, "two": 2.00,
    "three": 3.00, "four": 4.00,
}

eq := maps.EqualFunc(t, mFloat, equal)
fmt.Println("Is t equal to mFloat?", eq)
}
```

In this last part, we test the operation of maps.EqualFunc() by creating two maps, one that uses int values and the other that uses float64 values, and comparing them according to the equal() function that we have created earlier. In other words, the purpose of maps.EqualFunc() is to find out whether two maps contain the same key and value pairs by comparing them according to their function argument.

Running mapsPackage.go produces the following output:

```
$ go run mapsPackage.go
map[four:4 two:2]
Equal!
Before n: map[four:4 three:3 two:22] m: map[four:4 two:2]
After n: map[four:4 three:3 two:22] m: map[four:4 three:3 two:22]
Is t equal to mFloat? true
```

The maps.DeleteFunc(m, delete) statement deletes all key and value pairs where the value is odd leaving m with even values only. Additionally, the call to maps.Equal() returns true and the Equal! message is displayed on the screen. The maps.Copy(m, n) statement changes the value of m["two"] to 22 and adds the three key to m with a value of 3 as it was not present in m before the call to maps.Copy().

When to use generics

Generics is not a panacea and cannot replace good, accurate, and rational program design. Therefore, here are some principles and personal suggestions to keep in mind when thinking about using generics to solve a problem:

- Generics might be used when creating code that needs to work with multiple data types.
- Generics should be used when an implementation with interfaces and reflection makes the code more complex and more difficult to understand than necessary.
- Moreover, generics might be used when you expect to support more data types in the future.
- Once again, the goal of using anything while coding is code simplicity and easier maintenance, not bragging about your coding capabilities.
- Lastly, generics can be used when the developer is feeling comfortable with generics. There is no Go rule that makes the use of generics mandatory.

This section concludes this chapter. Keep in mind that in order to use the cmp, slices, and maps packages, you need Go version 1.21 or later.

Summary

This chapter presented generics and gave you the rationale behind the invention of generics. Additionally, it presented the Go syntax for generics as well as some issues that might come up if you use generics carelessly.

While the Go community is still trying to figure out how to use generics, two things are important: first, you do not have to use generics if you do not want to or if you do not feel comfortable with them, and second, when you use generics the right way, you will write less code for supporting multiple data types.

Although a function with generics is more flexible, code with generics usually runs slower than code that works with predefined static data types. So, the price you pay for flexibility is execution speed. Similarly, Go code with generics has a longer compilation time than equivalent code that does not use generics. Once the Go community begins working with generics in real-world scenarios, the cases where generics offer the highest productivity are going to become much more evident. At the end of the day, programming is about understanding the cost of your decisions. Only then can you consider yourself a programmer. So, understanding the cost of using generics instead of interfaces, reflection, or other techniques is important.

The next chapter is about type methods, which are functions attached to a data type, reflection, and interfaces. All these things will allow us to further improve the statistics application. Additionally, the next chapter will compare generics with interfaces and reflection as there is an overlap in their use.

Exercises

Try to solve the following exercises:

- Create a `PrintMe()` method in `structures.go` that prints all the elements of the linked list.
- Go 1.21 comes with a new function named `clear` that clears maps and slices. For maps, it deletes all entries whereas for slices it zeros all existing values. Experiment with it to learn how it works.
- Implement the `delete()` and `search()` functionality using generics for the linked list found in `structures.go`.
- Implement a doubly-linked list using generics starting with the code found in `structures.go`.

Additional resources

- Why Generics? https://blog.golang.org/why-generics
- An Introduction to Generics: https://go.dev/blog/intro-generics
- The Next Step for Generics: https://blog.golang.org/generics-next-step
- A Proposal for Adding Generics to Go: https://blog.golang.org/generics-proposal
- All your comparable types: https://go.dev/blog/comparable
- The constraints package: https://pkg.go.dev/golang.org/x/exp/constraints
- The cmp package: https://pkg.go.dev/cmp
- The slices package: https://pkg.go.dev/slices
- The maps package: https://pkg.go.dev/maps
- The official proposal for the slices package (similar proposals exist for other Go features): https://github.com/golang/go/issues/45955

Leave a review!

Enjoying this book? Help readers like you by leaving an Amazon review. Scan the QR code below to get a free eBook of your choice.

5

Reflection and Interfaces

You might wonder what happens if you want to sort user-defined data structures, such as phone records or numeric data, based on your own criteria, such as a surname or a statistical property such as the mean value of a dataset. What happens when you want to sort different datasets that share a common behavior without having to implement sorting from scratch for each one of the different data types using multiple functions? Also, imagine that you want to write a utility that sorts uncommon data. For example, imagine that you want to sort a slice that holds various kinds of 3D shapes based on their volume. Can this be performed easily and in a way that makes sense?

The answer to all these questions and concerns is the use of interfaces. However, interfaces are not just about data manipulation and sorting. Interfaces are about expressing abstractions and identifying and defining behaviors that can be shared among different data types. Once you have implemented an interface for a data type, a new world of functionality becomes available for the variables and the values of that type, which can save you time and increase your productivity. Interfaces work with *methods on types* or *type methods*, which are like functions attached to given data types, which, in Go, are usually structures. In Go, interfaces are satisfied implicitly. This means that you do not explicitly declare that a type implements an interface. Instead, a type is considered to implement an interface if it provides implementations for all the methods declared by that interface. Now, let us talk about the *empty interface*, which is represented by interface{}. The empty interface specifies zero methods, meaning that any type satisfies the empty interface. This can be powerful but also requires caution because it essentially says "I can hold a value of any type."

Another handy yet advanced Go feature is reflection, which allows you to examine the internal structure of a data type at execution time. However, as reflection is an advanced Go feature, you might not need to use it on a regular basis.

This chapter covers:

- Reflection
- Type methods
- Interfaces
- Object-oriented programming in Go
- Interfaces versus generics
- Reflection versus generics
- Updating the statistics application

Reflection

We begin this chapter with reflection, which is an advanced Go feature, not because it is an easy subject but because it is going to help you understand how Go works with different data types, including interfaces, and why it is needed.

You might be wondering how you can find out the names of the fields of a structure at execution time. In such cases, you need to use reflection. Apart from enabling you to print the fields and the values of a structure, reflection also allows you to explore and manipulate unknown structures like the ones created from decoding JSON data.

The two main questions that I asked myself when I was introduced to reflection for the first time were the following:

- Why is reflection included in Go?
- When should reflection be used?

To answer the first question, reflection allows you to dynamically learn the type of an arbitrary object along with information about its structure. Go provides the `reflect` package for working with reflection. The `fmt.Println()` function is clever enough to understand the data types of its parameters and act accordingly because, behind the scenes, the `fmt` package uses reflection to do that.

As far as the second question is concerned, reflection allows you to handle and work with data types that do not exist at the time at which you write your code but might exist in the future, which is when we use an existing package with new user-defined data types—Go functions can accept unknown data types with the use of the empty interface. Additionally, reflection might come in handy when you have to work with data types that do not implement a common interface and therefore have an uncommon or unknown behavior—this does not mean that they have bad or erroneous behavior, just uncommon/unusual behavior such as user-defined structures.

Interfaces are covered later in this chapter, so stay tuned for more!

 The introduction of generics in Go might make the use of reflection less frequent in some cases because, with generics, you can work with different data types more easily and without the need to know their exact data types in advance. However, nothing beats reflection for fully exploring the structure and the data types of a variable. We compare reflection with generics at the end of this chapter.

The most useful parts of the `reflect` package are two data types named `reflect.Value` and `reflect.Type`. `reflect.Value` is used for storing values of any type, whereas `reflect.Type` is used for representing Go types. There exist two functions named `reflect.TypeOf()` and `reflect.ValueOf()` that return `reflect.Type` and `reflect.Value` values, respectively. Note that `reflect.TypeOf()` returns the actual type of a variable—if we are examining a structure, it returns the name of the structure.

As structures are really important in Go, the `reflect` package offers the `reflect.NumField()` method for listing the number of fields in a structure as well as the `Field()` method for getting the `reflect.Value` value of a specific field of a structure.

The `reflect` package also defines the `reflect.Kind` data type, which is used for representing the specific data type of a variable: `int`, `struct`, etc. The documentation of the `reflect` package lists all possible values of the `reflect.Kind` data type. The `Kind()` function returns the kind of a variable.

Last, the `Int()` and `String()` methods return the integer and string value of `reflect.Value`, respectively.

Reflection code can look unpleasant and hard to read sometimes. Therefore, according to the Go philosophy, you should rarely use reflection unless it is necessary because, despite its cleverness, it does not create clean code.

Understanding the internal structure of a Go structure

The next utility shows how to use reflection to discover the internal structure and fields of a Go structure variable. Type it and save it as `reflection.go`.

```
package main
import (
    "fmt"
    "reflect"
)
```

```
type Secret struct {
    Username string
    Password string
}

type Record struct {
    Field1 string
    Field2 float64
    Field3 Secret
}
func main() {
    A := Record{"String value", -12.123, Secret{"Mihalis", "Tsoukalos"}}
```

We begin by defining a Record structure variable that contains another structure value
(Secret{"Mihalis", "Tsoukalos"}).

```
    r := reflect.ValueOf(A)
    fmt.Println("String value:", r.String())
```

This returns the reflect.Value of the A variable.

```
    iType := r.Type()
```

Using Type() is how we get the data type of a variable—in this case, variable A.

```
    fmt.Printf("i Type: %s\n", iType)
    fmt.Printf("The %d fields of %s are\n", r.NumField(), iType)
    for i := 0; i < r.NumField(); i++ {
```

The previous for loop allows the visiting of all fields of a structure and the examination of their
characteristics.

```
        fmt.Printf("\t%s ", iType.Field(i).Name)
        fmt.Printf("\twith type: %s ", r.Field(i).Type())
        fmt.Printf("\tand value _%v_\n", r.Field(i).Interface())
```

The previous fmt.Printf() statements return the name, the data type, and the value of the fields.

```
        // Check whether there are other structures embedded in Record
        k := reflect.TypeOf(r.Field(i).Interface()).Kind()
        // Need to convert it to string in order to compare it
        if k.String() == "struct" {
```

To check the data type of a variable with a string, we need to convert the data type into a `string` variable first.

```
            fmt.Println(r.Field(i).Type())
    }
    // Same as before but using the internal value
    if k == reflect.Struct {
```

You can also use the internal representation of a data type during checking.

```
            fmt.Println(r.Field(i).Type())
        }
    }
}
```

Running `reflection.go` produces the following output:

```
$ go run reflection.go
String value: <main.Record Value>
i Type: main.Record
The 3 fields of main.Record are
        Field1  with type: string       and value _String value_
        Field2  with type: float64      and value _-12.123_
        Field3  with type: main.Secret  and value _{Mihalis Tsoukalos}_
main.Secret
main.Secret
```

`main.Record` is the full unique name of the structure as defined by Go—`main` is the package name and `Record` is the `struct` name. This happens so that Go can differentiate between the elements of different packages.

The presented code does not modify any values of the structure. If you were to make changes to the values of the structure fields, you would use the `Elem()` method and pass the structure as a pointer to `ValueOf()`—remember that pointers allow you to make changes to actual variables. There exist methods for modifying existing values. In our case, we are going to use `SetString()` to modify a `string` field and `SetInt()` to modify an `int` field.

This technique is illustrated in the next subsection.

Changing structure values using reflection

Learning about the internal structure of a Go structure is handy, but what is more practical is being able to change values in the Go structure, which is the subject of this subsection. However, keep in mind that this approach is an exception and that the vast majority of Go programs should not need to implement this.

Type the following Go code and save it as setValues.go—it can also be found in the GitHub repository of the book inside the ch05 directory.

```
package main
import (
    "fmt"
    "reflect"
)
type T struct {
    F1 int
    F2 string
    F3 float64
}
func main() {
    A := T{1, "F2", 3.0}
```

A is the variable that is being examined in this program.

```
    fmt.Println("A:", A)
    r := reflect.ValueOf(&A).Elem()
```

With the use of Elem() and a pointer to variable A, variable A can be modified if needed.

```
    fmt.Println("String value:", r.String())
    typeOfA := r.Type()
    for i := 0; i < r.NumField(); i++ {
        f := r.Field(i)
        tOfA := typeOfA.Field(i).Name
        fmt.Printf("%d: %s %s = %v\n", i, tOfA, f.Type(), f.Interface())
        k := reflect.TypeOf(r.Field(i).Interface()).Kind()
        if k == reflect.Int {
            r.Field(i).SetInt(-100)
```

```
        } else if k == reflect.String {
            r.Field(i).SetString("Changed!")
        }
    }
}
```

We are using SetInt() to modify an integer value (reflect.Int) and SetString() to modify a string value (reflect.String). Integer values are set to -100 and string values are set to Changed!.

```
    fmt.Println("A:", A)
}
```

Running setValues.go creates the following output:

```
$ go run setValues.go
A: {1 F2 3}
String value: <main.T Value>
0: F1 int = 1
1: F2 string = F2
2: F3 float64 = 3
A: {-100 Changed! 3}
```

The first line of output shows the initial version of A, whereas the last line shows the final version of A with the modified fields. The main use of such code is for dynamically changing the values of the fields of a structure without knowing the internals of the structure in advance.

The three disadvantages of reflection

Without a doubt, reflection is a powerful Go feature. However, as with all tools, reflection should be used sparingly for three main reasons:

- The first reason is that extensive use of reflection will make your programs hard to read and maintain. A potential solution to this problem is good documentation, but developers are notorious for not having the time to write proper documentation.

- The second reason is that the Go code that uses reflection makes your programs slower. Generally speaking, *Go code that works with a particular data type is always faster than Go code that uses reflection to dynamically work with any Go data type*. Additionally, such dynamic code makes it difficult for tools to refactor or analyze your code.

- The last reason is that reflection errors cannot be caught at build time and are reported at runtime as panics, which means that reflection errors can potentially crash your programs. This can happen months or even years after the development of a Go program! One solution to this problem is extensive testing before a dangerous function call. However, this adds even more Go code to your programs, which makes them even slower.

With the disadvantages of reflection in mind, it is important to remember that reflection is needed for cases such as JSON and XML serialization, dynamic code generation, and dynamic mapping of Go structs to database tables.

Now that we know about reflection and what it can do for us, it is time to begin the discussion about type methods, which are necessary for understanding interfaces.

Type methods

A **type method** is a *function that is attached to a specific data type*. Although type methods (or methods on types) are functions, in reality, they are defined and used in a slightly different way.

 The methods on types feature gives some object-oriented capabilities to Go, which is very handy, and it's used extensively in Go. Additionally, interfaces require type methods to work.

Defining new type methods is as simple as creating new functions, provided that you follow certain rules that associate the function with a data type.

Creating type methods

So, imagine that you want to do calculations with 2x2 matrices. A very natural way of implementing that is by defining a new data type and defining type methods for adding, subtracting, and multiplying 2x2 matrices using that new data type. To make it even more interesting and generic, we are going to create a command line utility that accepts the elements of two 2x2 matrices as command line arguments, which are eight integer values in total, and performs all three calculations between them using the defined type methods.

By having a data type called ar2x2, you can create a type method named FunctionName for it as follows:

```
func (a ar2x2) FunctionName(parameters) <return values> {
    ...
}
```

The (a ar2x2) part is what makes the FunctionName() function a type method because it associ-ates FunctionName() with the ar2x2 data type. No other data type can use that function. However, you are free to implement FunctionName() for other data types or as a regular function. If you have an ar2x2 variable named varAr, you can invoke FunctionName() as varAr.FunctionName(...), which looks like selecting the field of a structure variable.

You are not obligated to develop type methods if you do not want to unless you are dealing with interfaces. Additionally, each type method can be rewritten as a regular function. Therefore, FunctionName() can be rewritten as follows:

```
func FunctionName(a ar2x2, parameters...) <return values> {
    ...
}
```

Bear in mind that, under the hood, the Go compiler does turn methods into regular function calls with the self-value as the first parameter. However, keep in mind that *interfaces require the use of type methods to work*.

 The expressions used for selecting a field of a structure or a type method of a data type, which would replace the ellipsis after the variable name above, are called *selectors*.

Performing calculations between matrices of a given predefined size is one of the rare cases where using an array instead of a slice makes more sense because you do not have to modify the size of the matrices. Some people might argue that using a slice instead of an array pointer is a better practice—you are allowed to use what makes more sense to you and the problem at hand. As a rule of thumb, arrays should be preferred to slices when a fixed-size, contiguous block of memory is required or when performance is a critical concern. So, it is common to use slices for most dynamic collections and arrays for situations where a fixed-size, performance-critical structure is needed.

Most of the time, the results of a type method are saved in the variable that invoked the type method—in order to implement that for the ar2x2 data type, we pass a pointer to the array that invoked the type method, like func (a *ar2x2).

Value and point receivers

As you already know, a method can be associated with a named type, and the receiver of the method can be either a value receiver or a pointer receiver. A value receiver is a receiver associated with a method that operates on a copy of the value rather than the actual value itself. A pointer receiver is a receiver associated with a method that operates directly on the value pointed to by the receiver, rather than on a copy of the value.

The choice between value and pointer receivers has implications for how the method behaves, particularly in terms of modifying the underlying value and performance considerations. In general, it is recommended to use a value receiver when the method does not need to modify the state of the receiver, when working with small, immutable types, or for methods that logically belong to the value itself, not a specific instance. On the other hand, you might prefer to use a pointer receiver when the method needs to modify the state of the receiver, when working with large data structures to avoid any copying overhead, or for methods that logically belong to a particular instance of the type.

The next subsection illustrates type methods in action.

Using type methods

This subsection shows the use of type methods using the ar2x2 data type as an example. The Add() function and the Add() method use the exact same algorithm for adding two matrices. The only difference between them is the way they are called and the fact that the function returns an array, whereas the method saves the result to the calling variable because of the use of a pointer.

Although adding and subtracting matrices is a straightforward process—you just add or subtract each element of the first matrix with the element of the second matrix that is located at the same position—matrix multiplication is a more complex process. This is the main reason that both addition and subtraction use for loops, which means that the code can also work with bigger matrices, whereas multiplication uses static code that cannot be applied to bigger matrices without major changes.

 If you are defining type methods for a structure, you should make sure that the names of the type methods do not conflict with any field name of the structure because the Go compiler will reject such ambiguities.

Type the following code and save it as methods.go.

```go
package main
import (
    "fmt"
    "os"
    "strconv"
)
type ar2x2 [2][2]int
```

```
// Traditional Add() function
func Add(a, b ar2x2) ar2x2 {
    c := ar2x2{}
    for i := 0; i < 2; i++ {
        for j := 0; j < 2; j++ {
            c[i][j] = a[i][j] + b[i][j]
        }
    }
    return c
}
```

Here, we have a traditional function that adds two ar2x2 variables and returns their result.

```
// Type method Add()
func (a *ar2x2) Add(b ar2x2) {
    for i := 0; i < 2; i++ {
        for j := 0; j < 2; j++ {
            a[i][j] = a[i][j] + b[i][j]
        }
    }
}
```

Here, we have a type method named Add() that is attached to the ar2x2 data type. The result of the addition is not returned. What happens is that the ar2x2 variable that called the Add() method is going to be modified and hold that result—this is the reason for using a pointer when defining the type method. If you do not want that behavior, you should modify the signature and the implementation of the type method to match your needs.

```
// Type method Subtract()
func (a *ar2x2) Subtract(b ar2x2) {
    for i := 0; i < 2; i++ {
        for j := 0; j < 2; j++ {
            a[i][j] = a[i][j] - b[i][j]
        }
    }
}
```

The previous method subtracts ar2x2 b from ar2x2 a and the result is saved in the a variable.

```
// Type method Multiply()
func (a *ar2x2) Multiply(b ar2x2) {
    a[0][0] = a[0][0]*b[0][0] + a[0][1]*b[1][0]
    a[1][0] = a[1][0]*b[0][0] + a[1][1]*b[1][0]
    a[0][1] = a[0][0]*b[0][1] + a[0][1]*b[1][1]
    a[1][1] = a[1][0]*b[0][1] + a[1][1]*b[1][1]
}
```

As we are working with small arrays, we do the multiplications without using any for loops.

```
func main() {
    if len(os.Args) != 9 {
        fmt.Println("Need 8 integers")
        return
    }
    k := [8]int{}
    for index, i := range os.Args[1:] {
        v, err := strconv.Atoi(i)
        if err != nil {
            fmt.Println(err)
            return
        }
        k[index] = v
    }
    a := ar2x2{{k[0], k[1]}, {k[2], k[3]}}
    b := ar2x2{{k[4], k[5]}, {k[6], k[7]}}
```

The main() function gets the input and creates two 2x2 matrices. After that, it performs the desired calculations with these two matrices.

```
    fmt.Println("Traditional a+b:", Add(a, b))
    a.Add(b)
    fmt.Println("a+b:", a)
    a.Subtract(a)
    fmt.Println("a-a:", a)
    a = ar2x2{{k[0], k[1]}, {k[2], k[3]}}
```

We calculate a+b using two different ways: using a regular function and using a type method. As both a.Add(b) and a.Subtract(a) change the value of a, we have to initialize a before using it again.

```
    a.Multiply(b)
    fmt.Println("a*b:", a)
    a = ar2x2{{k[0], k[1]}, {k[2], k[3]}}
    b.Multiply(a)
    fmt.Println("b*a:", b)
}
```

Last, we calculate a*b and b*a to show that they are different because the commutative property does not apply to matrix multiplication.

Running methods.go produces the following output:

```
$ go run methods.go 1 2 0 0 2 1 1 1
Traditional a+b: [[3 3] [1 1]]
a+b: [[3 3] [1 1]]
a-a: [[0 0] [0 0]]
a*b: [[4 6] [0 0]]
b*a: [[2 4] [1 2]]
```

The input here is two 2x2 matrices, [[1 2] [0 0]] and [[2 1] [1 1]], and the output is their calculations.

Now that we know about type methods, it is time to begin exploring interfaces as interfaces cannot be implemented without type methods.

Interfaces

An interface is a Go mechanism for defining behavior that is implemented using a set of methods. Interfaces have a core role in Go and can simplify the code of your programs when they have to deal with multiple data types that perform the same task—recall that fmt.Println() works for almost all data types.

But remember, interfaces should not be unnecessarily complex. If you decide to create your own interfaces, then you should begin with a common behavior that you want to be used by multiple data types. Additionally, you should not design your programs by defining interfaces. You should start designing your program and wait for common behaviors to reveal themselves and then convert those common behaviors into interfaces. Last, if the use of interfaces does not make your code simpler, consider removing some or all of your interfaces.

Interfaces define none, a single, or multiple type methods that need to be implemented. *As you already know, once you implement the required type methods of an interface, that interface is satisfied implicitly*. In simpler terms, once you implement the methods of an interface for a given data type, that interface is satisfied automatically for that data type.

 The empty interface is defined as just interface{}. As the empty interface has no methods, it means that it is already implemented by all data types. In Go generics terms, the empty interface is called any.

In a more formal way, a Go interface type defines (or describes) the behavior of other types by specifying a set of methods that need to be implemented to support that behavior. For a data type to satisfy an interface, it needs to implement all the type methods required by that interface. Therefore, interfaces are abstract types that specify a set of methods that need to be implemented so that another type can be considered an instance of the interface. So, an interface is two things: a set of methods and a data type. Bear in mind that small and well-defined interfaces are usually the most popular ones because they can be used in a much larger variety of cases.

As a rule of thumb, only create a new interface when you want to share a common behavior between two or more concrete data types. This is basically duck typing.

The biggest advantage you get from interfaces is that, if needed, you can pass a variable of a data type that implements a particular interface to any function that expects a parameter of that specific interface, which saves you from having to write separate functions for each supported data type. However, Go offers an alternative to this with the recent addition of generics.

Interfaces can also be used to provide a kind of polymorphism in Go, which is an object-oriented concept. *Polymorphism* offers a way of accessing objects of different types in the same uniform way when they share a common behavior.

Last, interfaces can be used for composition. In practice, this means that you can combine existing interfaces and create new ones that offer the combined behavior of the interfaces that were brought together. The next figure shows interface composition in a graphical way.

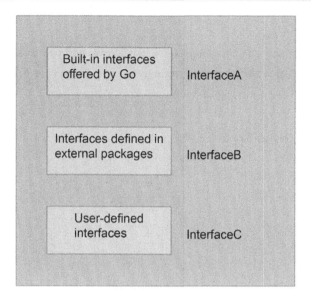

```
type ABC interface {
    InterfaceA
    InterfaceB
    InterfaceC
}
```

Figure 5.1: Interface composition

Put simply, the previous figure illustrates that because of its definition, satisfying interface ABC requires satisfying InterfaceA, InterfaceB, and InterfaceC. Additionally, any ABC variable can be used instead of an InterfaceA variable, an InterfaceB variable, or an InterfaceC variable because it supports all these three behaviors. Last, only ABC variables can be used where an ABC variable is expected. There is nothing prohibiting you from including additional methods in the definition of the ABC interface if the combination of existing interfaces does not describe the desired behavior accurately.

 When you combine existing interfaces, it is better that the interfaces do not contain methods with the same name.

What you should keep in mind is that there is no need for an interface to be impressive and require the implementation of a large number of methods. In fact, the fewer methods an interface has, the more generic and widely used it is going to be, which increases its usefulness and therefore its usage.

The subsection that follows illustrates the use of sort.Interface.

The sort.Interface interface

The sort package contains an interface named sort.Interface that allows you to sort slices according to your needs and your data, provided that you implement sort.Interface for the custom data types stored in your slices. The sort package defines the sort.Interface as follows:

```
type Interface interface {
    // Len is the number of elements in the collection.
    Len() int
    // Less reports whether the element with
    // index i should sort before the element with index j.
    Less(i, j int) bool
    // Swap swaps the elements with indexes i and j.
    Swap(i, j int)
}
```

What we can understand from the definition of sort.Interface is that in order to implement sort.Interface, we need to implement the following three type methods:

*   Len() int
*   Less(i, j int) bool
*   Swap(i, j int)

The Len() method returns the length of the slice that will be sorted and helps the interface to process all slice elements, whereas the Less() method, which compares and sorts elements in pairs, defines how elements, are going to be compared and therefore sorted. The return value of Less() is bool, which means that Less() only cares about whether the element at index i is bigger or not than the element at index j in the way that the two elements are being compared. Last, the Swap() method is used for swapping two elements of the slice, which is required for the sorting algorithm to work.

The following code, which can be found in sort.go, illustrates the use of sort.Interface.

```
package main
import (
    "fmt"
    "sort"
)

type Size struct {
```

```
    F1 int
    F2 string
    F3 int
}

// We want to sort Person records based on the value of Size.F1
// Which is Size.F1 as F3 is an Size structure
type Person struct {
    F1 int
    F2 string
    F3 Size
}
```

The Person structure includes a field named F3 that is of the Size data type, which is also a structure.

```
type Personslice []Person
```

You need to have a slice because all sorting operations work on slices. It is for this slice, which should be a new data type that in this case is called Personslice, that you are going to implement the three type methods of the sort.Interface.

```
// Implementing sort.Interface for Personslice
func (a Personslice) Len() int {
    return len(a)
}
```

Here is the implementation of Len() for the Personslice data type. It is usually that simple.

```
// What field to use when comparing
func (a Personslice) Less(i, j int) bool {
    return a[i].F3.F1 < a[j].F3.F1
}
```

Here is the implementation of Less() for the Personslice data type. This method defines the way elements get sorted. In this case, by using a field of the embedded data structure (F3.F1).

```
func (a Personslice) Swap(i, j int) {
    a[i], a[j] = a[j], a[i]
}
```

This is the implementation of the Swap() type method that defines the way to swap slice elements during sorting. It is usually that simple.

```go
func main() {
    data := []Person{
        Person{1, "One", Size{1, "Person_1", 10}},
        Person{2, "Two", Size{2, "Person_2", 20}},
        Person{-1, "Two", Size{-1, "Person_3", -20}},
    }

    fmt.Println("Before:", data)
    sort.Sort(Personslice(data))
    fmt.Println("After:", data)
    // Reverse sorting works automatically
    sort.Sort(sort.Reverse(Personslice(data)))
    fmt.Println("Reverse:", data)
}
```

Once you have implemented sort.Interface, you are going to see that sort.Reverse(), which is used for reverse sorting your slice, works automatically.

Running sort.go generates the following output:

```
$ go run sort.go
Before: [{1 One {1 Person_1 10}} {2 Two {2 Person_2 20}} {-1 Two {-1
Person_3 -20}}]
After: [{-1 Two {-1 Person_3 -20}} {1 One {1 Person_1 10}} {2 Two {2
Person_2 20}}]
Reverse: [{2 Two {2 Person_2 20}} {1 One {1 Person_1 10}} {-1 Two {-1
Person_3 -20}}]
```

The first line shows the elements of the slice as initially stored. The second line shows the sorted version, whereas the last line shows the reverse sorted version.

Let us now present the handy empty interface.

The empty interface

As mentioned before, the empty interface is defined as just interface{} and is already implemented by all data types. Therefore, variables of any data type can be put in the place of a parameter of the empty interface data type.

Therefore, a function with an interface{} parameter can accept variables of any data type in this place. However, if you intend to work with interface{} function parameters without examining their data type inside the function, you should process them with statements that work on all data types; otherwise, your code may crash or misbehave. Alternatively, you can use generics with proper constraints to avoid any undesired effects.

The program that follows defines two structures named S1 and S2 but just a single function named Print() for printing any of them. This is allowed because Print() requires an interface{} parameter that can accept both S1 and S2 variables. The fmt.Println(s) statement inside Print() can work with both S1 and S2.

If you create a function that accepts one or more interface{} parameters and you run a statement that can only be applied to a limited number of data types, things will not work out well. As an example, not all interface{} parameters can be multiplied by 5 or be used in fmt.Printf() with the %d control string.

The source code of empty.go is as follows:

```
package main
import "fmt"
type S1 struct {
    F1 int
    F2 string
}
type S2 struct {
    F1 int
    F2 S1
}
func Print(s interface{}) {
    fmt.Println(s)
}
func main() {
    v1 := S1{10, "Hello"}
    v2 := S2{F1: -1, F2: v1}
    Print(v1)
    Print(v2)
}
```

Although v1 and v2 are of different data types, Print() can work with both of them.

```
// Printing an integer
```

```
    Print(123)
    // Printing a string
    Print("Go is the best!")
}
```

Print() can also work with integers and strings.

Running empty.go produces the following output:

```
{10 Hello}
{-1 {10 Hello}}
123
Go is the best!
```

Using the empty interface is easy as soon as you realize that you can pass any type of variable in the place of an interface{} parameter and you can return any data type as an interface{} return value. However, with great power comes great responsibility—you should be very careful with interface{} parameters and their return values because, in order to use their real values, you have to be sure about their underlying data type. We are going to discuss this in the next section.

Type assertions and type switches

A *type assertion* is a mechanism for working with the underlying concrete value of an interface. This mainly happens because interfaces are virtual data types without their own values—interfaces just define behavior and do not hold data of their own. But what happens when you do not know the data type before attempting a type assertion? How can you differentiate between the supported data types and the unsupported ones? How can you choose a different action for each supported data type? The answer is by using type switches. Type switches use switch blocks for data types and allow you to differentiate between type assertion values, which are data types, and process each data type the way you want. Additionally, ***to use the empty interface in type switches, you need to use type assertions***.

 You can have type switches for all kinds of interfaces and data types in general. What is really important is to remember that the order of the case clauses in a switch statement is important as only the first match is going to be executed.

Therefore, the real work begins once you enter the function because this is where you need to define the supported data types and the actions that take place for each supported data type.

Type assertions use the x.(T) notation, where x is an interface type and T is a type, and help you extract the value that is hidden behind the empty interface. For a type assertion to work, x should not be nil and the dynamic type of x should be identical to the T type.

The following code can be found in typeSwitch.go.

```
package main
import "fmt"
type Secret struct {
    SecretValue string
}

type Entry struct {
    F1 int
    F2 string
    F3 Secret
}

func Teststruct(x interface{}) {
    // type switch
    switch T := x.(type) {
    case Secret:
        fmt.Println("Secret type")
    case Entry:
        fmt.Println("Entry type")
    default:
        fmt.Printf("Not supported type: %T\n", T)
    }
}
```

This is a type switch with direct support for the Secret and Entry data types only. The default case handles the remaining data types.

```
func Learn(x interface{}) {
    switch T := x.(type) {
    default:
        fmt.Printf("Data type: %T\n", T)
    }
}
```

The Learn() function prints the data type of its input parameter.

```go
func main() {
    A := Entry{100, "F2", Secret{"myPassword"}}
    Teststruct(A)
    Teststruct(A.F3)
    Teststruct("A string")
    Learn(12.23)
    Learn('€')
}
```

The last part of the code calls the desired functions to explore variable A. Running typeSwitch. go produces the following output:

```
$ go run typeSwitch.go
Entry type
Secret type
Not supported type: string
Data type: float64
Data type: int32
```

As you can see, we have managed to execute different code based on the data type of the variable passed to TestStruct() and Learn().

Strictly speaking, type assertions allow you to perform two main tasks. The first task is checking whether an interface value keeps a particular type. When used this way, a type assertion returns two values: the underlying value and a bool value. The underlying value is what you might want to use. However, it is the value of the bool variable that tells you whether the type assertion was successful or not and, therefore, whether you can use the underlying value or not. For example, checking whether a variable named aVar is of the int type requires the use of the aVar.(int) notation, which returns two values. If successful, it returns the real int value of aVar and true. Otherwise, it returns false as the second value, which means that the type assertion was not successful and that the real value could not be extracted. And the second task is using the concrete value stored in an interface or assigning it to a new variable. This means that if there is a float64 variable in an interface, a type assertion allows you to get that value.

 The functionality offered by the reflect package helps Go identify the underlying data type and the real value of an interface{} variable.

So far, we have seen a variation of the first case where we extract the data type stored in an empty interface variable. Now, we are going to learn how to extract the real value stored in an empty interface variable. As already explained, trying to extract the concrete value from an interface using a type assertion can have one of the following two outcomes:

- If you use the correct concrete data type, you get the underlying value without any issues.
- If you use an incorrect concrete data type, your program will panic.

All these are illustrated in assertions.go, which contains the next code as well as lots of code comments that explain the process.

```go
package main
import (
    "fmt"
)

func returnNumber() interface{} {
    return 12
}

func main() {
    anInt := returnNumber()
```

The returnNumber() function returns an int value that is *wrapped in an empty interface*.

```go
    Number, ok := anInt.(int)
    if ok {
        fmt.Println("Type assertion successful: ", number)
    } else {
        fmt.Println("Type assertion failed!")
    }
    number++
    fmt.Println(number)
```

In the previous code, we get the int value wrapped in an empty interface variable (anInt).

```go
    // The next statement would fail because there
    // is no type assertion to get the value:
    // anInt++

    // The next statement fails but the failure is under
```

```
// control because of the ok bool variable that tells
// whether the type assertion is successful or not
value, ok := anInt.(int64)
if ok {
    fmt.Println("Type assertion successful: ", value)
} else {
    fmt.Println("Type assertion failed!")
}

// The next statement is successful but
// dangerous because it does not make sure that
// the type assertion is successful.
// It just happens to be successful
i := anInt.(int)
fmt.Println("i:", i)

// The following will PANIC because anInt is not bool
_ = anInt.(bool)
}
```

The last statement panics the program because the anInt variable does not hold a bool value.
Running assertions.go generates the following output:

```
$ go run assertions.go
13
Type assertion failed!
i: 12
panic: interface conversion: interface {} is int, not bool

goroutine 1 [running]:
main.main()
    /Users/mtsouk/mGo4th/code/ch05/assertions.go:39 +0x130
exit status 2
```

The reason for the panic is written onscreen: panic: interface conversion: interface {}
is int, not bool. What else can the Go compiler do to help you?

Next, we discuss the map[string]interface{} map and its use.

The map[string]interface{} map

You have a utility that processes its command line arguments; if everything goes as expected, then you get the supported types of command line arguments and everything goes smoothly. But what happens when something unexpected occurs? In that case, the map[string]interface{} map is here to help, and this subsection shows how! This is just one of the cases where the handy map[string]interface{} map can be used.

Remember that the biggest advantage you get from using a map[string]interface{} map, or any map that stores an interface{} value in general, is that you still have your data in its original state and data type. If you use map[string]string instead, or anything similar, then any data you have is going to be converted into a string, which means that you are going to lose information about the original data type and the structure of the data you are storing in the map.

Nowadays, web services work by exchanging JSON records. If you get a JSON record in an anticipated format, then you can process it as expected and everything will be fine. However, there are times when you might get an erroneous record or a record in an unsupported JSON format. In these cases, using map[string]interface{} for storing these unknown JSON records (arbitrary data) is a good choice because map[string]interface{} is good at storing JSON records of unknown types. We are going to illustrate that using a utility named mapEmpty.go that processes arbitrary JSON records given as command line arguments. We process the input JSON record in two ways that are similar but not identical. There is no real difference between the exploreMap() and typeSwitch() functions apart from the fact that typeSwitch() generates a much richer output. The code of mapEmpty.go is as follows:

```go
package main
import (
    "encoding/json"
    "fmt"
    "os"
)

var JSONrecord = `{
    "Flag": true,
    "Array": ["a","b","c"],
    "Entity": {
      "a1": "b1",
      "a2": "b2",
```

```
        "Value": -456,
        "Null": null
      },
      "Message": "Hello Go!"
  }`
```

This global variable holds the default value of `JSONrecord`, in case there is no user input.

```
func typeSwitch(m map[string]interface{}) {
    for k, v := range m {
        switch c := v.(type) {
        case string:
            fmt.Println("Is a string!", k, c)
        case float64:
            fmt.Println("Is a float64!", k, c)
        case bool:
            fmt.Println("Is a Boolean!", k, c)
        case map[string]interface{}:
            fmt.Println("Is a map!", k, c)
            typeSwitch(v.(map[string]interface{}))
        default:
            fmt.Printf("...Is %v: %T!\n", k, c)
        }
    }
    return
}
```

The `typeSwitch()` function uses a type switch for differentiating between the values in its input map. If a map is found, then we recursively call `typeSwitch()` on the new map in order to examine it even more. The `for` loop allows you to examine all the elements of the `map[string]interface{}` map.

```
func exploreMap(m map[string]interface{}) {
    for k, v := range m {
        embMap, ok := v.(map[string]interface{})
        // If it is a map, explore deeper
        if ok {
            fmt.Printf("{\"%v\": \n", k)
```

```
            exploreMap(embMap)
            fmt.Printf("}\n")
        } else {
            fmt.Printf("%v: %v\n", k, v)
        }
    }
}
```

The `exploreMap()` function inspects the contents of its input map. If a map is found, then we call `exploreMap()` on the new map recursively in order to examine it on its own.

```
func main() {
    if len(os.Args) == 1 {
        fmt.Println("*** Using default JSON record.")
    } else {
        JSONrecord = os.Args[1]
    }
    JSONMap := make(map[string]interface{})
    err := json.Unmarshal([]byte(JSONrecord), &JSONMap)
```

As you will learn in *Chapter 7, Telling a UNIX System What To Do*, `json.Unmarshal()` processes JSON data and converts it into a Go value. Although this value is usually a Go structure, in this case, we are using a map as specified by the `map[string]interface{}` variable. Strictly speaking, the second parameter of `json.Unmarshal()` is of the empty interface data type, which means that its data type can be anything.

```
    if err != nil {
        fmt.Println(err)
        return
    }
    exploreMap(JSONMap)
    typeSwitch(JSONMap)
}
```

`map[string]interface{}` is extremely handy for storing JSON records when you do not know their schema in advance. In other words, `map[string]interface{}` is good at *storing arbitrary JSON data of unknown schema.*

Running mapEmpty.go produces the following output—bear in mind that you might see a different output since maps do not guarantee order:

```
$ go run mapEmpty.go
*** Using default JSON record.
Flag: true
Array: [a b c]
{"Entity":
a2: b2
Value: -456
Null: <nil>
a1: b1
}
Message: Hello Go!
...Is Array: []interface {}!
Is a map! Entity map[Null:<nil> Value:-456 a1:b1 a2:b2]
Is a float64! Value -456
...Is Null: <nil>!
Is a string! a1 b1
Is a string! a2 b2
Is a string! Message Hello Go!
Is a Boolean! Flag true
$ go run mapEmpty.go '{"Array": [3, 4], "Null": null, "String": "Hello
Go!"}'
Array: [3 4]
Null: <nil>
String: Hello Go!
...Is Array: []interface {}!
...Is Null: <nil>!
Is a string! String Hello Go!
$ go run mapEmpty.go '{"Array":"Error"'
unexpected end of JSON input
```

The first run is without any command line parameters, which means that the utility uses the default value of JSONrecord and therefore outputs the hardcoded data. The other two executions use user-specified data. First, valid data, and then data that does not represent a valid JSON record. The error message in the third execution is generated by json.Unmarshal() as it cannot understand the schema of the erroneous JSON record.

The error data type

As promised, we are revisiting the error data type because it is an interface defined as follows:

```
type error interface {
    Error() string
}
```

So, in order to satisfy the error interface, you just need to implement the Error() string type method. This does not change the way we use errors to find out whether the execution of a function or method was successful or not but shows how important interfaces are in Go as they are used transparently all the time. However, the crucial question is when you should implement the error interface on your own instead of using the default one. The answer to that question is when you want to give more context to an error condition.

Now, let us talk about the error interface in a more practical situation. When there is nothing more to read from a file, Go returns an io.EOF error, which, strictly speaking, is not an error condition but a logical part of reading a file. If a file is totally empty, you still get io.EOF when you try to read it for the first time. However, this might cause problems in some situations, and you might need to have a way of differentiating between a totally empty file and a file that has been read fully and there is nothing more to read. One way of dealing with that issue is with the help of the error interface.

The code example that is presented here is connected to file I/O. Putting it here might generate some questions about reading files in Go—however, I feel that this is the appropriate place to put it because it is connected to errors and error handling more than it is connected to file reading in Go.

The code of errorInt.go without the package and import blocks is as follows:

```
type emptyFile struct {
    Ended bool
    Read  int
}
```

emptyFile is a new data type that is used in the program.

```
// Implement error interface
func (e emptyFile) Error() string {
    return fmt.Sprintf("Ended with io.EOF (%t) but read (%d) bytes",
e.Ended, e.Read)
}
```

This is the implementation of the error interface for emptyFile.

```
// Check values
func isFileEmpty(e error) bool {
    // Type assertion
    v, ok := e.(emptyFile)
```

This is a type assertion for getting an emptyFile structure from the error variable.

```
    if ok {
        if v.Read == 0 && v.Ended == true {
            return true
        }
    }
    return false
}
```

This is a method for checking whether a file is empty or not. The if condition translates as: If you have read zero bytes (v.Read == 0) and you have reached the end of the file (v.Ended == true), then the file is empty.

If you want to deal with multiple error variables, you should add a type switch to the isFileEmpty() function after the type assertion.

```
func readFile(file string) error {
    var err error
    fd, err := os.Open(file)
    if err != nil {
        return err
    }
    defer fd.Close()
    reader := bufio.NewReader(fd)
    n := 0
    for {
        line, err := reader.ReadString('\n')
        n += len(line)
```

We read the input file line by line—you are going to learn more about file I/O in *Chapter 7, Telling a UNIX System What to Do.*

```
        if err == io.EOF {
```

```
                    // End of File: nothing more to read
                    if n == 0 {
                        return emptyFile{true, n}
                    }
```

If we have reached the end of a file (io.EOF) and we have read zero characters, then we are dealing with an empty file. This kind of context is added to the emptyFile structure and returned as an error value.

```
                    break
                } else if err != nil {
                    return err
                }
            }
        }
        return nil
    }


    func main() {
        flag.Parse()
        if len(flag.Args()) == 0 {
            fmt.Println("usage: errorInt <file1> [<file2> ...]")
            return
        }
        for _, file := range flag.Args() {
            err := readFile(file)
            if isFileEmpty(err) {
                fmt.Println(file, err)
```

This is where we check the error message of the readFile() function. The order we do the checking in is important because only the first match is executed. *This means that we must go from more specific cases to more generic ones*.

```
            } else if err != nil {
                fmt.Println(file, err)
            } else {
                fmt.Println(file, "is OK.")
            }
        }
    }
```

Running errorInt.go produces the following output—your output might differ:

```
$ go run errorInt.go /etc/hosts /tmp/doesNotExist /tmp/empty /tmp /tmp/
Empty.txt
/etc/hosts is OK.
/tmp/doesNotExist open /tmp/doesNotExist: no such file or directory
/tmp/empty open /tmp/empty: permission denied
/tmp read /tmp: is a directory
/tmp/Empty.txt Ended with io.EOF (true) but read (0) bytes
```

The first file (/etc/hosts) was read without any issues, whereas the second file (/tmp/doesNotExist) could not be found. The third file (/tmp/empty) was there but we did not have the required file permissions to read it, whereas the fourth file (/tmp) was, in reality, a directory. The last file (/tmp/Empty.txt) was there but was empty, which is the error situation that we wanted to catch in the first place.

Writing your own interfaces

In this section, we are going to learn how to write our own interfaces. Creating your own interfaces is easy. For reasons of simplicity, we include our own interface in the main package. However, this is rarely the case as we usually want to share our interfaces, which means that interfaces are usually included in Go packages other than main.

The following code excerpt defines a new interface.

```
type Shape2D interface {
    Perimeter() float64
}
```

This interface has the following properties:

- It is called Shape2D.
- It requires the implementation of a single method named Perimeter() that returns a float64 value.

Apart from being user-defined, there is nothing special about that interface compared to the built-in Go interfaces—you can use it as you do all other existing interfaces. So, in order for a data type to satisfy the Shape2D interface, it needs to implement a type method named Perimeter() that returns a float64 value.

Using a Go interface

The code that follows presents the simplest way of using an interface, which is by calling its method directly, as if it were a function, to get a result. Although this is allowed, it is rarely the case as we usually create functions that accept interface parameters in order for these functions to be able to work with multiple data types.

The code uses a handy technique for quickly finding out whether a given variable is of a given data type that was presented earlier in assertions.go. In this case, we examine whether a variable is of the Shape2D interface by using the interface{}(a).(Shape2D) notation, where a is the variable that is being examined and Shape2D is the data type against the variable being checked.

The next program is called Shape2D.go—its most interesting parts are the following:

```go
type Shape2D interface {
    Perimeter() float64
}
```

This is the definition of the Shape2D interface that requires the implementation of the Perimeter() type method.

```go
type circle struct {
    R float64
}

func (c circle) Perimeter() float64 {
    return 2 * math.Pi * c.R
}
```

This is where the circle type implements the Shape2D interface with the implementation of the Perimeter() type method.

```go
func main() {
    a := circle{R: 1.5}
    fmt.Printf("R %.2f -> Perimeter %.3f \n", a.R, a.Perimeter())

    _, ok := interface{}(a).(Shape2D)
    if ok {
        fmt.Println("a is a Shape2D!")
    }
```

```
    i := 12
    _, ok = interface{}(i).(Shape2D)
    if ok {
        fmt.Println("i is a Shape2D!")
    }
}
```

As stated before, the `interface{}(a).(Shape2D)` notation checks whether the a variable satisfies the `Shape2D` interface without using its underlying value (`circle{R: 1.5}`).

Running `Shape2D.go` creates the following output:

```
R 1.50 -> Perimeter 9.425
a is a Shape2D!
```

Object-oriented programming in Go

As Go does not support all object-oriented features, it cannot replace an object-oriented programming language fully. However, it can mimic some object-oriented concepts.

First, a Go structure with its type methods is like an object with its methods. Second, interfaces are like abstract data types that define behaviors and objects of the same class, which is similar to polymorphism. Third, Go supports encapsulation, which means it supports hiding data and functions from the user by making them private to the structure and the current Go package. Last, combining interfaces and structures is like composition in object-oriented terminology.

 If you really want to develop applications using the object-oriented methodology, then choosing Go might not be your best option. As I am not really into Java, I would suggest looking at C++ or Python instead. The general rule here is to choose the best tool for your job.

You have already seen some of these points earlier in this chapter—the next chapter discusses how to define private fields and functions. The example that follows, which is named `obj0.go`, illustrates composition and polymorphism as well as embedding an anonymous structure into an existing one to get all its fields.

```
package main
import (
    "fmt"
```

```
)

type IntA interface {
    foo()
}

type IntB interface {
    bar()
}

type IntC interface {
    IntA
    IntB
}
```

The IntC interface combines interfaces IntA and IntB. If you implement IntA and IntB for a data type, then this data type implicitly satisfies IntC.

```
type a struct {
    XX int
    YY int
}

type b struct {
    AA string
    XX int
}

type c struct {
    A a
    B b
}
```

This structure has two fields named A and B that are of the a and b data types, respectively.

```
func processA(s IntA) {
    fmt.Printf("%T\n", s)
}
```

This function works with data types that satisfy the IntA interface.

```
// Satisfying IntA
func (varC c) foo() {
    fmt.Println("Foo Processing", varC)
}
```

Structure c satisfies IntA as it implements foo().

```
// Satisfying IntB
func (varC c) bar() {
    fmt.Println("Bar Processing", varC)
}
```

Now, structure c satisfies IntB. As structure c satisfies both IntA and IntB, it implicitly satisfies IntC, which is a composition of the IntA and IntB interfaces.

```
// Structure compose gets the fields of structure a
type compose struct {
    field1 int
    a
}
```

This new structure uses an anonymous structure (a), which means that it gets the fields of that anonymous structure.

```
// Different structures can have methods with the same name
func (A a) A() {
    fmt.Println("Function A() for A")
}

func (B b) A() {
    fmt.Println("Function A() for B")
}

func main() {
    var iC c = c{a{120, 12}, b{"-12", -12}}
```

Here, we define a c variable that is composed of an a structure and a b structure.

```
    iC.A.A()
    iC.B.A()
```

Here, we access a method of the a structure (A.A()) and a method of the b structure (B.A()).

```
// The following will not work
// iComp := compose{field1: 123, a{456, 789}}
// iComp := compose{field1: 123, XX: 456, YY: 789}
iComp := compose{123, a{456, 789}}
fmt.Println(iComp.XX, iComp.YY, iComp.field1)
```

When using an anonymous structure inside another structure, as we do with a{456, 789}, you can access the fields of the anonymous structure, which is the a{456, 789} structure, directly as iComp.XX and iComp.YY.

```
    iC.bar()
    processA(iC)
}
```

Although processA() works with IntA variables, it can also work with IntC variables because the IntC interface satisfies IntA!

All the code in obj0.go is simplistic compared to the code of a real object-oriented programming language that supports abstract classes and inheritance. However, it is more than adequate for generating types and elements with an internal structure, as well as for having different data types with the same method names.

Running obj0.go produces the following output:

```
$ go run obj0.go
Function A() for A
Function A() for B
456 789 123
Bar Processing {{120 12} {-12 -12}}
main.c
```

The first two lines of the output show that two different structures can have methods with the same name. The third line proves that when using an anonymous structure inside one other structure, you can access the fields of the anonymous structure directly. The fourth line is the output of the iC.bar() call, where iC is a c variable accessing a method from the IntB interface. The last line is the output of processA(iC) that requires an IntA parameter and prints the real data type of its parameter, which, in this case, is main.c.

Evidently, although Go is not an object-oriented programming language, it can mimic some of the characteristics of object-oriented languages.

The next section discusses the differences between using interfaces and generics to support multiple data types.

Interfaces versus generics

This section presents a program that increments a numeric value by one using interfaces and generics so that you can compare the implementation details.

The code of genericsInterfaces.go illustrates the two techniques and contains the next code.

```
package main
import (
    "fmt"
)

type Numeric interface {
    int | int8 | int16 | int32 | int64 | float64
}
```

This is where we define a constraint named Numeric for limiting the permitted data types.

```
func Print(s interface{}) {
    // type switch
    switch s.(type) {
```

The Print() function uses the empty interface for getting input and a type switch to work with that input parameter.

Put simply, we are using a type switch to differentiate between the supported data types—in this case, the supported data types are just int and float64, which have to do with the implementation of the *type switch*. However, adding more data types requires code changes, which is not the most efficient solution when a large number of data types needs to be supported.

```
    case int:
        fmt.Println(s.(int)+1)
```

This branch is how we handle the int case.

```
case float64:
    fmt.Println(s.(float64)+1)
```

This branch is how we handle the float64 case.

```
default:
    fmt.Println("Unknown data type!")
    }
}
```

The default branch is how we handle all unsupported data types.

The biggest issue with Print() is that due to the use of the empty interface, it accepts all kinds of input. As a result, the function signature does not help us limit the allowed data types. The second issue with Print() is that we need to specifically handle each case—handling more cases means writing more code.

On the other hand, the compiler and the developer do not have to guess many things with that code, which is not the case with generics, where the compiler and the runtime have more work to do. This kind of work introduces delays in the execution time.

```
func PrintGenerics[T any](s T) {
    fmt.Println(s)
}
```

PrintGenerics() is a generic function that can handle all available data types simply and elegantly.

```
func PrintNumeric[T Numeric](s T) {
    fmt.Println(s+1)
}
```

The PrintNumeric() function supports all numeric data types with the use of the Numeric constraint. No need to specifically add code for supporting each distinct data type, as happens with Print().

```
func main() {
    Print(12)
    Print(-1.23)
    Print("Hi!")
```

The first part of main() uses Print() with various types of input: an int value, a float64 value, and a string value, respectively.

```
PrintGenerics(1)
PrintGenerics("a")
PrintGenerics(-2.33)
```

As stated before, PrintGenerics() works with all data types, including string values.

```
PrintNumeric(1)
PrintNumeric(-2.33)
}
```

The last part of main() uses PrintNumeric() with numeric values only, due to the use of the Numeric constraint.

Running genericsInterfaces.go produces the following output:

```
13
-0.22999999999999998
Unknown data type!
```

The preceding three lines of the output are from the Print() function, which uses the empty interface.

```
1
a
-2.33
```

The previous three lines of the output are from the PrintGenerics() function, which uses generics and supports all available data types. As a result, it should not blindly increase the value of its input because we do not know for sure that we are dealing with a numeric value. Therefore, it just prints the given input.

```
2
-1.33
```

The last two lines are generated by the two PrintNumeric() calls, which operate using the Numeric constraint.

So, in practice, when you have to support multiple data types, the use of generics might be a better choice than using interfaces. However, when we want to define and use a specific behavior, interfaces are better and more descriptive than generics. Such cases include reading data with the Reader interface or writing data with the Writer interface.

The next section discusses the use of reflection as a way of bypassing the use of generics.

Reflection versus generics

In this section, we develop a utility that prints the elements of a slice in two ways: first, using reflection, and second, using generics.

The code of genericsReflection.go is as follows:

```go
package main
import (
    "fmt"
    "reflect"
)

func PrintReflection(s interface{}) {
    fmt.Println("** Reflection")
    val := reflect.ValueOf(s)
    if val.Kind() != reflect.Slice {
        return
    }
    for i := 0; i < val.Len(); i++ {
        fmt.Print(val.Index(i).Interface(), " ")
    }
    fmt.Println()
}
```

Internally, the PrintReflection() function works with slices only. However, as we cannot express that in the function signature, we need to accept an empty interface parameter. Put simply, instead of specifying all kinds of slices, it makes much more sense to use the empty interface. Additionally, we have to write more code to get the desired output and prevent the function from crashing.

In more detail, first, we need to make sure that we are processing a slice (`reflect.Slice`), and second, we have to print the slice elements using a for loop, which is pretty ugly.

```
func PrintSlice[T any](s []T) {
    fmt.Println("** Generics")
    for _, v := range s {
        fmt.Print(v, " ")
    }
    fmt.Println()
}
```

Once again, *the implementation of the generic function is simpler and therefore easier to understand*. Moreover, the function signature specifies that only slices are accepted as function parameters—we do not have to perform any additional checks for that as this is a job for the Go compiler. Last, we use a simple for loop with range to print the slice elements.

```
func main() {
    PrintSlice([]int{1, 2, 3})
    PrintSlice([]string{"a", "b", "c"})
    PrintSlice([]float64{1.2, -2.33, 4.55})
    PrintReflection([]int{1, 2, 3})
    PrintReflection([]string{"a", "b", "c"})
    PrintReflection([]float64{1.2, -2.33, 4.55})
}
```

The `main()` function calls `PrintSlice()` and `PrintReflection()` with various kinds of input to test their operation.

Running `genericsReflection.go` generates the following output:

```
** Generics
1 2 3
** Generics
a b c
** Generics
1.2 -2.33 4.55
```

The first six lines are produced by taking advantage of generics and print the elements of a slice of int values, a slice of `string` values, and a slice of `float64` values.

```
** Reflection
```

```
1 2 3
** Reflection
a b c
** Reflection
1.2 -2.33 4.55
```

The last six lines of the output produce the same output but, this time, using reflection. There is no difference in the output—all differences are in the code found in the implementations of PrintReflection() and PrintSlice() for printing the output. As expected, *generics code is simpler and shorter than Go code that uses reflection*, especially when you must support lots of different data types. While generics in Go offer a powerful and type-safe way to write reusable code, there are scenarios where using reflection might be more suitable, including dynamic type handling, working with uncommon types, serialization and deserialization, and when implementing custom marshaling and unmarshaling.

Moving on, the last section of this chapter is about updating the statistics application by reading multiple files and sorting its output by a given statistical property.

Updating the statistics application

What we are going to do in this section is sort different datasets based on their mean value. As a result, the application is going to be able to read multiple files, which are going to be given as command line arguments to the utility—we are going to learn more about file I/O in *Chapter 7, Telling a UNIX System What to Do*.

We are going to create a structure that holds the statistical properties of each datafile, use a slice to store all such structures, and sort them based on the mean value of each dataset. The last functionality is going to be implemented using the sort.Interface. Using a structure for keeping the important information organized is a common practice. Additionally, we are going to use the slices.Min() and slices.Max() functions for finding the minimum and the maximum value in a slice, respectively, which saves us from having to sort the slice.

 Although such utilities look naïve at first, they can be the foundation of complex machine learning systems. In general, statistics is the foundation of machine learning.

The definition of the DataFile structure is the following:

```
type DataFile struct {
```

```
   Filename string
   Len       int
   Minimum   float64
   Maximum   float64
   Mean      float64
   StdDev    float64
}
```

We also need to define a new data type for a slice of DataFile structures, which is the following:

```
type DFslice []DataFile
```

It is for DFslice that we are going to implement the sort.Interface.

```
func (a DFslice) Len() int {
    return len(a)
}

func (a DFslice) Less(i, j int) bool {
    return a[i].Mean < a[j].Mean
}

func (a DFslice) Swap(i, j int) {
    a[i], a[j] = a[j], a[i]
}
```

The previous three methods satisfy the sort.Interface for DFslice.

The implementation of the main() function is presented in four parts, the first part being the following:

```
func main() {
    if len(os.Args) == 1 {
        fmt.Println("Need one or more file paths!")
        return
    }

    // Slice of DataFile structures
    files := DFslice{}
```

In this first part of main(), we make sure that we have at least one command line argument to process and we define a slice of DataFile structures variable for keeping the data of each file.

The second part of main() is as follows:

```
for i := 1; i < len(os.Args); i++ {
        file := os.Args[i]
        currentFile := DataFile{}
        currentFile.Filename = file

        values, err := readFile(file)
        if err != nil {
            fmt.Println("Error reading:", file, err)
            os.Exit(0)
        }
```

The presented for loop processes all input files unless there is an error. In case of error, the utility exits with a call to os.Exit(0). A different approach would have been to skip the erroneous input file and continue with the next. Additionally, the currentFile variable keeps the data of the current file in a DataFile structure.

The third part of main() contains the following code:

```
        currentFile.Len = len(values)
        currentFile.Minimum = slices.Min(values)
        currentFile.Maximum = slices.Max(values)
        meanValue, standardDeviation := stdDev(values)
        currentFile.Mean = meanValue
        currentFile.StdDev = standardDeviation

        files = append(files, currentFile)
    }
```

In the previous code, we compute all the required statistical properties and save them in the currentFile variable. Last, the current version of the currentFile variable is stored in the files slice before continuing with the next file, if any.

The last part of main() comes with the following code:

```
    sort.Sort(files)
    for _, val := range files {
```

```
        f := val.Filename
        fmt.Println(f,":",val.Len,val.Mean,val.Maximum,val.Minimum)
    }
}
```

The last part of the utility sorts the `files` slice and prints information about each one of the input files. You can print any data you want from the `files` slice.

Running `stats.go` using the simplistic data files found in the `ch05` directory produces the following output:

```
$ go run stats.go d1.txt d2.txt d3.txt
Mean value: 3.00000
Mean value: 18.20000
Mean value: 0.75000
d3.txt : 4 0.75 102 -300
d1.txt : 5 3 5 1
d2.txt : 5 18.2 100 -4
```

As the mean value of `d3.txt` is `0.75`, `d3.txt` is presented before `d1.txt`, which has a mean value of `3`, and `d2.txt`, which has a mean value of `18.2`.

Summary

In this chapter, we learned about interfaces, which are like contracts, and also about type methods, type assertion, and reflection. Although reflection is a very powerful Go feature, it might slow down your Go programs because it adds a layer of complexity at runtime. Furthermore, your Go programs could crash if you use reflection carelessly. However, reflection is not usually needed unless you want to perform low-level tasks with Go variables.

Remember that interfaces specify behavior, specify what you can do, and not what a data type is. Code that uses interfaces successfully is more readable, more extensible, and simpler to understand. Last, *keep in mind that interfaces are implemented implicitly once the required type methods are implemented*.

This chapter also discussed writing Go code that follows the principles of object-oriented programming. If you are going to remember just one thing from this chapter, it should be that Go is not an object-oriented programming language, but it can mimic some of the functionality offered by object-oriented programming languages, such as Java, Python, and C++. In the last section, we updated the statistics application to support the sorting of multiple datasets based on the mean value of a dataset.

The next chapter discusses semantic versioning, Go packages, functions, and workspaces.

Exercises

Try to do the following exercises:

- Create a slice of structures using a structure that you created and sort the elements of the slice using a field from the structure.
- Use the empty interface and a function that allows you to differentiate between two different structures that you have created.

Additional resources

- The documentation of the reflect package: https://pkg.go.dev/reflect
- The documentation of the sort package: https://pkg.go.dev/sort
- Working with errors in Go 1.13: https://blog.go.dev/go1.13-errors
- The implementation of the sort package: https://go.dev/src/sort/

Join our community on Discord

Join our community's Discord space for discussions with the authors and other readers:

https://discord.gg/FzuQbc8zd6

6

Go Packages and Functions

The focus of this chapter is on Go packages, which are the Go way of organizing, delivering, and using code. Packages are used to organize related functionality in your code. As the package author, you design the package, including the public API consisting of exported constants, variables, types, and functions. Go also supports modules, which contain one or more packages. Modules are versioned following SemVer, allowing the module author to release updates and even breaking changes using a `major.minor.patch` versioning scheme. This chapter will also explain the operation of `defer`, which is typically used for cleaning up and releasing resources.

Regarding the visibility of package elements, Go follows a simple rule which states that functions, variables, data types, structure fields, and so forth that begin with an uppercase letter are public, whereas functions, variables, types, and so forth that begin with a lowercase letter are private. This is the reason why `fmt.Println()` is named `Println()` instead of just `println()`. The same rule applies not only to the name of a struct variable but to the fields of a struct variable—in practice, this means that you can have a struct variable with both private and public fields. However, this rule does not affect package names, which are allowed to begin with either uppercase or lowercase letters. In fact, the names of packages, including `main`, are in lowercase.

There is a simple guideline that governs Go: ***Do not use any of its features prematurely***. This guideline applies to generics, interfaces, and packages. Put simply, do not create a package just because you can. Start developing your application in the `main` package and write your functions in the `main` package until you find out that the same code needs to be used from other Go applications or that you are writing too many functions that can be grouped in packages. In that case, grouping and putting related functionality in a separate package makes perfect sense. Other reasons for developing code in separate packages include the encapsulation, testing, and security of exposed functionality.

In summary, this chapter covers:

- Go packages
- Functions
- Big O complexity
- Developing your own packages
- Using GitHub to store Go packages
- Modules
- Creating better packages
- Creating documentation
- Workspaces
- Versioning utilities

Go packages

Everything in Go is delivered in the form of packages. A Go package is a Go source file that begins with the package keyword, followed by the name of the package.

Note that packages can have structure. For example, the net package has several subdirectories, named http, mail, rpc, smtp, textproto, and url, which should be imported as net/http, net/mail, net/rpc, net/smtp, net/textproto, and net/url, respectively.

Apart from the packages of the Go standard library, there are external packages that are imported using their full address and that should be downloaded on the local machine, before their first use. One such example is https://github.com/spf13/cobra, which is stored in GitHub.

Packages are mainly used for grouping *related* functions, variables, and constants so that you can transfer them easily and use them in your own Go programs. Note that apart from the main package, Go packages are not autonomous programs and cannot be compiled into executable files on their own. As a result, if you try to execute a Go package as if it were an autonomous program, you are going to be disappointed:

```
$ go run aPackage.go
go run: cannot run non-main package
```

Instead, packages need to be called directly or indirectly from the main package in order to be used, as we have shown in previous chapters.

About go get and go install

In this subsection, you will learn how to download external Go packages using `https://github.com/spf13/cobra` as an example. The go get command for downloading the cobra package is as follows:

```
$ go get github.com/spf13/cobra
```

However, as we are going to learn in a while, with all recent Go versions, the recommended way to download a package is with go install. You can learn more about that change at `https://go.dev/doc/go-get-install-deprecation`.

Note that you can download the package without using `https://` in its address. The results can be found inside the ~/go directory—the full path is ~/go/src/github.com/spf13/cobra. As the cobra package comes with a binary file that helps you structure and create command line utilities, you can find that binary file inside ~/go/bin as cobra.

The following output, which was created with the help of the tree(1) utility, shows a high-level view with 3 levels of detail of the structure of ~/go on my machine:

```
$ tree ~/go -L 3
/Users/mtsouk/go
├── bin
│   ├── benchstat
│   ├── client
│   ├── cobra
│   ├── dlv
│   ├── dlv-dap
│   ├── fillstruct
│   ├── go-outline
│   ├── go-symbols
│   ├── gocode
│   ├── gocode-gomod
│   ├── godef
│   ├── godoc
│   ├── godoctor
│   ├── golint
│   ├── gomodifytags
│   ├── gopkgs
```

```
│   ├── goplay
│   ├── gopls
│   ├── gorename
│   ├── goreturns
│   ├── gotests
│   ├── guru
│   ├── impl
│   └── staticcheck
├── pkg
│   ├── darwin_amd64
│   │   └── github.com
│   └── sumdb
│       └── sum.golang.org
└── src
    ├── document
    │   └── document.go
    ├── github.com
    │   ├── agext
    │   ├── apparentlymart
    │   ├── fsnotify
    │   ├── hashicorp
    │   ├── mactsouk
    │   ├── magiconair
    │   ├── mitchellh
    │   ├── pelletier
    │   ├── spf13
    │   ├── subosito
    │   └── zclconf
    ├── golang.org
    │   └── x
    └── gopkg.in
        ├── ini.v1
        └── yaml.v2

26 directories, 25 files
```

The x path, which is displayed near the end of the output, is used by the Go team for storing experiment packages that might become part of the standard Go library in the future.

Basically, there are three main directories under ~/go, with the following properties:

- The bin directory: This is where binary tools are placed.

- The pkg directory: This is where reusable packages are put. The darwin_amd64 directory, which can be found on macOS machines only, contains compiled versions of the
  installed packages. On a Linux machine, you can find a linux_amd64 directory instead
  of darwin_amd64.

- The src directory: This is where the source code of the packages is located. The underlying structure is based on the URL of the package you are looking for. So, the URL for the
  github.com/spf13/viper package is ~/go/src/github.com/spf13/viper. If a package
  is downloaded as a module, then it will be located under ~/go/pkg/mod.

Starting with Go 1.16, go install is the recommended way of building and installing packages
in module mode and you should only use that way. The use of go get is deprecated, but this
chapter uses go get because it is commonly used online and is worth knowing about. However,
most of the chapters in this book use go mod init and go mod tidy for downloading external
dependencies for your own source files, which is the recommended way.

If you want to upgrade an existing package, you should execute go get with the -u option. Additionally, if you want to see what is happening behind the scenes, add the -v option to the go
get command—in this case, we are using the Viper package as an example, but we abbreviate
the output:

```
$ go get -v github.com/spf13/viper
github.com/spf13/viper (download)
...
github.com/spf13/afero (download)
get "golang.org/x/text/transform": found meta tag get.
metaImport{Prefix:"golang.org/x/text", VCS:"git", RepoRoot:"https://
go.googlesource.com/text"} at //golang.org/x/text/transform?go-get=1
get "golang.org/x/text/transform": verifying non-authoritative meta tag
...
github.com/fsnotify/fsnotify
github.com/spf13/viper
```

What you can basically see in the output is the dependencies of the initial package being downloaded before the desired package—most of the time, you do not want to know that.

We will continue this chapter by looking at the most important package element: functions.

Functions

The main elements of packages are functions, which are the subject of this section.

 Type methods and functions are implemented in the same way and, sometimes, the terms functions and type methods are used interchangeably.

A piece of advice: functions must be as independent of each other as possible and must do one job (and only one job) well. So, if you find yourself writing functions that do multiple things, you might want to consider replacing them with multiple functions instead.

You should already know that all function definitions begin with the func keyword, followed by the function's signature and its implementation, and that functions accept none, one, or multiple arguments and return none, one, or multiple values back. The single most popular Go function is main(), which is used in every executable Go program—the main() function accepts no parameters and returns nothing, but it is the starting point of every Go program. Additionally, when the main() function ends along with the goroutine that executes it, the entire program ends as well.

Anonymous functions

Anonymous functions can be defined inline without the need for a name, and they are usually used for implementing things that require a small amount of code. In Go, a function can return an anonymous function or take an anonymous function as one of its arguments. Additionally, anonymous functions can be attached to Go variables. Note that anonymous functions are called *lambdas* in functional programming terminology. Similarly, a *closure* is a specific type of anonymous function that carries or closes over variables that are in the same lexical scope as the anonymous function that was defined.

It is considered a good practice for anonymous functions to have a small implementation and a local focus. If an anonymous function does not have a local focus, then you might need to consider making it a regular function. When an anonymous function is suitable for a job, it is extremely convenient and makes your life easier; just do not use too many anonymous functions in your programs without having a good reason. We will look at anonymous functions in action in a while.

Functions that return multiple values

As you already know from functions such as strconv.Atoi(), functions can return multiple distinct values, which saves you from having to create a dedicated structure for returning and receiving multiple values from a function. However, if you have a function that returns more than 3 values, you should reconsider that decision and maybe redesign it to use a single structure or slice for grouping and returning the desired values as a single entity—this makes handling the returned values simpler and easier. Functions, anonymous functions, and functions that return multiple values are all illustrated in functions.go, as shown in the following code:

```
package main
import "fmt"
func doubleSquare(x int) (int, int) {
    return x * 2, x * x
}
```

This function returns two int values, without the need for having separate variables to keep them—the returned values are created on the fly. Note the compulsory use of parentheses when a function returns more than one value.

```
// Sorting from smaller to bigger value
func sortTwo(x, y int) (int, int) {
    if x > y {
        return y, x
    }
    return x, y
}
```

The preceding function returns two int values as well.

```
func main() {
    n := 10
    d, s := doubleSquare(n)
```

The previous statement reads the two return values of doubleSquare() and saves them in d and s.

```
    fmt.Println("Double of", n, "is", d)
    fmt.Println("Square of", n, "is", s)
    // An anonymous function
    anF := func(param int) int {
```

```
        return param * param
   }
```

The anF variable holds an anonymous function that requires a single parameter as input and returns a single value. The only difference between an anonymous function and a regular one is that the name of the anonymous function is func() and that there is no func keyword.

```
     fmt.Println("anF of", n, "is", anF(n))
     fmt.Println(sortTwo(1, -3))
     fmt.Println(sortTwo(-1, 0))
 }
```

The last two statements print the return values of sortTwo(). Running functions.go produces the following output:

```
Double of 10 is 20
Square of 10 is 100
anF of 10 is 100
-3 1
-1 0
```

The subsection that follows illustrates functions that have named return values.

The return values of a function can be named

Unlike C, Go allows you to name the return values of a Go function. Additionally, when such a function has a return statement without any arguments, the function automatically returns the current value of each named return value, in the order in which they were declared in the function signature.

The following function is included in namedReturn.go:

```
func minMax(x, y int) (min, max int) {
    if x > y {
        min = y
        max = x
        return min, max
```

This return statement returns the values stored in the min and max variables—both min and max are defined in the function signature and not in the function body.

```
    }
    min = x
    max = y
    return
}
```

This return statement is equivalent to return min, max, which is based on the function signature and the use of named return values.

Running namedReturn.go produces the following output:

```
$ go run namedReturn.go 1 -2
-2 1
-2 1
```

Functions that accept other functions as parameters

Functions can accept other functions as parameters. The best example of a function that accepts another function as an argument can be found in the sort package. You can provide the sort. Slice() function with another function as an argument that specifies the way sorting is implemented. The signature of sort.Slice() is func Slice(slice interface{}, less func(i, j int) bool). This means the following:

- The sort.Slice() function does not return any data.

- The sort.Slice() function requires two arguments, a slice of type interface{} and another function—the slice variable is modified inside sort.Slice().

- The function parameter of sort.Slice() is named less and should have the func(i, j int) bool signature—there is no need for you to name the anonymous function. The name less is required because all function parameters should have a name.

- The i and j parameters of less are indexes of the slice parameter.

Similarly, there is another function in the sort package named sort.SliceIsSorted() that is defined as func SliceIsSorted(slice interface{}, less func(i, j int) bool) bool. sort.SliceIsSorted() returns a bool value and checks whether the slice parameter is sorted according to the rules of the second parameter, which is a function.

You are not obliged to use an anonymous function in either sort.Slice() or sort.SliceIsSorted(). You can define a regular function with the required signature and use that. However, using an anonymous function is more convenient.

The use of both sort.Slice() and sort.SliceIsSorted() is illustrated in the Go program that follows—the name of the source file is sorting.go:

```go
package main
import (
    "fmt"
    "sort"
)
type Grades struct {
    Name    string
    Surname string
    Grade   int
}
func main() {
    data := []Grades{{"J.", "Lewis", 10}, {"M.", "Tsoukalos", 7},
        {"D.", "Tsoukalos", 8}, {"J.", "Lewis", 9}}
    isSorted := sort.SliceIsSorted(data, func(i, j int) bool {
        return data[i].Grade < data[j].Grade
    })
```

The if else block that follows checks the bool value of sort.SliceIsSorted() to determine whether the slice was sorted or not:

```go
    if isSorted {
        fmt.Println("It is sorted!")
    } else {
        fmt.Println("It is NOT sorted!")
    }
    sort.Slice(data,
        func(i, j int) bool { return data[i].Grade < data[j].Grade })
    fmt.Println("By Grade:", data)
}
```

The call to sort.Slice() sorts the data according to the anonymous function that is passed as the second argument to sort.Slice().

Running sorting.go produces the following output:

```
It is NOT sorted!
By Grade: [{M. Tsoukalos 7} {D. Tsoukalos 8} {J. Lewis 9} {J. Lewis 10}]
```

Functions can return other functions

Apart from accepting functions as arguments, functions can also return anonymous functions, which can be handy when the returned function is not always the same but depends on the function's input or other external parameters. This is illustrated in returnFunction.go:

```
package main
import "fmt"
func funRet(i int) func(int) int {
    if i < 0 {
        return func(k int) int {
            k = -k
            return k + k
        }
    }
    return func(k int) int {
        return k * k
    }
}
```

The signature of funRet() declares that the function returns another function with the func(int) int signature. The implementation of the function is unknown, but it is going to be defined at runtime. Functions are returned using the return keyword. The developer should take care and save the returned function.

```
func main() {
    n := 10
    i := funRet(n)
    j := funRet(-4)
```

Note that n and -4 are only used for determining the anonymous functions that are going to be returned from funRet().

```
    fmt.Printf("%T\n", i)
    fmt.Printf("%T %v\n", j, j)
    fmt.Println("j", j, j(-5))
```

The first statement prints the signature of the function whereas the second statement prints the function signature and its memory address. The last statement also returns the memory address of j, because j is a pointer to the anonymous function and the value of j(-5).

```
    // Same input parameter but DIFFERENT
    // anonymous functions assigned to i and j
    fmt.Println(i(10))
    fmt.Println(j(10))
}
```

Although both i and j are called with the same input (10), they are going to return different values because they store different anonymous functions.

Running returnFunction.go generates the following output:

```
func(int) int
func(int) int 0x100d446c0
j 0x100d446c0 10
100
-20
```

The first line of the output shows the data type of the i variable that holds the return value of funRet(n), which is func(int) int as it holds a function. The second line of output shows the data type of j, as well as the memory address where the anonymous function is stored. The third line shows the memory address of the anonymous function stored in the j variable, as well as the return value of j(-5). The last two lines are the return values of i(10) and j(10), respectively.

So, in this subsection, we learned about functions returning functions. This allows Go to benefit from the functional programming paradigm and makes Go functions first-class citizens.

We are now going to examine variadic functions, which are functions with a variable number of parameters.

Variadic functions

Variadic functions are functions that can accept a variable number of parameters—you already know about fmt.Println() and append(), which are both variadic functions that are widely used. In fact, most functions found in the fmt package are variadic.

The general ideas and rules behind variadic functions are the following:

- Variadic functions use the pack operator, which consists of a ..., followed by a data type. So, for a variadic function to accept a variable number of int values, the pack operator should be ...int.
- The pack operator can only be used once in any given function.

- The variable that holds the pack operation is a slice and, therefore, is accessed as a slice inside the variadic function.
- The variable name that is related to the pack operator is always last in the list of function parameters.
- When calling a variadic function, you should put a list of values separated by , in the place of the variable with the pack operator or a slice with the unpack operator.

The pack operator can also be used with an empty interface. In fact, most functions in the fmt package use ...interface{} to accept a variable number of arguments of all data types. You can find the source code of the latest implementation of fmt at https://go.dev/src/fmt/.

However, there is a situation that needs special care here—I made that mistake when I was learning Go and I was wondering about the error message I was getting.

If you try to pass os.Args, which is a slice of strings ([]string), as ...interface{} to a variadic function, your code will not compile and will generate an error message similar to cannot use os.Args (type []string) as type []interface {} in argument to <function_name>. This happens because the two data types ([]string and []interface{}) do not have the same representations in memory—this applies to all data types. In practice, this means that you cannot write os.Args... to pass each individual value of the os.Args slice to a variadic function.

On the other hand, if you just use os.Args, it will work, but this passes the entire slice as a single entity instead of its individual values! This means that the everything(os.Args, os.Args) statement works but does not do what you want.

The solution to this problem is converting the slice of strings—or any other slice—into a slice of interface{}. One way to do that is by using the code that follows:

```
empty := make([]interface{}, len(os.Args[1:]))
for i, v := range os.Args {
    empty[i] = v
}
```

Now, you are allowed to use empty... as an argument to the variadic function. This is the only subtle point related to variadic functions and the pack operator.

This approach is an exception and should only be used if the user must provide the entire os.Args slice as a parameter to something like fmt.Println(). The main reason is that this removes some of the compiler guarantees.

As there is no standard library function to perform that conversion for you, you have to write your own code. Note that the conversion takes time as the code must visit all slice elements. The more elements the slice has, the more time the conversion will take. This topic is also discussed at https://github.com/golang/go/wiki/InterfaceSlice.

We are now ready to see variadic functions in action. Type the following Go code using your favorite text editor and save it as variadic.go:

```
package main
import (
    "fmt"
    "os"
)
```

As variadic functions are built into the grammar of the language, you do not need anything extra to support variadic functions.

```
func addFloats(message string, s ...float64) float64 {
```

This is a variadic function that accepts a string and an unknown number of float64 values. It prints the string variable and calculates the sum of the float64 values.

```
    fmt.Println(message)
    sum := float64(0)
    for _, a := range s {
        sum = sum + a
    }
```

This for loop accesses the pack operator as a slice, so there is nothing special here.

```
    s[0] = -1000
    return sum
}
```

You can also access individual elements of the s slice.

```
func everything(input ...interface{}) {
    fmt.Println(input)
}
```

This is another variadic function that accepts an unknown number of interface{} values.

```
func main() {
    sum := addFloats("Adding numbers...", 1.1, 2.12, 3.14, 4, 5, -1, 10)
```

You can put the arguments of a variadic function inline.

```
fmt.Println("Sum:", sum)
s := []float64{1.1, 2.12, 3.14}
```

But you usually use a slice variable with the unpack operator:

```
sum = addFloats("Adding numbers...", s...)
fmt.Println("Sum:", sum)
everything(s)
```

The previous code works because the content of s is not unpacked.

```
// Cannot directly pass []string as []interface{}
// You have to convert it first!
empty := make([]interface{}, len(os.Args[1:]))
```

You can convert []string into []interface{} in order to use the unpack operator.

```
for i, v := range os.Args[1:] {
    empty[i] = v
}
everything(empty...)
```

And now, we can unpack the contents of empty.

```
arguments := os.Args[1:]
empty = make([]interface{}, len(arguments))
for i := range arguments {
    empty[i] = arguments[i]
}
```

This is a slightly different way of converting []string into []interface{}.

```
everything(empty...)
str := []string{"One", "Two", "Three"}
everything(str, str, str)
}
```

The previous statement works because you are passing the entire str variable three times—not its contents. So, the slice contains three elements—each element is equal to the contents of the str variable.

Running `variadic.go` produces the following output:

```
$ go run variadic.go
Adding numbers...
Sum: 24.36
Adding numbers...
Sum: 6.36
[[-1000 2.12 3.14]]
[]
[]
[[One Two Three] [One Two Three] [One Two Three]]
```

The last line of the output shows that we have passed the `str` variable three times to the `everything()` function as three separate entities.

Variadic functions really come in handy when you want to have an unknown number of parameters in a function. The next subsection discusses the use of `defer`, which we have already used multiple times.

The defer keyword

So far, we have seen defer in `ch03/csvData.go`. But what does `defer` do? The `defer` keyword postpones the execution of a function until the surrounding function returns.

 Usually, `defer` is used in file I/O operations to keep the function call that closes an opened file close to the call that opened it, so that you do not have to remember to close a file that you have opened just before the function exits.

It is very important to remember that deferred functions are executed in **Last In, First Out (LIFO)** order after the surrounding function has been returned. Putting it simply, this means that if you defer function `f1()` first, function `f2()` second, and function `f3()` third in the same surrounding function, then when the surrounding function is about to return, function `f3()` will be executed first, function `f2()` will be executed second, and function `f1()` will be the last one to get executed.

In this section, we will discuss the dangers of careless use of `defer` using a simple program. The code for `defer.go` is as follows:

```go
package main
import (
    "fmt"
```

```
)
func d1() {
    for i := 3; i > 0; i-- {
        defer fmt.Print(i, " ")
    }
}
```

In d1(), defer is executed inside the function body with just a fmt.Print() call. Remember that these calls to fmt.Print() are executed just before function d1() returns.

```
func d2() {
    for i := 3; i > 0; i-- {
        defer func() {
            fmt.Print(i, " ")
        }()
    }
    fmt.Println()
}
```

In d2(), defer is attached to an anonymous function that does not accept any parameters. In practice, this means that the anonymous function should get the value of i on its own—this is dangerous because the current value of i depends on when the anonymous function is executed.

The anonymous function is a *closure*, and that is why it has access to variables that would normally be out of scope.

```
func d3() {
    for i := 3; i > 0; i-- {
        defer func(n int) {
            fmt.Print(n, " ")
        }(i)
    }
}
```

In this case, the current value of i is passed to the anonymous function as a parameter that initializes the n function parameter. This means that there are no ambiguities about the value that i has.

```
func main() {
    d1()
    d2()
    fmt.Println()
```

```
        d3()
        fmt.Println()
}
```

The task of main() is to call d1(), d2(), and d3().

Running defer.go produces the following output:

```
$ go run defer.go
1 2 3
0 0 0
1 2 3
```

You will most likely find the generated output complicated and challenging to understand, which proves that the operation and the results of the use of defer can be tricky if your code is not clear and unambiguous. Let me explain the results so that you get a better idea of how tricky defer can be if you do not pay close attention to your code.

Let us start with the first line of the output (1 2 3) that is generated by the d1() function. The values of i in d1() are 3, 2, and 1 in that order. The function that is deferred in s is the fmt.Print() statement; as a result, when the d1() function is about to return, you get the three values of the i variable of the for loop in reverse order. This is because *deferred functions are executed in LIFO order*.

Now, let me explain the second line of the output that is produced by the d2() function. It is really strange that we got three zeros instead of 1 2 3 in the output; however, there is a reason for that – note that this is not an issue with defer but with closures. After the for loop ends, the value of i is 0, because it is that value of i that made the for loop terminate. However, the tricky point here is that the deferred anonymous function is evaluated after the for loop ends because it has no parameters, which means that it is evaluated three times for an i value of 0, hence the generated output. This kind of confusing code is what might lead to the creation of nasty bugs in your projects, so try to avoid it. Go version 1.22 corrects this kind of errors.

Finally, we will talk about the third line of the output, which is generated by the d3() function. Due to the parameter of the anonymous function, each time the anonymous function is deferred, it gets and therefore uses the current value of i. As a result, each execution of the anonymous function has a different value to process without any ambiguities, hence the generated output.

After that, it should be clear that the best approach to using defer is the third one, which is exhibited in the d3() function, because you intentionally pass the desired variable in the anonymous function in an easy-to-read way. Now that we have learned about defer, it is time to discuss something completely different: the Big O notation.

Big O complexity

The computational complexity of an algorithm is usually denoted using the popular Big O notation. The Big O notation is used for expressing the worst-case scenario for the order of growth of an algorithm. It shows how the performance of an algorithm changes as the size of the data it processes grows.

$O(1)$ means constant time complexity, which does not depend on the amount of data at hand. $O(n)$ means that the execution time is proportional to n (linear time)—you cannot process data without accessing it, so $O(n)$ is considered good. $O(n^2)$ (quadratic time) means that the execution time is proportional to n^2. $O(n!)$ (factorial time) means that the execution time of the algorithm is directly proportional to the factorial of n. Simply put, if you have to process 100 values of some kind, then the $O(n)$ algorithm will do about 100 operations, $O(n^2)$ is going to perform about 10,000 operations, and the algorithm with the $O(n!)$ complexity 10^{158} operations!

Now that we have learned about the Big O notation, it is time to discuss developing your own packages.

Developing your own packages

At some point, you are going to need to develop your own packages to organize your code and distribute it if needed. As stated at the beginning of this chapter, everything that begins with an uppercase letter is considered public and can be accessed from outside its package, whereas all other elements are considered private. The only exception to this Go rule is package names—it is a best practice to use lowercase package names, even though uppercase package names are allowed.

Compiling a Go package can be done manually, if the package exists on the local machine, but it is also done automatically after you download the package from the internet, so there is no need to worry about that. Additionally, if the package you are downloading contains any errors, you will learn about them when you try to download it.

However, if you want to compile a package that has been saved in the sqlite06.go file (a combination of SQLite and Chapter 06) on your own, you can use the following command:

```
$ go build -o sqlite06.a sqlite06.go
```

So, the previous command compiles the sqlite06.go file and saves its output in the sqlite06.a file:

```
$ file sqlite06.a
```

```
sqlite06.a: current ar archive
The sqlite06.a file is an ar archive.
```

The main reason for compiling Go packages on your own is to check for syntax or other kinds of errors in your code without actually using them. Additionally, you can build Go packages as plugins (`https://pkg.go.dev/plugin`) or shared libraries. Discussing more about these is beyond the scope of this book.

The init() function

Each Go package can optionally have a private function named `init()` that is automatically executed at the beginning of execution time—`init()` runs when the package is initialized at the beginning of program execution. The `init()` function has the following characteristics:

- `init()` takes no arguments.
- `init()` returns no values.
- The `init()` function is optional.
- The `init()` function is called implicitly by Go.
- You can have an `init()` function in the `main` package. In that case, `init()` is executed before the `main()` function. In fact, all `init()` functions are always executed prior to the `main()` function.
- A source file can contain multiple `init()` functions—these are executed in the order of declaration.
- The `init()` function or functions of a package are executed *only once*, even if the package is imported multiple times.
- Go packages can contain multiple files. Each source file can contain one or more `init()` functions.
- The fact that the `init()` function is a private function by design means that it cannot be called from outside the package in which it is contained. Additionally, as the user of a package has no control over the `init()` function, you should think carefully before using an `init()` function in public packages or changing any global state in `init()`.

There are some exceptions where the use of init() makes sense:

- For initializing network connections that might take time prior to the execution of package functions or methods.
- For initializing connections to one or more servers prior to the execution of package functions or methods.
- For creating required files and directories.
- For checking whether required resources are available or not.

As the order of execution can be perplexing sometimes, in the next subsection, we will explain the order of execution in more detail.

Order of execution

This subsection illustrates how Go code is executed. As an example, if a main package imports package A and package A depends on package B, then the following will take place:

1. The process starts with the main package.
2. The main package imports package A.
3. Package A imports package B.
4. The global variables, if any, in package B are initialized.
5. The init() function or functions of package B, if they exist, run. This is the first init() function that gets executed.
6. The global variables, if any, in package A are initialized.
7. The init() function or functions of package A, if there are any, run.
8. The global variables in the main package are initialized.
9. The init() function or functions of the main package, if they exist, run.
10. The main() function of the main package begins its execution.

Notice that if the main package imports package B on its own, nothing is going to happen because everything related to package B is triggered by package A. This is because package A imported package B first.

The following diagram shows what is happening behind the scenes regarding the order of execution of Go code:

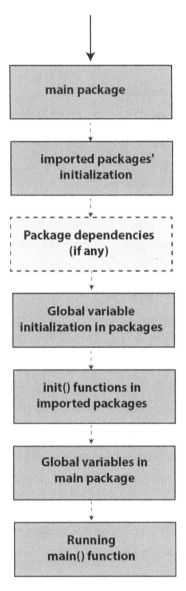

Figure 6.1: Go order of code execution

You can learn more about the order of execution by reading the Go Language Specification document at https://go.dev/ref/spec#Order_of_evaluation and about the package initialization process by reading https://go.dev/ref/spec#Package_initialization.

Using GitHub to store Go packages

This section will teach you how to create a GitHub repository where you can keep your Go package and make it available to the world.

First, you need to create the GitHub repository on your own. The easiest way to create a new GitHub repository is by visiting the GitHub website and going to the **Repositories** tab, where you can see your existing repositories and create new ones. Click the **New** button and type in the necessary information for creating a new GitHub repository. If you made your repository public, everyone will be able to see it—if it is a private repository, only the people you choose are going to be able to look into it.

Having a clear README.md file in your GitHub repository that explains the way the Go package works is considered a very good practice.

Next, you need to clone the repository on your local computer. I usually clone it using the git(1) utility. If the name of the repository is sqlite06 and the GitHub username is mactsouk, the git clone command is going to look as follows:

```
$ git clone git@github.com:mactsouk/sqlite06.git
```

After that, type cd sqlite06 and you are done! At this point, you just have to write the code of the Go package and remember to git commit and git push the changes to the GitHub repository.

 The best place to host, inspect, develop, or use a Go package is in the ~/go/src directory. Put simply, the purpose of ~/go/src is to store the source code of the packages you create or use.

The look of such a repository can be seen in *Figure 6.2*—you are going to learn more about the `sqlite06` repository in a while:

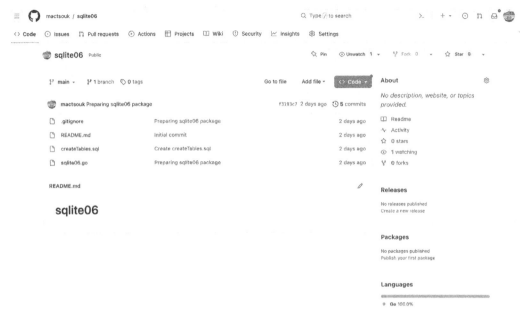

Figure 6.2: A GitHub repository with a Go package

  Using GitLab instead of GitHub for hosting your code does not require any changes to the way you work.

If you want to use that package, you just need to go get the package using its URL and include it in your `import` block—we will see this when we actually use it in a program. ***The previous process is about developing a Go package, not using a Go package***.

The next section presents a Go package that allows you to work with a database.

A package for working with SQLite

This section will develop a Go package for working with a given database schema stored on an SQLite database, with the end goal of demonstrating how to develop, store, and use a package. When interacting with specific schemas and tables in your application, you usually create separate packages with all the database-related functions—this also applies to NoSQL databases.

Go offers a generic package (`https://pkg.go.dev/database/sql`) for working with databases. However, each database requires a specific package that acts as the driver and allows Go to connect and work with that specific database.

The steps for creating the desired Go package are as follows:

- Downloading the necessary external Go packages for working with SQLite.
- Creating package files.
- Developing the required functions.
- Using the Go package for developing utilities and testing its functionality.
- Using CI/CD tools for automation (this is optional).

You might be wondering why we would create such a package for working with a database and not write the actual commands in our programs when needed. The reasons for this include the following:

- A Go package can be shared by all team members who work with the application.
- A Go package allows people to use the database in ways that are documented.
- The specialized functions you put in your Go package fit your needs a lot better.
- People do not need full access to the database—they just use the package functions and the functionality they offer.
- If you ever make changes to the database, people do not need to know about them, as long as the functions of the Go package remain the same.

Put simply, the functions you create can interact with a specific database schema, along with its tables and data—it would be almost impossible to work with an unknown database schema without knowing how the tables are connected to each other.

Apart from all these technical reasons, it is really fun to create Go packages that are shared among multiple developers!

Let us now continue by learning more about the SQLite database.

Working with SQLite3 and Go

You need to download an additional package for working with a database, such as Postgres, SQLite, MySQL, or MongoDB. In this case, we are using SQLite and therefore need to download a Go package that allows us to communicate with SQLite. The most popular Go package for working with SQLite3 is called `go-sqlite3` and can be found at `https://github.com/mattn/go-sqlite3`.

SQLite databases are single files that are accessed locally and, therefore, they do not need any TCP/IP services or other server processes running.

You can download that package by running go get github.com/mattn/go-sqlite3. However, this command no longer works outside of a module. The new way of installing the package is by running go install github.com/mattn/go-sqlite3@latest.

Bear in mind that this package uses cgo, which requires the gcc compiler installed on your computer. For more details, visit https://github.com/mattn/go-sqlite3.

After the successful execution of the previous command, ***the latest version of the package*** is going to be downloaded. In my case, the source code of the go-sqlite3 package can be found at ~/go/pkg/mod/github.com/mattn:

```
$ ls ~/go/pkg/mod/github.com/mattn
go-sqlite3@v1.14.22
```

Therefore, the version of the downloaded go-sqlite3 package is 1.14.22. Alternatively, you can let the go mod init and go mod tidy commands do the job for you.

Before doing any actual work with SQLite3, we are going to present a simple utility that just connects to a database and prints the version of SQLite3. Such utilities are really handy while troubleshooting as they perform simple yet critical tasks. As testSQLite.go uses an external package, it should be placed under ~/go/src during development and follow the go mod init and go mod tidy process. In my case, testSQLite.go is placed in the ~/go/src/github.com/mactsouk/mGo4th/ch06/testSQLite directory.

The code of testSQLite.go is presented in two parts. The first part is the following:

```go
package main

import (
    "database/sql"
    "fmt"
    "os"

    _ "github.com/mattn/go-sqlite3"
)
```

```go
func main() {
    // Connect or Create an SQLite database
    db, err := sql.Open("sqlite3", "test.db")
    if err != nil {
        fmt.Println("Error connecting:", err)
        return
    }
    defer db.Close()
```

As the package communicates with SQLite3, we import the `github.com/mattn/go-sqlite3` package and we use `_` in front of the package path. This happens because the imported package is *registering itself as the database handler* for the `sql` package, but it is not being directly used in the code. It is only being used through the `sql` package.

With the previous code, we use `sql.Open()` to connect to an SQLite3 database, which is called `test.db`. If the `test.db` file does not exist, it will be created.

The second part comes with the following Go code:

```go
    var version string
    err = db.QueryRow("SELECT SQLITE_VERSION()").Scan(&version)
    if err != nil {
        fmt.Println("Version:", err)
        return
    }

    fmt.Println("SQLite3 version:", version)
os.Remove("test.db")
}
```

In the second part, we query the SQLite database using `db.QueryRow()` in order to get information about its version number. `QueryRow()` is handy for executing queries that are expected to return at most one row, as in our case. The return value of the query is read using `Scan()` and saved in the variable that is the parameter of `Scan()` using a pointer. The `os.Remove()` statement deletes the `test.db` file—in general, this is not a good practice but it works in this particular case.

Do not forget to execute go `mod` `init` and go `mod` `tidy` before you execute `testSQLite.go` for the first time.

Running testSQLite.go produces the following output:

```
$ go run testSQLite.go
SQLite3 version: 3.42.0
```

Now, let us develop something more advanced. The connectSQLite3.go utility verifies that you can create an SQLite3 database along with some tables, get a list of the available tables, insert and update data in a table, select data from a table, delete data, and get the number of records. As the utility uses an external package, it should be placed under ~/go/src and follow the go mod init and go mod tidy process. In my case, connectSQLite3.go is placed in ~/go/src/github.com/mactsouk/mGo4th/ch06/connectSQLite3 but you can put it anywhere you want as long as it is under ~/go/src.

The code of connectSQLite3.go is going to be presented in six parts, the first part being the following:

```go
package main

import (
    "database/sql"
    "fmt"
    "os"
    "strconv"
    "time"


    _ "github.com/mattn/go-sqlite3"
)

var dbname = "ch06.db"

func insertData(db *sql.DB, dsc string) error {
    cT := time.Now().Format(time.RFC1123)
    stmt, err := db.Prepare("INSERT INTO book VALUES(NULL,?,?);")
    if err != nil {
        fmt.Println("Insert data table:", err)
        return err
    }

    _, err = stmt.Exec(cT, dsc)
```

```
        if err != nil {
            fmt.Println("Insert data table:", err)
            return err
        }


        return nil
    }
```

The insertData() function is used for inserting data into the database and is called by the main() function. We first use db.Prepare() to construct the INSERT SQL statement with the desired parameters and then we execute Exec() to actually insert the data. It is a common practice to use one or more ? while preparing an SQL statement and replace those question marks with the actual values when calling Exec().

The second part of connectSQLite3.go comes with the following code:

```
func selectData(db *sql.DB, n int) error {
    rows, err := db.Query("SELECT * from book WHERE id > ? ", n)
    if err != nil {
        fmt.Println("Select:", err)
        return err
    }
    defer rows.Close()

    for rows.Next() {
        var id int
        var dt string
        var description string

        err = rows.Scan(&id, &dt, &description)
        if err != nil {
            fmt.Println("Row:", err)
            return err
        }

        date, err := time.Parse(time.RFC1123, dt)
        if err != nil {
            fmt.Println("Date:", err)
            return err
```

```
        }
        fmt.Printf("%d %s %s\n", id, date, description)
    }
    return nil
}
```

In this second part, we show how to query SQLite3 data and read multiple rows. We use db.Query()
to construct the SELECT SQL query, which returns a *sql.Rows variable. We then read the rows
by calling Next() multiple times using a for loop, which automatically terminates when there
is no more data to read. As the time is stored as text in SQLite, we need to convert it into a proper
variable using time.Parse(). The selectData() function prints the data on its own instead of
returning it to the calling function.

 The db.Query() statement does not require Exec() to get executed. Therefore, we
replace ? with the actual values in the same statement.

The third part is the following:

```
func main() {
    // Delete database file
    os.Remove(dbname)

    // Connect and Create the SQLite database
    db, err := sql.Open("sqlite3", dbname)
    if err != nil {
        fmt.Println("Error connecting:", err)
        return
    }
    defer db.Close()

    // Create a table
    const create string = `
    CREATE TABLE IF NOT EXISTS book (
        id INTEGER NOT NULL PRIMARY KEY,
        time TEXT NOT NULL,
        description TEXT);`
```

```
    _, err = db.Exec(create)
    if err != nil {
        fmt.Println("Create table:", err)
        return
    }
```

In this part, we connect to the SQLite3 database and create a table named book. The table has three fields, named id, time, and description. The db.Exec() statement is used for executing the CREATE TABLE SQL command.

The fourth part of connectSQLite3.go contains the following code:

```
    // Insert 10 rows to the book table
    for i := 1; i < 11; i = i + 1 {
        dsc := "Description: " + strconv.Itoa(i)
        err = insertData(db, dsc)
        if err != nil {
            fmt.Println("Insert data:", err)
        }
    }

    // Select multiple rows
    err = selectData(db, 5)
    if err != nil {
        fmt.Println("Select:", err)
    }
```

The previous code inserts ten rows into the book table using the insertData() function and a for loop. After that, the selectData() function is called for selecting data from the book table.

The fifth part of connectSQLite3.go comes with the following Go code:

```
    time.Sleep(time.Second)
    // Update data
    cT := time.Now().Format(time.RFC1123)
    db.Exec("UPDATE book SET time = ? WHERE id > ?", cT, 7)

    // Select multiple rows
    err = selectData(db, 8)
```

```
if err != nil {
    fmt.Println("Select:", err)
    return
}

// Delete data
stmt, err := db.Prepare("DELETE from book where id = ?")
_, err = stmt.Exec(8)
if err != nil {
    fmt.Println("Delete:", err)
    return
}
```

In this part, we present the implementation of the UPDATE SQL statement, which is based on db.Exec()—once again, the values of the UPDATE SQL statement are passed to db.Exec(). After that, we call selectData() to see the changes we have made. Last, we use db.Prepare() to construct a DELETE statement, which is executed using Exec().

The last part of connectSQLite3.go is the following:

```
// Select multiple rows
err = selectData(db, 7)
if err != nil {
    fmt.Println("Select:", err)
    return
}

// Count rows in table
query, err := db.Query("SELECT count(*) as count from book")
if err != nil {
    fmt.Println("Select:", err)
    return
}
defer query.Close()

count := -100
for query.Next() {
    _ = query.Scan(&count)
}
```

```
    fmt.Println("count(*):", count)
}
```

In the last part of the utility, we use db.Query() to get the number of rows in the book table and print the results.

As expected, before you execute connectSQLite3.go, you should execute the following commands first:

```
$ go mod init
go: creating new go.mod: module github.com/mactsouk/mGo4th/ch06/
connectSQLite3
go: to add module requirements and sums:
    go mod tidy
$ go mod tidy
go: finding module for package github.com/mattn/go-sqlite3
go: found github.com/mattn/go-sqlite3 in github.com/mattn/go-sqlite3
v1.14.17
```

The last line of the output tells us that the github.com/mattn/go-sqlite3 package was found in our Go installation and therefore it was not downloaded—this is a result of the go get github.com/mattn/go-sqlite3 command we executed earlier.

Running connectSQLite3.go generates the following kind of output:

```
$ go run connectSQLite3.go
6 2023-08-16 21:12:00 +0300 EEST Description: 6
7 2023-08-16 21:12:00 +0300 EEST Description: 7
8 2023-08-16 21:12:00 +0300 EEST Description: 8
9 2023-08-16 21:12:00 +0300 EEST Description: 9
10 2023-08-16 21:12:00 +0300 EEST Description: 10
9 2023-08-16 21:12:01 +0300 EEST Description: 9
10 2023-08-16 21:12:01 +0300 EEST Description: 10
9 2023-08-16 21:12:01 +0300 EEST Description: 9
10 2023-08-16 21:12:01 +0300 EEST Description: 10
count(*): 9
```

 The main advantage of the connectSQLite3.go utility is that it illustrates how to perform a large number of tasks on an SQLite database—most of the presented code is going to be reused in the Go package that we are going to create in a while.

Now that we know how to access and query an SQLite3 database using Go, the next task should be to implement the Go package we want to develop.

Storing the Go package

As mentioned earlier, for reasons of simplicity, we will use a public Go repository for the Go module, which is named `sqilite06` and can be found at `https://github.com/mactsouk/sqlite06`.

To use that package on your machines, you should go get it first, either manually or with the help of `go mod init` and `go mod tidy`. However, during development, you should begin with `git clone git@github.com:mactsouk/sqlite06.git` to get the contents of the GitHub repository and make changes to it until its functionality is finalized and there are no bugs. This implies that you have ssh set up with GitHub, which is what I usually use. I am doing the development of the `sqilite06` package in `~/go/src/github.com/mactsouk/sqlite06`.

The design of the Go package

Figure 6.3 shows the database schema that the Go package works on. Remember that when working with a specific database and schema, you need to *include* the schema information in your Go code. Put simply, the Go code should know about the schema it works on:

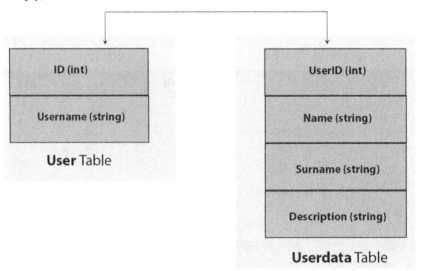

Figure 6.3: The two database tables the Go package works on

This is a simple schema that allows us to keep user data and update it. Apart from the Users table, there is also a table named Userdata that holds more detailed information about a user. What connects the two tables is the user ID, which should be unique. Additionally, the Username field on the Users table should also be unique as two or more users cannot share the same username. Once a record is entered in the Users table, it cannot be changed, it can only be deleted. What can change, however, is the data stored in the Userdata table.

 These two tables should already exist in SQLite, which means that the Go code assumes that the relevant tables are in the right place.

The tasks that the Go package should perform to make our lives easier are as follows:

- Create a new user.
- Delete an existing user.
- Update an existing user.
- List all users.

Each of these tasks should have one or more Go functions or methods to support it, which is what we are going to implement in the Go package:

- A function to initiate the SQLite3 connection. The helper function to initiate the connection is going to be private.
- A function that checks whether a given username exists—this is a helper function that is also going to be private.
- A function that inserts a new user into the database.
- A function that deletes an existing user from the database.
- A function for updating an existing user.
- A function for listing all users.

Now that we know the overall structure and functionality of the Go package, we should begin implementing it.

The implementation of the Go package

In this subsection, we will implement the Go package for working with the SQLite database and the given database schema. We will present each function separately—if you combine all these functions, then you have the functionality of the entire package.

During package development, you should regularly commit your changes to the GitHub or GitLab repository as a backup strategy.

All the code of the package is found in a Go source file named `sqlite06.go`. The preamble of the package is as follows:

```go
package sqlite06

import (
    "database/sql"
    "errors"
    "fmt"
    "strings"

    _ "github.com/mattn/go-sqlite3"
)

var (
    Filename = ""
)
```

The `Filename` variable holds the name of the database file—this is set by the applications that use `sqlite06`. For the first time in this book, you will see a package name different than `main`, which in this case is `sqlite06`.

The next element that you need in your Go package is one or more structures that can hold the data from the database tables. Most of the time, you need as many structures as there are database tables—we will begin with that and see how it goes. Therefore, we will define the following structures:

```go
type User struct {
    ID       int
    Username string
}

type Userdata struct {
    ID             int
```

```
    Name          string
    Surname       string
    Description string
}
```

If you think about this, you should see that there is no point in creating two separate Go structures in our case. This is because the User structure holds no real data, and there is no point in passing multiple structures to the functions that process data for the Users and Userdata SQLite tables. Therefore, we can create a single Go structure for holding all the data that has been defined, as follows:

```
type Userdata struct {
    ID            int
    Username      string
    Name          string
    Surname       string
    Description string
}
```

I have decided to name the structure after the database table for simplicity—however, in this case, this is not completely accurate as the Userdata structure has more fields than the Userdata database table.

Let us now begin presenting the functions of the package. The openConnection() function, which is private and only accessed within the scope of the package, is defined as follows:

```
func openConnection() (*sql.DB, error) {
    db, err := sql.Open("sqlite3", Filename)
    if err != nil {
        return nil, err
    }
    return db, nil
}
```

SQLite3 does not require a username or a password and does not operate over a TCP/IP network. Therefore, sql.Open() requires just a single parameter, which is the filename of the database.

Now, let us consider the exists() function, which is also private as it is a helper function:

```
// The function returns the User ID of the username
// -1 if the user does not exist
```

```go
func exists(username string) int {
    username = strings.ToLower(username)

    db, err := openConnection()
    if err != nil {
        fmt.Println(err)
        return -1
    }
    defer db.Close()

    userID := -1
    statement := fmt.Sprintf(`SELECT ID FROM Users where Username = '%s'`,
username)
    rows, err := db.Query(statement)
    defer rows.Close()
```

This is where we define the query that shows whether the provided username exists in the database or not. As all our data is kept in the database, we need to interact with the database all the time.

> This is one of the rare cases where returning an indication value from a function makes more sense as it makes the code less complex than returning an error value. However, returning an error value is still more robust and closer to the Go philosophy.

```go
    for rows.Next() {
        var id int
        err = rows.Scan(&id)
        if err != nil {
            fmt.Println("exists() Scan", err)
            return -1
        }
        userID = id
    }
```

If the rows.Scan(&id) call is executed without any errors, then we know that a result has been returned, which is the desired user ID.

```go
    return userID
}
```

The last part of exists() frees resources and returns the ID value of the username that was given as a parameter to exists().

Here is the implementation of the AddUser() function:

```go
// AddUser adds a new user to the database
// Returns new User ID
// -1 if there was an error
func AddUser(d Userdata) int {
    d.Username = strings.ToLower(d.Username)

    db, err := openConnection()
    if err != nil {
        fmt.Println(err)
        return -1
    }
    defer db.Close()
```

All usernames are converted into lowercase using strings.ToLower() to avoid duplicates. This is a design decision.

```go
    userID := exists(d.Username)
    if userID != -1 {
        fmt.Println("User already exists:", d.Username)
        return -1
    }

    insertStatement := `INSERT INTO Users values (NULL,?)`
```

This is how we construct an INSERT statement that accepts parameters. The presented statement requires one value as there is a single ?.

```go
    _, err = db.Exec(insertStatement, d.Username)
    if err != nil {
        fmt.Println(err)
        return -1
    }
```

With db.Exec() we pass the value of the parameter, which is kept as d.Username, into the insertStatement variable.

```
    userID = exists(d.Username)
    if userID == -1 {
  return userID
    }
```

After inserting a new user into the Users table, we make sure that everything went fine with the help of the exists() function, which also returns the user ID of the new user. That user ID is used for inserting the relevant data into the Userdata table.

```
    insertStatement = `INSERT INTO Userdata values (?, ?, ?, ?)`
    _, err = db.Exec(insertStatement, userID, d.Name, d.Surname,
  d.Description)
    if err != nil {
        fmt.Println("db.Exec()", err)
        return -1
    }
    return userID
}
```

The presented query needs four values that are signified by four ? characters. As we need to pass four variables to insertStatement, we will put four values in the db.Exec() call. This is the end of the function that adds a new user to the database.

The implementation of the DeleteUser() function is as follows.

```
func DeleteUser(id int) error {
    db, err := openConnection()
    if err != nil {
        return err
    }
    defer db.Close()

statement := fmt.Sprintf(`SELECT Username FROM Users WHERE ID = %d`, id)
    rows, err := db.Query(statement)
    defer rows.Close()
```

```go
    var username string
    for rows.Next() {
        err = rows.Scan(&username)
        if err != nil {
            return err
        }
    }

if exists(username) != id {
        return fmt.Errorf("User with ID %d does not exist", id)
    }
```

Here, we double-check whether the given user ID exists or not in the Users table before trying to delete it.

```go
    // Delete from Userdata
    deleteStatement := `DELETE FROM Userdata WHERE UserID = ?`
    _, err = db.Exec(deleteStatement, id)
    if err != nil {
        return err
    }

    // Delete from Users
    deleteStatement = `DELETE from Users where ID = ?`
    _, err = db.Exec(deleteStatement, id)
    if err != nil {
        return err
    }
    return nil
}
```

If the previously returned username exists and has the same user ID as the parameter to DeleteUser(), then we can continue the deletion process, which contains two steps: First, deleting the relevant user data from the Userdata table, and, second, deleting the data from the Users table.

During development, I included many `fmt.Println()` statements in the package code for debugging purposes. However, I have removed most of them in the final version of the Go package and replaced them with error values. These error values are passed to the program that uses the functionality of the package, which is responsible for deciding what to do with the error messages and error conditions. You can also use logging for this—the output can go to standard output or even `/dev/null` when not needed.

Now, let us examine the implementation of the `ListUsers()` function.

```go
func ListUsers() ([]Userdata, error) {
    Data := []Userdata{}
    db, err := openConnection()
    if err != nil {
        return nil, err
    }
    defer db.Close()
```

Once again, we need to open a connection to the database before executing any database queries.

```go
    rows, err := db.Query(`SELECT ID, Username, Name, Surname, Description
FROM Users, Userdata WHERE Users.ID = Userdata.UserID`)
    defer rows.Close()
    if err != nil {
        return Data, err
    }
```

This is the query that reads all data from the two tables. After that, we use the rows variable to get the results of the query:

```go
    for rows.Next() {
        var id int
        var username string
        var name string
        var surname string
        var desc string
        err = rows.Scan(&id, &username, &name, &surname, &desc)
        temp := Userdata{ID: id, Username: username, Name: name, Surname:
surname, Description: desc}
```

At this point, we will store the data we have received from the SELECT query in a Userdata structure. This is added to the slice that is going to be returned from the ListUsers() function. This
process continues until there is nothing left to read:

```
        Data = append(Data, temp)
        if err != nil {
            return nil, err
        }
    }
    return Data, nil
}
```

After updating the contents of the Data slice using append(), we end the query, and the function
returns the list of available users, as stored in the Data variable.

Lastly, let us examine the UpdateUser() function:

```
func UpdateUser(d Userdata) error {
    db, err := openConnection()
    if err != nil {
        return err
    }
    defer db.Close()

    userID := exists(d.Username)
    if userID == -1 {
        return errors.New("User does not exist")
    }
```

First, we need to make sure that the given username exists in the database—the update process
is based on the username.

```
d.ID = userID
    updateStatement := `UPDATE Userdata set Name = ?, Surname = ?,
Description = ? where UserID = ?`
    _, err = db.Exec(updateStatement, d.Name, d.Surname, d.Description,
d.ID)
    if err != nil {
        return err
    }
```

```
    return nil
}
```

The update statement stored in updateStatement that is executed using the desired parameters with the help of db.Exec() updates the user data.

After you finish writing your code, you should execute the following commands:

```
$ go mod init
go: creating new go.mod: module github.com/mactsouk/sqlite06
go: to add module requirements and sums:
    go mod tidy
```

The previous command tells Go that this is a package with external dependencies.

```
$ go mod tidy
go: finding module for package github.com/mattn/go-sqlite3
go: found github.com/mattn/go-sqlite3 in github.com/mattn/go-sqlite3
v1.14.17
```

The go mod tidy command downloads all required dependencies, if any.

Now that we know the details of how to implement each function in the sqlite06 package, it is time to begin using that package!

Testing the Go package

In order to test the package, we must develop a command line utility called sqliteGo.go. As sqliteGo.go uses an external package, even if we have developed that package, we should not forget to put it somewhere inside ~/go/src. If you download the GitHub repository of the book, you are going to find it in ch06/usePackage. As sqliteGo.go is used for testing purposes only, we hardcoded most of the data apart from the username of the user we put into the database. All usernames are randomly generated.

The code of sqliteGo.go is presented in six parts. The first part is the following:

```
package main

import (
    "fmt"
    "math/rand"
```

```
    "strings"
    "time"

    "github.com/mactsouk/sqlite06"
)
```

In this first part, we import the necessary Go packages, including our own sqlite06.

The second part of sqliteGo.go comes with the following code:

```
var MIN = 0
var MAX = 26

func random(min, max int) int {
    return rand.Intn(max-min) + min
}

func getString(length int64) string {
    startChar := "A"
    temp := ""
    var i int64 = 1
    for {
        myRand := random(MIN, MAX)
        newChar := string(startChar[0] + byte(myRand))
        temp = temp + newChar
        if i == length {
            break
        }
        i++
    }
    return temp
}
```

The previous code generates random strings of a given length. These strings contain regular characters in uppercase.

The third part of sqliteGo.go contains the following code:

```
func main() {
    sqlite06.Filename = "ch06.db"
```

```
data, err := sqlite06.ListUsers()
if err != nil {
    fmt.Println("ListUsers():", err)
    return
}

if len(data) != 0 {
    for _, v := range data {
        fmt.Println(v)
    }
}
```

This is where the implementation of main() begins. The first statement is where we define the name of the SQLite3 database. Although we are using an external package, the database is going to be created in the directory that we execute sqliteGo.go in.

After that, we call sqlite06.ListUsers() to get the list of available users.

The fourth part of sqliteGo.go is the following:

```
SEED := time.Now().Unix()
rand.Seed(SEED)
random_username := strings.ToLower(getString(5))

t := sqlite06.Userdata{
    Username:    random_username,
    Name:        "Mihalis",
    Surname:     "Tsoukalos",
    Description: "This is me!"}

fmt.Println("Adding username:", random_username)
id := sqlite06.AddUser(t)
if id == -1 {
    fmt.Println("There was an error adding user", t.Username)
}
```

The previous code generates a random username, creates and populates a Userdata structure, and calls sqlite06.AddUser() to add a new user.

The fifth part of `sqliteGo.go` contains the following code:

```
err = sqlite06.DeleteUser(id)
if err != nil {
    fmt.Println(err)
} else {
    fmt.Println("User with ID", id, "deleted!")
}


// Trying to delete the same user again!
err = sqlite06.DeleteUser(id)
if err != nil {
    fmt.Println(err)
}
```

In the previous code, we try to delete the same user twice by calling `sqlite06.DeleteUser()` two times. In this case, we expect the second attempt to fail.

The last part of `sqliteGo.go` is the following:

```
random_username = strings.ToLower(getString(5))
random_name := getString(7)
random_surname := getString(10)
dsc := time.Now().Format(time.RFC1123)
t = sqlite06.Userdata{
    Username:    random_username,
    Name:        random_name,
    Surname:     random_surname,
    Description: dsc}

id = sqlite06.AddUser(t)
if id == -1 {
    fmt.Println("There was an error adding user", t.Username)
}

dsc = time.Now().Format(time.RFC1123)
t.Description = dsc
err = sqlite06.UpdateUser(t)
if err != nil {
```

```
        fmt.Println(err)
    }
}
```

In this last part, we add another user with random data and then we update its description by calling sqlite06.UpdateUser().

You should create the two tables in the SQLIte3 database before using sqliteGo.go. Additionally, the name of the SQLite3 database file should be ch06.db, unless you change it in sqliteGo.go. The easiest way to be ready is by running the following commands using the sqlite3 utility:

```
$ sqlite3 ch06.db
SQLite version 3.39.5 2022-10-14 20:58:05
Enter ".help" for usage hints.
sqlite> .read createTables.sql
```

The first command creates the ch06.db database whereas the second command executes the code found in createTables.sql, which is included in the usePackage directory. The content of the createTables.sql file is the following:

```
DROP TABLE IF EXISTS Users;
DROP TABLE IF EXISTS Userdata;

CREATE TABLE Users (
    ID INTEGER PRIMARY KEY,
    Username TEXT
);

CREATE TABLE Userdata (
    UserID INTEGER NOT NULL,
    Name TEXT,
    Surname TEXT,
    Description TEXT
);
```

After you execute the createTables.sql file, you can verify its results as follows:

```
$ sqlite3 ch06.db
SQLite version 3.39.5 2022-10-14 20:58:05
Enter ".help" for usage hints.
sqlite> .tables
```

```
Userdata  Users
sqlite> .schema
CREATE TABLE Users (
    ID INTEGER PRIMARY KEY,
    Username TEXT
);
CREATE TABLE Userdata (
    UserID INTEGER NOT NULL,
    Name TEXT,
    Surname TEXT,
    Description TEXT
);
```

The .tables command just lists the available table names, whereas the .schema command also displays information about the available tables.

Now that we have the necessary infrastructure up and running, we can execute sqliteGo.go. But before that, we need to enable modules and download any package dependencies:

```
$ go mod init
go: creating new go.mod: module github.com/mactsouk/mGo4th/ch06/usePackage
go: to add module requirements and sums:
    go mod tidy
$ go mod tidy
go: finding module for package github.com/mactsouk/sqlite06
go: downloading github.com/mactsouk/sqlite06 v0.0.0-20230817125241-
55d77b17637d
go: found github.com/mactsouk/sqlite06 in github.com/mactsouk/sqlite06
v0.0.0-20230817125241-55d77b17637d
go: finding module for package github.com/mattn/go-sqlite3
go: found github.com/mattn/go-sqlite3 in github.com/mattn/go-sqlite3
v1.14.17
```

Working with sqliteGo.go creates the following kind of output:

```
$ go run sqliteGo.go
Adding username: yzpon
User with ID 1 deleted!
User with ID 1 does not exist
$ go run sqliteGo.go
```

```
{1 vjyps AWJTWCI YIXXXQHSQA Thu, 17 Aug 2023 23:26:40 EEST}
Adding username: cqrxf
User with ID 2 deleted!
User with ID 2 does not exist
```

The more times you execute it, the more data you are going to add to the relevant tables. Additionally, the previous output confirms that sqliteGo.go works as expected as it can connect to the database, add a new user, update a user, and delete an existing one. This also means that the sqlite06 package works as expected. Now that we know how to create Go packages, let us briefly discuss Go modules.

Modules

A Go module is like a Go package with a version—however, Go modules can consist of multiple packages. Go uses semantic versioning for versioning modules. This means that versions begin with the letter v, followed by the major.minor.patch version numbers. Therefore, you can have versions such as v1.0.0, v1.0.5, and v2.0.2. The v1, v2, and v3 parts signify the major version of a Go package that is usually not backward compatible. This means that if your Go program works with v1, it will not necessarily work with v2 or v3—it might work, but you cannot count on it. The second number in a version is about features. Usually, v1.1.0 has more features than v1.0.2 or v1.0.0, while being compatible with all older versions. Lastly, the third number is just about bug fixes without having any new features. Note that semantic versioning is also used for Go versions.

 Go modules were introduced in Go v1.11 but were finalized in Go v1.13.

If you want to learn more about modules, visit and read https://go.dev/blog/using-go-modules, which has five parts, as well as https://go.dev/doc/modules/developing. Just remember that a Go module is similar but not identical to a regular Go package with a version, and that a module can consist of multiple packages.

Creating better packages

This section provides handy advice that can help you develop better Go packages. Here are several good rules to follow to create high-class Go packages:

- The first unofficial rule of a successful package is that its ***elements must be connected in some way***. Thus, you can create a package for supporting cars, but it would not be a good idea to create a single package for supporting cars, bicycles, and airplanes. Put simply, it is better to split the functionality of a package unnecessarily into multiple packages than to add too much functionality to a single Go package.

- A second practical rule is that you should use your own packages first for a reasonable amount of time before making them public. This helps you discover bugs and make sure that your packages operate as expected. After that, give them to some fellow developers for additional testing before making them publicly available. Additionally, you should always write tests for any package you intend to be used by others.

- Next, make sure your package has a clear and useful API so that any consumer can be productive with it quickly.

- Try and limit the public API of your packages to only what is necessary. Additionally, give your functions descriptive but not very long names.

- Interfaces and generics can improve the usefulness of your functions, so when you think it is appropriate, use an interface or a generic data type instead of a single type as a function parameter or return type.

- When updating one of your packages, try not to break things and create incompatibilities with older versions unless it is absolutely necessary.

- When developing a new Go package, try to use multiple files in order to group similar tasks or concepts.

- Do not create a package that already exists from scratch. Make changes to the existing package and maybe create your own version of it.

- Nobody wants a Go package that prints logging information on the screen. It would be more professional to have a flag for turning on logging when needed. The Go code of your packages should be in harmony with the Go code of your programs. This means that if you look at a program that uses your packages and your function names stand out in the code in a bad way, it would be better to change the names of your functions. As the name of a package is used almost everywhere, try to use concise and expressive package names.

- It is more convenient if you put new Go type definitions near where they are used the first time because nobody, including yourself, wants to search huge source files for definitions of new data types.

- Try to create test files for your packages, because packages with test files are considered more professional than ones without them; small details make all the difference and give people confidence that you are a serious developer! Notice that writing tests for your packages is not optional and that you should avoid using packages that do not include tests. You will learn more about testing in *Chapter 12, Code Testing and Profiling*.

Always remember that apart from the fact that the actual Go code in a package should be bug-free, the next most important element of a successful package is its documentation, as well as some code examples that clarify its use and showcase the idiosyncrasies of the functions of the package. The next section discusses creating documentation in Go.

Generating documentation

This section discusses how to create documentation for your Go code using the code of the sqlite06 package as an example. The new package is renamed and is now called document—you can find it in ch06/document in the GitHub repository of the book.

Go follows a simple rule regarding documentation: in order to document a function, a method, a variable, or even the package itself, you can write comments, as usual, that should be located directly before the element you want to document, without any empty lines in between. You can use one or more single-line comments, which are lines beginning with //, or block comments, which begin with /* and end with */—everything in between is considered a comment.

 It is highly recommended that each Go package you create has a block comment preceding the package declaration that introduces developers to the package, and also explains what the package does.

Instead of presenting the entire code of the sqlite06 package, which has been renamed document, we will only present the important parts, which means that function implementations are going to be empty here (the actual file contains the full version). The new version of sqlite06.go is called document.go and comes with the following code and comments:

```
/*
The package works on 2 tables on an SQLite database.
The names of the tables are:
    * Users
    * Userdata
The definitions of the tables are:
    CREATE TABLE Users (
```

```
        ID INTEGER PRIMARY KEY,
        Username TEXT
    );

    CREATE TABLE Userdata (
        UserID INTEGER NOT NULL,
        Name TEXT,
        Surname TEXT,
        Description TEXT
    );
    This is rendered as code

This is not rendered as code
*/
package document
```

This is the first block of documentation that is located right before the name of the package. This is the appropriate place to document the functionality of the package, as well as other essential information. In this case, we are presenting the SQL CREATE TABLE commands that fully describe the database tables we are going to work on. Another important element is specifying the database server this package interacts with. Other information that you can put at the beginning of a package is the author, the license, and the version of the package.

 If a line in a block comment begins with a tab, then it is rendered differently in the graphical output, which is good for differentiating between various kinds of information in the documentation.

The BUG keyword is special when writing documentation. Go knows that bugs are part of the code and therefore should be documented as well. You can write any message you want after a BUG keyword, and you can place them anywhere you want—preferably close to the bugs they describe:

```
// BUG(1): Function ListUsers() not working as expected
// BUG(2): Function AddUser() is too slow
```

Next, we present the implementation details of the package.

```
import (
    "database/sql"
    "errors"
```

```
        "fmt"
        "strings"

        _ "github.com/mattn/go-sqlite3"
    )
```

This is the import block of the package—nothing special here.

The following code shows a way of documenting a global variable—this also works for multiple variables:

```
    /*
    This global variable holds the SQLite3 database filepath

        Filename: In the filepath to the database file
    */
    var (
        Filename = ""
    )
```

The good thing with this way is that you do not have to put a comment before each global variable and make the code less readable. The only downside of this method is that you should remember to update the comments, should you wish to make any changes to the code. However, documenting multiple variables at once might not end up rendering correctly in web-based godoc pages. For that reason, you might want to document each field independently.

The next excerpt shows how to document a Go structure—this is especially useful when you have lots of structures in a source file and you want to have a quick look at them:

```
    // The Userdata structure is for holding full user data
    // from the Userdata table and the Username from the
    // Users table
    type Userdata struct {
        ID          int
        Username    string
        Name        string
        Surname     string
        Description string
    }
```

When documenting a function, it is good to begin the first line of the comments with the function name. Apart from that, you can write any information that you consider important in the comments.

```
// openConnection() is for opening the SQLite3 connection
// in order to be used by the other functions of the package.
func openConnection() (*sql.DB, error) {
}
```

Next, we explain the return values of the exists() function as they have a special meaning.

```
// The function returns the User ID of the username
// -1 if the user does not exist
func exists(username string) int {
}
```

You can use block comments anywhere you want, not only at the beginning of a package, as in the following excerpt:

```
// AddUser adds a new user to the database
//
// Returns new User ID
// -1 if there was an error
func AddUser(d Userdata) int {
}
/*
DeleteUser deletes an existing user if the user exists.
It requires the User ID of the user to be deleted.
*/
func DeleteUser(id int) error {
}
```

When you request the documentation of the Userdata structure, Go automatically presents the functions that use Userdata, as happens with ListUsers().

```
// ListUsers() lists all users in the database.
//
// Returns a slice of Userdata to the calling function.
func ListUsers() ([]Userdata, error) {
    // Data holds the records returned by the SQL query
```

```
    Data := []Userdata{}
}
```

Similar to what we have seen so far is the documentation of the UpdateUser() function.

```
/*
UpdateUser() is for updating an existing user
given a Userdata structure.
The user ID of the user to be updated is found
inside the function.
*/
func UpdateUser(d Userdata) error {
}
```

We are not done yet because we need to see the documentation somehow. There are two ways to see the documentation of the package. The first one involves using go get, which also means creating a GitHub repository of the package, as we did with sqlite06. However, as this is for testing purposes, we are going to do things the easy way using the second way: as the package is already located under ~/go/src, we can access it from there—I am doing my development from ~/go/src/github.com/mactsouk/mGo4th/ch06/document. Therefore, the go doc command is going to work just fine with the document package.

```
$ go doc document.go
package document // import "command-line-arguments"

The package works on 2 tables on an SQLite database.

The names of the tables are:

  - Users
  - Userdata

The definitions of the tables are:

        CREATE TABLE Users (
            ID INTEGER PRIMARY KEY,
            Username TEXT
        );
```

```
        CREATE TABLE Userdata (
            UserID INTEGER NOT NULL,
            Name TEXT,
            Surname TEXT,
            Description TEXT
        );


        This is rendered as code

This is not rendered as code

var Filename = ""
func AddUser(d Userdata) int
func DeleteUser(id int) error
func UpdateUser(d Userdata) error
type Userdata struct{ ... }
    func ListUsers() ([]Userdata, error)

BUG: Function ListUsers() not working as expected

BUG: Function AddUser() is too slow
```

Please keep in mind that *only the documentation of public elements is displayed*.

If you want to see information about a specific function, you should use go doc, as follows:

```
$ go doc document.go ListUsers
package document // import "command-line-arguments"

func ListUsers() ([]Userdata, error)
    ListUsers() lists all users in the database.

    Returns a slice of Userdata to the calling function.
```

Workspaces

Workspaces is a relatively new Go feature. When you are working in workspace mode, you are allowed to work on multiple modules simultaneously. A Go Workspace contains both *source files and compiled binaries*. As usual, *you are not obliged to use workspaces if you do not want to*.

Fortunately, Go is flexible and allows the developer to make their own decisions. However, knowing the features of Go is important, even if you do not want to use them all the time. Not all Go features are for everyone.

When using Go workspaces, you control all dependencies using a file named go.work, which is located in the root directory of the workspace. Inside go.work, there exist use and replace directives that override the information found in the go.mod files of the directories of the workspace—this saves you from having to manually edit go.mod files.

Let us now look at an example of the use of workspaces. Imagine that we want to further develop the sqlite06 package while having the stable version present in our system. One way to do that is with the help of a workspace where we are going to keep a local copy of the sqlite06 package that we are going to modify and test. For reasons of simplicity, we are going to work with a single function only. More specifically, we are going to make the openConnection() function public, which means that we are going to rename it to OpenConnection().

First, we execute the following commands from the ch06 directory:

```
$ mkdir ws
$ cd ws
$ cp -r ~/go/src/github.com/mactsouk/sqlite06 .
$ cd sqlite06
$ rm go.mod go.sum
$ go mod init
$ go mod tidy
$ cd ..
```

The previous commands are for creating a local copy of the sqlite06 module. The version you are going to find inside ws is pretty minimal.

```
$ mkdir util
$ cp ~/go/src/github.com/mactsouk/mGo4th/ch06/usePackage/sqliteGo.go .
$ cd util
$ go mod init
$ go mod tidy
$ cd ..
```

The previous command is for copying the command line utility we have created for testing the sqlite06 module. As we are going to use a single function from sqlite06, we are also going to modify sqliteGo.go in order to call that function only.

The go work init . command creates the workspace.

```
$ go work use ./util
$ cat go.work
go 1.21.0

use ./util
```

The previous command says that we want to create a workspace for the modules in the ./util directory.

```
$ go work use ./sqlite06
$ cat go.work
go 1.21.0

use (
    ./sqlite06
    ./util
)
$
```

The previous command says that we want to use the local copies. There is another command missing from go.work, which is the following:

```
replace github.com/mactsouk/sqlite06 => ./sqlite06
```

This last command tells Go that *we want to replace* github.com/mactsouk/sqlite06 with the version of the module found in the ./sqlite06 directory, *which is the copy that we are actually changing*. This is the most important command of the process.

After that, we are ready to try running the modified version of ./util/sqliteGo.go.

```
$ go run ./util/sqliteGo.go
Connection string: &{{{} {} 0} {ch06.db 0x14000072020} {{} {} 0} {0
0} [] map[] 0 0 0x1400001c120 false map[] map[] 0 0 0 0 <nil> 0 0 0 0
0x1001512d0}
```

The output verifies that we executed the local and modified version of the sqlite06 module! This means that we can keep developing and changing the sqlite06 module and when we are done, we can replace the original one with the newer version!

If you want to learn about all the options of the go work command, type go help work.

The last section of this chapter is about versioning utilities and defining unique version strings.

Versioning utilities

One of the most difficult tasks is to automatically and uniquely version command line utilities, especially when using a CI/CD system. This section presents a technique that uses a GitHub value to version a command line utility on your local machine. You can apply the same technique to Git-Lab—just search for the available GitLab variables and values and choose one that fits your needs.

This technique is used by both the docker and kubectl utilities, among others:

```
$ docker version
Client:
 Version:           24.0.5
 API version:       1.43
 Go version:        go1.20.6
 Git commit:        ced0996600
 Built:             Wed Jul 26 21:44:58 2023
 OS/Arch:           linux/amd64
 Context:           default

Server:
 Engine:
  Version:          24.0.5
  API version:      1.43 (minimum version 1.12)
  Go version:       go1.20.6
  Git commit:       a61e2b4c9c
  Built:            Wed Jul 26 21:44:58 2023
  OS/Arch:          linux/amd64
  Experimental:     false
 containerd:
  Version:          v1.7.2
  GitCommit:        0cae528dd6cb557f7201036e9f43420650207b58.m
 runc:
```

```
  Version:              1.1.9
  GitCommit:
 docker-init:
  Version:              0.19.0
  GitCommit:            de40ad0
```

The previous output shows that docker uses the Git commit value for versioning—we are going to use a slightly different value that is longer than the one used by docker.

The utility that is used, which is saved as gitVersion.go, is implemented as follows:

```
package main
import (
    "fmt"
    "os"
)
var VERSION string
```

VERSION is the variable that is going to be set at runtime using the Go linker.

```
func main() {
    if len(os.Args) == 2 {
        if os.Args[1] == "version" {
            fmt.Println("Version:", VERSION)
        }
    }
}
```

The previous code says that if there is a command line argument and its value is version, print the version message with the help of the VERSION variable.

What we need to do is tell the Go linker that we are going to define the value of the VERSION variable. This happens with the help of the -ldflags flag, which stands for linker flags—this passes values to the cmd/link package, which allows us to change values in imported packages at build time. The -X value that is used requires a key/value pair, where the key is a variable name, and the value is the value that we want to set for that key. In our case, the key has the main.Variable form because we change the value of a variable in the main package. As the name of the variable in gitVersion.go is VERSION, the key is main.VERSION.

But first, we need to decide on the GitHub value that we are going to use as the version string. The git rev-list HEAD command returns a full list of commits for the current repository from the latest to the oldest. We only need the last one—the most recent—which we can get using git rev-list -1 HEAD or git rev-list HEAD | head -1. So, we need to assign that value to an environment variable and pass that environment variable to the Go compiler. As this value changes each time you make a commit and you always want to have the latest value, you should reevaluate it each time you execute go build—this will be shown in a while.

In order to provide gitVersion.go with the value of the desired environment variable, we should execute it as follows:

```
$ export VERSION=$(git rev-list -1 HEAD)
$ go build -ldflags "-X main.VERSION=$VERSION" gitVersion.go
```

 This works on both bash and zsh shells. If you are using a different shell, you should make sure that you are defining an environment variable the right way.

If you want to execute the two commands at the same time, you can do the following:

```
$ export VERSION=$(git rev-list -1 HEAD) && go build -ldflags "-X main.
VERSION=$VERSION" gitVersion.go
```

Running the generated executable, which is called gitVersion, produces the following output:

```
$ ./gitVersion version
Version: 4dc3d6b5fd030bf7075ed26f9ab471e8835a8a77
```

Your output is going to be different because your GitHub repository is going to be different. As GitHub generates random and unique values, you will not have the same version number twice!

Summary

This chapter presented two primary topics: functions and packages. Functions are first-class citizens in Go, which makes them powerful and handy. Remember that everything that begins with an uppercase letter is public. The only exception to this rule is package names. Private variables, functions, data type names, and structure fields can be strictly used and called internally in a package, whereas public ones are available to everyone. Additionally, we learned more about the defer keyword. Also, remember that Go packages are not like Java classes—a Go package can be as big as it needs to be. Regarding Go modules, keep in mind that a Go module is multiple packages with a version.

Finally, this chapter discussed creating documentation, which is an important part of development, workspaces, and versioning command line utilities.

The next chapter discusses systems programming as well as file I/O in more detail.

Exercises

- Can you write a function that sorts three int values? Try to write two versions of the function: one with named returned values and another without named return values. Which one do you think is better?

- The `sqlite06` package does not support searching by username. Can you implement that?

- Rewrite the `sqlite06` package so that it works with MySQL databases.

Additional resources

- How do you structure your Go apps? Talk by Kat Zien from GopherCon UK 2018: `https://www.youtube.com/watch?v=1rxDzs0zgcE`

- Get familiar with workspaces: `https://go.dev/blog/get-familiar-with-workspaces`

- Tutorial: Getting started with multi-module workspaces: `https://go.dev/doc/tutorial/workspaces`

- Experimenting with project templates: `https://go.dev/blog/gonew`

- SQLite: `https://www.sqlite.org/index.html`

- Go SQLite package: `https://github.com/mattn/go-sqlite3`

- The documentation of `database/sql`: `https://pkg.go.dev/database/sql`

- The documentation of the `cmd/link` package: `https://pkg.go.dev/cmd/link`

- `golang.org` moving to go.dev: `https://go.dev/blog/tidy-web`

Join our community on Discord

Join our community's Discord space for discussions with the authors and other readers:

`https://discord.gg/FzuQbc8zd6`

7

Telling a UNIX System What to Do

This chapter is about systems programming in Go. Systems programming involves working with files and directories, process control, signal handling, network programming, system files, configuration files, and file **input and output (I/O)**. If you recall from *Chapter 1, A Quick Introduction to Go*, the reason for writing system utilities with Linux in mind is that, often, Go software is executed in a Docker environment—Docker images use the Linux operating system, which means that you might need to develop your utilities with the Linux operating system in mind. However, as Go code is portable, most system utilities work on Windows machines without any changes or with minor modifications. The key idea to remember is that Go makes systems programming more portable. Additionally, in this chapter, we are going to improve the statistics application with the help of the cobra package.

 As already mentioned, starting with Go 1.16, the GO111MODULE environment variable defaults to on—this affects the use of Go packages that do not belong to the Go standard library. In practice, this means that you must put your code under ~/go/src.

This chapter covers:

- stdin, stdout, and stderr
- UNIX processes
- File I/O
- Reading plain text files
- Writing to a file

- Working with JSON
- The viper package
- The cobra package
- Important Go features
- Updating the statistics application

stdin, stdout, and stderr

Every UNIX operating system has three files open all the time for its processes. Remember that UNIX considers everything, even a printer or a mouse, as a file. UNIX uses file descriptors, which are positive integer values, as an internal representation to access open files, which is much prettier than using long paths. So, by default, all UNIX systems support three special and standard filenames: /dev/stdin, /dev/stdout, and /dev/stderr, which can also be accessed using the file descriptors 0, 1, and 2, respectively. These three file descriptors are also called standard input, standard output, and standard error, respectively. Additionally, the file descriptor 0 can be accessed as /dev/fd/0 on a macOS machine and as both /dev/fd/0 and /dev/pts/0 on a Debian Linux machine.

Go uses os.Stdin to access standard input, os.Stdout to access standard output, and os.Stderr to access standard error. Although you can still use /dev/stdin, /dev/stdout, and /dev/stderr or the related file descriptor values to access the same devices, it is better, safer, and more portable to stick with os.Stdin, os.Stdout, and os.Stderr.

UNIX processes

As Go servers, utilities, and Docker images are mainly executed on Linux, it is good to know about Linux processes and threads.

Strictly speaking, a process is an execution environment that contains instructions, user data and system data parts, and other types of resources that are obtained during runtime. On the other hand, a program is a binary file that contains instructions and data that are used to initialize the instruction and user data parts of a process. Each running UNIX process is uniquely identified by an unsigned integer, which is called the process ID of the process.

There are three process categories: user processes, daemon processes, and kernel processes. User processes run in user space and usually have no special access rights. Daemon processes are programs that can be found in the user space and run in the background without the need for a terminal. Kernel processes are executed in kernel space only and can fully access all kernel data structures.

The C way of creating new processes involves the calling of the fork(2) system call. The return value of fork(2) allows the programmer to differentiate between a parent and a child process. Although you can fork a new process in Go using the exec package, Go does not allow you to control threads—Go offers goroutines, which the user can create on top of threads that are created and handled by the Go runtime, which is partially controlled by the operating system.

Now, we need to learn how to read and write files in Go.

File I/O

This section discusses file I/O in Go, which includes the use of the io.Reader and io.Writer interfaces, buffered and unbuffered I/O, as well as the bufio package.

The io/ioutil package (https://pkg.go.dev/io/ioutil) has been deprecated since Go version 1.16. Existing Go code that uses the functionality of io/ioutil will continue to work, but it is better to stop using that package.

The io.Reader and io.Writer interfaces

This subsection presents the definitions of the popular io.Reader and io.Writer interfaces because these two interfaces are the basis of file I/O in Go—the former allows you to read from a file, whereas the latter allows you to write to a file. The definition of the io.Reader interface is the following:

```
type Reader interface {
    Read(p []byte) (n int, err error)
}
```

This definition, which should be revisited when we want one of our data types to satisfy the io.Reader interface, tells us the following:

- The Reader interface requires the implementation of a single method.
- The Read() method takes a byte slice as input, which will be filled with data up to its length.
- The Read() method returns the number of bytes read as well as an error variable.

The definition of the io.Writer interface is the following:

```
type Writer interface {
    Write(p []byte) (n int, err error)
}
```

The previous definition, which should be revisited when we want one of our data types to satisfy the io.Writer interface and write to a file, reveals the following information:

- The interface requires the implementation of a single method.
- The Write() method takes a byte slice, which contains the data that you want to write, as input.
- The Write() method returns the number of bytes written and an error variable.

Using and misusing io.Reader and io.Writer

The code that follows showcases the use of io.Reader and io.Writer for *custom data types*, which, in this case, are two Go structures named S1 and S2.

For the S1 structure, the presented code implements both interfaces in order to read user data from the terminal and print data to the terminal, respectively. Although this is redundant, as we already have fmt.Scanln() and fmt.Printf(), it is a good exercise that shows how versatile and flexible both interfaces are. In a different situation, you could have used io.Writer for writing to a log service, keeping a second backup copy of the written data, or anything else that fits your needs. However, this is also an example of interfaces allowing you to do crazy or, if you prefer, unusual things. It is up to the developer to create the desired functionality using the appropriate Go concepts and features!

The Read() method uses fmt.Scanln() to get user input from the terminal, whereas the Write() method prints the contents of its buffer parameter as many times as the value of the F1 field of the structure, using fmt.Printf()!

For the S2 struct, the presented code implements the io.Reader interface only, in the traditional way. The Read() method reads the text field of the S2 structure, which is a byte slice. When there is nothing left to read, the Read() method returns the expected io.EOF error, which in reality is not an error but an expected situation. Along with the Read() method, there exist two helper methods, named eof(), which declares that there is nothing more to read, and readByte(), which reads the text field of the S2 structure byte by byte. After the Read() method is done, the text field of the S2 structure, which is used as a buffer, is emptied.

With this implementation, the io.Reader for S2 can be used for reading in a traditional way, which, in this case, is with bufio.NewReader() and multiple Read() calls—the number of Read() calls depends on the size of the buffer that is used, which, in this case, is a byte slice with two places for data.

Type the following code and save it as ioInterface.go:

```
package main
import (
    "bufio"
    "fmt"
    "io"
)
```

The previous part shows that we are using the io and bufio packages to work with files.

```
type S1 struct {
    F1 int
    F2 string
}

type S2 struct {
    F1    S1
    text []byte
}
```

These are the two structures we are going to work with.

```
// Using pointer to S1 for changes to be persistent
func (s *S1) Read(p []byte) (n int, err error) {
    fmt.Print("Give me your name: ")
    fmt.Scanln(&p)
    s.F2 = string(p)
    return len(p), nil
}
```

In the preceding code, we implement the io.Reader interface for S1.

```
func (s *S1) Write(p []byte) (n int, err error) {
    if s.F1 < 0 {
        return -1, nil
    }
    for i := 0; i < s.F1; i++ {
        fmt.Printf("%s ", p)
    }
    fmt.Println()
    return s.F1, nil
}
```

The previous method implements the io.Writer interface for S1.

```go
func (s S2) eof() bool {
    return len(s.text) == 0
}


func (s *S2) readByte() byte {
    // this function assumes that eof() check was done before
    temp := s.text[0]
    s.text = s.text[1:]
    return temp
}
```

The previous function is an implementation of bytes.Buffer.ReadByte from the standard library.

```go
func (s *S2) Read(p []byte) (n int, err error) {
    if s.eof() {
        err = io.EOF
        return 0, err
    }
    l := len(p)
    if l > 0 {
        for n < l {
            p[n] = s.readByte()
            n++
            if s.eof() {
                s.text = s.text[0:0]
                break
            }
        }
    }
    return n, nil
}
```

The previous code reads from the given buffer until it is empty. When all data is read, the relevant structure field is emptied. The previous method implements io.Reader for S2. However, the operation of Read() is supported by eof() and readByte(), which are also user-defined.

Recall that Go allows you to name the return values of a function; in that case, a `return` statement without any additional arguments automatically returns the current value of each named return variable in the order they appear in the function signature. The `Read()` method could have used that feature, but in general, naked returns are considered bad practice.

```go
func main() {
    s1var := S1{4, "Hello"}
    fmt.Println(s1var)
```

We initialize an S1 variable that is named s1var.

```go
    buf := make([]byte, 2)
    _, err := s1var.Read(buf)
```

The previous line reads for the s1var variable using a buffer of two bytes. The block does not do what is expected because the implementation of the `Read()` method gets the value from the terminal—we are misusing Go interfaces here!

```go
    if err != nil {
        fmt.Println(err)
        return
    }
    fmt.Println("Read:", s1var.F2)
    _, _ = s1var.Write([]byte("Hello There!"))
```

In the previous line, we call the `Write()` method for s1var in order to write the contents of a byte slice.

```go
    s2var := S2{F1: s1var, text: []byte("Hello world!!")}
```

In the previous code, we initialize an S2 variable that is named s2var.

```go
    // Read s2var.text
    r := bufio.NewReader(&s2var)
```

We now create a reader for s2var.

```go
    for {
        n, err := r.Read(buf)
        if err == io.EOF {
            break
```

We keep reading from s2var until there is an io.EOF condition.

```
        } else if err != nil {
            fmt.Println("*", err)
            break
        }
        fmt.Println("**", n, string(buf[:n]))
    }
}
```

Running ioInterface.go produces the following output:

```
$ go run ioInterface.go
{4 Hello}
```

The first line of the output shows the contents of the s1var variable.

```
Give me your name: Mike
Calling the Read() method of the s1var variable.
Read: Mike
Hello There! Hello There! Hello There! Hello There!
The previous line is the output of s1var.Write([]byte("Hello There!")).
** 2 He
** 2 ll
** 2 o
** 2 wo
** 2 rl
** 2 d!
** 1 !
```

The last part of the output illustrates the reading process, using a buffer with a size of two. The next section discusses buffered and unbuffered operations.

Buffered and unbuffered file I/O

Buffered file I/O happens when there is a buffer to temporarily store data before reading data or writing data. Thus, instead of reading a file byte by byte, you read many bytes at once. You put the data in a buffer and wait for someone to read it in the desired way.

Unbuffered file I/O happens when there is no buffer to temporarily store data before reading or writing it—this can affect the performance of your programs.

The next question that you might ask is how to decide when to use buffered and when to use unbuffered file I/O. When dealing with critical data, unbuffered file I/O is generally a better choice because buffered reads might result in out-of-date data, and buffered writes might result in data loss when the power of your computer is interrupted. However, most of the time, there is no definitive answer to that question. This means that you can use whatever makes your tasks easier to implement. However, keep in mind that buffered readers can also improve performance by reducing the number of system calls needed to read from a file or socket, so there can be a real performance impact on what the programmer decides to use.

There is also the bufio package. As the name suggests, bufio is about buffered I/O. Internally, the bufio package implements the io.Reader and io.Writer interfaces, which it wraps in order to create the bufio.Reader and bufio.Writer types, respectively. The bufio package is very popular for working with plain text files, and you are going to see it in action in the next section.

Reading text files

In this section, you will learn how to read plain text files, as well as use the /dev/random UNIX device, which offers you a way of getting random numbers.

Reading a text file line by line

The function to read a file line by line is found in byLine.go and is named lineByLine(). The technique for reading a text file line by line is also used when reading a plain text file word by word, as well as when reading a plain text file character by character because you usually process plain text files line by line. The presented utility prints every line that it reads, which makes it a simplified version of the cat(1) utility.

First, you create a new reader for the desired file using a call to bufio.NewReader(). Then, you use that reader with bufio.ReadString() in order to read the input file line by line. The trick is done by the parameter of bufio.ReadString(), which is a character that tells bufio.ReadString() to keep reading until that character is found. Constantly calling bufio.ReadString() when that parameter is the newline character (\n) results in reading the input file line by line.

The implementation of lineByLine() is as follows:

```
func lineByLine(file string) error {
    f, err := os.Open(file)
    if err != nil {
        return err
    }
```

```
    defer f.Close()
    r := bufio.NewReader(f)
```

After making sure that you can open the given file for reading (os.Open()), you create a new
reader using bufio.NewReader().

```
    for {
        line, err := r.ReadString('\n')
```

bufio.ReadString() returns two values: the string that was read and an error variable.

```
        if err == io.EOF {
            if len(line) != 0 {
                    fmt.Println(line)
            }
            break
        }

        if err != nil {
            fmt.Printf("error reading file %s", err)
            return err
        }
        fmt.Print(line)
```

The use of fmt.Print() instead of fmt.Println() to print the input line shows that the newline
character is included in each input line.

```
    }
    return nil
}
```

Running byLine.go generates the following kind of output:

```
$ go run byLine.go ~/csv.data
Dimitris,Tsoukalos,2101112223,1600665563
Mihalis,Tsoukalos,2109416471,1600665563
Jane,Doe,0800123456,1608559903
```

The previous output shows the contents of ~/csv.data (use your own plain text file) presented
line by line with the help of byLine.go. The next subsection shows how to read a plain text file
word by word.

Reading a text file word by word

Reading a plain text file word by word is one of the most useful functions that you want to perform on a file because you usually want to process a file on a per-word basis—it is illustrated in this subsection, using the code found in byWord.go. The desired functionality is implemented in the wordByWord() function. The wordByWord() function uses *regular expressions* to separate the words found in each line of the input file. The regular expression defined in the regexp. MustCompile("[^\\s]+") statement states that we use whitespace characters to separate one word from another.

The implementation of the wordByWord() function is as follows:

```
func wordByWord(file string) error {
    f, err := os.Open(file)
    if err != nil {
        return err
    }
    defer f.Close()

    r := bufio.NewReader(f)
    re := regexp.MustCompile("[^\\s]+")
    for {
```

This is where we define the regular expression for splitting lines into words.

```
        line, err := r.ReadString('\n')
        if err == io.EOF {
            if len(line) != 0 {
                words := re.FindAllString(line, -1)
                for i := 0; i < len(words); i++ {
                    fmt.Println(words[i])
                }
            }
        }
        break
```

This is the tricky part of the program. If we reach the end of a file having a line that does not end with a newline character, we must also process it, but after that, we must exit the for loop, as there is nothing more to read from that file. The previous code takes care of it.

```
        } else if err != nil {
```

```
        fmt.Printf("error reading file %s", err)
        return err
    }
```

In this part of the program, we deal with potential error conditions that might come up and prevent us from reading the file.

```
        words := re.FindAllString(line, -1)
```

This is the place where we apply the regular expression to split the line variable into fields when the line that we have read ends with newline character.

```
        for i := 0; i < len(words); i++ {
            fmt.Println(words[i])
        }
```

This for loop just prints the fields of the words slice. If you want to know the number of words found in the input line, you can just find the value of the len(words) call.

```
    }
    return nil
}
```

Running byWord.go produces the following kind of output:

```
$ go run byWord.go ~/csv.data
Dimitris,Tsoukalos,2101112223,1600665563
Mihalis,Tsoukalos,2109416471,1600665563
Jane,Doe,0800123456,1608559903
```

As ~/csv.data does not contain any whitespace characters, each line is considered a single word!

Reading a text file character by character

In this subsection, you will learn how to read a text file character by character, which is a rare requirement unless you want to develop a text editor. You take each line that you read and split it using a for loop with a range, which returns two values. You discard the first, which is the location of the current character in the line variable, and you use the second. However, that value is a rune, which means that you have to convert it into a character using string().

The implementation of charByChar() is as follows:

```
func charByChar(file string) error {
```

```
    f, err := os.Open(file)
    if err != nil {
        return err
    }
    defer f.Close()

    r := bufio.NewReader(f)
    for {
        line, err := r.ReadString('\n')
        if err == io.EOF {
            if len(line) != 0 {
                for _, x := range line {
                    fmt.Println(string(x))
                }
```

Once again, we should take extra care with lines that end without a newline character. The conditions for catching such lines are that we have reached the end of the file that we are reading and that we still have text to process.

```
            }
            break
        } else if err != nil {
            fmt.Printf("error reading file %s", err)
            return err
        }

        for _, x := range line {
            fmt.Println(string(x))
        }
    }
    return nil
}
```

Note that, due to the fmt.Println(string(x)) statement, each character is printed in a distinct line, which means that the output of the program is going to be large. If you want a more compressed output, you should use the fmt.Print() function instead.

Running byCharacter.go and filtering it with head(1), without any parameters, produces the
following kind of output:

```
$ go run byCharacter.go ~/csv.data | head
D
...
,
T
```

 The use of the head(1) utility without any parameters limits the output to just 10
lines. Type man head to learn more about the head(1) utility.

The next section is about reading from /dev/random, which is a UNIX system file.

Reading from /dev/random

In this subsection, you will learn how to read from the /dev/random system device. The purpose
of the /dev/random system device is to generate random data, which you might use to test your
programs or, in this case, as the seed for a random number generator. Getting data from /dev/
random can be a little bit tricky, and this is the main reason for specifically discussing it here.

The code for devRandom.go is the following:

```go
package main
import (
    "encoding/binary"
    "fmt"
    "os"
)
```

You need encoding/binary because you read binary data from /dev/random that you convert
into integer values.

```go
func main() {
    f, err := os.Open("/dev/random")
    defer f.Close()
    if err != nil {
        fmt.Println(err)
        return
```

```
    }
    var seed int64
    binary.Read(f, binary.LittleEndian, &seed)
    fmt.Println("Seed:", seed)
}
```

There are two representations named *little endian* and *big endian* that relate to the byte order in the internal representation. In our case, we are using little endian. The endian-ness relates to the way different computing systems order multiple bytes of information.

 A real-world example of endian-ness is how different languages read text in different ways: European languages tend to be read from left to right, whereas Arabic texts are read from right to left.

In a big endian representation, bytes are read from left to right, while little endian reads bytes from right to left. For the 0x01234567 value, which requires 4 bytes for storing, the big endian representation is 01 | 23 | 45 | 67, whereas the little endian representation is 67 | 45 | 23 | 01.

Running devRandom.go creates the following kind of output:

```
$ go run devRandom.go
Seed: 422907465220227415
```

This means that the /dev/random device is a good place to get random data, including a seed value for your random number generator.

Reading a specific amount of data from a file

This subsection teaches you how to read a specific amount of data from a file. The presented utility can come in handy when you want to see a small part of a file. The numeric value that is given as a command line argument specifies the size of the buffer that is going to be used for reading. The most important code of readSize.go is the implementation of the readSize() function:

```
func readSize(f *os.File, size int) []byte {
    buffer := make([]byte, size)
    n, err := f.Read(buffer)
```

All the magic happens in the definition of the buffer variable, because this is where we define the maximum amount of data that it can hold. Therefore, each time we invoke readSize(), the function is going to read from f at most size characters.

```go
    // io.EOF is a special case and is treated as such
    if err == io.EOF {
        return nil
    }
    if err != nil {
        fmt.Println(err)
        return nil
    }
    return buffer[0:n]
}
```

The remaining code is about error conditions; io.EOF is a special and expected condition that should be treated separately and return the read characters as a byte slice to the caller function.

Running readSize.go produces the following kind of output.

```
$ go run readSize.go 12 readSize.go
package main
```

In this case, we read 12 characters from readSize.go itself because of the 12 parameter. Now that we know how to read files, it is time to learn how to write to files.

Writing to a file

So far, we have seen ways to read files. This subsection shows how to write data to files in four different ways and how to append data to an existing file. The code of writeFile.go is as follows:

```go
package main
import (
    "bufio"
    "fmt"
    "io"
    "os"
)
func main() {
    buffer := []byte("Data to write\n")
    f1, err := os.Create("/tmp/f1.txt")
```

os.Create() returns an *os.File value associated with the file path that is passed as a parameter. Note that if the file already exists, os.Create() truncates it.

```
    if err != nil {
        fmt.Println("Cannot create file", err)
        return
    }
    defer f1.Close()
    fmt.Fprintf(f1, string(buffer))
```

The fmt.Fprintf() function, which requires a string variable, helps you write data to your own files using the format you want. The only requirement is having an io.Writer to write to. In this case, a valid *os.File variable, which satisfies the io.Writer interface, does the job.

```
    f2, err := os.Create("/tmp/f2.txt")
    if err != nil {
        fmt.Println("Cannot create file", err)
        return
    }
    defer f2.Close()
    n, err := f2.WriteString(string(buffer))
```

WriteString() writes the contents of a string to a valid *os.File variable.

```
    fmt.Printf("wrote %d bytes\n", n)
    f3, err := os.Create("/tmp/f3.txt")
```

Here, we create a temporary file on our own.

 Go also offers os.CreateTemp() to create temporary files. Type go doc os.CreateTemp to learn more about it.

```
    if err != nil {
        fmt.Println(err)
        return
    }
    w := bufio.NewWriter(f3)
```

This function returns a bufio.Writer, which satisfies the io.Writer interface.

```
    n, err = w.WriteString(string(buffer))
    fmt.Printf("wrote %d bytes\n", n)
```

```
    w.Flush()
    f := "/tmp/f4.txt"
    f4, err := os.Create(f)
    if err != nil {
        fmt.Println(err)
        return
    }
    defer f4.Close()
    for i := 0; i < 5; i++ {
        n, err = io.WriteString(f4, string(buffer))
        if err != nil {
            fmt.Println(err)
            return
        }
        fmt.Printf("wrote %d bytes\n", n)
    }
    // Append to a file
    f4, err = os.OpenFile(f, os.O_APPEND|os.O_CREATE|os.O_WRONLY, 0644)
```

os.OpenFile() provides a better way to create or open a file for writing. os.O_APPEND says that if the file already exists, you should append to it instead of truncating it. os.O_CREATE states that if the file does not already exist, it should be created. Last, os.O_WRONLY says that the program should open the file for writing only.

```
    if err != nil {
        fmt.Println(err)
        return
    }
    defer f4.Close()
    // Write() needs a byte slice
    n, err = f4.Write([]byte("Put some more data at the end.\n"))
```

The Write() method gets its input from a byte slice, which is the Go way of writing. All previous techniques used strings, which is not the best way, especially when working with binary data. However, using strings instead of byte slices is more practical as it is more convenient to manipulate string values than the elements of a byte slice, especially when working with Unicode characters. On the other hand, using string values increases allocation and can cause a lot of garbage collection pressure.

```
    if err != nil {
        fmt.Println(err)
        return
    }
    fmt.Printf("wrote %d bytes\n", n)
}
```

Running writeFile.go generates some information output about the bytes written on disk. What is interesting is seeing the files created in the /tmp folder:

```
$ ls -l /tmp/f?.txt
-rw-r--r--@ 1 mtsouk  wheel   14 Aug  5 11:30 /tmp/f1.txt
-rw-r--r--@ 1 mtsouk  wheel   14 Aug  5 11:30 /tmp/f2.txt
-rw-r--r--@ 1 mtsouk  wheel   14 Aug  5 11:30 /tmp/f3.txt
-rw-r--r--@ 1 mtsouk  wheel  101 Aug  5 11:30 /tmp/f4.txt
```

The previous output shows that the same amount of information (14 bytes) has been written in f1.txt, f2.txt, and f3.txt, which means that the presented writing techniques are equivalent.

The next section shows how to work with JSON data in Go.

Working with JSON

The Go standard library includes encoding/json, which is for working with JSON data. Additionally, Go allows you to add support for JSON fields in Go structures using tags, which is the subject of the Structures and JSON subsection. Tags control the encoding and decoding of JSON records to and from Go structures. But first, we should talk about the *marshaling* and *unmarshaling* of JSON records.

Using Marshal() and Unmarshal()

Both the marshaling and unmarshaling of JSON data are important procedures for working with JSON data using Go structures. Marshaling is the process of converting a Go structure into a JSON record. You usually want that for transferring JSON data via computer networks or for saving it on disk. Unmarshaling is the process of converting a JSON record given as a byte slice into a Go structure. You usually want that when receiving JSON data via computer networks or when loading JSON data from disk files.

The number one bug when converting JSON records into Go structures, and vice versa, is not making the required fields of your Go structures exported, that is having their first letter in uppercase. When you have issues with marshaling and unmarshaling, begin your debugging process from there.

The code in encodeDecode.go illustrates both the marshaling and unmarshaling of JSON records using hardcoded data for simplicity:

```
package main
import (
    "encoding/json"
    "fmt"
)
type UseAll struct {
    Name    string `json:"username"`
    Surname string `json:"surname"`
    Year    int    `json:"created"`
}
```

What the previous metadata tells us is that the Name field of the UseAll structure is translated to username in the JSON record, and vice versa; the Surname field is translated to surname, and vice versa; and the Year structure field is translated to created in the JSON record, and vice versa. This information has to do with the marshaling and unmarshaling of JSON data. Other than this, you treat and use UseAll as a regular Go structure.

```
func main() {
    useall := UseAll{Name: "Mike", Surname: "Tsoukalos", Year: 2023}

    // Encoding JSON data: Convert Structure to JSON record with fields
    t, err := json.Marshal(&useall)
```

The json.Marshal() function requires a pointer to a structure variable—its real data type is an empty interface variable—and returns a byte slice with the encoded information and an error variable.

```
    if err != nil {
        fmt.Println(err)
    } else {
        fmt.Printf("Value %s\n", t)
```

```
        }

        // Decoding JSON data given as a string
        str := `{"username": "M.", "surname": "Ts", "created":2024}`
```

JSON data usually comes as a string.

```
        // Convert string into a byte slice
        jsonRecord := []byte(str)
```

However, as json.Unmarshal() requires a byte slice, you need to convert that string into a byte slice before passing it to json.Unmarshal().

```
        // Create a structure variable to store the result
        temp := UseAll{}
        err = json.Unmarshal(jsonRecord, &temp)
```

The json.Unmarshal() function requires the byte slice with the JSON record and a pointer to the Go structure variable that will store the JSON record, returning an error variable.

```
        if err != nil {
            fmt.Println(err)
        } else {
            fmt.Printf("Data type: %T with value %v\n", temp, temp)
        }
    }
```

Running encodeDecode.go produces the following output:

```
$ go run encodeDecode.go
Value {"username":"Mike","surname":"Tsoukalos","created":2023}
Data type: main.UseAll with value {M. Ts 2024}
```

The next subsection illustrates how to define the JSON tags in a Go structure in more detail.

Structures and JSON

Imagine that you have a Go structure that you want to convert into a JSON record without including any empty fields—the following code illustrates how to perform that task with the use of omitempty:

```
// Ignoring empty fields in JSON
type NoEmpty struct {
```

```
    Name     string `json:"username"`
    Surname string `json:"surname"`
    Year     int    `json:"creationyear,omitempty"`
}
```

Now, imagine that you have some sensitive data on some of the fields of a Go structure that you do not want to include in the JSON records. You can do that by including the – special value in the desired json: structure tags. This is shown in the following code excerpt:

```
// Removing private fields and ignoring empty fields
type Password struct {
    Name     string `json:"username"`
    Surname string `json:"surname,omitempty"`
    Year     int    `json:"creationyear,omitempty"`
    Pass     string `json:"-"`
}
```

So the Pass field is going to be ignored when converting a Password structure into a JSON record using json.Marshal().

These two techniques are illustrated in tagsJSON.go. Running tagsJSON.go produces the following output:

```
$ go run tagsJSON.go
noEmptyVar decoded with value {username":"Mihalis","surname":""}
password decoded with value {"username":"Mihalis"}
```

For the first line of output, we have the following: the value of noEmpty, which is converted into a NoEmpty structure variable named noEmptyVar, is NoEmpty{Name: "Mihalis"}. The noEmpty structure has the default values for the Surname and Year fields. However, as they are not specifically defined, json.Marshal() ignores the Year field because it has the omitempty tag but does not ignore the Surname field, which has the empty string value but not the omitempty tag.

For the second line of output, the value of the password variable is Password{Name: "Mihalis", Pass: "myPassword"}. When the password variable is converted into a JSON record, the Pass field is not included in the output. The remaining two fields of the Password structure, Surname and Year, are omitted because of the omitempty tag. So, what is left is the username field along with its value.

So far, we have seen working with single JSON records. But what happens when we have multiple records to process? Do we have to process them one by one? The next subsection answers these questions and many more!

Reading and writing JSON data as streams

Imagine that you have a slice of Go structures that represent JSON records that you want to process. Should you process the records one by one? It can be done but does it look efficient? The good thing is that Go supports the processing of multiple JSON records as streams instead of individual records. This subsection teaches how to perform that using the JSONstreams.go utility, which contains the following two functions:

```
// DeSerialize decodes a serialized slice with JSON records
func DeSerialize(e *json.Decoder, slice interface{}) error {
    return e.Decode(slice)
}
```

The DeSerialize() function is used for reading input in the form of JSON records, decoding it, and putting it into a slice. The function writes the slice, which is of the interface{} data type and is given as a parameter, and gets its input from the buffer of the *json.Decoder parameter. The *json.Decoder parameter, along with its buffer, is defined in the main() function in order to avoid allocating it all the time, and therefore, losing the performance gains and efficiency of using this type. The same applies to the use of *json.Encoder that follows:

```
// Serialize serializes a slice with JSON records
func Serialize(e *json.Encoder, slice interface{}) error {
    return e.Encode(slice)
}
```

The Serialize() function accepts two parameters, a *json.Encoder and a slice of any data type, hence the use of interface{}. The function processes the slice and writes the output to the buffer of the json.Encoder—this buffer is passed as a parameter to the encoder at the time of its creation.

 Both the Serialize() and DeSerialize() functions can work with any type of JSON record due to the use of interface{}.

You can replace both `Serialize()` and `DeSerialize()` with the `err := json.NewEncoder(buf).Encode(DataRecords)` and `err := json.NewEncoder(buf).Encode(DataRecords)` calls, respectively. Personally, I prefer using separate functions, but your taste might differ.

The `JSONstreams.go` utility generates random data. Running `JSONstreams.go` creates the following output:

```
$ go run JSONstreams.go
After Serialize:[{"key":"RESZD","value":63},{"key":"XUEYA","value":13}]
After DeSerialize:
0 {RESZD 63}
1 {XUEYA 13}
```

The input slice of structures, which is generated in `main()`, is serialized, as seen in the first line of the output. After that, it is deserialized into the original slice of structures.

Pretty printing JSON records

This subsection illustrates how to pretty print JSON records, which means printing JSON records in a pleasant and readable format without knowing the internals of the Go structure that holds the JSON records. As there exist two ways to read JSON records, individually and as a stream, there exist two ways to pretty print JSON data: as single JSON records and as a stream. Therefore, we are going to implement two separate functions named `prettyPrint()` and `JSONstream()`, respectively.

The implementation of the `prettyPrint()` function is the following:

```go
func PrettyPrint(v interface{}) (err error) {
    b, err := json.MarshalIndent(v, "", "\t")
    if err == nil {
        fmt.Println(string(b))
    }
    return err
}
```

All the work is done by `json.MarshalIndent()`, which applies indentation to format the output.

 Although both `json.MarshalIndent()` and `json.Marshal()` produce a JSON text result (byte slice), only `json.MarshalIndent()` allows applying customizable indentation, whereas `json.Marshal()` generates a more compact output.

For pretty printing streams of JSON data, you should use the `JSONstream()` function:

```
func JSONstream(data interface{}) (string, error) {
  buffer := new(bytes.Buffer)
  encoder := json.NewEncoder(buffer)
  encoder.SetIndent("", "\t")
```

The `json.NewEncoder()` function returns a new encoder that writes to a writer that is passed as a parameter to `json.NewEncoder()`. An encoder writes JSON values to an output stream. Similarly to `json.MarshalIndent()`, the `SetIndent()` method allows you to apply a customizable indent to a stream.

```
  err := encoder.Encode(data)
  if err != nil {
    return "", err
  }
  return buffer.String(), nil
}
```

After we are done configuring the encoder, we are free to process the JSON stream using `Encode()`.

These two functions are illustrated in `prettyPrint.go`, which generates JSON records using random data. Running `prettyPrint.go` produces the following kind of output:

```
Last record: {YJOML 63}
{
    "key": "YJOML",
    "value": 63
}
[
    {
        "key": "HXNIG",
        "value": 79
    },
    {
        "key": "YJOML",
        "value": 63
    }
]
```

The previous output shows the beautified output of a single JSON record followed by the beautified output of a slice with two JSON records—all JSON records are represented as Go structures.

And now, we are going to deal with something completely different, which is the development of a powerful command line utility—Go is really good at it.

The viper package

Flags are specially formatted strings that are passed into a program to control its behavior. Dealing with flags on your own might become very frustrating if you want to support multiple flags and options. Go offers the `flag` package to work with command line options, parameters, and flags. Although `flag` can do many things, it is not as capable as other external Go packages. Thus, if you are developing simple UNIX system command line utilities, you might find the `flag` package very interesting and useful. But you are not reading this book to create simple command line utilities! Therefore, I am going to skip the `flag` package and introduce you to an external package named `viper`, which is a powerful Go package that supports a plethora of options. `viper` uses the `pflag` package instead of `flag`, which is also illustrated in the code.

All `viper` projects follow a pattern. First, you initialize `viper` and then you define the elements that interest you. After that, you get these elements and read their values in order to use them. The desired values can be taken either directly, which happens when you use the `flag` package from the standard Go library, or indirectly using configuration files. When using formatted configuration files in the JSON, YAML, TOML, HCL, or Java properties format, `viper` does all the parsing for you, which saves you from having to write and debug lots of Go code. `viper` also allows you to extract and save values in Go structures. However, this requires that the fields of the Go structure match the keys of the configuration file.

The home page of `viper` is on GitHub (`https://github.com/spf13/viper`). Please note that you are not obliged to use every capability of `viper` in your tools, just the features that you want. However, if your command line utility requires too many command line parameters and flags, then it would be better to use a configuration file instead.

Using command line flags

The first example shows how to write a simple utility that accepts two values as command line parameters and prints them on screen for verification. This means that we are going to need two command line flags for these two parameters.

The relevant code is in `~/go/src/github.com/mactsouk/mGo4th/ch07/useViper`. You should replace `mGo4th` with the name of the actual GitHub repository of the book, or rename it `mGo4th`. Generally speaking, short directory names are more convenient.

After that, you must go to the ~/go/src/github.com/mactsouk/mGo4th/ch07/useViper directory and run the following commands:

```
$ go mod init
$ go mod tidy
```

Keep in mind that the previous two commands should be executed when useViper.go is ready and include all the required external packages. The GitHub repository of the book contains the final versions of all programs.

The implementation of useViper.go is as follows:

```
package main
import (
    "fmt"
    "github.com/spf13/pflag"
    "github.com/spf13/viper"
)
```

We need to import both the pflag and viper packages, as we are going to use their functionality.

```
func aliasNormalizeFunc(f *pflag.FlagSet, n string) pflag.NormalizedName {
    switch n {
    case "pass":
        n = "password"
        break
    case "ps":
        n = "password"
        break
    }
    return pflag.NormalizedName(n)
}
```

The aliasNormalizeFunc() function is used to create additional aliases for a flag, in this case, an alias for the --password flag. According to the existing code, the --password flag can be accessed as either --pass or –ps.

```
func main() {
    pflag.StringP("name", "n", "Mike", "Name parameter")
```

In the preceding code, we create a new flag called name that can also be accessed as -n. Its default value is Mike, and its description, which appears in the usage of the utility, is Name parameter.

```
pflag.StringP("password", "p", "hardToGuess", "Password")
pflag.CommandLine.SetNormalizeFunc(aliasNormalizeFunc)
```

We create another flag named password that can also be accessed as -p and has a default value of hardToGuess and a description. Additionally, we register a normalization function to generate aliases for the password flag.

```
pflag.Parse()
viper.BindPFlags(pflag.CommandLine)
```

The pflag.Parse() call should be used after all command line flags are defined. Its purpose is to parse the command line flags into the predefined flags.

Additionally, the viper.BindPFlags() call makes all flags available to the viper package. Strictly speaking, we say that the viper.BindPFlags() call binds an existing set of pflag flags (pflag.FlagSet) to viper.

```
name := viper.GetString("name")
password := viper.GetString("password")
```

The previous commands show that you can read the values of two string command line flags using viper.GetString().

```
fmt.Println(name, password)
// Reading an Environment variable
viper.BindEnv("GOMAXPROCS")
val := viper.Get("GOMAXPROCS")
if val != nil {
    fmt.Println("GOMAXPROCS:", val)
}
```

The viper package can also work with environment variables. We first need to call viper.BindEnv() to tell viper which environment variable interests us, and then we can read its value by calling viper.Get(). If GOMAXPROCS is not already set, which means that its value is nil, the fmt.Println() call will not get executed.

```
// Setting an Environment variable
viper.Set("GOMAXPROCS", 16)
val = viper.Get("GOMAXPROCS")
```

```
        fmt.Println("GOMAXPROCS:", val)
}
```

Similarly, we can change the value of an environment variable with `viper.Set()`.

The good thing is that `viper` automatically provides usage information:

```
$ go build useViper.go
$ ./useViper.go --help
Usage of ./useViper:
  -n, --name string       Name parameter (default "Mike")
  -p, --password string   Password (default "hardToGuess")
pflag: help requested
exit status 2
```

Using `useViper.go` without any command line arguments produces the following kind of output:

```
$ go run useViper.go
Mike hardToGuess
GOMAXPROCS: 16
```

However, if we provide values for the command line flags, the output is going to be slightly different.

```
$ go run useViper.go -n mtsouk -p d1ff1cultPAssw0rd
mtsouk d1ff1cultPAssw0rd
GOMAXPROCS: 16
```

In this second case, we used the shortcuts for the command line flags because it is faster to do so.

The next subsection discusses the use of JSON files to store configuration information in `viper`.

Reading JSON configuration files

The `viper` package can read JSON files to get its configuration, and this subsection illustrates how. Using text files to store configuration details can be very helpful when writing complex applications that require lots of data and setup. This is illustrated in `jsonViper.go`. Once again, we need to have `jsonViper.go` inside `~/go/src` as we did before: `~/go/src/github.com/mactsouk/mGo4th/ch07/jsonViper`. The code of `jsonViper.go` is as follows:

```
package main
import (
    "encoding/json"
```

```
        "fmt"
        "os"
        "github.com/spf13/viper"
)
type ConfigStructure struct {
    MacPass      string `mapstructure:"macos"`
    LinuxPass    string `mapstructure:"linux"`
    WindowsPass  string `mapstructure:"windows"`
    PostHost     string `mapstructure:"postgres"`
    MySQLHost    string `mapstructure:"mysql"`
    MongoHost    string `mapstructure:"mongodb"`
}
```

There is an important point here: although we are using a JSON file to store the configuration, the Go structure uses mapstructure instead of json for the fields of the JSON configuration file.

```
var CONFIG = ".config.json"
func main() {
    if len(os.Args) == 1 {
        fmt.Println("Using default file", CONFIG)
    } else {
        CONFIG = os.Args[1]
    }
    viper.SetConfigType("json")
    viper.SetConfigFile(CONFIG)
    fmt.Printf("Using config: %s\n", viper.ConfigFileUsed())
    viper.ReadInConfig()
```

The previous four statements declare that we are using a JSON file, let viper know the path to the default configuration file, print the configuration file used, and read and parse that configuration file.

Keep in mind that viper does not check whether the configuration file actually exists and is readable. If the file cannot be found or read, viper.ReadInConfig() acts like it is processing an empty configuration file.

```
    if viper.IsSet("macos") {
        fmt.Println("macos:", viper.Get("macos"))
    } else {
```

```
            fmt.Println("macos not set!")
    }
```

The viper.IsSet() call checks whether a key named macos can be found in the configuration. If it is set, it reads its value using viper.Get("macos") and prints it on screen.

```
    if viper.IsSet("active") {
        value := viper.GetBool("active")
        if value {
            postgres := viper.Get("postgres")
            mysql := viper.Get("mysql")
            mongo := viper.Get("mongodb")
            fmt.Println("P:", postgres, "My:", mysql, "Mo:", mongo)
        }
    } else {
        fmt.Println("active is not set!")
    }
```

In the aforementioned code, we check whether the active key can be found before reading its value. If its value is equal to true, then we read the values from three more keys, named postgres, mysql, and mongodb.

As the active key should hold a Boolean value, we use viper.GetBool() to read it.

```
    if !viper.IsSet("DoesNotExist") {
        fmt.Println("DoesNotExist is not set!")
    }
```

As expected, trying to read a key that does not exist fails.

```
    var t ConfigStructure
    err := viper.Unmarshal(&t)
    if err != nil {
        fmt.Println(err)
        return
    }
```

The call to viper.Unmarshal() allows you to put the information from the JSON configuration file into a properly defined Go structure—this is optional but handy.

```
    PrettyPrint(t)
}
```

The implementation of the `PrettyPrint()` function was presented in `prettyPrint.go` earlier on in this chapter.

Now, you need to download the dependencies of `jsonViper.go`:

```
$ go mod init
$ go mod tidy
```

The contents of the current directory are as follows:

```
$ ls -l
total 120
-rw-r--r--@ 1 mtsouk  staff    745 Aug 21 18:21 go.mod
-rw-r--r--@ 1 mtsouk  staff  48357 Aug 21 18:21 go.sum
-rw-r--r--@ 1 mtsouk  staff   1418 Aug  3 07:51 jsonViper.go
-rw-r--r--@ 1 mtsouk  staff    188 Aug 21 18:20 myConfig.json
```

The contents of the `myConfig.json` file used for testing are as follows:

```
{
    "macos": "pass_macos",
    "linux": "pass_linux",
    "windows": "pass_windows",
    "active": true,
    "postgres": "machine1",
    "mysql": "machine2",
    "mongodb": "machine3"
}
```

Running `jsonViper.go` on the preceding JSON file produces the following output:

```
$ go run jsonViper.go myConfig.json
Using config: myConfig.json
macos: pass_macos
P: machine1 My: machine2 Mo: machine3
DoesNotExist is not set!
{
  "MacPass": "pass_macos",
  "LinuxPass": "pass_linux",
  "WindowsPass": "pass_windows",
  "PostHost": "machine1",
```

```
    "MySQLHost": "machine2",
    "MongoHost": "machine3"
}
```

The previous output is generated by jsonViper.go when parsing myConfig.json and trying to find the desired information.

The next section discusses a Go package for creating powerful and professional command line utilities, such as docker and kubectl.

The cobra package

cobra is a very handy and popular Go package that allows you to develop command line utilities with commands, subcommands, and aliases. If you have ever used hugo, docker, or kubectl, you are going to realize immediately what the cobra package does, as all these tools are developed using cobra. Commands can have one or more aliases, which is very handy when you want to please both amateur and experienced users. cobra also supports persistent flags and local flags, which are flags that are available to all commands and flags that are available to given commands only, respectively. Also, by default, cobra uses viper for parsing its command line arguments.

All Cobra projects follow the same development pattern. You use the Cobra command line utility, you create commands, and then you make the desired changes to the generated Go source code files in order to implement the desired functionality. Depending on the complexity of your utility, you might need to make lots of changes to the created files. Although cobra saves you lots of time, you still have to write the code that implements the desired functionality for each command.

You need to take some extra steps in order to download the cobra binary the right way:

```
$ GO111MODULE=on go install github.com/spf13/cobra-cli@latest
```

The previous command downloads the cobra-cli binary—this is the new name for the cobra binary executable. It is not necessary to know about all of the supported environment variables such as GO111MODULE but, sometimes, they can help you resolve tricky problems with your Go installation. So if you want to learn about your current Go environment, you can use the go env command.

 As I prefer to work using shorter utility names, I renamed cobra-cli to cobra. If you do not know how to do that or if you prefer to use cobra-cli, replace ~/go/bin/cobra with ~/go/bin/cobra-cli in all commands.

For the purposes of this section, we are going to need a separate directory under ch07. As mentioned multiple times in this book, everything is going to be much easier if you put your code somewhere inside ~/go/src; the exact place depends on you, but it would be ideal if you use something like ~/go/src/github.com/mactsouk/mGo4th/ch07/go-cobra, where mGo4th is the name of the directory in which you keep the source code files from this book. Provided that you are going to use the aforementioned directory, you are going to need to execute the next commands (*if you have downloaded the source code of the book, you do not need to do anything, as everything is going to be there*):

```
$ cd ~/go/src/github.com/mactsouk/mGo4th/ch07/
$ mkdir go-cobra # only required if the directory is not there
$ cd go-cobra
$ go mod init
go: creating new go.mod: module github.com/mactsouk/mGo4th/ch07/go-cobra
$ ~/go/bin/cobra init
Using config file: /Users/mtsouk/.cobra.yaml
Your Cobra application is ready at
/Users/mtsouk/go/src/github.com/mactsouk/mGo4th/ch07/go-cobra
$ go mod tidy
go: finding module for package github.com/spf13/viper
go: finding module for package github.com/spf13/cobra
go: downloading github.com/spf13/cobra v1.7.0
...
go: downloading github.com/rogpeppe/go-internal v1.9.0
go: downloading github.com/kr/text v0.2.0
```

All output lines beginning with go: relate to Go modules and will appear only once. If you try to execute the utility, which is currently empty, you are going to get the following output:

```
$ go run main.go
A longer description that spans multiple lines and likely contains
examples and usage of using your application. For example:

Cobra is a CLI library for Go that empowers applications.
This application is a tool to generate the needed files
to quickly create a Cobra application.
```

The last lines are the default message of a cobra project. We are going to modify that message later on. You are now ready to begin working with the cobra tool and add commands to the command line utility we are developing.

A utility with three commands

This subsection illustrates the use of the cobra add command, which is used to add new commands to an existing cobra project. The names of the commands are one, two, and three:

```
$ ~/go/bin/cobra add one
Using config file: /Users/mtsouk/.cobra.yaml
one created at /Users/mtsouk/go/src/github.com/mactsouk/go-cobra
$ ~/go/bin/cobra add two
$ ~/go/bin/cobra add three
```

The previous commands create three new files in the cmd folder, named one.go, two.go, and three.go, which are the initial naïve implementations of the three commands.

The first thing you should usually do is delete any unwanted code from root.go and change the messages of the utility and each command, as described in the Short and Long fields. However, if you want, you can leave the source files unchanged.

The next subsection enriches the utility by adding command line flags to the commands.

Adding command line flags

We are going to create two global command line flags and one command line flag that is attached to a given command (two) and not supported by the other two commands. Global command line flags are defined in the ./cmd/root.go file. We are going to define two global flags, named directory, which is a string, and depth, which is an unsigned integer. Both global flags are defined in the init() function of ./cmd/root.go:

```
rootCmd.PersistentFlags().StringP("directory", "d", "/tmp", "Path")
rootCmd.PersistentFlags().Uint("depth", 2, "Depth of search")
viper.BindPFlag("directory", rootCmd.PersistentFlags().
Lookup("directory"))
viper.BindPFlag("depth", rootCmd.PersistentFlags().Lookup("depth"))
```

We use `rootCmd.PersistentFlags()` to define global flags, followed by the data type of the flag. The name of the first flag is `directory` and its shortcut is d, whereas the name of the second flag is `depth` and has no shortcut—if you want to add a shortcut to it, you should use the `UintP()` method, as the `depth` parameter is an unsigned integer. After defining the two flags, we pass their control to `viper` by calling `viper.BindPFlag()`. The first flag is a `string`, whereas the second one is a `uint` value. As both of them are available in the cobra project, we call `viper.GetString("directory")` to get the value of the `directory` flag and `viper.GetUint("depth")` to get the value of the `depth` flag. This is not the only way to read the value of a flag and use it. You are going to see an alternative way when we update the statistics application.

Last, we add a command line flag that is only available to the two command by adding the next line to the `init()` function of the `./cmd/two.go` file:

```
twoCmd.Flags().StringP("username", "u", "Mike", "Username")
```

The name of the flag is `username`, and its shortcut is u. As this is a local flag available to the two command only, we can get its value by calling `cmd.Flags().GetString("username")` inside the `./cmd/two.go` file only.

The next subsection creates command aliases for the existing commands.

Creating command aliases

In this subsection, we continue building on the code from the previous subsection by creating aliases for existing commands. This means that the commands one, two, and three will also be accessible as `cmd1`, `cmd2`, and `cmd3`, respectively.

In order to do that, you need to add an extra field named `Aliases` to the `cobra.Command` structure of each command. The data type of the `Aliases` field is *string slice*. So, for the one command, the beginning of the `cobra.Command` structure in `./cmd/one.go` will look as follows:

```
var oneCmd = &cobra.Command{
    Use:     "one",
    Aliases: []string{"cmd1"},
    Short:   "Command one",
```

You should make similar changes to `./cmd/two.go` and `./cmd/three.go`. Please keep in mind that the ***internal name*** of the one command is oneCmd and continues to be—the other commands have analogous internal names.

If you accidentally put the cmd1 alias, or any other alias, in multiple commands, the Go compiler will not complain. However, only its first occurrence gets executed.

The next subsection enriches the utility by adding subcommands for the one and two commands.

Creating subcommands

This subsection illustrates how to create two subcommands for the command named three. The names of the two subcommands will be list and delete. The way to create them using the cobra utility is as follows:

```
$ ~/go/bin/cobra add list -p 'threeCmd'
Using config file: /Users/mtsouk/.cobra.yaml
list created at /Users/mtsouk/go/src/github.com/mactsouk/mGo4th/ch07/go-
cobra
$ ~/go/bin/cobra add delete -p 'threeCmd'
Using config file: /Users/mtsouk/.cobra.yaml
delete created at /Users/mtsouk/go/src/github.com/mactsouk/mGo4th/ch07/go-
cobra
```

The previous commands create two new files inside ./cmd, named delete.go and list.go. The -p flag is followed by the internal name of the command you want to associate the subcommands with. The internal name of the three command is threeCmd. You can verify that these two commands are associated with the three command as follows (the default message of each command is displayed):

```
$ go run main.go three delete
delete called
$ go run main.go three list
list called
```

If you run go run main.go two list, Go considers list as a command line argument of two, and it will not execute the code in ./cmd/list.go. The final version of the go-cobra project has the following structure and contains the following files, as generated by the tree(1) utility:

```
$ tree
.
├── LICENSE
```

```
├── cmd
│   ├── delete.go
│   ├── list.go
│   ├── one.go
│   ├── root.go
│   ├── three.go
│   └── two.go
├── go.mod
├── go.sum
└── main.go

2 directories, 10 files
```

At this point, you might wonder what happens when you want to create two subcommands with the same name for two different commands. In that case, you create the first subcommand and rename its file before creating the second one.

The use of the `cobra` package is also illustrated in the final section, where we radically update the statistics application. The next section discusses some important additions that came with Go version 1.16.

Important Go features

Go 1.16 came with some new features, including embedding files in Go binaries as well as the introduction of the `os.ReadDir()` function, the `os.DirEntry` type, and the `io/fs` package.

As these features are related to systems programming, they are included and explored in the current chapter. We begin by presenting the embedding of files into Go binary executables.

Embedding files

This section presents a feature that allows you to *embed static assets into Go binaries*. The allowed data types to keep an embedded file are `string`, `[]byte`, and `embed.FS`. This means that a Go binary may contain a file that you do not have to manually download when you execute the Go binary! The presented utility embeds two different files that it can retrieve based on the given command line argument.

The code that follows, which is saved as `embedFiles.go`, illustrates this new Go feature:

```go
package main
import (
```

```
    _   "embed"
    "fmt"
    "os"
)
```

You need the embed package in order to embed any files in your Go binaries. As the embed package is not used directly, you need to put _ in front of it so that the Go compiler will not complain.

```
//go:embed static/image.png
var f1 []byte
```

You need to begin a line with //go:embed, which denotes a Go comment but is treated in a special way, followed by the path to the file you want to embed. In this case, we embed static/image. png, which is a binary file. The next line should define the variable that is going to hold the data of the embedded file, which, in this case, is a byte slice named f1. Using a byte slice is recommended for binary files because we are going to directly use that byte slice to save that binary file.

```
//go:embed static/textfile
var f2 string
```

In this case, we save the contents of a plain text file, which is static/textfile, in a string variable named f2.

```
func writeToFile(s []byte, path string) error {
    fd, err := os.OpenFile(path, os.O_CREATE|os.O_WRONLY, 0644)
    if err != nil {
        return err
    }
    defer fd.Close()
    n, err := fd.Write(s)
    if err != nil {
        return err
    }
    fmt.Printf("wrote %d bytes\n", n)
    return nil
}
```

The writeToFile() function is used to store a byte slice in a file and is a helper function that can be used in other cases as well.

```
func main() {
```

```go
arguments := os.Args
if len(arguments) == 1 {
    fmt.Println("Print select 1|2")
    return
}
fmt.Println("f1:", len(f1), "f2:", len(f2))
```

This statement prints the lengths of the f1 and f2 variables to make sure that they represent the size of the embedded files.

```go
switch arguments[1] {
case "1":
    filename := "/tmp/temporary.png"
    err := writeToFile(f1, filename)
    if err != nil {
        fmt.Println(err)
        return
    }
case "2":
    fmt.Print(f2)
default:
    fmt.Println("Not a valid option!")
}
```

The switch block is responsible for returning the desired file to the user—in the case of static/textfile, the file contents are printed on screen. For the binary file, we decided to store it as /tmp/temporary.png.

This time, we are going to compile embedFiles.go to make things more realistic, as it is the executable binary file that holds the embedded files. We build the binary file using go build embedFiles.go. Running embedFiles produces the following kind of output:

```
$ ./embedFiles 2
f1: 75072 f2: 14
Data to write
$ ./embedFiles 1
f1: 75072 f2: 14
wrote 75072 bytes
```

The following output verifies that temporary.png is located at the right path (/tmp/temporary.png):

```
$ ls -l /tmp/temporary.png
-rw-r--r--  1 mtsouk  wheel  75072 Feb 25 15:20 /tmp/temporary.png
```

Using the embedding functionality, we can create a utility that embeds its own source code and prints it on screen when it gets executed! This is a fun way of using embedded files. The source code of printSource.go is the following:

```
package main
import (
    _ "embed"
    "fmt"
)
//go:embed printSource.go
var src string
func main() {
    fmt.Print(src)
}
```

As before, the file that is being embedded is defined in the //go:embed line. Running printSource.go prints the aforementioned code on screen.

ReadDir and DirEntry

This section discusses os.ReadDir() and os.DirEntry. However, it begins by discussing the deprecation of the io/ioutil package—the functionality of the io/ioutil package has been transferred to other packages. So, we have the following:

- os.ReadDir(), which is a new function, returns []DirEntry. This means that it cannot directly replace ioutil.ReadDir(), which returns []FileInfo. Although neither os.ReadDir() nor os.DirEntry offer any new functionality, they make things faster and simpler, which is important.
- The os.ReadFile() function directly replaces ioutil.ReadFile().
- The os.WriteFile() function can directly replace ioutil.WriteFile().
- Similarly, os.MkdirTemp() can replace ioutil.TempDir() without any changes. However, as the os.TempDir() name was already taken, the new function name is different.

- The os.CreateTemp() function is the same as ioutil.TempFile(). Although the name os.TempFile() was not taken, the Go people decided to name it os.CreateTemp() in order to be on a par with os.MkdirTemp().

- Both os.ReadDir() and os.DirEntry can be found as fs.ReadDir() and fs.DirEntry in the io/fs package to work with the file system interface found in io/fs.

The ReadDirEntry.go utility illustrates the use of os.ReadDir(). Additionally, we are going to see fs.DirEntry in combination with fs.WalkDir() in action in the next section—io/fs only supports WalkDir(), which uses DirEntry by default. Both fs.WalkDir() and filepath.WalkDir() use DirEntry instead of FileInfo. This means that in order to see any performance improvements when walking directory trees, you need to change filepath.Walk() calls to filepath.WalkDir() calls.

The presented utility calculates the size of a directory tree using os.ReadDir(), with the help of the following function:

```
func GetSize(path string) (int64, error) {
    contents, err := os.ReadDir(path)
    if err != nil {
        return -1, err
    }
    var total int64
    for _, entry := range contents {
        // Visit directory entries
        if entry.IsDir() {
```

If the return value of entry.IsDir() is true, then we process a directory, which means that we need to keep digging.

```
            temp, err := GetSize(filepath.Join(path, entry.Name()))
            if err != nil {
                return -1, err
            }
            total += temp
            // Get size of each non-directory entry
        } else {
```

If we process a file, then we just need to get its size. This involves calling Info() to get general information about the file and then Size() to get its size:

```
        info, err := entry.Info()
        if err != nil {
            return -1, err
        }
        // Returns an int64 value
        total += info.Size()
    }
}
return total, nil
}
```

Running ReadDirEntry.go produces the next output, which indicates that the utility works as expected:

```
$ go run ReadDirEntry.go /usr/bin
Total Size: 240527817
```

Last, keep in mind that both ReadDir and DirEntry are copied from the Python programming language.

The next section introduces us to the io/fs package.

The io/fs package

This section illustrates the functionality of the io/fs package, which was also introduced in Go 1.16. As io/fs offers a unique kind of functionality, we begin this section by explaining what it can do. Put simply, io/fs offers a read-only file system interface named FS. Note that embed.FS implements the fs.FS interface, which means that embed.FS can take advantage of some of the functionality offered by the io/fs package. *This means that your applications can create their own internal file systems and work with their files.*

The code example that follows, which is saved as ioFS.go, creates a file system using embed by putting all the files of the ./static folder in there. ioFS.go supports the following functionality: list all files, search for a filename, and extract a file using list(), search(), and extract(), respectively. We begin by presenting the implementation of list():

```
func list(f embed.FS) error {
    return fs.WalkDir(f, ".", walkFunction)
}
```

Keep in mind that fs.WalkDir() works with regular file systems as well as embed.FS file systems. You can learn more about the signature of walkFunction() by running go doc fs.WalkDirFunc.

Here, we begin with the given directory of a file system and visit its contents. The file system is stored in f and the root directory is defined as ".". After that, all the magic happens in the walkFunction() function, which is implemented as follows:

```
func walkFunction(path string, d fs.DirEntry, err error) error {
    if err != nil {
        return err
    }
    fmt.Printf("Path=%q, isDir=%v\n", path, d.IsDir())
    return nil
}
```

The walkFunction() function processes every entry in the given root directory in the desired way. Keep in mind that the walkFunc() is *automatically called* by fs.WalkDir() to visit each file or directory.

Then, we present the implementation of the extract() function:

```
func extract(f embed.FS, filepath string) ([]byte, error) {
    s, err := fs.ReadFile(f, filepath)
    if err != nil {
        return nil, err
    }
    return s, nil
}
```

The ReadFile() function is used to retrieve a file, which is identified by its file path, from the embed.FS file system as a byte slice, which is returned from the extract() function.

Last, we have the implementation of the search() function, which is based on walkSearch():

```
func walkSearch(path string, d fs.DirEntry, err error) error {
    if err != nil {
        return err
    }
    if d.Name() == searchString {
```

searchString is a global variable that holds the search string. When a match is found, the matching path is printed on screen.

```
        fileInfo, err := fs.Stat(f, path)
        if err != nil {
            return err
        }
        fmt.Println("Found", path, "with size", fileInfo.Size())
        return nil
    }
```

Before printing a match, we make a call to fs.Stat() to get more details about it:

```
    return nil
}
```

The main() function specifically calls these three functions. Running ioFS.go produces the following kind of output:

```
$ go run ioFS.go
Path=".", isDir=true
Path="static", isDir=true
Path="static/file.txt", isDir=false
Path="static/image.png", isDir=false
Path="static/textfile", isDir=false
Found static/file.txt with size 14
wrote 14 bytes
```

Initially, the utility lists all files in the file system (lines beginning with Path). Then, it verifies that static/file.txt can be found in the file system. Last, it verifies that the writing of 14 bytes into a new file was successful, as all 14 bytes have been written.

So it turns out that Go version 1.16 introduced important functionality.

In the next section, we are going to improve the statistics application.

Updating the statistics application

In this section, we will change the format that the statistics application uses to store its data. This time, the statistics application is going to use the JSON format. Additionally, it uses the cobra package to implement the supported commands.

However, before continuing with the statistics application, we are going to learn more about the slog package.

The slog package

The log/slog package was added to the standard Go library with Go 1.21 in order to improve the original log package. You can find more information about it at https://pkg.go.dev/log/slog. The main reason for including it in this chapter is that it can create log entries in the JSON format, which is handy when you want to further process log entries.

The code of useSLog.go that illustrates the use of the log/slog package is going to be presented in three parts. The first part is the following:

```go
package main

import (
    "fmt"
    "log/slog"
    "os"
)

func main() {
    slog.Error("This is an ERROR message")
    slog.Debug("This is a DEBUG message")
    slog.Info("This ia an INFO message")
    slog.Warn("This is a WARNING message")
```

First, we need to import log/slog for using the slog package of the Go standard library. When using the default logger, we can send messages using Error(), Debug(), Info(), and Warn(), which is the simplest way of using the functionality of slog.

The second part contains the following code:

```go
        logLevel := &slog.LevelVar{}
        fmt.Println("Log level:", logLevel)

        // Text Handler
        opts := &slog.HandlerOptions{
            Level: logLevel,
        }
```

```
handler := slog.NewTextHandler(os.Stdout, opts)
logger := slog.New(handler)

logLevel.Set(slog.LevelDebug)
logger.Debug("This is a DEBUG message")
```

In this part of the program, we get the current log level using &slog.LevelVar{} and change it to the Debug level in order to also get the log entries issued with logger.Debug(). This is implemented with the logLevel.Set(slog.LevelDebug) statement.

The last part of useSLog.go comes with the following code:

```
// JSON Handler
logJSON := slog.New(slog.NewJSONHandler(os.Stdout, nil))
logJSON.Error("ERROR message in JSON")
}
```

The presented code creates a logger that writes JSON records.

Running useSLog.go produces the following output:

```
$ go run useSLog.go
2023/08/22 21:49:18 ERROR This is an ERROR message
2023/08/22 21:49:18 INFO This ia an INFO message
2023/08/22 21:49:18 WARN This is a WARNING message
```

The previous output is from the first four statements of main(). The slog.Debug() statement generated no output because the DEBUG level does not get printed by default.

```
Log level: LevelVar(INFO)
time=2023-08-22T21:49:18.474+03:00 level=DEBUG msg="This is a DEBUG
message"
```

The previous output shows that if we increase the logging level, we can get DEBUG messages printed—the default logging level was INFO.

```
{"time":"2023-08-22T21:49:18.474392+03:00","level":"ERROR","msg":"ERROR
message in JSON"}
```

The last line of the output shows logging information in the JSON format. This can be very handy if we want to store log entries in a regular or a time series database for further processing, visualization, or data analysis.

Sending logs to io.Discard

This subsection presents a trick that involves the use of io.Discard for sending log entries—
io.Discard discards all Write() calls without doing anything! Although we are going to apply
the trick to log files, it can also be used in other cases where writing data is involved. The implementation of the main() function in discard.go is the following:

```
func main() {
    if len(os.Args) == 1 {
        log.Println("Enabling logging!")
        log.SetOutput(os.Stderr)
    } else {
        log.SetOutput(os.Stderr)
        log.Println("Disabling logging!")
        log.SetOutput(io.Discard)
        log.Println("NOT GOING TO GET THAT!")
    }
}
```

The condition that enables or disables writing is simplistic: when there is a single command line
argument, logging is enabled; otherwise, it is disabled. The statement that disables logging is
log.SetOutput(io.Discard). However, before logging is disabled, we print a log entry stating so.

Running discard.go generates the following output:

```
$ go run discard.go
2023/08/22 21:35:17 Enabling logging!
$ go run discard.go 1
2023/08/22 21:35:21 Disabling logging!
```

In the second program execution, the log.Println("NOT GOING TO GET THAT!") statement
generates no output, as it went to io.Discard.

With all this information in mind, let us continue with the implementation of the statistics application with the help of cobra.

Using cobra

First, we need to create a place to host the cobra version of the statistics application. At this point,
you have two options: either create a separate GitHub repository or put the necessary files in a
directory under ~/go/src. This subsection is going to follow the latter option. As a result, all
relevant code is going to reside at ~/go/src/github.com/mactsouk/mGo4th/ch07/stats.

The project is already present in the `stats` directory. The presented steps make sense if you want to create it on your own.

First, we need to create and go to the relevant directory:

```
$ cd ~/go/src/github.com/mactsouk/mGo4th/ch07/stats
```

After that, we should declare that we want to use Go modules:

```
$ go mod init
go: creating new go.mod: module github.com/mactsouk/mGo4th/ch07/stats
```

After that, we need to run the `cobra init` command:

```
$ ~/go/bin/cobra init
Using config file: /Users/mtsouk/.cobra.yaml
Your Cobra application is ready at
/Users/mtsouk/go/src/github.com/mactsouk/mGo4th/ch07/stats
```

Then, we can execute go `mod tidy`:

```
$ go mod tidy
```

Then, we should create the structure of the application using the cobra (or `cobra-cli`) binary. *Once we have the structure, it is easy to know what we have to implement*. The structure of the application is based on the supported commands and functionality:

```
$ ~/go/bin/cobra add list
$ ~/go/bin/cobra add delete
$ ~/go/bin/cobra add insert
$ ~/go/bin/cobra add search
```

At this point, executing go `run main.go` is going to download any missing packages and generate the default cobra output.

We need to create a command line flag to enable and disable logging. We are going to be using the log/slog package. The flag is called `--log` and is going to be a Boolean variable. The relevant statement, which is located in root.go, is the following:

```
rootCmd.PersistentFlags().BoolVarP(&disableLogging, "log", "l", false,
"Logging information")
```

The previous statement is supported by a global variable, which is defined as follows:

```
var disableLogging bool
```

 This is a different approach regarding the use of the command line flags than what we did in the go-cobra project presented earlier.

So, the value of the disableLogging global variable holds the value of the --log flag. Although the disableLogging variable is global, you have to define *a separate logger variable in each one of the commands*.

The next subsection discusses the storing and loading of JSON data.

Storing and loading JSON data

This functionality of the saveJSONFile() helper function is implemented in ./cmd/root.go, using the following function:

```
func saveJSONFile(filepath string) error {
    f, err := os.Create(filepath)
    if err != nil {
        return err
    }
    defer f.Close()
    err = Serialize(&data, f)
    return err
}
```

Basically, all we have to do is serialize the slice of structures using Serialize() and save the result in a file. Next, we need to be able to load the JSON data from that file. The loading functionality is also implemented in ./cmd/root.go, using the readJSONFile() helper function:

```
func readJSONFile(filepath string) error {
    _, err := os.Stat(filepath)
    if err != nil {
        return err
    }

    f, err := os.Open(filepath)
```

```
        if err != nil {
            return err
        }
        defer f.Close()

        err = DeSerialize(&data, f)
        if err != nil {
            return err
        }
        return nil
    }
```

All we have to do is read the data file with the JSON data and put that data into a slice of structures by deserializing it.

Now, we are going to discuss the implementation of the `list` and `insert` commands. The other two commands (`delete` and `search`) have similar implementations.

Implementing the list command

The important code of `./cmd/list.go` is in the implementation of the `list()` function:

```go
func list() {
    sort.Sort(DFslice(data))
    text, err := PrettyPrintJSONstream(data)
    if err != nil {
        fmt.Println(err)
        return
    }
    fmt.Println(text)
```

The core functionality of `list` is included in the previous code, which sorts the data slice and pretty prints the JSON records using `PrettyPrintJSONstream(data)`.

```go
    logger = slog.New(slog.NewJSONHandler(os.Stderr, nil))
    if disableLogging == false {
        logger = slog.New(slog.NewJSONHandler(io.Discard, nil))
    }

    slog.SetDefault(logger)
    s := fmt.Sprintf("%d records in total.", len(data))
```

```
        logger.Info(s)
    }
```

The previous code deals with logging based on the value of disableLogging, which is based on the --log flag.

Implementing the insert command

The implementation of the insert command is as follows:

```
var insertCmd = &cobra.Command{
    Use:   "insert",
    Short: "Insert command",
    Long: `The insert command reads a datafile and stores
    its data into the application in JSON format.`,
    Run: func(cmd *cobra.Command, args []string) {
        logger = slog.New(slog.NewJSONHandler(os.Stderr, nil))
        // Work with logger
        if disableLogging == false {
            logger = slog.New(slog.NewJSONHandler(io.Discard, nil))
        }

        slog.SetDefault(logger)
```

First, we define a separate logger for the insert command based on the value of disableLogging.

```
        if file == "" {
            logger.Info("Need a file to read!")
            return
        }
        _, ok := index[file]
        if ok {
            fmt.Println("Found key:", file)
            delete(index, file)
        }

        // Now, delete it from data
        if ok {
            for i, k := range data {
                if k.Filename == file {
```

```
                    data = slices.Delete(data, i, i+1)
                    break
                }
            }
        }
```

Then, the previous code makes sure that the `file` variable, which is the path to the file that contains the data, is not empty. Additionally, if `file` is a key of the `index` map, it means that we have processed that file previously—*we assume that no two datasets have the same filename, as for us, the filename is what uniquely identifies the datasets*. In that case, we delete it from the `data` slice and the `index` map, and we process it again. This is similar to the update functionality, which is not directly supported by the application.

```
        err := ProcessFile(file)
        if err != nil {
            s := fmt.Sprintf("Error processing: %s", err)
            logger.Warn(s)
        }

        err = saveJSONFile(JSONFILE)
        if err != nil {
            s := fmt.Sprintf("Error saving data: %s", err)
            logger.Info(s)
        }
    },
}
```

The last part of the implementation of the `insert` command is about processing the given file, using `ProcessFile()`, and saving the updated version of the `data` slice, using `saveJSONFile()`.

Summary

This chapter was about working with environment variables, command line arguments, reading and writing plain text files, traversing file systems, working with JSON data, and creating powerful command line utilities using `cobra`. This is one of the most important chapters of this book because you cannot create any real-world utility without interacting with the operating system as well as the file system, and without reading and saving data.

The next chapter is about concurrency in Go, with the main subjects being goroutines, channels, and data sharing with safety. We are also going to talk about UNIX signal handling, as Go uses channels and goroutines for this purpose.

Exercises

- Use the functionality of byCharacter.go, byLine.go, and byWord.go in order to create a simplified version of the wc(1) UNIX utility.

- Create a full version of the wc(1) UNIX utility, using the viper package to process command line options.

- Create a full version of the wc(1) UNIX utility, using commands instead of command line options, with the help of the cobra package.

- Go offers bufio.Scanner to read files line by line. Try to rewrite byLine.go using bufio. Scanner.

- The bufio.Scanner in Go is designed to read input line by line, splitting it into tokens. If you need to read a file character by character, a common approach is to use bufio. NewReader in conjunction with Read() or ReadRune(). Implement the functionality of byCharacter.go this way.

- Make ioFS.go a cobra project.

- Update the statistics application cobra project in order to also store the normalized version of the dataset in data.json.

- The byLine.go utility uses ReadString('\n') to read the input file. Modify the code to use Scanner (https://pkg.go.dev/bufio#Scanner) for reading.

- Similarly, byWord.go uses ReadString('\n') to read the input file. Modify the code to use Scanner instead.

Additional resources

- The viper package: https://github.com/spf13/viper
- The cobra package: https://github.com/spf13/cobra
- The documentation for encoding/json: https://pkg.go.dev/encoding/json
- The documentation for io/fs: https://pkg.go.dev/io/fs
- Go slog package: http://gopherguides.com/articles/golang-slog-package
- A comprehensive guide to logging in Go with slog: https://betterstack.com/community/guides/logging/logging-in-go/
- Endian-ness: https://en.wikipedia.org/wiki/Endianness

Join our community on Discord

Join our community's Discord space for discussions with the authors and other readers:

https://discord.gg/FzuQbc8zd6

8

Go Concurrency

The key component of the Go concurrency model is the goroutine, which is the *minimum executable entity* in Go. To create a new goroutine, we must use the go keyword followed by a function call or an anonymous function—the two methods are equivalent. For a goroutine or a function to terminate the entire Go application, it should call os.Exit() instead of return. However, most of the time, we exit a goroutine or a function using return because what we really want is to exit that specific goroutine or function and not stop the entire application.

Everything in Go is executed as a goroutine, either transparently or consciously. Each executable Go program has at least one goroutine, which is used for running the main() function of the main package. Each goroutine is executed on a single OS thread according to the instructions of the Go scheduler, which is responsible for the execution of goroutines—the developer has no control over the amount of memory allocated to a goroutine. The OS scheduler does not dictate how many threads the Go runtime is going to create because the Go runtime will spawn enough threads to ensure that GOMAXPROCS threads are available to run the Go code.

However, *goroutines cannot communicate with each other directly*. Data sharing in Go is implemented using either channels, local sockets, or shared memory. *Channels* act as the glue that connects multiple goroutines. On the other hand, channels cannot process data or execute code but they can send data to and receive data from goroutines and have a special purpose like acting as signals or specifying the order of execution for goroutines.

When I first learned about channels, I thought that they were a great idea, much better than shared memory, and I wanted to use channels everywhere! However, nowadays *I only use channels when I have no other alternative*. Look at the implementation of the concurrent statistical application at the end of the chapter to realize that there exist designs that do not require the use of channels.

Although the use of channels to communicate and synchronize between goroutines is very typical and expected, channels might introduce deadlocks, overhead, and complexity to the design, as well as performance considerations, especially when low-latency communication is a priority.

When you combine multiple channels and goroutines, you can create data flows, which, in Go terminology, are called pipelines. So, you might have a goroutine that reads data from a database and sends it to a channel and a second goroutine that reads from that channel, processes that data, and sends it to another channel to be read from another goroutine, before making modifications to the data and storing it in another database.

This chapter covers:

- Processes, threads, and goroutines
- The Go scheduler
- Goroutines
- Channels
- Race conditions are bad
- The select keyword
- Timing out a goroutine
- Go channels revisited
- Handling UNIX signals
- Shared memory and shared variables
- Closured variables and the go statement
- The context package
- The semaphore package
- Making the statistics application concurrent

Processes, threads, and goroutines

A process is an OS representation of a running program, while a program is a binary file on a disk that contains all the information necessary for creating an OS process. The binary file is written in a specific format and contains all the instructions the CPU is going to run, as well as a plethora of other required sections. That program is loaded into memory and the instructions are executed, creating a running process. So, a process carries with it additional resources such as memory, opened file descriptions, and user data, as well as other types of resources that are obtained during runtime.

A thread is a smaller and lighter entity than a process. Processes consist of one or more threads that have their own flow of control and stack. A quick and simplistic way to differentiate a thread from a process is to consider a process as the running binary file and a thread as a subset of a process.

A goroutine is the minimum Go entity that can be executed concurrently. The use of the word *minimum* is very important here, as goroutines are not autonomous entities like UNIX processes—**goroutines live in OS threads that live in OS processes**. The good thing is that goroutines are lighter than threads, which, in turn, are lighter than processes—running thousands or hundreds of thousands of goroutines on a single machine is not a problem. Among the reasons that goroutines are lighter than threads are that they have a smaller stack that can grow, they have a faster startup time, and they can communicate with each other through channels with low latency. In practice, this means that a process can have multiple threads and lots of goroutines, whereas a goroutine needs the environment of a process to exist. So, to create a goroutine, you need to have a process with at least one thread. The OS takes care of the process and thread scheduling, while Go creates the necessary threads and the developer creates the desired number of goroutines.

Now that you know the basics of processes, programs, threads, and goroutines, let us talk a little bit about the Go scheduler.

The Go scheduler

The OS kernel scheduler is responsible for the execution of the threads of a program. Similarly, the Go runtime has its own scheduler, which is responsible for the execution of the goroutines using a technique known as *m:n scheduling*, where m goroutines are executed using n OS threads using multiplexing. The Go scheduler is the Go component responsible for the way and the order in which the goroutines of a Go program get executed. This makes the Go scheduler a really important part of the Go programming language. The Go scheduler is also executed as a goroutine.

 Be aware that as the Go scheduler only deals with the goroutines of a single program, its operation is much simpler, cheaper, and faster than the operation of the OS kernel scheduler.

Go uses the fork-join concurrency model. The *fork part* of the model, which should not be confused with the fork(2) system call, states that a child branch can be created at any point of a program. Analogously, the *join part* of the Go concurrency model is where the child branch ends and joins with its parent. Keep in mind that both sync.Wait() statements and channels that collect the results of goroutines are join points, whereas each new goroutine creates a child branch.

The fair scheduling strategy shares all load evenly among the available processors. At first, this might look like the perfect strategy because it does not have to take many things into consideration while keeping all processors equally occupied. However, it turns out that this is not exactly the case because most distributed tasks usually depend on other tasks. Therefore, some processors are underutilized or, equivalently, some processors are utilized more than others.

A goroutine is a task, whereas everything after the calling statement of a goroutine is a continuation. *In the work-stealing strategy used by the Go scheduler, a (logical) processor that is underutilized looks for additional work from other processors.* When it finds such jobs, it steals them from the other processor or processors, hence the name. Additionally, the work-stealing algorithm of Go queues and steals continuations. A stalling join, as is suggested by its name, is a point where a thread of execution stalls at a join and starts looking for other work to do.

Although both task stealing and continuation stealing have stalling joins, continuations happen more often than tasks; therefore, the Go scheduling algorithm works with continuations rather than tasks. The main disadvantage of continuation stealing is that it requires extra work from the compiler of the programming language. Fortunately, Go provides that extra help and, therefore, uses continuation stealing in its work-stealing algorithm. One of the benefits of continuation stealing is that you get the same results when using function calls instead of goroutines or a single thread with multiple goroutines. This makes perfect sense, as only one thing is executed at any given point in both cases.

The Go scheduler works using three main kinds of entities: OS threads (M), which are related to the OS in use, goroutines (G), and logical processors (P). The number of processors that can be used by a Go program is specified by the value of the GOMAXPROCS environment variable—at any given time, there are, at most, GOMAXPROCS processors. Now, let us return to the m:n scheduling algorithm used in Go. Strictly speaking, at any time, you have m goroutines that are executed and, therefore, scheduled to run, on n OS threads using, at most, GOMAXPROCS number of logical processors. You will learn more about GOMAXPROCS shortly.

Each goroutine can be in one of the following three stages: *executing*, *runnable*, or *waiting*. In the executing stage, the instructions of the goroutine are executed on an OS thread. In the runnable stage, the goroutine waits to be assigned to an OS thread for execution. Finally, in the waiting stage, the goroutine is blocked for some reason like waiting for a resource or a mutex to become available to go into one of the other two stages.

The following figure shows that there are two different kinds of queues—a global run queue and a local run queue—attached to each logical processor. Goroutines from the global queue are assigned to the queue of a logical processor in order to get executed at some point in the future.

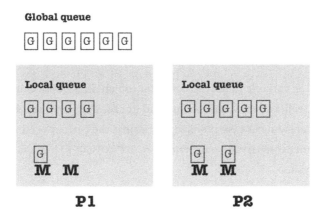

Figure 8.1: The operation of the Go scheduler

Each logical processor can have multiple threads, and the stealing occurs between the local queues of the available logical processors. Finally, keep in mind that the Go scheduler is allowed to create more OS threads when needed. OS threads are expensive in terms of resources and going from one status to another (*context switching*), which means that dealing too much with OS threads might slow down your Go applications.

Next, we discuss the meaning and the use of GOMAXPROCS.

The **GOMAXPROCS** environment variable

The GOMAXPROCS environment variable allows you to set the number of OS threads that can execute user-level Go code simultaneously; this does not limit the number of threads created but it does limit the number of threads that are actively running. Starting with Go version 1.5, the default value of GOMAXPROCS should be the number of logical cores available in your machine. There is also the runtime.GOMAXPROCS() function, which allows you to set and get the value of GOMAXPROCS programmatically.

If you decide to assign a value to GOMAXPROCS that is smaller than the number of cores in your machine, you might affect the performance of your program. However, using a GOMAXPROCS value that is larger than the number of available cores does not necessarily make your Go programs run faster due to the context switching of threads.

As mentioned earlier in this subsection, you can programmatically set and get the value of the GOMAXPROCS environment variable—this is illustrated in maxprocs.go, which will also show additional capabilities of the runtime package. The main() function is implemented as follows:

```
func main() {
```

```
        fmt.Print("You are using ", runtime.Compiler, " ")
        fmt.Println("on a", runtime.GOARCH, "machine")
        fmt.Println("Using Go version", runtime.Version())
```

The runtime.Compiler variable holds the compiler toolchain used for building the running binary. The two most well-known values are gc and gccgo. The runtime.GOARCH variable holds the current architecture and runtime.Version() returns the current version of the Go compiler. This information is not necessary for using runtime.GOMAXPROCS() but it is good to have a better knowledge of your system.

```
        fmt.Printf("GOMAXPROCS: %d\n", runtime.GOMAXPROCS(0))
    }
```

What happens with the runtime.GOMAXPROCS(0) call? It always returns the previous value of the maximum number of CPUs that can be executed simultaneously. When the parameter of runtime.GOMAXPROCS() is equal to or bigger than 1, then runtime.GOMAXPROCS() also changes the current setting. As we are using 0, our call does not alter the current setting.

Running maxprocs.go produces the following output:

```
You are using gc on a arm64 machine
Using Go version go1.21.0
GOMAXPROCS: 10
```

You can change the value of GOMAXPROCS on the fly using the following technique:

```
$ GOMAXPROCS=100; go run maxprocs.go
You are using gc on a amd64 machine
Using Go version go1.21.0
GOMAXPROCS: 100
```

The previous command temporarily changes the value of GOMAXPROCS to 100 and runs maxprocs.go.

Apart from testing the performance of your code using fewer cores, you will most likely not need to change GOMAXPROCS. The next subsection will explain the similarities and differences between concurrency and parallelism.

Concurrency and parallelism

It is a common misconception that concurrency is the same thing as parallelism—this is not true! Parallelism is the simultaneous execution of multiple entities of some kind, whereas concurrency is a way of structuring your components so that they can be executed independently when possible.

It is only when you build software components concurrently that you can safely execute them in parallel, when and if your OS and your hardware permit it. The Erlang programming language did this a long time ago—long before CPUs had multiple cores and computers had lots of RAM.

In a valid concurrent design, adding concurrent entities makes the whole system run faster because more things can be executed in parallel. So, the desired parallelism comes from a better concurrent expression and implementation of the problem. The developer is responsible for taking concurrency into account during the design phase of a system and will benefit from a potential parallel execution of the components of the system. So, the developer should not think about parallelism but about breaking things into independent components that solve the initial problem when combined.

Even if you cannot run your functions in parallel on your machine, a valid concurrent design still improves the design, data flow, and maintainability of your programs. In other words, concurrency is better than parallelism! Let us now talk about goroutines before looking into channels, which are the main components of the Go concurrency model.

Goroutines

You can define, create, and execute a new goroutine using the go keyword followed by a named function or an anonymous function call. The go keyword makes the function call return immediately, while the function starts running in the background as a goroutine and the rest of the program continues its execution. You cannot control or make any assumptions about the order in which your goroutines are going to be executed because that depends on the scheduler of the OS, the Go scheduler, and the load of the OS.

Creating a goroutine

In this subsection, you will learn how to create goroutines. The program that illustrates the technique is called create.go. The implementation of the main() function is as follows:

```
func main() {
    go func(x int) {
        fmt.Printf("%d ", x)
    }(10)
```

This is how you run an anonymous function as a goroutine. The (10) at the end is how you pass a parameter to an anonymous function. The previous anonymous function just prints a value. In general, it is more readable to pass parameters explicitly than to have the function close over the variables it uses.

```
    go printme(15)
```

This is how you execute a function as a goroutine. As a rule of thumb, the functions that you execute as goroutines should not return any values directly. *Exchanging data with goroutines happens via the use of shared memory or channels or some other mechanism*.

```
    time.Sleep(time.Second)
    fmt.Println("Exiting...")
}
```

As a Go program does not wait for its goroutines to end before exiting, we need to delay it manually, which is the purpose of the `time.Sleep()` call. We correct that shortly in order to wait for all goroutines to finish before exiting.

Running `create.go` produces the following output:

```
$ go run create.go
10 * 15
Exiting...
```

The 10 part in the output is from the anonymous function, whereas the * 15 part is from the go `printme(15)` statement. However, if you run `create.go` more than once, you might get a different output because the two goroutines are not always executed in the same order, as this depends on the Go scheduler:

```
$ go run create.go
* 15
10 Exiting...
```

The next subsection shows how to run a variable number of goroutines.

Creating multiple goroutines

In this subsection, you will learn how to create a variable number of goroutines. The program that illustrates the technique is called `multiple.go`. The number of goroutines is given as a command line argument to the program. The important code from the implementation of the `main()` function is the following:

```
fmt.Printf("Going to create %d goroutines.\n", count)
for i := 0; i < count; i++ {
```

There is nothing prohibiting you from using a `for` loop to create multiple goroutines, especially when you want to create lots of them.

```
    go func(x int) {
```

```
        fmt.Printf("%d ", x)
    }(i)
}
time.Sleep(time.Second)
fmt.Println("\nExiting...")
```

Once again, `time.Sleep()` prevents the `main()` function from exiting immediately.

Running `multiple.go` generates the following kind of output:

```
$ go run multiple.go 15
Going to create 15 goroutines.
3 0 8 4 5 6 7 11 9 12 14 13 1 2 10
Exiting...
```

If you run `multiple.go` many times, you are going to get different outputs. So, there is still room for improvement. The next subsection shows how to remove the call to `time.Sleep()` and make your programs wait for the goroutines to finish.

Waiting for all goroutines to finish

It is not enough to create multiple goroutines—you also need to wait for them to finish before the `main()` function ends. Therefore, this subsection shows a very popular technique that improves the code of `multiple.go`—the improved version is called `varGoroutines.go`. But first, we need to explain how this works.

The synchronization process begins by defining a `sync.WaitGroup` variable and using the `Add()`, `Done()`, and `Wait()` methods. If you look at the source code of the `sync` Go package, and more specifically at the `waitgroup.go` file, you see that the `sync.WaitGroup` type is nothing more than a structure with two fields:

```
type WaitGroup struct {
    noCopy noCopy
    state1 [3]uint32
}
```

Each call to `sync.Add()` increases a counter in the `state1` field, which is an array with three `uint32` elements. Notice that it is really important to call `sync.Add()` before the go statement in order to prevent any *race conditions*—we will learn about race conditions in the *Race conditions are bad* section. When each goroutine finishes its job, the `sync.Done()` function should be executed in order to decrease the same counter by one.

Behind the scenes, sync.Done() runs an Add(-1) call. The Wait() method waits until that counter becomes 0 in order to return. The return of Wait() inside the main() function means that main() is going to return and the program ends.

 You can call Add() with a positive integer value other than 1 in order to avoid calling Add(1) multiple times. This can be handy when you know the number of goroutines you are going to create in advance. Done() does not support that functionality.

The important part of varGoroutines.go is the following:

```
var waitGroup sync.WaitGroup
fmt.Printf("%#v\n", waitGroup)
```

This is where you create a sync.WaitGroup variable that you are going to use. The fmt.Printf() call prints the contents of the sync.WaitGroup structure—you do not usually do that but it is good for learning more about the sync.WaitGroup structure.

```
for i := 0; i < count; i++ {
    waitGroup.Add(1)
```

We call Add(1) just before we create the goroutine in order to avoid race conditions.

```
    go func(x int) {
        defer waitGroup.Done()
```

The Done() call is going to be executed just before the anonymous function returns because of the defer keyword.

```
        fmt.Printf("%d ", x)
    }(i)
}
fmt.Printf("%#v\n", waitGroup)
waitGroup.Wait()
```

The Wait() function waits for the counter in the waitGroup variable to become 0 before it returns, which is what we want to achieve.

```
fmt.Println("\nExiting...")
```

When the Wait() function returns, the fmt.Println() statement is executed. No need to call time.Sleep() any more!

Running varGoroutines.go produces the following output:

```
$ go run varGoroutines.go 15
Going to create 10 goroutines.
sync.WaitGroup{noCopy:sync.noCopy{}, state:atomic.Uint64{_:atomic.
noCopy{}, _:atomic.align64{}, v:0x0}, sema:0x0}
sync.WaitGroup{noCopy:sync.noCopy{}, state:atomic.Uint64{_:atomic.
noCopy{}, _:atomic.align64{}, v:0xa00000000}, sema:0x0}
14 8 9 10 11 5 0 4 1 2 3 6 13 12 7
Exiting...
```

Remember that using more goroutines in a program is not a panacea for performance, as more goroutines, in addition to the various calls to sync.Add(), sync.Wait(), and sync.Done(), might slow down your program due to the extra housekeeping that needs to be done by the Go scheduler and the Go garbage collector.

What if the number of Add() and Done() calls differ?

When the number of sync.Add() calls and sync.Done() calls are equal, everything is going to be fine in your programs. However, this subsection tells you what happens when these two numbers do not agree with each other.

Without giving any command line parameters to addDone.go, the number of Add() calls is going to be smaller than the number of Done() calls. With at least one command line argument, the number of Done() calls is going to be smaller than the number of Add() calls. You can look at the Go code of addDone.go on your own. What is important is the output it generates. Running addDone.go without any command line arguments produces the following error message:

```
$ go run addDone.go
Going to create 20 goroutines.
sync.WaitGroup{noCopy:sync.noCopy{}, state:atomic.Uint64{_:atomic.
noCopy{}, _:atomic.align64{}, v:0x0}, sema:0x0}
sync.WaitGroup{noCopy:sync.noCopy{}, state:atomic.Uint64{_:atomic.
noCopy{}, _:atomic.align64{}, v:0x1300000000}, sema:0x0}
19 3 4 5 6 7 8 9 10 11 12 13 14 15 16 2 1 17 18 0
Exiting...
panic: sync: negative WaitGroup counter

goroutine 20 [running]:
sync.(*WaitGroup).Add(0x1?, 0x1?)
```

```
    /opt/homebrew/Cellar/go/1.21.0/libexec/src/sync/waitgroup.go:62 +0x108
sync.(*WaitGroup).Done(0x0?)
    /opt/homebrew/Cellar/go/1.21.0/libexec/src/sync/waitgroup.go:87 +0x20
main.main.func1(0x0?)
    ~/go/src/github.com/mactsouk/mGo4th/ch08/addDone.go:26 +0x9c
created by main.main in goroutine 1
    ~/go/src/github.com/mactsouk/mGo4th/ch08/addDone.go:23 +0xec
exit status 2
```

The cause of the error message can be found in the output: panic: sync: negative WaitGroup
counter.

 Sometimes, addDone.go does not produce any error messages and terminates just
fine—***this mainly happens when the system is already busy***. This is an issue with concurrent programs in general—they do not always crash or misbehave as the order of
execution can change, which might change the behavior of the program. This makes
the debugging of concurrent software even more difficult.

Running addDone.go with one command line argument produces the following error message:

```
$ go run addDone.go 1
Going to create 20 goroutines.
sync.WaitGroup{noCopy:sync.noCopy{}, state:atomic.Uint64{_:atomic.
noCopy{}, _:atomic.align64{}, v:0x0}, sema:0x0}
sync.WaitGroup{noCopy:sync.noCopy{}, state:atomic.Uint64{_:atomic.
noCopy{}, _:atomic.align64{}, v:0x1500000000}, sema:0x0}
19 1 2 11 12 13 14 15 16 17 18 6 3 4 5 8 7 9 0 10 fatal error: all
goroutines are asleep - deadlock!

goroutine 1 [semacquire]:
sync.runtime_Semacquire(0x0?)
    /opt/homebrew/Cellar/go/1.21.0/libexec/src/runtime/sema.go:62 +0x2c
sync.(*WaitGroup).Wait(0x14000128030)
    /opt/homebrew/Cellar/go/1.21.0/libexec/src/sync/waitgroup.go:116 +0x78
main.main()
    ~/go/src/github.com/mactsouk/mGo4th/code/ch08/addDone.go:38 +0x230
exit status 2
```

Once again, the reason for the crash is printed on the screen: `fatal error: all goroutines are asleep - deadlock!`. This means that the program should wait indefinitely for a goroutine to finish—that is, for a `Done()` call that is never going to happen.

Creating multiple files with goroutines

As a practical example of the use of goroutines, this subsection presents a command line utility that creates multiple files populated with randomly generated data—such files can be used for testing file systems or generating data for testing. The crucial code of `randomFiles.go` is the following:

```
var waitGroup sync.WaitGroup
for i := start; i <= end; i++ {
    waitGroup.Add(1)

    go func(n int) {
        filepath := filepath.Join(path, fmt.Sprintf("%s%d", filename, n))
        defer waitGroup.Done()
        createFile(filepath)
    }(i)
}
waitGroup.Wait()
```

We first create a `sync.WaitGroup` variable in order to wait for all goroutines to finish in the right way. Each file is created by a single goroutine only. What is important here is that each file has a unique filename—this is implemented with the `filepath` variable that contains the value of the `for` loop counter. Multiple `createFile()` functions executed as goroutines create the files. This is a simple yet very efficient way of creating multiple files. Running `randomFiles.go` generates the following output:

```
$ go run randomFiles.go
Usage: randomFiles firstInt lastInt filename directory
```

So, the utility requires four parameters, which are the first and last values of the `for` loop as well as the filename and the directory in which the files are going to be written. So, let us run the utility with the correct number of parameters:

```
$ go run randomFiles.go 3 5 masterGo /tmp
/tmp/masterGo3 created!
/tmp/masterGo5 created!
/tmp/masterGo4 created!
```

Everything looks fine, and four files have been created according to our instructions! Now that we know about goroutines, let us continue with channels.

Channels

A channel is a communication mechanism that, among other things, allows goroutines to exchange data. Firstly, each channel allows the exchange of a particular data type, which is also called the element type of the channel, and secondly, for a channel to operate properly, you need someone to receive what is sent via the channel. You should declare a new channel using make() and the chan keyword (make(chan int)), and you can close a channel using the close() function. You can declare the size of a channel by writing something similar to make(chan int, 1). This statement creates a *buffered channel* that has a different use—buffered channels are explained later in this chapter.

 Just because we can use channels, it does not mean that we should. If a simpler solution exists that allows goroutines to get executed and save the generated information, we should also consider that. The purpose of every developer should be to create a simple design, not to use all the features of a programming language.

A pipeline is a virtual method for connecting goroutines and channels so that the output of one goroutine becomes the input of another goroutine using channels to transfer your data. One of the benefits that you get from using pipelines is that there is a constant data flow in your program, as no goroutine or channel has to wait for everything to be completed in order to start their execution. Additionally, you use fewer variables and, therefore, less memory space because you do not have to save everything as a variable. Finally, the use of pipelines simplifies the design of the program and improves its maintainability.

Writing to and reading from a channel

Writing a value (val) to a channel (ch) is as easy as writing ch <- val. The arrow shows the direction of the value, and you will have no problem with this statement as long as both var and ch are of the same data type.

You can read a single value from a channel named c by executing <-c. In this case, the direction is from the channel to the outer world. You can save that value into a new variable using aVar := <-c.

Both channel reading and writing are illustrated in channels.go, which comes with the following code:

```
package main
import (
    "fmt"
    "sync"
)
func writeToChannel(c chan int, x int) {
    c <- x
    close(c)
}
```

This function just writes a value to the channel and immediately closes it.

```
func printer(ch chan bool) {
    ch <- true
}
```

This function just sends the true value to a bool channel.

```
func main() {
    c := make(chan int, 1)
```

This channel is buffered with a size of 1. This means that as soon as we fill that buffer, we can close the channel and the goroutine is going to continue its execution and return. A channel that is unbuffered has a different behavior: when you try to send a value to that channel, it blocks forever because it is waiting for someone to fetch that value. In this case, we definitely want a buffered channel in order to avoid any blocking.

```
    var waitGroup sync.WaitGroup
    waitGroup.Add(1)
    go func(c chan int) {
        defer waitGroup.Done()
        writeToChannel(c, 10)
        fmt.Println("Exit.")
    }(c)
    fmt.Println("Read:", <-c)
```

Here, we read from the channel and print the value without storing it in a separate variable.

```
    _, ok := <-c
    if ok {
        fmt.Println("Channel is open!")
```

```
    } else {
        fmt.Println("Channel is closed!")
    }
```

The previous code shows a technique for determining whether a channel is closed or not. In this case, we are ignoring the read value—if the channel was open, then the read value would be discarded.

```
    waitGroup.Wait()
    var ch chan bool = make(chan bool)
    for i := 0; i < 5; i++ {
        go printer(ch)
    }
```

Here, we make an unbuffered channel and create five goroutines without any synchronization as we do not use any Add() calls.

```
    // Range on channels
    // IMPORTANT: As the channel ch is not closed,
    // the range loop does not exit on its own.
    n := 0
    for i := range ch {
```

The range keyword works with channels! However, a range loop on a channel only exits when the channel is closed or uses the break keyword.

```
        fmt.Println(i)
        if i == true {
            n++
        }
        if n > 2 {
            fmt.Println("n:", n)
            close(ch)
            break
        }
    }
```

We close the ch channel when a condition is met and exit the for loop using break. Note that it is never a good idea to close a channel on the receiving end—this is presented here for the sake of the example. You are going to see the consequences of this decision in a while.

```
    for i := 0; i < 5; i++ {
```

```
            fmt.Println(<-ch)
    }
}
```

When trying to read from a closed channel, we get the zero value of its data type, so this for loop works just fine and does not cause any issues.

Running `channels.go` generates the following output:

```
Exit.
Read: 10
```

After writing the value 10 to the channel using `writeToChannel(c, 10)`, we read that value back.

```
Channel is closed!
true
true
true
```

The for loop with the range exits after three iterations—each iteration prints true on screen.

```
n: 3
false
false
false
false
false
```

These five `false` values are printed by the last for loop of the program.

Although everything looks fine with `channels.go`, there is a logical issue with it, which we will explain and resolve in the *Race conditions are bad* section. Additionally, if we run `channels.go` multiple times, it might crash. However, most of the time, it does not, which makes debugging even more challenging.

Receiving from a closed channel

Reading from a closed channel returns the zero value of its data type. However, if you try to write to a closed channel, your program is going to crash in a bad way (panic). These two situations are explored in `readCloseCh.go` and, more specifically, in the implementation of the `main()` function:

```
func main() {
    willClose := make(chan complex64, 10)
```

If you make that an unbuffered channel, the program is going to crash.

```
// Write some data to the channel
willClose <- -1
willClose <- 1i
```

We write two values to the `willClose` channel.

```
// Read data and empty channel
<-willClose
<-willClose
close(willClose)
```

Then, we read and discard these two values and we close the channel.

```
// Read again - this is a closed channel
read := <-willClose
fmt.Println(read)
}
```

The last value that we read from the channel is the zero value of a `complex64` data type. Running `readCloseCh.go` generates the following output:

```
(0+0i)
```

So, we got back the zero value of the `complex64` data type. Now let us continue and discuss how to work with functions that accept channels as parameters.

Channels as function parameters

When using a channel as a function parameter, you can specify its direction—that is, whether it is going to be used for sending or receiving data only. In my opinion, if you know the purpose of a channel in advance, you should use this capability because it makes your programs more robust. You will not be able to send data accidentally to a channel from which you should only receive data, or receive data from a channel to which you should only be sending data.

 If you declare that a channel function parameter is going to be used for reading only and you try to write to it, you are going to get a compile error message that will most likely save you from nasty bugs in the future. This is the major benefit of this approach!

All these are illustrated in `channelFunc.go`—the implementation of the functions that accept channel parameters are the following:

```
func printer(ch chan<- bool) {
    ch <- true
}
```

The above function accepts a channel parameter that is available for writing only.

```
func writeToChannel(c chan<- int, x int) {
    fmt.Println("1", x)
    c <- x
    fmt.Println("2", x)
}
```

The channel parameter of the above function is available for reading only.

```
func f2(out <-chan int, in chan<- int) {
    x := <-out
    fmt.Println("Read (f2):", x)
    in <- x
    return
}
```

The last function accepts two channel parameters. However, `out` is available for reading, whereas `in` is offered for writing. If you try to perform an operation on a channel parameter that is not allowed, the Go compiler is going to complain. This happens even if the function is not being used.

The subject of the next section is race conditions—read it carefully in order to avoid undefined behaviors and unpleasant situations when working with multiple goroutines.

Race conditions are bad

A *data race condition* is a situation where two or more running elements, such as threads and goroutines, try to take control of or modify a shared resource or shared variable of a program. Strictly speaking, a data race occurs when two or more instructions access the same memory address, where at least one of them performs a write (change) operation. If all operations are read operations, then there is no race condition. In practice, this means that you might get different output if you run your program multiple times, and that is a bad thing.

Using the -race flag when running or building Go source files executes the Go race detector, which makes the compiler create a modified version of a typical executable file. This modified version can record all accesses to shared variables as well as all synchronization events that take place, including calls to sync.Mutex and sync.WaitGroup, which are presented later on in this chapter. After analyzing the relevant events, the race detector prints a report that can help you identify potential problems so that you can correct them.

The Go race detector

You can run the race detector tool with go run -race. If we test channels.go using go run -race, we are going to get the following output:

```
$ go run -race channels.go
Exit.
Read: 10
Channel is closed!
true
true
true
n: 3
==================
WARNING: DATA RACE
Write at 0x00c000094010 by main goroutine:
  runtime.recvDirect()
      /opt/homebrew/Cellar/go/1.21.0/libexec/src/runtime/chan.go:348 +0x7c
  main.main()
      ~/go/src/github.com/mactsouk/mGo4th/ch08/channels.go:54 +0x444

Previous read at 0x00c000094010 by goroutine 10:
  runtime.chansend1()
      /opt/homebrew/Cellar/go/1.21.0/libexec/src/runtime/chan.go:146 +0x2c
  main.printer()
      ~/go/src/github.com/mactsouk/mGo4th/ch08/channels.go:14 +0x34
  main.main.func3()
      ~/go/src/github.com/mactsouk/mGo4th/ch08/channels.go:40 +0x34

Goroutine 10 (running) created at:
  main.main()
      ~/go/src/github.com/mactsouk/mGo4th/ch08/channels.go:40 +0x2b8
```

```
====================
false
false
false
false
false
panic: send on closed channel

goroutine 36 [running]:
main.printer(0x0?)
    ~/go/src/github.com/mactsouk/mGo4th/ch08/channels.go:14 +0x38
created by main.main in goroutine 1
    ~/go/src/github.com/mactsouk/mGo4th/ch08/channels.go:40 +0x2bc
exit status 2
```

Therefore, although channels.go looks fine at first, there is a race condition waiting to happen. Let us now discuss where the problem with channels.go lies based on the previous output. There is a closing of a channel at channels.go on line 54, and there is a write to the same channel on line 14 that looks to be the root of the race condition situation. Line 54 is close(ch), whereas line 14 is ch <- true. The issue is that we cannot be sure about what is going to happen and in which order—this is the race condition. If you execute channels.go without the race detector, it might work, but if you try it multiple times, you might get a panic: send on closed channel error message—this mainly has to do with the order in which the Go scheduler is going to run the goroutines of the program. So, if the closing of the channel happens first, then writing to that channel is going to fail—race condition!

Fixing channels.go requires changing the code and, more specifically, the implementation of the printer() function. The corrected version of channels.go is named chRace.go and comes with the following code:

```
func printer(ch chan<- bool, times int) {
    for i := 0; i < times; i++ {
        ch <- true
    }
    close(ch)
}

func main() {
    // This is an unbuffered channel
```

```go
    var ch chan bool = make(chan bool)
    // Write 5 values to channel with a single goroutine
    go printer(ch, 5)
    // IMPORTANT: As the channel ch is closed,
    // the range loop is going to exit on its own.
    for val := range ch {
        fmt.Print(val, " ")
    }
    fmt.Println()
    for i := 0; i < 15; i++ {
        fmt.Print(<-ch, " ")
    }
    fmt.Println()
}
```

The first thing to notice is that instead of using multiple goroutines for writing to the desired channel, we use a single goroutine. *A single goroutine writing to a channel followed by the closing of that channel cannot create any race conditions because things happen sequentially*.

Running go run -race chRace.go produces the following output, which means that there is no longer a race condition:

```
true true true true true
false false false false false false false false false false false false
false false false
```

The next section is about the important and powerful select keyword.

The select keyword

The select keyword is really important because it allows you to *listen to multiple channels at the same time*. A select block can have multiple cases and an optional default case, which mimics the switch statement. It is good for select blocks to have a timeout option just in case. Lastly, a select without any cases (select{}) waits forever.

In practice, this means that select allows a goroutine to wait on multiple communication operations. So, select gives you the power to listen to multiple channels using a single select block. Consequently, you can have non-blocking operations on channels, provided that you have implemented your select blocks appropriately.

A select statement is *not evaluated sequentially*, as all of its channels are examined simultaneously. If none of the channels in a select statement are ready, the select statement blocks (waits) until one of the channels is ready. If multiple channels of a select statement are ready, then the Go runtime *makes a random selection* from the set of these ready channels.

The code in select.go presents a simple use of select running in a goroutine that has three cases. But first, let us see how the goroutine that contains select is executed:

```
wg.Add(1)
go func() {
    gen(0, 2*n, createNumber, end)
    wg.Done()
}()
```

The previous code tells us that for wg.Done() to get executed, gen() should return first. So, let us see the implementation of gen():

```
func gen(min, max int, createNumber chan int, end chan bool) {
    time.Sleep(time.Second)
    for {
        select {
        case createNumber <- rand.Intn(max-min) + min:
        case <-end:
            fmt.Println("Ended!")
            // return
```

The right thing to do here is to add the return statement for gen() to finish. Let us imagine that you have forgotten to add the return statement. This means that the function is not going to finish after the select branch associated with the end channel parameter is executed—createNumber is not going to end the function as it has no return statement. Therefore, the select block keeps waiting for more. The solution can be found in the code that follows:

```
        case <-time.After(4 * time.Second):
            fmt.Println("time.After()!")
            return
        }
    }
}
```

So, what is really happening in the code of the entire select block? This particular `select` statement has three cases. As stated earlier, `select` does not require a `default` branch. You can consider the third branch of the `select` statement as a clever `default` branch. This happens because `time.After()` waits for the specified duration (4 * `time.Second`) to elapse and then prints a message and properly ends `gen()` with `return`. This unblocks the `select` statement in case all of the other channels are blocked for some reason. Although omitting `return` from the second branch is a bug, this shows that having an exit strategy is always a good thing.

Running `select.go` produces the following output:

```
$ go run select.go 10
Going to create 10 random numbers.
13 0 2 8 12 4 13 15 14 19 Ended!
time.After()!
Exiting...
```

We are going to see `select` in action in the remainder of the chapter, starting from the next section, which discusses how to time out goroutines. What you should remember is that `select` allows us to *listen to multiple channels from a single point*.

Timing out a goroutine

There are times when goroutines take more time than expected to finish—in such situations, we want to time out the goroutines so that we can unblock the program. This section presents two such techniques.

Timing out a goroutine inside main()

This subsection presents a simple technique for timing out a goroutine. The relevant code can be found in the `main()` function of `timeOut1.go`:

```go
func main() {
    c1 := make(chan string)
    go func() {
        time.Sleep(3 * time.Second)
        c1 <- "c1 OK"
    }()
```

The `time.Sleep()` call is used for emulating the time it normally takes for a function to finish its operation. In this case, the anonymous function that is executed as a goroutine takes about three seconds before writing a message to the `c1` channel.

```
    select {
    case res := <-c1:
        fmt.Println(res)
    case <-time.After(time.Second):
        fmt.Println("timeout c1")
    }
```

The purpose of the time.After() call is to wait for the desired time before being executed—if another branch is executed, the waiting time resets. In this case, we are not interested in the actual value returned by time.After() but in the fact that the time.After() branch was executed, which means that the waiting time has passed. In this case, as the value passed to the time.After() function is smaller than the value used in the time.Sleep() call that was executed previously, you will most likely get a timeout message. The reason for saying "most likely" is that Linux is not a real-time OS and, sometimes, the OS scheduler plays strange games, especially when it has to deal with a high load and has to schedule lots of tasks—this means that you should not make any assumptions about the operation of the OS scheduler.

```
    c2 := make(chan string)
    go func() {
        time.Sleep(3 * time.Second)
        c2 <- "c2 OK"
    }()
    select {
    case res := <-c2:
        fmt.Println(res)
    case <-time.After(4 * time.Second):
        fmt.Println("timeout c2")
    }
}
```

The preceding code executes a goroutine that takes about three seconds to execute because of the time.Sleep() call and defines a timeout period of four seconds in select using time.After(4 * time.Second). If the time.After(4 * time.Second) call returns after you get a value from the c2 channel found in the first case of the select block, then there will be no timeout; otherwise, you will get a timeout. However, in this case, the value of the time.After() call provides enough time for the time.Sleep() call to return, so you will most likely not get a timeout message here.

Let us now verify our thoughts. Running timeOut1.go produces the following output:

```
$ go run timeOut1.go
timeout c1
c2 OK
```

As expected, the first goroutine timed out, whereas the second one did not. The subsection that follows presents another timeout technique.

Timing out a goroutine outside main()

This subsection illustrates another technique for timing out goroutines. The select statement can be found in a separate function. Additionally, the timeout period is given as a command line argument.

The interesting part of timeOut2.go is the implementation of timeout():

```
func timeout(t time.Duration) {
    temp := make(chan int)
    go func() {
        time.Sleep(5 * time.Second)
        defer close(temp)
    }()
    select {
    case <-temp:
        result <- false
    case <-time.After(t):
        result <- true
    }
}
```

In timeout(), the time duration that is used in the time.After() call is a function parameter, which means that it can vary. Once again, the select block supports the logic of the timeout. Any timeout period longer than 5 seconds will most likely give the goroutine enough time to finish. If timeout() writes false to the result channel, then there is no timeout, whereas if it writes true, there is a timeout. Running timeOut2.go produces the following output:

```
$ go run timeOut2.go 100
Timeout period is 100ms
Time out!
```

The timeout period is 100 milliseconds, which means that the goroutine did not have enough time to finish, hence the timeout message.

```
$ go run timeOut2.go 5500
Timeout period is 5.5s
OK
```

This time, the timeout is 5,500 milliseconds, which means that the goroutine had enough time to finish.

The next section revisits and presents advanced concepts related to channels.

Go channels revisited

So far, we have seen the basic usages of channels—this section presents the definition and the usage of nil channels, signal channels, and buffered channels.

 Although channels seem like an interesting concept, they are not the answer to every concurrency problem as there exist times when they can be replaced by mutexes and shared memory. So, *do not force the use of channels*.

It helps to remember that the zero value of the channel type is nil, and if you send a message to a closed channel, the program panics. However, if you try to read from a closed channel, you get the zero value of the type of that channel. So, after closing a channel, you can no longer write to it but you can still read from it. To be able to close a channel, the channel must not be receive-only.

Additionally, a nil channel always blocks, which means that both reading and writing from nil channels block. This property of channels can be very useful when you want to disable a branch of a select statement by assigning the nil value to a channel variable. Finally, if you try to close a nil channel, your program is going to panic. This is best illustrated in the closeNil.go program:

```
package main
func main() {
    var c chan string
```

The previous statement defines a nil channel named c of the type string.

```
    close(c)
}
```

Running `closeNil.go` generates the following output:

```
panic: close of nil channel

goroutine 1 [running]:
main.main()
    ~/go/src/github.com/mactsouk/mGo4th/ch08/closeNil.go:5 +0x20
exit status 2
```

The previous output shows the message you are going to get if you try to close a `nil` channel. Let us now discuss buffered channels.

Buffered channels

Unlike unbuffered channels, which have a capacity of 0 and require a sender to have a corresponding receiver ready at the other end, buffered channels allow a certain number of values to be sent into the channel before a receiver is needed.

These channels allow us to put jobs in a queue quickly to be able to deal with more requests and process requests later on. Moreover, you can use buffered channels as semaphores to limit the throughput of your application.

The presented technique works as follows: all incoming requests are forwarded to a channel, which processes them one by one. When the channel is done processing a request, it sends a message to the original caller saying that it is ready to process a new one. So, *the capacity of the buffer of the channel restricts the number of simultaneous requests that it can keep*. Bear in mind that it is not the channel that processes the requests or sends the messages.

Also, bear in mind that a buffered channel keeps accepting data until it blocks due to its limited capacity. However, in the presented example, the implementation is what cancels remaining requests after the channel buffer is full due to the `select` statement, not the channel itself. The source file that implements the technique is named `bufChannel.go` and contains the following code:

```
package main
import (
    "fmt"
)
func main() {
    numbers := make(chan int, 5)
```

The `numbers` channel can store up to five integers because it is a buffer channel with a capacity of 5.

```
    counter := 10
    for i := 0; i < counter; i++ {
        select {
        // This is where the processing takes place
        case numbers <- i * i:
            fmt.Println("About to process", i)
        default:
            fmt.Print("No space for ", i, " ")
        }
```

We begin putting data into numbers—however, when the channel is full, it is not going to store more data and the default branch is going to be executed. This is not because of the way channels work but because of the specific implementation with select.

```
    }
    fmt.Println()
    for {
        select {
        case num := <-numbers:
            fmt.Print("*", num, " ")
        default:
            fmt.Println("Nothing left to read!")
            return
        }
    }
}
```

Similarly, we try to read data from numbers using a for loop. When all data from the channel is read, the default branch is going to be executed and will terminate the program with its return statement—when main() returns, the entire program will be terminated.

Running bufChannel.go produces the following output:

```
$ go run bufChannel.go
About to process 0
. . .
About to process 4
No space for 5 No space for 6 No space for 7 No space for 8 No space for 9
*0 *1 *4 *9 *16 Nothing left to read!
```

Let us now discuss nil channels.

nil channels

nil channels *always block*! Therefore, you should use them when you want that behavior on purpose! The code that follows illustrates nil channels:

```
package main
import (
    "fmt"
    "math/rand"
    "sync"
    "time"
)
var wg sync.WaitGroup
```

We are making wg a global variable in order to be available from anywhere in the code and avoid passing it to every function that needs it as a parameter. This is not idiomatic Go and some people might dislike that approach, despite its simpler implementation. An alternative would be to declare wg in main() and pass a pointer to each function that needs it—you can implement that as an exercise.

```
func add(c chan int) {
    sum := 0
    t := time.NewTimer(time.Second)
    for {
        select {
        case input := <-c:
            sum = sum + input
        case <-t.C:
            c = nil
            fmt.Println(sum)
            wg.Done()
        }
    }
}
```

The send() function keeps sending random numbers to channel c. Do not confuse channel c, which is a (channel) function parameter, with channel t.C, which is part of timer t—you can change the name of the c variable but not the name of the C field of a timer. When the time of timer t expires, the timer sends a value to the t.C channel.

This triggers the execution of the relevant branch of the select statement, which assigns the value nil to channel c and prints the value of the sum variable, and wg.Done() is executed, which is going to unblock wg.Wait() found in the main() function. Additionally, as c becomes nil, it stops/blocks send() from sending more data to it.

```go
func send(c chan int) {
    for {
        c <- rand.Intn(10)
    }
}
func main() {
    c := make(chan int)
    rand.Seed(time.Now().Unix())
    wg.Add(1)
    go add(c)
    go send(c)
    wg.Wait()
}
```

Running nilChannel.go produces the following output:

```
$ go run nilChannel.go
11168960
```

Since the number of times that the first branch of the select statement in add() is going to be executed is not fixed, you get different results each time you execute nilChannel.go.

The next subsection discusses worker pools.

Worker pools

A worker pool is a *set of threads that process jobs assigned to them*. The Apache web server and the net/http package of Go more or less work this way: the main process accepts all incoming requests, which are forwarded to worker processes to get served. Once a worker process has finished its job, it is ready to serve a new client.

As Go does not have threads, the presented implementation is going to use goroutines instead of threads. Additionally, threads do not usually die after serving a request because the cost of ending a thread and creating a new one is too high, whereas goroutines do die after finishing their job. Worker pools in Go are implemented with the help of buffered channels, as they allow you to limit the number of goroutines running at the same time.

The presented utility implements a simple task: it processes integers and prints their square values using a single goroutine for serving each request. The code of wPools.go is as follows:

```go
package main
import (
    "fmt"
    "os"
    "runtime"
    "strconv"
    "sync"
    "time"
)
type Client struct {
    id      int
    integer int
}
```

The Client structure is used for keeping track of the requests that the program is going to process.

```go
type Result struct {
    job    Client
    square int
}
```

The Result structure is used for keeping the data of each Client as well as the results generated by the client. Put simply, the Client structure holds the input data of each request, whereas Result holds the results of a request—if you want to process more complex data, you should modify these structures.

```go
var size = runtime.GOMAXPROCS(0)
var clients = make(chan Client, size)
var data = make(chan Result, size)
```

The clients and data buffered channels are used to get new client requests and write the results, respectively. If you want your program to run faster, you can increase the value of size.

```go
func worker(wg *sync.WaitGroup) {
    for c := range clients {
        square := c.integer * c.integer
        output := Result{c, square}
        data <- output
```

```
            time.Sleep(time.Second)
        }
        wg.Done()
    }
}
```

The worker() function processes requests by reading the clients channel. Once the processing is complete, the result is written to the data channel. The delay that is introduced with time.Sleep() is not necessary but it gives you a better sense of the way that the generated output is printed.

```
func create(n int) {
    for i := 0; i < n; i++ {
        c := Client{i, i}
        clients <- c
    }
    close(clients)
}
```

The purpose of the create() function is to create all requests properly and then send them to the clients buffered channel for processing. Note that the clients channel is read by worker().

```
func main() {
    if len(os.Args) != 3 {
        fmt.Println("Need #jobs and #workers!")
        return
    }
    nJobs, err := strconv.Atoi(os.Args[1])
    if err != nil {
        fmt.Println(err)
        return
    }
    nWorkers, err := strconv.Atoi(os.Args[2])
    if err != nil {
        fmt.Println(err)
        return
    }
```

In the preceding code, you read the command line parameters that define the number of jobs and workers. If the number of jobs is greater than the number of workers, the jobs are served in smaller chunks.

```
    go create(nJobs)
```

The create() call mimics the client requests that you are going to process.

```
finished := make(chan interface{})
```

The finished channel is used for blocking the program and, therefore, needs no particular data type.

```
go func() {
    for d := range data {
        fmt.Printf("Client ID: %d\tint: ", d.job.id)
        fmt.Printf("%d\tsquare: %d\n", d.job.integer, d.square)
    }
    finished <- true
```

The finished <- true statement is used for unblocking the program as soon as the for range loop ends. The for range loop ends when the data channel is closed, which happens after wg.Wait(), which means after all workers have finished.

```
}()
var wg sync.WaitGroup
for i := 0; i < nWorkers; i++ {
    wg.Add(1)
    go worker(&wg)
}
wg.Wait()
close(data)
```

The purpose of the previous for loop is to generate the required number of worker() goroutines to process all requests.

```
fmt.Printf("Finished: %v\n", <-finished)
}
```

The <-finished statement in fmt.Printf() blocks until the finished channel is closed.

Running wPools.go creates the following kind of output:

```
$ go run wPools.go 8 5
Client ID: 0    int: 0    square: 0
Client ID: 1    int: 1    square: 1
Client ID: 2    int: 2    square: 4
```

```
Client ID: 3      int: 3      square: 9
Client ID: 4      int: 4      square: 16
Client ID: 5      int: 5      square: 25
Client ID: 6      int: 6      square: 36
Finished: true
```

The previous output shows that all requests were processed. This technique allows you to serve a given number of requests, which saves you from server overload. The price you pay for that is having to write more code.

The next subsection introduces signal channels and shows a technique for using them to define the order of execution for a small number of goroutines.

Signal channels

A signal channel is one that is used just for signaling. Put simply, you can use a signal channel when you want to inform another goroutine about something. Signal channels should not be used for data transferring. You are going to see signal channels in action in the next subsection where we specify the order of execution of goroutines.

Specifying the order of execution for your goroutines

This subsection presents a technique for specifying the order of execution of goroutines using signal channels. However, keep in mind that this technique works best when you are dealing with a small number of goroutines. The presented code example has four goroutines that we want to execute in the desired order—first, the goroutine for function A(), then function B(), then C(), and finally, D().

The code of defineOrder.go without the package statement and import block is the following:

```go
var wg sync.WaitGroup
func A(a, b chan struct{}) {
    <-a
    fmt.Println("A()!")
    time.Sleep(time.Second)
    close(b)
}
```

Function A( ) is going to be blocked until channel a, which is passed as a parameter, is closed. Just before it ends, it closes channel b, which is passed as a parameter. This is going to unblock the next goroutine, which is going to be function B( ).

```
func B(a, b chan struct{}) {
    <-a
    fmt.Println("B()!")
    time.Sleep(3 * time.Second)
    close(b)
}
```

Similarly, function B( ) is going to be blocked until channel a, which is passed as a parameter, is closed. Just before B( ) ends, it closes channel b, which is passed as a parameter. As before, this is going to unblock the following function:

```
func C(a, b chan struct{}) {
    <-a
    fmt.Println("C()!")
    close(b)
}
```

As it happened with functions A( ) and B( ), the execution of function C( ) is blocked by channel a. Just before it ends, it closes channel b.

```
func D(a chan struct{}) {
    <-a
    fmt.Println("D()!")
    wg.Done()
}
```

This is the last function that is going to be executed. Therefore, although it is blocked, it does not close any channels before exiting. Additionally, being the last function means that it can be executed more than once, which is not true for functions A( ), B( ), and C( ) because a channel can be closed only once.

```
func main() {
    x := make(chan struct{})
    y := make(chan struct{})
    z := make(chan struct{})
    w := make(chan struct{})
```

We need to have as many channels as the number of functions we want to execute as goroutines.

```
wg.Add(1)
go func() {
    D(w)
}()
```

This proves that the order of execution dictated by the Go code does not matter as D() is going to be executed last.

```
wg.Add(1)
go func() {
    D(w)
}()
go A(x, y)
wg.Add(1)
go func() {
    D(w)
}()
go C(z, w)
go B(y, z)
```

Although we run C() before B(), C() is going to finish after B() has finished.

```
wg.Add(1)
go func() {
    D(w)
}()
// This triggers the process
close(x)
```

The closing of the first channel is what triggers the execution of the goroutines because this unblocks A().

```
    wg.Wait()
}
```

Running defineOrder.go produces the following output:

```
$ go run defineOrder.go
A()!
B()!
```

```
C()!
D()! D()! D()! D()!
```

So, the four functions, which are executed as goroutines, are executed in the desired order, and, in the case of the last function, the desired number of times.

Handling UNIX signals

UNIX signals offer a very handy way of interacting asynchronously with applications and server processes. UNIX signal handling in Go requires the use of channels that are used exclusively for this task. The presented program handles SIGINT (which is called syscall.SIGINT in Go) and SIGINFO separately and uses a default case in a switch block for handling the remaining signals. The implementation of that switch block allows you to differentiate between the various signals according to your needs.

There exists a dedicated channel that receives all signals, as defined by the signal.Notify() function. Go channels can have a capacity—the capacity of this particular channel is 1 in order to be able to receive and keep *one signal at a time*. This makes perfect sense as a signal can terminate a program and there is no need to try to handle another signal at the same time. There is usually an anonymous function that is executed as a goroutine and performs the signal handling and nothing else. The main task of that goroutine is to listen to the channel for data. Once a signal is received, it is sent to that channel, read by the goroutine, and stored into a variable—at this point, the channel can receive more signals. That variable is processed by a switch statement.

 Some signals cannot be caught, and the operating system cannot ignore them. So, the SIGKILL and SIGSTOP signals cannot be blocked, caught, or ignored; the reason for this is that they allow privileged users as well as the UNIX kernel to terminate any process they desire.

Create a text file by typing the following code—a good filename for it would be signals.go.

```
package main
import (
    "fmt"
    "os"
    "os/signal"
    "syscall"
    "time"
```

```
)
func handleSignal(sig os.Signal) {
    fmt.Println("handleSignal() Caught:", sig)
}
```

handleSignal() is a separate function for handling signals. However, you can also handle signals inline, in the branches of a switch statement.

```
func main() {
    fmt.Printf("Process ID: %d\n", os.Getpid())
    sigs := make(chan os.Signal, 1)
```

We create a channel with data of the type os.Signal because all channels must have a type.

```
    signal.Notify(sigs)
```

The previous statement means handling all signals that can be handled.

```
    start := time.Now()
    go func() {
        for {
            sig := <-sigs
```

Wait until you read data (<-) from the sigs channel and store it in the sig variable.

```
            switch sig {
```

Depending on the read value, act accordingly. This is how you differentiate between signals.

```
            case syscall.SIGINT:
                duration := time.Since(start)
                fmt.Println("Execution time:", duration)
```

For the handling of syscall.SIGINT, we calculate the time that has passed since the beginning of the program execution and print it on the screen.

```
            case syscall.SIGINFO:
                handleSignal(sig)
```

The code of the syscall.SIGINFO case calls the handleSignal() function—it is up to the developer to decide on the details of the implementation.

On Linux machines, you should replace syscall.SIGINFO with another signal such as syscall.SIGUSR1 or syscall.SIGUSR2 because syscall.SIGINFO is not available on Linux (https://github.com/golang/go/issues/1653).

```go
        // do not use return here because the goroutine exits
        // but the time.Sleep() will continue to work!
        os.Exit(0)
    default:
        fmt.Println("Caught:", sig)
    }
```

If there is no match, the default case handles the rest of the values and just prints a message.

```go
        }
    }()
    for {
        fmt.Print("+")
        time.Sleep(10 * time.Second)
    }
}
```

The endless for loop at the end of the main() function is for emulating the operation of a real program. Without an endless for loop, the program exits almost immediately.

Running signals.go and interacting with it creates the following kind of output:

```
$ go run signals.go
Process ID: 70153
+^CExecution time: 631.533125ms
+Caught: user defined signal 1
+Caught: urgent I/O condition
+signal: killed
```

The second line of output was generated by pressing *Ctrl + C* on the keyboard, which, on UNIX machines, sends the syscall.SIGINT signal to the program. The third line of output was caused by executing kill -USR1 74252 on a different terminal. The last line of the output was generated by the kill -9 74252 command. As the KILL signal (which is also represented by the number 9) cannot be handled, it terminates the program, and the shell prints the killed message.

Handling two signals

If you want to handle a limited number of signals instead of all of them, you should replace the `signal.Notify(sigs)` statement with a statement like the following:

```
signal.Notify(sigs, syscall.SIGINT, syscall.SIGINFO)
```

After that, you need to make the appropriate changes to the code of the goroutine responsible for signal handling in order to identify and handle `syscall.SIGINT` and `syscall.SIGINFO`—the current version (`signals.go`) already handles both of them.

The next section talks about shared memory and shared variables, which is a very handy way of making goroutines communicate with each other with the use of channels.

Shared memory and shared variables

Shared memory and shared variables are huge topics in concurrent programming and the most common ways for UNIX threads to communicate with each other. The same principles apply to Go and goroutines, which is what this section is about. *A mutex variable, which is the abbreviation for a mutual exclusion variable, is mainly used for thread synchronization and for protecting shared data when multiple writes or a write and a read can occur at the same time*. A mutex works like a buffered channel with a capacity of one, which allows, at most, one goroutine to access a shared variable at any given time. This means that there is no way for two or more goroutines to be able to update that variable simultaneously. Go offers the `sync.Mutex` and `sync.RWMutex` data types.

A *critical section* of a concurrent program is the code that cannot be executed simultaneously by all processes, threads, or, in this case, goroutines. It is the code that needs to be protected by mutexes. Therefore, identifying the critical sections of your code makes the whole programming process so much simpler that you should pay particular attention to this task. A critical section cannot be embedded into another critical section when both critical sections use the same `sync.Mutex` or `sync.RWMutex` variable. However, *avoid at almost any cost the spreading of mutexes across functions because that makes it really hard to see whether you are embedding or not*.

The sync.Mutex type

The `sync.Mutex` type is the Go implementation of a mutex. Its definition, which can be found in the `mutex.go` file of the `sync` directory, is as follows (you do not need to know the definition of `sync.Mutex` in order to use it):

```
type Mutex struct {
    state int32
```

```
        sema  uint32
}
```

The definition of sync.Mutex is nothing special. All of the interesting work is done by the sync. Lock() and sync.Unlock() functions, which can lock and unlock a sync.Mutex variable, respectively. Locking a mutex means that nobody else can lock it until it has been released using the sync.Unlock() function. All these are illustrated in mutex.go, which contains the following code:

```go
package main
import (
        "fmt"
        "os"
        "strconv"
        "sync"
        "time"
)
var m sync.Mutex
var v1 int
func change() {
        m.Lock()
        defer m.Unlock()
```

This function makes changes to the value of v1. The critical section begins here.

```go
        time.Sleep(time.Second)
        v1 = v1 + 1
        if v1 == 10 {
                v1 = 0
                fmt.Print("* ")
        }
```

This is the end of the critical section. Now, another goroutine can lock the mutex.

```go
}
func read() int {
        m.Lock()
        a := v1
        defer m.Unlock()
        return a
}
```

This function is used for reading the value of v1—therefore, it should use a mutex to make the process concurrently safe. Most specifically, we want to make sure that nobody is going to change the value of v1 while we are reading it. The rest of the program contains the implementation of the main() function—feel free to see the entire code of mutex.go in the GitHub repository of the book.

Running mutex.go produces the following output:

```
$ go run -race mutex.go 10
0 -> 1-> 2-> 3-> 4-> 5-> 6-> 7-> 8-> 9* -> 0-> 0
```

The previous output shows that due to the use of a mutex, goroutines cannot access shared data and, therefore, there are no hidden race conditions.

The next subsection shows what could happen if we forget to unlock a mutex.

What happens if you forget to unlock a mutex?

Forgetting to unlock a sync.Mutex mutex creates a panic situation, even in the simplest kind of a program. The same applies to the sync.RWMutex mutex, which is presented in the next section. Let us now see a code example to understand this unpleasant situation a lot better—this is part of forgetMutex.go:

```
var m sync.Mutex
var w sync.WaitGroup
func function() {
    m.Lock()
    fmt.Println("Locked!")
}
```

Here, we lock a mutex without releasing it afterward. This means that if we run function() as a goroutine more than once, all instances after the first one are going to be blocked waiting to Lock() the shared mutex. In our case, we run two goroutines—feel free to see the entire code of forgetMutex.go for more details. Running forgetMutex.go generates the following output:

```
Locked!
fatal error: all goroutines are asleep - deadlock!

goroutine 1 [semacquire]:
sync.runtime_Semacquire(0x140000021a0?)
    /opt/homebrew/Cellar/go/1.21.0/libexec/src/runtime/sema.go:62 +0x2c
sync.(*WaitGroup).Wait(0x100fa1710)
```

```
    /opt/homebrew/Cellar/go/1.21.0/libexec/src/sync/waitgroup.go:116 +0x74
main.main()
    ~/go/src/github.com/mactsouk/mGo4th/ch08/forgetMutex.go:29 +0x5c

goroutine 34 [sync.Mutex.Lock]:
sync.runtime_SemacquireMutex(0x0?, 0x0?, 0x0?)
    /opt/homebrew/Cellar/go/1.21.0/libexec/src/runtime/sema.go:77 +0x28
sync.(*Mutex).lockSlow(0x100fa1520)
    /opt/homebrew/Cellar/go/1.21.0/libexec/src/sync/mutex.go:171 +0x174
sync.(*Mutex).Lock(...)
    /opt/homebrew/Cellar/go/1.21.0/libexec/src/sync/mutex.go:90
main.function()
    ~/go/src/github.com/mactsouk/mGo4th/ch08/forgetMutex.go:12 +0x84
main.main.func1()
    ~/go/src/github.com/mactsouk/mGo4th/ch08/forgetMutex.go:20 +0x50
created by main.main in goroutine 1
    ~/go/src/github.com/mactsouk/mGo4th/ch08/forgetMutex.go:18 +0x34
exit status 2
```

As expected, the program crashes because of the deadlock. To avoid such situations, always re-member to unlock any mutexes created in your program as soon as possible.

Let us now discuss sync.RWMutex, which is an improved version of sync.Mutex.

The sync.RWMutex type

The sync.RWMutex data type is an improved version of sync.Mutex and is defined in the rwmutex.go file of the sync directory of the Go Standard library as follows:

```
type RWMutex struct {
    w           Mutex
    writerSem   uint32
    readerSem   uint32
    readerCount int32
    readerWait  int32
}
```

In other words, sync.RWMutex is based on sync.Mutex with the necessary additions and improvements. So, you might ask, how does sync.RWMutex improve sync.Mutex? Although a single function is allowed to perform write operations with a sync.RWMutex mutex, you can have multiple readers owning a sync.RWMutex mutex—this means that read operations are usually faster with sync.RWMutex. However, there is one important detail that you should be aware of: until all of the readers of a sync.RWMutex mutex unlock it, you cannot lock it for writing, which is the small price you have to pay for the performance improvement you get for allowing multiple readers.

The functions that can help you work with sync.RWMutex are RLock() and RUnlock(), which are used for locking and unlocking the mutex for reading purposes, respectively. The Lock() and Unlock() functions used in sync.Mutex should still be used when you want to lock and unlock a sync.RWMutex mutex for writing purposes. Finally, it should be apparent that you should not make changes to any shared variables inside an RLock() and RUnlock() block of code.

All these are illustrated in rwMutex.go—the important code is the following:

```go
var Password *secret
var wg sync.WaitGroup
type secret struct {
    RWM      sync.RWMutex
    password string
}
```

This is the shared variable of the program—you can share any type of variable you want.

```go
func Change(pass string) {
    if Password == nil {
        fmt.Println("Password is nil!")
        return
    }
    fmt.Println("Change() function")
    Password.RWM.Lock()
```

This is the beginning of the critical section.

```go
    fmt.Println("Change() Locked")
    time.Sleep(4 * time.Second)
    Password.password = pass
    Password.RWM.Unlock()
```

This is the end of the critical section.

```
    fmt.Println("Change() UnLocked")
}
```

The Change() function makes changes to the shared variable Password and, therefore, needs to use the Lock() function, which can be held by a single writer only.

```
func show () {
    defer wg.Done()
    defer Password.RWM.RUnlock()
    Password.RWM.RLock()
    fmt.Println("Show function locked!")
    time.Sleep(2 * time.Second)
    fmt.Println("Pass value:", Password.password)
}
```

The show() function reads the shared variable Password and therefore it is allowed to use the RLock() function, which can be held by multiple readers. Inside main(), three show() functions are executed as goroutines before a call to the Change() function, which also runs as a goroutine. The key point here is that no race conditions are going to happen. Running rwMutex.go produces the following output:

```
$ go run rwMutex.go
Change() function
```

The Change() function is executed but cannot acquire the mutex because it is already taken by one or more show() goroutines.

```
Show function locked!
Show function locked!
```

The previous output verifies that two show() goroutines have successfully taken the mutex for reading.

```
Change() function
```

Here, we can see a second Change() function running and waiting to get the mutex.

```
Pass value: myPass
Pass value: myPass
```

This is the output from the two show() goroutines.

```
Change() Locked
Change() UnLocked
```

Here we see that one Change() goroutine finishes its job.

```
Show function locked!
Pass value: 54321
```

After that another show() goroutine finishes.

```
Change() Locked
Change() UnLocked
Current password value: 123456
```

Lastly, the second Change() goroutine finishes. The last output line is for making sure that the password value has changed—please look at the full code of rwMutex.go for more details.

Bear in mind that the output you are going to get might be different due to the way the scheduler works. This is the nature of concurrent programming and these programs do not have any mechanism to ensure the show() function should be scheduled first.

The next subsection discusses the use of the atomic package for avoiding race conditions.

The atomic package

An atomic operation is an operation that is completed in a single step relative to other threads or, in this case, to other goroutines. *This means that an atomic operation cannot be interrupted in the middle of it.* The Go Standard library offers the atomic package, which, in some simple cases, can help you avoid using a mutex. With the atomic package, you can have atomic counters accessed by multiple goroutines without synchronization issues and without worrying about race conditions. However, mutexes are more versatile than atomic operations.

As illustrated in the code that follows, when using an atomic variable, all reading and writing operations of an atomic variable must be done using the functions provided by the atomic package in order to avoid race conditions.

The code in atomic.go is as follows, which is made smaller by hardcoding some values:

```
package main
import (
    "fmt"
```

```
    "sync"
    "sync/atomic"
)
type atomCounter struct {
    val int64
}
```

This is a structure for holding the desired `int64` atomic variable.

```
func (c *atomCounter) Value() int64 {
    return atomic.LoadInt64(&c.val)
}
```

This is a helper function that returns the current value of an `int64` atomic variable using `atomic.LoadInt64()`.

```
func main() {
    X := 100
    Y := 4
    var waitGroup sync.WaitGroup
    counter := atomCounter{}
    for i := 0; i < X; i++ {
```

We are creating lots of goroutines that change the shared variable—as stated before, the use of the `atomic` package for working with the shared variable offers a simple way of avoiding race conditions when changing the value of the shared variable.

```
        waitGroup.Add(1)
        go func() {
            defer waitGroup.Done()
            for i := 0; i < Y; i++ {
                atomic.AddInt64(&counter.val, 1)
            }
```

The `atomic.AddInt64()` function changes the value of the `val` field of the counter structure variable in a safe way.

```
        }()
    }
    waitGroup.Wait()
    fmt.Println(counter.Value())
}
```

Running `atomic.go` while checking for race conditions produces the following kind of output:

```
$ go run -race atomic.go
400
```

So, the atomic variable is modified by multiple goroutines without any issues.

The next subsection shows how to share memory using goroutines.

Sharing memory using goroutines

This subsection illustrates how to share data using a dedicated goroutine. Although shared memory is the traditional way that threads communicate with each other, Go comes with built-in synchronization features that allow a single goroutine to own a shared piece of data. This means that other goroutines must send messages to this single goroutine that owns the shared data, which prevents the corruption of the data. Such a goroutine is called a monitor goroutine. In Go terminology, *this is sharing by communicating instead of communicating by sharing*.

Personally, I prefer to use a monitor goroutine instead of traditional shared memory techniques because the implementation with the monitor goroutine is safer, closer to the Go philosophy, and easier to understand.

The logic of the program can be found in the implementation of the `monitor()` function. More specifically, the `select` statement orchestrates the operation of the entire program. When you have a read request, the `read()` function attempts to read from the `readValue` channel, which is controlled by the `monitor()` function.

This returns the current value of the value variable. On the other hand, when you want to change the stored value, you call `set()`. This writes to the `writeValue` channel, which is also handled by the same `select` statement. As a result, no one can deal with the shared variable without using the `monitor()` function, which is in charge.

The code of `monitor.go` is as follows:

```go
package main
import (
    "fmt"
    "math/rand"
    "os"
    "strconv"
    "sync"
    "time"
```

```
    )
    var readValue = make(chan int)
    var writeValue = make(chan int)
    func set(newValue int) {
        writeValue <- newValue
    }
```

This function sends data to the writeValue channel.

```
    func read() int {
        return <-readValue
    }
```

When the read() function is called, it reads from the readValue channel—this reading happens inside the monitor() function.

```
    func monitor() {
        var value int
        for {
            select {
            case newValue := <-writeValue:
                value = newValue
                fmt.Printf("%d ", value)
            case readValue <- value:
            }
        }
    }
```

The monitor() function contains the logic of the program with the endless for loop and the select statement. The first case receives data from the writeValue channel, sets the value variable accordingly, and prints that new value. The second case sends the value of the value variable to the readValue channel. As all traffic goes through monitor() and its select block, there is no way to have a race condition because there is a single instance of monitor() running.

```
    func main() {
        if len(os.Args) != 2 {
            fmt.Println("Please give an integer!")
            return
        }
        n, err := strconv.Atoi(os.Args[1])
```

```
        if err != nil {
            fmt.Println(err)
            return
        }
        fmt.Printf("Going to create %d random numbers.\n", n)
        rand.Seed(time.Now().Unix())
        go monitor()
```

It is important that the monitor() function is executed first because that is the goroutine that orchestrates the flow of the program.

```
        var wg sync.WaitGroup
        for r := 0; r < n; r++ {
            wg.Add(1)
            go func() {
                defer wg.Done()
                set(rand.Intn(10 * n))
            }()
        }
```

When the for loop ends, it means that we have created the desired number of random numbers.

```
        wg.Wait()
        fmt.Printf("\nLast value: %d\n", read())
    }
```

Lastly, we wait for all set() goroutines to finish before printing the last random number.

Running monitor.go produces the following output:

```
$ go run monitor.go 10
Going to create 10 random numbers.
98 22 5 84 20 26 45 36 0 16
Last value: 16
```

So, 10 random numbers are created by 10 goroutines and all these goroutines send their output to the monitor() function, which is also executed as a goroutine. Apart from receiving the results, the monitor() function prints them on the screen, so all this output is generated by monitor().

The next section discusses the go statement in more detail.

Closured variables and the go statement

In this section, we are going to talk about closured variables, which are variables inside closures, and the go statement. Notice that closured variables in goroutines are evaluated when the goroutine actually runs and when the go statement is executed in order to create a new goroutine. This means that closured variables are going to be replaced by their values when the Go scheduler decides to execute the relevant code. This is illustrated in the main() function of goClosure.go:

```
func main() {
    for i := 0; i <= 20; i++ {
        go func() {
            fmt.Print(i, " ")
        }()
    }
    time.Sleep(time.Second)
    fmt.Println()
}
```

Running goClosure.go produces the following output:

```
$ go run goClosure.go
3 7 21 21 21 21 21 21 21 21 21 21 21 21 21 21 21 21 21 21 21
```

The program mostly prints the number 21, which is the last value of the variable of the for loop, and not the other numbers. As i is a closured variable, it is evaluated at the time of execution. As the goroutines begin but wait for the Go scheduler to allow them to get executed, the for loop ends, so the value of i that is being used is 21. Lastly, the same issue also applies to Go channels, so be careful.

Running goClosure.go with the Go race detector reveals the issue:

```
$ go run -race goClosure.go
5 4 5 5 ===================
WARNING: DATA RACE
Read at 0x00c00011e028 by goroutine 6:
  main.main.func1()
      ~/go/src/github.com/mactsouk/mGo4th/ch08/goClosure.go:11 +0x34

Previous write at 0x00c00011e028 by main goroutine:
  main.main()
```

```
        ~/go/src/github.com/mactsouk/mGo4th/ch08/goClosure.go:9 +0x5c

Goroutine 6 (running) created at:
  main.main()
        ~/go/src/github.com/mactsouk/mGo4th/ch08/goClosure.go:10 +0x44
===================
8 8 6 10 12 11 15 15 15 18 20 20 21 15 21 21 21
Found 1 data race(s)
exit status 66
```

Now, let us correct goClosure.go and present it to you—the new name is goClosureCorrect.go and its main() function is as follows:

```go
func main() {
    for i := 0; i <= 20; i++ {
        i := i
        go func() {
            fmt.Print(i, " ")
        }()
    }
}
```

This is one way of correcting the issue. The valid yet bizarre i := i statement creates a new instance of the variable for the goroutine that holds the correct value. Although this is a valid approach, this kind of variable shadowing is not considered a good practice.

 Variable shadowing in Go occurs when a variable declared in a nested scope has the same name as a variable in an outer scope. While variable shadowing can be intentional and useful in certain situations, it can also lead to confusion and introduce subtle bugs. In practice, it is recommended to avoid unnecessary variable shadowing and choose meaningful variable names that minimize the likelihood of unintentional shadowing.

```go
    time.Sleep(time.Second)
    fmt.Println()
    for i := 0; i <= 20; i++ {
        go func(x int) {
            fmt.Print(x, " ")
        }(i)
    }
}
```

This is a totally different way of correcting the race condition: pass the current value of i to the anonymous function as a parameter and everything is OK. As explained in *Chapter 15, Changes in Recent Go Versions*, this issue does not exist in Go 1.22.

```
    time.Sleep(time.Second)
    fmt.Println()
}
```

Testing goClosureCorrect.go with the race detector generates the expected output:

```
$ go run -race goClosureCorrect.go
0 1 2 4 3 5 6 9 8 7 10 11 13 12 14 16 15 17 18 20 19
0 1 2 3 4 5 6 7 8 10 9 12 13 11 14 15 16 17 18 19 20
```

The next section presents the functionality of the context package.

The context package

The main purpose of the context package is to define the Context type and support cancellation. Yes, you heard that right; there are times when, for some reason, you want to abandon what you are doing. However, it would be very helpful to be able to include some extra information about your cancellation decisions. The context package allows you to do exactly that.

If you take a look at the source code of the context package, you will realize that its implementation is pretty simple—even the implementation of the Context type is pretty simple, yet the context package is very important.

The Context type is an interface with four methods: Deadline(), Done(), Err(), and Value(). The good news is that you do not need to implement all of these functions of the Context interface—you just need to modify a Context variable using methods such as context.WithCancel(), context.WithDeadline(), and context.WithTimeout().

All three of these methods return a derived Context (the child) and a CancelFunc() function. Calling the CancelFunc() function removes the parent's reference to the child and stops any associated timers. As a side effect, this means that the Go garbage collector is free to garbage collect the child goroutines that no longer have associated parent goroutines. For garbage collection to work correctly, the parent goroutine needs to keep a reference to each child goroutine. If a child goroutine ends without the parent knowing about it, then a memory leak occurs until the parent is canceled as well.

The example that follows showcases the use of the context package. The program contains four functions, including the main() function. Functions f1(), f2(), and f3() each require just one parameter (which is a time delay) because everything else they need is defined inside their function body. In this example, we use context.Background() to initialize an empty Context. The other function that can create an empty Context is context.TODO(), which is presented later on in this chapter.

```go
package main
import (
    "context"
    "fmt"
    "os"
    "strconv"
    "time"
)
func f1(t int) {
    c1 := context.Background()
    c1, cancel := context.WithCancel(c1)
    defer cancel()
```

The WithCancel() method returns a copy of the parent context with a new Done channel. Notice that the cancel variable, which is a function, is one of the return values of context.CancelFunc(). The context.WithCancel() function uses an existing Context and creates a child with cancellation. The context.WithCancel() function also returns a Done channel that can be closed, either when the cancel() function is called, as shown in the preceding code, or when the Done channel of the parent context is closed.

```go
    go func() {
        time.Sleep(4 * time.Second)
        cancel()
    }()
    select {
    case <-c1.Done():
        fmt.Println("f1() Done:", c1.Err())
        return
    case r := <-time.After(time.Duration(t) * time.Second):
        fmt.Println("f1():", r)
    }
```

```
        return
    }
```

The f1() function creates and executes a goroutine. The time.Sleep() call simulates the time it would take a real goroutine to do its job. In this case, it is 4 seconds, but you can put any time period you want. If the c1 context calls the Done() function in less than 4 seconds, the goroutine will not have enough time to finish.

```
func f2(t int) {
    c2 := context.Background()
    c2, cancel := context.WithTimeout(c2, time.Duration(t)*time.Second)
    defer cancel()
```

The cancel variable in f2() comes from context.WithTimeout(), which requires two parameters: a Context parameter and a time.Duration parameter. When the timeout period expires, the cancel() function is called automatically.

```
    go func() {
        time.Sleep(4 * time.Second)
        cancel()
    }()
    select {
    case <-c2.Done():
        fmt.Println("f2() Done:", c2.Err())
        return
    case r := <-time.After(time.Duration(t) * time.Second):
        fmt.Println("f2():", r)
    }
    return
}
func f3(t int) {
    c3 := context.Background()
    deadline := time.Now().Add(time.Duration(2*t) * time.Second)
    c3, cancel := context.WithDeadline(c3, deadline)
    defer cancel()
```

The cancel variable in f3() comes from context.WithDeadline(), which requires two parameters: a Context variable and a time in the future that signifies the deadline of the operation. When the deadline passes, the cancel() function is called automatically.

```
        go func() {
            time.Sleep(4 * time.Second)
            cancel()
        }()
        select {
        case <-c3.Done():
            fmt.Println("f3() Done:", c3.Err())
            return
        case r := <-time.After(time.Duration(t) * time.Second):
            fmt.Println("f3():", r)
        }
        return
    }
```

The logic of f3() is the same as in f1() and f2()—the select block orchestrates the process.

```
func main() {
    if len(os.Args) != 2 {
        fmt.Println("Need a delay!")
        return
    }
    delay, err := strconv.Atoi(os.Args[1])
    if err != nil {
        fmt.Println(err)
        return
    }
    fmt.Println("Delay:", delay)
    f1(delay)
    f2(delay)
    f3(delay)
}
```

The three functions are executed in sequence by the main() function. Running useContext.go produces the following kind of output:

```
$ go run useContext.go 3
Delay: 3
f1(): 2023-08-28 16:23:22.300595 +0300 EEST m=+3.001225751
f2(): 2023-08-28 16:23:25.302122 +0300 EEST m=+6.002730959
f3(): 2023-08-28 16:23:28.303326 +0300 EEST m=+9.00391262
```

The long lines of the output are the return values of time.After() and show the times that After() sent the current time on the returned channel. All of them denote a normal operation of the program.

If you define a bigger delay, then the output is going to be similar to the following:

```
$ go run useContext.go 13
Delay: 13
f1() Done: context canceled
f2() Done: context canceled
f3() Done: context canceled
```

The point here is that the operation of the program is canceled when there are delays in its execution.

About context.WithCancelCause

The context.WithCancelCause() method was introduced in Go 1.21. Its main advantage is that it gives you customization capabilities, which are not offered by the other methods of the context package. Apart from that, it behaves like WithCancel().

 Similar to context.WithCancelCause(), there exists context.WithTimeoutCause() and context.WithDeadlineCause().

The withCancelCause.go program illustrates the use of context.WithCancelCause().

```go
func main() {
    ctx := context.Background()
    ctx, cancel := context.WithCancelCause(ctx)
    cancel(errors.New("Canceled by timeout"))

    err := takingTooLong(ctx)
    if err != nil {
        fmt.Println(err)
        return
    }
}
```

The implementation of main() contains two important elements. First, we call context. WithCancelCause(), which returns a context, and a CancelCauseFunc() function, which behaves like CancelFunc() while allowing us to define and customize the cancellation cause giving clearer context to the error situation—in this case, the cancellation cause is defined as errors. New("Canceled by timeout"). After that, we call takingTooLong() with the context that we have just defined. If takingTooLong() returns an error that is not nil, we print that error.

```go
func takingTooLong(ctx context.Context) error {
    select {
    case <-time.After(3 * time.Second):
        fmt.Println("Done!")
        return nil
    case <-ctx.Done():
        fmt.Println("Canceled!")
        return context.Cause(ctx)
    }
}
```

The previous function returns either nil or context.Cause(ctx).

Running withCancelCause.go produces the following output:

```
$ go run withCancelCause.go
Canceled!
Canceled by timeout
```

So, as the second part of the select block is executed, takingTooLong() prints Canceled! and main() prints the cancellation reason according to the initialization of context.WithCancelCause().

We are not completely done with context as the next chapter is going to use it to timeout HTTP interactions on the client side of the connection. The next section discusses the semaphore package, which is not part of the standard library.

The semaphore package

This last section of this chapter presents the semaphore package, which is provided by the Go team. A semaphore is a construct that can limit or control the access to a shared resource. As we are talking about Go, *a semaphore can limit the access of goroutines to a shared resource* but, originally, semaphores were used for limiting access to threads. Semaphores can have weights that limit the number of threads or goroutines that can have access to a resource.

The process is supported via the Acquire() and Release() methods, which are defined as follows:

```
func (s *Weighted) Acquire(ctx context.Context, n int64) error
func (s *Weighted) Release(n int64)
```

The second parameter of Acquire() defines the weight of the semaphore. As we are going to use an external package, we need to put the code inside ~/go/src in order to use Go modules: ~/go/src/github.com/mactsouk/mGo4th/ch08/semaphore.

Now, let us present the code of semaphore.go, which shows an implementation of a worker pool using semaphores:

```
package main
import (
    "context"
    "fmt"
    "os"
    "strconv"
    "time"
    "golang.org/x/sync/semaphore"
)
var Workers = 4
```

The Workers variable specifies the maximum number of goroutines that can be executed by this program.

```
var sem = semaphore.NewWeighted(int64(Workers))
```

This is where we define the semaphore with a weight identical to the maximum number of goroutines that can be executed concurrently. This means that no more than Workers goroutines can acquire the semaphore at the same time.

```
func worker(n int) int {
    square := n * n
    time.Sleep(time.Second)
    return square
}
```

The worker() function is run as part of a goroutine. However, as we are using a semaphore, there is no need to return the results to a channel.

```
func main() {
```

```
    if len(os.Args) != 2 {
        fmt.Println("Need #jobs!")
        return
    }
    nJobs, err := strconv.Atoi(os.Args[1])
    if err != nil {
        fmt.Println(err)
        return
    }
```

The previous code reads the number of jobs that we want to run.

```
    // Where to store the results
    var results = make([]int, nJobs)
    // Needed by Acquire()
    ctx := context.TODO()
    for i := range results {
        err = sem.Acquire(ctx, 1)
        if err != nil {
            fmt.Println("Cannot acquire semaphore:", err)
            break
        }
```

In this part, we try to acquire the semaphore as many times as the number of jobs defined by nJobs. If nJobs is bigger than Workers, then the Acquire() call is going to block and wait for Release() calls in order to unblock.

```
        go func(i int) {
            defer sem.Release(1)
            temp := worker(i)
            results[i] = temp
        }(i)
    }
```

This is where we run the goroutines that do the job and write the results to the results slice. As each goroutine writes to a different slice element, there are not any race conditions.

```
    err = sem.Acquire(ctx, int64(Workers))
    if err != nil {
```

```
        fmt.Println(err)
    }
```

This is a clever trick: we acquire all of the tokens so that the sem.Acquire() call blocks until all workers/goroutines have finished. This is similar in functionality to a Wait() call.

```
    for k, v := range results {
        fmt.Println(k, "->", v)
    }
}
```

The last part of the program is about printing the results. After writing the code, we need to run the following commands to get the required Go modules:

```
$ go mod init
$ go mod tidy
$ mod download golang.org/x/sync
```

Apart from the first command, these commands were indicated by the output of go mod init, so you do not have to remember anything.

Lastly, running semaphore.go produces the following output:

```
$ go run semaphore.go 3
0 -> 0
1 -> 1
2 -> 4
```

Each line in the output shows the input value and the output value separated by ->. The use of the semaphore keeps things in order.

Making the statistics application concurrent

In this section of this chapter, we are going to convert the statistics application into a concurrent application that uses goroutines. However, instead of using channels, we are going to use a different approach that prevents deadlocks, while making the overall design of the program much simpler. Apart from that, there is also a version of stats.go named statsNC.go that does not create any goroutines and processes the input files sequentially.

We are only going to present the implementation of the `main()` function of `stats.go` because this is where the logic of the utility is found. However, minor additional changes exist for taking advantage of goroutines. The most time-consuming part of `stats.go` is the normalization of the time series.

 What is impressive is that we converted `stats.go` into a concurrent application using a minimal amount of changes that mainly have to do with goroutine synchronization—this is a good indication of great design.

The implementation of `main()` is the following:

```
func main() {
    if len(os.Args) == 1 {
        fmt.Println("Need one or more file paths!")
        return
    }

    var waitGroup sync.WaitGroup
    files = make(DFslice, len(os.Args))
```

So far, we have a `sync.WaitGroup` variable for synchronizing the goroutines. Additionally, we have a slice variable named `files` that has as many elements as the length of the `os.Args` slice—`files[0]` is not going to be used.

The remaining code of `main()` is the following:

```
    for i := 1; i < len(os.Args); i++ {
        waitGroup.Add(1)

        go func(x int) {
            process(os.Args[x], x)
            defer waitGroup.Done()
        }(i)
    }

    waitGroup.Wait()
}
```

What do we have here? There is an anonymous function that runs as a goroutine. That anonymous function requires a single parameter, which is *the index of the command line argument that is being processed*. There is a handy property that comes with that index: that index is unique, which means that we can use that unique index when we put data into the files slice—this process takes place inside process(). This resolves any potential race conditions as each goroutine uses a different place in files. Keep in mind that files[0] is not being used but we have decided to make files bigger than needed in order to put the data for the first command line argument in files[1], and so on.

Apart from that, we use sync to wait for all goroutines to finish before exiting the program.

In order to compare stats.go with statsNC.go, we are going to use bigger datasets, which are all stored in the ./ch08/dataset directory. The sizes of the three data files can be seen in the following output:

```
$ wc dataset/*
 1518653 1518653 4119086 dataset/1.5M
 2531086 2531086 6918628 dataset/2.5M
 4049739 4049739 11037714 dataset/4.0M
 8099478 8099478 22075428 total
```

A quick and dirty way to calculate the execution time of a program is using the time(1) UNIX utility. Using that utility, we are going to compare the execution time of ./ch05/stats.go with ./ch05/stats.go and see what happens:

```
$ time go run stats.go ./dataset/* ./dataset/* ./dataset/*
real    0m1.240s
user    0m6.259s
sys     0m0.528s
$ time go run statsNC.go ./dataset/* ./dataset/* ./dataset/*
real    0m3.267s
user    0m7.766s
sys     0m0.535s
```

What is important in the output is the values in the lines that begin with real. The concurrent version is about *three times faster* than the non-concurrent version when processing nine files. Imagine using even bigger datasets and having to process 1,000 datasets instead of just nine!

Summary

In this important chapter, we talked about Go concurrency, goroutines, channels, the `select` keyword, shared memory, and mutexes, as well as timing out goroutines and the use of the `context` package. Bear in mind that although goroutines can process data and execute commands, they cannot communicate with each other directly but they can communicate in other ways, including channels, local sockets, and shared memory.

Remember that OS threads are controlled by the OS scheduler, whereas goroutines executed in one or more OS threads are controlled by the Go runtime. The correct terminology for when a goroutine or an OS thread is executed and then paused is *context-switched on and off*, respectively. Keep in mind that the Go scheduler checks the global queue from time to time in order to find out whether there are any goroutines waiting to be assigned to a local queue. If both the global queue and a given local queue are empty, then *work-stealing* takes place.

The main advantage of concurrency is that it allows the splitting of bigger tasks into smaller ones and the execution of each smaller task concurrently. Additionally, concurrency does a great job in distributing multiple HTTP requests among different goroutines. Lastly, concurrency makes better use of modern CPUs with multiple cores and virtual environments. However, concurrency adds complexity to the software design and the code, which affects readability and maintainability. For that reason, you might need to add concurrency last in your code, as we did with the statistics application. One other concern of concurrency is the risk of consuming all available resources making other services unreliable or even unavailable. Lastly, concurrent code is harder to benchmark—if you want to compare two concurrent implementations, it is better to compare their sequential versions that tell more about the actual algorithms and code efficiency.

What is important to remember is that the rational use of concurrency and goroutines is going to allow you to write powerful Go applications. Feel free to experiment with the concepts and the examples of this chapter to better understand goroutines, channels, and shared memory.

The next chapter is all about web services and working with the HTTP protocol in Go. Among other things, we are going to convert the statistics application into a web service.

Exercises

- Try to implement a concurrent version of wc(1) that uses a buffered channel.
- Try to implement a concurrent version of wc(1) that uses shared memory.
- Try to implement a concurrent version of wc(1) that uses semaphores.
- Try to implement a concurrent version of wc(1) that saves its output to a file.

Additional resources

- The documentation page of sync: `https://pkg.go.dev/sync`
- Learn about the `semaphore` package: `https://pkg.go.dev/golang.org/x/sync/semaphore`
- Coroutines for Go: `https://research.swtch.com/coro`
- Learn more about the Go scheduler by reading a series of posts: `https://www.ardanlabs.com/blog/2018/08/scheduling-in-go-part1.html`
- The implementation of the Go scheduler: `https://go.dev/src/runtime/proc.go`

Join our community on Discord

Join our community's Discord space for discussions with the authors and other readers:

`https://discord.gg/FzuQbc8zd6`

9

Building Web Services

The core subject of this chapter is working with HTTP using the net/http package—keep in mind that all web services require a web server to operate. Additionally, in this chapter, we are going to convert the statistics application into a web application that accepts HTTP connections and create a command line client to work with it. In the last part of the chapter, we are going to learn how to time out HTTP connections.

In more detail, this chapter covers:

- The net/http package
- Creating a web server
- Updating the statistics application
- Developing web clients
- Creating a client for the statistics service
- Timing out HTTP connections

The net/http package

The net/http package offers functions that allow you to develop web servers and clients. For example, http.Get() and http.NewRequest() are used by clients to make HTTP requests, whereas http.ListenAndServe() is used to start web servers by specifying the IP address and the TCP port that the server listens to. Additionally, http.HandleFunc() defines supported URLs as well as the functions that are going to handle these URLs.

The next three subsections describe three important data structures of the net/http package—you can use these descriptions as a reference while reading this chapter.

The http.Response type

The http.Response struct embodies the response from an HTTP request—both http.Client and http.Transport return http.Response values once the response headers have been received. Its definition can be found at https://go.dev/src/net/http/response.go:

```
type Response struct {
    Status     string // e.g. "200 OK"
    StatusCode int    // e.g. 200
    Proto      string // e.g. "HTTP/1.0"
    ProtoMajor int    // e.g. 1
    ProtoMinor int    // e.g. 0
    Header Header
    Body io.ReadCloser
    ContentLength int64
    TransferEncoding []string
    Close bool
    Uncompressed bool
    Trailer Header
    Request *Request
    TLS *tls.ConnectionState
}
```

You do not have to use all the structure fields, but it is good to know that they exist. However, some of them, such as Status, StatusCode, and Body, are more important than others. The Go source file, as well as the output of go doc http.Response, contains more information about the purpose of each field, which is also the case with most struct data types found in the standard Go library.

The http.Request type

The http.Request structure represents an HTTP request as constructed by a client in order to be sent or received by an HTTP server. The public fields of http.Request are as follows:

```
type Request struct {
    Method string
    URL *url.URL
    Proto  string
    ProtoMajor int
    ProtoMinor int
    Header Header
```

```
        Body io.ReadCloser
        GetBody func() (io.ReadCloser, error)
        ContentLength int64
        TransferEncoding []string
        Close bool
        Host string
        Form url.Values
        PostForm url.Values
        MultipartForm *multipart.Form
        Trailer Header
        RemoteAddr string
        RequestURI string
        TLS *tls.ConnectionState
        Cancel <-chan struct{}
        Response *Response
    }
```

The Body field holds the body of the request. After reading the body of a request, you are allowed to call GetBody(), which returns a new copy of the body—this is optional.

Let us now present the http.Transport structure.

The http.Transport type

The definition of http.Transport, which gives you more control over your HTTP connections, is fairly long and complex:

```
type Transport struct {
    Proxy func(*Request) (*url.URL, error)
    DialContext func(ctx context.Context, network, addr string) (net.Conn,
error)
    Dial func(network, addr string) (net.Conn, error)
    DialTLSContext func(ctx context.Context, network, addr string) (net.
Conn, error)
    DialTLS func(network, addr string) (net.Conn, error)
    TLSClientConfig *tls.Config
    TLSHandshakeTimeout time.Duration
    DisableKeepAlives bool
    DisableCompression bool
    MaxIdleConns int
```

```
    MaxIdleConnsPerHost int
    MaxConnsPerHost int
    IdleConnTimeout time.Duration
    ResponseHeaderTimeout time.Duration
    ExpectContinueTimeout time.Duration
    TLSNextProto map[string]func(authority string, c *tls.Conn)
RoundTripper
    ProxyConnectHeader Header
    GetProxyConnectHeader func(ctx context.Context, proxyURL *url.URL,
target string) (Header, error)
    MaxResponseHeaderBytes int64
    WriteBufferSize int
    ReadBufferSize int
    ForceAttemptHTTP2 bool
}
```

Keep in mind that http.Transport is *low-level* compared to http.Client. The latter implements
a high-level HTTP client—each http.Client contains a Transport field. If its value is nil, then
DefaultTransport is used. You do not need to use http.Transport in all of your programs, and you
are not required to deal with all of its fields all the time. To learn more about DefaultTransport,
type go doc http.DefaultTransport.

Let us now learn how to develop a web server.

Creating a web server

This section presents a simple web server developed in Go to better understand the principles
behind such applications. Although a web server programmed in Go can do many things effi-
ciently and securely, if what you really need is a powerful web server that supports modules,
multiple websites, and virtual hosts, then you would be better off using a web server such as
Apache, Nginx, or Caddy that is written in Go. Those powerful web servers typically are in front
of Go application servers.

You might ask why the presented web server uses HTTP instead of secure HTTP (HTTPS). The
answer to this question is simple: most Go web servers are deployed as Docker images and are
hidden behind web servers, such as Caddy and Nginx, that provide the secure HTTP operation
part using the appropriate security credentials. It does not make any sense to use the secure HTTP
protocol along with the required security credentials without knowing how, and under which
domain name, an application is going to be deployed.

This is a common practice in microservices as well as regular web applications that are deployed as Docker images. So this is a design decision that is a common practice for such cases. However, your requirements might differ.

The net/http package offers functions and data types that allow you to develop powerful web servers and clients. The http.Set() and http.Get() methods can be used to make HTTP and HTTPS requests, whereas http.ListenAndServe() is used for creating web servers given the user-specified handler function or functions that handle incoming requests. As most web services require support for multiple endpoints, you end up needing multiple discrete functions to handle incoming requests, which also leads to the better design of your services.

 The simplest way to define the supported endpoints, as well as the handler function that responds to each client request, is with the use of http.HandleFunc(), which can be called multiple times.

After this quick and somewhat theoretical introduction, it is time to begin talking about more practical topics, beginning with the implementation of a simple web server, as illustrated in wwwServer.go:

```go
package main
import (
    "fmt"
    "net/http"
    "os"
    "time"
)

func myHandler(w http.ResponseWriter, r *http.Request) {
    fmt.Fprintf(w, "Serving: %s\n", r.URL.Path)
    fmt.Printf("Served: %s\n", r.Host)
}
```

This is a handler function that sends a message back to the client using the w http.ResponseWriter, which is an interface that implements io.Writer and is used to send the server response.

```go
func timeHandler(w http.ResponseWriter, r *http.Request) {
    t := time.Now().Format(time.RFC1123)
    Body := "The current time is:"
    fmt.Fprintf(w, "<h1 align=\"center\">%s</h1>", Body)
```

```
        fmt.Fprintf(w, "<h2 align=\"center\">%s</h2>\n", t)
        fmt.Fprintf(w, "Serving: %s\n", r.URL.Path)
        fmt.Printf("Served time for: %s\n", r.Host)

}
```

This is another handler function called `timeHandler` that returns the current time in the HTML format. All `fmt.Fprintf()` calls send data back to the HTTP client, whereas the output of `fmt.Printf()` is printed on the terminal that the web server runs on. The first argument of `fmt.Fprintf()` is the `w http.ResponseWriter`, which implements `io.Writer` and, therefore, can accept data for writing.

```
func main() {
    PORT := ":8001"
```

This is where you define the port number that your web server is going to listen to.

```
        arguments := os.Args
        if len(arguments) != 1 {
            PORT = ":" + arguments[1]
        }
        fmt.Println("Using port number: ", PORT)
```

 If you use port number 0, you are going to get a randomly selected free port, which is pretty handy for testing or when you do not want to specify the port yourself.

If you do not want to use the predefined port number (8001), then you should provide `wwwServer.go` with your own port number as a command line argument.

```
        http.HandleFunc("/time", timeHandler)
        http.HandleFunc("/", myHandler)
```

So, the web server supports the `/time` URL as well as `/`. The `/` path matches every URL not matched by other handlers. The fact that we associate `myHandler()` with `/` makes `myHandler()` the default handler function.

```
        err := http.ListenAndServe(PORT, nil)
        if err != nil {

            fmt.Fprintln(os.Stderr, err)
```

```
        os.Exit(1)
    }
}
```

The http.ListenAndServe() call begins the HTTP server using the predefined port number. As there is no hostname given in the PORT string, the web server is going to listen to all available network interfaces. The port number and the hostname should be separated with a colon (:), which should be there even if there is no hostname—in that case, the server listens to all available network interfaces and, therefore, all supported hostnames. This is the reason that the value of PORT is :8001 instead of just 8001.

Part of the net/http package is the ServeMux struct (go doc http.ServeMux), which is an HTTP request multiplexer that provides a slightly different way of defining handler functions and endpoints than the default one, which is used in wwwServer.go. So if we do not create and configure our own ServeMux variable, then http.HandleFunc() uses DefaultServeMux, which is the default ServeMux. So in this case, we are going to implement the web service using the default Go router—this is the reason that the second parameter of http.ListenAndServe() is nil.

Running wwwServer.go and interacting with it using curl(1) produces the following output:

```
$ go run wwwServer.go
Using port number:  :8001
Served: localhost:8001
Served time for: localhost:8001
Served: localhost:8001
```

Note that as wwwServer.go does not terminate automatically, you need to stop it on your own.

On the curl(1) side, the interaction looks as follows:

```
$ curl localhost:8001
Serving: /
```

In this first case, we visit the / path of the web server, and we are served by myHandler().

```
$ curl localhost:8001/time
<h1 align="center">The current time is:</h1><h2 align="center">Thu, 31 Aug
2023 22:37:37 EEST</h2>
Serving: /time
```

In this case, we visit /time, and we get HTML output back from `timeHandler()`.

```
$ curl localhost:8001/doesNotExist
Serving: /doesNotExist
```

In this last case, we visit /doesNotExist, which does not exist. As this cannot be matched by any other path, it is served by the default handler, which is the `myHandler()` function.

The next section is about making the statistics application a web application!

Updating the statistics application

This time, the statistics application is going to work as a web service. The two main tasks that need to be performed are defining the API along with the endpoints and implementing the API. A third task that needs to be determined concerns data exchange between the application server and its clients. There exist many approaches regarding data exchange between the server and its clients. We are going to discuss the following four ways:

- Using plain text
- Using HTML
- Using JSON
- Using a hybrid approach that combines plain text and JSON data

As JSON is explored in *Chapter 11, Working with REST APIs*, and HTML might not be the best option for a service because you need to separate the data from the HTML tags and parse the data, we are going to use the first approach. Therefore, the service is going to work with plain text data. We begin by defining the API that supports the operation of the statistics application.

Defining the API

The API has support for the following URLs:

- /list: This lists all available entries.
- /insert/name/d1/d2/d3/.../: This inserts a new dataset. Later in this chapter, we are going to see how to extract the desired information from a URL that contains user data and parameters. The key point here is that the number of elements in a dataset varies so the URL is going to contain a variable number of values.
- /delete/name/: This deletes an entry based on the name of the dataset.
- /search/name/: This searches for an entry based on the dataset name.
- /status: This is an extra URL that returns the number of entries in the statistics application.

The list of endpoints does not follow standard REST conventions—all these are going to be presented in *Chapter 11, Working with REST APIs*.

This time, ***we are not using the default Go router***, which means that we define and configure our own `http.NewServeMux()` variable. This changes the way we provide handler functions: a handler function with the `func(http.ResponseWriter, *http.Request)` signature has to be converted into an `http.HandlerFunc` type and used by the `ServeMux` type and its own `Handle()` method. Therefore, when using a different `ServeMux` than the default one, we should do that conversion explicitly by calling `http.HandlerFunc()`, which makes the `http.HandlerFunc` type act as an adapter that allows the use of ordinary functions as HTTP handlers, provided that they have the required signature. This is not a problem when using the default Go router (`DefaultServeMux`) because the `http.HandleFunc()` function does that conversion automatically and internally. However, you can also use the `HandleFunc()` method from the `ServeMux` type to do the same implicit conversion.

> To make things clearer, the `http.HandlerFunc` type has support for a method named `HandlerFunc()`—both the type and method are defined in the `http` package. The similarly named `http.HandleFunc()` function (without an r) is used with the default Go router.

As an example, for the `/time` endpoint and the `timeHandler()` handler function, you should call `mux.Handle()` as `mux.Handle("/time", http.HandlerFunc(timeHandler))`. If you were using `http.HandleFunc()` and, as a consequence, `DefaultServeMux`, then you should have called `http.HandleFunc("/time", timeHandler)` instead.

The subject of the next subsection is the implementation of the HTTP endpoints.

Implementing the handlers

The new version of the statistics application is going to be created inside `~/go/src`: `~/go/src/github.com/mactsouk/mGo4th/ch09/server`. As expected, you also need to do the following:

```
$ cd ~/go/src/github.com/mactsouk/mGo4th/ch09/server
$ touch handlers.go
$ touch stats.go
```

> If you use the GitHub repository of the book, you are not going to need to create the server from scratch, as the Go code is already there.

The stats.go file holds the code that defines the operation of the web server. Usually, handlers are put in a separate external package, but for reasons of simplicity, we have decided to put handlers in a separate file named handlers.go within the same package. The contents of the handlers.go file, which contains all functionality related to the serving of the clients, are as follows:

```go
package main
import (
    "fmt"
    "log"
    "net/http"
    "strconv"
    "strings"
)
```

All required packages for handlers.go are imported, even if some of them have already been imported by stats.go. Note that the name of the package is main, which is also the case for stats.go.

```go
const PORT = ":1234"
```

This is the default port number that the HTTP server listens to.

```go
func defaultHandler(w http.ResponseWriter, r *http.Request) {
    log.Println("Serving:", r.URL.Path, "from", r.Host)
    w.WriteHeader(http.StatusOK)
    body := "Thanks for visiting!\n"
    fmt.Fprintf(w, "%s", body)
}
```

This is the default handler, which serves all requests that are not a match for any of the other handlers. Next is the handler for deleting entries:

```go
func deleteHandler(w http.ResponseWriter, r *http.Request) {
    // Get dataset
    paramStr := strings.Split(r.URL.Path, "/")
    fmt.Println("Path:", paramStr)
    if len(paramStr) < 3 {
        w.WriteHeader(http.StatusNotFound)
        fmt.Fprintln(w, "Not found:", r.URL.Path)
        return
    }
```

This is the handler function for the /delete path, which begins by splitting the URL in order to read the desired information. If we do not have enough parameters, we should send an error message back to the client with the appropriate HTTP code, which in this case is http.StatusNotFound. You can use any HTTP code you want as long as it makes sense. The WriteHeader() method sends back a header with the provided status code, before writing the body of the response.

```
log.Println("Serving:", r.URL.Path, "from", r.Host)
```

This is where the HTTP server sends data to log files—this mainly happens for debugging reasons.

```
dataset := paramStr[2]
err := deleteEntry(dataset)
if err != nil {
    fmt.Println(err)
    Body := err.Error() + "\n"
    w.WriteHeader(http.StatusNotFound)
    fmt.Fprintf(w, "%s", Body)
    return
}
```

As the delete process is based on the dataset name, all that is required is a valid dataset name. This is where the parameter is read after splitting the provided URL. If the deleteEntry() function returns an error, then we construct a fitting response and send it to the client.

```
    body := dataset + " deleted!\n"
    w.WriteHeader(http.StatusOK)
    fmt.Fprintf(w, "%s", body)
}
```

At this point, we know that the delete operation was successful, so we send a proper message to the client as well as the http.StatusOK status code. Type go doc http.StatusOK for the list of codes.

Next up is the implementation of listHandler():

```
func listHandler(w http.ResponseWriter, r *http.Request) {
    log.Println("Serving:", r.URL.Path, "from", r.Host)
    w.WriteHeader(http.StatusOK)
    body := list()
    fmt.Fprintf(w, "%s", body)
}
```

The list() helper function that is used in the /list path cannot fail. Therefore, http.StatusOK is always returned when serving /list. However, sometimes the return value of list() can be the empty string.

Next, we implement statusHandler():

```go
func statusHandler(w http.ResponseWriter, r *http.Request) {
    log.Println("Serving:", r.URL.Path, "from", r.Host)
    w.WriteHeader(http.StatusOK)
    body := fmt.Sprintf("Total entries: %d\n", len(data))
    fmt.Fprintf(w, "%s", body)
}
```

The preceding code defines the handler function for /status. It just returns information about the total number of entries found in the statistics application. It can be used to verify that the web service works fine.

Next, we present the implementation of the insertHandler() handler:

```go
func insertHandler(w http.ResponseWriter, r *http.Request) {
    paramStr := strings.Split(r.URL.Path, "/")
    fmt.Println("Path:", paramStr)

    if len(paramStr) < 4 {
        w.WriteHeader(http.StatusBadRequest)
        fmt.Fprintln(w, "Not enough arguments: "+r.URL.Path)
        return
    }
```

As before, we need to split the given URL in order to extract the information. In this case, we need at least four elements, as we are trying to insert a new dataset into the statistics service.

```go
    dataset := paramStr[2]

    // These are string values
    dataStr := paramStr[3:]
    data := make([]float64, 0)

    for _, v := range dataStr {
        val, err := strconv.ParseFloat(v, 64)
        if err == nil {
```

```
                data = append(data, val)
        }
    }
```

In the previous code, we initialize the `dataset` variable and read the data elements, which have a variable length. In this case, we also need to convert the data elements into `float64` values because they are read as text.

```
    entry := process(dataset, data)
    err := insert(&entry)

    if err != nil {
        w.WriteHeader(http.StatusNotModified)
        Body := "Failed to add record\n"
        fmt.Fprintf(w, "%s", Body)
    } else {
        Body := "New record added successfully\n"
        w.WriteHeader(http.StatusOK)
        fmt.Fprintf(w, "%s", Body)
    }

    log.Println("Serving:", r.URL.Path, "from", r.Host)
}
```

This is the end of the handler for `/insert`. The last part of the implementation of `insertHandler()` deals with the return value of `insert()`. If there was not an error, then `http.StatusOK` is sent to the client. In the opposite case, `http.StatusNotModified` is returned to signify that there was not a change in the statistics application. It is the job of the client to examine the status code of the interaction, but it is the job of the server to send an appropriate status code back to the client.

Next, we implement `searchHandler()`:

```
func searchHandler(w http.ResponseWriter, r *http.Request) {
    // Get Search value from URL
    paramStr := strings.Split(r.URL.Path, "/")
    fmt.Println("Path:", paramStr)

    if len(paramStr) < 3 {
        w.WriteHeader(http.StatusNotFound)
        fmt.Fprintln(w, "Not found: "+r.URL.Path)
```

```
        return
    }
    var body string
    dataset := paramStr[2]
```

At this point, we extract the dataset name from the URL, as we did with /delete.

```
    t := search(dataset)
    if t == nil {
        w.WriteHeader(http.StatusNotFound)
        body = "Could not be found: " + dataset + "\n"
    } else {
        w.WriteHeader(http.StatusOK)
        body = fmt.Sprintf("%s %d %f %f\n", t.Name, t.Len, t.Mean,
t.StdDev)
    }

    log.Println("Serving:", r.URL.Path, "from", r.Host)
    fmt.Fprintf(w, "%s", body)
}
```

The last function of handlers.go ends here and is about the /search endpoint. The search() helper function checks whether the given input exists in the data records or not and acts accordingly.

Additionally, the implementation of the main() function, which can be found in stats.go, is the following:

```
func main() {
    err := readJSONFile(JSONFILE)
    if err != nil && err != io.EOF {
        fmt.Println("Error:", err)
        return
    }
    createIndex()
```

This first part of main() relates to the proper initialization of the statistics application. Internally, data is stored in the JSON format.

```
    mux := http.NewServeMux()
    s := &http.Server{
```

```
        Addr:        PORT,
        Handler:     mux,
        IdleTimeout: 10 * time.Second,
        ReadTimeout: time.Second,
        WriteTimeout: time.Second,
    }
```

Here, we store the parameters of the HTTP server in the `http.Server` structure and use our own `http.NewServeMux()` instead of the default one.

```
    mux.Handle("/list", http.HandlerFunc(listHandler))
    mux.Handle("/insert/", http.HandlerFunc(insertHandler))
    mux.Handle("/insert", http.HandlerFunc(insertHandler))
    mux.Handle("/search", http.HandlerFunc(searchHandler))
    mux.Handle("/search/", http.HandlerFunc(searchHandler))
    mux.Handle("/delete/", http.HandlerFunc(deleteHandler))
    mux.Handle("/status", http.HandlerFunc(statusHandler))
    mux.Handle("/", http.HandlerFunc(defaultHandler))
```

This is the list of the supported URLs. Note that /search and /search/ are both handled by the same handler function even though /search is going to fail, as it does not include the required data. On the other hand, /delete/ is handled differently—this will be apparent when testing the application. As we are using `http.NewServeMux()` and not the default Go router, we need to use `http.HandlerFunc()` when defining the handler functions.

```
    fmt.Println("Ready to serve at", PORT)
    err = s.ListenAndServe()
    if err != nil {
        fmt.Println(err)
        return
    }
}
```

 As mentioned earlier in this chapter, each `mux.Handle()` call can be replaced by an equivalent `mux.HandleFunc()` call. So `mux.Handle("/list", http.HandlerFunc(listHandler))` is going to become `mux.HandleFunc("/list", listHandler)`. The same applies to all the other `mux.Handle()` calls.

The ListenAndServe() method starts the HTTP server using the parameters defined previously in the http.Server structure. The rest of stats.go contains helper functions related to the operation of the web service. Note that it is important to save and update the contents of the application as often as possible because this is a live application, and you might lose data if it crashes.

The next command allows you to execute the application—you need to provide both files in go run:

```
$ go run stats.go handlers.go
Ready to serve at :1234
2023/08/31 17:10:10 Serving: /list from localhost:1234
Path: [ delete d1]
2023/08/31 17:10:20 Serving: /delete/d1 from localhost:1234
Path: [ delete d2]
2023/08/31 17:10:22 Serving: /delete/d2 from localhost:1234
Path: [ delete d1]
2023/08/31 17:10:23 Serving: /delete/d1 from localhost:1234
d1 cannot be found!
2023/08/31 17:11:01 Serving: /status from localhost:1234
Path: [ search d3]
2023/08/31 17:11:26 Serving: /search/d3 from localhost:1234
Path: [ search d2]
2023/08/31 17:11:29 Serving: /search/d2 from localhost:1234
Path: [ search d5]
2023/08/31 17:11:30 Serving: /search/d5 from localhost:1234
Path: [ search d4]
2023/08/31 17:11:32 Serving: /search/d4 from localhost:1234
Path: [ insert v1 1.0 2 3 4 5 ]
2023/08/31 17:16:23 Serving: /insert/v1/1.0/2/3/4/5/ from localhost:1234
Path: [ insert v1 1.0 2 3 4 5 ]
2023/08/31 17:16:34 Serving: /insert/v1/1.0/2/3/4/5/ from localhost:1234
Path: [ insert v2 1.0 2 3 4 5 -5 -3 ]
2023/08/31 17:17:21 Serving: /insert/v2/1.0/2/3/4/5/-5/-3/ from
localhost:1234
```

On the client side, which is curl(1), we have the following interactions:

```
$ curl localhost:1234/list
d6    4    2.325000    1.080220
d4    5    2.860000    1.441666
d1    6    2.216667    1.949715
```

```
d2    9    1.000000    0.000000
d0    12   0.333333    0.942809
```

Here, we get all entries from the statistics application by visiting /list:

```
$ curl localhost:1234/delete/d1
d1 deleted!
```

The previous command is going to work if d1 is in the list of existing datasets. If your list is empty or d1 does not exist, you should include it before deleting it.

```
$ curl localhost:1234/delete/d2
d2 deleted!
$ curl localhost:1234/delete/d1
d1 cannot be found!
```

In the previous part, we tried to delete the d1 and d2 datasets. Trying to delete d1 again fails.

```
$ curl localhost:1234/status
Total entries: 3
```

Next, we visit /status and get back the expected output:

```
$ curl localhost:1234/search/d3
Could not be found: d3
$ curl localhost:1234/search/d4
d4 5 2.860000 1.44166
```

First, we search for d3, which does not exist, and then for d4, which exists. In the latter case, the web service returns the data of d4. Now, let us try and visit /delete instead of /delete/:

```
$ curl localhost:1234/delete
<a href="/delete/">Moved Permanently</a>.
```

The presented message was generated by the Go router and tells us that we should try /delete/ instead because /delete was moved permanently. This is the kind of message that we get by not specifically defining both /delete and /delete/ in the routes.

Now, let us insert two datasets:

```
$ curl localhost:1234/insert/v1/1.0/2/3/4/5/
New record added successfully
$ curl localhost:1234/insert/v2/1.0/2/3/4/5/-5/-3/
New record added successfully
```

The previous commands are going to work if both v1 and v2 do not already exist. If we try to insert a dataset with a name that already exists, we get no response back other than 304 - Not Modified.

Everything looks like it is working OK. We can now put the statistics web service online and interact with it using multiple HTTP requests, as the http package uses multiple goroutines to interact with clients—in practice, this means that the statistics application runs concurrently! However, in its current version, there is no protection against data races, which might take place if we try to insert the same dataset more than once at the exact same time.

Later in this chapter, we are going to create a command line client for the statistics server. Additionally, *Chapter 12, Code Testing and Profiling*, shows how to test your code.

The next section shows how to build Docker images for server applications.

Creating a Docker image

This section shows how to convert a Go application into a Docker image—the kind of application we are going to use is an HTTP server that interacts with the outer world. In our case, it is going to be the statistical web service that we have just developed.

The contents of buildDocker, which contains the steps to create a Docker image, are as follows:

```
FROM golang:alpine AS builder


# Install git.
# Git is required for fetching the dependencies.
RUN apk update && apk add --no-cache git


RUN mkdir $GOPATH/src/server
ADD ./stats.go $GOPATH/src/server
ADD ./handlers.go $GOPATH/src/server
WORKDIR $GOPATH/src/server
RUN go mod init
RUN go mod tidy
RUN mkdir /pro
RUN go build -o /pro/server stats.go handlers.go


FROM alpine:latest


RUN mkdir /pro
COPY --from=builder /pro/server /pro/server
```

```
EXPOSE 1234
WORKDIR /pro
CMD ["/pro/server"]
```

After that, we can use the `buildDocker` file to build a Docker image, named goapp, as follows:

```
$ docker build -f buildDocker -t goapp .
. . .
Successfully built 56d0b84b0ab5
Successfully tagged goapp:latest
```

The contents of `docker-compose.yml`, which allows us to use a Docker image, are as follows:

```
version: "3"

services:
  goapp:
    image: goapp
    container_name: goapp
    restart: always
    ports:
      - 1234:1234
    networks:
      - services

networks:
  services:
    driver: bridge
```

What is important in the `docker-compose.yml` file is to use the goapp image name that was created in the previous step.

Having the `docker-compose.yml` at hand, we can use it as follows:

```
$ docker-compose up
[+] Running 2/0
  Network server_services  Created  0.0s
  Container goapp          Created  0.0s
Attaching to goapp
goapp  | Ready to serve at :1234
goapp  | 2023/08/31 13:32:54 Serving: /status from think:1234
```

After that, we are free to interact with the web service using curl(1) or any other similar tool. When done, we can use *Ctrl + C* to stop the Docker image from running.

 The main disadvantage of this particular web service is that once you disable the Docker image, all data is lost—the solution to this problem is simple. You can either store the data in an external database or link the internal Docker data file to a file in the local filesystem. Implementing either of these two solutions is beyond the scope of this chapter.

After learning about HTTP servers, the next section shows how to develop HTTP clients.

Developing web clients

This section shows how to develop HTTP clients, starting with a simplistic version and continuing with a more advanced one. In this simplistic version, all of the work is done by the http.Get() call, which is pretty convenient when you do not want to deal with lots of options and parameters. However, this type of call gives you no flexibility over the process. Notice that http.Get() returns an http.Response value. All this is illustrated in simpleClient.go:

```
package main

import (
    "fmt"
    "io"
    "net/http"
    "os"
    "path/filepath"
)

func main() {
    if len(os.Args) != 2 {
        fmt.Printf("Usage: %s URL\n", filepath.Base(os.Args[0]))
        return
    }
```

The filepath.Base() function returns the last element of a path. When given os.Args[0] as its parameter, it returns the name of the executable binary file.

```
    URL := os.Args[1]
    data, err := http.Get(URL)
```

In the previous two statements, we get the URL and its data using `http.Get()`, which returns an `*http.Response` and an error variable. The `*http.Response` value contains all the information, so you do not need to make any additional calls to `http.Get()`.

```
if err != nil {
    fmt.Println(err)
    return
}
_, err = io.Copy(os.Stdout, data.Body)
```

The `io.Copy()` function reads from the `data.Body` reader, which contains the body of the server response, and writes the data to `os.Stdout`. As `os.Stdout` is always open, you do not need to open it for writing. Therefore, all data is written to standard output, which is usually the terminal window:

```
if err != nil {
    fmt.Println(err)
    return
}
data.Body.Close()
}
```

Last, we close the `data.Body` reader to make the work of garbage collection easier.

Working with `simpleClient.go` produces the following kind of output, which in this case is abbreviated:

```
$ go run simpleClient.go https://www.golang.org
<!DOCTYPE html>
<html lang="en" data-theme="auto">
<head>
<link rel="preconnect" href="https://www.googletagmanager.com">
...
</body>
</html>
```

Although `simpleClient.go` does the job of verifying that the given URL exists and is reachable, it offers no control over the process. The next subsection develops an advanced HTTP client that processes the server response.

Using http.NewRequest() to improve the client

As the web client of the previous section is relatively simplistic and does not give you any flexibility, in this subsection, you will learn how to read a URL without using the http.Get() function and by having more options. However, the extra flexibility comes at a cost, as you must write more code.

The code of wwwClient.go is as follows:

```go
package main

import (
    "fmt"
    "net/http"
    "net/http/httputil"
    "net/url"
    "os"
    "path/filepath"
    "strings"
    "time"
)

func main() {
    if len(os.Args) != 2 {
        fmt.Printf("Usage: %s URL\n", filepath.Base(os.Args[0]))
        return
    }
```

Although using filepath.Base() is not necessary, it makes your output more professional.

```go
    URL, err := url.Parse(os.Args[1])
    if err != nil {
        fmt.Println("Error in parsing:", err)
        return
    }
```

The url.Parse() function parses a string into a URL structure. This means that if the given argument is not a valid URL, url.Parse() is going to notice. As usual, we need to check the error variable.

```go
    c := &http.Client{
        Timeout: 15 * time.Second,
```

```
        }
        request, err := http.NewRequest(http.MethodGet, URL.String(), nil)
        if err != nil {
            fmt.Println("Get:", err)
            return
        }
```

The `http.NewRequest()` function returns an `http.Request` object when provided with a method, a URL, and an optional body. The `http.MethodGet` parameter defines that we want to retrieve the data using a GET HTTP method, whereas `URL.String()` returns the `string` value of an `http.URL` variable.

```
        httpData, err := c.Do(request)
        if err != nil {
            fmt.Println("Error in Do():", err)
            return
        }
```

The `http.Do()` function sends an HTTP request (`http.Request`) using an `http.Client` and gets an `http.Response` back. So `http.Do()` does the job of `http.Get()` in a more detailed way:

```
        fmt.Println("Status code:", httpData.Status)
```

`httpData.Status` holds the HTTP status code of the response—this is important because it allows you to understand what really happened with the request.

```
        header, _ := httputil.DumpResponse(httpData, false)
        fmt.Print(string(header))
```

The `httputil.DumpResponse()` function is used here to get the response from the server and is mainly used for debugging purposes. The second argument of `httputil.DumpResponse()` is a Boolean value that specifies whether the function is going to include the body or not in its output—in our case, it is set to `false`, which excludes the response body from the output and only prints the header. If you want to do the same on the server side, you should use `httputil.DumpRequest()`.

```
        contentType := httpData.Header.Get("Content-Type")
        characterSet := strings.SplitAfter(contentType, "charset=")
        if len(characterSet) > 1 {
            fmt.Println("Character Set:", characterSet[1])
        }
```

Here, we find out about the character set of the response by searching the value of Content-Type:

```
if httpData.ContentLength == -1 {
    fmt.Println("ContentLength is unknown!")
} else {
    fmt.Println("ContentLength:", httpData.ContentLength)
}
```

Next, we try to get the content length from the response by reading httpData.ContentLength. However, if the value is not set, we print a relevant message:

```
length := 0
var buffer [1024]byte
r := httpData.Body
for {
    n, err := r.Read(buffer[0:])
    if err != nil {
        fmt.Println(err)
            break
    }
    length = length + n
}
fmt.Println("Calculated response data length:", length)
}
```

In the last part of the program, we use a technique for discovering the size of the server HTTP response on our own. If we wanted to display the HTML output on our screen, we could have printed the contents of the r buffer variable.

Working with wwwClient.go and visiting https://www.golang.org produces the following output:

```
$ go run wwwClient.go https://www.golang.org
Status code: 200 OK
```

The previous is the output of fmt.Println("Status code:", httpData.Status).

Next, we see the output of the fmt.Print(string(header)) statement with the header data of the HTTP server response:

```
HTTP/2.0 200 OK
Cache-Control: private
```

```
Content-Security-Policy: connect-src 'self' www.google-analytics.com
stats.g.doubleclick.net ; default-src 'self' ; font-src 'self' fonts.
googleapis.com fonts.gstatic.com data: ; frame-ancestors 'self' ;
frame-src 'self' www.google.com feedback.googleusercontent.com www.
googletagmanager.com scone-pa.clients6.google.com www.youtube.com player.
vimeo.com ; img-src 'self' www.google.com www.google-analytics.com ssl.
gstatic.com www.gstatic.com gstatic.com data: * ; object-src 'none' ;
script-src 'self' 'sha256-n6OdwTrm52KqKm6aHYgD0TFUdMgww4a0GQlIAVrMz
ck=' 'sha256-4ryYrf7Y5daLOBv0CpYtyBIcJPZkRD2eBPdfqsN3r1M=' 'sha256-sVK
X08+SqOmnWhiySYk3xC7RDUgKyAkmbXV2GWts4fo=' www.google.com apis.google.
com www.gstatic.com gstatic.com support.google.com www.googletagmanager.
com www.google-analytics.com ssl.google-analytics.com tagmanager.google.
com ; style-src 'self' 'unsafe-inline' fonts.googleapis.com feedback.
googleusercontent.com www.gstatic.com gstatic.com tagmanager.google.com ;
Content-Type: text/html; charset=utf-8
Date: Fri, 01 Sep 2023 19:12:13 GMT
Server: Google Frontend
Strict-Transport-Security: max-age=31536000; includeSubDomains; preload
Vary: Accept-Encoding
X-Cloud-Trace-Context: 63a0ba25023e0ff4d5b5ccb87ef286bc
```

The last part of the output is about the character set of the interaction (utf-8) and the content length of the response (61870), as calculated by the code:

```
Character Set: utf-8
ContentLength is unknown!
EOF
Calculated response data length: 61870
```

Let us now see a technique to fetch multiple addresses concurrently.

Using errGroup

In this section, we are going to use the errGroup package to fetch multiple URLs concurrently, using the golang.org/x/sync/errgroup external package. For that reason, eGroup.go is located at ~/go/src/github.com/mactsouk/mGo4th/ch09/eGroup.

The code of eGroup.go is presented in two parts. The first part is the following:

```
package main

import (
```

```
    "fmt"
    "net/http"
    "os"

    "golang.org/x/sync/errgroup"
)

func main() {
    if len(os.Args) == 1 {
        fmt.Println("Not enough arguments!")
        return
    }

    g := new(errgroup.Group)
```

We use the errgroup.Group variable, which is a collection of goroutines that work on parts of the same bigger task. In general, the errgroup package provides synchronization, error propagation, and Context cancelation for goroutines that work on subtasks of the same task that we want to treat as a group.

The second part of eGroup.go comes with the following code:

```
    for _, url := range os.Args[1:] {
        url := url
        g.Go(func() error {
            resp, err := http.Get(url)
            if err != nil {
                return err
            }
            defer resp.Body.Close()
            fmt.Println(url, "is OK.")
            return nil
        })
    }

    err := g.Wait()
    if err != nil {
        fmt.Println("Error:", err)
        return
```

```
        }

    fmt.Println("Everything went fine!")
}
```

In this part, we use g.Go() to call the desired function as a goroutine. Additionally, we use a *closured variable* for the url variable so that each goroutine processes the desired URL correctly.

As expected, we need to run the following two commands first:

```
$ go mod init
$ go mod tidy
```

Running eGroup.go on my macOS machine generates the following output:

```
$ go run eGroup.go https://golang.org https://www.mtsoukalos.eu/
https://www.mtsoukalos.eu/ is OK.
https://golang.org is OK.
Everything went fine!
```

Running the same command on my Arch Linux machine produces a different output:

```
$ go run eGroup.go https://golang.org https://www.mtsoukalos.eu/
https://golang.org is OK.
Error: Get "https://www.mtsoukalos.eu/": tls: failed to verify
certificate: x509: certificate signed by unknown authority
```

The next section shows how to create a command line client for the statistics web service we developed earlier.

Creating a client for the statistics service

In this subsection, we create a command line utility that interacts with the statistics web service that was developed earlier in this chapter. This version of the statistics client is going to be created using the cobra package, and as expected, it is going to go under ~/go/src: ~/go/src/ github.com/mactsouk/mGo4th/ch09/client. The previous directory contains the final version of the client. The initial steps for creating the client are the following:

```
$ cd ~/go/src/github.com/mactsouk/mGo4th/ch09/client
$ go mod init
$ ~/go/bin/cobra init
$ ~/go/bin/cobra add search
```

```
$ ~/go/bin/cobra add insert
$ ~/go/bin/cobra add delete
$ ~/go/bin/cobra add status
$ ~/go/bin/cobra add list
```

So, we have a command line utility with five commands, named search, insert, delete, status, and list. After that, we need to implement the commands and define their local parameters in order to interact with the statistics server.

Now, let us see the implementations of the commands, starting from the implementation of the init() function of the root.go file because this is where the global command line parameters are defined:

```
func init() {
    rootCmd.PersistentFlags().StringP("server", "S", "localhost",
"Server")
    rootCmd.PersistentFlags().StringP("port", "P", "1234", "Port number")
    viper.BindPFlag("server", rootCmd.PersistentFlags().Lookup("server"))
    viper.BindPFlag("port", rootCmd.PersistentFlags().Lookup("port"))
}
```

So, we define two global parameters named server and port, which are the hostname and the port number of the server, respectively. Both parameters have an alias and are handled by viper.

Let us now examine the implementation of the status command as found in status.go:

```
SERVER := viper.GetString("server")
PORT := viper.GetString("port")
```

All commands read the values of the server and port command line parameters to get information about the server, and the status command is no exception:

```
// Create request
URL := "http://" + SERVER + ":" + PORT + "/status"
```

After that, we construct the full URL of the request.

```
data, err := http.Get(URL)
if err != nil {
    fmt.Println(err)
    return
}
```

Then, we send a GET request to the server using `http.Get()`.

```
// Check HTTP Status Code
if data.StatusCode != http.StatusOK {
    fmt.Println("Status code:", data.StatusCode)
    return
}
```

After that, we check the HTTP status code of the request to make sure that everything is OK.

```
// Read data
responseData, err := io.ReadAll(data.Body)
if err != nil {
    fmt.Println(err)
    return
}
fmt.Print(string(responseData))
```

If everything is OK, we read the entire body of the server response, which is a byte slice, and print it onscreen as a string. The implementation of `list` is almost identical to the implementation of `status`. The only differences are that the implementation is found in `list.go` and that the full URL is constructed as follows:

```
URL := "http://" + SERVER + ":" + PORT + "/list"
```

After that, let us see how the `delete` command is implemented in `delete.go`:

```
SERVER := viper.GetString("server")
PORT := viper.GetString("port")

dataset, _ := cmd.Flags().GetString("dataset")
if dataset == "" {
    fmt.Println("Number is empty!")
    return
}
```

Apart from reading the values of the `server` and `port` global parameters, we read the value of the `dataset` parameter. If `dataset` has no value, the command returns this.

```
URL := "http://" + SERVER + ":" + PORT + "/delete/" + dataset
```

Once again, we construct the full URL of the request before connecting to the server.

```
data, err := http.Get(URL)
if err != nil {
    fmt.Println(err)
    return
}
```

The previous code sends the client request to the server.

```
if data.StatusCode != http.StatusOK {
    fmt.Println("Status code:", data.StatusCode)
    return
}
```

If there is an error in the server response, the delete command prints the HTTP error and terminates.

```
responseData, err := io.ReadAll(data.Body)
if err != nil {
    fmt.Println(err)
    return
}

fmt.Print(string(responseData))
```

If everything was fine, the server response text is printed on the screen.

 The init() function of delete.go contains the definition of the local dataset command line parameter to get the dataset name to delete.

Next, let us learn more about the search command and how it is implemented in search.go. The implementation is the same as in delete except for the full request URL:

```
URL := "http://" + SERVER + ":" + PORT + "/search/" + dataset
```

The search command also supports the dataset command line parameter in getting the dataset name to search for—this is defined in the init() function of search.go.

The last command that is presented is the `insert` command, which supports two local command line parameters that are defined in the `init()` function in `insert.go`:

```
insertCmd.Flags().StringP("dataset", "d", "", "Dataset name")
insertCmd.Flags().StringP("values", "v", "", "List of values")
```

These two parameters are needed to get the required user input. However, the value of the `values` parameter is expected to be a comma-separated list of floating-point values—this is the way we define how to get all the elements of a dataset.

The `insert` command is implemented using the following code:

```
SERVER := viper.GetString("server")
PORT := viper.GetString("port")
```

First, we read the server and port global parameters.

```
dataset, _ := cmd.Flags().GetString("dataset")
if dataset == "" {
    fmt.Println("Dataset is empty!")
    return
}

values, _ := cmd.Flags().GetString("values")
if values == "" {
    fmt.Println("No data!")
    return
}
```

Then, we get the values of the two local command line parameters. If either one of them has an empty value, the command returns without sending the request to the server.

```
VALS := strings.Split(values, ",")
vSend := ""
for _, v := range VALS {
    _, err := strconv.ParseFloat(v, 64)
    if err == nil {
        vSend = vSend + "/" + v
    }
}
```

The previous code is very important, as it checks whether the given dataset elements are valid float64 values, and then it creates a string of the /value1/value2/. . ./valueN/ form. This string value is attached to the end of the URL that holds the server request.

```
URL := "http://" + SERVER + ":" + PORT + "/insert/"
URL = URL + "/" + dataset + "/" + vSend + "/"
```

Here, we create the server request in two steps for readability.

```
data, err := http.Get(URL)
if err != nil {
    fmt.Println("**", err)
    return
}
```

Then, we send the request to the server.

```
if data.StatusCode != http.StatusOK {
    fmt.Println("Status code:", data.StatusCode)
    return
}
```

Checking the HTTP status code is always a good practice. Therefore, if everything is OK with the server response, we continue by reading the data. Otherwise, we print the status code, and we exit.

```
responseData, err := io.ReadAll(data.Body)
if err != nil {
    fmt.Println("*", err)
    return
}
fmt.Print(string(responseData))
```

After reading the body of the server response, which is stored in a byte slice, we print it onscreen as a string using string(responseData).

The client application generates the following kind of output:

```
$ go run main.go list
List of entries:
d6    4    2.325000    1.080220
d4    5    2.860000    1.441666
d2    9    1.000000    0.000000
```

```
v1     5     3.000000     1.414214
v2     7     1.000000     3.422614
```

This is the output of the `list` command.

```
$ go run main.go status
Total entries: 5
```

The output of the `status` command informs us about the number of entries in the application.

```
$ go run main.go search -d v1
v1 5 3.000000 1.414214
```

The previous output shows the use of the `search` command when successfully finding a dataset.

```
$ go run main.go search -d notThere
Status code: 404
```

The previous output shows the use of the `search` command when not finding a dataset.

```
$ go run main.go delete -d v1
v1 deleted!
```

This is the output of the `delete` command.

```
$ go run main.go insert -d n1 -v 1,2,3,-4,0,0
New record added successfully
```

This is the operation of the `insert` command. If you try to insert the same dataset name more than once, the server output is going to be `Status code: 304`.

The next section explains how to time out HTTP connections.

Timing out HTTP connections

This section presents techniques for timing out HTTP connections that take too long to finish and work either on the server or the client side.

Using SetDeadline()

The `SetDeadline()` function is used by `net` to set the read and write deadlines of network connections. Due to the way that `SetDeadline()` works, you need to call `SetDeadline()` before any read or write operation. Keep in mind that Go uses deadlines to implement timeouts, so you do not need to reset the timeout every time your application receives or sends any data.

The use of `SetDeadline()` is illustrated in `withDeadline.go` and, more specifically, in the implementation of the `Timeout()` function:

```
var timeout = time.Duration(time.Second)
func Timeout(network, host string) (net.Conn, error) {
    conn, err := net.DialTimeout(network, host, timeout)
    if err != nil {
        return nil, err
    }
    conn.SetDeadline(time.Now().Add(timeout))
    return conn, nil
}
```

The `timeout` global variable defines the timeout period used in the `SetDeadline()` call. The previous function is used in the following code inside `main()`:

```
t := http.Transport{
    Dial: Timeout,
}
client := http.Client{
        Transport: &t,
}
```

So, `http.Transport` uses `Timeout()` in the `Dial` field, and `http.Client` uses `http.Transport`. When you call the `client.Get()` method with the desired URL, which is not shown here, `Timeout` is automatically used because of the `http.Transport` definition. So, if the `Timeout` function returns before the server response is received, we have a timeout.

Using `withDeadline.go` produces the following kind of output:

```
$ go run withDeadline.go http://www.golang.org
Timeout value: 1s
<!DOCTYPE html>
...
```

The call was successful and took less than 1 second to finish, so there was no timeout.

```
$ go run withDeadline.go http://localhost:80
Timeout value: 1s
Get "http://localhost:80": read tcp 127.0.0.1:52492->127.0.0.1:80: i/o
timeout
```

This time, we have a timeout, as the server took too long to answer.

Next, we show how to time out a connection using the `context` package.

Setting the timeout period on the client side

This section presents a technique for timing out network connections that take too long to finish *on the client side*. So if the client does not receive a response from the server in the desired time, it closes the connection. The `timeoutClient.go` source file illustrates the technique.

```
package main
import (
    "context"
    "fmt"
    "io"
    "net/http"
    "os"
    "strconv"
    "time"
)

var delay int = 5
```

In the previous code, we define a global variable named `delay` that holds the delay value.

```
func main() {
    if len(os.Args) == 1 {
        fmt.Println("Need a URL and a delay!")
        os.Exit(1)
    }

    url := os.Args[1]
    if len(os.Args) == 3 {
      t, err := strconv.Atoi(os.Args[2])
      if err != nil {
          fmt.Println(err)
          return
      }
      delay = t
    }
```

```
      fmt.Println("Delay:", delay)
```

The URL is read directly because it is already a string value, whereas the delay period is converted into a numeric value using strconv.Atoi().

The rest of the main() implementation is the following:

```
      ctx, cncl := context.WithTimeout(context.Background(), time.Second *
   time.Duration(delay))
      defer cncl()

      req, err := http.NewRequestWithContext(ctx, http.MethodGet, url, nil)
      if err != nil {
          fmt.Println(err)
          return
      }

      res, err := http.DefaultClient.Do(req.WithContext(ctx))
      if err != nil {
          fmt.Println(err)
          return
      }

      defer res.Body.Close()

      body, err := io.ReadAll(res.Body)
      if err != nil {
          fmt.Println(err)
          return
      }
      fmt.Println(string(body))
   }
```

First, we initialize the ctx context, and then we associate that context with the HTTP request using http.NewRequestWithContext(). If the timeout period is exceeded, the context.Context created with WithTimeout() is going to expire.

Working with timeoutClient.go and having a timeout situation generates the following kind of output:

```
$ go run timeoutClient.go http://localhost:1234 5
Delay: 5
Get "http://localhost:1234": context deadline exceeded
```

The next subsection shows how to time out an HTTP request on the server side.

Setting the timeout period on the server side

This section presents a technique for timing out network connections that take too long to finish *on the server side*. This is much more important than the client side, as a server with too many open connections might not be able to process additional requests unless some of the already open connections close. This usually happens for two reasons. The first reason is software bugs, and the second reason is when a server experiences a **Denial of Service (DoS)** attack!

The `main()` function in `timeoutServer.go` shows the technique:

```go
func main() {
    PORT := ":8001"
    arguments := os.Args
    if len(arguments) != 1 {
        PORT = ":" + arguments[1]
    }
    fmt.Println("Using port number: ", PORT)
    m := http.NewServeMux()
    srv := &http.Server{
        Addr:         PORT,
        Handler:      m,
        ReadTimeout:  3 * time.Second,
        WriteTimeout: 3 * time.Second,
    }
```

This is where the timeout periods are defined. Note that you can define timeout periods for both reading and writing processes. The value of the `ReadTimeout` field specifies the maximum duration allowed to read the entire client request, including the body, whereas the value of the `WriteTimeout` field specifies the maximum time duration before timing out the sending of the client response.

```go
    m.HandleFunc("/time", timeHandler)
    m.HandleFunc("/", myHandler)
    err := srv.ListenAndServe()
    if err != nil {
```

```
        fmt.Println(err)
        return
    }
}
```

Apart from the parameters in the definition of http.Server, the rest of the code is as usual: it contains the handler functions and calls ListenAndServe() to start the HTTP server.

Working with timeoutServer.go generates no output. However, if a client connects to it without sending any requests, the client connection will end after 3 seconds. The same will happen if it takes the client more than 3 seconds to receive the server response.

Summary

In this chapter, we learned how to work with HTTP and how to create Docker images from Go code, as well as how to develop HTTP clients and servers. We have also converted the statistics application into a web application and programmed a command line client for it. Additionally, we learned how to time out HTTP connections.

We are now ready to begin developing powerful and concurrent HTTP applications —however, we are not done yet with HTTP. *Chapter 11, Working with REST APIs*, is going to connect the dots and show how to develop powerful RESTful servers and clients.

But first, we need to learn about working with TCP/IP, TCP, UDP, and WebSocket, which are the subjects of the next chapter.

Exercises

- Modify wwwClient.go to save the HTML output to an external file.
- Use sync.Mutex in order to avoid race conditions in the statistics application.
- Implement a simple version of ab(1) using goroutines and channels. ab(1) is an Apache HTTP server benchmarking tool.

Additional resources

- Caddy server: https://caddyserver.com/
- Nginx server: https://nginx.org/en/
- The net/http package: https://pkg.go.dev/net/http
- Official Docker Go images: https://hub.docker.com/_/golang/

Join our community on Discord

Join our community's Discord space for discussions with the authors and other readers:

`https://discord.gg/FzuQbc8zd6`

10

Working with TCP/IP and WebSocket

TCP/IP is the foundation of the Internet and, therefore, being able to create TCP/IP servers and clients is essential when developing network services. This chapter teaches you how to work with the lower-level protocols of TCP/IP, which are TCP and UDP, with the help of the net package, so that you can develop TCP/IP servers and clients and have more control over their functionality. The Go code of the TCP and UDP utilities included in this chapter allows us to create our own advanced TCP/IP services as the core principles and logic of TCP/IP remain the same.

Additionally, this chapter illustrates the development of servers and clients for the WebSocket protocol, which is based on HTTP, and shows how to interact with RabbitMQ, which is an open-source *message broker*.

The WebSocket protocol provides full-duplex communication channels over a single TCP connection. On the other hand, message brokers such as RabbitMQ and Apache Kafka are famous for their speed, which is the main reason for including them in a workflow that processes lots of data.

In more detail, this chapter covers:

- TCP/IP
- The net package
- Developing a TCP client
- Developing a TCP server
- Developing a UDP client

- Developing a UDP server
- Developing concurrent TCP servers
- Creating a WebSocket server
- Creating a WebSocket client
- Working with RabbitMQ

TCP/IP

TCP/IP is a family of protocols that help the Internet operate. Its name comes from its two most well-known protocols: TCP and IP.

TCP stands for Transmission Control Protocol. TCP software transmits data between machines using segments, which are also called TCP packets. The main characteristic of TCP is that it is a *reliable protocol*, which means that it makes sure that every packet is delivered without requiring any extra code from the programmer. If there is no proof of packet delivery, TCP resends that packet. Among other things, TCP packets can be used to establish connections, transfer data, send acknowledgments, and close connections.

When a TCP connection is established between two machines, a full-duplex virtual circuit, similar to a telephone call, is created between those two machines. The two machines constantly communicate to make sure that data is sent and received correctly. If the connection fails for some reason, the two machines try to find the problem and report it to the relevant application. The TCP header of each packet includes the source port and destination port fields. These two fields, plus the source and destination IP addresses, are combined to uniquely identify every single TCP connection. All these details are handled by TCP/IP, as long as you provide the required details without any extra effort.

 When creating TCP/IP server processes, remember that port numbers 0-1024 have restricted access and can only be used by the root user, which means that you need administrative privileges to use any port in that range. Running a process with root privileges is a security risk and must be avoided.

IP stands for Internet Protocol. The main characteristic of IP is that it is not a reliable protocol by nature. IP encapsulates the data that travels over a TCP/IP network because it is responsible for delivering packets from the source host to the destination host according to the IP addresses. IP must find an addressing method for sending a packet to its destination effectively. Although there are dedicated devices, called routers, that perform IP routing, every TCP/IP device has to perform some basic routing.

The first version of the IP protocol is now called IPv4 to differentiate it from the latest version of the IP protocol, which is called IPv6. The main problem with IPv4 is that it is about to run out of available IP addresses, which is the main reason for creating the IPv6 protocol. This happened because an IPv4 address is represented using 32 bits only, which allows a total number of 2^{32} (4,294,967,296) different IP addresses. On the other hand, IPv6 uses 128 bits to define each one of its addresses. The format of an IPv4 address is 10.20.32.245 (four parts with values from 0 to 255 separated by dots), while the format of an IPv6 address is 3fce:1706:4523:3:150:f8ff:fe 21:56cf (eight parts separated by colons).

UDP (User Datagram Protocol) is based on IP, which means that it is also unreliable. UDP is simpler than TCP, mainly because UDP is not reliable by design. As a result, UDP messages can be lost, duplicated, or arrive out of order. Furthermore, packets can arrive faster than the recipient can process them. So, UDP is used when speed is more important than reliability.

This chapter implements both TCP and UDP software—TCP and UDP services are the basis of the Internet. But first, let us talk about the handy nc(1) utility.

The nc(1) command line utility

The nc(1) utility, which is also called netcat(1), is very convenient when you want to test TCP/IP servers and clients: nc(1) is a utility for everything that involves TCP and UDP as well as IPv4 and IPv6, including but not limited to opening TCP connections, sending and receiving UDP messages, and acting as a TCP server.

You can use nc(1) as a client for a TCP service that runs on a machine with the 10.10.1.123 IP address and listens to port number 1234, as follows:

```
$ nc 10.10.1.123 1234
```

The -l option tells netcat(1) to act as a server, which means that when the -l option is given, netcat(1) starts listening for incoming connections at the given port number. By default, nc(1) uses the TCP protocol. However, if you execute nc(1) with the -u flag, it uses the UDP protocol, either as a client or as a server. Finally, the -v and -vv options tell netcat(1) to generate verbose output, which can be practical when you want to troubleshoot network connections.

The net package

The net package of the Go Standard Library is all about TCP/IP, UDP, domain name resolution, and UNIX domain sockets. The net.Dial() function is used to connect to a network as a client, whereas the net.Listen() function is used to tell a Go program to accept incoming network connections and thus act as a server.

The return value for both net.Dial() and net.Listen() is of the net.Conn data type, which implements the io.Reader and io.Writer interfaces—this means that you can both read and write to a net.Conn connection using code related to file I/O. The first parameter of both net.Dial() and net.Listen() is the network type, but this is where their similarities end.

The net.Dial() function is used to connect to a remote server. The first parameter of the net.Dial() function defines the network protocol that is going to be used, while the second parameter defines the server address, which must also include the port number. Valid values for the first parameter are tcp, tcp4 (IPv4-only), tcp6 (IPv6-only), udp, udp4 (IPv4-only), udp6 (IPv6-only), ip, ip4 (IPv4-only), ip6 (IPv6-only), unix (UNIX sockets), unixgram, and unixpacket. On the other hand, valid values for net.Listen() are tcp, tcp4, tcp6, unix, and unixpacket.

Execute the go doc net.Listen and go doc net.Dial commands for detailed information regarding these two functions.

Developing a TCP client

This section is about developing TCP clients. The two subsections that follow present two equivalent ways of developing TCP clients.

Developing a TCP client with net.Dial()

First, we are going to present the most widely used way, which is implemented in tcpC.go:

```
package main
import (
    "bufio"
    "fmt"
    "net"
    "os"
    "strings"
)
```

The import block contains packages such as bufio and fmt that also work with file I/O operations.

```
func main() {
    arguments := os.Args
    if len(arguments) == 1 {
        fmt.Println("Please provide host:port.")
        return
    }
```

First, we read the details of the TCP server we want to connect to.

```
connect := arguments[1]
c, err := net.Dial("tcp", connect)
if err != nil {
    fmt.Println(err)
    os.Exit(5)
}
```

With the connection details, we call net.Dial()—its first parameter is the protocol we want to use, which in this case is tcp, and its second parameter contains the connection details. A successful net.Dial() call returns an open connection (a net.Conn interface), which is a generic stream-oriented network connection.

```
reader := bufio.NewReader(os.Stdin)
for {
    fmt.Print(">> ")
    text, _ := reader.ReadString('\n')
    fmt.Fprintf(c, "%s\n", text)
    message, _ := bufio.NewReader(c).ReadString('\n')
    fmt.Print("->: " + message)
    if strings.TrimSpace(string(text)) == "STOP" {
        fmt.Println("TCP client exiting...")
        return
    }
}
}
```

The last part of the TCP client keeps reading user input until the word STOP is given as input—in this case, the client waits for the server response before terminating after STOP because this is how the for loop is constructed. This mainly happens because the server might have a useful answer for us, and we do not want to miss that. All given user input is sent (written) to the open TCP connection using fmt.Fprintf(), whereas bufio.NewReader() is used to read data from the TCP connection, just like you would do with a regular file.

 Bear in mind that the reason for not checking the error value returned by reader. ReadString('\n') is simplicity. We should never ignore errors.

Using `tcpC.go` to connect to a TCP server, which in this case is implemented with `nc(1)` as `nc -l 1234`, produces the next kind of output:

```
$ go run tcpC.go localhost:1234
>> Hello!
->: Hi from nc -l 1234
>> STOP
->: Bye!
TCP client exiting...
```

Lines beginning with `>>` denote user input, whereas lines beginning with `->` signify server messages. After sending `STOP`, we wait for the server response and then the client ends the TCP connection. The previous code demonstrates how to create a proper TCP client in Go with some extra logic and functionality in it (the `STOP` keyword).

The next subsection shows a different way of creating a TCP client.

Developing a TCP client that uses net.DialTCP()

This subsection presents an alternative way to develop a TCP client. The difference lies in the Go functions that are being used to establish the TCP connection, which are `net.DialTCP()` and `net.ResolveTCPAddr()`, and not in the functionality of the client.

The code of `otherTCPclient.go` is as follows:

```
package main
import (
    "bufio"
    "fmt"
    "net"
    "os"
    "strings"
)
```

Although we are working with TCP/IP connections, we need packages such as `bufio` because UNIX treats network connections as files, so we are basically working with I/O operations over networks.

```
func main() {
    arguments := os.Args
    if len(arguments) == 1 {
```

```
                fmt.Println("Please provide a server:port string!")
                return
        }
```

We need to read the details of the TCP server we want to connect to, including the desired port number. The utility cannot operate with default parameters when working with TCP/IP unless we are developing a very specialized TCP client.

```
        connect := arguments[1]
        tcpAddr, err := net.ResolveTCPAddr("tcp4", connect)
        if err != nil {
                fmt.Println("ResolveTCPAddr:", err)
                return
        }
```

The net.ResolveTCPAddr() function is specific to TCP connections, hence its name, and resolves the given address to a *net.TCPAddr value, which is a structure that represents the address of a TCP endpoint—in this case, the endpoint is the TCP server we are going to connect to.

```
        conn, err := net.DialTCP("tcp4", nil, tcpAddr)
        if err != nil {
                fmt.Println("DialTCP:", err)
                return
        }
```

With the TCP endpoint at hand, we call net.DialTCP() to connect to the server. Apart from the use of net.ResolveTCPAddr() and net.DialTCP(), the rest of the code that has to do with the TCP client and TCP server interaction is exactly the same.

```
        reader := bufio.NewReader(os.Stdin)
        for {
                fmt.Print(">> ")
                text, _ := reader.ReadString('\n')
                fmt.Fprintf(conn, text+"\n")
                message, _ := bufio.NewReader(conn).ReadString('\n')
                fmt.Print("->: " + message)
                if strings.TrimSpace(string(text)) == "STOP" {
                        fmt.Println("TCP client exiting...")
                        conn.Close()
```

```
            return
        }
    }
}
```

Lastly, an infinite for loop is used to interact with the TCP server. The TCP client reads user data, which is sent to the server. After that, it reads data from the TCP server. Once again, the STOP keyword terminates the TCP connection on the client side using the Close() method.

Working with otherTCPclient.go and interacting with a TCP server process produces the next kind of output:

```
$ go run otherTCPclient.go localhost:1234
>> Hello!
->: Hi from nc -l 1234
>> STOP
->: Thanks for connecting!
TCP client exiting...
```

The interaction is the same as with tcpC.go—we have just learned a different way of developing TCP clients. If you want my opinion, I prefer the implementation found in tcpC.go because it uses more generic functions. However, this is just personal taste.

The next section shows how to program TCP servers.

Developing a TCP server

This section presents two ways of developing TCP servers that can interact with TCP clients, just as we did with the TCP client.

Developing a TCP server with net.Listen()

The TCP server presented in this section, which uses net.Listen(), returns the current date and time to the client in a single network packet. In practice, this means that after accepting a client connection, the server gets the time and date from the operating system and sends that data back to the client. The net.Listen() function listens for connections, whereas the net.Accept() method waits for the next connection and returns a generic net.Conn variable with the client information. The code of tcpS.go is as follows:

```
package main
import (
    "bufio"
```

```
        "fmt"
        "net"
        "os"
        "strings"
        "time"
)
func main() {
    arguments := os.Args
    if len(arguments) == 1 {
        fmt.Println("Please provide port number")
        return
    }
```

The TCP server should know about the port number it is going to use—this is given as a command line argument.

```
    PORT := ":" + arguments[1]
    l, err := net.Listen("tcp", PORT)
    if err != nil {
        fmt.Println(err)
        return
    }
    defer l.Close()
```

The net.Listen() function listens for connections and is what makes that particular program a server process. If the second parameter of net.Listen() contains a port number without an IP address or a hostname, net.Listen() listens to all available IP addresses of the local system, which is the case here.

 This is a personal preference; although it is considered a bad practice to have variable names such as PORT and SERVER, this is my own way of signifying important or global variables.

```
    c, err := l.Accept()
    if err != nil {
        fmt.Println(err)
        return
    }
```

We call Accept() and wait for a client connection—Accept() blocks until a new connection comes. There is something unusual with this particular TCP server: it can only serve the first TCP client that is going to connect to it because the Accept() call is outside of the for loop and therefore is *called only once*. Each individual client should be served by a different Accept() call, which is not happening here. Correcting that is left as an exercise for the reader.

```
for {
    netData, err := bufio.NewReader(c).ReadString('\n')
    if err != nil {
        fmt.Println(err)
        return
    }
    if strings.TrimSpace(string(netData)) == "STOP" {
        fmt.Println("Exiting TCP server!")
        return
    }
    fmt.Print("-> ", string(netData))
    t := time.Now()
    myTime := t.Format(time.RFC3339) + "\n"
    c.Write([]byte(myTime))
}
}
```

This endless for loop keeps interacting with the same TCP client until the word STOP is sent from the client. As it happened with the TCP clients, bufio.NewReader() is used to read data from the network connection, whereas Write() is used to send data to the TCP client.

Running tcpS.go and interacting with a TCP client produces the next kind of output:

```
$ go run tcpS.go 1234
-> Hello!
-> Have to leave now!
Exiting TCP server!
```

The server connection ended automatically with the client connection because the for loop concluded when bufio.NewReader(c).ReadString('\n') had nothing more to read. The client was nc(1), which produced the next output:

```
$ nc localhost 1234
Hello!
```

```
2023-10-09T20:02:55+03:00
Have to leave now!
2023-10-09T20:03:01+03:00
STOP
```

We have ended the connection using the STOP keyword.

So, we now know how to develop a TCP server in Go. As with the TCP client, there is an alternative way to develop a TCP server, which is presented in the next subsection.

Developing a TCP server that uses net.ListenTCP()

This time, this alternative version of the TCP server implements the echo service. Put simply, the TCP server sends back to the client the data that was received by the client.

The code of otherTCPserver.go is as follows:

```go
package main
import (
    "fmt"
    "net"
    "os"
    "strings"
)
func main() {
    arguments := os.Args
    if len(arguments) == 1 {
        fmt.Println("Please provide a port number!")
        return
    }
    SERVER := "localhost" + ":" + arguments[1]
    s, err := net.ResolveTCPAddr("tcp", SERVER)
    if err != nil {
        fmt.Println(err)
        return
    }
```

The previous code gets the TCP port number value as a command line argument, which is used in net.ResolveTCPAddr()—this is required for defining the TCP port number the TCP server is going to listen to.

That function only works with TCP, hence its name.

```
l, err := net.ListenTCP("tcp", s)
if err != nil {
    fmt.Println(err)
    return
}
```

Similarly, net.ListenTCP() only works with TCP and is what makes that program a TCP server ready to accept incoming connections.

```
buffer := make([]byte, 1024)
conn, err := l.Accept()
if err != nil {
    fmt.Println(err)
    return
}
```

As before, due to the place where Accept() is called, this particular implementation can work with a single client only. This is used for reasons of simplicity. The concurrent TCP server that is developed later on in this chapter puts the Accept() call inside an endless for loop.

```
for {
    n, err := conn.Read(buffer)
    if err != nil {
        fmt.Println(err)
        return
    }
    if strings.TrimSpace(string(buffer[0:n])) == "STOP" {
        fmt.Println("Exiting TCP server!")
        conn.Close()
        return
    }
```

You need to use strings.TrimSpace() in order to remove any space characters from your input and compare the result with STOP, which has a special meaning in this implementation. Once the STOP keyword is received from the client, the server closes the connection using the Close() method.

```
fmt.Print("> ", string(buffer[0:n-1]), "\n")
_, err = conn.Write(buffer)
if err != nil {
```

```
                    fmt.Println(err)
                    return
            }
        }
}
```

All previous code is for interacting with the TCP client until the client decides to close the connection. Running `otherTCPserver.go` and interacting with a TCP client produces the following kind of output:

```
$ go run otherTCPserver.go 1234
> Hello from the client!
Exiting TCP server!
```

The first line that begins with > is the client message, whereas the second line is the server output when getting the STOP message from the client. Therefore, the TCP server processes client requests as programmed and exits when it gets the STOP message, which is the desired behavior.

The next section is about developing UDP clients.

Developing a UDP client

This section demonstrates how to develop a UDP client that can interact with UDP services. The code of `udpC.go` is as follows:

```
package main
import (
    "bufio"
    "fmt"
    "net"
    "os"
    "strings"
)
func main() {
    arguments := os.Args
    if len(arguments) == 1 {
        fmt.Println("Please provide a host:port string")
        return
    }
    CONNECT := arguments[1]
```

This is how we get the UDP server details from the user.

```
s, err := net.ResolveUDPAddr("udp4", CONNECT)
c, err := net.DialUDP("udp4", nil, s)
```

The previous two lines declare that we are using UDP and that we want to connect to the UDP server that is specified by the return value of net.ResolveUDPAddr(). The actual connection is initiated using net.DialUDP().

```
if err != nil {
    fmt.Println(err)
    return
}
fmt.Printf("The UDP server is %s\n", c.RemoteAddr().String())
defer c.Close()
```

This part of the program finds the details of the UDP server by calling the RemoteAddr() method.

```
reader := bufio.NewReader(os.Stdin)
for {

    fmt.Print(">> ")
    text, _ := reader.ReadString('\n')
    data := []byte(text + "\n")
    _, err = c.Write(data)
```

Data is read from the user using bufio.NewReader(os.Stdin) and is written to the UDP server using Write().

```
    if strings.TrimSpace(string(data)) == "STOP" {
        fmt.Println("Exiting UDP client!")
        return
    }
```

If the input read from the user is the STOP keyword, then the connection is terminated.

```
    if err != nil {
        fmt.Println(err)
        return
    }
    buffer := make([]byte, 1024)
    n, _, err := c.ReadFromUDP(buffer)
```

Data is read from the UDP connection using the ReadFromUDP() method.

```
        if err != nil {
            fmt.Println(err)
            return
        }
        fmt.Printf("Reply: %s\n", string(buffer[0:n]))
    }
}
```

The for loop is going to keep going forever until the STOP keyword is received as input or the program is terminated in some other way.

Working with udpC.go is as simple as follows—the client side is implemented using nc(1):

```
$ go run udpC.go localhost:1234
The UDP server is 127.0.0.1:1234
```

127.0.0.1:1234 is the value of c.RemoteAddr().String(), which shows the details of the UDP server we have connected to.

```
>> Hello!
Reply: Hi from the server.
```

Our client sent Hello! to the UDP server and received Hi from the server. back.

```
>> Have to leave now :)
Reply: OK - bye from nc -l -u 1234
```

Our client sent Have to leave now :) to the UDP server and received OK - bye from nc -l -u 1234 back. The UDP server started using nc -l -u 1234.

```
>> STOP
Exiting UDP client!
```

Finally, after sending the STOP keyword to the server, the client prints Exiting UDP client! and terminates—the message is defined in the Go code and can be anything you want.

The next section is about programming a UDP server.

Developing a UDP server

This section shows how to develop a UDP server, which generates and returns random numbers to its clients. The code for the UDP server (udpS.go) is as follows:

```
package main
```

```
import (
    "fmt"
    "math/rand"
    "net"
    "os"
    "strconv"
    "strings"
    "time"
)

func random(min, max int) int {
    return rand.Intn(max-min) + min
}

func main() {
    arguments := os.Args
    if len(arguments) == 1 {
        fmt.Println("Please provide a port number!")
        return
    }
    PORT := ":" + arguments[1]
```

The UDP port number the server is going to listen to is provided as a command line argument.

```
    s, err := net.ResolveUDPAddr("udp4", PORT)
    if err != nil {
        fmt.Println(err)
        return
    }
```

The net.ResolveUDPAddr() function creates a UDP endpoint that the UDP server is going to listen to.

```
    connection, err := net.ListenUDP("udp4", s)
    if err != nil {
        fmt.Println(err)
        return
    }
```

The net.ListenUDP("udp4", s) function call makes this process a server for the udp4 protocol using the details specified by its second parameter.

```
defer connection.Close()
buffer := make([]byte, 1024)
```

The buffer variable stores a byte slice with 1024 bytes and is used to read data from the connection with the UDP client.

```
rand.Seed(time.Now().Unix())
for {
    n, addr, err := connection.ReadFromUDP(buffer)
    fmt.Print("-> ", string(buffer[0:n-1]))
```

The ReadFromUDP() and WriteToUDP() methods are used to read data from a UDP connection and write data to a UDP connection, respectively. Additionally, due to the way UDP operates, the UDP server can serve multiple clients.

```
if strings.TrimSpace(string(buffer[0:n])) == "STOP" {
    fmt.Println("Exiting UDP server!")
    return
}
```

The UDP server terminates when any one of the clients sends the STOP message. Aside from this, the for loop is going to keep running forever.

```
data := []byte(strconv.Itoa(random(1, 1001)))
fmt.Printf("data: %s\n", string(data))
```

A byte slice is stored in the data variable and used to write the desired data to the client.

```
    _, err = connection.WriteToUDP(data, addr)
    if err != nil {
        fmt.Println(err)
        return
    }
    }
}
```

Working with udpS.go is as simple as the following:

```
$ go run udpS.go 1234
```

```
-> Hello from client!
data: 403
```

Lines beginning with -> show data coming from a client. Lines beginning with data: show random numbers generated by the UDP server—in this case, 403.

```
-> Going to terminate the connection now.
data: 154
```

The previous two lines show another interaction with a UDP client.

```
-> STOP
Exiting UDP server!
```

Once the UDP server receives the STOP keyword from the client, it closes the connection and exits.

On the client side, which uses udpC.go, we have the following interaction:

```
$ go run udpC.go localhost:1234
The UDP server is 127.0.0.1:1234
>> Hello from client!
Reply: 403
```

The client sends the Hello from client! message to the server and receives 403.

```
>> Going to terminate the connection now.
Reply: 154
```

The client sends Going to terminate the connection now. to the server and receives the random number 154.

```
>> STOP
Exiting UDP client!
```

When the client gets STOP as user input, it terminates the UDP connection and exits.

The next section shows how to develop a concurrent TCP server that uses goroutines for serving its clients.

Developing concurrent TCP servers

This section teaches you a pattern for developing concurrent TCP servers, which are servers that use separate goroutines to serve their clients following a successful Accept() call. Therefore, such servers can serve multiple TCP clients at the same time. This is how real-world production servers and services are implemented.

The code of concTCP.go is as follows:

```go
package main
import (
    "bufio"
    "fmt"
    "net"
    "os"
    "strconv"
    "strings"
)
var count = 0
func handleConnection(c net.Conn, myCount int) {
    fmt.Print(".")
```

The previous statement is not required—it just informs us that a new client has been connected.

```go
    netData, err := bufio.NewReader(c).ReadString('\n')
    if err != nil {
        fmt.Println(err)
        return
    }
    for {

        temp := strings.TrimSpace(string(netData))
        if temp == "STOP" {
            break
        }
        fmt.Println(temp)
        counter := "Client number: " + strconv.Itoa(myCount) + "\n"
        c.Write([]byte(string(counter)))
    }
```

The for loop makes sure that handleConnection() is not going to exit automatically. Once again, the STOP keyword stops the goroutine of the current client connection—however, the server process, as well as all other active client connections, is going to keep running.

```go
    defer c.Close()
}
```

This is the end of the function that is executed as a goroutine to serve clients. All you need in order to serve a client is a net.Conn parameter with the TCP client details. After reading the client data, the server sends back a message to the current TCP client indicating the total number of TCP clients that have been served so far.

```go
func main() {
    arguments := os.Args
    if len(arguments) == 1 {
        fmt.Println("Please provide a port number!")

        os.Exit(5)
    }
    PORT := ":" + arguments[1]
    l, err := net.Listen("tcp4", PORT)
    if err != nil {
        fmt.Println(err)
        return
    }
    defer l.Close()
    for {
        c, err := l.Accept()
        if err != nil {
            fmt.Println(err)
            return
        }
        go handleConnection(c, count)
        count++
    }
}
```

Each time a new client connects to the server, the count variable is increased. Each TCP client is served by a separate goroutine that executes the handleConnection() function. This frees the server process and allows it to accept new connections. Put simply, while multiple TCP clients are being served, the TCP server is free to interact with more TCP clients. As before, new TCP clients are connected using the Accept() function.

Working with concTCP.go produces the next kind of output:

```
$ go run concTCP.go 1234
```

```
.Hello
.Hi from  nc localhost 1234
```

The first line of output is from the first TCP client, whereas the second line is from the second TCP client. This means that the concurrent TCP server works as expected. Therefore, when you want to be able to serve multiple TCP clients in your TCP services, you can use the presented technique and code as a template for developing your own concurrent TCP servers.

The sections that follow concern the WebSocket protocol.

Creating a WebSocket server

The WebSocket protocol is a computer communications protocol that provides full-duplex (transmission of data in two directions simultaneously) communication channels over a single TCP connection. The WebSocket protocol is defined in RFC 6455 (`https://tools.ietf.org/html/rfc6455`) and uses `ws://` and `wss://` instead of `http://` and `https://`, respectively. Therefore, the client should begin a WebSocket connection by using a URL that starts with `ws://`.

In this section, we are going to develop a small yet fully functional WebSocket server using the `gorilla/websocket` (`https://github.com/gorilla/websocket`) module. The server implements the echo service, which means that it automatically returns the client input back to the client.

> The `https://pkg.go.dev/golang.org/x/net/websocket` package offers another way of developing WebSocket clients and servers. However, based on its documentation, `pkg.go.dev/golang.org/x/net/websocket` lacks some features and it is advised to use either `https://pkg.go.dev/github.com/gorilla/websocket`, the one used here, or `https://pkg.go.dev/nhooyr.io/websocket` instead.

You might ask why to use the WebSocket protocol instead of HTTP. The advantages of the WebSocket protocol include the following:

- A WebSocket connection is a full-duplex, bidirectional communications channel. This means that a server does not need to wait to read from a client to send data to the client and vice versa.
- WebSocket connections are raw TCP sockets, which means that they do not have the overhead required to establish an HTTP connection.
- WebSocket connections can also be used to send HTTP data. However, plain HTTP connections cannot work as WebSocket connections.

- WebSocket connections live until they are killed, so there is no need to reopen them all the time.

- WebSocket connections can be used for real-time web applications.

- Data can be sent from the server to the client at any time, without the client even requesting it.

- WebSocket is part of the HTML5 specification, which means that it is supported by all modern web browsers.

Before showing the server implementation, it would be good for you to know that the websocket. Upgrader method of the gorilla/websocket package upgrades an HTTP server connection to the WebSocket protocol and allows you to define the parameters of the upgrade. After that, your HTTP connection is a WebSocket connection, which means that you will not be allowed to execute statements that work with the HTTP protocol.

The next subsection shows the implementation of the server.

The implementation of the server

This subsection presents the implementation of the WebSocket server that implements the echo service, which can be really handy when testing network connections.

The code is put inside ~/go/src/github.com/mactsouk/mGo4th/ch10/ws. The server directory contains the implementation of the server whereas the client directory contains the implementation of the WebSocket client.

The implementation of the WebSocket server can be found in server.go:

```
package main
import (
    "fmt"
    "log"
    "net/http"
    "os"
    "time"
    "github.com/gorilla/websocket"
)
```

This is the external package used for working with the WebSocket protocol.

```
var PORT = ":1234"
var upgrader = websocket.Upgrader{
```

```
    ReadBufferSize:  1024,
    WriteBufferSize: 1024,
    CheckOrigin: func(r *http.Request) bool {
        return true
    },
}
```

This is where the parameters of websocket.Upgrader are defined. They are going to be used shortly.

```
func rootHandler(w http.ResponseWriter, r *http.Request) {
    fmt.Fprintf(w, "Welcome!\n")
    fmt.Fprintf(w, "Please use /ws for WebSocket!")
}
```

This is a regular HTTP handler function.

```
func wsHandler(w http.ResponseWriter, r *http.Request) {
    log.Println("Connection from:", r.Host)
    ws, err := upgrader.Upgrade(w, r, nil)
    if err != nil {
        log.Println("upgrader.Upgrade:", err)
        return
    }
    defer ws.Close()
```

A WebSocket server application calls the Upgrader.Upgrade method to get a WebSocket connection from an HTTP request handler. After a successful call to Upgrader.Upgrade, the server begins working with the WebSocket connection and the WebSocket client.

```
    for {
        mt, message, err := ws.ReadMessage()
        if err != nil {
            log.Println("From", r.Host, "read", err)
            break
        }
        log.Print("Received: ", string(message))
        err = ws.WriteMessage(mt, message)
        if err != nil {
            log.Println("WriteMessage:", err)
            break
        }
    }
```

```
        }
    }
```

The for loop in wsHandler() handles all incoming messages for /ws—you can use any technique you want to serve incoming requests. Additionally, in the presented implementation, only the client is allowed to close an existing WebSocket connection unless there is a network issue, or the server process is killed.

Last, remember that in a WebSocket connection, you cannot use fmt.Fprintf() statements to send data to the WebSocket client—if you use any of these, or any other call that can implement the same functionality, the WebSocket connection fails and you are not going to be able to send or receive any data. Therefore, the only way to send and receive data in a WebSocket connection implemented with gorilla/websocket is through WriteMessage() and ReadMessage() calls, respectively. Of course, you can always implement the desired functionality on your own by working with raw network data, but implementing this goes beyond the scope of this book.

```
func main() {
    arguments := os.Args
    if len(arguments) != 1 {
        PORT = ":" + arguments[1]
    }
```

If there is not a command line argument, the default port number stored in the PORT global variable is used. Otherwise, the given value is used.

```
    mux := http.NewServeMux()
    s := &http.Server{
        Addr:         PORT,
        Handler:      mux,
        IdleTimeout:  10 * time.Second,
        ReadTimeout:  time.Second,
        WriteTimeout: time.Second,
    }
```

These are the details of the HTTP server that also handles WebSocket connections.

```
    mux.Handle("/", http.HandlerFunc(rootHandler))
    mux.Handle("/ws", http.HandlerFunc(wsHandler))
```

The endpoint used for WebSocket can be anything you want—in this case, it is /ws. Additionally, you can have multiple endpoints that work with the WebSocket protocol.

```
    log.Println("Listening to TCP Port", PORT)
    err := s.ListenAndServe()
    if err != nil {
        log.Println(err)
        return
    }
}
```

The presented code uses `log.Println()` instead of `fmt.Println()` for printing messages—as this is a server process, using `log.Println()` is a much better choice than `fmt.Println()` because logging information is sent to files that can be examined at a later time. However, during development, you might prefer `fmt.Println()` calls and avoid writing to your log files because you can see your data on screen immediately without having to look elsewhere. Additionally, if you are going to run the server as a Docker image, using `fmt.Println()` makes more sense. However, you should bear in mind that the `log` package also prints to the screen by default.

The server implementation is short, yet fully functional. The single most important call in the code is `Upgrader.Upgrade` because this is what upgrades an HTTP connection to a WebSocket connection.

Getting and running the code from GitHub requires the following steps—most of the steps have to do with module initialization and downloading the required packages:

```
$ go mod init
$ go mod tidy
$ go run server.go
```

To test that server, we need to have a client. As we have not developed our own client so far, we are going to test the WebSocket server using the `websocat` utility.

Using websocat

`websocat` is a command line utility that can help you test WebSocket connections. However, as `websocat` is not installed by default, you need to install it on your machine using your package manager of choice. You can use it as follows, provided that there is a WebSocket server at the desired address:

```
$ websocat ws://localhost:1234/ws
Hello from websocat!
```

This is what we type and send to the server.

```
Hello from websocat!
```

This is what we get back from the WebSocket server, which implements the echo service—different WebSocket servers implement different functionality.

```
Bye!
```

Again, the previous line is user input given to websocat.

```
Bye!
```

And the last line is the data sent back from the server. The connection was closed by pressing *Ctrl + D* on the websocat client.

Should you wish for verbose output from websocat, you can execute it with the -v flag:

```
$ websocat -v ws://localhost:1234/ws
[INFO  websocat::lints] Auto-inserting the line mode
[INFO  websocat::stdio_threaded_peer] get_stdio_peer (threaded)
[INFO  websocat::ws_client_peer] get_ws_client_peer
[INFO  websocat::ws_client_peer] Connected to ws
Hello from websocat!
Hello from websocat!
Bye!
Bye!
[INFO  websocat::sessionserve] Forward finished
[INFO  websocat::ws_peer] Received WebSocket close message
[INFO  websocat::sessionserve] Reverse finished
[INFO  websocat::sessionserve] Both directions finished
```

In both cases, the output from our WebSocket server should be similar to the following:

```
$ go run server.go
2023/10/09 20:29:16 Listening to TCP Port :1234
2023/10/09 20:29:24 Connection from: localhost:1234
2023/10/09 20:29:31 Received: Hello from websocat!
2023/10/09 20:29:53 Received: Bye!
2023/10/09 20:30:01 From localhost:1234 read websocket: close 1005 (no status)
```

The next subsection shows how to develop a WebSocket client in Go.

Creating a WebSocket client

This subsection shows how to program a WebSocket client in Go. The client reads user data, sends it to the server, and reads the server response. The client directory contains the implementation of the WebSocket client. The gorilla/websocket package is going to help us develop the WebSocket client.

The code of ./client/client.go is as follows:

```go
package main
import (
    "bufio"
    "fmt"
    "log"
    "net/url"
    "os"
    "os/signal"
    "syscall"
    "time"
    "github.com/gorilla/websocket"
)

var (
    SERVER       = ""
    PATH         = ""
    TIMESWAIT    = 0
    TIMESWAITMAX = 5
    in           = bufio.NewReader(os.Stdin)
)
```

The in variable is just a shortcut for bufio.NewReader(os.Stdin).

```go
func getInput(input chan string) {
    result, err := in.ReadString('\n')
    if err != nil {
        log.Println(err)
        return
    }
    input <- result
}
```

The getInput() function, which is executed as a goroutine, gets user input that is transferred to the main() function via the input channel. Each time the program reads some user input, the old goroutine ends and a new getInput() goroutine begins in order to get new user input.

```go
func main() {
    arguments := os.Args
    if len(arguments) != 3 {
        fmt.Println("Need SERVER + PATH!")
        return
    }
    SERVER = arguments[1]
    PATH = arguments[2]
    fmt.Println("Connecting to:", SERVER, "at", PATH)
    interrupt := make(chan os.Signal, 1)
    signal.Notify(interrupt, os.Interrupt)
```

The WebSocket client handles UNIX interrupts with the help of the interrupt channel. When the appropriate signal is caught (syscall.SIGINT), the WebSocket connection with the server is closed with the help of the websocket.CloseMessage message. This is how professional tools work!

```go
    input := make(chan string, 1)
    go getInput(input)
    URL := url.URL{Scheme: "ws", Host: SERVER, Path: PATH}
    c, _, err := websocket.DefaultDialer.Dial(URL.String(), nil)
    if err != nil {
        log.Println("Error:", err)
        return
    }
    defer c.Close()
```

The WebSocket connection begins with a call to websocket.DefaultDialer.Dial(). Everything that goes to the input channel is transferred to the WebSocket server using the WriteMessage() method.

```go
    done := make(chan struct{})
    go func() {
        defer close(done)
        for {
            _, message, err := c.ReadMessage()
```

```
            if err != nil {
                log.Println("ReadMessage() error:", err)
                return
            }
            log.Printf("Received: %s", message)
        }
    }()
```

Another goroutine, which this time is implemented using an anonymous Go function, is responsible for reading data from the WebSocket connection using the ReadMessage() method.

```
    for {
        select {
        case <-time.After(4 * time.Second):
            log.Println("Please give me input!", TIMESWAIT)
            TIMESWAIT++
            if TIMESWAIT > TIMESWAITMAX {
                syscall.Kill(syscall.Getpid(), syscall.SIGINT)
            }
```

The syscall.Kill(syscall.Getpid(), syscall.SIGINT) statement sends the interrupt signal to the program using Go code. According to the logic of client.go, the interrupt signal makes the program close the WebSocket connection with the server and terminate its execution. This only happens if the current number of timeout periods is bigger than a predefined global value, which in this case is equal to 5.

```
        case <-done:
            return
        case t := <-input:
            err := c.WriteMessage(websocket.TextMessage, []byte(t))
            if err != nil {
                log.Println("Write error:", err)
                return
            }
            TIMESWAIT = 0
```

If you get user input, the current number of the timeout periods (TIMESWAIT) is reset and the new input is read.

```
        go getInput(input)
```

```
        case <-interrupt:
            log.Println("Caught interrupt signal - quitting!")
            err := c.WriteMessage(websocket.CloseMessage, websocket.
  FormatCloseMessage(websocket.CloseNormalClosure, ""))
```

Just before we close the client connection, we send websocket.CloseMessage to the server in order to end the connection the right way.

```
        if err != nil {
            log.Println("Write close error:", err)
            return
        }
        select {
        case <-done:
        case <-time.After(2 * time.Second):
        }
        return
    }
  }
}
```

As ./client/client.go is in a separate directory, we need to run the next commands in order to collect the required dependencies and run it:

```
$ cd client
$ go mod init
$ go mod tidy
```

Interacting with the WebSocket server produces the next kind of output:

```
$ go run client.go localhost:1234 ws
Connecting to: localhost:1234 at ws
Hello there!
2023/10/09 20:36:25 Received: Hello there!
```

The previous two lines show user input as well as the server response.

```
2023/10/09 20:36:29 Please give me input! 0
2023/10/09 20:36:33 Please give me input! 1
2023/10/09 20:36:37 Please give me input! 2
```

```
2023/10/09 20:36:41 Please give me input! 3
2023/10/09 20:36:45 Please give me input! 4
2023/10/09 20:36:49 Please give me input! 5
2023/10/09 20:36:49 Caught interrupt signal - quitting!
2023/10/09 20:36:49 ReadMessage() error: websocket: close 1000 (normal)
```

The last lines of output show how the automatic timeout process works.

The WebSocket server generated the following output for the previous interaction:

```
2023/10/09 20:36:22 Connection from: localhost:1234
2023/10/09 20:36:25 Received: Hello there!
2023/10/09 20:36:49 From localhost:1234 read websocket: close 1000
(normal)
```

However, if a WebSocket server cannot be found at the address provided, the WebSocket client produces the next output:

```
$ go run client.go localhost:1234 ws
Connecting to: localhost:1234 at ws
2023/10/09 08:11:20 Error: dial tcp [::1]:1234: connect: connection
refused
```

The `connection refused` message indicates that there is no process listening to port number 1234 on `localhost`.

The next section of the chapter is about working with the RabbitMQ message broker.

Working with RabbitMQ

In the last section of this chapter, we are going to learn how to work with RabbitMQ. RabbitMQ is an open-source message broker that is particularly handy when you want to exchange information asynchronously and need a place where messages can be stored safely until they are read. RabbitMQ enables you to exchange information, which is the main reason that you do not need to use it directly unless you want to perform administrative tasks.

RabbitMQ uses the AMQP protocol. AMQP, which stands for Advanced Message Queuing Protocol, is an open protocol for message-oriented middleware. The characteristic features of AMQP are message orientation, queuing, routing, reliability, and security. AMQP works with binary data and transmits data in frames. There exist nine types of frames (open connection, close connection, transfer data, etc.) depending on the task that you want to perform.

If you must choose between RabbitMQ and Kafka, which both do a similar job, you should begin by considering their differences. First, Kafka is faster than RabbitMQ. Second, RabbitMQ works with the push model whereas Kafka works with a pull-based approach. Third, Kafka offers support for batching whereas RabbitMQ does not. Last, RabbitMQ does not have a limit on the payload size whereas Kafka has some restrictions on the payload size. The key thing to remember is that if speed is your main concern, then Kafka might be a better choice, whereas if payload size and simplicity are your main concerns, then RabbitMQ is a more rational choice.

Data is stored in queues. A queue in RabbitMQ is a FIFO (First In, First Out) structure that supports two operations: adding elements and getting elements. Queues have names, which means that you should know the name of the queue you want to interact with either as a message producer or a message consumer.

The `github.com/rabbitmq/amqp091-go` Go module does the job of connecting to RabbitMQ using the AMQP protocol, provided that you supply the correct connection details.

All files for this section, including source files and a `docker-compose.yml` file for running Rabbit-MQ, are located in `~/go/src/github.com/mactsouk/mGo4th/ch10/MQ`.

Running RabbitMQ

In this first subsection, we are going to learn how to execute RabbitMQ using Docker—this is the cleanest solution for running RabbitMQ on your machine because it only requires the use of a single Docker image. The contents of the `docker-compose.yml` file, which can be found inside `~/go/src/github.com/mactsouk/mGo4th/ch10/MQ/`, are the following:

```
version: "3.6"

services:
  rabbitmq:
    image: 'rabbitmq:3.12-management'
    container_name: rabbit
    ports:
      - '5672:5672'
      - '15672:15672'
    environment:
      AMQP_URL: 'amqp://rabbitmq?connection_attempts=5&retry_delay=5'
```

```
        RABBITMQ_DEFAULT_USER: "guest"
        RABBITMQ_DEFAULT_PASS: "guest"
      networks:
        - rabbit

  networks:
    rabbit:
      driver: bridge
```

Running docker-compose.yml is as simple as using docker-compose up from inside ~/go/src/ github.com/mactsouk/mGo4th/ch10/MQ/. If the relevant Docker image is not present on the active machine, it is going to be downloaded first.

Now that we have RabbitMQ up and running, let us learn how to send data to RabbitMQ (producer) and read data from a RabbitMQ queue (consumer).

Writing to RabbitMQ

The code of the RabbitMQ producer is named sendMQ.go and is located under the producer directory. The sendMQ.go source file is presented in two parts. The first part contains the following code:

```go
package main

import (
    "fmt"

    amqp "github.com/rabbitmq/amqp091-go"
)

func main() {
    fmt.Println("RabbitMQ producer")

    conn, err := amqp.Dial("amqp://guest:guest@localhost:5672/")
    if err != nil {
        fmt.Println("amqp.Dial():", err)
        return
    }

    ch, err := conn.Channel()
```

```go
    if err != nil {
        fmt.Println(err)
        return
    }
    defer ch.Close()
```

The amqp.Dial() call initiates a connection to RabbitMQ, whereas the Channel() call opens a channel to that connection and makes it ready for use.

The connection string (amqp://guest:guest@localhost:5672/) can be split into three logical parts. The first part (amqp://) is the protocol that is used, the second part contains the user credentials, and the third part contains the name of the server and the port number (localhost:5672/).

The second part comes with the following code:

```go
    q, err := ch.QueueDeclare("Go", false, false, false, false, nil)
    if err != nil {
        fmt.Println(err)
        return
    }
    fmt.Println("Queue:", q)

    message := "Writing to RabbitMQ!"
    err = ch.PublishWithContext(nil, "", "Go", false, false,
        amqp.Publishing{ContentType: "text/plain", Body: []byte(message)},
    )

    if err != nil {
        fmt.Println(err)
        return
    }

    fmt.Println("Message published to Queue!")
}
```

The QueueDeclare() defines the queue that we are going to use. If the queue name specified by QueueDeclare() does not already exist, it is going to be created. This means that typos in queue names are not caught. In this case, the queue is named Go.

The plain text data we want to send is kept in the `message` variable. After that, we specify the format of the data we are going to put in the `amqp.Publishing{}` structure, which in this case is plain text (the JSON format is also supported). The contents of the `message` variable are converted into a byte slice and put into the `Body` field of an anonymous `amqp.Publishing{}` structure.

That `amqp.Publishing{}` structure is one of the parameters of the `ch.PublishWithContext()` call, which sends the structure to RabbitMQ.

The current version of `sendMQ.go` just writes a message to the predefined queue using `Publish()` and exits. This means that in order to send multiple messages to RabbitMQ, we have to execute `sendMQ.go` multiple times.

Running `sendMQ.go` generates the following kind of output:

```
$ go run sendMQ.go
RabbitMQ producer
Queue: {Go 0 0}
Message published to Queue!
$ go run sendMQ.go
RabbitMQ producer
Queue: {Go 1 0}
Message published to Queue!
```

The `{Go 1 0}` output means that we currently have two messages in the RabbitMQ queue.

The next subsection shows how to consume messages from a RabbitMQ queue.

Reading from RabbitMQ

The code of the RabbitMQ consumer is named `readMQ.go` and is located under the `consumer` directory. The `readMQ.go` source file is also presented in two parts. The first part contains the following code:

```
package main

import (
    "fmt"

    amqp "github.com/rabbitmq/amqp091-go"
)
```

```
func main() {
    fmt.Println("RabbitMQ consumer")

    conn, err := amqp.Dial("amqp://guest:guest@localhost:5672/")
    if err != nil {
        fmt.Println("Failed Initializing Broker Connection")
        panic(err)
    }

    ch, err := conn.Channel()
    if err != nil {
        fmt.Println(err)
    }
    defer ch.Close()
```

As in sendMQ.go, we define the connection details, and we open the connection.

The second part is the following:

```
    msgs, err := ch.Consume("Go", "", true, false, false, false, nil)
    if err != nil {
        fmt.Println(err)
    }

    forever := make(chan bool)
    go func() {
        for d := range msgs {
            fmt.Printf("Received: %s\n", d.Body)
        }
    }()

    fmt.Println("Connected to the RabbitMQ server!")
    <-forever
}
```

The Consume() method reads messages from the Go queue using a goroutine. The forever channel blocks the program and prevents it from exiting. The Body field of the received message, which is a structure, contains the data we want.

Running `readMQ.go`, after `sendMQ.go` has put some messages in RabbitMQ, generates the following kind of output:

```
$ go run readMQ.go
RabbitMQ consumer
Connected to the RabbitMQ server!
Received: Writing to RabbitMQ!
Received: Writing to RabbitMQ!
```

The `readMQ.go` utility keeps running and waits for new messages, which means that we need to end it on our own by pressing *Ctrl + C*.

How to remove a module

This is not directly related to RabbitMQ, but it is a useful tip. The current version of `go.mod` in the consumer directory is the following:

```
module github.com/mactsouk/mGo4th/ch10/MQ/consumer
go 1.21.1
require github.com/rabbitmq/amqp091-go v1.8.1
```

You can remove a module from `go.mod` using none as follows:

```
$ go get github.com/rabbitmq/amqp091-go@none
go: removed github.com/rabbitmq/amqp091-go v1.8.1
```

After that, `go.mod` is going to look as follows:

```
module github.com/mactsouk/mGo4th/ch10/MQ/consumer
go 1.21.1
```

If you want to bring `go.mod` back into its previous state, you can run go `mod tidy`.

Summary

This chapter was all about the `net` package, TCP/IP, TCP, and UDP, which implement low-level connections, as well as WebSocket and RabbitMQ.

WebSocket gives us an alternative way of creating services. As a rule of thumb, WebSocket is better when we want to exchange lots of data, and we want the connection to remain open all the time and exchange data in full duplex. However, if we are not sure about what to choose, it is recommended to begin with a TCP/IP service and see how it goes before upgrading it to the WebSocket protocol.

Lastly, RabbitMQ is a rational choice when we want to store and retrieve a large amount of data to an external data store.

Go can help you create all kinds of concurrent servers and clients.

We are now ready to begin developing our own services! The next chapter is about REST APIs, exchanging JSON data over HTTP, and developing RESTful clients and servers—Go is widely used for developing RESTful clients and servers.

Exercises

- Develop a concurrent TCP server that generates random numbers in a predefined range.
- Develop a concurrent TCP server that generates random numbers in a range that is given by the TCP client. This can be used as a way of randomly picking values from a set.
- Add UNIX signal processing to the concurrent TCP server developed in this chapter to gracefully stop the server process when a given signal is received.
- Write a client program that reads a message from a RabbitMQ server and posts it to a TCP server.
- Develop a WebSocket server that creates a variable number of random integers that are sent to the client. The number of random integers is specified by the client in the initial client message.

Additional resources

- The WebSocket protocol: `https://tools.ietf.org/rfc/rfc6455.txt`
- Wikipedia WebSocket: `https://en.wikipedia.org/wiki/WebSocket`
- Gorilla WebSocket package: `https://github.com/gorilla/websocket`
- Gorilla WebSocket docs: `https://www.gorillatoolkit.org/pkg/websocket`
- RabbitMQ Go module: `https://github.com/rabbitmq/amqp091-go`
- Learn more about AMQP at `https://www.amqp.org/` and `https://en.wikipedia.org/wiki/Advanced_Message_Queuing_Protocol`

Leave a review!

Enjoying this book? Help readers like you by leaving an Amazon review. Scan the QR code below to get a free eBook of your choice.

11

Working with REST APIs

The subject of this chapter is the development of RESTful servers and clients with the Go programming language, which is one of the many areas where Go excels.

REST is an acronym for *REpresentational State Transfer* and is primarily an architecture for designing web services that offers a standardized efficient way for clients to access data and use the provided server functionality.

RESTful services usually use the JSON format to exchange information, which is well supported by Go. REST is not tied to any operating system or system architecture and is not a protocol; however, to implement a RESTful service, we need to use a protocol such as HTTP or HTTPS as REST is an API convention built on the HTTP(S) protocol.

Although we are already familiar with most of the presented Go code, the ideas behind REST and the way Go code serves them are going to be new. The epicenter of the development of RESTful servers is the definition of the appropriate Go structures and the execution of the necessary marshaling and unmarshaling operations for supporting the exchange of JSON data between the clients and the server.

This truly important and practical chapter covers:

- An introduction to REST
- Developing RESTful servers and clients
- Creating a functional RESTful server
- Creating a RESTful client

An introduction to REST

Most modern web applications work by exposing their APIs and allowing clients to use these APIs to interact and communicate with them. Although REST is not tied to HTTP, most web services use HTTP as their underlying protocol. Additionally, although REST can work with any data format, usually REST means *JSON over HTTP* because most of the time, data is exchanged in JSON format in RESTful services. There are also times when data is exchanged in plain text format, usually when the exchanged data is simple and there is no practical need for JSON records. Due to the way a RESTful service works, it should have an architecture that follows the subsequent principles:

- Client-server design
- Stateless implementation (each interaction does not depend on previous ones)
- Cacheable
- Uniform interface
- Layered system

According to the HTTP protocol, we can perform the following operations on an HTTP server:

- POST: This is used for creating new resources.
- GET: This is used for reading (getting) existing resources.
- PUT: This is used for updating existing resources. As a convention, a PUT request should contain the full and updated version of an existing resource.
- DELETE: This is used for deleting existing resources.
- PATCH: This is used for updating existing resources. A PATCH request only contains the modifications to an existing resource.

The important thing here is that everything you do, especially when it is out of the ordinary, must be well documented. As a reference, keep in mind that the HTTP methods supported by Go are defined as constants in the net/http package:

```
const (
    MethodGet     = "GET"
    MethodHead    = "HEAD"
    MethodPost    = "POST"
    MethodPut     = "PUT"
    MethodPatch   = "PATCH" // RFC 5789
    MethodDelete  = "DELETE"
```

```
    MethodConnect = "CONNECT"
    MethodOptions = "OPTIONS"
    MethodTrace   = "TRACE"
)
```

There also exist conventions regarding the returning HTTP status code of each client request. The most popular HTTP status codes as well as their meanings are the following:

- 200 means that everything went well and the specified action was executed successfully.

- 201 means that the wanted resource was created.

- 202 means that the request was accepted and is currently being processed. This is usually used when an action takes too much time to complete.

- 301 means that the requested resource has been moved permanently—the new URI should be part of the response. This is rarely used in RESTful services because API versioning is used instead.

- 400 means that there was a bad request and that you should change your initial request before sending it again.

- 401 means that the client tried to access a protected request without authorization.

- 403 means that the client does not have the required permissions for accessing a resource even though the client is properly authorized. In UNIX terminology, 403 means that the current user does not have the required privileges to perform an action.

- 404 means that the resource was not found.

- 405 means that the client used a method that is not allowed by the type of resource.

- 500 means internal server error—it probably indicates a server failure.

 If you want to learn more about the HTTP protocol, you should visit RFC 7231 at https://datatracker.ietf.org/doc/html/rfc7231.

Now, let me tell you a personal story. A couple of years ago, I was developing a small RESTful client for a project I was working on. The client connected to a given server in order to get a list of usernames. For each username, I had to get a list of login and logout times by hitting another endpoint.

What I can tell you from my personal experience is that most of the Go code was not about interacting with the RESTful server but about taking care of the data, transforming it to the desired format, and storing it in a database—the two most tricky tasks that I needed to perform were getting a date and time in UNIX epoch format and truncating the information about the minutes and seconds from that epoch time, as well as inserting a new record into a database table after making sure that a record with the same data was not already stored in that database. So, expect that most of the code you are going to write is going to be about confronting the logic of the service, which is true not only for RESTful services but for all services in general.

The first section of this chapter contains general yet essential information about programming RESTful servers and clients.

Developing RESTful servers and clients

This section is going to develop a RESTful server and a client for that server using the functionality of the Go standard library to understand how things really work behind the scenes. The functionality of the server is described in the following list of endpoints:

- `/add`: This endpoint is for adding new entries to the server.
- `/delete`: This endpoint is used for deleting an existing entry.
- `/get`: This endpoint is for getting information about an entry that already exists.
- `/time`: This endpoint returns the current date and time and is mainly used for testing the operation of the RESTful server.
- `/`: This endpoint is used for serving any request that is not a match to any other endpoint.

An alternative and more professional way of defining the endpoints would have been the following:

- `/users/` with the `GET` method: Get a list of all users.
- `/users/:id` with the `GET` method: Get information about the user with the given ID value.
- `/users/:id` with the `DELETE` method: Delete the user with the given ID.
- `/users/` with the `POST` method: Create a new user.
- `/users/:id` with either the `PATCH` or the `PUT` method: Update the user with the given ID value.

The implementation of the alternative way is left as an exercise for the reader—it should not be that difficult to implement it given that the Go code for the handlers is going to be the same and you must only redefine the part where we specify the handling of the endpoints.

The next subsection presents the implementation of the RESTful server.

A RESTful server

The purpose of the presented implementation is to understand how things work behind the scenes because the principles behind REST services remain the same.

The logic behind each handler function is simple. Each function reads user input and decides whether the given input and HTTP method are the desired ones before processing any data.

The principles of each client interaction are also simple: The server should send appropriate error messages and HTTP codes back to the client so that everyone knows what really happened. Lastly, everything should be documented to communicate in a common language.

The code of the server, which is saved as rServer.go, is the following:

```
package main
import (
    "encoding/json"
    "fmt"
    "io"
    "log"
    "net/http"
    "os"
    "time"
)

type User struct {
    Username string `json:"user"`
    Password string `json:"password"`
}
```

This is a structure that holds user data, so the use of JSON tags is mandatory as the JSON data format is different from the one we use in Go.

```
var user User
```

The user global variable holds the user data of the current interaction—this is the input for the /add, /get, and /delete endpoints and their simplistic implementations. As this global variable is shared by the entire program, our code is not concurrently safe, which is fine for a RESTful server used as a proof of concept.

```
// PORT is where the web server listens to
```

```
var PORT = ":1234"
```

A RESTful server is just an HTTP server, so we need to define the TCP port number the server listens to.

```
// DATA is the map that holds User records
var DATA = make(map[string]string)
```

The preceding code defines a global variable named DATA that holds the data of the service.

```
func defaultHandler(w http.ResponseWriter, r *http.Request) {
    log.Println("Serving:", r.URL.Path, "from", r.Host)
    w.WriteHeader(http.StatusNotFound)
    body := "Thanks for visiting!\n"
    fmt.Fprintf(w, "%s", body)
}
```

This is the default handler of the service. On a production server, the default handler might print instructions about the operation of the server as well as the list of available endpoints.

```
func timeHandler(w http.ResponseWriter, r *http.Request) {
    log.Println("Serving:", r.URL.Path, "from", r.Host)
    t := time.Now().Format(time.RFC1123)
    body := "The current time is: " + t + "\n"
    fmt.Fprintf(w, "%s", body)
}
```

timeHandler() is another simple handler that returns the current date and time—such modest handlers are usually used for testing the health of the server and are usually removed in the production version. A very popular endpoint with a similar purpose is /health, which is usually present in modern REST APIs with the purpose of providing a health status for the server, even in production.

```
func addHandler(w http.ResponseWriter, r *http.Request) {
    log.Println("Serving:", r.URL.Path, "from", r.Host, r.Method)
    if r.Method != http.MethodPost {
        fmt.Fprintf(w, "%s\n", "Method not allowed!")
        http.Error(w, "Error:", http.StatusMethodNotAllowed)
        return
    }
```

This is the first time that you are seeing the http.Error() function. The http.Error() function sends a reply to the client request that includes the specified error message, which should be in plain text, as well as the desired HTTP code. You still need to write the data you want to send back to the client using an fmt.Fprintf() statement. However, http.Error() needs to be called last as we should not perform any more writes to w after using http.Error().

```
d, err := io.ReadAll(r.Body)
if err != nil {
    http.Error(w, "Error:", http.StatusBadRequest)
    return
}
```

We try to read all data from the client at once using io.ReadAll() and we make sure that we read the data without any errors by checking the value of the d variable returned by io.ReadAll(r. Body).

```
err = json.Unmarshal(d, &user)
if err != nil {
    log.Println(err)
    http.Error(w, "Error:", http.StatusBadRequest)
    return
}
```

After reading the data from the client, we put it into the user global variable – although using global variables is not considered a good practice, I personally prefer to use global variables for important settings or data that needs to be shared among a Go source file when dealing with relatively small Go source code files. Where you want to store the data and what to do with it is decided by the server. There is no rule on how to interpret the data. Therefore, *the client should communicate with the server according to the wishes of the server*.

```
if user.Username == "" {
    http.Error(w, "Error:", http.StatusBadRequest)
    return
}
DATA[user.Username] = user.Password
log.Println(DATA)
w.WriteHeader(http.StatusCreated)
}
```

If the given Username field is not empty, add the new structure to the DATA map. Data persistence is not implemented for this sample server—each time you restart the RESTful server, the DATA map is initialized from scratch.

If the value of the username field is empty, then we cannot add it to the DATA map and the operation fails with an http.StatusBadRequest code.

```go
func getHandler(w http.ResponseWriter, r *http.Request) {
    log.Println("Serving:", r.URL.Path, "from", r.Host, r.Method)
    if r.Method != http.MethodGet {
        http.Error(w, "Error:", http.StatusMethodNotAllowed)
        fmt.Fprintf(w, "%s\n", "Method not allowed!")
        return
    }
```

For the /get endpoint, we need to use http.MethodGet, so we have to make sure that this condition is met (if r.Method != http.MethodGet).

```go
    d, err := io.ReadAll(r.Body)
    if err != nil {
        http.Error(w, "ReadAll - Error", http.StatusBadRequest)
        return
    }
```

After that, we still need to make sure that we can read the data from the client request without any issues.

```go
    err = json.Unmarshal(d, &user)
    if err != nil {
        log.Println(err)
        http.Error(w, "Unmarshal - Error", http.StatusBadRequest)
        return
    }
    fmt.Println(user)
```

Then, we use the client data and put it into a User structure (the user global variable). Once again, I have to mention that using a global variable for storing the data is a personal preference that works well for smaller source code files but should be avoided for larger programs.

```go
    _, ok := DATA[user.Username]
    if ok && user.Username != "" {
```

```
        log.Println("Found!")
        w.WriteHeader(http.StatusOK)
        fmt.Fprintf(w, "%s\n", d)
```

If the desired user record is found, we send it back to the client using the data stored in the d variable—remember that d was initialized in the io.ReadAll(r.Body) call and already contains a JSON record that is marshaled.

```
    } else {
        log.Println("Not found!")
        w.WriteHeader(http.StatusNotFound)
        http.Error(w, "Map - Resource not found!", http.StatusNotFound)
    }
    return
}
```

Otherwise, we inform the client that the desired record was not found and return http. StatusNotFound.

```
func deleteHandler(w http.ResponseWriter, r *http.Request) {
    log.Println("Serving:", r.URL.Path, "from", r.Host, r.Method)
    if r.Method != http.MethodDelete {
        fmt.Fprintf(w, "%s\n", "Method not allowed!")
        http.Error(w, "Error:", http.StatusMethodNotAllowed)
        return
    }
```

The DELETE HTTP method looks like a rational choice when deleting a resource, hence the r.Method != http.MethodDelete check.

```
    d, err := io.ReadAll(r.Body)
    if err != nil {
        http.Error(w, "ReadAll - Error", http.StatusBadRequest)
        return
    }
```

Again, we read the client input and store it in the d variable.

```
    err = json.Unmarshal(d, &user)
    if err != nil {
        log.Println(err)
```

```
        http.Error(w, "Unmarshal - Error", http.StatusBadRequest)
        return
    }
    log.Println(user)
```

It is considered a good practice to keep additional logging information when deleting resources.

```
    _, ok := DATA[user.Username]
    if ok && user.Username != "" {
        if user.Password == DATA[user.Username] {
```

For the delete process, we make sure that both the given username and password values are the same as the ones that exist in the DATA map before deleting the relevant entry.

```
            delete(DATA, user.Username)
            w.WriteHeader(http.StatusOK)
            fmt.Fprintf(w, "%s\n", d)
            log.Println(DATA)
        }
    } else {
        log.Println("User", user.Username, "Not found!")
        w.WriteHeader(http.StatusNotFound)
        http.Error(w, "Resource not found!", http.StatusNotFound)
    }
    return
}

func main() {
    arguments := os.Args
    if len(arguments) != 1 {
        PORT = ":" + arguments[1]
    }
```

The previous code presents a technique for defining the TCP port number of a web server while having a default value at hand. So, if there are no command line arguments, the default value will be used. Otherwise, the value given as a command line argument is used.

```
    mux := http.NewServeMux()
    s := &http.Server{
        Addr:           PORT,
```

```
        Handler:      mux,
        IdleTimeout:  10 * time.Second,
        ReadTimeout:  time.Second,
        WriteTimeout: time.Second,
    }
}
```

The preceding code block includes the details and the options for the web server.

```
    mux.Handle("/time", http.HandlerFunc(timeHandler))
    mux.Handle("/add", http.HandlerFunc(addHandler))
    mux.Handle("/get", http.HandlerFunc(getHandler))
    mux.Handle("/delete", http.HandlerFunc(deleteHandler))
    mux.Handle("/", http.HandlerFunc(defaultHandler))
```

The previous code defines the endpoints of the web server—nothing special here as a RESTful server implements an HTTP server behind the scenes.

```
    fmt.Println("Ready to serve at", PORT)
    err := s.ListenAndServe()
    if err != nil {
        fmt.Println(err)
        return
    }
}
```

The last step is about running the web server with the predefined options, which is common practice. After that, we test the RESTful server using the `curl(1)` utility, which is very handy when we do not have a client and we want to test the operation of a RESTful server—the good thing is that `curl(1)` can send and receive JSON data.

> When working with a RESTful server, we need to add `-H 'Content-Type: application/json'` to `curl(1)` to specify that we are going to work using the JSON format. The `-d` option is used for passing data to a server and is equivalent to the `--data` option, whereas the `-v` option generates more verbose output if we need more details to understand what is going on.

```
$ curl localhost:1234/
Thanks for visiting!
```

The first interaction with the RESTful server is to make sure that the server works as expected. The next interaction is for adding a new user to the server—the details of the user are in the {"user": "mtsouk", "password" : "admin"} JSON record:

```
$ curl -H 'Content-Type: application/json' -d '{"user": "mtsouk", "pass-
word" : "admin"}' http://localhost:1234/add -v
*   Trying ::1...
* TCP_NODELAY set
* Connected to localhost (::1) port 1234 (#0)
```

The previous output shows that curl(1) has successfully connected to the server (localhost) using the desired TCP port (1234).

```
> POST /add HTTP/1.1
> Host: localhost:1234
> User-Agent: curl/7.64.1
> Accept: */*
> Content-Type: application/json
> Content-Length: 40
```

The previous output shows that curl(1) is going to send data using the POST method and the length of the data is 40 bytes.

```
>
< HTTP/1.1 200 OK
< Date: Sat, 28 Oct 2023 19:56:45 GMT
< Content-Length: 0
```

The previous output tells us that the data was sent and that the body of the server response is 0 bytes.

```
<
* Connection #0 to host localhost left intact
```

The last part of the output tells us that after sending the data to the server, the connection was closed.

If we try to add the same user, the RESTful server is not going to complain:

```
$ curl -H 'Content-Type: application/json' -d '{"user": "mtsouk", "pass-
word" : "admin"}' http://localhost:1234/add
```

Although this behavior might not be perfect, it is good if it is documented. This is not allowed on a production server, but it is acceptable when experimenting. So, we are diverting from a standard practice here and you should not do that in production.

```
$ curl -H 'Content-Type: application/json' -d '{"user": "mihalis", "pass-
word" : "admin"}' http://localhost:1234/add
```

With the preceding command, we add another user as specified by {"user": "mihalis", "password" : "admin"}.

```
$ curl -H -d '{"user": "admin"}' http://localhost:1234/add
curl: (3) URL using bad/illegal format or missing URL
Error:
Method not allowed!
```

The previous output shows an erroneous interaction where -H is not followed by a value. Although the request is sent to the server, it is rejected because /add does not use the default HTTP method.

```
$ curl -H 'Content-Type: application/json' -d '{"user": "admin", "pass-
word": "admin"}' http://localhost:1234/get
Error:
Method not allowed!
```

This time, the curl command is correct, but the HTTP method used is not set correctly. Therefore, the request is not served.

```
$ curl -X GET -H 'Content-Type: application/json' -d '{"user": "admin",
"password" : "admin"}' http://localhost:1234/get
Map - Resource not found!
$ curl -X GET -H 'Content-Type: application/json' -d '{"user": "mtsouk",
"password" : "admin"}' http://localhost:1234/get
{"user": "mtsouk", "password" : "admin"}
```

The previous two interactions use /get to get information about an existing user. However, only the second user is found.

```
$ curl -H 'Content-Type: application/json' -d '{"user": "mtsouk", "pass-
word" : "admin"}' http://localhost:1234/delete -X DELETE
{"user": "mtsouk", "password" : "admin"}
```

The last interaction successfully deletes the user specified by {"user": "mtsouk", "password" : "admin"}.

The output generated by the server process for all previous interactions would look like the following:

```
$ go run rServer.go
Ready to serve at :1234
2023/10/28 22:56:36 Serving: / from localhost:1234
2023/10/28 22:56:45 Serving: /add from localhost:1234 POST
2023/10/28 22:56:45 map[mtsouk:admin]
2023/10/28 22:57:44 Serving: /add from localhost:1234 POST
2023/10/28 22:57:44 map[mtsouk:admin]
2023/10/28 22:59:29 Serving: /add from localhost:1234 POST
2023/10/28 22:59:29 map[mihalis:admin mtsouk:admin]
2023/10/28 22:59:47 Serving: /add from localhost:1234 GET
2023/10/28 23:00:08 Serving: /get from localhost:1234 POST
2023/10/28 23:00:17 Serving: /get from localhost:1234 GET
{admin admin}
2023/10/28 23:00:17 Not found!
2023/10/28 23:00:32 Serving: /get from localhost:1234 GET
{mtsouk admin}
2023/10/28 23:00:32 Found!
2023/10/28 23:00:45 Serving: /delete from localhost:1234 DELETE
2023/10/28 23:00:45 {mtsouk admin}
2023/10/28 23:00:45 map[mihalis:admin]
2023/10/28 23:00:45 After: map[mihalis:admin]
```

So far, we have a working RESTful server that has been tested with the help of the `curl(1)` utility. The next section is about developing a command line client for the RESTful server.

A RESTful client

This subsection illustrates the development of a client for the RESTful server developed previously. However, in this case, the client acts as a testing program that tries the capabilities of the RESTful server—later in this chapter, you are going to learn how to write proper clients using the cobra library. So, the code of the client, which can be found in `rClient.go`, is as follows:

```
package main
import (
    "bytes"
    "encoding/json"
```

```
    "fmt"
    "io"
    "net/http"
    "os"
    "time"
)

type User struct {
    Username string `json:"user"`
    Password string `json:"password"`
}
```

This same structure is found in the server implementation and is used for data exchange.

```
var u1 = User{"admin", "admin"}
var u2 = User{"tsoukalos", "pass"}
var u3 = User{"", "pass"}
```

Here, we predefine three User variables that are going to be used during testing.

```
const addEndPoint = "/add"
const getEndPoint = "/get"
const deleteEndPoint = "/delete"
const timeEndPoint = "/time"
```

The previous constants define the endpoints that are going to be used.

```
func deleteEndpoint(server string, user User) int {
    userMarshall, err := json.Marshal(user)
    if err != nil {
        fmt.Println("Error in req: ", err)
        return http.StatusInternalServerError
    }
    u := bytes.NewReader(userMarshall)
    req, err := http.NewRequest(http.MethodDelete, server+deleteEndPoint,
u)
```

We prepare a request that is going to access /delete using the DELETE HTTP method.

```
    if err != nil {
        fmt.Println("Error in req: ", err)
```

```
        return http.StatusBadRequest
    }
    req.Header.Set("Content-Type", "application/json")
```

This is the correct way to specify that we want to use JSON data when interacting with the server.

```
    c := &http.Client{
        Timeout: 15 * time.Second,
    }
    resp, err := c.Do(req)
```

Then, we send the request and wait for the server response using the Do() method with a 15-second timeout.

```
    if err != nil {
        fmt.Println("Error:", err)
    }
    defer resp.Body.Close()
    if resp == nil {
        return http.StatusBadRequest
    }


    data, err := io.ReadAll(resp.Body)
    fmt.Print("/delete returned: ", string(data))
```

The reason for putting that fmt.Print() here is that we want to get informed about the server response even if there is an error in the interaction.

```
    if err != nil {
        fmt.Println("Error:", err)
    }
    return resp.StatusCode
}
```

The resp.StatusCode value specifies the response HTTP code from /delete.

```
func getEndpoint(server string, user User) int {
    userMarshall, err := json.Marshal(user)
    if err != nil {
        fmt.Println("Error in unmarshalling: ", err)
        return http.StatusBadRequest
```

```
    }

    u := bytes.NewReader(userMarshall)
    req, err := http.NewRequest(http.MethodGet, server+getEndPoint, u)
```

The previous code is going to access /get using the GET HTTP method.

```
    if err != nil {
        fmt.Println("Error in req: ", err)
        return http.StatusBadRequest
    }
    req.Header.Set("Content-Type", "application/json")
```

We specify that we are going to interact with the server using the JSON format using Header.Set().

```
    c := &http.Client{
        Timeout: 15 * time.Second,
    }
```

The previous statements define a timeout period for the HTTP client in case the server is too busy responding.

```
    resp, err := c.Do(req)
    if err != nil {
        fmt.Println("Error:", err)
    }
    defer resp.Body.Close()
    if resp == nil {
        return resp.StatusCode
    }
```

The previous code sends the client request to the server using c.Do(req) and saves the server response in resp and the error value in err. If the value of resp is nil, then the server response is empty, which is an error condition.

```
    data, err := io.ReadAll(resp.Body)
    fmt.Print("/get returned: ", string(data))
    if err != nil {
        fmt.Println("Error:", err)
    }
    return resp.StatusCode
}
```

The value of resp.StatusCode, which is specified and transferred by the RESTful server, determines whether the interaction was successful in an HTTP sense (logically) or not.

```go
func addEndpoint(server string, user User) int {
    userMarshall, err := json.Marshal(user)
    if err != nil {
        fmt.Println("Error in unmarshalling: ", err)
        return http.StatusBadRequest
    }
    u := bytes.NewReader(userMarshall)
    req, err := http.NewRequest("POST", server+addEndPoint, u)
```

We are going to access /add using the POST HTTP method. We can use http.MethodPost instead of POST. As stated earlier in this chapter, there exist relevant global variables in http for the remaining HTTP methods (http.MethodGet, http.MethodDelete, http.MethodPut, etc.) and it is recommended that we use them for portability.

```go
    if err != nil {
        fmt.Println("Error in req: ", err)
        return http.StatusBadRequest
    }
    req.Header.Set("Content-Type", "application/json")
```

As before, we specify that we are going to interact with the server using the JSON format.

```go
    c := &http.Client{
        Timeout: 15 * time.Second,
    }
```

Once again, we define a timeout period for the client in case the server is too busy replying.

```go
    resp, err := c.Do(req)
     if resp == nil || (resp.StatusCode == http.StatusNotFound) {
        return resp.StatusCode
    }
    defer resp.Body.Close()

    return resp.StatusCode
}
```

The addEndpoint() function is for testing the /add endpoint using the POST method.

```
func timeEndpoint(server string) (int, string) {
    req, err := http.NewRequest(http.MethodPost, server+timeEndPoint, nil)
```

We are going to access the /time endpoint using the POST HTTP method.

```
    if err != nil {
        fmt.Println("Error in req: ", err)
        return http.StatusBadRequest, ""
    }
    c := &http.Client{
        Timeout: 15 * time.Second,
    }
```

As before, we define a timeout period for the client in case the server is too busy responding.

```
    resp, err := c.Do(req)
    if resp == nil || (resp.StatusCode == http.StatusNotFound) {
        return resp.StatusCode, ""
    }
    defer resp.Body.Close()

    data, _ := io.ReadAll(resp.Body)
    return resp.StatusCode, string(data)
}
```

The timeEndpoint() function is for testing the /time endpoint—note that this endpoint does not require any data from the client, so the client request is empty. The server is going to return a string with the current time and date of the server.

```
func slashEndpoint(server, URL string) (int, string) {
    req, err := http.NewRequest(MethodPost, server+URL, nil)
```

We are going to access / using the POST HTTP method.

```
    if err != nil {
        fmt.Println("Error in req: ", err)
        return http.StatusBadRequest, ""
    }
    c := &http.Client{
        Timeout: 15 * time.Second,
    }
```

It is considered a good practice to have a timeout period on the client side in case there are delays in the server response.

```go
    resp, err := c.Do(req)
    if resp == nil {
        return resp.StatusCode, ""
    }
    defer resp.Body.Close()

    data, _ := io.ReadAll(resp.Body)
    return resp.StatusCode, string(data)
}
```

The slashEndpoint() function is for testing the default endpoint in the server—note that this endpoint does not require any data from the client.

The next step is the implementation of the main() function, which uses all previous functions to visit the RESTful server endpoints:

```go
func main() {
    if len(os.Args) != 2 {
        fmt.Println("Wrong number of arguments!")
        fmt.Println("Need: Server URL")
        return
    }
    server := os.Args[1]
```

The server variable holds the server address and the port number that are going to be used.

```go
    fmt.Println("/add")
    httpCode := addEndpoint(server, u1)
    if HTTPcode != http.StatusOK {
        fmt.Println("u1 Return code:", httpCode)
    } else {
        fmt.Println("u1 Data added:", u1, httpCode)
    }
    httpCode = addEndpoint(server, u2)
    if httpCode != http.StatusOK {
        fmt.Println("u2 Return code:", httpCode)
    } else {
```

```
        fmt.Println("u2 Data added:", u2, httpCode)
    }
    httpCode = addEndpoint(server, u3)
    if httpCode != http.StatusOK {
        fmt.Println("u3 Return code:", httpCode)
    } else {
        fmt.Println("u3 Data added:", u3, httpCode)
    }
```

All the previous code is used for testing the /add endpoint using various types of data.

```
    fmt.Println("/get")
    httpCode = getEndpoint(server, u1)
    fmt.Println("/get u1 return code:", httpCode)
    httpCode = getEndpoint(server, u2)
    fmt.Println("/get u2 return code:", httpCode)
    httpCode = getEndpoint(server, u3)
    fmt.Println("/get u3 return code:", httpCode)
```

All the previous code is used for testing the /get endpoint using various types of input. We only test for the return code because the HTTP code specifies the success or failure of the operation.

```
    fmt.Println("/delete")
    httpCode = deleteEndpoint(server, u1)
    fmt.Println("/delete u1 return code:", httpCode)
    httpCode = deleteEndpoint(server, u1)
    fmt.Println("/delete u1 return code:", httpCode)
    httpCode = deleteEndpoint(server, u2)
    fmt.Println("/delete u2 return code:", httpCode)
    httpCode = deleteEndpoint(server, u3)
    fmt.Println("/delete u3 return code:", httpCode)
```

All the previous code is used for testing the /delete endpoint using various types of input. Once again, we print the HTTP code of the interaction because the value of the HTTP code specifies the success or failure of the client request.

```
    fmt.Println("/time")
    httpCode, myTime := timeEndpoint(server)
    fmt.Print("/time returned: ", httpCode, " ", myTime)
    time.Sleep(time.Second)
```

```
httpCode, myTime = timeEndpoint(server)
fmt.Print("/time returned: ", httpCode, " ", myTime)
```

The previous code tests the /time endpoint—it prints the HTTP code as well as the rest of the server response.

```
fmt.Println("/")
URL := "/"
httpCode, response := slashEndpoint(server, URL)
fmt.Print("/ returned: ", httpCode, " with response: ", response)
fmt.Println("/what")
URL = "/what"
httpCode, response = slashEndpoint(server, URL)
fmt.Print(URL, " returned: ", httpCode, " with response: ", response)
}
```

The last part of the program tries to connect to an endpoint that does not exist to verify the correct operation of the default handler function.

Running rClient.go and interacting with rServer.go produces the next kind of output:

```
$ go run rClient.go http://localhost:1234
/add
u1 Data added: {admin admin} 200
u2 Data added: {tsoukalos pass} 200
u3 Return code: 400
```

The previous part is related to the testing of the /add endpoint. The first two users were successfully added, whereas the third user (var u3 = User{"", "pass"}) was not added because it does not contain all the required information.

```
/get
/get returned: {"user":"admin","password":"admin"}
/get u1 return code: 200
/get returned: {"user":"tsoukalos","password":"pass"}
/get u2 return code: 200
/get returned: Map - Resource not found!
/get u3 return code: 404
```

The previous part is related to the testing of the /get endpoint. The data of the first two users with the usernames admin and tsoukalos was successfully returned, whereas the user stored in the u3 variable was not found.

```
/delete
/delete returned: {"user":"admin","password":"admin"}
/delete u1 return code: 200
/delete returned: Delete - Resource not found!
/delete u1 return code: 404
/delete returned: {"user":"tsoukalos","password":"pass"}
/delete u2 return code: 200
/delete returned: Delete - Resource not found!
/delete u3 return code: 404
```

The previous output is related to the testing of the /delete endpoint. The admin and tsoukalos users were deleted. However, trying to delete admin for the second time failed.

```
/time
/time returned: 200 The current time is: Sat, 28 Oct 2023 23:03:39 EEST
/time returned: 200 The current time is: Sat, 28 Oct 2023 23:03:40 EEST
```

Similarly, the previous part is related to the testing of the /time endpoint.

```
/
/ returned: 404 with response: Thanks for visiting!
/what
/what returned: 404 swith response: Thanks for visiting!
```

The last part of the output is related to the operation of the default handler.

 It is important to realize that rClient.go can successfully interact with every RESTful server that supports the same endpoints without knowing the implementation details of the RESTful server.

So far, both the RESTful server and the client can interact with each other. However, neither of them performs a real job. The next section shows how to develop a real-world RESTful server using gorilla/mux and a database backend for storing data.

Creating a functional RESTful server

This section illustrates how to develop a RESTful server in Go given a REST API. The biggest difference between the presented RESTful service and the statistics application created in *Chapter 9, Building Web Services*, is that the RESTful service uses JSON messages for interacting with its clients, whereas the statistics application interacts and works using plain text messages.

If you are thinking of using net/http for the implementation of the RESTful server, please do not do so without first thinking about the requirements of your server! This implementation uses the gorilla/mux package, which is a much better choice because it supports subrouters – more about that in the *Using gorilla/mux* subsection. However, net/http is still powerful and can be useful for many REST requirements.

The purpose of the RESTful server is to implement a login/authentication system. The purpose of the login system is to keep track of the users who are logged in, as well as their permissions. The system comes with a default administrator user named admin—the default password is also admin and you should change it. The application stores its data in an SQLite3 database, which means that if you restart it, the list of existing users is read from that database and is not lost.

The REST API

The API of an application helps you implement the functionality that you have in mind. However, this is a job for the client, not the server. The job of the server is to facilitate the job of its clients as much as possible by supporting a simple yet fully working functionality through a properly defined and implemented REST API. Make sure that you understand that before trying to develop and use a RESTful server.

We are going to define the endpoints that are going to be used, the HTTP codes that are going to be returned, as well as the allowed method or methods. Creating a RESTful server based on a REST API for production is a serious job that should not be taken lightly. Creating a prototype to test and validate your ideas and designs is going to save you lots of time in the long run. Always begin with a prototype.

The supported endpoints as well as the supported HTTP methods and the parameters are as follows:

- /: This is used for catching and serving everything that is not a match. This endpoint works with all HTTP methods.

- /getall: This is used for getting the full contents of the database. Using this requires a user with administrative privileges. This endpoint might return multiple JSON records and works with the GET HTTP method.

- /getid/username: This is used for getting the ID of a user identified by their username, which is passed to the endpoint. This command should be issued by a user with administrative privileges and supports the GET HTTP method.

- /username/ID: This is used for deleting or getting information about the user with an ID equal to ID, depending on the HTTP method used. Therefore, the actual action that is going to be performed depends on the HTTP method used. The DELETE method deletes the user, whereas the GET method returns the user information. This endpoint should be issued by a user with administrative privileges.

- /logged: This is used for getting a list of all logged-in users. This endpoint might return multiple JSON records and requires the use of the GET HTTP method.

- /update: This is used for updating the username, password, or admin status of a user—the ID of the user in the database remains the same. This endpoint works with the PUT HTTP method only and the search for the user is based on the username.

- /login: This is used for logging a user into the system, given a username and a password. This endpoint works with the POST HTTP method.

- /logout: This is used for logging out a user, given a username and a password. This endpoint works with the POST HTTP method.

- /add: This is used for adding a new user to the database. This endpoint works with the POST HTTP method and is issued by a user with administrative privileges.

- /time: This is an endpoint used mainly for testing purposes. It is the only endpoint that does not work with JSON data, does not require a valid account, and works with all HTTP methods.

Now, let us discuss the capabilities and the functionality of the gorilla/mux package.

Using gorilla/mux

The gorilla/mux package (https://github.com/gorilla/mux) is a popular and powerful alternative to the default Go router that allows you to match incoming requests to their respective handler. Although there exist many differences between the default Go router (http.ServeMux) and mux.Router (the gorilla/mux router), the main difference is that mux.Router supports multiple conditions when matching a route with a handler function. This means that you can write less code to handle some options such as the HTTP method used.

Let us begin by presenting some matching examples—this functionality is not supported by the default Go router:

- `r.HandleFunc("/url", UrlHandlerFunction)`: The previous command calls the `UrlHandlerFunction` function each time /url is visited.

- `r.HandleFunc("/url", UrlHandlerFunction).Methods(http.MethodPut)`: This example shows how you can tell Gorilla to match a specific HTTP method (`PUT` in this case, which is defined by the use of `http.MethodPut`), which saves you from having to write code to do that manually.

- `mux.NotFoundHandler = http.HandlerFunc(handlers.DefaultHandler)`: With Gorilla, the right way to match anything that is not a match by any other path is by using `mux.NotFoundHandler`.

- `mux.MethodNotAllowedHandler = notAllowed`: If a method is not allowed for an existing route, it is handled with the help of `MethodNotAllowedHandler`. This is specific to `gorilla/mux`.

- `s.HandleFunc("/users/{id:[0-9]+}"), HandlerFunction)`: This last example shows that you can define a variable in a path using a name (`id`) and a pattern – Gorilla does the matching for you! If there is not a regular expression, then the match is going to be anything from the beginning slash to the next slash in the path.

Now, let us talk about another capability of `gorilla/mux`, which is subrouters.

The use of subrouters

The server implementation uses subrouters. A *subrouter* is a nested route that will only be examined for potential matches if the parent route matches the parameters of the subrouter. The good thing is that the parent route can contain conditions that are common among all paths that are defined under a subrouter, which includes hosts, path prefixes, and, as it happens in our case, HTTP request methods. As a result, our subrouters are divided based on the common request method of the endpoints that follow. Not only does this optimize the request matchings, but it also makes the structure of the code easier to understand.

As an example, the subrouter for the `DELETE` HTTP method is as simple as the following:

```
deleteMux := mux.Methods(http.MethodDelete).Subrouter()
deleteMux.HandleFunc("/username/{id:[0-9]+}", handlers.DeleteHandler)
```

The first statement is for defining the common characteristics of the subrouter, which in this case is the `http.MethodDelete` HTTP method, whereas the remaining statement, which in this case is the `deleteMux.HandleFunc(...)` one, is for defining the supported paths.

Yes, gorilla/mux might be more difficult to use than the default Go router, but by now you should understand the benefits of the gorilla/mux package for working with HTTP services.

The next subsection briefly presents the Gin framework, which is an alternative to the gorilla/mux package.

The Gin HTTP framework

Gin is an open source web framework written in Go that can help you write powerful HTTP services. The Gin GitHub repository can be found at https://github.com/gin-gonic/gin. Gin uses httprouter as its HTTP router because httprouter is optimized for high performance and small memory usage. httprouter is an HTTP router, just like the default mux from the net/http package or the more advanced gorilla/mux. You can learn more about it at https://github.com/julienschmidt/httprouter and at https://pkg.go.dev/github.com/julienschmidt/httprouter.

Gin versus Gorilla

The biggest difference between Gin and gorilla/mux is that gorilla/mux is just an HTTP router and nothing more, whereas Gin can do what gorilla/mux can plus JSON marshaling and unmarshaling, validation, customized response writing, and so on. Put simply, Gin can do many more things than gorilla/mux. In practice, you can consider Gin as being a higher-level framework than gorilla/mux with more capabilities.

So, the question here is which one should you choose. It is not bad to try both starting with gorilla/mux. If gorilla/mux cannot do your job, then you definitely need to use Gin. Put simply, if performance is critical, if you want middleware support, or if want minimalistic and fast routing, then use Gin.

Working with the database

In this subsection, we will show you how we work with the SQLite database that supports the functionality of the RESTful server. The relevant file is ./server/restdb.go.

The RESTful server itself knows nothing about the SQLite database. All related functionality is kept in the restdb.go file, which means that if you change the database, the handler functions do not have to know about it.

The database name, the database table, and the admin user are created using the next create_
db.sql SQL file:

```
DROP TABLE IF EXISTS users;

CREATE TABLE users (
    UserID INTEGER PRIMARY KEY,
    username TEXT NOT NULL,
    password TEXT NOT NULL,
    lastlogin INTEGER,
    admin INTEGER,
    active INTEGER
);

INSERT INTO users (username, password, lastlogin, admin, active) VALUES
('admin', 'admin', 1620922454, 1, 1);
```

You can use create_db.sql as follows:

```
$ sqlite3 REST.db
SQLite version 3.39.5 2022-10-14 20:58:05
Enter ".help" for usage hints.
sqlite> .read create_db.sql
```

We can verify that the users table is created and contains the desired entry as follows:

```
$ sqlite3 REST.db
SQLite version 3.39.5 2022-10-14 20:58:05
Enter ".help" for usage hints.
sqlite> .schema
CREATE TABLE users (
    UserID INTEGER PRIMARY KEY,
    username TEXT NOT NULL,
    password TEXT NOT NULL,
    lastlogin INTEGER,
    admin INTEGER,
    active INTEGER
);
sqlite> select * from users;
1|admin|admin|1620922454|1|1
```

We are going to present the most important database-related functions, beginning with OpenConnection():

```go
func OpenConnection() *sql.DB {
    db, err := sql.Open("sqlite3", Filename)
    if err != nil {
        fmt.Println("Error connecting:", err)
        return nil
    }
    return db
}
```

As we need to interact with SQLite3 all the time, we created a helper function that returns an *sql. DB variable, which is an open connection to SQLite3. Filename is a global variable that specifies the SQLite3 database file that is going to be used.

Next, we present the DeleteUser() function:

```go
func DeleteUser(ID int) bool {
    db := OpenConnection()
    if db == nil {
        log.Println("Cannot connect to SQLite3!")
        return false
    }
    defer db.Close()
```

The preceding code is how we use OpenConnection() to get a database connection to work with.

```go
    t := FindUserID(ID)
    if t.ID == 0 {
        log.Println("User", ID, "does not exist.")
        return false
    }
```

Here, we use the FindUserID() helper function to make sure that the user with the given user ID exists in the database. If the user does not exist, the function stops and returns false.

```go
    stmt, err := db.Prepare("DELETE FROM users WHERE UserID = $1")
    if err != nil {
        log.Println("DeleteUser:", err)
        return false
    }
```

This is the actual SQL statement for deleting the user. We use Prepare() to construct the required SQL statement that we execute using Exec(). The $1 in Prepare() denotes a parameter that is going to be given in Exec(). If we wanted to have more parameters, we should have named them $2, $3, and so on.

```
    _, err = stmt.Exec(ID)
    if err != nil {
        log.Println("DeleteUser:", err)
        return false
    }
    return true
}
```

This is where the implementation of the DeleteUser() function ends. The execution of the stmt. Exec(ID) statement is what deletes a user from the database.

The ListAllUsers() function, which is presented next, returns a slice of User elements, which holds all users found in the RESTful server:

```
func ListAllUsers() []User {
    db := OpenConnection()
    if db == nil {
        fmt.Println("Cannot connect to SQLite3!")
        return []User{}
    }
    defer db.Close()

    rows, err := db.Query("SELECT * FROM users \n")
    if err != nil {
        log.Println(err)
        return []User{}
    }
}
```

As the SELECT query requires no parameters, we use Query() to run it instead of Prepare() and Exec(). Keep in mind that this is a query that most likely returns multiple records.

```
    all := []User{}
    var c1 int
    var c2, c3 string
    var c4 int64
```

```
    var c5, c6 int
    for rows.Next() {
        err = rows.Scan(&c1, &c2, &c3, &c4, &c5, &c6)
        if err != nil {
            log.Println(err)
            return []User{}
        }
```

This is how we read the values from a single record returned by the SQL query. First, we define multiple variables for each one of the returned values and then we pass their pointers to Scan(). The rows.Next() method keeps returning records as long as there are new results in the database.

```
        temp := User{c1, c2, c3, c4, c5, c6}
        all = append(all, temp)
    }
    log.Println("All:", all)
    return all
}
```

So, as mentioned before, a slice of User structures is returned from ListAllUsers().

Lastly, we are going to present the implementation of IsUserValid():

```
func IsUserValid(u User) bool {
    db := OpenConnection()
    if db == nil {
        fmt.Println("Cannot connect to SQLite3!")
        return false
    }
    defer db.Close()
```

This is a common pattern: we call OpenConnection() and wait to get a connection to use before continuing.

```
    rows, err := db.Query("SELECT * FROM users WHERE username = $1 \n",
u.Username)
    if err != nil {
        log.Println(err)
        return false
    }
```

Here, we pass our parameter to Query() without using Prepare() and Exec().

```go
temp := User{}
var c1 int
var c2, c3 string
var c4 int64
var c5, c6 int
```

Next, we create the required parameters to keep the return values of the SQL query.

```go
// If there exist multiple users with the same username,
// we will get the FIRST ONE only.
for rows.Next() {
    err = rows.Scan(&c1, &c2, &c3, &c4, &c5, &c6)
    if err != nil {
        log.Println(err)
        return false
    }
    temp = User{c1, c2, c3, c4, c5, c6}
}
```

Once again, the for loop keeps running for as long as rows.Next() returns new records.

```go
if u.Username == temp.Username && u.Password == temp.Password {
    return true
}
```

This is an important point: not only should the given user exist, but the given password should be the same as the one stored in the database for the given user to be valid.

```go
    return false
}
```

You can view the rest of the restdb.go source code on your own. Most functions are like the ones presented here. The code of restdb.go is going to be used in the implementation of the RESTful server that is presented next.

Implementing the RESTful server

We are now ready to begin explaining the implementation of the RESTful server. The server code is split into three files that belong to the main package. So, apart from restdb.go, we have main. go and handlers.go.

The main reason for doing so is to not have to work with huge source code files and to separate the functionality of the server logically.

The most important part of `main.go`, which belongs to the `main()` function, is the following:

```
rMux.NotFoundHandler = http.HandlerFunc(DefaultHandler)
```

So, we define the default handler function. Although this is not necessary, it is a good practice to have such a handler.

```
notAllowed := notAllowedHandler{}
rMux.MethodNotAllowedHandler = notAllowed
```

The `MethodNotAllowedHandler` handler is executed when you try to visit an endpoint using an unsupported HTTP method. The actual implementation of the handler is found in `handlers.go`.

```
rMux.HandleFunc("/time", TimeHandler)
```

The `/time` endpoint is supported by all HTTP methods, so it does not belong to any subrouter.

```
// Define Handler Functions
// Register GET
getMux := rMux.Methods(http.MethodGet).Subrouter()
getMux.HandleFunc("/getall", GetAllHandler)
getMux.HandleFunc("/getid/{username}", GetIDHandler)
getMux.HandleFunc("/logged", LoggedUsersHandler)
getMux.HandleFunc("/username/{id:[0-9]+}", GetUserDataHandler)
```

First, we define a subrouter for the `GET` HTTP method along with the supported endpoints. Remember that `gorilla/mux` is responsible for making sure that only `GET` requests are going to be served by the getMux subrouter.

```
// Register PUT
// Update User
putMux := rMux.Methods(http.MethodPut).Subrouter()
putMux.HandleFunc("/update", UpdateHandler)
```

After that, we define a subrouter for PUT requests.

```
// Register POST
// Add User + Login + Logout
postMux := rMux.Methods(http.MethodPost).Subrouter()
postMux.HandleFunc("/add", AddHandler)
```

```
postMux.HandleFunc("/login", LoginHandler)
postMux.HandleFunc("/logout", LogoutHandler)
```

Then, we define the subrouter for POST requests.

```
// Register DELETE
// Delete User
deleteMux := rMux.Methods(http.MethodDelete).Subrouter()
deleteMux.HandleFunc("/username/{id:[0-9]+}", DeleteHandler)
```

The last subrouter is for DELETE HTTP methods. The code in gorilla/mux is responsible for choosing the correct subrouter based on the details of the client request.

```
go func() {
    log.Println("Listening to", PORT)
    err := s.ListenAndServe()
    if err != nil {
        log.Printf("Error starting server: %s\n", err)
        return
    }
}()
```

The HTTP server is executed as a goroutine because the program supports signal handling—refer to *Chapter 8, Go Concurrency*, for more details.

```
sigs := make(chan os.Signal, 1)
signal.Notify(sigs, os.Interrupt)
sig := <-sigs
log.Println("Quitting after signal:", sig)
time.Sleep(5 * time.Second)
s.Shutdown(nil)
```

Last, we add signal handling for gracefully terminating the HTTP server. The sig := <-sigs statement prevents the main() function from exiting unless an os.Interrupt signal is received.

The handlers.go file contains the implementations for the handler functions and is also part of the main package—its most important parts are the following:

```
// AddHandler is for adding a new user
func AddHandler(rw http.ResponseWriter, r *http.Request) {
    log.Println("AddHandler Serving:", r.URL.Path, "from", r.Host)
```

```
    d, err := io.ReadAll(r.Body)
    if err != nil {
        rw.WriteHeader(http.StatusBadRequest)
        log.Println(err)
        return
    }
```

This handler is for the /add endpoint. The server reads the client input using io.ReadAll() and makes sure that the io.ReadAll() call was successful.

```
    if len(d) == 0 {
        rw.WriteHeader(http.StatusBadRequest)
        log.Println("No input!")
        return
    }
```

Then, the code makes sure that the body of the client request is not empty.

```
    // We read two structures as an array:
    // 1. The user issuing the command
    // 2. The user to be added
    users := []User{}
    err = json.Unmarshal(d, &users)
    if err != nil {
        log.Println(err)
        rw.WriteHeader(http.StatusBadRequest)
        return
    }
```

As the /add endpoint requires two User structures, the previous code uses json.Unmarshal() to put them into a []User variable—this means that the client should send these two JSON records using an array.

```
    log.Println(users)
    if !IsUserAdmin(users[0]) {
        log.Println("Issued by non-admin user:", users[0].Username)
        rw.WriteHeader(http.StatusBadRequest)
        return
    }
```

If the user issuing the command does not have administrative privileges, then the request fails. IsUserAdmin() is implemented in restdb.go as it has to do with the data stored in the database.

```go
        result := InsertUser(users[1])
        if !result {
            rw.WriteHeader(http.StatusBadRequest)
        }
    }
```

Otherwise, InsertUser() inserts the desired user into the database.

Last, we present the handler for the /getall endpoint.

```go
    // GetAllHandler is for getting all data from the user database
    func GetAllHandler(rw http.ResponseWriter, r *http.Request) {
        log.Println("GetAllHandler Serving:", r.URL.Path, "from", r.Host)
        d, err := io.ReadAll(r.Body)
        if err != nil {
            rw.WriteHeader(http.StatusBadRequest)
            log.Println(err)
            return
        }
```

Once again, we read the data from the client using io.ReadAll(r.Body) and we make sure that the process is error-free by examining the err variable.

```go
        if len(d) == 0 {
            rw.WriteHeader(http.StatusBadRequest)
            log.Println("No input!")
            return
        }
        user := User{}
        err = json.Unmarshal(d, &user)
        if err != nil {
            log.Println(err)
            rw.WriteHeader(http.StatusBadRequest)
            return
        }
```

Here, we put the client data into a User variable. The /getall endpoint requires a single User record as input.

```
if !IsUserAdmin(user) {
    log.Println("User", user, "is not an admin!")
    rw.WriteHeader(http.StatusBadRequest)
    return
}
```

Only admin users can visit /getall and get the list of all users, hence the use of IsUserAdmin().

```
    err = SliceToJSON(ListAllUsers(), rw)
    if err != nil {
        log.Println(err)
        rw.WriteHeader(http.StatusBadRequest)
        return
    }
}
```

The last part of the code is about getting the desired data from the database and sending it to the client using the SliceToJSON(ListAllUsers(), rw) call.

Feel free to put each handler into a separate Go file. The general idea is that if you have many handler functions, using a separate file for each handler function is a good practice. Among other things, it allows multiple developers to work on multiple handler functions without bothering each other.

Before developing a proper command line client, it would be a good idea to test the RESTful server using curl(1).

Testing the RESTful server

This subsection shows how to test the RESTful server using the curl(1) utility. You should test the RESTful server as much and as extensively as possible to find bugs or unwanted behavior. As we use three files for the server implementation, we need to run it as go run main.go restdb. go handlers.go. We begin by testing the /time handler, which works with all HTTP methods:

```
$ curl localhost:1234/time
The current time is: Mon, 30 Oct 2023 19:38:21 EET
```

Next, we test the default handler:

```
$ curl localhost:1234/
/ is not supported. Thanks for visiting!
$ curl localhost:1234/doesNotExist
/doesNotExist is not supported. Thanks for visiting!
```

Last, we see what happens if we use an unsupported HTTP method with a supported endpoint—in this case, the /getall endpoint that works with GET only:

```
$ curl -s -X PUT -H 'Content-Type: application/json' localhost:1234/getall
Method not allowed!
```

Although the /getall endpoint requires a valid user to operate, the fact that we are using an HTTP method that is not supported by that endpoint takes precedence and the call fails for the right reasons.

 It is important to look at the output of the RESTful server and the log entries that it generates during testing. Not all information can be sent back to a client, but the server process is allowed to print anything we want. This can be very helpful for debugging a server process such as our RESTful server.

The next subsection tests all of the handlers that support the GET HTTP method.

Testing GET handlers

First, we test the /getall endpoint—your output might vary depending on the contents of the SQLite database:

```
$ curl -s -X GET -H 'Content-Type: application/json' -d '{"username": "admin", "password" : "justChanged"}' localhost:1234/getall
[{"id":1,"username":"admin","password":"justChanged","lastlogin":1620922454,"admin":1,"active":1},{"id":2,"username":"","password":"admin","lastlogin":0,"admin":0,"active":0},{"id":3,"username":"mihalis","password":"admin","lastlogin":0,"admin":0,"active":0},{"id":4,"username":"newUser","password":"aPass","lastlogin":0,"admin":0,"active":0}]
```

The previous output is a list of all existing users found in the database in JSON format. You can always process the generated output with the jq(1) utility for a better-looking output.

Then, we test the /logged endpoint:

```
$ curl -X GET -H 'Content-Type: application/json' -d '{"username": "ad-
min", "password" : "justChanged"}' localhost:1234/logged
[{"id":1,"username":"admin","password":"justChanged","lastlog-
in":1620922454,"admin":1,"active":1}]
```

After that, we test the /username/{id} endpoint:

```
$ curl -X GET -H 'Content-Type: application/json' -d '{"username": "ad-
min", "password" : "justChanged"}' localhost:1234/username/3
{"id":3,"username":"mihalis","password":"admin","lastlogin":0,"admin-
":0,"active":0}
```

Last, we test the /getid/{username} endpoint:

```
$ curl -X GET -H 'Content-Type: application/json' -d '{"username": "ad-
min", "password" : "justChanged"}' localhost:1234/getid/mihalis
{"id":3,"username":"mihalis","password":"admin","lastlogin":0,"admin-
":0,"active":0}
```

So, user mihalis has a user ID of 3.

So far, we can get a list of existing users and a list of logged-in users and get information about specific users—all of these endpoints use the GET method. The next subsection tests all of the handlers that support the POST method.

Testing POST handlers

First, we test the /add endpoint by adding the packt user, which does not have admin privileges:

```
$ curl -X POST -H 'Content-Type: application/json' -d '[{"username": "ad-
min", "password" : "justChanged", "admin":1}, {"username": "packt", "pass-
word" : "admin", "admin":0} ]' localhost:1234/add
```

The previous call passes an array of two JSON records to the server. The second record comes with the details of the packt user. The command is issued by the admin user as specified by the data in the first JSON record.

If we try to add the same username more than once, the process is going to fail—this is revealed with the use of -v in the curl(1) command. The relevant error message is going to be HTTP/1.1 400 Bad Request.

Additionally, if we try to add a new user using the credentials of a user that is not an administrator, the server is going to generate the `Command issued by non-admin user: packt` message.

Next, we test the `/login` endpoint:

```
$ curl -X POST -H 'Content-Type: application/json' -d '{"username":
"packt", "password" : "admin"}' localhost:1234/login
```

The previous command is used for logging in the `packt` user.

Last, we test the `/logout` endpoint:

```
$ curl -X POST -H 'Content-Type: application/json' -d '{"username":
"packt", "password" : "admin"}' localhost:1234/logout
```

The previous command is used for logging out the `packt` user. You can use the `/logged` endpoint to verify the results of the previous two interactions.

Let us now test the only endpoint that supports the PUT HTTP method.

Testing the PUT handler

First, we test the `/update` endpoint as follows:

```
$ curl -X PUT -H 'Content-Type: application/json' -d '[{"username": "ad-
min", "password" : "admin", "admin":1}, {"username": "admin", "password" :
"justChanged", "admin":1} ]' localhost:1234/update
```

The previous command changes the password of the `admin` user from `admin` to `justChanged`.

Then, we try to change a user password using the credentials of a non-admin user (`packt`):

```
$ curl -X PUT -H 'Content-Type: application/json' -d '[{"Username":"pack-
t","Password":"admin"}, {"username": "admin", "password" : "justChanged",
"admin":1} ]' localhost:1234/update
```

The generated log message is `Command issued by non-admin user: packt`.

We might consider the fact that a non-admin user cannot even change their password as a flaw—it might be, but this is the way the RESTful server is implemented. The idea is that non-admin users should not issue dangerous commands directly. Additionally, this flaw can be easily fixed as follows: Generally speaking, regular users are not going to interact in this way with the server and are going to be offered a web interface for doing so. After that, an admin user can send the user request to the server. Therefore, this can be implemented in a different way that is more secure and does not give unnecessary privileges to regular users.

Lastly, we are going to test the DELETE HTTP method.

Testing the DELETE handler

For the DELETE HTTP method, we need to test the /username/{id} endpoint. As this endpoint does not return any output, using -v in curl(1) is going to reveal the returned HTTP status code:

```
$ curl -X DELETE -H 'Content-Type: application/json' -d '{"username": "ad-
min", "password" : "justChanged"}' localhost:1234/username/4 -v
```

The HTTP/1.1 200 OK status code verifies that the user was deleted successfully. If we try to delete the same user again, the request is going to fail, and the returned message is going to be HTTP/1.1 404 Not Found.

So far, we know that the RESTful server works as expected. However, curl(1) is far from perfect for working with the RESTful server on a daily basis. The next section shows how to develop a command line client for the RESTful server.

Creating a RESTful client

Creating a RESTful client is much easier than programming a server mainly because you do not have to work with the database on the client side. The only thing that the client needs to do is send the right amount and kind of data to the server and receive back and interpret the server response. The full RESTful client implementation can be found in ./ch11/client of the book GitHub repository.

The supported first-level cobra commands are going to be the following:

- list: This command accesses the /getall endpoint and returns the list of all available users.
- time: This command is for visiting the /time endpoint.
- update: This command is for updating user records—the user ID cannot change.
- logged: This command lists all logged-in users.
- delete: This command deletes an existing user.
- login: This command is for logging in a user.
- logout: This command is for logging out a user.
- add: This command is for adding a new user to the system.
- getid: This command returns the ID of a user, identified by their username.
- search: This command displays information about a given user, identified by their ID.

A client like the one we are about to present is much better than working with curl(1) because it can process the received information but, most importantly, it can interpret the HTTP return codes and preprocess data before sending it to the server. The price you pay is the extra time needed for developing and debugging the RESTful client.

There exist two command line flags for passing the username and the password of the user issuing the command: username and password. As you are going to see in their implementations, they have the -u and -p shortcuts, respectively. Additionally, as the JSON record that holds user information has a small number of fields, all the fields are going to be given using the data flag or the -d shortcut—this is implemented in ./cmd/root.go. Each command is going to read the desired flags only and the desired fields of the input JSON record—this is implemented in the source code file of each command. Lastly, the utility is going to return JSON records, when this makes sense, or a text message related to the endpoint that was visited. Now, let us continue with the structure of the client and the implementation of the commands.

Creating the structure of the command line client

This subsection uses the cobra utility to create the structure for the command line utility. But first, we are going to create a proper cobra project with Go modules:

```
$ cd ~/go/src/github.com/mactsouk/mGo4th/ch11
$ mkdir client
$ cd client
$ go mod init
$ ~/go/bin/cobra init
$ go mod tidy
$ go run main.go
```

You do not need to execute the last command, but it makes sure that everything is fine so far. After that, we are ready to define the commands that the utility is going to support by running the following cobra commands:

```
$ ~/go/bin/cobra add add
$ ~/go/bin/cobra add delete
$ ~/go/bin/cobra add list
$ ~/go/bin/cobra add logged
$ ~/go/bin/cobra add login
```

```
$ ~/go/bin/cobra add logout
$ ~/go/bin/cobra add search
$ ~/go/bin/cobra add getid
$ ~/go/bin/cobra add time
$ ~/go/bin/cobra add update
```

Now that we have the desired structure, we can begin implementing the commands and maybe remove some of the comments inserted by cobra, which is the subject of the next subsection.

Implementing the RESTful client commands

As there is no point in displaying the entire code, we are going to present the most characteristic code found in some of the commands, starting with root.go, which is where the next global variables are defined:

```
var SERVER string
var PORT string
var data string
var username string
var password string
```

These global variables hold the values of the command line options of the utility and are accessible from anywhere in the utility code.

```
type User struct {
    ID        int      `json:"id"`
    Username  string `json:"username"`
    Password  string `json:"password"`
    LastLogin int64    `json:"lastlogin"`
    Admin     int      `json:"admin"`
    Active    int      `json:"active"`
}
```

We define the User structure for sending and receiving data.

```
func init() {
    rootCmd.PersistentFlags().StringVarP(&username, "username", "u", "us-
ername", "The username")
    rootCmd.PersistentFlags().StringVarP(&password, "password", "p", "ad-
min", "The password")
```

```
    rootCmd.PersistentFlags().StringVarP(&data, "data", "d", "{}", "JSON
Record")

    rootCmd.PersistentFlags().StringVarP(&SERVER, "server", "s", "http://
localhost", "RESTful server hostname")
    rootCmd.PersistentFlags().StringVarP(&PORT, "port", "P", ":1234",
"Port of RESTful Server")
}
```

We present the implementation of the init() function that holds the definitions of the command line options. The values of the command line flags are automatically stored in the variables that are passed as the first argument to rootCmd.PersistentFlags().StringVarP(). So, the username flag, which has the -u alias, stores its value in the username global variable.

The next part is the implementation of the list command as found in list.go:

```
var listCmd = &cobra.Command{
    Use:   "list",
    Short: "List all available users",
    Long:  `The list command lists all available users.`,
```

This part is about the help messages that are displayed for the command. Although they are optional, it is good to have an accurate description of the command. We continue with the actual implementation:

```
    Run: func(cmd *cobra.Command, args []string) {
        endpoint := "/getall"
        user := User{Username: username, Password: password}
```

First, we construct a User variable named user that holds the username and the password of the user issuing the command—the user variable is going to be passed to the server.

```
        // bytes.Buffer is both a Reader and a Writer
        buf := new(bytes.Buffer)
        err := user.ToJSON(buf)
        if err != nil {
            fmt.Println("JSON:", err)

            os.Exit(1)
        }
```

We need to encode the user variable before transferring it to the RESTful server, which is the purpose of the ToJSON() method. The implementation of the ToJSON() method is found in root.go.

```go
req, err := http.NewRequest(http.MethodGet,
                        SERVER+PORT+endpoint, buf)
if err != nil {
    fmt.Println("GetAll - Error in req: ", err)
    return
}
req.Header.Set("Content-Type", "application/json")
```

Here, we create the request using the SERVER and PORT global variables followed by the endpoint, using the desired HTTP method (http.MethodGet), and declare that we are going to send JSON data using the Header.Set() statement.

```go
c := &http.Client{
    Timeout: 15 * time.Second,
}
resp, err := c.Do(req)
if err != nil {
    fmt.Println("Do:", err)
    return
}
```

After that, we send our data to the server using Do() and get the server response.

```go
if resp.StatusCode != http.StatusOK {
    fmt.Println(resp)
    return
}
```

If the status code of the response is not http.StatusOK, then the request has failed.

```go
users := []User{}
SliceFromJSON(&users, resp.Body)
if err != nil {
    fmt.Println(err)
    return
}
data, err := PrettyJSON(users)
if err != nil {
```

```
            fmt.Println(err)
            return
        }
        fmt.Print(data)
    },
}
```

If the status code is http.StatusOK, then we prepare to read a slice of User variables. As these variables hold JSON records, we need to decode them using SliceFromJSON(), which is defined in root.go.

Last is the code of the add command, as found in add.go. The difference between add and list is that the add command needs to send two JSON records to the RESTful server; the first one holds the data of the user issuing the command, and the second holds the data for the user that is about to be added to the system. The username and password flags hold the data for the Username and Password fields of the first record, whereas the data command line flag holds the data for the second record.

```
var addCmd = &cobra.Command{
    Use:    "add",
    Short: "Add a new user",
    Long:   `Add a new user to the system.`,
    Run: func(cmd *cobra.Command, args []string) {
        endpoint := "/add"
        u1 := User{Username: username, Password: password}
```

As before, we get the information about the user issuing the command and put it into a structure.

```
        // Convert data string to User Structure
        var u2 User
        err := json.Unmarshal([]byte(data), &u2)
        if err != nil {
            fmt.Println("Unmarshal:", err)

            os.Exit(1)
        }
```

As the data command line flag holds a string value, we need to convert that string value to a User structure—this is the purpose of the json.Unmarshal() call.

```
users := []User{}
users = append(users, u1)
users = append(users, u2)
```

Then, we create a slice of User variables that are going to be sent to the server. The order you put the structures in that slice is important: first, the user issuing the command, and then the data of the user that is going to be created. This was decided by the RESTful server.

```
buf := new(bytes.Buffer)
err = SliceToJSON(users, buf)
if err != nil {
    fmt.Println("JSON:", err)
    return
}
```

Then, we encode that slice before sending it to the RESTful server through the HTTP request.

```
req, err := http.NewRequest(http.MethodPost,
                            SERVER+PORT+endpoint, buf)
if err != nil {
    fmt.Println("GetAll - Error in req: ", err)
    return
}

req.Header.Set("Content-Type", "application/json")
c := &http.Client{
    Timeout: 15 * time.Second,
}
resp, err := c.Do(req)
if err != nil {
    fmt.Println("Do:", err)
    return
}
```

We prepare the request and send it to the server. The server is responsible for decoding the provided data and acting accordingly, in this case, by adding a new user to the system. The client just needs to visit the correct endpoint using the appropriate HTTP method (`http.MethodPost`) and check the returned HTTP status code.

```
if resp.StatusCode != http.StatusOK {
```

```
        fmt.Println("Status code:", resp.Status)
    }
    fmt.Println("User", u2.Username, "added.")
    }
},
}
```

The add command does not return any data back to the client—what interests us is the HTTP status code because this is what determines the success or failure of the command.

The rest of the commands have a similar implementation, which is not presented here. Feel free to look at the Go source code files in the cmd directory.

Using the RESTful client

We are now going to use the command line utility to interact with the RESTful server. This type of utility can be used for administering a RESTful server, creating automated tasks, and carrying out CI/CD jobs. For reasons of simplicity, the client and the server reside on the same machine, and we mostly work with the default user (admin)—this makes the presented commands shorter. Additionally, we execute go build -o rest-cli to create a binary executable and avoid using go run main.go all the time.

First, we get the time from the server:

```
$ ./rest-cli time
The current time is: Wed, 01 Nov 2023 07:37:49 EET
```

Next, we list all users. As the output depends on the contents of the database, we print a small part of the output. Note that the list command needs to be issued by a user with admin privileges:

```
$ ./rest-cli list -u admin -p admin
[
    {
        "id": 3,
        "username": "mihalis",
        "password": "admin",
        "lastlogin": 0,
        "admin": 0,
        "active": 0
    }
```

Keep in mind that you should use the active password of the admin user for the previous command to be executed correctly. In my case, the active password was also admin but this depends on your current status of the database.

Next, we test the logged command when issued with an invalid password:

```
$ ./rest-cli logged -u admin -p notPass
&{400 Bad Request 400 HTTP/1.1 1 1 map[Content-Length:[0] Date:[Wed, 01
Nov 2023 05:39:38 GMT]] 0x14000204020 0 [] false false map[] 0x14000132c00
<nil>}
```

As expected, the command fails—this output is used for debugging purposes. After making sure that the command works as expected, you might want to print a more appropriate error message.

After that, we test the add command:

```
$ ./rest-cli add -u admin -p admin --data '{"Username":"newUser", "Pass-
word":"aPass"}'
User newUser added.
```

Trying to add the same user again is going to fail:

```
$ ./rest-cli add -u admin -p admin --data '{"Username":"newUser", "Pass-
word":"aPass"}'
Status code: 400 Bad Request
```

Next, we are going to delete newUser—but first, we need to find the user ID of newUser:

```
$ ./rest-cli getid -u admin -p admin --data '{"Username":"newUser"}'
User newUser has ID: 4
$ ./rest-cli delete -u admin -p admin --data '{"ID":4}'
User with ID 4 deleted.
```

Feel free to continue testing the RESTful client and let me know if you find any bugs!

Working with multiple REST API versions

A REST API can change and evolve over time. There exist various approaches on how to implement REST API versioning, including the following:

- Using a custom HTTP header (version-used) to define the version used
- Using a different subdomain for each version (v1.servername and v2.servername)

- Using a combination of `Accept` and `Content-Type` headers—this method is based on content negotiation

- Using a different path for each version (`/v1` and `/v2` if the RESTful server supports two REST API versions)

- Using a query parameter to reference the desired version (`..../endpoint?version=v1` or `..../endpoint?v=1`)

There is no correct answer for how to implement REST API versioning. Use what seems more natural to you and your users. What is important is to be consistent and use the same approach everywhere. Personally, I prefer to use `/v1/...` for supporting the endpoints of version 1, and `/v2/...` for supporting the endpoints of version 2, and so on.

The development of our RESTful servers and clients has come to an end here. With the knowledge presented in this chapter, you can create powerful RESTful services!

Summary

Go is widely used for developing RESTful clients and servers and this chapter illustrated how to program professional RESTful clients and servers in Go. Although you can develop a RESTful server using the Standard Go library, this can be a really tedious task. External packages such as `gorilla/mux`, which was used in this chapter, and Gin can save you time by providing advanced features that would otherwise require lots of code when implemented with the functionality offered by the standard Go library.

Remember that defining a proper REST API and implementing a server and clients for it is a process that takes time and requires small adjustments and modifications.

Behind an efficient and productive RESTful service are properly defined JSON records and HTTP endpoints that support the desired operations. Given these two items, the Go code should offer support for the exchange of the JSON records between the server and the clients.

The next chapter is about code testing, profiling, cross-compilation, and creating example functions. Among other things, we are going to write code for testing the HTTP handlers developed in this chapter.

Exercises

- Try to make `rServer.go` use Gin instead of `net/http`. Does `rClient.go` still work with the updated `rServer.go`? Why? Is that a good thing?

- Change the `server/restdb.go` file to support PostgreSQL instead of SQLite.

- Change the `server/restdb.go` file to support MySQL instead of SQLite.
- Put the handler functions from `server/handlers.go` into separate files.

Additional resources

- You can find more about `gorilla/mux` at `https://github.com/gorilla/mux` and `https://www.gorillatoolkit.org/pkg/mux`
- The `go-querystring` library is for encoding Go structures into URL query parameters: `https://github.com/google/go-querystring`
- Tutorial: Developing a RESTful API with Go and Gin: `https://go.dev/doc/tutorial/web-service-gin`
- If you want to validate JSON input, have a look at the Go `validator` package at `https://github.com/go-playground/validator`
- You might find the `jq(1)` command line utility pretty handy when working with JSON records: `https://stedolan.github.io/jq/` and `https://jqplay.org/`

Join our community on Discord

Join our community's Discord space for discussions with the authors and other readers:

`https://discord.gg/FzuQbc8zd6`

12

Code Testing and Profiling

Programming is both an art and a science, and as such, it needs tools that help the developer generate better software and understand why some aspects of their code do not work as expected. This chapter primarily addresses code testing and code profiling with the Go programming language. The provided code profiling tools are about improving the performance of Go programs by finding and understanding bottlenecks and discovering bugs.

Code optimization is the process where one or more developers try to make certain parts of a program run faster, be more efficient, or use fewer resources. Put simply, code optimization is about eliminating the bottlenecks of a program where and when it matters. The discussion about code optimization is going to continue in *Chapter 14, Efficiency and Performance*, where we talk about benchmarking code.

Code testing is about making sure that your code does what you want it to do. In this chapter, we are experiencing the Go way of code testing. The best time to write test code is during development, as this can help to reveal bugs in the code as early as possible. *Code profiling* relates to measuring certain aspects of a program to get a detailed understanding of the way the code works. The results of code profiling may help you to decide which parts of your code need to change.

Keep in mind that when writing code, we should focus on its correctness as well as other desirable properties, such as readability, simplicity, and maintainability, not its performance. Once we are sure that the code is correct, then we might need to focus on its performance. A good trick for performance is to execute the code on machines that are a bit slower than the ones that are going to be used in production.

This chapter covers:

- Optimizing code
- Rewriting the `main()` function for better testing
- Profiling code
- The `go tool trace` utility
- Tracing a web server
- Testing Go code
- The govulncheck tool
- Cross-compilation
- Using `go:generate`
- Creating example functions

Optimizing code

Code optimization is both an art and a science. This means that there is no deterministic way to help you optimize your code and that you should use your brain and try many things, algorithms and techniques, if you want to make your code faster. However, the general principle regarding code optimization is ***first make it correct, then make it fast***. Always remember what Donald Knuth said about optimization:

> *"The real problem is that programmers have spent far too much time worrying about efficiency in the wrong places and at the wrong times; premature optimization is the root of all evil (or at least most of it) in programming."*

Also, remember what the late Joe Armstrong, one of the developers of Erlang, said about optimization:

> *"Make it work, then make it beautiful, then if you really, really have to, make it fast. 90 percent of the time, if you make it beautiful, it will already be fast. So really, just make it beautiful!"*

Code testing helps you make your program work correctly and code profiling reveals bottlenecks.

If you are really into code optimization, you might want to read *Compilers: Principles, Techniques, and Tools,* by Alfred V. Aho, Monica S. Lam, Ravi Sethi, and Jeffrey D. Ullman (Pearson Education Limited, 2014), which focuses on compiler construction. Additionally, all volumes in the *The Art of Computer Programming* series by Donald Knuth (Addison-Wesley Professional, 1998) are great resources for all aspects of programming if you have the time to read them.

The next section shows a technique for rewriting main() to make testing easier.

Rewriting the main() function for better testing

There exists a clever way that you can rewrite each main() function in order to make testing (and benchmarking) a lot easier. The main() function has a restriction, which is that you cannot call it from test code—this technique presents a solution to that problem using the code found in main. go. The import block is omitted to save space.

```go
func main() {
    err := run(os.Args, os.Stdout)
    if err != nil {
        fmt.Printf("%s\n", err)
        return
    }
}
```

As we cannot have an executable program without a main() function, we have to create a minimalistic one. What main() does is call run(), which is our own customized version of main(), send the desired os.Args to it, and collect the return value of run():

```go
func run(args []string, stdout io.Writer) error {
    if len(args) == 1 {
        return errors.New("No input!")
    }
    // Continue with the implementation of run()
    // as you would have with main()
    return nil
}
```

As discussed before, the run() function, or any other function that is called by main() in the same way, provides a new top-level, root-type function like main() with the additional benefit of being able to be called by test functions. Put simply, the run() function contains the code that would have been located in main()—the only difference is that run() returns an error variable, which is not possible with main(), which can only return exit codes to the operating system when used with os.Exit(). You might say that this creates a slightly bigger stack because of the extra function call but the benefits are far more important than the added memory usage. Although, technically, both parameters of run() can be removed as they are globally available by default, passing these two parameters explicitly allows the programmer to pass other values during testing.

Running main.go produces the next output:

```
$ go run main.go
No input!
$ go run main.go some input
```

There is nothing special in the way main.go operates. The good thing is that you can call run() from anywhere you want, including the code you write for testing, and pass the desired parameters to run()! It is good to have that technique in mind because it might save you when you want to write tests for a program with certain command line arguments or other input.

The next section is about profiling Go code.

Profiling code

Profiling is a process of dynamic program analysis that measures various values related to program execution to give you a better understanding of the program behavior. In this section, we are going to learn how to profile Go code to understand it better, which can be used to improve its performance. Sometimes, code profiling can even reveal bugs in the code, such as endless loops or functions that never return. However, profiling would be better for memory leak bugs and things of that nature.

The runtime/pprof standard Go package is used for profiling all kinds of applications apart from HTTP servers. The high-level net/http/pprof package should be used when you want to profile a web application. What net/http/pprof does is provide HTTP endpoints for profiling data, which means that it can also be used for any long-running application. You can see the help page of the pprof tool by executing go tool pprof -help.

This next subsection is going to illustrate how to profile a command line application, and the following subsection shows the profiling of an HTTP server.

Profiling a command line application

The code of the application is saved as profileCla.go and collects CPU and memory profiling data. What is interesting is the implementation of main() because this is where the collection of the profiling data takes place:

```go
func main() {
    fmt.Println(os.TempDir())
    cpuFilename := path.Join(os.TempDir(), "cpuProfileCla.out")
    cpuFile, err := os.Create(cpuFilename)
    if err != nil {
        fmt.Println(err)
        return
    }
    pprof.StartCPUProfile(cpuFile)
    defer pprof.StopCPUProfile()
```

The previous code is about collecting CPU profiling data. pprof.StartCPUProfile() starts collecting data, which is stopped with the pprof.StopCPUProfile() call. All data is saved into a file named cpuProfileCla.out under the os.TempDir() directory—the value returned by os.TempDir() depends on the OS used and makes the code portable. The use of defer means that pprof.StopCPUProfile() is going to get called just before main() exits—if you want to stop data collection at another point, you should put the pprof.StopCPUProfile() call at the desired place.

```go
    total := 0
    for i := 2; i < 100000; i++ {
        n := N1(i)
        if n {
            total = total + 1
        }
    }
    fmt.Println("Total primes:", total)
    total = 0
    for i := 2; i < 100000; i++ {
        n := N2(i)
        if n {
            total = total + 1
        }
    }
```

```
    fmt.Println("Total primes:", total)
    for i := 1; i < 90; i++ {
        n := fibo1(i)
        fmt.Print(n, " ")
    }
    fmt.Println()
    for i := 1; i < 90; i++ {
        n := fibo2(i)
        fmt.Print(n, " ")
    }
    fmt.Println()
    runtime.GC()
```

All the previous code performs lots of CPU-intensive calculations for the CPU profiler to have data to collect—this is where your actual code usually goes.

```
    // Memory profiling!
    memoryFilename := path.Join(os.TempDir(), "memoryProfileCla.out")
    memory, err := os.Create(memoryFilename)
    if err != nil {
        fmt.Println(err)
        return
    }
    defer memory.Close()
```

After the CPU-intensive code, we are going to put code that uses lots of memory. For that, we create a second file named memoryFilename for collecting memory-related profiling data.

```
    for i := 0; i < 10; i++ {
        s := make([]byte, 50000000)
        if s == nil {
            fmt.Println("Operation failed!")
        }
        time.Sleep(50 * time.Millisecond)
    }
    err = pprof.WriteHeapProfile(memory)
    if err != nil {
        fmt.Println(err)
```

```
        return
    }
}
```

The pprof.WriteHeapProfile() function writes the memory data into the specified file. Once again, we allocate lots of memory for the memory profiler to have data to collect.

Running profileCla.go using go run is going to create two files in the folder returned by os.TempDir()—usually, we move them into a different folder. Feel free to change the code of profileCla.go and put the profiling files in a different place.

In my case, running on a macOS Sonoma machine, the temporary directory is going to be /var/folders/sk/1tk8cnw50lzdtr2hxcj5sv2m0000gn/T/. So, I am going to move the cpuProfileCla.out and memoryProfileCla.out files from there into the ch12 directory—you are not going to be able to find them because the .gitignore file of the GitHub repository of the book ignores both of them.

So, what do we do next? We should use go tool pprof to process these two files:

```
$ go tool pprof cpuProfileCla.out
Type: cpu
Time: Dec 13, 2023 at 6:35pm (EET)
Duration: 14.85s, Total samples = 650ms ( 4.38%)
Entering interactive mode (type "help" for commands, "o" for options)
(pprof) top
Showing nodes accounting for 630ms, 96.92% of 650ms total
Showing top 10 nodes out of 47
      flat  flat%   sum%        cum   cum%
     300ms 46.15% 46.15%      330ms 50.77%  main.N2 (inline)
     120ms 18.46% 64.62%      120ms 18.46%  main.N1 (inline)
      40ms  6.15% 70.77%       40ms  6.15%  runtime.kevent
      40ms  6.15% 76.92%       40ms  6.15%  runtime.pthread_cond_signal
      40ms  6.15% 83.08%       40ms  6.15%  runtime.pthread_cond_wait
      30ms  4.62% 87.69%       30ms  4.62%  runtime.asyncPreempt
      30ms  4.62% 92.31%       30ms  4.62%  runtime.madvise
      10ms  1.54% 93.85%       10ms  1.54%  internal/poll.(*pollDesc).
prepare
      10ms  1.54% 95.38%      480ms 73.85%  main.main
      10ms  1.54% 96.92%       10ms  1.54%  runtime.memclrNoHeapPointers
```

The top command returns a summary of the top 10 entries.

```
(pprof) top10 -cum
Showing nodes accounting for 440ms, 67.69% of 650ms total
Showing top 10 nodes out of 47
      flat  flat%   sum%        cum   cum%
      10ms  1.54%  1.54%      480ms 73.85%  main.main
         0     0%  1.54%      480ms 73.85%  runtime.main
     300ms 46.15% 47.69%      330ms 50.77%  main.N2 (inline)
     120ms 18.46% 66.15%      120ms 18.46%  main.N1 (inline)
         0     0% 66.15%      120ms 18.46%  runtime.mcall
      10ms  1.54% 67.69%      120ms 18.46%  runtime.schedule
         0     0% 67.69%      110ms 16.92%  runtime.park_m
         0     0% 67.69%       80ms 12.31%  runtime.findRunnable
         0     0% 67.69%       50ms  7.69%  runtime.notewakeup
         0     0% 67.69%       50ms  7.69%  runtime.semawakeup
```

The top10 -cum command returns the cumulative time for each function.

```
(pprof) list main.N1
Total: 650ms
ROUTINE ======================== main.N1 in /Users/mtsouk/go/src/github.
com/mactsouk/mGo4th/ch12/profileCla.go
     120ms      120ms (flat, cum) 18.46% of Total
         .          .     36:func N1(n int) bool {
         .          .     37:     k := math.Floor(float64(n/2 + 1))
         .          .     38:     for i := 2; i < int(k); i++ {
     120ms      120ms     39:         if (n % i) == 0 {
         .          .     40:             return false
         .          .     41:         }
         .          .     42:     }
         .          .     43:     return true
         .          .     44:}
```

Last, the list command shows information about a given function. The previous output shows that the if (n % i) == 0 statement is responsible for all the time it takes N1() to run!

Try the profile commands on your own in your own code to see their full output. Visit https://go.dev/blog/pprof from the Go blog to learn more about profiling.

You can also create PDF output of the profiling data from the shell of the Go profiler using the pdf command. Personally, most of the time, I begin with this command because it gives me a rich and clear overview of the collected data.

Now, let us discuss how to profile an HTTP server, which is the subject of the next subsection.

Profiling an HTTP server

As discussed, the net/http/pprof package should be used when you want to collect profiling data for a Go application that runs an HTTP server or any other long-running program where you want to periodically collect profiling data. To that end, importing net/http/pprof installs various handlers under the /debug/pprof/ path. You are going to see more on this in a short while.

The technique is illustrated in profileHTTP.go, which comes with the following code:

```
package main
import (
    "fmt"
    "net/http"
    "net/http/pprof"
    "os"
    "time"
)
```

As discussed earlier, you should import the net/http/pprof package. However, although net/http/pprof is imported, it is not used directly. The import is for the side effects of registering the HTTP handlers, as explained in https://pkg.go.dev/net/http/pprof.

```
func myHandler(w http.ResponseWriter, r *http.Request) {
    fmt.Fprintf(w, "Serving: %s\n", r.URL.Path)
    fmt.Printf("Served: %s\n", r.Host)
}

func timeHandler(w http.ResponseWriter, r *http.Request) {
    t := time.Now().Format(time.RFC1123)
    Body := "The current time is:"
    fmt.Fprintf(w, "%s %s", Body, t)
    fmt.Fprintf(w, "Serving: %s\n", r.URL.Path)
    fmt.Printf("Served time for: %s\n", r.Host)
}
```

The previous two functions implement two handlers that are going to be used in our naïve HTTP server. myHandler() is the default handler function, whereas timeHandler() returns the current time and date on the server.

```
func main() {
    PORT := ":8001"
    arguments := os.Args
    if len(arguments) == 1 {
        fmt.Println("Using default port number: ", PORT)
    } else {
        PORT = ":" + arguments[1]
        fmt.Println("Using port number: ", PORT)
    }
    r := http.NewServeMux()
    r.HandleFunc("/time", timeHandler)
    r.HandleFunc("/", myHandler)
```

Up to this point, there is nothing special as we just register the handler functions.

All of the previous statements install the handlers for the HTTP profiler—you can access them using the hostname and port number of the web server. You do not have to use all handlers.

```
    err := http.ListenAndServe(PORT, r)
    if err != nil {
        fmt.Println(err)
        return
    }
}
```

Last, you start the HTTP server as usual.

What is next? First, you run the HTTP server (go run profileHTTP.go). After that, you run the next command *in a different terminal window* to collect profiling data while interacting with the HTTP server:

```
$ go tool pprof http://localhost:8001/debug/pprof/profile
Fetching profile over HTTP from http://localhost:8001/debug/pprof/profile
Saved profile in /Users/mtsouk/pprof/pprof.samples.cpu.001.pb.gz
Type: cpu
Time: Dec 13, 2023 at 6:44pm (EET)
Duration: 30.02s, Total samples = 30ms ( 0.1%)
Entering interactive mode (type "help" for commands, "o" for options)
(pprof) %
```

The previous output shows the initial screen of the HTTP profiler—the available commands are the same as when profiling a command line application.

You can either exit the shell and analyze your data later using go tool pprof or continue giving profiler commands. This is the general idea behind profiling HTTP servers in Go.

The next subsection discusses the web interface of the Go profiler.

The web interface of the Go profiler

The good news is that, starting with Go version 1.10, go tool pprof comes with a web interface that you can start as go tool pprof -http=[host]:[port] aProfile.out—do not forget to set your desired values to -http.

 I have executed the previous command as go tool pprof -http=127.0.0.1:1234 cpuProfileCla.out.

A part of the web interface of the profiler is seen in the next figure, which shows how the program execution time was spent—it is now the job of the developer to find out whether there is something wrong with the performance or not.

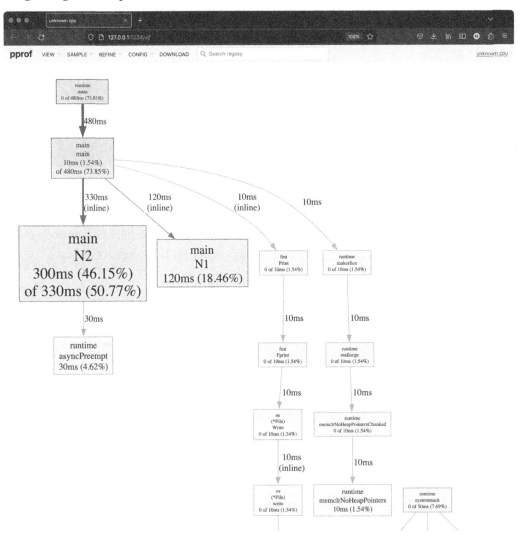

Figure 12.1: The web interface of the Go profiler

Feel free to browse the web interface and see the various options and menus that are offered. Unfortunately, talking more about profiling is beyond the scope of this chapter. As always, if you are really interested in code profiling, experiment with it as much as possible.

The next section is about code tracing, which gives you information about the operation of the Go internals.

The go tool trace utility

Code tracing is a process that allows you to learn information such as the operation of the garbage collector, the lifetime of goroutines, the activity of each logical processor, and the number of operating system threads used. The go tool trace utility is a tool for viewing the data stored in trace files, which can be generated in any one of the following three ways:

- With the runtime/trace package
- With the net/http/pprof package
- With the go test -trace command

This section illustrates the use of the first technique using the code of traceCLA.go:

```
package main
import (
    "fmt"
    "os"
    "path"
    "runtime/trace"
    "time"
)
```

The runtime/trace package is required for collecting all kinds of tracing data—there is no point in selecting specific tracing data as all tracing data is interconnected.

```
func main() {
    filename := path.Join(os.TempDir(), "traceCLA.out")
    f, err := os.Create(filename)
    if err != nil {
        panic(err)
    }
    defer f.Close()
```

As we did for profiling, we need to create a file to store tracing data. In this case, the file is called traceCLA.out and is stored inside the temporary directory of your operating system.

```
    err = trace.Start(f)
    if err != nil {
```

```
        fmt.Println(err)
        return
    }
    defer trace.Stop()
```

This part is all about acquiring data for go tool trace, and it has nothing to do with the purpose of the program. We start the tracing process using trace.Start(). When we are done, we call the trace.Stop() function. The defer call means that we want to terminate tracing when the main() function returns.

```
    for i := 0; i < 3; i++ {
        s := make([]byte, 50000000)
        if s == nil {
            fmt.Println("Operation failed!")
        }
    }
    for i := 0; i < 5; i++ {
        s := make([]byte, 100000000)
        if s == nil {
            fmt.Println("Operation failed!")
        }
        time.Sleep(time.Millisecond)
    }
}
```

All the previous code is about allocating memory to trigger the operation of the garbage collector and generate more tracing data—you can learn more about the Go garbage collector in *Appendix A, Go Garbage Collector*. The program is executed as usual. However, when it finishes, it populates traceCLA.out with tracing data. After that, we should process the tracing data as follows:

```
$ go tool trace /path/ToTemporary/Directory/traceCLA.out
2023/12/14 18:12:06 Parsing trace...
2023/12/14 18:12:06 Splitting trace...
2023/12/14 18:12:06 Opening browser. Trace viewer is listening on
http://127.0.0.1:52829
```

The last command automatically starts a web server (http://127.0.0.1:52829) and opens the web interface of the trace tool on your default web browser—you can run it on your own computer to play with the web interface of the trace tool.

The View trace link shows information about the goroutines of your program and the operation of the garbage collector—if your code uses multiple goroutines, this is the best place to understand their behavior.

 Keep in mind that although go tool trace is very handy and powerful, it cannot solve every kind of performance problem. There are times when go tool pprof is more appropriate, especially when we want to reveal where our code spends most of its time.

As with profiling, collecting tracing data for an HTTP server is a slightly different process, which is explained in the next subsection.

Tracing a web server from a client

This section shows how to trace a web server application using net/http/httptrace. The package allows you to trace the phases of an HTTP request from a client. The code of traceHTTP.go that interacts with web servers is as follows:

```
package main
import (
    "fmt"
    "net/http"
    "net/http/httptrace"
    "os"
)
```

As expected, we need to import net/http/httptrace before being able to enable HTTP tracing.

```
func main() {
    if len(os.Args) != 2 {
        fmt.Printf("Usage: URL\n")
        return
    }
    URL := os.Args[1]
    client := http.Client{}
    req, _ := http.NewRequest("GET", URL, nil)
```

Up to this point, we have prepared the client request to the web server as usual.

```
    trace := &httptrace.ClientTrace{
```

```
        GotFirstResponseByte: func() {
            fmt.Println("First response byte!")
        },
        GotConn: func(connInfo httptrace.GotConnInfo) {
            fmt.Printf("Got Conn: %+v\n", connInfo)
        },
        DNSDone: func(dnsInfo httptrace.DNSDoneInfo) {
            fmt.Printf("DNS Info: %+v\n", dnsInfo)
        },
        ConnectStart: func(network, addr string) {
            fmt.Println("Dial start")
        },
        ConnectDone: func(network, addr string, err error) {
            fmt.Println("Dial done")
        },
        WroteHeaders: func() {
            fmt.Println("Wrote headers")
        },
    }
```

The preceding code is all about tracing HTTP requests. The httptrace.ClientTrace structure defines the events that interest us, which are GotFirstResponseByte, GotConn, DNSDone,
ConnectStart, ConnectDone, and WroteHeaders. When such an event occurs, the relevant code
is executed. You can find more information about the supported events and their purpose in the
documentation of the net/http/httptrace package.

```
    req = req.WithContext(httptrace.WithClientTrace(req.Context(), trace))
    fmt.Println("Requesting data from server!")
    _, err := http.DefaultTransport.RoundTrip(req)
    if err != nil {
        fmt.Println(err)
        return
    }
```

The httptrace.WithClientTrace() function returns a new context value based on the given
parent context, while http.DefaultTransport.RoundTrip() wraps the request with the context
value in order to keep track of the request.

Keep in mind that Go HTTP tracing has been designed to trace the events of a single `http.Transport.RoundTrip`.

```
    _, err = client.Do(req)
    if err != nil {
        fmt.Println(err)
        return
    }
}
```

The last part sends the client request to the server for the tracing to begin.

Running `traceHTTP.go` generates the next output:

```
$ go run traceHTTP.go https://go.dev
Requesting data from server!
DNS Info: {Addrs:[{IP:2001:4860:4802:32::15 Zone:}
{IP:2001:4860:4802:34::15 Zone:} {IP:2001:4860:4802:36::15
Zone:} {IP:2001:4860:4802:38::15 Zone:} {IP:216.239.32.21 Zone:}
{IP:216.239.34.21 Zone:} {IP:216.239.36.21 Zone:} {IP:216.239.38.21
Zone:}] Err:<nil> Coalesced:false}
Dial start
Dial done
Got Conn: {Conn:0x1400018e000 Reused:false WasIdle:false IdleTime:0s}
Wrote headers
First response byte!
Got Conn: {Conn:0x1400018e000 Reused:true WasIdle:false IdleTime:0s}
Wrote headers
First response byte!
```

The previous output helps you understand the progress of the connection in more detail and is handy when troubleshooting. Unfortunately, talking more about tracing is beyond the scope of this book. The next subsection shows how to visit all the routes of a web server to make sure that they are properly defined.

Visiting all routes of a web server

The gorilla/mux package offers a Walk() function that can be used to visit all the registered routes of a router—this can be very handy when you want to make sure that every route is registered and is working.

The code of walkAll.go, which contains lots of empty handler functions because its purpose is not to test handling functions but to visit them, is as follows (nothing prohibits you from using the same technique on a fully implemented web server):

```
package main
import (
    "fmt"
    "net/http"
    "strings"
    "github.com/gorilla/mux"
)
```

As we are using an external package, the running of walkAll.go should take place somewhere under ~/go/src—in our case, under ./ch12/walkAll.

```
func handler(w http.ResponseWriter, r *http.Request) {
    return
}
```

This empty handler function is shared by all endpoints for reasons of simplicity.

```
func (h notAllowedHandler) ServeHTTP(rw http.ResponseWriter, r *http.
Request) {
    handler(rw, r)
}
```

The notAllowedHandler handler also calls the handler() function.

```
type notAllowedHandler struct{}
func main() {
    r := mux.NewRouter()
    r.NotFoundHandler = http.HandlerFunc(handler)
    notAllowed := notAllowedHandler{}
    r.MethodNotAllowedHandler = notAllowed
    // Register GET
    getMux := r.Methods(http.MethodGet).Subrouter()
```

```
getMux.HandleFunc("/time", handler)
getMux.HandleFunc("/getall", handler)
getMux.HandleFunc("/getid", handler)
getMux.HandleFunc("/logged", handler)
getMux.HandleFunc("/username/{id:[0-9]+}", handler)
// Register PUT
// Update User
putMux := r.Methods(http.MethodPut).Subrouter()
putMux.HandleFunc("/update", handler)
// Register POST
// Add User + Login + Logout
postMux := r.Methods(http.MethodPost).Subrouter()
postMux.HandleFunc("/add", handler)
postMux.HandleFunc("/login", handler)
postMux.HandleFunc("/logout", handler)
// Register DELETE
// Delete User
deleteMux := r.Methods(http.MethodDelete).Subrouter()
deleteMux.HandleFunc("/username/{id:[0-9]+}", handler)
```

The previous part is about defining the routes and the HTTP methods that we want to support.

```
err := r.Walk(func(route *mux.Route, router *mux.Router, ancestors
[]*mux.Route) error {
```

The previous statements illustrate how we call the Walk() method.

```
        pathTemplate, err := route.GetPathTemplate()
        if err == nil {
            fmt.Println("ROUTE:", pathTemplate)
        }
        pathRegexp, err := route.GetPathRegexp()
        if err == nil {
            fmt.Println("Path regexp:", pathRegexp)
        }
        qT, err := route.GetQueriesTemplates()
        if err == nil {
            fmt.Println("Queries templates:", strings.Join(qT, ","))
        }
```

```
        qRegexps, err := route.GetQueriesRegexp()
        if err == nil {
            fmt.Println("Queries regexps:", strings.Join(qRegexps, ","))
        }
        methods, err := route.GetMethods()
        if err == nil {
            fmt.Println("Methods:", strings.Join(methods, ","))
        }
        fmt.Println()
        return nil
    })
```

For each visited route, the program collects the desired information. Feel free to remove some of the fmt.Println() calls if it does not help your purpose.

```
    if err != nil {
        fmt.Println(err)
    }
    http.Handle("/", r)
}
```

So, the general idea behind walkAll.go is that you assign an empty handler to each route that you have in your server and then you call mux.Walk() to visit all routes. Enabling Go modules and running walkAll.go generates the next output:

```
$ go mod init
$ go mod tidy
$ go run walkAll.go
Queries templates:
Queries regexps:
Methods: GET
ROUTE: /time
Path regexp: ^/time$
Queries templates:
Queries regexps:
Methods: GET
```

The output shows the HTTP methods that each route supports as well as the format of the path. So, the /time endpoint works with GET and its path is /time because the value of Path regexp means that /time is between the beginning (^) and the end of the path ($).

```
ROUTE: /getall
Path regexp: ^/getall$
Queries templates:
Queries regexps:
Methods: GET
ROUTE: /getid
Path regexp: ^/getid$
Queries templates:
Queries regexps:
Methods: GET
ROUTE: /logged
Path regexp: ^/logged$
Queries templates:
Queries regexps:
Methods: GET
ROUTE: /username/{id:[0-9]+}
Path regexp: ^/username/(?P<v0>[0-9]+)$
Queries templates:
Queries regexps:
Methods: GET
```

In the case of /username, the output includes the regular expressions associated with the endpoint that is used for selecting the value of the id variable.

```
Queries templates:
Queries regexps:
Methods: PUT
ROUTE: /update
Path regexp: ^/update$
Queries templates:
Queries regexps:
Methods: PUT
Queries templates:
Queries regexps:
Methods: POST
ROUTE: /add
Path regexp: ^/add$
Queries templates:
```

```
Queries regexps:
Methods: POST
ROUTE: /login
Path regexp: ^/login$
Queries templates:
Queries regexps:
Methods: POST
ROUTE: /logout
Path regexp: ^/logout$
Queries templates:
Queries regexps:
Methods: POST
Queries templates:
Queries regexps:
Methods: DELETE
ROUTE: /username/{id:[0-9]+}
Path regexp: ^/username/(?P<v0>[0-9]+)$
Queries templates:
Queries regexps:
Methods: DELETE
```

Although visiting the routes of a web server is a kind of testing, it is not the official Go way of testing. The main thing to look for in such output is the absence of an endpoint, the use of the wrong HTTP method, or the absence of a parameter from an endpoint.

The next section discusses the testing of Go code.

Testing Go code

The subject of this section is the testing of Go code by *writing test functions*. Software testing is a very large subject and cannot be covered in a single section of a chapter in a book. So, this section tries to present as much practical information as possible.

Go allows you to write tests for your Go code to detect bugs. However, software testing can only show the presence of one or more bugs, not the absence of bugs. This means that you can never be 100% sure that your code contains no bugs!

Strictly speaking, this section is about automated testing, which involves writing extra code to verify whether the real code—that is, the production code—works as expected or not. Thus, the result of a test function is either PASS or FAIL.

You will see how this works shortly. Although the Go approach to testing might look simple at first, especially if you compare it with the testing practices of other programming languages, it is very efficient and effective because it does not require too much of the developer's time.

Go follows certain conventions regarding testing (and benchmarking). The most important convention is that the name of a test function must begin with Test. After the Test word, we must put an underscore or an uppercase letter. Therefore, both TestFunctionName() and Test_functionName() are valid test functions, whereas Testfunctionname() is not. If you prefer idiomatic Go, then use TestFunctionName(). All such functions are put in files that end with _test.go. All test functions must have a t *testing.T parameter and return no values. Lastly, packages that contain testing code should include the testing package.

Once the testing code is correct, the go test subcommand does all the dirty work for you, which includes scanning all *_test.go files for special functions, generating a proper temporary main package, calling these special functions, getting the results, and generating the final output.

Now, let us present testing by revisiting the matchInt() function from *Chapter 3, Composite Data Types.*

Writing tests for ./ch03/intRE.go

In this subsection, we write tests for the matchInt() function, which was implemented in intRE.go back in *Chapter 3, Composite Data Types.* First, we create a new file named intRE_test.go, which is going to contain all tests. Then, we rename the package from main to testRE and remove the main() function—this is an optional step. After that, we must decide what we are going to test and how. The main steps in testing include writing tests for expected input, unexpected input, empty input, and edge cases. All these are going to be seen in the code. Additionally, we are going to generate random integers, convert them into strings, and use them as input for matchInt(). Generally speaking, a good way to test functions that work with numeric values is by using random numbers, or random values in general, as input and see how your code behaves and handles these values.

The relevant code, which includes the original version of intRE.go, can be found inside ~/go/src/github.com/mactsouk/mGo4th/ch12/intRE and is composed of two test functions. The two test functions of intRE_test.go are the following:

```
func TestMatchInt(t *testing.T) {
    if matchInt("") {
        t.Error(`matchInt("") != false`)
    }
```

The matchInt("") call should return false, so if it returns true, it means that the function does not work as expected.

```
if matchInt("00") == false {
    t.Error(`matchInt("00") != true`)
}
```

The matchInt("00") call should return true because 00 is a valid integer, so if it returns false, it means that the function does not work as expected.

```
if matchInt("-00") == false {
    t.Error(`matchInt("-00") != true`)
}

if matchInt("+00") == false {
    t.Error(`matchInt("+00") != true`)
}
}
```

This first test function uses static input to test the correctness of matchInt(). As discussed earlier, a testing function requires a single *testing.T parameter and returns no values.

```
func TestWithRandom(t *testing.T) {
    n := strconv.Itoa(random(-100000, 19999))
    if matchInt(n) == false {
        t.Error("n = ", n)
    }
}
```

The second test function uses a random but valid input to test matchInt()—that random input is generated by the random() function, which is also implemented in intRE_test.go. Therefore, the given input should always pass the test. Running the two test functions with go test creates the next output:

```
$ go test -v *.go
=== RUN   TestMatchInt
--- PASS: TestMatchInt (0.00s)
=== RUN   TestWithRandom
--- PASS: TestWithRandom (0.00s)
PASS
ok      command-line-arguments      0.580s
```

So, all tests passed, which means that everything is fine with matchInt()—in general, the simpler the operation of a function is, the easier it is to test it. The -v parameter creates verbose output and can be omitted.

The next subsection shows how to test UNIX signals.

Testing UNIX signals

There exists a technique for testing UNIX signals. Why do system signals need special treatment? The main reason is that it is difficult to send a UNIX signal to a running UNIX process, which means that it is also difficult to manually test a process that handles UNIX signals. The other tricky reason is that there is a possibility that you exit your running tests by accident when you receive a signal that is defined to do so.

The relevant code can be found inside ch12/testSignals, which contains two files named signalsTest.go and signalsTest_test.go.

The structure of signalsTest.go is as follows:

```
package mySignals

func HandleSignal(sig os.Signal) {
    fmt.Println("handleSignal() Caught:", sig)
}

func Listener() {
    // Function implementation
}
```

So, signalsTest.go does not include a main() function as it does not implement the main package. This happens because such an implementation makes testing easier. After you make sure that your code works as expected, you can either include it in the main package or convert the existing file into the main package. In that case, you just need to change the package statement and rename the Listener() function to main().

The code of signalsTest_test.go is presented in two parts. The first part contains the following code:

```
package mySignals

import (
```

```
        "fmt"
        "syscall"
        "testing"
        "time"
    )

    func TestAll(t *testing.T) {
        go Listener()
        time.Sleep(time.Second)
        test_SIGUSR1()
        time.Sleep(time.Second)
        test_SIGUSR2()
        time.Sleep(time.Second)
        test_SIGHUP()
        time.Sleep(time.Second)
    }
```

The TestAll() function is the only testing function found in signalsTest_test.go, which means
that it is the only one that is going to get executed by go test. Therefore, it would be responsible
for calling the other functions signalsTest_test.go as well as the Listener() function from
signalsTest.go, which is responsible for the handling of the UNIX signals. If you forget to call the
Listener() function, all tests will fail. Additionally, Listener() needs to be called as a goroutine
because, otherwise, all tests will stall as Listener() never returns.

> Bear in mind that if the Listener() goroutine stops handling signals for some
> reason and the program continues to run, the test will still return PASS when it
> actually failed to handle the signal. One possible way for this to happen is if the
> anonymous function in Listener() returns prematurely. However, normally, this
> should never happen.

The time.Sleep() calls give enough time to the test_SIGUSR1(), test_SIGUSR2(), and test_
SIGHUP() functions to send the UNIX signal and the Listener() function to handle them sequentially. The purpose of the last time.Sleep() call is to give Listener() time to process the
last signal before all tests end.

The second part of signalsTest_test.go comes with the next code:

```
    func test_SIGUSR1() {
```

```
    fmt.Println("Sending syscall.SIGUSR1")
    syscall.Kill(syscall.Getpid(), syscall.SIGUSR1)
}

func test_SIGUSR2() {
    fmt.Println("Sending syscall.SIGUSR2")
    syscall.Kill(syscall.Getpid(), syscall.SIGUSR2)
}

func test_SIGHUP() {
    fmt.Println("Sending syscall.SIGHUP")
    syscall.Kill(syscall.Getpid(), syscall.SIGHUP)
}
```

Each one of the test_SIGUSR1(), test_SIGUSR2(), and test_SIGHUP() functions sends a different signal to the running UNIX process—the process ID of the running UNIX process is discovered using a call to syscall.Getpid().

Running the tests produces the following output:

```
$ go test -v *.go
=== RUN    TestAll
Process ID: 22100
Sending syscall.SIGUSR1
handleSignal() Caught: user defined signal 1
Execution time: 1.001762208s
Sending syscall.SIGUSR2
handleSignal() Caught: user defined signal 2
Sending syscall.SIGHUP
Caught: hangup
--- PASS: TestAll (4.00s)
PASS
ok      command-line-arguments    4.411s
```

All tests finish successfully, which means that all signals are handled successfully without the Listener() function exiting prematurely.

If you run the previous test multiple times, you might get a last line that looks like the following:

```
ok      command-line-arguments    (cached)
```

The word cached in the output tells us that Go used existing testing results to make running the tests faster and did not execute the testing functions, which is not always the desired behavior. The next subsection shows how to clear or disable the cache when testing.

Disabling test caching

Testing and caching are not always a good combination, mainly because you get the same results all the time. However, it has its benefits if the test inputs and the test subject do not change—this makes it a completely valid condition in several situations. There exist two ways to avoid getting results using test caching. The first one requires running go clean -testcache, which cleans the entire testing cache, whereas the second one requires running your tests using -count=1, which prevents Go from saving any testing cache for the given testing execution.

The next subsection discusses the use of the TempDir() method, which is handy when you want to create a temporary place for data during testing or benchmarking.

The testing.TempDir() function

The testing.TempDir() method works with both testing and benchmarking. Its purpose is to create a temporary directory that will be used during testing (or benchmarking). Each call to testing.TempDir() returns a unique directory. Go *automatically removes* that temporary directory when the test and its subtests or the benchmarks are about to finish with the help of the CleanUp() method—this is arranged by Go and you do not need to use and implement CleanUp() on your own.

> You should not confuse testing.TempDir() with os.TempDir(). We already saw the use of the os.TempDir() method in profileCla.go and traceCLA.go at the beginning of this chapter. os.TempDir() returns the default directory to use for temporary files, whereas testing.TempDir() returns a temporary directory for the current test to use.

The exact place where the temporary directory is going to be created depends on the operating system used. On macOS, it is under /var/folders, whereas on Linux, it is under /tmp. We are going to illustrate testing.TempDir() in the next subsection, where we also talk about Cleanup().

The Cleanup() function

Although we present the Cleanup() method in a testing scenario, Cleanup() works for both testing and benchmarking. Its name reveals its purpose, which is to clean up some things that we have created when testing or benchmarking a package. However, it is we who need to tell Cleanup() what to do—the parameter of Cleanup() is a function that does the cleaning up.

That function is usually implemented inline as an anonymous function, but you can also create it elsewhere and call it by its name.

The `cleanup.go` file contains a dummy function named `Foo()`—as it contains no real code, there is no point in presenting it. On the other hand, all important code can be found in `cleanup_test.go`.

```go
func myCleanUp() func() {
    return func() {
        fmt.Println("Cleaning up!")
    }
}
```

The `myCleanUp()` function is going to be used as a parameter to `CleanUp()` and should have that specific signature. Apart from the signature, you can put any kind of code in the implementation of `myCleanUp()`.

```go
func TestFoo(t *testing.T) {
    t1 := path.Join(os.TempDir(), "test01")
    t2 := path.Join(os.TempDir(), "test02")
```

The `t1` and `t2` variables hold the paths of two directories that we are going to create.

```go
    err := os.Mkdir(t1, 0755)
    if err != nil {
        t.Error("os.Mkdir() failed:", err)
        return
    }
```

The previous code creates a directory using `os.Mkdir()`—we manually specify its path. Therefore, it is our duty to delete that directory when it is no longer needed.

```go
    defer t.Cleanup(func() {
        err = os.Remove(t1)
        if err != nil {
            t.Error("os.Mkdir() failed:", err)
        }
    })
```

After `TestFoo()` finishes, `t1` is deleted by the code of the anonymous function that is passed as a parameter to `t.CleanUp()`.

```go
    err = os.Mkdir(t2, 0755)
```

```
    if err != nil {
        t.Error("os.Mkdir() failed:", err)
        return
    }
}
```

We create another directory with os.Mkdir()—however, in this case, we are not deleting that directory. Therefore, after TestFoo() finishes, t2 is not going to be deleted.

```
func TestBar(t *testing.T) {
    t1 := t.TempDir()
```

Because of the use of the testing.TempDir() method, the value (directory path) of t1 is assigned by the operating system. Additionally, that directory path is ***automatically deleted*** when the test function is about to finish.

```
    fmt.Println(t1)
    t.Cleanup(myCleanUp())
}
```

Here we use myCleanUp() as the parameter to Cleanup(). This is handy when you want to perform the same cleanup multiple times. Running the tests creates the next output:

```
$ go test -v *.go
=== RUN    TestFoo
--- PASS: TestFoo (0.00s)
=== RUN    TestBar
/var/folders/sk/1tk8cnw50lzdtr2hxcj5sv2m0000gn/T/TestBar1090994662/001
```

This is the temporary directory that was created with TempDir() on a macOS machine.

```
Cleaning up!
--- PASS: TestBar (0.00s)
PASS
ok      command-line-arguments          0.493s
```

Checking whether the directories created by TempDir() are there shows that they have been successfully deleted. On the other hand, the directory stored in the t2 variable of TestFoo() has not been deleted. Running the same tests again (remember to disable caching) is going to fail because the test02 file already exists and cannot be created:

```
$ go test -v *.go -count=1
```

```
=== RUN     TestFoo
    cleanup_test.go:34: os.Mkdir() failed: mkdir /var/folders/sk/
ltk8cnw50lzdtr2hxcj5sv2m0000gn/T/test02: file exists
--- FAIL: TestFoo (0.00s)
=== RUN     TestBar
/var/folders/sk/ltk8cnw50lzdtr2hxcj5sv2m0000gn/T/TestBar1703429008/001
Cleaning up!
--- PASS: TestBar (0.00s)
FAIL
FAIL    command-line-arguments    0.310s
FAIL
```

The `/var/folders/sk/ltk8cnw50lzdtr2hxcj5sv2m0000gn/T/test02: file exists` error message reveals the root of the problem. So, ***clean up your tests properly***.

The next subsection discusses the use of the `testing/quick` package.

The testing/quick package

There are times when you need to create testing data without human intervention. The Go standard library offers the `testing/quick` package, which can be used for *black-box testing* (a software testing method that checks the functionality of an application or function without any prior knowledge of its internal working) and is somewhat related to the `QuickCheck` package found in the Haskell programming language—both packages implement utility functions to help you with black-box testing. With the help of `testing/quick`, Go generates random values of built-in types that you can use for testing, which saves you from having to generate all these values manually.

The code of `quickT.go` is the following:

```
package quickt

type Point2D struct {
    X, Y int
}

func Add(x1, x2 Point2D) Point2D {
    temp := Point2D{}
    temp.X = x1.X + x2.X
    temp.Y = x1.Y + x2.Y
    return temp
}
```

The previous code implements a single function that adds two `Point2D` variables—this is the function that we are going to test.

The code of `quickT_test.go` is as follows:

```go
package quickt

import (
    "testing"
    "testing/quick"
)

var N = 1000000

func TestWithItself(t *testing.T) {
    condition := func(a, b Point2D) bool {
        return Add(a, b) == Add(b, a)
    }
    err := quick.Check(condition, &quick.Config{MaxCount: N})
    if err != nil {
        t.Errorf("Error: %v", err)
    }
}
```

The call to `quick.Check()` automatically generates random numbers based on the signature of its first argument, which is a function defined earlier. There is no need to create these random numbers on your own, which makes the code easy to read and write. The actual tests happen in the `condition` function. Put simply, we start by defining a property function that represents a condition that we want to hold true for a range of inputs. This function takes the input values and returns a Boolean value indicating whether the property holds for those values or not.

```go
func TestThree(t *testing.T) {
    condition := func(a, b, c Point2D) bool {
        return Add(Add(a, b), c) == Add(a, b)
    }
```

This implementation is wrong on purpose. To correct the implementation, we should replace `Add(Add(a, b), c)` == `Add(a, b)` with `Add(Add(a, b), c)` == `Add(c, Add(a, b))`. We did that to see the output that is generated when a test fails.

```
        err := quick.Check(condition, &quick.Config{MaxCount: N})
        if err != nil {
            t.Errorf("Error: %v", err)
        }
    }
}
```

Running the created tests generates the next output:

```
$ go test -v *.go
=== RUN    TestWithItself
--- PASS: TestWithItself (0.86s)
```

As expected, the first test was successful.

```
=== RUN    TestThree
    quickT_test.go:28: Error: #1: failed on input quickT.
Point2D{X:-8079189616506550499, Y:-6176385978113309642}, quickT.
Point2D{X:9017849222923794558, Y:-7161977443830767080}, quickT.
Point2D{X:-714979330681957566, Y:-4578147860393889265}
--- FAIL: TestThree (0.00s)
FAIL
FAIL    command-line-arguments  0.618s
FAIL
```

However, as expected, the second test generated an error. The good thing is that the input that caused the error is presented onscreen so that you can see the input that caused your function to fail.

The next subsection tells us how to time out tests that take too long to finish.

Timing out tests

If the go test tool takes too long to finish or, for some reason, never ends, the -timeout parameter can help you.

To illustrate that, we are using the code from the previous subsection as well as the -timeout and -count command line flags. While the former specifies the maximum allowed time duration for the tests, the latter specifies the number of times the tests are going to be executed.

Running go test -v *.go -timeout 1s tells go test that all tests should take at most one second to finish—on my machine, the tests did take less than a second to finish.

However, running the following generates a different output:

```
$ go test -v *.go -timeout 1s -count 2
=== RUN    TestWithItself
--- PASS: TestWithItself (0.87s)
=== RUN    TestThree
    quickT_test.go:28: Error: #1: failed on input quickT.
Point2D{X:-312047170140227400, Y:-5441930920566042029}, quickT.
Point2D{X:7855449254220087092, Y:7437813460700902767}, quickT.
Point2D{X:4838605758154930957, Y:-7621852714243790655}
--- FAIL: TestThree (0.00s)
=== RUN    TestWithItself
panic: test timed out after 1s
```

The actual output is longer than the presented one—the rest of the output has to do with gorou-tines being terminated before they have finished. The key thing here is that the go test command timed out the process due to the use of -timeout 1s.

So far, we have seen the use of Errorf() when a test fails. The next subsection discusses the use of testing.T.Fatalf() and testing.T.Fatal().

Testing using testing.T.Fatal() and testing.T.Fatalf()

This subsection discusses the use of testing.T.Fatalf() and testing.T.Fatal(). The core idea behind the use of T.Fatal() and T.Fatalf() instead of T.Error() and T.Errorf() is that you should use T.Fatal() or T.Fatalf() when it makes sense to stop testing the code that comes because the previous failure is going to cause more failures. On the other hand, you should use the appropriate T.Error() variant when a condition failure is not going to cause more failures due to various dependencies.

 Two real-world cases for using t.Fatalf() are when a database connection re-quired for testing fails or when a network connection required for testing cannot be established.

The relevant code can be found in code.go and code_test.go, which are both located inside ch12/testFatal.

The contents of code.go are the following:

```
package server
```

```
var DATA = map[string]string{}

func init() {
    DATA["server"] = "127.0.0.1"
}
```

The server package initializes the DATA map using the init() function by defining the value for the "server" key.

The contents of code_test.go are the following:

```
package server

import (
    "testing"
)

func TestMap(t *testing.T) {
    key := "server"
    server, ok := DATA[key]
    if !ok {
        t.Fatalf("Key %s not found!", key)
    }

    key = "port"
    port, ok := DATA[key]
    if !ok {
        t.Fatalf("Key %s not found!", key)
    }

    t.Log("Connecting to", server, "@port", port)
}
```

In this case, there is no point in executing the t.Log() call as the "port" key is not defined in the DATA map. In this case, we use t.Fatalf(), which terminates the testing process.

Running the tests generates the following output:

```
$ go test -v *.go
```

```
=== RUN    TestMap
    code_test.go:17: Key port not found!
--- FAIL: TestMap (0.00s)
FAIL
FAIL    command-line-arguments    0.412s
FAIL
```

So, as expected, t.Log() is never executed and the test fails.

The next subsection talks about table-driven testing.

Table-driven tests

Table-driven tests are tests that have many input scenarios. The main advantage of table-driven testing is that a developer can cover lots of testing cases by reusing existing code, which saves time and energy. In order to have the parameters of the various tests in the same place, we usually use a slice of structures and iterate over its elements to run the tests.

All relevant code of the example can be found in the ch12/table directory, which contains two files. The first file is called table.go, whereas the source code file that is used for testing is called table_test.go.

The table.go file contains the following code:

```
package division

func intDiv(a, b int) int {
    return a / b
}

func floatDiv(a, b int) float64 {
    return float64(a) / float64(b)
}
```

The Go package that we are going to test contains two functions that implement integer division (intDiv()) and floating-point division between two integers (floatDiv()), respectively. As you might recall from your mathematics classes, integer division between two integers gives different results from regular division. As an example, dividing 2 by 4 gives 0 as a result in integer division and 0.5 in regular division. This means that integer division ignores the remainder and produces integer results only, hence the function signature of intDiv().

The table_test.go file is going to be presented in two parts. The first part comes with the following code:

```go
package division
import (
    "testing"
)

type myTest struct {
    a        int
    b        int
    resInt   int
    resFloat float64
}

var tests = []myTest{
    {a: 1, b: 2, resInt: 0, resFloat: 0.5},
    {a: 5, b: 10, resInt: 0, resFloat: 0.5},
    {a: 2, b: 2, resInt: 1, resFloat: 1.0},
    {a: 4, b: 2, resInt: 2, resFloat: 2.0},
    {a: 5, b: 2, resInt: 2, resFloat: 2.5},
    {a: 5, b: 4, resInt: 1, resFloat: 1.2},
}
```

The number of entries in the tests structure, which can have any name you want, signifies the number of tests that we are going to perform. The last entry has an intentional error in it as 5 divided by 4 equals 1.25 instead of 1.2, which means that the respective test is going to fail.

 The biggest advantage of table-driven testing is that adding a new test is just as simple as adding an entry to the structure that holds the existing tests. In a different case, you would need to add an additional test function.

The second part of table_test.go is the following:

```go
func TestAll(t *testing.T) {
    t.Parallel()

    for _, test := range tests {
```

```
        intResult := intDiv(test.a, test.b)
        if intResult != test.resInt {
            t.Errorf("Expected %d, got %d", test.resInt, intResult)
        }

        floatResult := floatDiv(test.a, test.b)
        if floatResult != test.resFloat {
            t.Errorf("Expected %f, got %f", test.resFloat, floatResult)
        }
    }
}
```

The Test_all() testing function iterates over the contents of the tests structure and runs the tests. The t.Parallel() statement allows the tests to run in parallel, which makes the process faster. Execute go doc testing.T.Parallel in the shell for more information about its usage. However, in this case, t.Parallel() has no effect since no other tests are marked as parallel.

 In general, float comparison like the one presented here is, generally, unreliable. For the purposes of the book, it is fine, but you should not rely on float comparison in your test functions. More about that can be found at https://medium.com/p/9872fe6de17f.

Running the tests produces the following results:

```
$ go test -v *.go
=== RUN   TestAll
    table_test.go:33: Expected 1.200000, got 1.250000
--- FAIL: TestAll (0.00s)
FAIL
FAIL    command-line-arguments    0.332s
FAIL
```

All tests were successful apart from the last one. The next subsection shows how to find information about the code coverage of your software.

Testing code coverage

In this section, we are going to learn how to find information about the code coverage of our programs to discover blocks of code or single code statements that are not being executed by testing functions.

Among other things, seeing the code coverage of programs can reveal logical issues and bugs in the code, so do not underestimate its usefulness. However, the code coverage test complements unit testing without replacing it. The only thing to remember is that you should make sure that the testing functions try to cover all cases and, therefore, try to run all available code. If the testing functions do not try to cover all cases, then the issue might be with them, not the code that is being tested.

All relevant files can be found in `ch12/coverage`. The code of `coverage.go`, which has some intentional issues in order to show how unreachable code is identified, is as follows:

```go
package coverage
import "fmt"

func f1() {
    if true {
        fmt.Println("Hello!")
    } else {
        fmt.Println("Hi!")
    }
}
```

The issue with this function is that the first branch of `if` is always true and, therefore, the `else` branch is never going to get executed.

```go
func f2(n int) int {
    if n >= 0 {
        return 0
    } else if n == 1 {
        return 1
    } else {
        return f2(n-1) + f2(n-2)
    }
}
```

There exist two issues with `f2()`. The first one is that it does not work well with negative integers and the second one is that all positive integers are handled by the first `if` branch. Code coverage can only help you with the second issue. The code of `coverage_test.go` is the following—these are regular test functions that try to run all available code:

```go
package coverage
```

```
import "testing"
func Test_f1(t *testing.T) {
    f1()
}
```

This test function naively tests the operation of f1().

```
func Test_f2(t *testing.T) {
    _ = f2(123)
}
```

The second test function checks the operation of f2() by running f2(123).

First, we should run go test as follows—the code coverage task is done by the s flag:

```
$ go test -cover *.go
ok      command-line-arguments      0.420s      coverage: 50.0% of statements
```

The previous output shows that we have 50% code coverage, which is not a good thing! However, we are not done yet as we can generate a test coverage report. The next command generates the code coverage report:

```
$ go test -coverprofile=coverage.out *.go
```

The contents of coverage.out are as follows—yours might vary a little depending on your username and the folder used:

```
$ cat coverage.out
mode: set
~/go/src/github.com/mGo4th/ch12/coverage/coverage.go:5.11,6.10 1 1
~/go/src/github.com/mactsouk/mGo4th/ch12/coverage/coverage.go:6.10,8.3 1 1
~/go/src/github.com/mactsouk/mGo4th/ch12/coverage/coverage.go:8.8,10.3 1 0
~/go/src/github.com/mactsouk/mGo4th/ch12/coverage/coverage.go:13.20,14.12
1 1
~/go/src/github.com/mactsouk/mGo4th/ch12/coverage/coverage.go:14.12,16.3 1
1
~/go/src/github.com/mactsouk/mGo4th/ch12/coverage/coverage.go:16.8,16.19 1
0
~/go/src/github.com/mactsouk/mGo4th/ch12/coverage/coverage.go:16.19,18.3 1
0
~/go/src/github.com/mactsouk/mGo4th/ch12/coverage/coverage.go:18.8,20.3 1
0
```

The format and the fields in each line of the coverage file are `name.go:line.column,line.column` `numberOfStatements count`. The last field is a flag that tells you whether the statements specified by `line.column,line.column` are covered or not. So, when you see 0 in the last field, it means that the code is not covered.

Lastly, the HTML output can be seen in your favorite web browser by running `go tool cover` `-html=coverage.out`. If you used a different filename than `coverage.out`, modify the command accordingly. The next figure shows the generated output—if you are reading the printed version of the book, you might not be able to see the colors. Red lines denote code that is not being executed, whereas green lines show code that was executed by the tests.

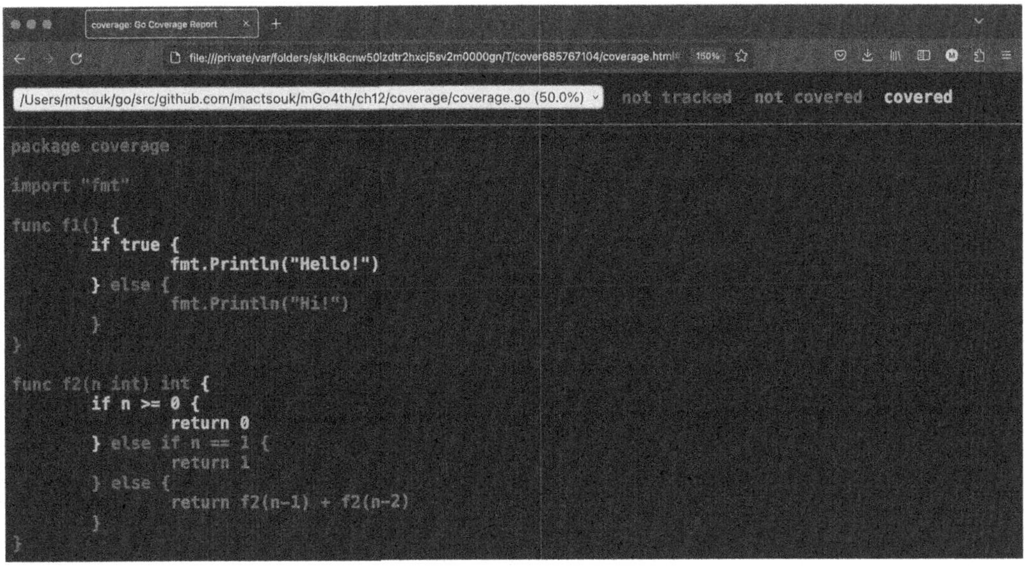

Figure 12.2: Code coverage report

Some of the code is marked as not tracked (gray in color) because this is code that cannot be processed by the code coverage tool. The generated output clearly shows the code issues with both `f1()` and `f2()`. You just have to correct them now!

The next subsection discusses unreachable code and how to discover it.

Finding unreachable Go code

Sometimes, a wrongly implemented `if` or a misplaced `return` statement can create blocks of code that are unreachable, that is, blocks of code that are not going to be executed at all. As this is a logical kind of error, which means that it is not going to get caught by the compiler, we need to find a way of discovering it.

Fortunately, the go vet tool, which examines Go source code and reports suspicious constructs, can help with that—the use of go vet is illustrated with the help of the cannotReach.go source code file, which contains the next two functions:

```
func S2() {
    return
    fmt.Println("Hello!")
}
```

There is a logical error here because S2() returns before printing the desired message.

```
func S1() {
    fmt.Println("In S1()")
    return
    fmt.Println("Leaving S1()")
}
```

Similarly, S1() returns without giving the fmt.Println("Leaving S1()") statement a chance to be executed.

Running go vet on cannotReach.go creates the next output:

```
$ go vet cannotReach.go
# command-line-arguments
./cannotReach.go:9:2: unreachable code
./cannotReach.go:16:2: unreachable code
```

The first message points to the fmt.Println() statement of S2() and the second one to the second fmt.Println() statement of S1(). In this case, go vet did a great job. However, go vet is not particularly sophisticated and cannot catch every possible type of logical error. If you need a more advanced tool, have a look at staticcheck (https://staticcheck.io/), which can also be integrated with Microsoft Visual Studio Code (https://code.visualstudio.com/), Neovim (!), and Zed (https://zed.dev/)—the next figure shows that Zed underlines the unreachable code. Visual Studio Code works in a similar way.

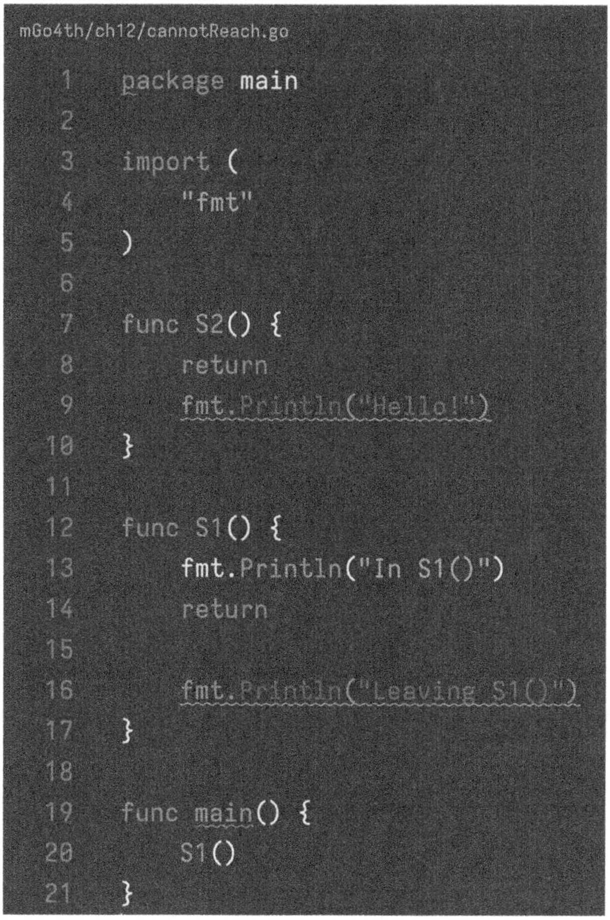

```
mGo4th/ch12/cannotReach.go
1    package main
2
3    import (
4        "fmt"
5    )
6
7    func S2() {
8        return
9        fmt.Println("Hello!")
10   }
11
12   func S1() {
13       fmt.Println("In S1()")
14       return
15
16       fmt.Println("Leaving S1()")
17   }
18
19   func main() {
20       S1()
21   }
```

Figure 12.3: Viewing unreachable code in Zed

As a rule of thumb, it does not hurt to include go vet in your workflow. You can find more information about the capabilities of go vet by running go doc cmd/vet.

The next subsection illustrates how to test an HTTP server with a database backend.

Testing an HTTP server with a database backend

An HTTP server is a different kind of animal because it should already run for tests to get executed. Thankfully, the net/http/httptest package can help—you do not need to run the HTTP server on your own as the net/http/httptest package does the work for you, but you need to have the database server up and running. We are going to test the REST API server we developed in *Chapter 11, Working with REST APIs*. All relevant files are located inside ch12/testHTTP.

The code of server_test.go, which holds the test functions for the HTTP service, is the following:

```go
package main
import (
    "bytes"
    "net/http"
    "net/http/httptest"
    "strconv"
    "strings"
    "testing"
    "time"
    "github.com/gorilla/mux"
)
```

The only reason for including github.com/gorilla/mux is the use of mux.SetURLVars() later on.

```go
func TestTimeHandler(t *testing.T) {
    req, err := http.NewRequest("GET", "/time", nil)
    if err != nil {
        t.Fatal(err)
    }
    rr := httptest.NewRecorder()
    handler := http.HandlerFunc(TimeHandler)
    handler.ServeHTTP(rr, req)
    status := rr.Code
    if status != http.StatusOK {
        t.Errorf("handler returned wrong status code: got %v want %v",
            status, http.StatusOK)
    }
}
```

The `http.NewRequest()` function is used to define the HTTP request method and the endpoint and to send data to the endpoint when needed. The `http.HandlerFunc(TimeHandler)` call specifies the handler function that is being tested.

```
func TestMethodNotAllowed(t *testing.T) {
    req, err := http.NewRequest("DELETE", "/time", nil)
    if err != nil {
        t.Fatal(err)
    }
    rr := httptest.NewRecorder()
    handler := http.HandlerFunc(MethodNotAllowedHandler)
```

We are testing `MethodNotAllowedHandler` in this test function.

```
    handler.ServeHTTP(rr, req)
    status := rr.Code
    if status != http.StatusNotFound {
        t.Errorf("handler returned wrong status code: got %v want %v",
            status, http.StatusOK)
    }
}
```

We know that this interaction is going to fail as we are testing `MethodNotAllowedHandler`. Therefore, we expect to get an `http.StatusNotFound` response code back—if we get a different code, the test function is going to fail.

```
func TestLogin(t *testing.T) {
    UserPass := []byte(`{"Username": "admin", "Password": "admin"}`)
```

Here we store the desired fields of a `User` structure in a byte slice. For the tests to work, the `admin` user should have `admin` as the password because this is what is used in the code—modify `server_test.go` in order to have the correct password for the `admin` user, or any other user with admin privileges, of your installation.

In general, and mainly for critical applications or projects that involve more than a single developer, this is not a good practice. Ideally, everything needed for the tests should be contained within the tests. One possible solution is to provide a separate database or a separate machine used just for testing purposes.

```
    req, err := http.NewRequest("POST", "/login", bytes.
NewBuffer(UserPass))
```

```
    if err != nil {
        t.Fatal(err)
    }
    req.Header.Set("Content-Type", "application/json")
```

The previous lines of code construct the desired request, which is about logging in to the service.

```
    rr := httptest.NewRecorder()
    handler := http.HandlerFunc(LoginHandler)
    handler.ServeHTTP(rr, req)
```

`NewRecorder()` returns an initialized `ResponseRecorder` that is used in `ServeHTTP()`—`ServeHTTP()` is the method that performs the request. The response is saved in the `rr` variable.

There is also a test function for the `/logout` endpoint, which is not presented here as it is almost identical to `TestLogin()`. In this case, running the tests in a random order might create issues with testing because `TestLogin()` should always get executed before `TestLogout()`.

```
    status := rr.Code
    if status != http.StatusOK {
        t.Errorf("handler returned wrong status code: got %v want %v",
            status, http.StatusOK)
        return
    }
}
```

If the status code is `http.StatusOK`, it means that the interaction worked as expected.

```
func TestAdd(t *testing.T) {
    now := int(time.Now().Unix())
    username := "test_" + strconv.Itoa(now)
    users := `[{"Username": "admin", "Password": "admin"}, {"Username":"`
+ username + `", "Password": "myPass"}]`
```

For the Add() handler, we need to pass an array of JSON records, which is constructed here. As we do not want to create the same username every time, we append the current timestamp to the _test string.

```
    UserPass := []byte(users)
    req, err := http.NewRequest("POST", "/add", bytes.NewBuffer(UserPass))
    if err != nil {
        t.Fatal(err)
```

```
        }
        req.Header.Set("Content-Type", "application/json")
```

This is where we construct the slice of JSON records (UserPass) and create the request.

```
        rr := httptest.NewRecorder()
        handler := http.HandlerFunc(AddHandler)
        handler.ServeHTTP(rr, req)
        // Check the HTTP status code is what we expect.
        if status := rr.Code; status != http.StatusOK {
            t.Errorf("handler returned wrong status code: got %v want %v",
                status, http.StatusOK)
            return
        }
    }
```

If the server response is http.StatusOK, then the request is successful and the test passes.

```
func TestGetUserDataHandler(t *testing.T) {
    UserPass := []byte(`{"Username": "admin", "Password": "admin"}`)
    req, err := http.NewRequest("GET", "/username/1", bytes.
NewBuffer(UserPass))
```

Although we use /username/1 in the request, this does not add any value to the Vars map. There-fore, we need to use the SetURLVars() function to change the values in the Vars map—this is illustrated next:

```
    if err != nil {
        t.Fatal(err)
    }
    req.Header.Set("Content-Type", "application/json")
    vars := map[string]string{
        "id": "1",
    }
    req = mux.SetURLVars(req, vars)
```

The gorilla/mux package provides the SetURLVars() function for testing purposes—this func-tion allows you to add elements to the Vars map. In this case, we need to set the value of the id key to 1. You can add as many key/value pairs as you want.

```
        rr := httptest.NewRecorder()
```

```
    handler := http.HandlerFunc(GetUserDataHandler)
    handler.ServeHTTP(rr, req)
    if status := rr.Code; status != http.StatusOK {
        t.Errorf("handler returned wrong status code: got %v want %v",
            status, http.StatusOK)
        return
    }
expected := `{"id":1,"username":"admin","password":"admin",
"lastlogin":1702577035,"admin":1,"active":0}`
```

The expected variable holds the record we expect to get back from our request.

Using the same value for lastlogin does not make any sense. Therefore, we might be dealing with a bug here. Additionally, if we cannot guess the value of lastlogin in the server response, we might need to replace it with 0 in both expected and serverResponse. An alternative would have been to marshal the result into a structure and only compare what is relevant for the test.

```
    serverResponse = strings.TrimSpace(serverResponse)
```

The previous statement removes any spaces from the HTTP server response.

```
    if serverResponse != expected {
        t.Errorf("handler returned unexpected body: got %v but wanted %v",
serverResponse, expected)
    }
}
```

The last part of the code contains the standard Go way of checking whether we have received the expected answer or not.

Creating tests for HTTP services is easy once you understand the presented examples. This mainly happens because most of the code is repeated among test functions.

Running the tests generates the next output:

```
$ go test -v server_test.go main.go handlers.go restdb.go
```

```
=== RUN    TestTimeHandler
2023/12/14 22:12:30 TimeHandler Serving: /time from
--- PASS: TestTimeHandler (0.00s)
=== RUN    TestMethodNotAllowed
2023/12/14 22:12:30 Serving: /time from  with method DELETE
--- PASS: TestMethodNotAllowed (0.00s)
=== RUN    TestLogin
```

This is the output from visiting the /time endpoint with the DELETE HTTP method. Its result is PASS because we were expecting this request to fail as it uses the wrong HTTP method.

```
2023/12/14 22:12:30 LoginHandler Serving: /login from
2023/12/14 22:12:30 Input user: {0 admin admin 0 0 0}
2023/12/14 22:12:30 Found user: {1 admin admin 1702577035 1 0}
2023/12/14 22:12:30 Logging in: {1 admin admin 1702577035 1 0}
2023/12/14 22:12:30 Updating user: {1 admin admin 1702577825 1 1}
2023/12/14 22:12:30 Affected: 1
2023/12/14 22:12:30 User updated: {1 admin admin 1702577728 1 1}
--- PASS: TestLogin (0.00s)
```

This is the output from TestLogin() that tests the /login endpoint. All lines beginning with the date and time are generated by the REST API server and show the progress of the request.

```
=== RUN    TestLogout
2023/12/14 22:12:30 LogoutHandler Serving: /logout from
2023/12/14 22:12:30 Found user: {1 admin admin 1702577035 1 1}
2023/12/14 22:12:30 Logging out: admin
2023/12/14 22:12:30 Updating user: {1 admin admin 1702577035 1 0}
2023/12/14 22:12:30 Affected: 1
2023/12/14 22:12:30 User updated: {1 admin admin 1702577035 1 0}
--- PASS: TestLogout (0.00s)
```

This is the output from TestLogout() that tests the /logout endpoint, which also has the PASS result.

```
=== RUN    TestAdd
2023/12/14 22:12:30 AddHandler Serving: /add from
2023/12/14 22:12:30 [{0 admin admin 0 0 0} {0 test_1702577728 myPass 0 0
0}]
```

This is the output from the `TestAdd()` test function. The name of the new user that is created is `test_1702577728` and it should be different each time the test is executed.

```
--- PASS: TestAdd (0.00s)
=== RUN    TestGetUserDataHandler
2023/12/14 22:12:30 GetUserDataHandler Serving: /username/1 from
2023/12/14 22:12:30 Found user: {1 admin admin 1702577035 1 0}
--- PASS: TestGetUserDataHandler (0.00s)
PASS
ok      command-line-arguments      0.329s
```

Lastly, this is the output from the `TestGetUserDataHandler()` test function that was also executed without any issues.

The next section presents the `govulncheck` tool, which is used to find vulnerabilities in project dependencies.

The govulncheck tool

The purpose of the `govulncheck` tool is to find vulnerabilities in project dependencies. This means that it is there to make your Go binaries and Go modules more secure.

Installing the tool

You can install `govulncheck` by running the following command:

```
$ go install golang.org/x/vuln/cmd/govulncheck@latest
$ cd ~/go/bin
$ ls -lh govulncheck
-rwxr-xr-x@ 1 mtsouk  staff   11M Dec  9 19:41 govulncheck
```

As expected, the `govulncheck` binary is going to be installed in `~/go/bin`.

The relevant Go code can be found inside `ch12/vulcheck`—the source code file is called `vul.go` and contains the following code:

```go
package main

import (
    "fmt"
    "golang.org/x/text/language"
)
```

```
func main() {
    greece := language.Make("el")
    en := language.Make("en")
    fmt.Println(greece.Region())
    fmt.Println(en.Region())
}
```

Running vul.go requires executing the following commands first:

```
$ go mod init
$ go mod tidy
go: finding module for package golang.org/x/text/language
go: downloading golang.org/x/text v0.14.0
go: found golang.org/x/text/language in golang.org/x/text v0.14.0
```

Based on the previous output of go mod tidy, the contents of go.mod are the following:

```
$ cat go.mod
module github.com/mactsouk/mGo4th/ch12/vulcheck
go 1.21.5
require golang.org/x/text v0.14.0
```

So, we are using version v0.14.0 of the golang.org/x/text package.

Running govulncheck against vul.go produces the following results:

```
$ ~/go/bin/govulncheck ./...
Scanning your code and 47 packages across 1 dependent module for known
vulnerabilities...


No vulnerabilities found.


Share feedback at https://go.dev/s/govulncheck-feedback
```

Now, let us change the contents of go.mod to include a package version with known vulnerabilities *on purpose*. This requires executing the following commands:

```
$ go get golang.org/x/text@v0.3.5
go: downloading golang.org/x/text v0.3.5
go: downgraded golang.org/x/text v0.14.0 => v0.3.5
```

The purpose of the previous command is to download an older version of the golang.org/x/text package with known vulnerabilities.

The contents of go.mod are now the following:

```
module github.com/mactsouk/mGo4th/ch12/vulcheck

go 1.21.5

require golang.org/x/text v0.3.5
```

So, we are now using version v0.3.5 of the golang.org/x/text package.

This time, running govulncheck against vul.go produces the following output:

```
$ ~/go/bin/govulncheck ./...
Scanning your code and 47 packages across 1 dependent module for known
vulnerabilities...

=== Informational ===

Found 2 vulnerabilities in packages that you import, but there are no call
stacks leading to the use of these vulnerabilities. You may not need to
take any action. See https://pkg.go.dev/golang.org/x/vuln/cmd/govulncheck
for details.

Vulnerability #1: GO-2022-1059
    Denial of service via crafted Accept-Language header in
    golang.org/x/text/language
  More info: https://pkg.go.dev/vuln/GO-2022-1059
  Module: golang.org/x/text
    Found in: golang.org/x/text@v0.3.5
    Fixed in: golang.org/x/text@v0.3.8

Vulnerability #2: GO-2021-0113
    Out-of-bounds read in golang.org/x/text/language
  More info: https://pkg.go.dev/vuln/GO-2021-0113
  Module: golang.org/x/text
    Found in: golang.org/x/text@v0.3.5
```

```
      Fixed in: golang.org/x/text@v0.3.7

No vulnerabilities found.

Share feedback at https://go.dev/s/govulncheck-feedback
```

This time, *we found vulnerabilities in the modules that we are using*. The solution to that is to upgrade to the latest version of the golang.org/x/text package by running the following command:

```
$ go get golang.org/x/text@latest
go: upgraded golang.org/x/text v0.3.5 => v0.14.0
```

If you want to get the output in JSON format, you can run govulncheck with the -json flag, which is illustrated in the following output:

```
$ ~/go/bin/govulncheck -json ./...
{
  "config": {
    "protocol_version": "v1.0.0",
    "scanner_name": "govulncheck",
    "scanner_version": "v1.0.1",
    "db": "https://vuln.go.dev",
    "db_last_modified": "2023-12-11T21:16:41Z",
    "go_version": "go1.21.5",
    "scan_level": "symbol"
  }
}
{
  "progress": {
    "message": "Scanning your code and 47 packages across 1 dependent
module for known vulnerabilities..."
  }
}
```

You should definitely make a habit of using govulncheck in your projects.

The next section discusses a handy Go feature, cross-compilation, because after testing your code, you usually want to distribute it!

Cross-compilation

Cross-compilation is the process of generating a binary executable file for a different architecture than the one that we are working on without having access to other machines. The main benefit that we receive from cross-compilation is that we do not need a second or third machine to create and distribute executable files for different architectures. This means that we basically need just a single machine for our development. Fortunately, Go has built-in support for cross-compilation.

To cross-compile a Go source file, we need to set the GOOS and GOARCH environment variables to the target operating system and architecture, respectively, which is not as difficult as it sounds.

> You can find a list of available values for the GOOS and GOARCH environment variables at https://go.dev/doc/install/source. Keep in mind, however, that not all GOOS and GOARCH combinations are valid. You can find a list of all valid combinations using go tool dist list.

The code of crossCompile.go is the following:

```go
package main
import (
    "fmt"
    "runtime"
)

func main() {
    fmt.Print("You are using ", runtime.GOOS, " ")
    fmt.Println("on a(n)", runtime.GOARCH, "machine")
    fmt.Println("with Go version", runtime.Version())
}
```

Running it on a macOS machine with Go version 1.21.5 generates the next output:

```
$ go run crossCompile.go
You are using darwin on a(n) arm64 machine
with Go version go1.21.5
```

Compiling crossCompile.go for the Linux OS that runs on a machine with an amd64 processor is as simple as running the next command on a macOS machine:

```
$ env GOOS=linux GOARCH=amd64 go build crossCompile.go
```

```
$ file crossCompile
crossCompile: ELF 64-bit LSB executable, x86-64, version 1 (SYSV),
statically linked, Go BuildID=28hWIc2cet8-kmHxC-W6/Y7DEXRrm3CrFgqVvflBA/
KWqCcnUNgUozkElJHidj/Geqp0vSmfLgkLrZ_-7cX, with debug_info, not stripped
```

Transferring that file to an Arch Linux machine and running it generates the next output:

```
$ ./crossCompile
You are using linux on a(n) amd64 machine
with Go version go1.21.5
```

One thing to notice here is that the cross-compiled binary file of crossCompile.go prints the Go version of the machine used for compiling it—this makes perfect sense as the target machine might not even have Go installed on it!

Cross-compilation is a great Go feature that can come in handy when you want to generate multiple versions of your executables through a CI/CD system and distribute them.

The next subsection discusses go:generate.

Using go:generate

Although go:generate is not directly connected to testing or profiling, it is a handy and advanced Go feature, and I believe that this chapter is the perfect place for discussing it as it can also help you with testing. The go:generate directive is associated with the go generate command, which was added in Go 1.4 in order to help with automation, and allows you to run commands described by directives within existing files.

The go generate command supports the -v, -n, and -x flags. The -v flag prints the names of packages and files as they are processed, whereas the -n flag prints the commands that would be executed. Lastly, the -x flag prints commands as they are executed—this is great for debugging go:generate commands.

The main reasons that you might need to use go:generate are the following:

- You want to download dynamic data from the internet or some other source prior to the execution of the Go code.
- You want to execute some code prior to running the Go code.
- You want to generate a version number or other unique data before code execution.
- You want to make sure that you have sample data to work with. For example, you can put data into a database using go:generate.

As using go:generate is not considered a good practice because it hides things from the developer and creates additional dependencies, I try to avoid it when I can, and I usually can. On the other hand, if you really need it, you will know it!

The use of go:generate is illustrated in goGenerate.go, which is found in ./ch12/generate and has the following content:

```
package main
import "fmt"
//go:generate ./echo.sh
```

This executes the echo.sh script, which should be available in the current directory.

```
//go:generate echo GOFILE: $GOFILE
//go:generate echo GOARCH: $GOARCH
//go:generate echo GOOS: $GOOS
//go:generate echo GOLINE: $GOLINE
//go:generate echo GOPACKAGE: $GOPACKAGE
```

$GOFILE, $GOARCH, $GOOS, $GOLINE, and $GOPACKAGE are special variables and are translated at the time of execution.

```
//go:generate echo DOLLAR: $DOLLAR
//go:generate echo Hello!
//go:generate ls -l
//go:generate ./hello.py
```

This executes the hello.py Python script, which should be available in the current directory.

```
func main() {
    fmt.Println("Hello there!")
}
```

The go generate command is not going to run the fmt.Println() statement or any other statements found in a Go source file. Lastly, keep in mind that go generate is not executed automatically and must be run explicitly.

Working with goGenerate.go from within ./ch12/generate generates the next output:

```
$ go mod init
$ go mod tidy
$ go generate
```

```
Hello world!
GOFILE: goGenerate.go
GOARCH: arm64
GOOS: darwin
GOLINE: 10
GOPACKAGE: main
```

This is the output of the $GOFILE, $GOARCH, $GOOS, $GOLINE, and $GOPACKAGE variables, which shows the values of these variables defined at runtime.

```
DOLLAR: $
```

There is also a special variable named $DOLLAR for printing a dollar character in the output because $ has a special meaning in the OS environment.

```
Hello!
total 32
-rwxr-xr-x@ 1 mtsouk  staff   32 Nov 10 22:22 echo.sh
-rw-r--r--  1 mtsouk  staff   59 Dec 14 20:25 go.mod
-rw-r--r--@ 1 mtsouk  staff  383 Nov 10 22:22 goGenerate.go
-rwxr-xr-x@ 1 mtsouk  staff   52 Nov 10 22:22 hello.py
```

This is the output of the ls -l command, which shows the files found in the current directory at the time of the code execution. This can be used to test whether some necessary files are present at the time of execution or not.

```
Hello from Python!
```

Running go generate with -n shows the commands that are going to be executed:

```
$ go generate -n
./echo.sh
echo GOFILE: goGenerate.go
echo GOARCH: arm64
echo GOOS: darwin
echo GOLINE: 10
echo GOPACKAGE: main
echo DOLLAR: $
echo Hello!
ls -l
./hello.py
```

So, go:generate can help you work with the OS ***before program execution***. However, as it hides things from the developer, its usage should be limited.

The last section of this chapter talks about example functions.

Creating example functions

Part of the documentation process is generating example code that showcases the use of some or all the functions and data types of a package. Example functions have many benefits, including the fact that they are executable tests that are executed by go test. Therefore, if an example function contains an // Output: line, the go test tool checks whether the calculated output matches the values found after the // Output: line. Although we should include example functions in Go files that end with _test.go, we do not need to import the testing Go package for example functions. Moreover, the name of each example function must begin with Example. Lastly, example functions take no input parameters and return no results.

We are going to illustrate example functions using the code of exampleFunctions.go and exampleFunctions_test.go. The content of exampleFunctions.go is as follows:

```
package exampleFunctions
func LengthRange(s string) int {
    i := 0
    for _, _ = range s {
        i = i + 1
    }
    return i
}
```

The previous code presents a regular package that contains a single function named LengthRange(). The contents of exampleFunctions_test.go, which includes the example functions, are the following:

```
package exampleFunctions

import "fmt"

func ExampleLengthRange() {
    fmt.Println(LengthRange("Mihalis"))
    fmt.Println(LengthRange("Mastering Go, 4th edition!"))
    // Output:
```

```
    // 7
    // 7
}
```

What the comment lines say is that the expected output is 7 and 7, which is obviously wrong. This is going to be seen after we run go test:

```
$ go test -v exampleFunctions*
=== RUN   ExampleLengthRange
--- FAIL: ExampleLengthRange (0.00s)
got:
7
26
want:
7
7
FAIL
FAIL    command-line-arguments  0.410s
FAIL
```

As expected, there is an error in the generated output—the second generated value is 26 instead of the expected 7. If we make the necessary corrections, the output is going to look as follows:

```
$ go test -v exampleFunctions*
=== RUN   ExampleLengthRange
--- PASS: ExampleLengthRange (0.00s)
PASS
ok      command-line-arguments  0.572s
```

Example functions can be a great tool both for learning the capabilities of a package and for testing the correctness of functions, so I suggest that you include both test code and example functions in your Go packages. As a bonus, your test functions appear in the documentation of the package, if you decide to generate package documentation.

Summary

This chapter discussed go:generate, code profiling and tracing, and testing Go code. You might find the Go way of testing boring, but this happens because Go is boring and predictable in general and that is a good thing! Remember that writing bug-free code is important, whereas writing the fastest code possible is not always that important.

Most of the time, you need to be able to write fast-enough code. So, spend more time writing tests than benchmarks, unless your code runs really slowly. You have also learned how to find unreachable code and how to cross-compile Go code.

Although the discussions of the Go profiler and go `tool trace` are far from complete, you should understand that with topics such as profiling and code tracing, nothing can replace experimenting and trying new techniques on your own!

The next chapter is about fuzz testing, which is a modern way of testing Go code in addition to the testing techniques presented in this chapter. We will also look at observability in Go.

Exercises

- Create test functions for a package that calculates numbers in the Fibonacci sequence. Do not forget to implement the package.
- The code in `testHTTP/server_test.go` uses the same value for `lastlogin` in the expected variable. This is clearly a bug in `restdb.go` as the value of `lastlogin` should be updated. After correcting the bug, modify `testHTTP/server_test.go` to take into account the different values of the `lastlogin` field.
- Try to find the value of `os.TempDir()` in various operating systems.
- Type go `doc os/signal.NotifyContext` to see that you can handle signals in a `context.Context` environment. Try to create an example that uses `signal.NotifyContext`.

Additional resources

- The generate package: `https://pkg.go.dev/cmd/go/internal/generate`
- Generating code: `https://go.dev/blog/generate`
- The code of testing: `https://go.dev/src/testing/testing.go`
- About net/http/httptrace: `https://pkg.go.dev/net/http/httptrace`
- Profile-guided optimization in Go 1.21: `https://go.dev/blog/pgo`
- Govulncheck v1.0.0 is released: `https://go.dev/blog/govulncheck`
- The govulncheck tool: `https://pkg.go.dev/golang.org/x/vuln/cmd/govulncheck`
- A govulncheck tutorial: `https://go.dev/doc/tutorial/govulncheck`
- Build more secure apps with Go and Google: `https://www.youtube.com/watch?v=HSt6FhsPT8c`
- Introducing HTTP Tracing by Jaana Dogan: `https://go.dev/blog/http-tracing`
- GopherCon 2019: Dave Cheney—Two Go Programs, Three Different Profiling Techniques: `https://youtu.be/nok0aYiGiYA`

Join our community on Discord

Join our community's Discord space for discussions with the authors and other readers:

`https://discord.gg/FzuQbc8zd6`

13

Fuzz Testing and Observability

The subject of this chapter is twofold. First, we are going to talk about *fuzz testing*, which is a recent Go feature that improves the testing process, and second, we are going to talk about *observability*, which can help you understand what is going on when everything is working as expected but slower than desired.

With fuzz testing, we bring the unexpected to testing. The main benefit is that you get to test your code using random and unpredicted values and data, which might lead to detecting unknown vulnerabilities. This also leads to improved test coverage, better automation and efficiency in testing, better continuous testing, improved software quality, and cost-effective security testing.

Observability refers to the ability to understand, measure, and analyze the internal state and behavior of a system based on its external outputs or observable signals. In the context of computer systems and software applications, observability is crucial for monitoring, troubleshooting, and maintaining the health and performance of the system. So, observability helps us find out more about the unseen sides of a program.

The first rule of observability is ***knowing what you are looking for***. This means that if you do not know what to look for, you might end up collecting the wrong data, overlook the useful metrics, and concentrate on the irrelevant ones!

Additionally, reading metrics without storing and visualizing them is not effective. Therefore, this chapter also illustrates how to expose your metrics to Prometheus and how to visualize data stored in Prometheus using Grafana. Keep in mind that Prometheus is not the only software for storing time series data. One alternative to Prometheus is Elasticsearch. In that case, you might need to use Kibana instead of Grafana. What is important is that the key ideas remain the same.

In this chapter, we will cover the following topics:

- Fuzz testing
- Observability
- Exposing metrics to Prometheus

We begin this chapter with fuzz testing.

Fuzz testing

As software engineers, we worry , not when things go as expected, but when unexpected things happen. One way to deal with the unexpected is fuzzing. Fuzzing (or fuzz testing) is a testing technique that generates invalid, unexpected, or random data on ***programs that require input***.

Fuzz testing is good at discovering security and vulnerability issues with code—manual testing is not always ideal as those tests may not account for all potential untrusted inputs, specifically invalid inputs that may break a system. However, fuzz testing cannot replace unit testing. This means that fuzz testing is not a panacea and cannot replace all other testing techniques. So, fuzz testing is more suitable for ***testing code that parses input***, which includes cases such as buffer overflow and SQL injection.

The main advantages of fuzzing include the following:

- You can make sure that the code can handle invalid or random input.
- Bugs that are discovered with fuzzing may be severe and might indicate security risks.
- Malicious attackers often use fuzzing to locate vulnerabilities, so it is good to be prepared.

With fuzzing comes the `testing.F` data type in the same way that we use `testing.T` for testing and `testing.B` for benchmarking—benchmarking Go code is covered in *Chapter 14, Efficiency and Performance*. Additionally, fuzz testing functions begin with `Fuzz` just like testing functions begin with `Test`.

When a fuzz testing run fails, the data that generated the issue is saved on disk under the `testdata` directory, and after that, even regular tests are going to fail—because they are going to use that data automatically—until we correct the relevant issues or bugs. Feel free to delete that `testdata` directory if you need to rerun your regular tests.

The next subsection presents a simple example of fuzz testing.

A simple fuzz testing example

In this subsection, we are going to create a simple example that uses fuzz testing in order to better understand it. The relevant code is found under `ch13/fuzz`.

For the purposes of this simple example, we are going to see code that tests a simple Go function that is found in `code.go`. The contents of `code.go` are the following:

```
package main

import (
    "fmt"
)

func AddInt(x, y int) int {
    for i := 0; i < x; i++ {
        y = y + 1
    }

    return y
}

func main() {
    fmt.Println(AddInt(5, 4))
}
```

There is an issue here: `AddInt()` is not implemented properly because the `for` loop is not going to work when the `x` parameter has a negative value.

The `code_test.go` file with the tests is going to be presented in two parts. The first part comes with the following code:

```
package main

import (
    "testing"
)

func TestAddInt(t *testing.T) {
```

```
    testCases := []struct {
        x, y, want int
    }{
        {1, 2, 3},
        {1, 0, 1},
        {100, 10, 110},
    }

    for _, tc := range testCases {
        result := AddInt(tc.x, tc.y)
        if result != tc.want {
            t.Errorf("X: %d, Y: %d, want %d", tc.x, tc.y, tc.want)
        }
    }
}
```

This first part implements a testing function in the usual way. However, in this case, we are only testing AddInt() using positive integers (natural numbers), which means that it is going to work without any issues.

The second part of code_test.go contains the following code:

```
func FuzzAddInt(f *testing.F) {
    testCases := []struct {
        x, y int
    }{
        {0, 1},
        {0, 100},
    }

    for _, tc := range testCases {
        f.Add(tc.x, tc.y)
    }
}
```

This part implements a fuzz testing function named FuzzAddInt(), which can be verified by the use of the testing.F data type as well as its name beginning with Fuzz. The testing.F data type provides the Add() and Fuzz() methods, which are used for providing the (optional) starting input and for running the actual fuzz tests, respectively.

The *corpus* is a collection of inputs that guide the fuzz testing process and is composed of two parts. The first part is the *seed corpus*, and the second part is the *generated corpus*. The *seed corpus* can be provided by Add() function calls and/or data in the testdata/fuzz directory. The *generated corpus* is completely machine generated. It is not mandatory to have a seed corpus.

The Add() function adds data to the *seed corpus* and can be called as many times as you want—in this case, we call Add() two times.

```
f.Fuzz(func(t *testing.T, x, y int) {
    result := AddInt(x, y)

    if result != x+y {
        t.Errorf("X: %d, Y: %d, Result %d, want %d", x, y, result,
x+y)
    }
})
}
```

After the (optional) Add() function, we need to call Fuzz(), which requires a *testing.T variable as well as a list of fuzzing arguments, which should be the same number and have the same data type as the ones used in Add(), which are usually the same as the number of arguments in the function that is being tested.

Put simply, we embed regular testing functions in fuzz testing functions—it is the input for those regular testing functions that are provided by the fuzz testing process based on the generated corpus.

So, we tell f.Fuzz() that we need two additional int parameters apart from the compulsory *testing.T, which are named x and y. These two parameters are the input of the tests. Because of that, the f.Add() call should also have two parameters.

Running the regular tests is as simple as executing the following command:

```
$ go test *.go
ok      command-line-arguments    0.427s
```

So, the testing function revealed no issues with AddInt().

Running the fuzz test requires the use of the -fuzz command line parameter followed by the name of the fuzz function. So, we need to execute the following command:

```
$ go test -fuzz=FuzzAddInt *.go
fuzz: elapsed: 0s, gathering baseline coverage: 0/2 completed
fuzz: elapsed: 0s, gathering baseline coverage: 2/2 completed, now fuzzing
with 10 workers
fuzz: elapsed: 0s, execs: 6 (410/sec), new interesting: 2 (total: 4)
--- FAIL: FuzzAddInt (0.02s)
    --- FAIL: FuzzAddInt (0.00s)
        code_test.go:40: X: -63, Y: 32, Result 32, want -31

    Failing input written to testdata/fuzz/FuzzAddInt/b403d5353f8afe03
    To re-run:
    go test -run=FuzzAddInt/b403d5353f8afe03
FAIL
exit status 1
FAIL    command-line-arguments    0.222s
```

So, the fuzz test caught the error with AddInt(). Put simply, the fuzz testing process included negative integers in the testing and caught a logical error generated by the use of the for loop—we did not!

The contents of testdata/fuzz/FuzzAddInt/b403d5353f8afe03 are the following:

```
$ cat testdata/fuzz/FuzzAddInt/b403d5353f8afe03
go test fuzz v1
int(-63)
int(32)
```

Fixing AddInt() is left as an exercise for you—as a hint, consider using different code when the parameter used in the for loop is negative. In our case, the function parameter that causes the error condition is x.

The next subsection presents a more practical fuzz testing example.

An advanced fuzz testing example

In this subsection, we present a more advanced fuzz testing example. The relevant code is found under ch13/reverse. The code in reverse.go is the following:

```
package main
```

```
// This version has bugs

import (
    "fmt"
)

func R1(s string) []byte {
    sAr := []byte(sAr)
    rev := make([]byte, len(s))

    l := len(sAr)
    for i := 0; i < l; i++ {
        rev[i] = sAr[l-1-i]
    }

    return rev
}
```

In this first part, we implement a function named R1() that reverses a string. Internally, the function converts the input string value into a byte slice and returns a byte slice.

```
func R2(s string) string {
    b := []byte(s)
    for i, j := 0, len(b)-1; i < len(b)/2; i, j = i+1, j-1 {
        b[i], b[j] = b[j], b[i]
    }

    return string(b)
}
```

In this part, we implement a function named R2() that also reverses a string. Internally, the function works with a byte slice but returns a string value.

```
func main() {
    str := "1234567890"
    fmt.Println(string(R1(str)))
    fmt.Println(R2(str))
}
```

The `main()` function calls both `R1()` and `R2()` in order to reverse the "1234567890" string—this is a naive way of testing the implemented functionality.

Running `reverse.go` generates the following output:

```
$ go run reverse.go
0987654321
0987654321
```

So, at first, the code looks correct and produces the expected output. Now, let us write some tests for the two functions in `reverse.go`.

The code in `reverse_test.go` is presented in three parts. The first part is the following:

```go
package main

import (
    "testing"
    "unicode/utf8"
)

func TestR1(t *testing.T) {
    testCases := []struct {
        in, want string
    }{
        {" ", " "},
        {"!12345@", "@54321!"},
        {"Mastering Go", "oG gniretsaM"},
    }

    for _, tc := range testCases {
        rev := R1(tc.in)
        if string(rev) != tc.want {
            t.Errorf("Reverse: %q, want %q", rev, tc.want)
        }
    }
}
```

The preceding is a test function for `R1()`.

```go
func TestR2(t *testing.T) {
```

```
    testCases := []struct {
        in, want string
    }{
        {" ", " "},
        {"!12345@", "@54321!"},
        {"Mastering Go", "oG gniretsaM"},
    }
    for _, tc := range testCases {
        rev := R2(tc.in)
        if rev != tc.want {
            t.Errorf("Reverse: %q, want %q", rev, tc.want)
        }
    }
}
```

The preceding is a test function for R2().

Both TestR1() and TestR2() are regular testing functions that use user-defined tests, which are stored in the testCases structure. The first field is the original string, whereas the second field is the reversed string.

The second part contains the fuzz testing functions and is the following:

```
func FuzzR1(f *testing.F) {
    testCases := []string{"Hello, world", " ", "!12345"}
    for _, tc := range testCases {
        f.Add(tc)
    }

    f.Fuzz(func(t *testing.T, orig string) {
        rev := R1(orig)
        doubleRev := R1(string(rev))
        if orig != string(doubleRev) {
            t.Errorf("Before: %q, after: %q", orig, doubleRev)
        }

        if utf8.ValidString(orig) && !utf8.ValidString(string(rev)) {
            t.Errorf("Reverse: invalid UTF-8 string %q", rev)
```

```
        }
    })
}
```

This is a fuzz testing function for testing R1(). We add three strings to the seed corpus, which are saved in the testCases slice.

The last part of reverse_test.go contains the code for testing R2():

```go
func FuzzR2(f *testing.F) {
    testCases := []string{"Hello, world", " ", "!12345"}
    for _, tc := range testCases {
        f.Add(tc)
    }

    f.Fuzz(func(t *testing.T, orig string) {
        rev := R2(orig)
        doubleRev := R2(rev)
        if orig != doubleRev {
            t.Errorf("Before: %q, after: %q", orig, doubleRev)
        }

        if utf8.ValidString(orig) && !utf8.ValidString(rev) {
            t.Errorf("Reverse: invalid UTF-8 string %q", rev)
        }
    })
}
```

This is a fuzz testing function for testing R2(). As before, we add three strings to the seed corpus using the values stored in the testCases slice.

 Both fuzz testing functions reverse the given string two times and compare it with orig itself to make sure that they are the same. This happens because, when you reverse a string twice, you should get the original string back.

Running tests without fuzzing produces the following results:

```
$ go test *.go
ok    command-line-arguments    0.103s
```

So, it looks like everything is working as expected. But is this the case?

Let us run tests with fuzzing. First, we are going to run FuzzR1() as follows:

```
$ go test -fuzz=FuzzR1 *.go
fuzz: elapsed: 0s, gathering baseline coverage: 0/7 completed
fuzz: elapsed: 0s, gathering baseline coverage: 7/7 completed, now fuzzing
with 10 workers
fuzz: minimizing 30-byte failing input file
fuzz: elapsed: 0s, minimizing
--- FAIL: FuzzR1 (0.03s)
    --- FAIL: FuzzR1 (0.00s)
        reverse_test.go:55: Reverse: invalid UTF-8 string "\x94\xd4"

    Failing input written to testdata/fuzz/FuzzR1/a256ceb5e3bf582f
    To re-run:
    go test -run=FuzzR1/a256ceb5e3bf582f
FAIL
exit status 1
FAIL    command-line-arguments    0.493s
```

So, in this case, the fuzz test found an issue with the code. The failing input is saved in testdata/fuzz/FuzzR1/42f418307d5ef745.

The contents of testdata/fuzz/FuzzR1/a256ceb5e3bf582f are the following:

```
$ cat testdata/fuzz/FuzzR1/a256ceb5e3bf582f
go test fuzz v1
string("Ӿ")
```

Put simply, the string stored in testdata/fuzz/FuzzR1/a256ceb5e3bf582f is not being reversed successfully.

Next, we are going to run FuzzR2() with fuzzing:

```
$ go test -fuzz=FuzzR2 *.go
--- FAIL: FuzzR1 (0.00s)
    --- FAIL: FuzzR1/a256ceb5e3bf582f (0.00s)
        reverse_test.go:55: Reverse: invalid UTF-8 string "\x94\xd4"
FAIL
exit status 1
FAIL    command-line-arguments    0.253s
```

As there exists a testdata directory from the failure of FuzzR1(), the second fuzz testing fails because of the data found in the testdata directory. In the subsection that follows, we are going to correct the bug.

Correcting the bug

What we should do now is *correct the bug*. The improved version of reverse.go is called correct. go and is found in ch13/reverse/correct. Its code is as follows:

```go
package main

import (
    "errors"
    "fmt"
    "unicode/utf8"
)

func R1(s string) (string, error) {
    if !utf8.ValidString(s) {
        return s, errors.New("Invalid UTF-8")
    }

    a := []byte(s)
    for i, j := 0, len(s)-1; i < j; i++ {
        a[i], a[j] = a[j], a[i]
        j--
    }
    return string(a), nil
}

func R2(s string) (string, error) {
    if !utf8.ValidString(s) {
        return s, errors.New("Invalid UTF-8")
    }
    r := []rune(s)
    for i, j := 0, len(r)-1; i < len(r)/2; i, j = i+1, j-1 {
        r[i], r[j] = r[j], r[i]
```

```
        }
        return string(r), nil
}
```

Notice that in the implementation of R2(), we now work with **runes instead of bytes**. Additionally, both R1() and R2() verify that we are dealing with a valid UTF-8 string using the functionality of utf8.ValidString() prior to doing any processing. When the input is an invalid UTF-8 string, an error message is returned—we did not do that in reverse.go, which is what caused the bug.

The remaining code is about the implementation of main():

```
func main() {
        str := "1234567890"

        R1ret, _ := R1(str)
        fmt.Println(R1ret)

        R2ret, _ := R2(str)
        fmt.Println(R2ret)
}
```

As explained earlier, the main difference in this improved version is that the two functions also return an error variable to make sure that we are dealing with valid UTF-8 strings. However, this also means that the test functions as well as the fuzz testing functions should be modified in order to adjust to the change in the function signatures.

Running correct.go produces the following output:

```
$ go run correct.go
0987654321
0987654321
```

So, it looks like the basic functionality is still implemented correctly.

The improved test version is called correct_test.go and is also found in ch13/reverse/correct—it is going to be presented in two parts. The first part of correct_test.go contains the following code:

```
package main

import (
```

```go
        "testing"
        "unicode/utf8"
)

func TestR1(t *testing.T) {
    testCases := []struct {
        in, want string
    }{
        {" ", " "},
        {"!12345@", "@54321!"},
        {"Mastering Go", "oG gniretsaM"},
    }

    for _, tc := range testCases {
        rev, err := R1(tc.in)
        if err != nil {
            return
        }

        if rev != tc.want {
            t.Errorf("Reverse: %q, want %q", rev, tc.want)
        }
    }
}

func TestR2(t *testing.T) {
    testCases := []struct {
        in, want string
    }{
        {" ", " "},
        {"!12345@", "@54321!"},
        {"Mastering Go", "oG gniretsaM"},
    }

    for _, tc := range testCases {
        rev, err := R2(tc.in)
        if err != nil {
```

```
            return
        }

        if rev != tc.want {
            t.Errorf("Reverse: %q, want %q", rev, tc.want)
        }
    }
}
```

The logic of both TestR1() and TestR2() is the same as before: we use the values stored in a slice of structures (testCases) to verify the correctness of R1() and R2(). However, this time, we take into consideration the error value returned by R1() and R2(). If there is an error with R1() or R2(), both test functions return immediately, which makes the test successful.

The second part of correct_test.go is the implementation of the fuzz testing functions:

```
func FuzzR1(f *testing.F) {
    testCases := []string{"Hello, world", " ", "!12345"}
    for _, tc := range testCases {
        f.Add(tc)
    }

    f.Fuzz(func(t *testing.T, orig string) {
        rev, err := R1(orig)
        if err != nil {
            return
        }

        doubleRev, err := R1(rev)
        if err != nil {
            return
        }

        if orig != doubleRev {
            t.Errorf("Before: %q, after: %q", orig, doubleRev)
        }

        if utf8.ValidString(orig) && !utf8.ValidString(string(rev)) {
```

```
                t.Errorf("Reverse: invalid UTF-8 string %q", rev)
        }
    })
}
```

FuzzR1() uses the error value returned by R1() to make sure that we are dealing with a valid string. If the string is not valid, then it returns. Additionally, it reverses the given string—which is stored in the automatically generated orig parameter—two times and compares it with orig itself to make sure that they are the same.

```
func FuzzR2(f *testing.F) {
    testCases := []string{"Hello, world", " ", "!12345"}
    for _, tc := range testCases {
        f.Add(tc)
    }

    f.Fuzz(func(t *testing.T, orig string) {
        rev, err := R2(orig)
        if err != nil {
            return
        }
        doubleRev, err := R2(string(rev))
        if err != nil {
            return
        }

        if orig != doubleRev {
            t.Errorf("Before: %q, after: %q", orig, doubleRev)
        }

        if utf8.ValidString(orig) && !utf8.ValidString(rev) {
            t.Errorf("Reverse: invalid UTF-8 string %q", rev)
        }
    })
}
```

FuzzR2() also uses the error value returned by R2() to make sure that we are dealing with a valid string. If the string is not valid, then it also returns. The remaining implementation follows the logic of FuzzR1().

Running the regular tests produces the following output:

```
$ go test *.go
ok    command-line-arguments    0.609s
```

Performing the fuzzing test for R1() generates the following output:

```
$ go test -fuzz=FuzzR1 *.go -fuzztime 10s
fuzz: elapsed: 0s, gathering baseline coverage: 0/15 completed
fuzz: elapsed: 0s, gathering baseline coverage: 15/15 completed, now fuzz-
ing with 10 workers
fuzz: elapsed: 3s, execs: 1129701 (376437/sec), new interesting: 31 (to-
tal: 46)
fuzz: elapsed: 6s, execs: 2527522 (466068/sec), new interesting: 34 (to-
tal: 49)
fuzz: elapsed: 9s, execs: 3808349 (426919/sec), new interesting: 37 (to-
tal: 52)
fuzz: elapsed: 11s, execs: 4208389 (199790/sec), new interesting: 37 (to-
tal: 52)
PASS
ok    command-line-arguments    11.508s
```

The use of -fuzztime 10s makes sure that the tests are going to stop after they exceed the given time limit or when there is an error.

Running the fuzzing test for R2() generates the following output:

```
$ go test -fuzz=FuzzR2 *.go -fuzztime 10s
fuzz: elapsed: 0s, gathering baseline coverage: 0/3 completed
fuzz: elapsed: 0s, gathering baseline coverage: 3/3 completed, now fuzzing
with 10 workers
fuzz: elapsed: 3s, execs: 1271973 (423844/sec), new interesting: 38 (to-
tal: 41)
fuzz: elapsed: 6s, execs: 2638924 (455741/sec), new interesting: 39 (to-
tal: 42)
fuzz: elapsed: 9s, execs: 4044955 (468745/sec), new interesting: 39 (to-
tal: 42)
fuzz: elapsed: 10s, execs: 4495553 (413586/sec), new interesting: 39 (to-
tal: 42)
PASS
ok    command-line-arguments    10.396s
```

So, everything works as expected and the bug was corrected!

The next section is about observability, which is a systematic way of collecting data related to the efficiency and the internals of a system.

Observability

Observability is the measurement of the internal state of a system in relation to external operations. In practical terms, observability is about understanding how well the resources of a computer system are being utilized while a given software or application is being executed on a system.

In Go terminology, and in relation to the content of this book, observability is about learning *how Go uses the available resources and how an application performs while the application is executed* in order to understand the efficiency of the Go application as well as the Go runtime itself. The purpose of this process is to improve the efficiency of a Go application and maybe modify the resources available to that particular Go application in order to improve its overall operation.

If it is still unclear, let me explain it in a more practical way. Let us say that a Go application runs slow. We need to discover why this happens. For that, we measure the appropriate internal Go metrics as well as application-specific metrics and try to make sense of them.

The key components of observability include:

- **Logs**: Recording events, activities, and messages generated by a system. Logs provide a historical record of what has happened and are useful for debugging and auditing.

- **Metrics**: Quantitative measurements that provide insight into the system's performance and behavior. Metrics examples include response times, error rates, and resource utilization.

- **Traces**: Sequences of events or transactions that allow you to trace the flow of a request through a system. Tracing helps in understanding the latency and dependencies between different components.

- **Monitoring**: Continuous tracking of metrics and logs to identify patterns, anomalies, and potential issues. Monitoring systems can generate alerts when predefined thresholds are exceeded. This is a complex task, especially when having to deal with a large number of metrics.

- **Alerting**: Notification mechanisms that inform administrators or operators about potential issues or irregularities in the system. Alerts help in responding quickly to problems and minimizing downtime.

- **Distributed tracing**: Tracking and visualizing requests as they traverse through various components in a distributed system. This is particularly important in microservices architectures and is extremely challenging.

This chapter is going to deal with metrics. Code profiling and tracing were covered in *Chapter 12, Code Testing and Profiling*. Additionally, logging was covered in *Chapter 1, A Quick Introduction to Go*, and *Chapter 7, Telling a UNIX System What to Do*. Dealing with the remaining components is beyond the scope of this book.

We begin by explaining the use of the `runtime/metrics` package, which provides Go runtime-related metrics.

The runtime/metrics package

The `runtime/metrics` package makes metrics exported by the Go runtime available to the developer. Each metric name is specified by a path. As an example, the number of live goroutines is accessed as `/sched/goroutines:goroutines`. However, if you want to collect all available metrics, you should use `metrics.All()`—this saves you from having to write lots of code in order to collect each individual metric.

Metrics are saved using the `metrics.Sample` data type. The definition of the `metrics.Sample` data structure is as follows:

```
type Sample struct {
    Name string
    Value Value
}
```

The `Name` value must correspond to the name of one of the metric descriptions returned by `metrics.All()`. If you already know the metric description, there is no need to use `metrics.All()`.

The use of the `runtime/metrics` package is illustrated in `metrics.go`. The presented code gets the value of `/sched/goroutines:goroutines` and prints it on screen:

```
package main
import (
    "fmt"
    "runtime/metrics"
    "sync"
    "time"
)
```

```
func main() {
    const nGo = "/sched/goroutines:goroutines"
```

The nGo variable holds the path of the metric we want to collect.

```
    getMetric := make([]metrics.Sample, 1)
    getMetric[0].Name = nGo
```

After that, we create a slice of type metrics.Sample in order to keep the metric value. The initial
size of the slice is 1 because we are only collecting values for a single metric. We set the Name value
to /sched/goroutines:goroutines as stored in nGo.

```
    var wg sync.WaitGroup
    for i := 0; i < 3; i++ {
        wg.Add(1)
        go func() {
            defer wg.Done()
            time.Sleep(4 * time.Second)
        }()
```

Here, we manually create three goroutines so that the program has relevant data to collect.

```
        // Get actual data
        metrics.Read(getMetric)
        if getMetric[0].Value.Kind() == metrics.KindBad {
            fmt.Printf("metric %q no longer supported\n", nGo)
        }
```

The metrics.Read() function collects the desired metrics based on the data in the getMetric slice.

```
        mVal := getMetric[0].Value.Uint64()
        fmt.Printf("Number of goroutines: %d\n", mVal)
    }
```

After reading the desired metric, we convert it into a numeric value (unsigned int64 here) in
order to use it in our program.

```
    wg.Wait()
    metrics.Read(getMetric)
    mVal := getMetric[0].Value.Uint64()
    fmt.Printf("Before exiting: %d\n", mVal)
}
```

The last lines of the code verify that, after all goroutines have finished, the value of the metric is going to be 1, which is the goroutine used for running the main() function.

Running metrics.go produces the next output:

```
$ go run metrics.go
Number of goroutines: 2
Number of goroutines: 3
Number of goroutines: 4
Before exiting: 1
```

We have created three goroutines and we already have a goroutine for running the main() function. Therefore, the maximum number of goroutines is indeed four.

The following subsection presents a technique for measuring the execution time of a Go function, which is not something that is directly supported by Go.

Measuring the execution time of a function

The runtime/metrics package provides a list of metrics that you can find on the help page of the package. However, there are times when we want to measure the time of a specific operation, which is a request not supported by the runtime/metrics package. In our example, we are going to do exactly that and store the information in a log entry.

In this example, we are going to use the log/slog package of the standard library. You can use any logging package you want as long as it is simple and readable, but most importantly, as long as it is efficient and does not introduce extra load to the system.

The code of functionTime.go is presented in two parts. The first part is the following:

```go
package main

import (
    "log/slog"
    "os"
    "time"
)

func myFunction() {
    j := 0
    for i := 1; i < 100000000; i++ {
```

```
        j = j % i
    }
}
```

This is where we define the function that we want to measure—this can be any function or operation you want.

The second part of functionTime.go comes with the following code:

```
func main() {
    handler := slog.NewTextHandler(os.Stdout, nil)
    logger := slog.New(handler)
    logger.Debug("This is a DEBUG message")

    for i := 0; i < 5; i++ {
        now := time.Now()
        myFunction()
        elapsed := time.Since(now)
        logger.Info(
            "Observability",
            slog.Int64("time_taken", int64(elapsed)),
        )
    }
}
```

The use of time.Now() and time.Since() calls that surround the execution of myFunction() is how we measure the execution time of myFunction().

Remember that the time.Duration data type holds nanoseconds and is, in reality, an int64 value, hence the use of slog.Int64() as well as the int64(elapsed) cast for converting the time. Duration value into an int64 one.

Running functionTime.go generates the following kind of output:

```
$ go run functionTime.go
time=2023-12-30T11:33:36.471+02:00 level=INFO msg=Observability time_tak-
en=51243083
time=2023-12-30T11:33:36.505+02:00 level=INFO msg=Observability time_tak-
en=34088708
time=2023-12-30T11:33:36.536+02:00 level=INFO msg=Observability time_tak-
en=31203083
```

```
time=2023-12-30T11:33:36.568+02:00 level=INFO msg=Observability time_tak-
en=31224625
time=2023-12-30T11:33:36.599+02:00 level=INFO msg=Observability time_tak-
en=31206208
```

Keep in mind that on a busy system, the time_taken values are not going to be so similar because of the OS scheduler as well as the Go scheduler operations.

The next subsection is a handy introduction to the expvar package.

The expvar package

The expvar package allows you to expose variables and functions to servers, which includes custom metrics. The expvar package exposes these variables via HTTP at /debug/vars in JSON format.

The code of expvarUse.go is presented in two parts. The first part is the following:

```go
package main

import (
    "expvar"
    "fmt"
    "net/http"
)

func main() {
    intVar := expvar.NewInt("intVar")
    intVar.Set(1234)

    expvar.Publish("customFunction", expvar.Func(func() interface{} {
        return "Hi from Mastering Go!"
    }))
```

The previous code does two things. First, it registers an integer variable named intVar to be exposed and, second, it registers a function named customFunction to be exposed using expvar. NewInt() and expvar.Publish(), respectively. The Publish() function takes two arguments in its signature, which are the name of the variable that the function is going to expose and the function that we want to expose. In this case, we use an anonymous function that is implemented inline.

The second part of expvarUse.go is the following:

```go
    http.Handle("/debug/expvars", expvar.Handler())
```

```go
go func() {
    fmt.Println("HTTP server listening on :8080")
    err := http.ListenAndServe(":8080", nil)
    if err != nil {
        fmt.Println("Error starting HTTP server:", err)
    }
}()

intVar.Add(10)

select {}
}
```

The http.Handle() function allows us to install an additional handler in a non-standard location, which, in this case, is /debug/expvars. So, we use the /debug/expvars path to also access the registered variable and function, we start the HTTP server that listens on port number 8080, we modify intVar using intVar.Add(), and we use select {} to prevent the program from terminating because it blocks the program.

In this case, we mimic the application logic, which we should replace with our own logic, by updating the value of intVar manually using intVar.Add(10).

Running expvarUse.go is not going to produce any output but it is going to start the HTTP server. We can access the exposed variable and function by visiting http://localhost:8080/debug/vars or http://localhost:8080/debug/expvars in a web browser or by making an HTTP GET request using a tool such as curl(1) or wget(1).

In our case, we are going to use curl(1) and we are going to get the following kind of output (some output is omitted for brevity):

```
$ curl -X GET http://localhost:8080/debug/expvars
{
"cmdline": ["/var/folders/sk/1tk8cnw50lzdtr2hxcj5sv2m0000gn/T/go-
build4228023601/b001/exe/expvarUse"],
"customFunction": "Hi from Mastering Go!",
"intVar": 1244,
```

The next subsection covers learning about the CPU of a machine and its characteristics.

Learning about CPU characteristics

There are times when we need to learn about the details of the CPU at runtime and maybe expose them in order to collect the relevant metrics. For such times, the https://github.com/klauspost/ cpuid package can really come in handy.

We are going to put all relevant code inside ~/go/src/github.com/mactsouk/mGo4th/ch13/cpuid because we are going to utilize an external package.

The Go code of cpuid.go is the following:

```go
package main

import (
    "fmt"
    "strings"

    . "github.com/klauspost/cpuid/v2"
)

func main() {
    // Print basic CPU information:
    fmt.Println("Name:", CPU.BrandName)
    fmt.Println("PhysicalCores:", CPU.PhysicalCores)
    fmt.Println("LogicalCores:", CPU.LogicalCores)
    fmt.Println("ThreadsPerCore:", CPU.ThreadsPerCore)
    fmt.Println("Family", CPU.Family, "Model:", CPU.Model, "Vendor ID:",
CPU.VendorID)

    fmt.Println("Features:", strings.Join(CPU.FeatureSet(), ","))
    fmt.Println("Cacheline bytes:", CPU.CacheLine)
    fmt.Println("L1 Data Cache:", CPU.Cache.L1D, "bytes")
    fmt.Println("L1 Instruction Cache:", CPU.Cache.L1I, "bytes")
    fmt.Println("L2 Cache:", CPU.Cache.L2, "bytes")
    fmt.Println("L3 Cache:", CPU.Cache.L3, "bytes")
    fmt.Println("Frequency", CPU.Hz, "hz")
}
```

The code is standard, and you should not need to make any changes to it.

Running `cpuid.go` on my macOS machine with a M1 Max CPU produces the following output:

```
Name: Apple M1 Max
PhysicalCores: 10
LogicalCores: 10
ThreadsPerCore: 1
Family 458787763 Model: 0 Vendor ID: VendorUnknown
Features: AESARM,ASIMD,ASIMDDP,ASIMDHP,ASIMDRDM,ATOMICS,CRC32,DCPOP,FC-
MA,FP,FPHP,GPA,JSCVT,LRCPC,PMULL,SHA1,SHA2,SHA3,SHA512
Cacheline bytes: 128
L1 Data Cache: 65536 bytes
L1 Instruction Cache: 131072 bytes
L2 Cache: 4194304 bytes
L3 Cache: -1 bytes
Frequency 0 hz
```

Running `cpuid.go` on a Linux machine with an Intel i7 processor produces the following output:

```
Name: Intel(R) Core(TM) i7-10510U CPU @ 1.80GHz
PhysicalCores: 4
LogicalCores: 8
ThreadsPerCore: 2
Family 6 Model: 142 Vendor ID: Intel
Features: ADX,AESNI,AVX,AVX2,BMI1,BMI2,CLMUL,CMOV,CMPXCHG8,CX-
16,ERMS,F16C,FLUSH_L1D,FMA3,FXSR,FXSROPT,HTT,IA32_ARCH_CAP,IBP-
B,LAHF,LZCNT,MD_CLEAR,MMX,MOVBE,MPX,NX,OSXSAVE,POPCNT,RDRAND,RD-
SEED,RDTSCP,SGX,SPEC_CTRL_SSBD,SSE,SSE2,SSE3,SSE4,SSE42,SSSE3,S
TIBP,SYSCALL,SYSEE,VMX,X87,XGETBV1,XSAVE,XSAVEC,XSAVEOPT,XSAVES
Cacheline bytes: 64
L1 Data Cache: 32768 bytes
L1 Instruction Cache: 32768 bytes
L2 Cache: 262144 bytes
L3 Cache: 8388608 bytes
Frequency 2300000000 hz
```

By comparing the outputs, we can see that `cpuid` works better on the Linux machine with the Intel CPU as it displays the frequency of the CPU, which is not the case for the MacBook Pro machine.

The next section is about how to expose metrics to Prometheus and how to plot the metrics in Grafana.

Exposing metrics to Prometheus

Imagine that you have an application that writes files to disk and you want to get metrics for that application to better understand how the writing of multiple files influences the general performance—you need to gather performance data to understand the behavior of your application. A good way to store such metrics is by using Prometheus.

The list of supported data types for metrics by Prometheus is the following:

- **Counter**: This is a cumulative value that is used for representing increasing counters—the value of a counter can stay the same, go up, or be reset to zero, but it cannot decrease. Counters are usually used for representing cumulative values such as the number of requests served so far, the total number of errors, and so on.
- **Gauge**: This is a single numerical value that is allowed to increase or decrease. Gauges are usually used for representing values that can go up or down such as the number of requests and time durations.
- **Histogram**: A histogram is used for sampling observations and creating counts and buckets. Histograms are usually used for counting request durations, response times, and so on.
- **Summary**: A summary is like a histogram but can also calculate quantiles over sliding windows that work with times.

Both histograms and summaries are useful for performing statistical calculations and properties. Usually, a counter or a gauge is all that you need for storing your system metrics.

The subsections that follow illustrate how to make any metric you collect available to Prometheus.

Exposing metrics

Collecting metrics is a totally different task from exposing them for Prometheus to collect them. This subsection shows how to make the metrics available to Prometheus for collection. For reasons of simplicity, the presented application is going to generate random values.

The code of `samplePro.go` is as follows:

```
package main
import (
    "fmt"
    "net/http"
    "math/rand"
    "time"
```

```
    "github.com/prometheus/client_golang/prometheus"
    "github.com/prometheus/client_golang/prometheus/promhttp"
)
```

We need to use two external packages for communicating with Prometheus.

```
var PORT = ":1234"
var counter = prometheus.NewCounter(
    prometheus.CounterOpts{
        Namespace: "mtsouk",
        Name:      "my_counter",
        Help:      "This is my counter",
    })
```

 Bear in mind that I use global variables here to denote important settings and that is a personal preference and my way of easily finding those settings. The same applies for the use of all caps for naming the PORT variable.

This is how we define a new counter variable and specify the desired options. The Namespace field is very important as it allows you to group metrics in sets. The name of the first metric is my_counter.

```
var gauge = prometheus.NewGauge(
    prometheus.GaugeOpts{
        Namespace: "mtsouk",
        Name:      "my_gauge",
        Help:      "This is my gauge",
    })
```

This is how we define a new gauge variable and specify the desired options—the name of the metric is my_gauge.

```
var histogram = prometheus.NewHistogram(
    prometheus.HistogramOpts{
        Namespace: "mtsouk",
        Name:      "my_histogram",
        Help:      "This is my histogram",
    })
```

This is how we define a new histogram variable and specify the desired options.

```
var summary = prometheus.NewSummary(
    prometheus.SummaryOpts{
        Namespace: "mtsouk",
        Name:      "my_summary",
        Help:      "This is my summary",
    })
```

This is how we define a new summary variable and specify the desired options. However, as you are going to see, defining a metric variable is not enough. You also need to register it.

```
func main() {
    prometheus.MustRegister(counter)
    prometheus.MustRegister(gauge)
    prometheus.MustRegister(histogram)
    prometheus.MustRegister(summary)
```

In these four prometheus.MustRegister() statements, you register the four metric variables. Now, when Prometheus connects to the server and the namespace, it is going to know about them.

```
    go func() {
        for {
            counter.Add(rand.Float64() * 5)
            gauge.Add(rand.Float64()*15 - 5)
            histogram.Observe(rand.Float64() * 10)
            summary.Observe(rand.Float64() * 10)
            time.Sleep(2 * time.Second)
        }
    }()
```

This goroutine runs for as long as the web server runs with the help of the endless for loop. In this goroutine, the metrics are updated every 2 seconds due to the use of the time.Sleep(2 * time.Second) statement.

```
    http.Handle("/metrics", promhttp.Handler())
    fmt.Println("Listening to port", PORT)
    fmt.Println(http.ListenAndServe(PORT, nil))
}
```

As you already know, each URL is handled by a handler function that you usually implement on your own. However, in this case, we are using the `promhttp.Handler()` handler function that comes with the `github.com/prometheus/client_golang/prometheus/promhttp` package—this saves us from having to write our own code. However, we still need to register the `promhttp.Handler()` handler function using `http.Handle()` before we start the web server. Note that the metrics are found under the `/metrics` path—Prometheus knows how to find that.

With `samplePro.go` running, getting the list of metrics that belong to the `mtsouk` namespace is as simple as running the next `curl(1)` command:

```
$ curl localhost:1234/metrics --silent | grep mtsouk
# HELP mtsouk_my_counter This is my counter
# TYPE mtsouk_my_counter counter
mtsouk_my_counter 19.948239343027772
```

This is the output from a `counter` variable. If the `| grep mtsouk` part is omitted, then you are going to get the list of all available metrics.

```
# HELP mtsouk_my_gauge This is my gauge
# TYPE mtsouk_my_gauge gauge
mtsouk_my_gauge 29.335329668135287
```

This is the output from a gauge variable.

```
# HELP mtsouk_my_histogram This is my histogram
# TYPE mtsouk_my_histogram histogram
mtsouk_my_histogram_bucket{le="0.005"} 0
mtsouk_my_histogram_bucket{le="0.01"} 0
mtsouk_my_histogram_bucket{le="0.025"} 0
. . .
mtsouk_my_histogram_bucket{le="5"} 4
mtsouk_my_histogram_bucket{le="10"} 9
mtsouk_my_histogram_bucket{le="+Inf"} 9
mtsouk_my_histogram_sum 44.52262035556937
mtsouk_my_histogram_count 9
```

This is the output from a `histogram` variable. Histograms contain buckets, hence the large number of output lines.

```
# HELP mtsouk_my_summary This is my summary
# TYPE mtsouk_my_summary summary
```

```
mtsouk_my_summary_sum 19.407554729772105
mtsouk_my_summary_count 9
```

The last lines of the output are for the summary data type.

So, the metrics are there and ready to be pulled by Prometheus—in practice, this means that every production Go application can export metrics that can be used for measuring its performance and discovering its bottlenecks. However, we are not done yet as we need to learn about building Docker images for Go applications.

Creating a Docker image for a Go server

This subsection shows how to create a Docker image for a Go application. The main benefit you get from this is that you can deploy it in a Docker environment without worrying about compiling it and having the required resources—everything is included in the Docker image.

Still, you might ask, "Why not use a normal Go binary instead of a Docker image?" The answer is simple: Docker images can be put in docker-compose.yml files and can be deployed using Kubernetes. The same is not true for Go binaries. Additionally, Docker images can provide consistent shared libraries when this is needed.

When creating a new Docker image, you usually start with a base Docker image that already includes Go and create the desired binary in there. The key point here is that samplePro.go uses an external package that should be downloaded in the Docker image before building the executable binary.

The process must start with go mod init and go mod tidy. The contents of the relevant Docker file, which is named dFilev2, are as follows:

```
FROM golang:alpine AS builder
RUN apk update && apk add --no-cache git
```

As golang:alpine uses the latest Go version, which does not come with git, we install git manually.

```
RUN mkdir $GOPATH/src/server
ADD ./samplePro.go $GOPATH/src/server
```

If you want to use Go modules, you should put your code in $GOPATH/src, which is what we do here.

```
WORKDIR $GOPATH/src/server
RUN go mod init
RUN go mod tidy
```

```
RUN go mod download
RUN mkdir /pro
RUN go build -o /pro/server samplePro.go
```

We download the required dependencies using various go mod commands. The building of the binary file is the same as before.

```
FROM alpine:latest
RUN mkdir /pro
COPY --from=builder /pro/server /pro/server
EXPOSE 1234
WORKDIR /pro
CMD ["/pro/server"]
```

In this second stage, we put the binary file into the desired location (/pro) and expose the desired port, which, in this case, is port number 1234. The port number depends on the code in samplePro.go.

The previous process is a ***two-step process that makes the final Docker image smaller in size***, hence the use of the second FROM command with a Docker image that does not include the Go tools and is just used for running the generated Go binary.

Building a Docker image using dFilev2 is as simple as running the next command:

```
$ docker build -f dFilev2 -t go-app122 .
```

 Although previous versions of Docker used the docker build command for building images, recent versions of Docker also support the use of buildx for the same task. You might need to install the buildkit and docker-buildx packages to enable the buildx command.

So, if you want to go the docker buildx way, you should execute the following command instead:

```
$ docker buildx build -f dFilev2 -t go-app122 .
```

The results from both docker build and docker buildx are exactly the same.

Once the Docker image has been successfully created, there is no difference in the way you should use it in a docker-compose.yml file—a relevant entry in a docker-compose.yml file would look as follows:

```
goapp:
```

```
    image: go-app122
    container_name: goapp-int
    restart: always
    ports:
      - 1234:1234
    networks:
      - monitoring
```

The name of the Docker image is go-app122, whereas the internal name of the container would be goapp-int. So, if a different container from the monitoring network wants to access that container, it should use the goapp-int hostname. Last, the only open port is port number 1234.

The next subsection illustrates how you can expose the chosen metrics to Prometheus.

Specifying the metrics to expose

This section illustrates how to expose the desired metrics from the runtime/metrics package to Prometheus. In our case, we use /sched/goroutines:goroutines and /memory/classes/total:bytes. You already know about the former, which is the total number of goroutines. The latter metric is the amount of memory mapped by the Go runtime into the current process as read-write.

As the presented code uses external packages, it should be put inside ~/go/src and Go modules should be enabled using go mod init. In our case, the code can be found in ch13/prom/.

The Go code of prometheus.go is as follows:

```
package main

import (
    "log"
    "math/rand"
    "net/http"
    "runtime"
    "runtime/metrics"
    "time"
    "github.com/prometheus/client_golang/prometheus"
    "github.com/prometheus/client_golang/prometheus/promhttp"
)
```

The first external package is the Go client library for Prometheus and the second package is for using the default handler function (promhttp.Handler()).

```
var PORT = ":1234"
var nGoroutines = prometheus.NewGauge(
    prometheus.GaugeOpts{
        Namespace: "packt",
        Name:      "n_goroutines",
        Help:      "Number of goroutines"})
var nMemory = prometheus.NewGauge(
    prometheus.GaugeOpts{
        Namespace: "packt",
        Name:      "n_memory",
        Help:      "Memory usage"})
```

Here, we define the two Prometheus metrics.

```
func main() {
    prometheus.MustRegister(nGoroutines)
    prometheus.MustRegister(nMemory)
    const nGo = "/sched/goroutines:goroutines"
    const nMem = "/memory/classes/heap/free:bytes"
```

This is where you register the variables for the metrics in Prometheus and define the metrics you want to read from the runtime/metrics package.

```
    getMetric := make([]metrics.Sample, 2)
    getMetric[0].Name = nGo
    getMetric[1].Name = nMem
    http.Handle("/metrics", promhttp.Handler())
```

This is where you register the handler function for the /metrics path. We use promhttp.Handler().

```
    go func() {
        for {
            for i := 1; i < 4; i++ {
                go func() {
                    _ = make([]int, 1000000)
                    time.Sleep(time.Duration(rand.Intn(10)) * time.Second)
                }()
            }
```

Note that such a program should definitely have at least two goroutines: one for running the HTTP server and another one for collecting the metrics. Usually, the HTTP server is on the goroutine that runs the `main()` function and the metric collection happens in a user-defined goroutine.

The outer `for` loop makes sure that the goroutine runs forever, whereas the inner `for` loop creates additional goroutines so that the value of the `/sched/goroutines:goroutines` metric changes all the time.

```
                runtime.GC()
                metrics.Read(getMetric)
                goVal := getMetric[0].Value.Uint64()
                memVal := getMetric[1].Value.Uint64()
                time.Sleep(time.Duration(rand.Intn(15)) * time.Second)
                nGoroutines.Set(float64(goVal))
                nMemory.Set(float64(memVal))
        }
    }()
```

The `runtime.GC()` function tells the Go garbage collector to run and is called for changing the `/memory/classes/heap/free:bytes` metric. The two `Set()` calls update the values of the metrics.

You can read more about the operation of the Go garbage collector in *Appendix A, Go Garbage Collector*.

```
    log.Println("Listening to port", PORT)
    log.Println(http.ListenAndServe(PORT, nil))
}
```

The last statement runs the web server using the default Go router. Running `prometheus.go` from the `ch13/prom` directory requires executing the next commands:

```
$ go mod init
$ go mod tidy
$ go mod download
$ go run prometheus.go
2024/01/01 19:18:11 Listening to port :1234
```

Although `prometheus.go` generates no output apart from the previous line, the next subsection illustrates how to read the desired metrics from it using `curl(1)`.

Getting the metrics

You can get a list of the available metrics from prometheus.go using curl(1) in order to make sure that the application works as expected. I always test the operation of such an application with curl(1) or some other similar utility such as wget(1) before trying to get the metrics with Prometheus.

```
$ curl localhost:1234/metrics --silent | grep packt
# HELP packt_n_goroutines Number of goroutines
# TYPE packt_n_goroutines gauge
packt_n_goroutines 6
# HELP packt_n_memory Memory usage
# TYPE packt_n_memory gauge
packt_n_memory 4.8799744e+07
```

The previous command assumes that curl(1) is executed on the same machine as the HTTP server and that the server listens to TCP port number 1234.

Next, we must enable Prometheus to pull the metrics—it is much easier to run Prometheus from a Docker image. The easiest way for a Prometheus Docker image to be able to see the Go application with the metrics is to execute both as Docker images. We are going to use the following Dockerfile (which is similar to dFilev2 used previously) to convert prometheus.go into a Docker image:

```
FROM golang:alpine AS builder
```

This is the name of the base Docker image that is used for building the binary. golang:alpine always contains the latest Go version as long as you update it regularly.

```
RUN apk update && apk add --no-cache git
RUN mkdir $GOPATH/src/server
ADD ./prometheus.go $GOPATH/src/server
WORKDIR $GOPATH/src/server
RUN go mod init
RUN go mod tidy
RUN go mod download
```

The previous commands download the required dependencies before trying to build the binary.

```
RUN mkdir /pro
RUN go build -o /pro/server prometheus.go

FROM alpine:latest
RUN mkdir /pro
COPY --from=builder /pro/server /pro/server
EXPOSE 1234
WORKDIR /pro
CMD ["/pro/server"]
```

Building the desired Docker image, which is going to be named goapp, is as simple as running the next command:

```
$ docker build -f Dockerfile -t goapp .
```

If you prefer to use docker buildx, you should execute the following command instead:

```
$ docker buildx build -f Dockerfile -t goapp .
```

As usual, the output of docker images verifies the successful creation of the goapp Docker image—in my case, the relevant entry looks as follows:

```
goapp              latest            6f63d9a27185   2 minutes ago   17.8MB
```

Let us now discuss how to configure Prometheus to pull the desired metrics.

Putting the metrics in Prometheus

To be able to pull the metrics, Prometheus needs a proper configuration file that specifies the source of the metrics. The configuration file that is going to be used is as follows:

```
# prometheus.yml
scrape_configs:
  - job_name: GoServer
    scrape_interval: 5s
    static_configs:
      - targets: ['goapp:1234']
```

We tell Prometheus to connect to a host named goapp using port number 1234. Prometheus pulls data every five seconds, according to the value of the scrape_interval field. You should put prometheus.yml in the prometheus directory, which should be under the same root directory as the docker-compose.yml file that is presented next.

Prometheus, as well as Grafana and the Go application, are going to run as Docker containers using the next docker-compose.yml file:

```
version: "3"
services:
  goapp:
    image: goapp
    container_name: goapp
    restart: always
    ports:
      - 1234:1234
    networks:
      - monitoring
```

This is the part that deals with the Go application that collects the metrics. The Docker image name, as well as the internal hostname of the Docker container, is goapp. You should define the port number that is going to be open for connections. In this case, both the internal and external port numbers are 1234. The internal one is mapped to the external one. Additionally, you should put all Docker images under the same network, which, in this case, is called monitoring and is defined in a while.

```
  prometheus:
    image: prom/prometheus:latest
    container_name: prometheus
    restart: always
    user: "0"
    volumes:
      - ./prometheus/:/etc/prometheus/
```

This is how you pass your own copy of prometheus.yml to the Docker image to be used by Prometheus. So, ./prometheus/prometheus.yml from the local machine can be accessed as /etc/prometheus/prometheus.yml from within the Docker image.

```
    - ./prometheus_data/:/prometheus/
  command:
    - '--config.file=/etc/prometheus/prometheus.yml'
```

This is where you tell Prometheus which configuration file to use.

```
    - '--storage.tsdb.path=/prometheus'
    - '--web.console.libraries=/etc/prometheus/console_libraries'
    - '--web.console.templates=/etc/prometheus/consoles'
    - '--storage.tsdb.retention.time=200h'
    - '--web.enable-lifecycle'
  ports:
    - 9090:9090
  networks:
    - monitoring
```

This is where the definition of the Prometheus part of the scenario ends. The Docker image used is called prom/prometheus:latest and the internal name of it is prometheus. Prometheus listens to port number 9090.

Last, we present the Grafana part. Grafana listens to port number 3000:

```
grafana:
  image: grafana/grafana
  container_name: grafana
  depends_on:
    - prometheus
  restart: always
  user: "0"
  ports:
    - 3000:3000
  environment:
    - GF_SECURITY_ADMIN_PASSWORD=helloThere
```

This is the current password of the admin user (helloThere)—you need that for connecting to Grafana.

```
        - GF_USERS_ALLOW_SIGN_UP=false
        - GF_PANELS_DISABLE_SANITIZE_HTML=true
        - GF_SECURITY_ALLOW_EMBEDDING=true
    networks:
        - monitoring
    volumes:
        - ./grafana_data/:/var/lib/grafana/
volumes:
    grafana_data: {}
    prometheus_data: {}
```

The preceding two lines in combination with the two volumes fields allow both Grafana and Prometheus to save their data locally so that data is not lost each time you restart the Docker images.

```
networks:
  monitoring:
    driver: bridge
```

Internally, all three containers are known by the value of their container_name field. However, externally, you can connect to the open ports from your local machine as http://localhost:port or from another machine using http://hostname:port—the second way is not very secure and should be blocked by a firewall. Lastly, you need to run docker-compose up and you are done! The Go application begins exposing data and Prometheus begins collecting it.

The next figure shows the Prometheus UI (http://hostname:9090) displaying a simple plot of packt_n_goroutines:

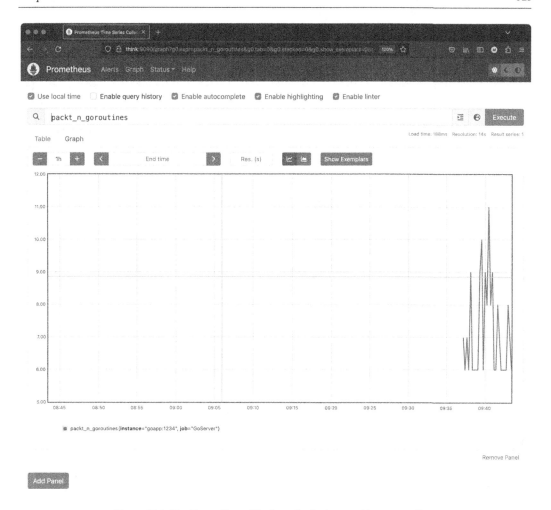

Figure 13.1: The Prometheus UI when displaying packt_n_goroutines

This output, which shows the values of the metrics in a graphical way, is very handy for debugging purposes, but it is far from being truly professional as Prometheus is not a visualization tool. The next subsection shows how you can connect Prometheus with Grafana and use Grafana to create impressive plots.

Visualizing Prometheus metrics in Grafana

There is no point in collecting metrics without doing something with them, and by something, I mean visualizing them. Prometheus and Grafana work very well together, so we are going to use Grafana for the visualization part. The single most important task that you should perform in Grafana is connecting it with your Prometheus instance. In Grafana terminology, you should create a Grafana data source that allows Grafana to get data from Prometheus.

The steps for creating a data source with our Prometheus installation are the following:

1. First, go to `http://localhost:3000` to connect to Grafana, because Grafana needs to learn about the data stored in Prometheus.

2. The username of the administrator is `admin`, whereas the password is defined in the value of the `GF_SECURITY_ADMIN_PASSWORD` parameter of the `docker-compose.yml` file.

3. Then, select **Add your first data source**. From the list of data sources, select **Prometheus**, which is usually at the top of the list.

4. Put `http://prometheus:9090` in the **URL** field and then press the **Save & Test** button. Due to the internal network that exists between the Docker images, the Grafana container knows the Prometheus container by the `prometheus` hostname—this is the value of the `container_name` field. As you already know, you can also connect to Prometheus from your local machine using `http://localhost:9090`.

We are done! The name of the data source is `Prometheus`.

After these steps, create a new dashboard from the initial Grafana screen and put a new visualization on it. Select **Prometheus** as the data source of the panel if it is not already selected. Then, go to the **Metrics** drop-down menu and select the desired metrics. Click **Save** and you are done. Create as many panels as you want.

The next figure shows Grafana visualizing two metrics from Prometheus as exposed by `prometheus. go`.

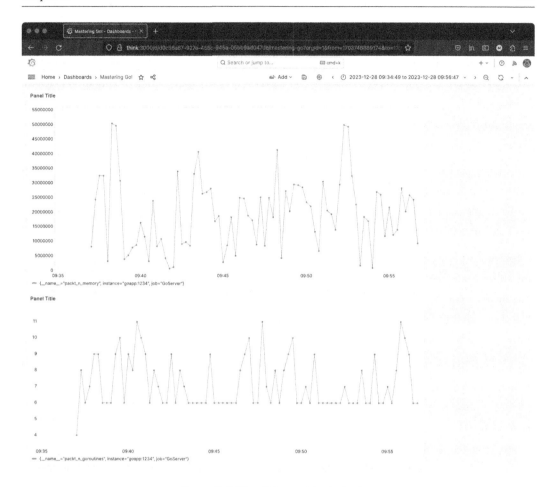

Figure 13.2: Visualizing metrics in Grafana

Grafana has many more capabilities than the ones presented here—if you are working with system metrics and want to check the performance of your Go applications, Prometheus and Grafana are good and popular choices.

In this section, we learned how to send metrics to Prometheus from a Go application and how to visualize the metrics in Grafana. However, nothing is going to make sense if we do not know what metrics to collect, what a metric means, or how to collect metrics without sacrificing the overall performance of an application.

Summary

This chapter was about a recent addition to Go testing, which is fuzz testing. Fuzz testing can help you find bugs in your code by generating test data on its own. While fuzz testing offers several benefits, it is important to note that it is not a silver bullet. This means that it should be used in conjunction with other testing techniques and security practices to ensure comprehensive coverage and robust security measures.

You might say that after making sure that your software has no bugs, you may need to make it faster. In such cases, you need to understand how your resources are being used—observability is about collecting performance-related information that helps you identify the behavior of your application.

Observability is crucial in modern, complex systems where traditional monitoring methods may fall short. It enables engineers and operators to gain insights into the inner workings of a system, diagnose problems, and improve the overall system reliability and performance. The concept is closely related to DevOps and **Site Reliability Engineering** (**SRE**) practices, emphasizing the importance of understanding, and managing systems in real-world, production environments.

In the next chapter, which is about efficiency and performance, we are going to learn how to avoid memory leaks, how to benchmark Go code, and about Go memory management.

Exercises

Try to do the following exercises on your own:

- Run cpuid.go on your own machine and see the capabilities and features of your hardware.
- Create a version of cpuid.go that writes the desired information in logs.
- Fix the AddInt() function from fuzz/code.go.
- Create a function for integer multiplication that uses a for loop in its implementation. Write testing functions and fuzz testing functions for it.

Additional resources

- The runtime/metrics package: https://pkg.go.dev/runtime/metrics
- The expvar package: https://pkg.go.dev/expvar
- Prometheus: https://prometheus.io/
- Grafana: https://grafana.com/
- Kibana: https://www.elastic.co/kibana/
- Elasticsearch: https://www.elastic.co/

Leave a review!

Enjoying this book? Help readers like you by leaving an Amazon review. Scan the QR code below to get a free eBook of your choice.

14

Efficiency and Performance

Every story has a villain. For developers, that villain is usually time. They must write code in a given time frame and ideally, the code must run as fast as possible. Most of the errors and bugs are a result of fighting with time constraints, both realistic and imaginary ones! So, this chapter is here to help you fight with the second aspect of time: efficiency and performance. For the first aspect of time, you need a good manager with technical skills.

The first part of the chapter is about benchmarking Go code using benchmark functions that measure the performance of a function or an entire program. Thinking that the implementation of a function is faster than a different implementation is not enough. We need to be able to prove it.

After that, we talk about how Go manages memory and how careless Go code can introduce memory leaks. A memory leak in Go occurs when memory that is no longer needed is not properly released, causing the program's memory usage to grow over time. Understanding the memory model is crucial for writing efficient, correct, and concurrent Go programs. In practice, when our code uses large amounts of memory, which is not usually the case, we need to take extra care with our code for better performance.

Lastly, we show how to use eBPF with Go. eBPF, which stands for Extended Berkeley Packet Filter, is a technology that enables programmability in the *Linux kernel*. It originated as an extension of the traditional **Berkeley Packet Filter** (**BPF**), which was designed for packet filtering within the kernel. eBPF, however, is a more general-purpose and flexible framework that allows the execution of user-supplied programs within the kernel space without requiring changes to the kernel itself.

We will cover the following topics:

- Benchmarking code

- Buffered versus unbuffered file I/O
- Wrongly defined benchmark functions
- Go memory management
- Memory leaks
- Working with eBPF

The section that follows is about benchmarking Go code, which helps you determine what is faster and what is slower in your code—this makes it a perfect place to begin your search for efficiency.

Benchmarking code

Benchmarking measures the performance of a function or a program, allowing you to compare different implementations and understand the performance impact of code changes. Using that information, you can easily reveal the part of the code that needs to be rewritten to improve its performance. It goes without saying that you should not benchmark Go code on a busy machine that is currently being used for other, more important, purposes unless you have a very good reason to do so! Otherwise, you might interfere with the benchmarking process and get inaccurate results, but most importantly, you might generate performance issues on the machine.

Most of the time, the load of the operating system plays a key role in the performance of your code. Let me tell you a story here: a Java utility I developed for a project performs lots of computations and finishes in 6,242 seconds (roughly 1.7 hours) when running on its own. It took about a day for four instances of the same Java command line utility to run on the same Linux machine! If you think about it, running them one after the other would have been faster than running them at the same time!

Go follows certain conventions regarding benchmarking (and testing). The most important convention is that the name of a benchmark function must begin with Benchmark. After the Benchmark word, we can put an underscore or an uppercase letter. Therefore, both BenchmarkFunctionName() and Benchmark_functionName() are valid benchmark functions, whereas Benchmarkfunctionname() is not. By convention such functions are put in files that end with _test.go. Once the benchmarking is correct, the go test subcommand does all the dirty work for you, which includes scanning all *_test.go files for special functions, generating a proper temporary main package, calling these special functions, getting the results, and generating the final output.

Benchmark functions use testing.B variables, whereas testing functions use testing.T variables. It is easy to remember.

Starting from Go 1.17, we can shuffle the execution order of both tests and benchmarks with the help of the shuffle parameter (go test -shuffle=on). The shuffle parameter accepts a value (which is the seed for the random number generator) and can be useful when you want to replay an execution order. Its default value is off. *The logic behind this capability is that, sometimes, the order in which tests and benchmarks are executed affects their results.*

The next subsection presents a simple benchmarking scenario where we try to optimize slice initializations.

A simple benchmark scenario

We begin by presenting a scenario that tests the performance of two functions that do the same thing but with a different implementation. We want to be able to initialize slices with consecutive values that start from 0 and go up to a predefined value. So, given a slice named mySlice, mySlice[0] is going to have the value of 0, mySlice[1] is going to have the value of 1, and so on. The relevant code can be found inside ch14/slices, which contains two files named initialize. go and initialize_test.go. The Go code of initialize.go is presented in two parts. The first part is the following:

```
package main

import (
    "fmt"
)

func InitSliceNew(n int) []int {
    s := make([]int, n)
    for i := 0; i < n; i++ {
    s[i] = i
    }
    return s
}
```

In the previous code, we see the implementation of the desired functionality that uses make() to pre-allocate the desired memory space.

The second part of initialize.go is the following:

```
func InitSliceAppend(n int) []int {
    s := make([]int, 0)
```

```
        for i := 0; i < n; i++ {
         s = append(s, i)
        }
        return s
    }

    func main() {
        fmt.Println(InitSliceNew(10))
        fmt.Println(InitSliceAppend(10))
    }
```

In `InitSliceAppend()`, we see a different implementation of the desired functionality that starts with an empty slice and uses multiple `append()` calls to populate it. The purpose of the `main()` function is to naively test the functionality of `InitSliceNew()` and `InitSliceAppend()`.

The implementation of the benchmarking functions is found in `initialize_test.go` and is the following:

```
    package main

    import (
        "testing"
    )

    var t []int

    func BenchmarkNew(b *testing.B) {
        for i := 0; i < b.N; i++ {
         t = InitSliceNew(i)
        }
    }

    func BenchmarkAppend(b *testing.B) {
        for i := 0; i < b.N; i++ {
         t = InitSliceAppend(i)
        }
    }
```

Here, we have two benchmarking functions that benchmark `InitSliceNew()` and `InitSliceAppend()`. The global parameter t is used to prevent Go from optimizing the for loops by preventing the return values of `InitSliceNew()` and `InitSliceAppend()` from being ignored.

 Keep in mind that the benchmarking process takes place inside the for loop. This means that, when needed, we can declare new variables, open network connections, and so on, outside that for loop.

And now some important information regarding benchmarking: *each benchmark function is executed for at least one second by default*—this duration also includes the execution time of the functions that are called by a benchmark function. If the benchmark function returns in a time that is less than one second, the value of b.N is increased, and the function runs again as many times in total as the value of b.N. The first time the value of b.N is 1, then it becomes 2, then 5, then 10, then 20, then 50, and so on. This happens because the faster the function, the more times Go needs to run it to get accurate results.

Benchmarking the code on a macOS M1 Max laptop produces the following kind of output—your output might vary:

```
$ go test -bench=. *.go
goos: darwin
goarch: arm64
BenchmarkNew-10              255704          79712 ns/op
BenchmarkAppend-10           86847         143459 ns/op
PASS
ok      command-line-arguments    33.539s
```

There are two important points here. First, the value of the -bench parameter specifies the benchmark functions that are going to be executed. The . value used is a regular expression that matches all valid benchmark functions. The second point is that if you omit the -bench parameter, no benchmark function is going to be executed.

The generated output shows that `InitSliceNew()` is faster than `InitSliceAppend()` because `InitSliceNew()` was executed 255704 times, each time taking 79712 ns, whereas `InitSliceAppend()` was executed 86847 times, each time taking 143459 ns. This makes perfect sense as `InitSliceAppend()` needs to allocate memory all the time—this means that both the length and the capacity of the slice change, whereas `InitSliceNew()` allocates the prerequisite memory once and for all.

Understanding how append() works is going to help you make sense of the results. If the underlying array has sufficient capacity, then the length of the resulting slice is increased by the number of elements appended and its capacity remains the same. This means that there are no new memory allocations. However, if the underlying array does not have sufficient capacity, a new array is created, which means that a new memory space is allocated, with a larger capacity. After that, the slice is updated to reference the new array, and its length and capacity are adjusted accordingly.

The subsection that follows shows a benchmarking technique that allows us to reduce the number of allocations.

Benchmarking the number of memory allocations

In this second benchmarking scenario, we are going to deal with a performance issue that has to do with the number of memory allocations that take place during the operation of a function. We present two versions of the same program to illustrate the differences between the slow version and the improved ones. All the relevant code can be found in two directories inside ch14/alloc named base and improved.

Initial version

The purpose of the function that is being benchmarked is to write a message to a buffer. This version contains no optimizations. The code of this first version is found in ch14/alloc/base, which contains two Go source code files. The first one is named allocate.go and comes with the following code:

```
package allocate

import (
    "bytes"
)

func writeMessage(msg []byte) {
    b := new(bytes.Buffer)
    b.Write(msg)
}
```

The writeMessage() function just writes the given message in a new buffer (bytes.Buffer). As we are only concerned about its performance, we do not deal with error handling.

The second file, which is called `allocate_test.go`, contains benchmarks and comes with the following code:

```
package allocate

import (
    "testing"
)

func BenchmarkWrite(b *testing.B) {
    msg := []byte("Mastering Go!")
    for i := 0; i < b.N; i++ {
        for k := 0; k < 50; k++ {
            writeMessage(msg)
        }
    }
}
```

Benchmarking the code using the `-benchmem` command line flag, which also displays memory allocations, produces the following kind of output:

```
$ go test -bench=. -benchmem *.go
goos: darwin
goarch: arm64
BenchmarkWrite-10       1148637      1024 ns/op      3200 B/op      50 allocs/op
PASS
ok      command-line-arguments      2.256s
```

Each execution of the benchmarking function requires 50 memory allocations. This means that there is room for improvement regarding the number of memory allocations that are taking place. We are going to try to reduce them in the subsection that follows.

Improving the number of memory allocations

In this subsection, we present three different functions that all implement the writing of a message to a buffer. However, this time, the buffer is given as a function parameter instead of being initialized internally.

The code of the improved version is found in ch14/alloc/improved and contains two Go source code files. The first one is named improve.go and contains the following code:

```go
package allocate

import (
    "bytes"
    "io"
)

func writeMessageBuffer(msg []byte, b bytes.Buffer) {
    b.Write(msg)
}

func writeMessageBufferPointer(msg []byte, b *bytes.Buffer) {
    b.Write(msg)
}

func writeMessageBufferWriter(msg []byte, b io.Writer) {
    b.Write(msg)
}
```

What we have here are three functions that all implement the writing of a message to a buffer. However, writeMessageBuffer() passes the buffer by value, whereas writeMessageBufferPointer() passes a pointer to the buffer variable. Lastly, writeMessageBufferWriter() uses an io.Writer interface variable, which also supports bytes.Buffer variables.

The second file is named improve_test.go and is going to be presented in three parts. The first part comes with the following code:

```go
package allocate

import (
    "bytes"
    "testing"
)

func BenchmarkWBuf(b *testing.B) {
    msg := []byte("Mastering Go!")
```

```
    buffer := bytes.Buffer{}

    for i := 0; i < b.N; i++ {
        for k := 0; k < 50; k++ {
            writeMessageBuffer(msg, buffer)
        }
    }
}
```

This is the benchmarking function for `writeMessageBuffer()`. The buffer is allocated only once and is being used in all benchmarks by passing it to the relevant function.

The second part is the following:

```
func BenchmarkWBufPointerNoReset(b *testing.B) {
    msg := []byte("Mastering Go!")
    buffer := new(bytes.Buffer)

    for i := 0; i < b.N; i++ {
        for k := 0; k < 50; k++ {
            writeMessageBufferPointer(msg, buffer)
        }
    }
}
```

This is the benchmarking function for `writeMessageBufferPointer()`. Once again, the used buffer is allocated only once and is being shared by all benchmarks.

The last part of `improve_test.go` contains the following code:

```
func BenchmarkWBufPointerReset(b *testing.B) {
    msg := []byte("Mastering Go!")
    buffer := new(bytes.Buffer)

    for i := 0; i < b.N; i++ {
        for k := 0; k < 50; k++ {
            writeMessageBufferPointer(msg, buffer)
            buffer.Reset()
        }
    }
}
```

```
    }

func BenchmarkWBufWriterReset(b *testing.B) {
    msg := []byte("Mastering Go!")
    buffer := new(bytes.Buffer)

    for i := 0; i < b.N; i++ {
        for k := 0; k < 50; k++ {
            writeMessageBufferWriter(msg, buffer)
            buffer.Reset()
        }
    }
}
```

Here, we see the use of `buffer.Reset()` in the two benchmarking functions. The purpose of the `buffer.Reset()` function is to reset the buffer so it has no content. The `buffer.Reset()` function has the same results as `buffer.Truncate(0)`. `Truncate(n)` discards all but the first n unread bytes from the buffer. We use `buffer.Reset()` thinking it might improve performance. However, this remains to be seen.

Benchmarking the improved version produces the following kind of output:

```
$ go test -bench=. -benchmem *.go
goos: darwin
goarch: arm64
BenchmarkWBuf-10                   1128193    1056 ns/op    3200 B/op 50 allocs/op
BenchmarkWBufPointerNoReset-10 4050562    337.1 ns/op   2120 B/op 0 allocs/
op
BenchmarkWBufPointerReset-10    7993546    150.7 ns/op   0 B/op        0
allocs/op
BenchmarkWBufWriterReset-10     7851434    151.8 ns/op   0 B/op    0 allocs/
op
PASS
ok      command-line-arguments    7.667s
```

As presented by the results of the `BenchmarkWBuf()` benchmarking function, the use of a buffer as a parameter to the function does not automatically speed up the process, even if we share the same buffer during benchmarking. However, this is not the case with the remaining benchmarks.

The use of a pointer to the buffer saves us from having to copy the buffer before passing it to the function—this explains the results of the BenchmarkWBufPointerNoReset() function where we have no additional memory allocations. However, we still need to use 2,120 bytes per operation.

The output with the -benchmem command line parameter includes two additional columns. The fourth column shows the amount of memory that was allocated on average in each execution of the benchmark function. The fifth column shows the number of allocations used to allocate the memory value of the fourth column.

Lastly, it turns out that resetting the buffer using buffer.Reset() after calling writeMessageBufferPointer() and writeMessageBufferWriter() speeds up the process. A possible explanation for that is that an empty buffer is easier to work with. So, when buffer. Reset() is used, we have both 0 memory allocations and 0 bytes per operation. As a result, BenchmarkWBufPointerReset() and BenchmarkWBufWriterReset() need 150.7 and 151.8 nano-seconds per operation, respectively, which is a huge speed up from the 1,056 and 337.1 nanoseconds per operation required by BenchmarkWBuf() and BenchmarkWBufPointerNoReset(), respectively.

Using buffer.Reset() can be more efficient for one or a combination of the following reasons:

- **Reuse of allocated memory**: When you call buffer.Reset(), the underlying byte slice used by the bytes.Buffer is not deallocated. Instead, it is reused. The length of the buffer is set to zero, making the existing memory available for new data to be written.

- **Reduced allocation overhead**: Creating a new buffer involves allocating a new underlying byte slice. This allocation comes with overhead, including managing the memory, updating the memory allocator's data structures, and possibly invoking the garbage collector.

- **Avoiding garbage collection**: Creating and discarding many small buffers can lead to increased pressure on the Garbage Collector, especially in scenarios with high-frequency buffer creation. By reusing the buffer with Reset(), you reduce the number of short-lived objects, potentially reducing the impact on garbage collection.

The subject of the next section is benchmarking buffered writing.

Buffered versus unbuffered file I/O

In this section, we are going to compare buffered and unbuffered operations while reading and writing files.

In this section, we are going to test whether the size of the buffer plays a key role in the performance of write operations. The relevant code can be found in ch14/io. Apart from the relevant files, the directory includes a testdata directory, which was first seen in *Chapter 13, Fuzz Testing and Observability*, and is used for storing data related to the testing process.

The code of table.go is not presented here—feel free to look at it. The code of table_test.go is the following:

```
package table

import (
    "fmt"
    "os"
    "path"
    "strconv"
    "testing"
)

var ERR error
var countChars int

func benchmarkCreate(b *testing.B, buffer, filesize int) {
    filename := path.Join(os.TempDir(), strconv.Itoa(buffer))
    filename = filename + "-" + strconv.Itoa(filesize)
    var err error
    for i := 0; i < b.N; i++ {
        err = Create(filename, buffer, filesize)
    }
    ERR = err
```

The reason for storing the return value of Create() in a variable named err and using another global variable named ERR afterward is tricky. We want to prevent the compiler from doing any optimizations that might exclude the function that we want to measure from being executed because its results are never used.

```
    err = os.Remove(filename)
    if err != nil {
        fmt.Println(err)
```

```
        }
        ERR = err
    }
```

Neither the signature nor the name of benchmarkCreate() makes it a benchmark function. This is a helper function that allows you to call Create(), which creates a new file on disk; its implementation can be found in table.go, with the proper parameters. Its implementation is valid, and it can be used by benchmark functions.

```
func BenchmarkBuffer4Create(b *testing.B) {
    benchmarkCreate(b, 4, 1000000)
}


func BenchmarkBuffer8Create(b *testing.B) {
    benchmarkCreate(b, 8, 1000000)
}


func BenchmarkBuffer16Create(b *testing.B) {
    benchmarkCreate(b, 16, 1000000)
}
```

These are three correctly defined benchmark functions that all call benchmarkCreate(). Benchmark functions require a single *testing.B variable and return no values. In this case, the numbers at the end of the function name indicate the size of the buffer.

```
func BenchmarkRead(b *testing.B) {
    buffers := []int{1, 16, 96}
    files := []string{"10.txt", "1000.txt", "5k.txt"}
```

This is the code that defines the array structures that are going to be used in the table tests. This saves us from having to implement (3x3=) 9 separate benchmark functions.

```
    for _, filename := range files {
        for _, bufSize := range buffers {
            name := fmt.Sprintf("%s-%d", filename, bufSize)
            b.Run(name, func(b *testing.B) {
                for i := 0; i < b.N; i++ {
                    t := CountChars("./testdata/"+filename, bufSize)
                    countChars = t
```

```
                }
            })
        }
    }
}
```

The b.Run() method, which allows you to run one or more sub-benchmarks within a benchmark function, accepts two parameters. First, the name of the sub-benchmark, which is displayed on the screen, and second, the function that implements the sub-benchmark. This is an efficient way to run multiple benchmarks with the use of table tests and know their parameters. Just remember to define a proper name for each sub-benchmark because this is going to be displayed on the screen.

Running the benchmarks generates the next output:

```
$ go test -bench=. -benchmem *.go
goos: darwin
goarch: arm64
BenchmarkBuffer4Create-10        382740    2915 ns/op    384 B/op    5 allocs/
op
BenchmarkBuffer8Create-10        444297    2400 ns/op    384 B/op    5 allocs/
op
BenchmarkBuffer16Create-10       491230    2165 ns/op    384 B/op  5 allocs/op
```

The previous three lines are the results of the BenchmarkBuffer4Create(), BenchmarkBuffer8Create(), and BenchmarkBuffer16Create() benchmark functions, respectively, and indicate their performance.

```
BenchmarkRead/10.txt-1-10        146298    8180 ns/op    168 B/op    6 allocs/
op
BenchmarkRead/10.txt-16-10       197534    6024 ns/op    200 B/op    6 allocs/
op
BenchmarkRead/10.txt-96-10       197245    6148 ns/op    440 B/op    6 allocs/
op
BenchmarkRead/1000.txt-1-10      4382        268204 ns/op  168 B/op    6
allocs/op
BenchmarkRead/1000.txt-16-10     32732     36684 ns/op    200 B/op    6 allocs/
op
BenchmarkRead/1000.txt-96-10     105078    11337 ns/op    440 B/op        6
allocs/op
```

```
BenchmarkRead/5k.txt-1-10        912      1308924 ns/op   168 B/op         6
allocs/op
BenchmarkRead/5k.txt-16-10      7413       159638 ns/op   200 B/op         6
allocs/op
BenchmarkRead/5k.txt-96-10     36471        32841 ns/op   440 B/op      6
allocs/op
```

The previous results are from the table tests with the 9 sub-benchmarks.

```
PASS
ok       command-line-arguments     24.518s
```

So, what does this output tell us? First, the -10 at the end of each benchmark function signifies the number of goroutines used for its execution, which is essentially the value of the GOMAXPROCS environment variable. Similarly, you can see the values of GOOS and GOARCH, which show the operating system and the architecture of the machine in the generated output. The second column in the output displays the number of times that the relevant function was executed. Faster functions are executed more times than slower functions. As an example, BenchmarkBuffer4Create() was executed 382740 times, while BenchmarkBuffer16Create() was executed 491230 times because it is faster! The third column in the output shows the average time of each run and is measured in nanoseconds per benchmark function execution (ns/op). The higher the value of the third column, the slower the benchmark function is. *A large value in the third column is an indication that a function might need to be optimized*.

So far, we have learned how to create benchmark functions to test the performance of our own functions to better understand potential bottlenecks that might need to be optimized. You might ask, how often do we need to create benchmark functions? The answer is simple. When something runs slower than needed and/or when you want to choose between two or more implementations.

The next subsection shows how to compare benchmark results.

The benchstat utility

Now imagine that you have benchmarking data, and you want to compare it with the results that were produced in another computer or with a different configuration. The benchstat utility can help you here. The utility can be found in the https://pkg.go.dev/golang.org/x/perf/cmd/benchstat package and can be downloaded using go install golang.org/x/perf/cmd/benchstat@latest. Go puts all binary files in ~/go/bin, and benchstat is no exception to that rule.

The benchstat utility replaces the benchcmp utility, which can be found at https://pkg.go.dev/golang.org/x/tools/cmd/benchcmp.

So, imagine that we have two benchmark results for `table_test.go` saved in `r1.txt` and `r2.txt`—you should remove all lines from the go `test` output that do not contain benchmarking results, which leaves all lines that begin with `Benchmark`. You can use `benchstat` as follows:

```
$ ~/go/bin/benchstat r1.txt r2.txt
                      |       r1.txt       |                      r2.txt                       |
                      |      sec/op        |        sec/op       vs base                       |
Buffer4Create-8        10472.0n ± ∞ ¹      830.8n ± ∞ ¹         ~ (p=0.667 n=1+2) ²
Buffer8Create-8         6884.0n ± ∞ ¹      798.9n ± ∞ ¹         ~ (p=0.667 n=1+2) ²
Buffer16Create-8        5010.0n ± ∞ ¹      770.5n ± ∞ ¹         ~ (p=0.667 n=1+2) ²
Read/10.txt-1-8         14.955µ ± ∞ ¹      3.987µ ± ∞ ¹         ~ (p=0.667 n=1+2) ²
Read/10.txt-16-8        12.172µ ± ∞ ¹      2.583µ ± ∞ ¹         ~ (p=0.667 n=1+2) ²
Read/10.txt-96-8        11.925µ ± ∞ ¹      2.612µ ± ∞ ¹         ~ (p=0.667 n=1+2) ²
Read/1000.txt-1-8       381.3µ ± ∞ ¹       175.8µ ± ∞ ¹         ~ (p=0.667 n=1+2) ²
Read/1000.txt-16-8      54.05µ ± ∞ ¹       22.68µ ± ∞ ¹         ~ (p=0.667 n=1+2) ²
Read/1000.txt-96-8      19.115µ ± ∞ ¹      6.225µ ± ∞ ¹         ~ (p=1.333 n=1+2) ²
Read/5k.txt-1-8         1812.5µ ± ∞ ¹      895.7µ ± ∞ ¹         ~ (p=0.667 n=1+2) ²
Read/5k.txt-16-8        221.8µ ± ∞ ¹       107.7µ ± ∞ ¹         ~ (p=0.667 n=1+2) ²
Read/5k.txt-96-8        51.53µ ± ∞ ¹       21.52µ ± ∞ ¹         ~ (p=0.667 n=1+2) ²
geomean                 36.91µ             9.717µ               -73.68%
¹ need >= 6 samples for confidence interval at level 0.95
² need >= 4 samples to detect a difference at alpha level 0.05
```

 You can save the results from benchmarks by simply redirecting the generated output into a file. For example, you can run go `test -bench=. > output.txt`.

If the value of the last column is ~, as it happens to be here, it means that there was no significant change in the results. The previous output shows no differences between the two results. Discussing more about `benchstat` is beyond the scope of the book. Type `benchstat -h` to learn more about the supported parameters.

The next section touches on a sensitive subject, which is incorrectly defined benchmark functions.

Wrongly defined benchmark functions

You should be very careful when defining benchmark functions because you might define them incorrectly. Look at the Go code of the following benchmark function:

```go
func BenchmarkFiboI(b *testing.B) {
    for i := 0; i < b.N; i++ {
        _ = fibo1(i)
    }
}
```

The BenchmarkFibo() function has a valid name and the correct signature. The bad news is that this benchmark function is logically wrong and is not going to produce any results. The reason for this is that as the b.N value grows in the way described earlier, the runtime of the benchmark function also increases because of the for loop. This fact prevents BenchmarkFiboI() from converging to a stable number, which prevents the function from completing and, therefore, returning any results. For analogous reasons, the next benchmark function is also wrongly implemented:

```go
func BenchmarkfiboII(b *testing.B) {
    for i := 0; i < b.N; i++ {
        _ = fibo1(b.N)
    }
}
```

On the other hand, there is nothing wrong with the implementation of the following two benchmark functions:

```go
func BenchmarkFiboIV(b *testing.B) {
    for i := 0; i < b.N; i++ {
        _ = fibo1(10)
    }
}
```

```go
func BenchmarkFiboIII(b *testing.B) {
    _ = fibo1(b.N)
}
```

Correct benchmark functions are a tool for identifying bottlenecks in your code that you should put in your own projects, especially when working with file I/O or CPU-intensive operations—as I am writing this, I have been waiting three days for a Python program to finish its operation to test the performance of the brute-force method of a mathematical algorithm.

Enough with benchmarking. The next section discusses the Go way of working with memory.

Go memory management

The subject of this section is Go memory management. We are going to begin by stating a fact that you should already be familiar with: Go sacrifices visibility and total control over memory management for the sake of simplicity and the use of the **Garbage Collector (GC)**. Although the GC operation introduces an overhead to the speed of a program, it saves us from having to manually deal with memory, which is a huge advantage and saves us from lots of bugs.

There exist two types of allocations that take place during program execution: *dynamic allocations* and *automatic allocations*. Automatic allocations are the allocations whose lifespan can be inferred by the compiler before the program starts its execution. For example, all local variables, the return arguments of functions, and function arguments have a given lifespan, which means that they can be automatically allocated by the compiler. All other allocations are performed dynamically, which also includes data that must be available outside the scope of a function.

We continue our discussion on Go memory management by talking about the heap and the stack because this is where most of the allocations take place.

Heap and stack

The *heap* is the place where programming languages store global variables—the heap is where garbage collection takes place. The *stack* is the place where programming languages store temporary variables used by functions—each function has its own stack. As goroutines are located in user space, the Go runtime is responsible for the rules that govern their operation. Additionally, **each goroutine has its own stack,** whereas the heap is "shared" among goroutines.

 Dynamic allocations take place in the heap, whereas automatic allocations are stored in the stack. The Go compiler performs a process that is called *escape analysis* to find out whether a memory needs to be allocated at the heap or should stay within the stack.

In C++, when you create new variables using the new operator, you know that these variables are going to the heap. This is not the case with Go and the use of new() and make() functions. In Go, the compiler decides where a new variable is going to be placed based on its size and the result of escape analysis. This is the reason that we can return pointers to local variables from Go functions. Although we have not seen new() in this book frequently, keep in mind that new() returns pointers to initialized memory.

If you want to know where the variables of a program are allocated by Go, you can use the -m gc flag with go run. This is illustrated in allocate.go—this is a regular program that needs no modifications in order to display the extra output as all details are handled by Go.

```go
package main

import "fmt"

const VAT = 24

type Item struct {
    Description string
    Value       float64
}

func Value(price float64) float64 {
    total := price + price*VAT/100
    return total
}

func main() {
    t := Item{Description: "Keyboard", Value: 100}
    t.Value = Value(t.Value)
    fmt.Println(t)

    tP := &Item{}
    *&tP.Description = "Mouse"
    *&tP.Value = 100
    fmt.Println(tP)
}
```

Running allocate.go generates the next output—the output is a result of the use of -gcflags '-m', which modifies the generated executable. You should not create executable binaries that go to production with the use of -gcflags flags.

```
$ go run -gcflags '-m' allocate.go
# command-line-arguments
./allocate.go:12:6: can inline Value
./allocate.go:19:17: inlining call to Value
```

```
./allocate.go:20:13: inlining call to fmt.Println
./allocate.go:25:13: inlining call to fmt.Println
./allocate.go:20:13: ... argument does not escape
./allocate.go:20:14: t escapes to heap
./allocate.go:22:8: &Item{} escapes to heap
./allocate.go:25:13: ... argument does not escape
{Keyboard 124}
&{Mouse 100}
```

The t escapes to heap message means that t escapes the function. Put simply, it means that t is used outside of the function and does not have a local scope (because it is passed outside the function). However, this does not necessarily mean that the variable has moved to the heap. On other occasions, you can see the message moved to heap. This message shows that the compiler decided to move a variable to the heap because it might be used outside of the function. The does not escape message indicates that the relevant argument does not escape to the heap.

Ideally, we should write our algorithms in order to use the stack instead of the heap, but this is impossible as stacks cannot allocate too-large objects and cannot store variables that live longer than a function. So, it is up to the Go compiler to decide.

The last two lines of the output consist of the output generated by the two fmt.Println() statements.

If you want to get a more detailed output, you can use -m twice:

```
$ go run -gcflags '-m -m' allocate.go
# command-line-arguments
./allocate.go:12:6: can inline Value with cost 13 as: func(float64)
float64 { total := price + price * VAT / 100; return total }
./allocate.go:17:6: cannot inline main: function too complex: cost 199
exceeds budget 80
./allocate.go:19:17: inlining call to Value
./allocate.go:20:13: inlining call to fmt.Println
./allocate.go:25:13: inlining call to fmt.Println
./allocate.go:22:8: &Item{} escapes to heap:
./allocate.go:22:8:   flow: tP = &{storage for &Item{}}:
./allocate.go:22:8:       from &Item{} (spill) at ./allocate.go:22:8
./allocate.go:22:8:       from tP := &Item{} (assign) at ./allocate.go:22:5
./allocate.go:22:8:   flow: {storage for ... argument} = tP:
```

```
./allocate.go:22:8:       from tP (interface-converted) at ./allocate.
go:25:14
./allocate.go:22:8:       from ... argument (slice-literal-element) at ./
allocate.go:25:13
./allocate.go:22:8:   flow: fmt.a = &{storage for ... argument}:
./allocate.go:22:8:       from ... argument (spill) at ./allocate.go:25:13
./allocate.go:22:8:       from fmt.a := ... argument (assign-pair) at ./
allocate.go:25:13
./allocate.go:22:8:   flow: {heap} = *fmt.a:
./allocate.go:22:8:       from fmt.Fprintln(os.Stdout, fmt.a...) (call
parameter) at ./allocate.go:25:13
./allocate.go:20:14: t escapes to heap:
./allocate.go:20:14:   flow: {storage for ... argument} = &{storage for
t}:
./allocate.go:20:14:       from t (spill) at ./allocate.go:20:14
./allocate.go:20:14:       from ... argument (slice-literal-element) at ./
allocate.go:20:13
./allocate.go:20:14:   flow: fmt.a = &{storage for ... argument}:
./allocate.go:20:14:       from ... argument (spill) at ./allocate.go:20:13
./allocate.go:20:14:       from fmt.a := ... argument (assign-pair) at ./
allocate.go:20:13
./allocate.go:20:14:   flow: {heap} = *fmt.a:
./allocate.go:20:14:       from fmt.Fprintln(os.Stdout, fmt.a...) (call
parameter) at ./allocate.go:20:13
./allocate.go:20:13: ... argument does not escape
./allocate.go:20:14: t escapes to heap
./allocate.go:22:8: &Item{} escapes to heap
./allocate.go:25:13: ... argument does not escape
{Keyboard 124}
&{Mouse 100}
```

Although more detailed, I find this output too crowded. Usually, using -m just once reveals what is happening behind the scenes regarding the program heap and stack.

What you should remember is that the heap is where the largest amounts of memory are usually stored. In practice, this means that *measuring the heap size is usually enough for understanding and counting the memory usage of a Go process*. As a result, the Go GC spends most of its time working with the heap, which means the heap is the first element to be analyzed when we want to optimize the memory usage of a program.

The next subsection discusses the main elements of the Go memory model.

The main elements of the Go memory model

In this section, we are going to discuss the main elements of the Go memory model in order to have a better understanding of what is happening behind the scenes.

The Go memory model works with the following main elements:

- **Program code**: Program code is memory mapped by the OS when the process is about to run, so Go has no control over that part. This kind of data is read-only.

- **Global data**: Global data is also memory mapped by the OS in read-only status.

- **Uninitialized data**: Uninitialized data is stored in anonymous pages by the OS. By uninitialized data, we mean data such as the global variables of a package. Although we might not know their values before the program starts, we know that we are going to need to allocate memory for them when the program starts its execution. This kind of memory space is allocated once and is never freed. So, the GC has no control over it.

- **Heap**: As discussed earlier in this chapter, this is the heap used for dynamic allocations.

- **Stacks**: These are the stacks used for automatic allocations.

You do not need to know all the gory details of all these components of the Go memory model. What you need to remember is that problems arise when we either purposely or unintentionally put objects into the heap without letting the GC release them and, therefore, free their respective memory space. We are going to see cases related to memory leaks that have to do with slices and maps in a while.

There also exists an internal Go component that performs memory allocations called the *Go allocator*. It can dynamically allocate memory blocks in order for Go objects to work properly and it is optimized to prevent memory fragmentation and locking. The Go allocator is implemented and maintained by the Go team and, as such, its operation details can change.

The next section discusses memory leaks, which have to do with not properly freeing memory space.

Memory leaks

In the subsections that follow, we are going to talk about ***memory leaks in slices and maps***. A *memory leak* happens when a memory space is allocated without being completely freed afterward.

We are going to begin with memory leaks caused by wrongly used slices.

Slices and memory leaks

In this subsection, we are going to showcase code that uses slices and produces memory leaks and then illustrate a way to avoid such memory leaks. One common scenario for memory leaks with slices involves holding a reference to a larger underlying array even after the slice is no longer needed. This prevents the GC from reclaiming the memory associated with the array.

The code in slicesLeaks.go is the following:

```
package main

import (
    "fmt"
    "time"
)

func createSlice() []int {
    return make([]int, 1000000)
}

func getValue(s []int) []int {
    val := s[:3]
    return val
}

func main() {
    for i := 0; i < 15; i++ {
        message := createSlice()
        val := getValue(message)
        fmt.Print(len(val), " ")
        time.Sleep(10 * time.Millisecond)
    }
}
```

The createSlice() function creates a slice with a large underlying array, which means that it requires lots of memory. The getValue() function takes the first five elements of its input slice and returns those elements as a slice. However, it does that while referencing the original input slice, which means that that input slice cannot be freed by the GC. Yes, this is a problem!

Running slicesLeaks.go with some extra command line arguments produces the following output:

```
$ go run -gcflags '-m -l' slicesLeaks.go
# command-line-arguments
./slicesLeaks.go:9:13: make([]int, 1000000) escapes to heap
./slicesLeaks.go:12:15: leaking param: s to result ~r0 level=0
./slicesLeaks.go:21:12: ... argument does not escape
./slicesLeaks.go:21:16: len(val) escapes to heap
./slicesLeaks.go:21:23: " " escapes to heap
3 3 3 3 3 3 3 3 3 3 3 3 3 3 3
```

The output indicates that there is a leaking parameter. A *leaking parameter* means that this function somehow keeps its parameter alive after it returns—this is where the memory leak takes place. However, this does not mean it is being moved to the stack, as most *leaking parameters* are allocated on the heap.

An improved version of slicesLeaks.go can be found in slicesNoLeaks.go. The only difference is in the implementation of the getValue() function:

```
func getValue(s []int) []int {
    returnVal := make([]int, 3)
    copy(returnVal, s)
    return returnVal
}
```

This time we create a copy of the slice part that we want to return, which means that the function no longer references the initial slice. As a result, the GC is going to be allowed to free its memory.

Running slicesNoLeaks.go produces the following output:

```
$ go run -gcflags '-m -l' slicesNoLeaks.go
# command-line-arguments
./slicesNoLeaks.go:9:13: make([]int, 1000000) escapes to heap
./slicesNoLeaks.go:12:15: s does not escape
./slicesNoLeaks.go:13:19: make([]int, 3) escapes to heap
./slicesNoLeaks.go:22:12: ... argument does not escape
./slicesNoLeaks.go:22:16: len(val) escapes to heap
./slicesNoLeaks.go:22:23: " " escapes to heap
3 3 3 3 3 3 3 3 3 3 3 3 3 3 3
```

So, we get no message about leaking parameters, which means that the issue has been resolved.

Next, we are going to discuss memory leaks and maps.

Maps and memory leaks

This subsection is about memory leaks introduced by maps as illustrated in mapsLeaks.go. The code in mapsLeaks.go is the following:

```go
package main

import (
    "fmt"
    "runtime"
)

func printAlloc() {
    var m runtime.MemStats
    runtime.ReadMemStats(&m)
    fmt.Printf("%d KB\n", m.Alloc/1024)
}

func main() {
    n := 2000000
    m := make(map[int][128]byte)
    printAlloc()

    for i := 0; i < n; i++ {
    m[i] = [128]byte{}
    }
    printAlloc()

    for i := 0; i < n; i++ {
    delete(m, i)
    }

    runtime.GC()
    printAlloc()
    runtime.KeepAlive(m)
```

```
    m = nil
    runtime.GC()
    printAlloc()
}
```

The printAlloc() is a helper function for printing information about the memory, whereas the runtime.KeepAlive(m) statement keeps a reference to m so that the map is not garbage collected.

Running mapsLeaks.go produces the following output:

```
$ go run -gcflags '-m -l' mapsLeaks.go
# command-line-arguments
./mapsLeaks.go:11:12: ... argument does not escape
./mapsLeaks.go:11:31: m.Alloc / 1024 escapes to heap
./mapsLeaks.go:16:11: make(map[int][128]byte) does not escape
111 KB
927931 KB
600767 KB
119 KB
```

The make(map[int][128]byte) statement allocates 111 KB of memory only. However, when we populate the map, it allocates 927,931 KB of memory. After that, we delete all the elements of the map, and we somehow expect the used memory to shrink. However, the empty map requires 600,767 KB of memory! The reason for that is that by design the number of buckets in a map cannot shrink. As a result, when we remove all maps elements, we do not reduce the number of existing buckets; we just zero the slots in the buckets.

However, using m = nil allows the GC to free the memory that was previously occupied by m and now only 119 KB of memory are allocated. As a result, giving nil values to unused objects is a good practice.

Lastly, we are going to present a technique that can reduce memory allocations.

Memory pre-allocation

Memory pre-allocation refers to the act of reserving memory space for data structures before they are needed. Although pre-allocating memory is not a panacea, it can be beneficial in certain situations to avoid frequent memory allocations and deallocations, which can lead to improved performance and reduced memory fragmentation.

It is essential to consider pre-allocation when you have a good estimate of the required capacity or size, you expect a significant number of insertions or appends, or when you want to reduce memory reallocations and improve performance. However, pre-allocation makes more sense when dealing with large amounts of data.

The implementation of the `main()` function of `preallocate.go` is presented in two parts. The first part comes with the following code:

```go
func main() {
    mySlice := make([]int, 0, 100)

    for i := 0; i < 100; i++ {
    mySlice = append(mySlice, i)
    }

    fmt.Println(mySlice)
```

In this example, the `make()` function is used to create a slice with a length of 0 and a capacity of 100. This pre-allocates memory for the slice, and as elements are appended, the slice can grow without the need for repeated reallocation, which slows down the process.

The second part is the following:

```go
    myMap := make(map[string]int, 10)

    for i := 0; i < 10; i++ {
    key := fmt.Sprintf("k%d", i)
    myMap[key] = i
    }

    fmt.Println(myMap)
}
```

As before, by providing an initial capacity, we reduce the chances of the map being resized frequently as elements are added, leading to more efficient memory usage.

The next section discusses the use of eBPF from Go—as *eBPF is available on Linux only*, the presented code can be executed on Linux machines only.

Working with eBPF

BPF stands for Berkeley Packet Filter and eBPF for Extended BPF. BPF was introduced back in 1992 to improve the performance of packet capture tools. Back in 2013, Alexei Starovoitov did a major rewrite of BPF that was included in the Linux kernel in 2014 and replaced BPF. With this rewrite, BPF, which is now called eBPF, became more versatile and can be used for a variety of tasks other than network packet capture.

eBPF software can be programmed in BCC, bpftrace, or using LLVM. The LLVM compiler can compile BPF programs into BPF bytecode using a supported programming language such as C or the LLVM intermediate representation. As both ways are difficult to program because of the use of low-level code, using BCC or bpftrace makes things simpler for the developer.

What is eBPF?

It is really difficult to describe precisely what eBPF can do because it has so many capabilities. It is much easier to describe how we can use eBPF. eBPF can be used in three main areas: networking, security, and observability. This section focuses on the observability capabilities (tracing) of eBPF.

You can consider eBPF as a virtual machine located inside the Linux kernel that can execute eBPF commands, which is custom BPF code. So, eBPF makes the Linux kernel programmable to help you solve real-world problems. Keep in mind that eBPF (as well as all programming languages) does not solve problems on its own. eBPF just gives you the tools to solve your problems! eBPF programs are executed by the Linux kernel eBPF runtime.

In more detail, the key features and aspects of eBPF include the following:

- **Programmability**: eBPF allows users to write and load small programs into the kernel, which can be attached to various hooks or entry points within the kernel code. These programs run in a restricted virtual machine environment, ensuring safety and security.

- **In-kernel execution**: eBPF programs are executed within the kernel in a secure way, making it possible to perform efficient and low-overhead operations directly in kernel space.

- **Dynamic attach points**: eBPF programs can be attached to various hooks or attach points in the kernel, allowing developers to extend and customize kernel behavior dynamically. Examples include networking, tracing, and security-related hooks.

- **Observability and tracing**: eBPF is widely used for observability and tracing purposes as it allows developers to instrument the kernel to gather insights into system behavior, performance, and interactions. Tools like bpftrace and perf use eBPF to provide advanced tracing capabilities.

- **Networking**: eBPF is extensively used in networking for tasks such as packet filtering, traffic monitoring, and load balancing. It enables the creation of efficient and customizable networking solutions without requiring modifications to the kernel.

- **Performance analysis**: eBPF provides a powerful framework for performance analysis and profiling. It allows developers and administrators to collect detailed information about system performance without significant overhead.

The main advantage of eBPF compared to traditional performance tools is that it is efficient, production-safe, and part of the Linux kernel. In practice, this means that we can use eBPF without the need to add or load any other components to the Linux kernel.

About observability and eBPF

Most Linux applications are executed in user space, which is a layer without too many privileges. Although using user space is safer and more secure, it has restrictions and requires using system calls to ask the kernel for access to privileged resources. Even the simplest commands use a large amount of system calls when executed. In practice, this means that if we are able to observe the system calls of our applications, we can learn more information about the way they behave and operate.

When things operate as expected and the performance of our applications is good, we usually do not care much about performance and the executed system calls. But when things go wrong, we desperately need to understand more about the operation of our applications. Putting special code in the Linux kernel or developing a module in order to understand the operation of our applications is a difficult task that might require a long period of time. This is where observability and eBPF come into play. eBPF, its language, and its tools allow us to dynamically see what happens behind the scenes without the need to change the entire Linux operating system.

All you need to communicate with eBPF is a programming language that supports `libbpf` (`https://github.com/libbpf/libbpf`). Apart from C, Go also offers support for the `libbpf` library (`https://github.com/aquasecurity/libbpfgo`).

The next subsection shows how to create an eBPF tool in Go.

Creating an eBPF tool in Go

As gobpf is an external Go package and the fact that, by default, all recent Go versions use modules, all source code should be put somewhere under `~/go/src`. The presented utility records the user ID of each user by tracing the `getuid(2)` system call and keeps a count for each user ID.

The code of the uid.go utility is going to be presented in four parts. The first part comes with the following code:

```go
package main

import (
    "encoding/binary"
    "flag"
    "fmt"
    "os"
    "os/signal"

    bpf "github.com/iovisor/gobpf/bcc"
)

import "C"

const source string = `
#include <uapi/linux/ptrace.h>
BPF_HASH(counts);

int count(struct pt_regs *ctx) {
    if (!PT_REGS_PARM1(ctx))
        return 0;

    u64 *pointer;
    u64 times = 0;
    u64 uid;

    uid = bpf_get_current_uid_gid() & 0xFFFFFFFF;
    pointer = counts.lookup(&uid);
        if (pointer !=0)
            times = *pointer;

    times++;
        counts.update(&uid, &times);

    return 0;
```

```
    }
```

If you are familiar with the C programming language, you should recognize that the source variable *holds C code*—this is the code that communicates with the Linux kernel to get the desired information. However, this code is called from a Go program.

The second part of the utility is the following:

```go
func main() {
    pid := flag.Int("pid", -1, "attach to pid, default is all processes")
    flag.Parse()
    m := bpf.NewModule(source, []string{})
    defer m.Close()
```

In this second part, we define a command line argument named pid and initialize a new eBPF module named m.

The third part of the utility contains the following code:

```go
        Uprobe, err := m.LoadUprobe("count")
        if err != nil {
            fmt.Fprintf(os.Stderr, "Failed to load uprobe count: %s\n", err)
            return
        }

        err = m.AttachUprobe("c", "getuid", Uprobe, *pid)
        if err != nil {
            fmt.Fprintf(os.Stderr, "Failed to attach uprobe to getuid: %s\n",
err)
            return
        }

        table := bpf.NewTable(m.TableId("counts"), m)
        fmt.Println("Tracing getuid()... Press Ctrl-C to end.")
```

The m.LoadUprobe("count") statement loads the count() function. The handling of the probe is initiated with the m.AttachUprobe() call. The AttachUprobe() method says that we want to trace the getuid(2) system call using Uprobe. The bpf.NewTable() statement is what gives us access to the counts hash defined in the C code. Remember that the eBPF program is written in C code that is held in a string variable.

The last part of the utility contains the following code:

```
sig := make(chan os.Signal, 1)
signal.Notify(sig, os.Interrupt)
<-sig

fmt.Printf("%s\t%s\n", "User ID", "COUNT")
for it := table.Iter(); it.Next(); {
    k := binary.LittleEndian.Uint64(it.Key())
    v := binary.LittleEndian.Uint64(it.Leaf())
    fmt.Printf("%d\t\t%d\n", k, v)
}
}
```

The previous code uses channels and UNIX signal handling to block the program. Once *Ctrl + C* is pressed, the `sig` channel unblocks the program and prints the desired information with the help of the `table` variable. As the data in the `table` variable is in the binary format, we need to decode it using two `binary.LittleEndian.Uint64()` calls.

 In order to execute the program, you need a C compiler and the BPF libraries to be installed, which depends on your Linux variant. Please refer to your Linux variant documentation for instructions on how to install eBPF. If you have any issues running the program, ask in relevant forums.

Running `uid.go` creates the following kind of output:

```
$ go run uid.go
Tracing getuid()... Press Ctrl-C to end.
User ID    COUNT
979        4
0          3
```

You can use the code in `uid.go` as a template when writing your own eBPF utilities in Go.

The section that follows discusses the `rand.Seed()` function and why it is not necessary to use it, starting from Go version 1.20.

Summary

In this chapter of the book, we presented various advanced Go topics related to benchmarking, performance, and efficiency. Remember that benchmark results can be influenced by various factors such as hardware, compiler optimizations, and workload. It is important to *interpret the results carefully and rationally* while considering the specific conditions under which the benchmarks are run.

In this chapter, we learned that Go has automatic memory management, which means that the language runtime takes care of memory allocation and deallocation for you. The primary components of Go's memory management are garbage collection, automatic memory allocation, and a runtime scheduler.

This chapter also presented a very powerful technology, eBPF. If you are using Linux machines, then you should definitely learn more about eBPF and how to use it with Go. The eBPF framework has gained popularity due to its versatility and the ability to address a wide range of use cases within the Linux kernel. When working with eBPF, you should first think like a system administrator, not as a programmer. Put simply, start by trying the existing eBPF tools instead of writing your own. However, if you have an actual issue that cannot be solved by existing eBPF tools, then you might need to start acting like a developer.

The next chapter is about Go 1.21 and Go 1.22 and the changes they introduced.

Exercises

Try to do the following exercises:

- Create three different implementations of a function that copies binary files and benchmark them to find the faster one. Can you explain why this function is faster?

- Write a version of `BenchmarkWBufWriterReset()` that does not use `buffer.Reset()` and see how fast it performs.

- This is a really difficult task: Create a machine learning library in Go. Keep in mind that, behind the scenes, ML uses statistics and matrix operations.

Additional resources

- gobpf: `https://github.com/iovisor/gobpf`
- The smallest Go binary: `https://totallygamerjet.hashnode.dev/the-smallest-go-binary-5kb`

- Working with Go execution traces (gotraceui): `https://gotraceui.dev/`

- How to troubleshoot memory leaks in Go with Grafana Pyroscope: `https://grafana.com/blog/2023/04/19/how-to-troubleshoot-memory-leaks-in-go-with-grafana-pyroscope/`

- *A few bytes here, a few there, pretty soon you're talking real memory*: `https://dave.cheney.net/2021/01/05/a-few-bytes-here-a-few-there-pretty-soon-youre-talking-real-memory`

Join our community on Discord

Join our community's Discord space for discussions with the authors and other readers:

`https://discord.gg/FzuQbc8zd6`

15

Changes in Recent Go Versions

This chapter is about the changes introduced in the latest Go versions.

First, we will see what has changed about the random number generation capabilities of Go. More specifically, we will talk about `rand.Seed()`.

The remainder of the chapter is about Go 1.21 and Go 1.22, which at the time of writing are the latest Go versions. *We should not forget that a programming language is also a piece of software developed by programmers.* Therefore, programming languages and compilers are being improved all the time with new functionality, better code generation, code optimizations, and faster operation. We close this chapter by discussing the most important improvements introduced in Go versions 1.21 and 1.22.

We will cover the following topics:

- About `rand.Seed()`
- What is new in Go 1.21?
- What is new in Go 1.22?

The first section discusses the `rand.Seed()` function and why it is not necessary to use it, starting from Go version 1.20.

About rand.Seed()

As of Go 1.20, there is no reason for calling `rand.Seed()` using a random value to initiate the random number generator. However, using `rand.Seed()` is not going to break existing code. To get a specific sequence of numbers, it is recommended to call `New(NewSource(seed))` instead.

This is illustrated in ch15/randSeed.go—the relevant Go code is the following:

```
src := rand.NewSource(seed)
r := rand.New(src)
for i := 0; i < times; i++ {
    fmt.Println(r.Uint64())
}
```

The rand.NewSource() call returns a new (pseudo) random source based on the given seed. Therefore, if called with the same seed, it is going to return the same sequence of values. The rand.New() call returns a new *rand.Rand variable, which is what generates the (pseudo) random values. Due to the call to Uint64(), we are generating unsigned int64 values.

Running randSeed.go produces the following output:

```
$ go run randSeed.go 1
Using seed: 1
5577006791947779410
8674665223082153551
$ go run randSeed.go 1
Using seed: 1
5577006791947779410
8674665223082153551
```

The next section introduces the changes introduced with Go 1.21.

What is new in Go 1.21?

In this section, we are going to talk about two new features that came with Go 1.21: The sync.OnceFunc() function of the standard library and the built-in function clear, which deletes or zeroes out all elements of a map, a slice, or a *type parameter* type.

We are going to begin with the sync.OnceFunc() function.

The sync.OnceFunc() function

The sync.OnceFunc() function is a helper function of the sync package. Its full signature is func OnceFunc(f func()) func(), which means that it accepts a function as a parameter and returns another function. In more detail, sync.OnceFunc() returns a function that invokes function f *only once*—the important detail here is the *only once*.

This might look unclear now but the presented code, which is saved as syncOnce.go, is going to shed some light on the use of sync.OnceFunc(). The code of syncOnce.go is presented in two parts. The first part is the following:

```
package main

import (
    "fmt"
    "sync"
    "time"
)

var x = 0

func initializeValue() {
    x = 5
}
```

The initializeValue() function is used for initializing the value of the x global variable. Let us make certain that initializeValue() gets executed only once.

The second part comes with the following code:

```
func main() {
    function := sync.OnceFunc(initializeValue)

    for i := 0; i < 10; i++ {
        go function()
    }
    time.Sleep(time.Second)

    for i := 0; i < 10; i++ {
        x = x + 1
    }
    fmt.Printf("x = %d\n", x)

    for i := 0; i < 10; i++ {
        go function()
    }
}
```

```
    time.Sleep(time.Second)
    fmt.Printf("x = %d\n", x)
}
```

The sync.OnceFunc(initializeValue) call is used for making sure that initializeValue() is going to be executed only once, despite the fact that function() is executed multiple times. In other words, we make sure that initializeValue() is going to be executed *by the first goroutine only*.

Running syncOnce.go produces the next output:

```
$ go run syncOnce.go
x = 15
x = 15
```

The output shows that the value of the x variable has been initialized only once. This means that sync.OnceFunc() might be used for initializing variables, connections, or files with the assurance that the initialization process is going to be executed only once.

Now, it is time to learn about the clear function.

The clear function

In this subsection, we are going to present the use of the clear function when working with maps and arrays. When used on a map object, clear() clears all the elements of the map object. When used on a slice object, clear() resets all the elements of the slice to the zero value of its data type while keeping the same slice length and capacity—this is totally different from what happens with a map object.

The name of the relevant program is clr.go—the important Go code is the following:

```
func main() {
    m := map[string]int{"One": 1}
    m["Two"] = 2
    fmt.Println("Before clear:", m)
    clear(m)
    fmt.Println("After clear:", m)

    s := make([]int, 0, 10)
    for i := 0; i < 5; i++ {
        s = append(s, i)
    }
```

```
        fmt.Println("Before clear:", s, len(s), cap(s))
        clear(s)
        fmt.Println("After clear:", s, len(s), cap(s))
    }
```

In the previous code, we create a map variable named m and a slice variable named s. After putting some data in them, we call the clear() function.

Running clr.go produces the following output:

```
$ go run clr.go
Before clear: map[One:1 Two:2]
After clear: map[]
Before clear: [0 1 2 3 4] 5 10
After clear: [0 0 0 0 0] 5 10
```

So, what has just happened? After calling clear(), m is an empty map and s is a slice with the same length and capacity as before with all its elements reset to the zero element of its data type, which is int.

The next section presents the most important changes introduced in Go 1.22.

What is new in Go 1.22?

While finishing the writing of this book, Go 1.22 was officially released. In this section, we are going to present the most interesting new features and improvements of Go 1.22.

- There is no more sharing in the variables of loops.
- Functions that shrink the size of a slice (Delete(), DeleteFunc(), Compact(), CompactFunc(), and Replace()) now zero the elements between the new length and the old length.
- There is an updated version of math/rand, which is called math/rand/v2.

Keep in mind that in Go 1.22 the HTTP routing capabilities of the standard library are improved. In practice, this means that the patterns used by net/http.ServeMux have been enhanced to accept methods and wildcards. You can find more about that at https://pkg.go.dev/net/http@master#ServeMux.

We'll begin by presenting the changes in the slices package.

Changes in slices

Apart from the changes in the functions that shrink the size of a slice, there is also the addition of slices.Concat(), which *concatenates multiple slices*. All these are illustrated in sliceChanges.go. The code of the main() function is presented in two parts.

The code of the first part of sliceChanges.go is the following:

```go
func main() {
    s1 := []int{1, 2}
    s2 := []int{-1, -2}
    s3 := []int{10, 20}
    conCat := slices.Concat(s1, s2, s3)
    fmt.Println(conCat)
```

In the previous code, we use slices.Concat() to concatenate three slices.

The rest of sliceChanges.go contains the following code:

```go
    v1 := []int{-1, 1, 2, 3, 4}
    fmt.Println("v1:", v1)
    v2 := slices.Delete(v1, 1, 3)
    fmt.Println("v1:", v1)
    fmt.Println("v2:", v2)
}
```

As mentioned earlier, slices.Delete() zeros the deleted elements of the slice that is given as its parameter, and returns a slice without the deleted slice elements—so v1 has the same length as before but v2 is smaller in length.

Running sliceChanges.go produces the following output:

```
$ go run sliceChanges.go
[1 2 -1 -2 10 20]
v1: [-1 1 2 3 4]
v1: [-1 3 4 0 0]
v2: [-1 3 4]
```

The first line shows the contents of the concatenated slice (conCat). The second line contains the initial version of v1, whereas the third line shows the contents of v1 after the call to slices.Delete(). The last line contains the return value of slices.Delete() as stored in the v2 slice.

Next, we are going to look at the changes in for loops.

Changes in for loops

Go 1.22 introduced some changes in for loops, which we are going to present in this subsection using changesForLoops.go. The code of the main() function of changesForLoops.go is going to be presented in two parts. The first part is the following:

```go
func main() {
    for x := range 5 {
        fmt.Print(" ", x)
    }
    fmt.Println()
```

So, starting with Go 1.22, for loops can range over integers.

The last part of changesForLoops.go is the following:

```go
    values := []int{1, 2, 3, 4, 5}
    for _, val := range values {
        go func() {
            fmt.Printf("%d ", val)
        }()
    }
    time.Sleep(time.Second)
    fmt.Println()
}
```

So, starting with Go 1.22, each time the for loop is executed, *a new variable is allocated*. This means that there is no more sharing of loop variables, which means that it is safe to use a loop variable inside a goroutine without having to worry about race conditions.

 This also means that ch08/goClosure.go is not going to have any issues with its execution. However, writing clear code is always considered a good practice.

Running changesForLoops.go produces the following output:

```
$ go run changesForLoops.go
 0 1 2 3 4
 5 3 4 1 2
```

The first line of output shows that loops can range over integers. The second line of output verifies that each goroutine that is created with the help of the for loop uses a different, separate copy of the loop variable.

Last, we present the new capabilities of the updated version of the math/rand package.

The math/rand/v2 package

Go 1.22 introduced an update to the math/rand package named math/rand/v2. The capabilities of this package are illustrated in randv2.go, which is presented in three parts. The first part of randv2.go is the following:

```go
package main

import (
    "fmt"
    "math/rand/v2"
)

func Read(p []byte) (n int, err error) {
    for i := 0; i < len(p); {
        val := rand.Uint64()
        for j := 0; j < 8 && i < len(p); j++ {
            p[i] = byte(val & 0xff)
            val >>= 8
            i++
        }
    }
    return len(p), nil
}
```

One of the most important changes is the deprecation of the Read() method from math/rand. However, a custom Read() function is implemented using the Uint64() method.

The second part comes with the next code:

```go
func main() {
    str := make([]byte, 3)

    nChar, err := Read(str)
```

```
    if err != nil {
        fmt.Println("Error:", err)
    } else {
        fmt.Printf("Read %d random bytes\n", nChar)
        fmt.Printf("The 3 random bytes are: %v\n", str)
    }
```

In this part, we call the previously implemented Read() to get 3 random bytes.

The last part of randv2.go contains the following code:

```
    var max int = 100
    n := rand.N(max)
    fmt.Println("integer n =", n)

    var uMax uint = 100
    uN := rand.N(uMax)
    fmt.Println("unsigned int uN =", uN)
}
```

There is the introduction of generic functions that work for any integer type. In the previous code, we use rand.N() to get an int value as well as a uint value. The parameter of rand.N() is what specifies the type of value that it is going to return.

 rand.N() also works for time durations as time.Duration is based on int64.

Running randv2.go with Go 1.22 or newer produces the following kind of output:

```
$ go run randv2.go
Read 3 random bytes
The 3 random bytes are: [71 215 175]
integer n = 0
unsigned int uN = 2
```

This subsection concludes this chapter, which is also the last chapter of this book! Thank you for reading the entire book and thank you for choosing my book to learn Go!

Summary

In this final chapter of the book, we presented the interesting and important changes introduced in Go 1.21 and Go 1.22 in order to have a clearer understanding of how the Go language keeps improving and evolving.

So, what does the future look like for Go developers? In short, it looks wonderful! You should already be enjoying programming in Go, and you should continue to do so as the language evolves. If you want to know about the latest and greatest of Go, you should definitely visit the official GitHub page of the Go team at `https://github.com/golang`.

Go helps you to create great software! So, go and create great software! And remember that *we are most productive when we are enjoying what we do!*

Exercises

Try to do the following exercises:

- Make the necessary changes to `./ch02/genPass.go` to remove the call to `rand.Seed()` and replace it with `rand.New(rand.NewSource(seed))`.
- Similarly, make the necessary changes to `./ch02/randomNumbers.go` to replace the call to `rand.Seed()` with `rand.New(rand.NewSource(seed))`.

Additional resources

- Rob Pike—What We Got Right, What We Got Wrong talk from GopherConAU 2023: `https://www.youtube.com/watch?v=yE5Tpp2BSGw`
- Meet the authors of Go: `https://youtu.be/3yghHvvZQmA`
- This is a video of Brian Kernighan interviewing Ken Thompson—not directly related to Go: `https://youtu.be/EY6q5dv_B-o`
- Brian Kernighan on successful language design—not directly related to Go: `https://youtu.be/Sg4U4r_AgJU`
- Brian Kernighan: UNIX, C, AWK, AMPL, and Go Programming from the Lex Fridman Podcast: `https://youtu.be/O9upVbGSBFo`
- Go 1.21 release notes: `https://go.dev/doc/go1.21`
- Go 1.22 release notes: `https://go.dev/doc/go1.22`

A note from the author

Being a good programmer is hard, but it can be done. Keep improving and—who knows—you might become famous and have a movie made about you!

Thank you for reading this book. Feel free to contact me with suggestions, questions, or maybe ideas for other books!

Soli Deo gloria

Join our community on Discord

Join our community's Discord space for discussions with the authors and other readers:

`https://discord.gg/FzuQbc8zd6`

Appendix

The Go Garbage Collector

The subject of this appendix is the operation of the Go **Garbage Collector** (**GC**). It is important to note that the details and performance characteristics of the GC may evolve with each new Go release.

Developers generally do not need to interact directly with the GC, as *it operates automatically in the background in its own goroutine*. However, understanding its behavior can be beneficial for optimizing memory usage and avoiding common pitfalls related to memory management. For the most up-to-date and detailed information, it is recommended to refer to the official Go documentation and release notes.

First, let us discuss garbage collection in general. Following that, we will dig deeper into the nuances of the Go GC.

Garbage collection

Garbage collection is the process of freeing up memory space that is not being used. In other words, the GC sees which objects are out of scope and cannot be referenced anymore and frees the memory space they consume. This process happens in a concurrent way while a Go program is running and not before or after the execution of the program. The documentation of the Go GC implementation states the following:

> *"The GC runs concurrently with mutator threads, is type accurate (also known as precise), allows multiple GC threads to run in parallel. It is a concurrent mark and sweep that uses a write barrier. It is non-generational and non-compacting. Allocation is done using size segregated per P allocation areas to minimize fragmentation while eliminating locks in the common case."*

The key characteristics of the Go GC

The key characteristics of the Go garbage collector are the following:

- **Concurrent and parallel**: The Go GC operates concurrently with the execution of Go programs. It runs concurrently with the application's threads, meaning that the GC can perform its work without stopping the application that is being executed. Additionally, certain phases of the GC can be parallelized to take advantage of multiple CPU cores and modern CPUs.

- **Generational collector**: The Go GC uses a generational garbage collection strategy, dividing objects into two generations: young and old. Most objects are allocated to the young generation, and most garbage collection work is focused there. The old generation contains longer-lived objects, which are less likely to get garbage collected.

- **Tri-color mark and sweep algorithm**: The Go GC uses a tri-color mark-and-sweep algorithm. This algorithm uses three colors (white, gray, and black) to track the state of objects during the marking phase. White objects are not yet visited, gray objects are in the process of being visited, and black objects have been visited.

- **Write barrier**: Go uses a write barrier to keep track of pointers that are updated in the heap in order to maintain consistency during garbage collection. The write barrier ensures that the GC is aware of changes to pointers, allowing it to trace object dependencies accurately.

- **Garbage collection triggers**: The Go GC is triggered based on memory allocation and heap size. When the allocated memory reaches a certain threshold or the heap size grows beyond a specified limit, the GC is triggered to reclaim unused memory.

- **Manual control**: While the GC is designed to be automatic and transparent to developers, there are ways to provide hints and control certain aspects of the garbage collection process. For example, the `runtime.GC()` function can be used to request an explicit garbage collection cycle.

We are going to revisit most of the characteristics of the GC in a while.

Learning more about the Go GC

The Go standard library offers functions that allow you to study the operation of the GC and learn more about what the GC covertly does. These functions are illustrated in the gColl.go utility. The source code of gColl.go is presented here in chunks.

```
package main
```

```
import (
    "fmt"
    "runtime"
    "time"
)
```

We need the runtime package because it allows us to get information about the Go runtime system, which among other things includes information about the operation of the GC.

```
func printStats(mem runtime.MemStats) {
    runtime.ReadMemStats(&mem)
    fmt.Println("mem.Alloc:", mem.Alloc)
    fmt.Println("mem.TotalAlloc:", mem.TotalAlloc)
    fmt.Println("mem.HeapAlloc:", mem.HeapAlloc)
    fmt.Println("mem.NumGC:", mem.NumGC, "\n")
}
```

The main purpose of printStats() is to avoid writing the same Go code multiple times. The runtime.ReadMemStats() call gets the latest garbage collection statistics for you.

```
func main() {
    var mem runtime.MemStats
    printStats(mem)

    for i := 0; i < 10; i++ {
        s := make([]byte, 50000000)
        if s == nil {
            fmt.Println("Operation failed!")
        }
    }
    printStats(mem)
```

In this part, we have a for loop that creates 10 byte slices with 50,000,000 bytes each. The reason for this is that by allocating large amounts of memory, we can trigger the GC.

```
    for i := 0; i < 10; i++ {
        s := make([]byte, 100000000)
        if s == nil {
            fmt.Println("Operation failed!")
```

```
        }
        time.Sleep(5 * time.Second)
    }
    printStats(mem)
}
```

The last part of the program makes even bigger memory allocations—this time, each byte slice has 100,000,000 bytes.

Running gColl.go on a macOS Sonoma machine with 32 GB of RAM produces the following kind of output:

```
$ go run gColl.go
mem.Alloc: 114960
mem.TotalAlloc: 114960
mem.HeapAlloc: 114960
mem.NumGC: 0

mem.Alloc: 50123152
mem.TotalAlloc: 500163016
mem.HeapAlloc: 50123152
mem.NumGC: 9

mem.Alloc: 121472
mem.TotalAlloc: 1500246248
mem.HeapAlloc: 121472
mem.NumGC: 20
```

The value of mem.Alloc is the bytes of allocated heap objects—all the objects that the GC has not yet freed. mem.TotalAlloc shows the cumulative bytes allocated for heap objects—this number does not decrease when objects are freed, which means that it keeps increasing. Therefore, it shows the total number of bytes allocated for heap objects during program execution. mem.HeapAlloc is the same as mem.Alloc. Last, mem.NumGC *shows the total number of completed garbage collection cycles*. The bigger that value is, the more you have to consider how you allocate memory in your code and if there is a way to optimize that.

If you want even more verbose output about the operation of the GC, you can combine go run gColl.go with GODEBUG=gctrace=1. Apart from the regular program output, you get some extra metrics—this is illustrated in the following output:

```
$ GODEBUG=gctrace=1 go run gColl.go
gc 1 @0.004s 2%: 0.008+0.34+0.042 ms clock, 0.081+0.063/0.51/0.18+0.42 ms
cpu, 3->3->0 MB, 4 MB goal, 0 MB stacks, 0 MB globals, 10 P
gc 2 @0.009s 3%: 0.097+0.93+0.049 ms clock, 0.97+0.20/1.0/0.84+0.49 ms
cpu, 3->3->1 MB, 4 MB goal, 0 MB stacks, 0 MB globals, 10 P
.

.

.

gc 18 @35.101s 0%: 0.13+0.15+0.009 ms clock, 1.3+0/0.22/0.007+0.095 ms
cpu, 95->95->0 MB, 95 MB goal, 0 MB stacks, 0 MB globals, 10 P
gc 19 @40.107s 0%: 0.091+0.38+0.011 ms clock, 0.91+0/0.54/0+0.11 ms cpu,
95->95->0 MB, 95 MB goal, 0 MB stacks, 0 MB globals, 10 P
gc 20 @45.111s 0%: 0.095+0.26+0.009 ms clock, 0.95+0/0.38/0+0.092 ms cpu,
95->95->0 MB, 95 MB goal, 0 MB stacks, 0 MB globals, 10 P
mem.Alloc: 121200
mem.TotalAlloc: 1500245792
mem.HeapAlloc: 121200
mem.NumGC: 20
```

As before, we have the same number of completed garbage collection cycles (20). However, we get extra information about the heap size of each cycle. So, for garbage collection cycle 20 (gc 20), we get the following:

```
gc 20 @45.111s 0%: 0.095+0.26+0.009 ms clock, 0.95+0/0.38/0+0.092 ms cpu,
95->95->0 MB, 95 MB goal, 0 MB stacks, 0 MB globals, 10 P
```

Now let us explain the 95->95->0 MB triplet in the previous line of output. The first value (95) is the heap size when the GC is about to run. The second value (95) is the heap size when the GC ends its operation. The last value is the size of the live heap (0).

The tri-color algorithm

As mentioned earlier, the operation of the Go GC is based on the tri-color algorithm. Note that the tri-color algorithm is not unique to Go and can be used in other programming languages as well.

Strictly speaking, the official name for the algorithm used in Go is the *tri-color mark-and-sweep algorithm*. It works concurrently with the program and uses a write barrier. This means that while a Go program runs, the Go scheduler is responsible for the scheduling of the application as well as the GC, which also runs as a goroutine. This is as if the Go scheduler must deal with a regular application with multiple goroutines!

The core idea behind this algorithm came from Edsger W. Dijkstra, Leslie Lamport, A. J. Martin, C. S. Scholten, and E. F. M. Steffens and was first illustrated in a paper named *On-the-Fly Garbage Collection: An Exercise in Cooperation*.

The primary principle behind the tri-color mark-and-sweep algorithm is that it divides the objects of the heap into three different sets according to their color, which is assigned by the algorithm and can be black, gray, or white. The objects in the black set are guaranteed to have no pointers to any object in the white set. On the other hand, an object in the white set can point to an object in the black set because this has no effect on the operation of the GC. The objects in the gray set might have pointers to some objects in the white set. Finally, the objects in the white set are the candidates for garbage collection.

So, when the garbage collection begins, all objects are white, and the GC visits all the root objects and colors them gray. The roots are the objects that can be directly accessed by the application, which includes global variables and other things on the stack. These objects mostly depend on the Go code of a particular program.

After that, the GC picks a gray object, makes it black, and starts looking at whether that object has pointers to other objects in the white set or not. Therefore, when an object in the gray set is scanned for pointers to other objects, it is colored black. If that scan discovers that this particular object has one or more pointers to a white object, it puts that white object in the gray set. This process keeps going for as long as there exist objects in the gray set. After that, the objects in the white set are unreachable and their memory space can be reused. Therefore, at this point, the elements in the white set are said to be garbage collected. Please note that no object can go directly from the black set to the white set, which allows the algorithm to operate and be able to clear the objects in the white set. As mentioned before, no object in the black set can directly point to an object in the white set. Additionally, if an object in the gray set becomes unreachable at some point in a garbage collection cycle, it will not be collected in that garbage collection cycle but in the next one! Although this is not an optimal situation, it is not that bad.

During this process, the running application is called the mutator. The mutator runs a small function named **write barrier**, which is executed each time a pointer in the heap is modified. If the pointer of an object in the heap is modified, this means that this object is now reachable—the write barrier colors it gray and puts it in the gray set. The mutator is responsible for the invariant that no element of the black set has a pointer to an element of the white set. This is accomplished with the help of the write barrier function. Failing to accomplish this invariant will ruin the garbage collection process and will most likely crash your program in a pretty bad and undesirable way!

So, to summarize, there are three different colors: black, white, and gray. When the algorithm begins, all objects are colored white. As the algorithm keeps going, white objects are moved into one of the other two sets. The objects that are left in the white set are the ones that are going to be cleared at some point. The next figure displays the three color sets with objects in them.

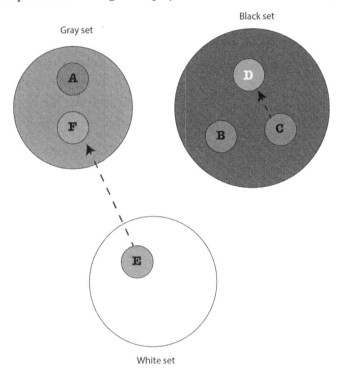

Figure A.1: The Go garbage collector represents the heap of a program as a graph

While object **E**, which is in the white set, can access object **F**, it cannot be accessed by any other object because no other object points to object **E**, which makes it a perfect candidate for garbage collection! Additionally, objects **A**, **B**, and **C** are root objects and are always reachable; therefore, they cannot be garbage collected.

Can you guess what happens next? Well, the algorithm will have to process the remaining elements of the gray set, which means that both objects **A** and **F** will go to the black set. Object **A** goes to the black set because it is a root element and **F** goes to the black set because it does not point to any other object while it is in the gray set.

After object **E** is garbage collected, object **F** will become unreachable and will be garbage collected in the next cycle of the GC because an unreachable object cannot magically become reachable in the next iteration of the garbage collection cycle.

Go garbage collection can also be applied to variables such as channels. When the GC finds out that a channel is unreachable, which is when the channel variable cannot be accessed anymore, it will free its resources even if the channel has not been closed.

Go allows you to manually initiate garbage collection cycles by putting a `runtime.GC()` statement in your Go code. However, keep in mind that `runtime.GC()` blocks the caller and it might block the entire program, especially if you are running a very busy Go program with many objects. This mainly happens because you cannot perform garbage collections while everything else is rapidly changing, as this will not give the GC the opportunity to clearly identify the members of the white, black, and gray sets. This garbage collection status is also called a garbage collection safe point.

You can find the long and relatively advanced Go code of the GC at `https://github.com/golang/go/blob/master/src/runtime/mgc.go`, which you can study if you want to learn even more information about the garbage collection operation. You can even make changes to that code if you are brave enough!

More about the operation of the Go GC

This section talks more about the Go GC and presents additional information about its activities. The main concern of the Go GC is low latency, which basically means short pauses in its operation in order to have real-time operation. On the other hand, what a program does is create new objects and manipulate existing objects with pointers all the time. This process can end up creating objects that cannot be accessed anymore because there are no pointers pointing to these objects. These objects are then garbage and wait for the GC to clean them up and free their memory space. After that, the memory space that has been freed is ready to be used again.

The mark-and-sweep algorithm is the simplest algorithm used. The algorithm stops the program execution (*stop-the-world GC*) in order to visit all the accessible objects of the heap of a program and marks them. After that, it sweeps the inaccessible objects. During the mark phase of the algorithm, each object is marked as white, gray, or black. The children of a gray object are colored gray, whereas the original gray object is then colored black. The sweep phase begins when there are no more gray objects to examine. This technique works because there are no pointers from the black set to the white set, which is a fundamental invariant of the algorithm.

Although the mark-and-sweep algorithm is simple, it suspends the execution of the program while it is running, which means that it adds latency to the actual process. Go tries to lower that latency by running the GC as a concurrent process and by using the tri-color algorithm described in the previous section. However, other processes can move pointers or create new objects while the GC runs concurrently. This fact can make things difficult for the GC.

As a result, the basic principle that will allow the tri-color algorithm to operate concurrently while maintaining the fundamental invariant of the mark-and-sweep algorithm is that no object in the black set can point to an object in the white set.

The solution to this problem is fixing all the cases that can cause a problem for the algorithm. Therefore, new objects must go to the gray set because, this way, the fundamental invariant of the mark-and-sweep algorithm cannot be altered. Additionally, when a pointer of the program is moved, you color the object that the pointer points to as gray. The gray set acts like a barrier between the white set and the black set. Finally, each time a pointer is moved, some Go code gets automatically executed, which is the write barrier mentioned earlier, which does some recoloring. The latency introduced by the execution of the write barrier code is the price we have to pay for being able to run the GC concurrently.

Note that the Java programming language has many garbage collectors that are highly configurable with the help of multiple parameters. One of these Java garbage collectors is called G1 and it is recommended for low-latency applications. Although Go does not have multiple garbage collectors, it does have knobs that you can use to tune the garbage collector for your applications.

The section that follows discusses maps and slices from a garbage collection perspective because sometimes the way we handle variables influences the operation of the GC.

Maps, slices, and the Go GC

In this section, we discuss the operation of the Go GC in relation to maps and slices. The purpose of this section is to let you write code that makes the work of the GC easier.

Using slices

The example in this section uses a slice to store a large number of structures in order to show how slice allocation is related to the operation of the GC. Each structure stores two integer values. This is implemented in `sliceGC.go` as follows:

```
package main

import (
    "runtime"
)
```

```
type data struct {
    i, j int
}

func main() {
    var N = 80000000
    var structure []data
    for i := 0; i < N; i++ {
        value := int(i)
        structure = append(structure, data{value, value})
    }

    runtime.GC()
    _ = structure[0]
}
```

The last statement, (_ = structure[0]), is used to prevent the GC from garbage collecting the structure variable too early, as it is not referenced or used outside of the for loop. The same technique will be used in the three Go programs that follow. Apart from this important detail, a for loop is used for putting all values into structures that are stored in the structure slice variable. An equivalent way of doing that is the use of runtime.KeepAlive(). The program generates no output—it just triggers the GC using a call to runtime.GC().

Using maps with pointers

In this subsection, we use a map for storing pointers. This time, the map uses integer keys that reference the pointers. The name of the program is mapStar.go and contains the following Go code:

```
package main

import (
    "runtime"
)

func main() {
    var N = 80000000
    myMap := make(map[int]*int)
    for i := 0; i < N; i++ {
```

```
        value := int(i)
        myMap[value] = &value
    }

    runtime.GC()
    _ = myMap[0]
}
```

The operation of the program is the same as in sliceGC.go from the previous section. What differs is the use of a map (make(map[int]*int)) for storing the pointers to int. As before, the program produces no output.

Using maps without pointers

In this subsection, we use a map that stores integer values directly instead of pointers to integers. The important code of mapNoStar.go is the following:

```
func main() {
    var N = 80000000
    myMap := make(map[int]int)
    for i := 0; i < N; i++ {
        value := int(i)
        myMap[value] = value
    }
    runtime.GC()
    _ = myMap[0]
}
```

Once again, the program produces no output.

Splitting a map

In this last program, we use a different technique called sharding where we split one long map into a map of maps. The implementation of the main() function of mapSplit.go is as follows:

```
func main() {
    var N = 80000000

    split := make([]map[int]int, 2000)
    for i := range split {
        split[i] = make(map[int]int)
```

```
    }

    for i := 0; i < N; i++ {
        value := int(i)
        split[i%2000][value] = value
    }
    runtime.GC()
    _ = split[0][0]
}
```

The code uses two for loops, one for creating the map of maps and the other one for storing the desired data values in the map of maps.

As all four programs are using huge data structures, they are consuming large amounts of memory. Programs that consume lots of memory space trigger the Go GC more often. The next subsection presents an evaluation of the presented techniques.

Comparing the performance of the presented techniques

In this subsection, we compare the performance of each one of these four implementations using the time command of zsh(1), which is pretty similar to the time(1) UNIX command. The purpose of the comparison is to understand how the allocation technique and the data structure used affect the performance of a program.

```
$ time go run sliceGC.go
go run sliceGC.go   0.61s user 0.52s system 92% cpu 1.222 total
$ time go run mapStar.go
go run mapStar.go   23.86s user 1.02s system 176% cpu 14.107 total
$ time go run mapNoStar.go
go run mapNoStar.go   10.01s user 0.53s system 98% cpu 10.701 total
$ time go run mapSplit.go
go run mapSplit.go   11.22s user 0.44s system 100% cpu 11.641 total
```

It turns out that *all map versions are slower than the slice version*. Unfortunately for maps, the map version will always be slower than the slice version because of the execution of the hash function and the fact that the data is not contiguous. *In maps, data is stored in a bucket determined by the output of the hash function.*

Additionally, the first map program (mapStar.go) may trigger some GC slowdown because taking the address of &value will cause it to escape to the heap. Every other program is just using the stack for those locals. ***When variables escape to the heap, they cause more garbage collection pressure***.

Accessing an element of a map or a slice has O(1) runtime, which means that the access time does not depend on the number of elements found in the map or the slice. However, the way these structures work affects the overall speed.

Additional resources

- Go FAQ: How do I know whether a variable is allocated on the heap or the stack? `https://go.dev/doc/faq#stack_or_heap`
- The list of available -gcflags options: `https://pkg.go.dev/cmd/compile`
- If you want to learn more about garbage collection, you should visit `http://gchandbook.org/`

Leave a review!

Enjoyed this book? Help readers like you by leaving an Amazon review. Scan the QR code below to get a free eBook of your choice.

packt.com

Subscribe to our online digital library for full access to over 7,000 books and videos, as well as industry leading tools to help you plan your personal development and advance your career. For more information, please visit our website.

Why subscribe?

- Spend less time learning and more time coding with practical eBooks and Videos from over 4,000 industry professionals
- Improve your learning with Skill Plans built especially for you
- Get a free eBook or video every month
- Fully searchable for easy access to vital information
- Copy and paste, print, and bookmark content

At www.packt.com, you can also read a collection of free technical articles, sign up for a range of free newsletters, and receive exclusive discounts and offers on Packt books and eBooks.

Other Books You May Enjoy

If you enjoyed this book, you may be interested in these other books by Packt:

Effective Concurrency in Go

Burak Serdar

ISBN: 9781804619070

- Understand basic concurrency concepts and problems
- Learn about Go concurrency primitives and how they work
- Learn about the Go memory model and why it is important
- Understand how to use common concurrency patterns
- See how you can deal with errors in a concurrent program
- Discover useful techniques for troubleshooting

Functional Programming in Go

Dylan Meeus

ISBN: 9781801811163

- Gain a deeper understanding of functional programming through practical examples
- Build a solid foundation in core FP concepts and see how they apply to Go code
- Discover how FP can improve the testability of your code base
- Apply functional design patterns for problem solving
- Understand when to choose and not choose FP concepts
- Discover the benefits of functional programming when dealing with concurrent code

Packt is searching for authors like you

If you're interested in becoming an author for Packt, please visit authors.packtpub.com and apply today. We have worked with thousands of developers and tech professionals, just like you, to help them share their insight with the global tech community. You can make a general application, apply for a specific hot topic that we are recruiting an author for, or submit your own idea.

Share your thoughts

Now you've finished *Mastering Go, Fourth Edition*, we'd love to hear your thoughts! Scan the QR code below to go straight to the Amazon review page for this book and share your feedback or leave a review on the site that you purchased it from.

https://packt.link/r/1805127144

Your review is important to us and the tech community and will help us make sure we're delivering excellent quality content.

Index

Download a free PDF copy of this book

Thanks for purchasing this book!

Do you like to read on the go but are unable to carry your print books everywhere?

Is your eBook purchase not compatible with the device of your choice?

Don't worry, now with every Packt book you get a DRM-free PDF version of that book at no cost.

Read anywhere, any place, on any device. Search, copy, and paste code from your favorite technical books directly into your application.

The perks don't stop there, you can get exclusive access to discounts, newsletters, and great free content in your inbox daily

Follow these simple steps to get the benefits:

1. Scan the QR code or visit the link below

https://packt.link/free-ebook/9781805127147

2. Submit your proof of purchase

3. That's it! We'll send your free PDF and other benefits to your email directly

Made in United States
North Haven, CT
01 April 2024

50764956R00402